Catholic Legal Perspectives

Catholic Legal Perspectives

THIRD EDITION

Bill Piatt
PROFESSOR OF LAW
ST. MARY'S UNIVERSITY SCHOOL OF LAW

CAROLINA ACADEMIC PRESS
Durham, North Carolina

ISBN 978-1-5310-0901-4
eISBN 978-1-53100-902-1
LCCN 2018944010

Carolina Academic Press, LLC
700 Kent Street
Durham, North Carolina 27701
Telephone (919) 489-7486
Fax (919) 493-5668
www.cap-press.com

Printed in the United States of America

To my mom, Betty

To my wife, Chris

To my children:
Seana, Bob, Alicia

To my grandchildren:
Fallyn, Max, Rory, William, Julia, Noah, Caroline, Eva, and baby Spence

To my honorary granddaughter, Sophia

And, to my great-great niece, Kyara

Contents

Acknowledgments

I am grateful to my research assistant Katja Wolf, LL.M., and to my administrative assistant Maria Vega, for their assistance.

The following entities and publications granted permission to reprint portions of previously-published material included in this book. I wish to thank them for the permission, and for their cooperation and assistance:

- Archdiocese of San Antonio, Texas
- The Journal of Catholic Social Thought
- The Scholar: St. Mary's Law Review on Race and Social Justice
- United States Conference of Catholic Bishops
- Albany Law Review
- Capital University Law Review
- Regent University Law Review

Catholic Legal Perspectives

Chapter 1

Introduction to the Sources of Law and Catholic Perspectives

A. Our Purpose

Catholic undergraduate and law schools often struggle with how to identify themselves as both Catholic institutions and institutions of higher learning. The concern is that in addition to the traditional learning experience at other institutions, Catholic schools should offer their students an opportunity to examine curricular material in light of Catholic teaching. This book affords the opportunity to examine our system of justice, identifying in several critical areas how Catholic principles and legal principles overlap and diverge.

Those who read this work whether they are lawyers, law students, undergraduate students or others, should be able to obtain an appreciation of both the law and the Catholic perspectives on that law. It is not expected or required that the reader agree, in every instance, with either the law or the Catholic perspectives. Nonetheless, the hope is that everyone who examines these materials will come away with an understanding of both. Critiques and responses regarding both the law and the Catholic perspectives are included throughout the book. Each chapter concludes with a "For Further Thought" section asking the reader to consider, apply, and examine the principles discussed in that chapter. Law students and lawyers are asked to reflect on whether these principles will, or should, affect their representation of clients, or the way judges should approach cases brought before them. This approach will offer some understanding of why a continuing interest and examination of these topics should be critical in Catholic institutions of higher learning.

Law students are very familiar with the sources of American law. They are able to identify statutes, case law, regulations, and other sources, and identify which are the most current and applicable. However, as law students are also aware, there is great divergence regarding whether particular principles are applicable in every instance, or to what extent. Major pronouncements of the Supreme Court of the United States carry important dissenting views, meaning that there is not absolute consensus on the law or its direction. It should come as no surprise that this is true in examining Catholic perspectives on the law as well.

B. Introduction to the Extent and Limits of Papal Infallibility

Many Catholics and non-Catholics alike lack an accurate understanding of the role of the Pope. While pronouncements by the Pope reflect the ultimate authority within the Catholic Church, not all such messages are delivered with the force of a mandatory interpretation.

It is critical from the outset to appreciate how misunderstandings of the role of the Pope and the Vatican have framed the American legal system's approach to Catholics and the Catholic Church. These misunderstandings are more than academic. They have resulted in horrific violence against Catholics. They continue to invite political attacks against the Pope and the Church. Moreover, the complicated treatment of the Vatican under domestic and international law has resulted in a need for the Church to utilize the services of very skilled legal talent. This author attempted to shed some light on these and related issues in an article published in 2015 by the Capital Law Review: *If the Pope is Infallible, Why Does He Need Lawyers?*[1] The article is reprinted in its entirety, maintaining its original footnotes.

IF THE POPE IS INFALLIBLE, WHY DOES HE NEED LAWYERS?

Bill Piatt*

"The Pope is not an oracle." Pope Benedict XVI[1]

I. Introduction

One of the most widely misunderstood teachings of the Catholic Church involves the doctrine of papal infallibility.[2] As a theological matter, papal infallibility is quite narrow. It does not mean the Pope cannot sin.[3] It does not mean the Pope cannot make errors in his administration of the Church. It does not mean the Pope cannot err during ordinary discussions of theological matters.[4] The widespread

---

1. Bill Piatt, *If the Pope is Infallible, Why Does He Need Lawyers?*, 43 Cap. U. L. Rev. 555 (2015). Copyright © 2015, Bill Piatt
  * Professor of law and former Dean (1998–2007), St. Mary's University School of Law. I would like to thank my research assistants, Sean Cohen and Jonathan Greiner. I would also like to thank Maria Vega for her clerical and technical assistance.
  1. John Thavis, The Vatican Diaries: A Behind-the-Scenes Look at the Power, Personalities and Politics at the Heart of the Catholic Church 305 (2014).
  2. *See* discussion *infra* Part II.
  3. *See* Bill Piatt, Catholic Legal Perspectives 3–5 (2d ed. 2014).
  4. *See id.*

misconception that all Catholics must believe their Pope cannot make mistakes helped create resentment against Catholics for centuries.[5] In the United States, this resentment took the form of physical attacks, political exclusion, and virulent anti-Catholic propaganda.[6] The next section of the article will examine the extent of such resentment.[7]

While the Catholic Church is no longer under direct physical attack, contemporaneous efforts seek to hold the Pope and the Church civilly and criminally liable in various contexts.[8] Most recently, sexual abuse allegations prompted domestic and international attempts to hold the Pope and his Church accountable to civil authorities.[9] Papal infallibility offers no insulation from these attempts.

Under some circumstances, however, the Pope acting as the head of the Catholic religion in implementing theological practices of the Catholic Church is afforded civil protection.[10] As will be discussed, these matters are extremely complicated. The Pope needs legal representation in these situations, particularly in light of the lingering resentment some hold against the papacy and the Vatican.

While invoking papal infallibility in theological matters provides limited insulation from private claims, another—legal—doctrine affords additional protection. That doctrine involves the "head of state" and related immunity against private civil claims recognized under international law.[11] Part III of this article will explore the efforts to hold the Pope liable for civil torts in the United States, and the application of this "head of state" immunity to these claims.[12]

What if the attempt to pursue an action against the Pope and Vatican is brought not by individual litigants in a civil arena, but rather, by another nation or body of nations against the nation-state that is the Vatican? It is apparent that the Pope needs counsel and representation in these arenas as well. Some international efforts directly challenge the religious teachings of the Church, even on a subject covered by a papal infallibility pronouncement.[13]

Who then provides the representation? And how are those attorneys selected? After examining the doctrine of papal infallibility, its political equivalent in the "head of

---

5. Robert Lockwood, *The Evolution of Anti-Catholicism in the United States*, *in* ANTI-CATHOLICISM IN AMERICAN CULTURE 15, 21 (Robert Lockwood ed., 2000).

6. *Id.* at 29.

7. *See* discussion *infra* Part II.A.

8. *The Catholic Church and Child Abuse: Looming Shadows*, ECONOMIST (May 17, 2014), http://www.economist.com/news/international/21602248-bid-hold-catholic-leadership-responsible-paedophile-priests-looming-shadows.

9. *Id.*

10. *See* discussion *infra* Part III.

11. *See* discussion *infra* Parts III.A, III.C.

12. *See* discussion *infra* Part III.C.

13. *See Vatican 'Must Immediately Remove' Child Abusers—UN*, BBC (Feb. 5, 2014 11:36 PM), http://www.bbc.com/news/world-europe-26044852.

state" immunity, and the unique status of the Holy See, an attempt will be made to identify those who provide—and will provide—the Pope with legal representation.[14] To do this, this Article will enter some murky areas of theology, politics, law, and sometimes plain old human bureaucracy and disorganization.

II. Papal Infallibility

A. *Some Historical Perspective and Resentment*

The first "murky" area, as promised in the Introduction, involves the history of the infallibility doctrine. As Brian Tierney, a noted historian has observed, the development of the doctrine of infallibility has a long, complicated, and contradictory background.[15] Adding to the complication is that "[t]here is no authoritative or agreed list of the infallible pronouncements made before 1870."[16]

One scholar, August Hasler, addressed the controversy surrounding the development of the dogma. He notes that supporters of papal infallibility within the Church argued that an infallible leader was necessary to prevent error in matters of faith and to prevent fragmentation.[17] Opponents argued that papal infallibility would create a double, and perhaps contradictory, infallibility of both the Church and Pope.[18] In any event, papal infallibility was not asserted by the Pope during the Church's first millennia.[19] It gradually came to be formally implemented as a response to both external and internal pressure challenging the authority of the Church.[20] Another scholar, Peter Chirico, argues that papal infallibility was adopted as a defensive posture by the Church to protect against threats from Protestants, atheists, and secularists.[21]

Regardless, the Catholic Church adopted the doctrine and enforced it from the mid-1300s.[22] The Church felt so strongly about this view that Martin Luther was excommunicated, in part, for his refusal to recant his assertion that neither Popes nor Church councils were infallible.[23] The refusal by Protestants thereafter to accept papal infallibility, even as it was widely misunderstood by Catholics and Protestants

---

14. *See* discussion *infra* Part IV.

15. Brian Tierney, Origins of Papal Infallibility, 1150–1350: A Study on the Concepts of Infallibility, Sovereignty and Tradition in the Middle Ages 273–81 (1972).

16. *Id.* at 3.

17. August Bernhard Hasler, How the Pope Became Infallible 172 (Peter Heinegg trans., 1981).

18. *Id.*

19. *Id.* at 8–9.

20. *Id.* at 38–44.

21. Peter Chirico, Infallibility: The Crossroads of Doctrine xiv (1983).

22. *See generally* Tierney, *supra* note 15.

23. Richard Marius, Luther 85 (1975). Luther elaborated on his objections to papal infallibility in Part II, Article IV of his "Smalcald Articles," published in 1537. *Available at* http://bookofconcord.org/smalcald.php (last visited Feb. 17, 2014).

alike, led to theological differences, legal disputes within the United States, and even to intense acts of violence within this country during the 1800s.[24]

Anti-Catholic resentment, based in large part on mistrust of the role of the Pope, found its way into the fabric of the American legal system. The framers of the Constitution sought to preserve religious liberties from actions of the federal government.[25] The Constitution of the United States guaranteed that "no religious Test shall ever be required as a Qualification to any Office or public Trust under the United States."[26] To further prohibit the federal government from infringing upon the religious liberties of its citizens, the First Amendment to the Constitution provided that "Congress shall make no law respecting an establishment of religion, or prohibiting the free exercise thereof."[27]

The religious liberty guaranteed by the First Amendment, however, initially operated as a limitation only on the action of the federal government and not of the states.[28] As a result, many of the overt and covert anti-Catholic provisions in the laws and constitutions of the states remained in effect well into the 19th century.[29] For example, until 1844, the New Jersey Constitution implicitly protected civil rights of Protestants but not Catholics:

> [N]o Protestant inhabitant of this colony shall be denied the enjoyment of any civil right merely on account of his religious principles, but that all persons professing a belief in the faith of any Protestant sect, who shall demean themselves peaceably under the government, as hereby established, shall be capable of being elected into any office of profit or trust, or being a member of either branch of the Legislature, and shall fully and freely enjoy every privilege and immunity enjoyed by others their fellow-subjects.[30]

New Jersey's Constitution was amended in 1844 to provide that: "no religious test shall be required as a qualification for any office or public trust; and no person shall be denied the enjoyment of any civil right merely on account of his religious principles."[31]

---

24. Lou Baldwin, *Pious Prejudice: Catholicism and the American Press Over Three Centuries, in* Anti-Catholicism in American Culture 55, 64 (Robert P. Lockwood ed., 2000).

25. *See* U.S. Const. amend. I.

26. U.S. Const. art. VI, cl. 3.

27. U.S. Const. amend. I.

28. *See* David Yassky, *Eras of the First Amendment*, 91 Colum. L. Rev. 1699, 1706, 1713 (1991).

29. *See* Richard W. Garnett, *The Theology of the Blaine Amendments*, 2 First Amend. L. Rev. 45 (2004).

30. *New Jersey—Catholic Encyclopedia*, Catholic Online, http://www.catholic.org/encyclopedia /view.php?id=8420 (last visited Mar. 2, 2015) (citations omitted) (referencing the Provincial Congress held at Burlington on July 2, 1776 and quoting the First Constitution of the State of New Jersey).

31. *See id.* (citations omitted) (indicating a proposed amendment to the Constitution, from a convention in Trenton, was ratified on 13 Aug. 13, 1844).

It was not until 1877 that New Hampshire allowed Catholics to hold office in that state.[32] A person of no less prominence than John Jay was able to include language in the New York Constitution prohibiting foreign-born Catholics from becoming citizens unless they would first "renounce all allegiance to the Pope in matters ecclesiastical."[33] This language remained in place until 1821.[34] Jay went on to serve as Chief Justice of the Supreme Court of the United States.[35]

The attempts to remove anti-Catholic provisions from state laws were hindered by the early Federalist Party.[36]

> [The early Federalists] strove to preserve the political ascendency of Protestantism in the States both by Federal legislation affecting the naturalization of emigrants and by preventing legislation in their respective States for the relief of Catholics from their religious disabilities, which was necessary to give effect to the liberal spirit and purpose of the Constitution.[37]

Even as the legal obstacles directed at Catholics began to be removed, or perhaps in part because of that action, resentment against Catholics and their allegiance to the Pope intensified in other areas.[38]

In addition to state-sanctioned resentment against Catholics, many newspapers were published in New England to warn about the "evils of Popery."[39] Catholics and the Pope were regularly denounced from the pulpit by Protestant preachers.[40] The angry anti-Catholic and anti-papacy rhetoric turned to violence.[41] Anti-Catholic rioting took place in 1844 in Philadelphia.[42] The Bishop of Philadelphia closed all Catholic churches on May 12, 1844 after St. Augustine's Church and St. Michael's Church were burned to the ground.[43] Protestants set fire to Catholic homes, and they shot and killed Catholics on their doorsteps.[44] Anti-Catholic fervor resulted in the creation of the "National Council of the United States of North America."[45] Members were sworn to secrecy and required to answer any inquiries about the organization

---

32. *New Hampshire — Catholic Encyclopedia*, Catholic Online, http://www.catholic.org /encyclopedia/view.php?id=8418 (last visited Mar. 2, 2015) (citations omitted).

33. *Knownotingism*, Catholic Encyclopedia, http://www.newadvent.org/cathen/08677a.htm (last visited Mar. 2, 2015).

34. *Id.*

35. *Id.*

36. *Id.*

37. *Id.* (quoting U.S. Catholic Historical Soc'y, Historical Records and Studies volume III 95 (1904)).

38. *Knownothingism, supra* note 33.

39. *Id.*

40. *Id.*

41. *Id.*

42. *Id.*

43. *Id.*

44. *Id.*

45. *Id.*

with: "I don't know."[46] As a result, the party came to be known as the "Knownothings."[47] Membership was only open to native-born Protestant citizens who were not married to a Catholic.[48] Knownothings were required by oath to "not vote, nor give your influence for any man for any office in the gift of the people, unless he be an American-born citizen, in favor of Americans ruling America, nor if he be a Roman Catholic."[49] As ridiculous as this oath might seem today, the activities of the Knownothings were effective and deadly serious.

By 1855, Knownothing governors held office in Connecticut, New Hampshire, and Rhode Island.[50] In December 1855, seventy-five Knownothing members were elected to the 35th Congress.[51] Their activities, however, were not limited to political endeavors.[52] In 1851, Knownothings attacked a convent in Providence, Rhode Island.[53] The civil authorities refused to provide assistance.[54] As a result, Bishop O'Reilly organized a contingent of Irish parishioners to physically protect the convent from attack.[55] Other attacks occurred in Cincinnati in 1853 and in Newark in 1854.[56] Houses of Irish Catholics were attacked as was St. Ann's Church in Manchester, New Hampshire in 1854.[57] A mob set fire to a church in Bath Maine.[58] Churches in Sydney and Massillon, Ohio were also attacked.[59] A church in Endorser, Massachusetts was destroyed.[60] Other attacks occurred in Norwalk, Connecticut and at the church of St. Peter and Paul in Brooklyn.[61]

In 1855, Knownothings agitated a crowd in Louisville to the extent that the ensuing riot — on August 5, 1855 — became known as bloody Monday.[62] Bishop Spalding wrote, "We have just passed through a reign of terror surpassed only by the Philadelphia riots. Nearly one hundred poor Irish have been butchered or burned and some twenty houses have been consumed in the flames. The City authorities, all

---

46. *Id.*
47. *Id.*
48. *Id.*
49. *Id.*
50. *Id.*
51. *See id.*
52. *Id.*
53. *Id.*
54. *Id.* The Knownothing attackers dispersed after finding the convent guarded by the Catholic defenders. *Id.*
55. *Id.*
56. *Id.*
57. *Id.*
58. *Id.*
59. *Id.*
60. *Id.*
61. *Id.*
62. *Id.*

Knownothings, looked calmly on and they are now endeavoring to lay the blame on the Catholics."[63]

One incident in particular highlights the resentment in this country against the Pope. In 1853, the Pope sent a papal "Nuncio" (representative) to the United States.[64] Hostile demonstrations against him, some including bloodshed, took place in Boston, Baltimore, St. Louis, Wheeling, and Cincinnati.[65] Some six hundred armed men marched to the cathedral in Cincinnati, intending to burn it, and to hang the Nuncio.[66] In this case, police acted to disperse the mob in an exchange of gunfire.[67]

The resentment and violence that Catholics, particularly Irish-American Catholics, experienced led many to have serious concerns about the nation to which they immigrated. During the war with Mexico, one group of Irish-American Catholic soldiers, seeing the destruction of the Catholic communities in Mexico by the United States, went over to the side of the enemy.[68] The St. Patrick's Battalion, as the group became known, fought with Mexican forces against the United States.[69] Ultimately, many of them were captured and executed as deserters.[70]

Eventually the Irish Catholic immigrants became assimilated. The Civil War placed other issues at the forefront. Many Irish Catholics enlisted in the armed forces of the United States during the Civil War,[71] and much of the anti-Catholic rhetoric and violence subsided.[72] Anti-Pope and anti-Catholic resentment, however, never completely went away.

B. *Contemporary View of Infallibility*

1. Vatican I's Explanation

On July 18, 1870 Vatican Council I formally announced the doctrine of infallibility:

> Therefore faithfully adhering to the tradition received from the beginning of the Christian faith, . . . We teach and define that it is a dogma divinely revealed: that the Roman Pontiff, when he speaks *ex cathedra*, that is, when in discharge of the office of Pastor and Doctor of all Christians, by virtue of his supreme Apostolic authority defines a doctrine regarding faith or

---

63. *Id.* (quoting J. L. SPALDING, The LIFE OF THE MOST REV. M. J. SPALDING, D.D. ARCHBISHOP OF BALTIMORE 185 (1873)).

64. *Id.*

65. *Id.*

66. *Id.*

67. *Id.*

68. Christopher Minster, *The Saint Patrick's Battalion*, ABOUT.COM, http://latinamericanhistory.about.com/od/Mexican-AmericanWar/a/The-Saint-Patricks-Battalion.htm (last visited Mar. 2, 2015).

69. *Id.*

70. *Id.*

71. *Knownothingism, supra* note 33.

72. *Id.*

morals to be held by the Universal Church, by the divine assistance promised to him in blessed Peter, is possessed of that infallibility with which the
divine Redeemer willed that His Church should be endowed for defining
doctrine regarding faith or morals: and that therefore such definitions of
the Roman Pontiff are irreformable of themselves, and not from the consent of the Church. (Vatican Council I, July 18, 180)[73]

While "[p]ronouncements by the Pope reflect the ultimate authority within the
Catholic Church[,] . . . [n]ot all such messages are delivered with the force of a mandatory interpretation. The *Catechism of the Catholic Church* (Catechism) offers this
summary:"[74]

891 "The Roman Pontiff, head of the college of bishops, enjoys this infallibility in virtue of his office, when, as supreme pastor and teacher of all the
faithful—who confirms his brethren in the faith—he proclaims by a definitive act a doctrine pertaining to faith or morals. . . . The infallibility promised to the Church is also present in the body of bishops when, together with
Peter's successor, they exercise the supreme Magisterium," above all in an
Ecumenical Council. When the Church through its supreme Magisterium
proposes a doctrine "for belief as being divinely revealed," and as the teaching of Christ, the definitions "must be adhered to with the obedience of
faith." This infallibility extends as far as the deposit of divine Revelation
itself.[75]

In other words, not every pronouncement of the pope is regarded as infallible.[76]
"A summary of the doctrine of papal infallibility, stamped under '*Nihil Obstat*' and
'*Imprimatur*,' including the teaching that it also belongs to the bishops within the
Church under some circumstances, is set forth at Catholic Answers."[77]

2. Vatican II's Explanation

Vatican II's explanation of the doctrine of infallibility is put best by a segment
which appears in "Catholic Answers" with an imprimatur by Bishop Robert H. Brom:

[A]lthough the individual bishops do not enjoy the prerogative of infallibility, they can nevertheless proclaim Christ's doctrine infallibly. This is
so, even when they are dispersed around the world, provided that while
maintaining the bond of unity among themselves and with Peter's successor, and while teaching authentically on a matter of faith or morals, they concur in a single viewpoint as the one which must be held conclusively. This

---

73. Tierney, *supra* note 15, at 1.
74. Bill Piatt, Catholic Legal Perspectives 4 (2d ed. 2014).
75. Catechism of the Catholic Church 235–36 (2d ed. 2001), *available at* http://www.usccb
.org/beliefs-and-teachings/what-we-believe/catechism/catechism-of-the-catholic-church/epub
/index.cfm.
76. *See id.*
77. Piatt, *supra* note 74, at 4.

authority is even more clearly verified when, gathered together in an ecumenical council, they are teachers and judges of faith and morals for the universal Church. Their definitions must then be adhered to with the submission of faith (Lumen Gentium 25).

Infallibility belongs in a special way to the pope as head of the bishops (Matt. 16:17–19; John 21:15–17). As Vatican II remarked, it is a charism the pope "enjoys in virtue of his office, when, as the supreme shepherd and teacher of all the faithful, who confirms his brethren in their faith (Luke 22:32), he proclaims by a definitive act some doctrine of faith or morals. Therefore his definitions, of themselves, and not from the consent of the Church, are justly held irreformable, for they are pronounced with the assistance of the Holy Spirit, an assistance promised to him in blessed Peter."

The infallibility of the pope is not a doctrine that suddenly appeared in Church teaching; rather, it is a doctrine which was implicit in the early Church. It is only our understanding of infallibility which has developed and been more clearly understood over time. In fact, the doctrine of infallibility is implicit in these Petrine texts: John 21:15–17 ("Feed my sheep . . ."), Luke 22:32 ("I have prayed for you that your faith may not fail"), and Matthew 16:18 ("You are Peter . . .").[78]

Under what circumstances are such pronouncements issued? "An infallible pronouncement—whether made by the pope alone or by an ecumenical council—usually is made only when some doctrine has been called into question. Most doctrines have never been doubted by the large majority of Catholics."[79] A complete explanation of the doctrine can be found in the Decree of the First Vatican Council.[80] And, a very understandable approach to the issue is that of Dr. Jeffrey Mirus, a contributor to EWTN.[81]

There is some confusion among Catholics and non-Catholics alike regarding the issue of papal infallibility. Some important considerations, as explained on the "Catholic Answers" website,[82] include the realities that infallibility does not mean that the Pope cannot sin.[83] It is not a charism exclusively belonging to the Pope; it also resides in the body of bishops (but not individual bishops).[84] Popes may disagree with each

---

78. Robert H. Brom, *Papal Infallibility*, Catholic Answers (Aug. 10, 2004), http://www.catholic.com/tracts/papal-infallibility.

79. *Id.*

80. Decrees of the Ecumenical Councils (*Conciliorum oecumenicorum decreta*), vol. 2, First Vatican Council, Session IV, Jul. 18, 1870-First Dogmatic Constitution on the Church of Christ, Ch. 4, 812–16 (Norman P. Tanner, SJ ed., 1990), *available at* http://www.papalencyclicals.net/Councils/ecum20.htm#SESSION (last visited May 18, 2015).

81. Jeffrey Mirus, *Papal Infallibility*, EWTN, http://www.ewtn.com/faith/teachings/papac2.htm (last visited May 18, 2015).

82. *See* Brom, *supra* note 78.

83. *See id.*

84. *Id.*

other on unofficial announcements concerning morals and faith without violating the infallibility doctrine because that doctrine only applies to the formal, official teachings of the Church.[85] Similarly, the doctrine does not preclude Popes from disagreeing with each other on disciplinary decisions.[86] The doctrine does not mean that the Pope automatically knows the "truth" regarding a theological matter, he must learn what is true through study, reflection and prayer — the same way his fellow members of the Church do.[87] As Pope, with the ability to consult with the bishops of the Church and role as the head of the Church, he has a distinct advantage. Moreover, Catholics teach that the Pope is precluded from officially teaching error by the Holy Spirit.[88]

> According to Father John Leies, it is relatively simple to identify statements issued under the infallibility doctrine. Those statements, which are relatively rare, are issued under a heading of "solemn form" or "*ex cathedra*," literally "from the chair." They are issued only by ecumenical councils or by the Pope after communion with the bishops. Vatican I issued only one and it is the infallibility doctrine itself. That decree was presented on July 18, 1870. . . . [89]

There have been very few such pronouncements. An important pronouncement, relevant to Part III, involves the issue of abortion.[90] On March 25, 1995, Pope John Paul II announced: "I declare that direct abortion, that is, abortion willed as an end or as a means, always constitutes a grave moral disorder, since it is the deliberate killing of an innocent human being."[91]

C. *Anti-Catholic/Anti-Pope Rhetoric Continues*

The resentment against the misunderstood role of the Pope and his Church continues in the United States. According to Robert P. Lockwood, "[Anti-Catholicism] is not only America's most persistent prejudice but also it's most accepted."[92] "Anti-Catholicism is deeply embedded in the fabric of America — so much so that Harvard historian Arthur Schlesinger, Sr., once termed it 'the deepest bias in the history of the American people.'"[93] Rick Hinshaw observed:

> Not a day goes by that the Catholic League is not confronted by ridicule of Catholic practices, defamation of that which Catholics hold sacred, and even

---

85. *Id.*
86. *Id.*
87. *Id.*
88. *Id.*
89. PIATT, *supra* note 74, at 5.
90. POPE JOHN PAUL II, EVANGELIUM VITAE: ON THE VALUE AND INVIOLABILITY OF HUMAN LIFE 63 (Mar. 25, 1995), *available at* http://www.catholic-pages.com/documents/evangelium_vitae.pdf.
91. *Id.* at 63, 108.
92. Robert P. Lockwood, *Introduction, in* ANTI-CATHOLICISM IN AMERICAN CULTURE 5, 5 (Robert P. Lockwood ed., 2000).
93. Rick Hinshaw, *Anti-Catholicism Today, in* ANTI-CATHOLICISM IN AMERICAN CULTURE 89, 89 (Robert P. Lockwood ed., 2000).

blatant challenges to the basic rights of Catholics in America. Moreover — even as social pressures and government regulations are aggressively employed to extinguish other expressions of hate — anti-Catholic bigotry is defended and even celebrated as a legitimate exercise of free speech.[94]

A study of the coverage of matters related to the Catholic Church by national media outlets concludes: "On most controversies involving Catholic teachings, the Church came out on the losing side of the issue debate reported in the media."[95] "[L]ong-term trends in the coverage have been unfavorable to the Church. Over time, official Church teachings were reported less frequently and were challenged more often when they did appear."[96] In Andrew M. Greeley's book *An Ugly Little Secret*, he discusses unexposed prejudice in American life that is termed "Anti-Catholic nativism."[97]

In his book, *The New Anti-Catholicism*, Philip Jenkins points out the anti-Catholicism which arose after September 11, 2001:

> [P]olitical leaders, the mass media, and civil liberties groups allied to resist attacks on Islam. Any public remark suggesting that Islam was intrinsically connected with violence and terrorism was deemed racist, prejudiced, and unacceptable, while sporadic assaults on Muslim institutions met with widespread condemnation. As with anti-Semitism, public opinion was expected to reject any attempt to denounce a religion on the grounds of the misdeeds of some of its members. Commonly, this kind of bigotry is seen as a fundamental betrayal of American values. . . . Ironically, the September massacres resulted in some remarkable tirades not against the religion of Islam but against Catholicism, though the actual Catholic linkage to the attacks was nonexistent. In the *New York Press*, Michelangelo Signorile somehow used Islamist fanatic Osama bin Laden as a means of denouncing "the gay-bashing Pope." John Paul, too, was "another omnipotent religious zealot, one who equally condemns us Western sinners and incites violence with his incendiary rhetoric. . . . [The Pope was a] Christian fundamentalist extraordinaire and a man who inspires thugs across the globe who commit hate crimes against homosexuals, a form of terrorism if the ever was one. Signorile later included the Catholic cardinals among the religious right who constituted "the real American Taliban."[98]

The Pope bashing continues, even by respected media outlets and Presidential advisors. As noted below, in Part III.B, misunderstandings and ignorance of the

---

94. *Id.*

95. Linda S. Lichter et al., *Media Coverage of the Catholic Church — Executive Summary, 1991 Report, in* Anti-Catholicism in American Culture 151, 152 (Robert P. Lockwood ed., 2000).

96. *Id.* at 153.

97. Andrew M. Greeley, An Ugly Little Secret: Anti-Catholicism in North America 2 (1977).

98. Philip Jenkins, The New Anti-Catholicism: The Last Acceptable Prejudice 9 (2003).

Church's position regarding the use of condoms led a New York Times editorial in 2009 to announce that the Pope "deserves no credence when he distorts scientific findings."[99] Harry Knox, who soon thereafter became an advisor to President Obama, claimed that the Pope was "hurting people in the name of Jesus."[100] The internet is replete with attacks on the Pope and his infallibility.[101] The vitriol that continues to be directed at the Pope is reminiscent of the rhetoric of the "Knownothings."

III. "Head of State" (What State?) Immunity

A. *Church, State, or Both?*

Is the Pope the head of a nation, a religion, or both? The answers produce significant legal consequences. If the Pope qualifies as a head of state, he is immune from civil liability[102] and effectively becomes "infallible" in a very real, legal sense. Those seeking to hold him and his Church liable in a civil or criminal court see a structure that is different from the view that the Pope urges courts and the United Nations to adopt.[103] First, consider what visitors to the Vatican observe.

On a trip to Rome during the summer of 2014, my wife and I stayed at a beautiful little hotel almost directly across the street from the entrance to the Vatican Museum. From our third floor vantage point, we could observe the hustle below as tourists lined up to wait for up to several hours to enter the vast museum. Those pilgrims who preferred not to wait in the long lines outside could pay a "skip the line" guide who could lead them directly to the entrance. Once inside, however, there was no skipping the crush of tourists moving slowly from room to room through some of the most interesting collections in the world. This hustle produces some very real benefits to the Vatican and is critical to its functioning. Most of the operating revenue of the Vatican government is derived from those fees and sales at the museum (and presumably from a portion of the "skip the line" fees collected by the guides).[104] The rest of the cost of governance is generated by the other minor commercial ventures including the sale of postage, coins, and from the sales in the Vatican stores.[105] (For obvious reasons, I hesitate to comment upon the profit that might be earned by the Vatican's money exchange, located within the gift shop area.)

There were also vendors gathered outside the entrance offering scarves, religious items, hats, t-shirts, and other items to the tourists. During the heat of the day, cold

---

99. *See* Thavis, *supra* note 1, at 257.

100. *Id.*

101. *See, e.g.*, Rand Winburn, *Lechery in the Church of Rome Exposed*, Iconbusters.com, http://www.iconbusters.com/iconbusters/htm/sex_crimes/sex_crimes.html (last visited Mar. 3, 2015); Peter De Rosa, *The Hillarious History of Papal Infallibility*, Jesuswouldbefurious.com, http://jesuswouldbefurious.org/Catholic/papalinfallibility.html (last visited Mar. 3, 2015).

102. *See* Philip Pullella, *Pope Immunity: Vatican Will Protect Benedict from Sexual Abuse Prosecution*, Huffington Post (Feb. 17, 2013, 10:10PM), http://www.huffingtonpost.com/2013/02/17/pope-immunity_n_2708518.html.

103. *Id.*

104. *See* Thavis, *supra* note 1, at 120.

105. *Id.*

bottles of water were a big seller. The pace was frenetic, and the money quickly changed hands. The walls of the Vatican loomed above the pilgrims and hawkers. Behind those walls — in what are now the Vatican Gardens — the emperor Nero once held magnificent parties, lighting the outdoor events with the bodies of Christians burning on high poles.[106] St. Peter was crucified here.[107] A basilica was built in 329 AD by the Emperor Constantine, and it was expanded into what is now St. Peter's basilica in the 1500s.[108] But the building of the new Cathedral was not without tremendous cost. Martin Luther objected to the raising of money from the poor, particularly by the selling of indulgences, to build a vast cathedral and was subsequently excommunicated.[109]

St. Peter's Cathedral is magnificent; the surrounding walls and gardens are beautiful; and the Museum contains a trove of historical collections. It is not the architecture, the collections, nor even the secular history that draws millions of visitors to this tiny enclave in the middle of Rome each year. It is tiny — we ran around the entire Vatican City, which consists of less than 109 acres,[110] in fifteen minutes or so. Rather, the fact that it is the seat of the Pope and of the Catholic Church, that accounts for the draw.[111] So is this beautiful little enclave a nation, or just the headquarters of a religion? Is the Pope only a spiritual leader, albeit of a billion people, or is he also the sovereign head of a state? As one might imagine, the answers to these questions carry significant legal and international consequences. The Pope's lawyers press for an interpretation and characterization that most benefits the Church in any given situation, while his detractors and their lawyers take the opposite approach in trying to pry financial and political concessions from him.

How is the Vatican viewed by other observers? One organization, "Catholics for Choice," is very much opposed to the church's position on abortion.[112] Undoubtedly, this perspective influences the way that organization views the legal categorization of the Pope and Church. In its publication *The Catholic Church at the United Nations: Church or State?*, Catholics for Choice argue that none of the three entities known as Vatican City, the Holy See, or the Roman Catholic Church fulfills the requirements for being characterized as a nation.[113] This same organization argues the

---

106. FLORENCE EDYTHE BLAKE-HEDGES, THE STORY OF THE CATACOMBS, 34–35 (1909).

107. *History*, VATICAN CITY STATE, http://www.vaticanstate.va/content/vaticanstate/en/monumenti/basilica-di-s-pietro/storia.paginate.1.html (last visited Mar. 3, 2015).

108. *Id.*

109. *See* WORKS OF MARTIN LUTHER 29–38 (Adolph Spaeth et al. trans. & eds., 1915), *available at* http://bookofconcord.org/95theses.php.

110. *See* CATHOLICS FOR CHOICE, THE CATHOLIC CHURCH AT THE UNITED NATIONS: CHURCH OR STATE? 2 (2013), *available at* http://www.catholicsforchoice.org/topics/politics/documents/CFC_See_Change_2013.pdf.

111. Stephanie Rosenbloom, *How to See the New Pope in Rome*, N.Y. TIMES, Apr. 23, 2013, http://www.nytimes.com/2013/04/28/travel/how-to-see-the-new-pope-in-rome.html?_r=0.

112. *Abortion*, CATHOLICS FOR CHOICE, http://www.catholicsforchoice.org/topics/abortion/default.asp (last visited May 12, 2015).

113. CATHOLICS FOR CHOICE, *supra* note 110, at 2.

temporal government of the Church is referred to as the Holy See.[114] The Holy See includes the Pope and the Roman Curia (administrative entity of the Vatican and the Church).[115] Catholics for Choice further identifies Vatican City as the "temporal location of both the Holy See and the headquarters of the Roman Catholic Church."[116]

Catholics for Choice argue that none of these entities can be considered a state under the United Nations' requirements for a state,[117] as defined in the Montevideo Convention on the Rights and Duties of States, Article 1. That Convention requires that a state have a defined territory.[118] It requires that a state have a government, ability to enter into relations with other states, and a permanent population.[119] The organization notes that the population of Vatican City is less than 600 citizens, mostly employees, and Vatican City citizenship terminates when a citizen moves out of its confines.[120] It notes that unlike most other countries, Vatican City citizenship is not obtained by being born in the territory or by inheritance.[121] Catholics for Choice argue that as a result, Vatican City should not be allowed to participate in the United Nations as a state.[122]

The United Nations, however, takes a different view. In April 1964, the Holy See was designated a Nonmember State Permanent Observer to the United Nations by then United Nations Secretary General U Thant.[123] Since 2004, the Holy See has been able to intervene in debates at the U.N., circulate its documents to members, and engage in formal replies.[124] The Holy See indicates it does not want full member status because it would not want to participate in the military defense obligations required of members.[125]

The Holy See became a Permanent Observer at the Organization of America States in 1978 and a full member of the World Trade Organization in 1997.[126] The Catholics for Choice publication contains an extensive history of the international involvement of the Vatican, including the fixation of its current territory through its 1870 agreement with Italy.[127] Catholics for Choice argues that no other religion has the status of a state.[128] It believes its own church—the Catholic Church—should not either, but its conclusions seem more oriented toward the goal of depriving the

---

114. *Id.*
115. *Id.*
116. *Id.* at 2.
117. *Id.*
118. *Id.*
119. *Id.*
120. *Id.*
121. *Id.*
122. *Id.* at 21.
123. *Id.* at 5.
124. *Id.*
125. *Id.* at 4.
126. *Id.* at 5.
127. *Id.*
128. *Id.* at 4.

Catholic Church of an international forum to present its religious views, including its teaching that abortion is a moral wrong.[129]

How does the American legal system view the status of these three entities? The United States Court of Appeals for the Second Circuit concluded in 2013: "The Vatican State is the territory over which the Holy See of the Roman Catholic Church exercises sovereignty."[130] For purposes of the Foreign Sovereign Immunities Act (FSIA),[131] discussed below, courts determined the Holy See is to be treated as a foreign sovereign.[132] Some commentators and critics struggle with these characterizations, but it is clear that for both domestic and international law purposes the Holy See is a recognized sovereign nation—albeit a tiny one.[133] Although its physical size is small, the one billion adherents to the Catholic faith worldwide[134] substantiate its role as a nation.

B. *Governance and Confusion*

Just because the Holy See is a nation, however, does not mean that its governance is similar to that of any other country. While the Pope is the head of the Church, his role, the roles of the Cardinals, and the roles of those in the administration of the Vatican are often operating in an unusually disjointed fashion.[135] One commentator identifies, "an amazing lack of internal communication and coordination in the Roman Curia, which operates more as a network of jealous bureaucratic enclaves than as a cohesive force in the church's evangelizing mission."[136] Thavis makes this point by identifying many situations where this is the case.[137] One in particular, involving the Church's position on the use of condoms, illustrates not only the bureaucratic murkiness but the external misperceptions and misrepresentations of the Pope's views by the press.[138]

Thavis notes that as of 2003, despite the public impression, no pope, speaking on behalf of the church, "had ever indicated that using condoms to prevent AIDS was morally wrong, . . . the . . . Catechism of the Catholic Church was silent on the matter and . . . the whole question remained a gray area."[139] Some Cardinals were quoted as stating the use of condoms was inherently wrong,[140] those position statements were misunderstood by the press to represent the position of the entire Church.[141]

---

129. *Id.* at 11.

130. MAGI XXI, Inc. v. Stato Della Citta Del Vaticano, 714 F.3d 714, 718 (2d Cir. 2013).

131. Foreign Sovereign Immunities Act of 1976, Pub. L. No. 94-583, 90 Stat. 2891 (codified as amended in scattered sections of 28 U.S.C.).

132. *See MAGI XXI*, 714 F.3d at 718; Doe v. Holy See, 557 F.3d 1066, 1098 (9th Cir. 2009); O'Bryan v. Holy See, 556 F.3d 361, 369 (6th Cir. 2009).

133. *MAGI XXI*, 714 F.3d at 718; *Doe*, 557 F.3d at 1098; *O'Bryan*, 556 F.3d at 369.

134. CATHOLICS FOR CHOICE, *supra* note 110, at 2.

135. *See* THAVIS, *supra* note 1, at 5.

136. *Id.* at 4.

137. *See id.* at 4–6.

138. *Id.* at 251–60.

139. *Id.* at 252.

140. *Id.* at 252–54.

141. *Id.* at 252.

In 2009, Pope Benedict took a trip to Africa.[142] Meeting with the press on the flight, he fielded a question about whether the Church's position on AIDS was "unrealistic and ineffective."[143] In a relatively lengthy response, the Pope stated that distributing condoms makes the problem worse without a spiritual dimension.[144] The Pope, admittedly, never addressed the issue of whether the use of condoms to prevent the spread of disease was immoral. Nonetheless, journalists ran headlines worldwide attacking the Pope for banning condoms.[145] For example, a New York Times editorial severely criticized him by stating the Pope "deserves no credence when he distorts scientific findings."[146] Harry Knox, who soon thereafter became an advisor to President Obama, claimed that the Pope was "hurting people in the name of Jesus."[147] Meanwhile, the Pope's public relations officials within his Secretariat of State attempted to clarify the Pope's remarks.[148] They cited Edward C. Green of the Harvard Center for Population in Development Studies, who reported that "the best evidence we have supports the pope's comments" in that condoms led to riskier behavior involving multiple partners.[149]

In 2010, Pope Benedict again criticized overreliance on the use of condoms to stop HIV/AIDS.[150] He did note, however, that under some circumstances the use of a condom might actually be the morally correct action.[151] A sexual transaction involving a prostitute was one example.[152] The Pope was asked, "Are you saying, then, that the Catholic Church is actually not opposed in principle to the use of condoms?"[153] Pope Benedict responded: "She of course does not regard it as a real or moral solution, but, in this or that case, there can be nonetheless, in the intention of reducing the risk of infection, a first step in a movement toward a different way, a more human way, of living sexuality."[154] The Pope was repeating what his own theologians quietly concluded for years in internal discussions that had not filtered out of the Vatican.[155] Liberals praised the "change" in the Church's position.[156] Conservatives condemned it.[157] What started as a theological work in progress within the Vatican

---

142. *Id.* at 256.

143. *Id.*

144. *Id.*

145. *Id.*; *Pope Visits Africa, Reaffirms Ban on Condoms*, CNN (Mar. 18, 2009), http://edition.cnn.com/2009/WORLD/africa/03/17/cameroon.pope.index.html?iref=topnews.

146. Thavis, *supra* note 1, at 257 (quoting Editorial, *The Pope on Condoms and AIDS*, N.Y. Times, Mar. 18, 2009, at A26).

147. *Id.*

148. *Id.*

149. *Id.* at 258.

150. *Id.*

151. *Id.*

152. *Id.*

153. *Id.*

154. *Id.*

155. *Id.* at 259.

156. *Id.*

157. *Id.*

became an illustration of the murkiness inherent within the workings of the church, the misunderstandings of the pronouncements by some church officials, and even the misunderstanding of the role of the Pope.

C. *Attempts to Hold the Holy See Liable in the Sex Abuse Scandal*

Over the last two decades, the Catholic Church within the United States witnessed a scandal involving the sexual abuse of children by its priests along with the alleged cover ups of those wrongful activities by bishops and other church officials.[158] The extent of these horrible acts has led various archdioceses, dioceses, religious orders, and individuals to pay out more than $3 billion in judgments and settlements over the last few years.[159] The largest of these include the Diocese of Los Angeles ($660 million, 2007), San Diego (approximately $200 million, 2007), Oregon Province of Jesuits (approximately $150 million, 2011), Orange County, California ($100 million, 2004), and Boston (approximately $85 million, 2003).[160] In these cases, the defendants were represented by counsel selected by the Archdioceses, the religious orders, and their insurers.[161]

In addition to the pursuit of these cases against individual priests, bishops, and archdioceses within the United States, plaintiffs sought to pursue actions against the Pope himself.[162] A judgment against the Pope and the Holy See would produce a deeper pocket for recovery, and it would have a much greater impact upon the Church itself. Litigants, thus far, have encountered the obstacle of the Foreign Sovereign Immunities Act (FSIA).[163] That act grants foreign sovereigns immunity from liability and also from the jurisdiction of courts in the United States.[164] The Holy See is considered to be a foreign state under the FSIA.[165] The Holy See cannot be sued under the FSIA even if plaintiffs allege that it is acting as a non-sovereign association or as the head of an international religious organization.[166]

The FSIA does allow, however, for jurisdiction of American courts over the Holy See under certain narrow exceptions set out in 28 U.S.C. § 1605(a).[167] One important exception, relevant in the sex abuse liability cases, precludes immunity in cases

---

158. *Sexual Abuse by U.S. Catholic Clergy Settlements and Monetary Awards in Civil Suits*, BishopAccountability.org, http://www.bishop-accountability.org/settlements/ (last visited Mar. 3, 2015).

159. *Id.*

160. *Id.*

161. Jack Hammel, *The Role of the Diocesan In-House Counsel Attorney*, *in* Restoring Trust: A Pastoral Response to Sexual Abuse 1–2 (1994), *available at* http://www.bishopaccountability .org/reports/1994_11_NCCB_Restoring_Trust/rt94_complete_optimized.pdf.

162. Luiza Oleszczuk, *Sex Abuse Victims Sue Pope at International Criminal Court*, CP World (Sep. 14, 2011, 12:01 AM), http://www.christianpost.com/news/sex-abuse-victims-sue-pope-at -international-criminal-court-55563/.

163. *See* 28 U.S.C. § 1602 (2012).

164. § 1604.

165. O'Bryan v. Holy See, 556 F.3d 361, 373 (6th Cir. 2008).

166. *Id.*

167. *See* 28 U.S.C. § 1605(a) (2012).

where "money damages are sought against a foreign state for personal injury . . . occurring in the United States and caused by the tortious act or omission of that foreign state or of any official or employee of that foreign state while acting within the scope of his office or employment."[168] The foreign sovereign retains its immunity if the tortious act was either "based upon the exercise or performance or the failure to exercise or perform a discretionary function."[169]

In the *O'Bryan* case, plaintiffs relied on a 1962 Policy of the Holy See requiring bishops to impose secrecy on the handling of sexual abuse allegations.[170] According to the plaintiffs, the policy was secret until 2003.[171] The *O'Bryan* court held that the promulgation of the Policy occurred abroad, and therefore, the claim against the Holy See could not proceed under the FSIA.[172] While the claim would not survive against the Holy See for its own failures to warn or report (which would have occurred abroad),[173] the claim against the Holy See for tortious supervisory conduct by its employees in the U.S. would fall within the exception to the FSIA, and it would, therefore, be within the jurisdiction of a U.S. court.[174] The case was eventually dismissed.[175]

In another case, *Doe v. Holy See*,[176] the Ninth Circuit held that there was no jurisdiction over the Holy See for negligent hiring and retention of an allegedly abusive priest under the discretionary acts exception to the FSIA.[177] However, the Court determined that the Holy See would not be immune from a tort claim where the allegation was that the priest was an "employee" of a foreign state acting within the scope of his employment.[178] The case was remanded to the trial court where discovery was limited.[179] A more recent decision, however, prevented the federal judiciary from reviewing a determination by the Holy See regarding whether someone is or is not a member of a religious order within the Roman Catholic Church.[180]

Other barriers to bringing an action against the pope, or the Vatican are also in place. In a matter unrelated to the sex abuse allegations against the Holy See, the 7th Circuit ruled that the FSIA does not apply to heads of states.[181] Any immunity to be granted to such a head of state relies upon the determination of such by the

---

168. § 1605(a)(5).
169. § 1605(a)(5)(A).
170. *O'Bryan*, 556 F.3d at 370.
171. *Id.*
172. *Id.* at 387.
173. *Id.* at 388.
174. *Id.*
175. Jacob William Neu, *"Workers of God": The Holy See's Liability for Clerical Sexual Abuse*, 63 Vand. L. Rev. 1507, 1518 (2010).
176. 557 F.3d 1066 (9th Cir. 2009).
177. *Id.* at 1069.
178. *Id.* at 1083.
179. *See* Doe v. Holy See, No. CV 02-430-MO, 2011 WL 1541275, at *1 (D. Or. Apr. 21, 2011).
180. McCarthy v. Fuller, 714 F.3d 971, 978 (7th Cir. 2013).
181. Ye v. Zemin, 383 F.3d 620, 625 (7th Cir. 2004).

Executive Branch of the U.S. government.[182] Yet, it is difficult to see a set of circumstances where an American President would waive this immunity and allow an action to proceed against the Pope. And in a case where victims of crimes committed during World War II sued, among others, the Vatican Bank and the Franciscan Order — alleging that those entities collaborated with the Nazis in depriving them of their property, the Ninth Circuit declined to hear the case.[183] The Ninth Circuit determined that those claims were non-justiciable political questions given the war power was vested in the President and Executive Branch, and courts could not intrude on policy determinations made by the Executive not to prosecute those defendants.[184] It appears the Pope is not always infallible, but the Pope is very likely going to continue to remain immune from American judicial proceedings.

The obstacles for litigants in the sex abuse matters caused a reaction against the notion of granting any immunity to the Holy See and the Pope.[185] Criticism originated from both outside and within the Church. Catholics for Choice explicitly call for removing the Holy See's and Pope's recognition as a nation sovereign.[186] Indeed, Catholics for Choice even allude to the imposition of criminal responsibility on the Pope.[187]

D. International Action Against the Vatican

The role of the Holy See as a nation, with the Pope as its head, is a double-edged sword for the Church. As a nation, the Holy See signed onto treaties of the United Nations protecting children and against torture.[188] Both of these treaties require reports from its signatories regarding implementation of the treaties.[189] In 2013, United Nations Committee on the Rights of the Child publicized the Vatican's alleged

---

182. *See id.*

183. Alperin v. Vatican Bank, 410 F.3d 532, 538, 562 (9th Cir. 2005).

184. *Id.* at 559.

185. *See* Neu, *supra* note 175, at 1508; Dina Aversano, Comment, *Can the Pope Be a Defendant in American Courts? The Grant of Head of State Immunity and the Judiciary's Role to Answer this Question*, 18 PACE INT'L L. REV. 495, 496 (2006); Geoffrey Robertson, *Put the Pope in the Dock*, GUARDIAN (Apr. 2, 2010, 3:30 PM), http://www.theguardian.com/commentisfree/libertycentral/2010/apr/02/pope-legal-immunity-international-law; Philip Pullella, *Pope Will Have Security, Immunity by Remaining in the Vatican*, REUTERS (Feb. 15, 2013, 1:59 PM), http://www.reuters.com/article/2013/02/15/us-pope-resignation-immunity-idUSBRE91E0ZI20130215; Eamonn McCann, *Why the Vatican's Diplomatic Immunity Days Are Numbered*, BELEFAST TELEGRAPH (Sept. 8, 2010), http://www.belfasttelegraph.co.uk/opinion/columnists/eamonn-mccann/why-the-vaticans-diplomatic-immunity-days-are-numbered-28557346.html; Lucian C. Martinez, Jr., *Sovereign Impunity: Does the Foreign Sovereign Immunities Act Bar Lawsuits Against the Holy See in Clerical Sexual Abuse Cases?*, 44 TEX. INT'L L.J. 123, 123 (2008).

186. *See* CATHOLICS FOR CHOICE, *supra* note 110, at 19, 21.

187. *See id.* at 18.

188. Convention on the Rights of the Child, G.A. Res. 44/25, U.N. Doc. A/RES/44/25 (Nov. 20, 1989), *available at* http://www.ohchr.org/Documents/ProfessionalInterest/crc.pdf.

189. Meredith Somers, *U.N. Finally gets Action . . . from the Pope as Vatican Forced to Reveal Punishment for Pedophiles*, WASH. TIMES, May 6, 2014, http://www.washingtontimes.com/news/2014/may/6/vatican-reveals-punishments-pedophile-priests-firs/?page=all.

violations of the U.N. Convention on the Rights of the Child.[190] In addition to requiring the Vatican to provide "detailed information on all cases of child sexual abuse committed by members of the clergy, brothers and nuns," the Vatican was requested to identify how it was responding to perpetrators and victims of abuse; the Vatican was required to report on other matters related to the scandal.[191]

In May 2014, the Vatican provided details regarding how it addressed the issue of child sexual abuse.[192] Since 2004, the Vatican identified more than 3,400 sexual abuse cases.[193] Eight hundred forty-eight priests were expelled, and 2,572 clergy members received other sanctions according to Archbishop Silvano Tomasi, who serves as the permanent Observer of the Vatican to the United Nations.[194] The Vatican also promised that it would learn from these mistakes.[195] By doing so, it likely opened itself to additional civil liability under the anti-torture and child protection treaties of the United Nations.[196] Prior to 2010, the Vatican did not require its bishops to report abuse to civil authorities.[197] According to Tomasi, that policy changed.[198]

The United Nations Committee on the Rights of the Child also criticized the Catholic Church's prohibition regarding abortion, birth control, premarital sex, and its stand on homosexuality.[199] The Committee stated:

> 55. The Committee urges the Holy See to review its position on abortion, which places obvious risks on the life and health of pregnant girls, and to amend Canon 1398 relating to abortion with a view to identifying circumstances under which access to abortion services may be permitted.[200]

Recall that the prohibition against abortion was issued as an *ex cathedra* pronouncement, under the full weight of the Church's infallibility doctrine, as noted above in part I of this article.[201] Thus, the U.N. Committee chose to directly challenge the position of the Pope and the Catholic Church on a religious matter of deep import and concern to the Church.[202] That action led the Vatican to counterattack with the

---

190. *U.N. Asks Vatican to Account for Every Abuse Allegation it has Received*, Catholic Herald, July 12, 2013, http://www.catholicherald.co.uk/news/2013/07/12/un-asks-vatican-to-account-for-every-abuse-allegation-it-has-received.

191. *Id.*

192. *See* Somers, *supra* note 189.

193. *Id.*

194. *Id.*

195. *Id.*

196. *Id.*

197. *Id.*

198. *Id.*

199. Comm. on the Rights of the Child, Concluding Observations on the Second Report of the Holy See adopted at its 65th Sess., Jan. 13–31, 2014, ¶ 55, Doc. CRC/C/VAT/CO/2 (Feb. 24, 2014), *available at* http://tbinternet.ohchr.org/Treaties/CRC/Shared%20 Documents/VAT/CRC_C_VAT _CO_2_16302_E.pdf.

200. *Id.*

201. Pope John Paul II, *supra* note 90.

202. *See id.*

assertion that the United Nations was violating its own religious freedom guarantees as set forth in the Universal Declaration of Human Rights by the United Nations.[203] The Vatican stated, "[t]he Holy See takes note of the concluding observations . . . which will be submitted to a thorough study and examination . . . according to international law and practice."[204] However, it added that the Church "regrets to see in some points of the concluding observations an attempt to interfere with Catholic Church teaching on the dignity of human person and in the exercise of religious freedom," and the Church "reiterates its commitment to defending and protecting the rights of the child . . . according to the moral and religious values offered by Catholic doctrine."[205]

In an Op-Ed piece published in the New York Times on February 11, 2014, Paul Valley noted that contrary to the implications of the United Nations report, the Vatican took "significant steps" to address the scandal.[206] For example, the Vatican insisted, since 2001, that all child abuse matters be handled in Rome.[207] By 2010, however, Pope Benedict changed this position and ordered dioceses to "report suspect priest to the police and order local bishops to draw up new guidelines to protect children."[208] Valley believes that the attempt by the U.N. Committee to attack Church doctrine was a mistake because it takes the focus away from the abuse scandal and might tend to make some Vatican insiders attempt to circle the wagons against external pressures to combat the horrors of child abuse.[209]

The attention this scandal garnered is unlikely to recede. Among the 400,000 priests and 5,000 bishops serving the 1.196 billion Catholics worldwide, approximately 400 abuse cases are being reported to and handled by the Vatican each year.[210] The attempts by Catholics for Choice and others to remove the Vatican's recognition

---

203. Article 2 of Universal Declaration of Human Rights provides: "Everyone is entitled to all the rights and freedoms set forth in this Declaration, without distinction of any kind, such as race, colour, sex, language, religion, political or other opinion, natural or social origin, property, birth, or other status." Universal Declaration of Human Rights, G.A. Res. 217 (III) A, U.N. Doc. A/RES/217(III) (Dec. 10, 1948). Article 18 provides: "Everyone has the right to freedom of thought, conscience and religion; this right includes freedom to change his religion or belief, and freedom, either alone or in community with others and in public or private, to manifest his religion or belief in teaching, practice, worship and observance." *Id.*

204. *Vatican 'Must Immediately Remove' Child Abusers—UN*, BBC (Feb. 5, 2014 11:36 PM), http://www.bbc.com/news/world-europe-26044852.

205. *Id.*

206. Paul Vallely, *Vatican Missteps and U.N. Blunders*, N.Y. TIMES, Feb. 11, 2014, http://www.nytimes.com/2014/02/12/opinion/vatican-missteps-and-un-blunders.html?_r=0.

207. *Id.*

208. *Id.* The reluctance of the Catholic Church to turn alleged abusers over to civil authorities might have roots in the Talmudic prohibition of "mesirah," which is the turning over of one Jew by another to civil authorities. "Mesirah" was meant to protect Jews and the entire Jewish community from anti-Semitic governments. "Mesirah" still has some adherents today. Rachel Aviv, *The Outcasts*, NEW YORKER, Nov. 10, 2014, at 46.

209. *See* Vallely, *supra* note 206.

210. *See* Somers, *supra* note 189.

as a state—effectively expelling it from the U.N. reporting required from signatories to its conventions—appears to be counterproductive to the goal of reducing child abuse. In any event, it highlights the Pope's and Vatican's need for legal and diplomatic counsel.

IV. The Pope's Lawyers

Each diocese or archdiocese in the Catholic Church in the United States selects its own counsel to represent it and its employees in church-related matters.[211] The United States Conference of Catholic Bishops in Washington DC maintains a staff of attorneys who assist the Conference in legal matters and in preparing position statements.[212] Within the Vatican itself, matters of church law or canon law are handled by canon lawyers trained at the Vatican or the Catholic University of America.[213] Regarding the equivalent of diplomatic relations, those matters are handled by the Secretariat of State office within the Vatican, and as of this writing, by the Most Rev. Bernadito C. Auza, the Apostolic Nuncio and Permanent Observer of the Hole See to the United Nations and to the Organization of American States.[214] Archbishop Auza was appointed to these positions by the Pope in July 2014.[215]

How is counsel selected to represent the Holy See in the United States? Once again, a somewhat murky realm must be entered. In the past five years, the main attorney for the Holy See in the United States has been Jeffrey Lena.[216] Lena is a solo practitioner, and was the main—and often only—attorney representing the Holy See in a number of cases cited throughout this article.[217]

His office is in Berkeley, California.[218] Lena graduated from the University of California at Santa Cruz in 1982.[219] In 1986 he obtained his MA degree at the University of California at Berkeley in history.[220] In 1988 he married a woman from Milan, Italy and enrolled in a PhD program in history, but he never completed his thesis.[221] He began teaching history at the University of Maryland and at Berkeley.[222] In 1993, however, Lena enrolled in Hastings College of the Law.[223] He became friends with one of

---

211. Christopher Beam, *Objection, Your Holiness!*, Slate, (Apr. 1, 2010, 2:45 PM), http://www .slate.com/articles/news_and_politics/explainer/2010/04/objection_your_holiness.html.

212. General Counsel, U.S. Conf. Catholic Bishops, http://www.usccb.org/about/general -counsel/ (last visited Mar. 10, 2015).

213. *See* Beam, *supra* note 211.

214. *The Permanent Observer*, Holy See Mission, http://www.holyseemission.org/about/the -permenant-observer.aspx (last visited Mar. 10, 2015).

215. *Id.*

216. Jason Horowitz, *Jeffrey Lena: California lawyer is the voice of the Vatican, Pope Benedict in U.S. court*, Wash. Post, Apr. 19, 2010, at C1.

217. *Id.* at C1, C9.

218. *Id.* at C9.

219. *Id.*

220. *Id.*

221. *Id.*

222. *Id.*

223. *Id.*

the law faculty members, Ugo Mattei.[224] Lena transferred to Berkeley and also studied at the University of Milan.[225] In 1996 Lena graduated from law school and returned to Italy to serve as a visiting professor.[226]

How did Lena become the Pope's lawyer? In 2000, while he was teaching at the University of Turin, he was asked for his opinion and advice regarding the Alperin suit, which had just been filed in San Francisco.[227] He later identified "academic and professional associations in Italy" as the link which landed him the role as the Pope's lawyer.[228] Lena repeatedly declines to provide any additional information regarding those professional associations.[229] Professor Mattei claimed to be the connection.[230] The two have since had a falling out.[231] Another writer suggests that the contact was an Italian attorney by the name of Franzo Grande Stevens.[232] So, it is unclear—and likely will remain unclear—exactly how Mr. Lena came to be the Pope's attorney.

While the overwhelming number of lawsuits against the Holy See in the United States were handled and are being handled by Mr. Lena, he is not the only advocate for the Pope in this country. Another attorney, Mr. David Dunn of the law firm of Hogan Lovells, LLP of New York, represented the Holy See in the case of *MAGI XXI, Inc.*[233] When a research assistant on this article, Sean Cohen, asked Mr. Dunn in October 2014 how he was selected to handle this case, Mr. Dunn hesitated. He would only indicate that he was appointed by referral through another lawyer in Rome. He did not go into any other detail. When Mr. Dunn was asked how other attorneys were selected to represent the Pope in the United States, he guessed that it was done through local cardinals and other members of the hierarchy, but he could not and would not confirm this. He said he did not take part in the hiring process of any other attorneys.

The author of this article made numerous direct and indirect attempts to determine who is selecting the Pope's lawyers in the United States to no avail. Throughout 2014, we communicated with various Church officials, both inside the United States and inside the Vatican. The persons with whom we communicated did not know how the Vatican's lawyers were selected and did not know who would know. The lengthy records of these attempts are on file. Finally, this author attempted to set up a face-to-face meeting with Vatican representatives within the Secretariat of

---

224. *Id.*

225. *Id.*

226. *Id.*

227. Nicole Winfield, *Jeffrey Lena, Lawyer for Pope, Talks About His Role*, Huffington Post (June 17, 2010 5:12 AM), http://www.huffingtonpost.com/2010/04/18/jeffrey-lena-lawyer-for-pope _n_541835.html (last visited Mar. 10, 2015).

228. Horowitz, *supra* note 216, at C9.

229. *Id.*

230. *Id.*

231. *Id.*

232. Winfield, *supra* note 227.

233. MAGI XXI, Inc. v. Stato Della Citta del Vaticano, 714 F.3d 714, 717 (2d Cir. 2013).

State at the Vatican in July 2014. After clearing several levels of security within the Vatican, I met with an official who told me that all of the people I needed to speak with were on vacation. He did, however, wish me well in my endeavors.

Of course, there are very good reasons for the Vatican to maintain a protective stance regarding these matters. As a result of its willingness to concede errors in the handling of child abuse cases, the Holy See now faces potential liability in lawsuits brought directly against it and perhaps even against the Pope. It does not seem likely that plaintiffs will give up on their attempts. The Church does not need to allow external interference or pressure in the selection process of its counsel, upon those who would select the Pope's lawyers, or upon the lawyers themselves. After all, Jeffrey Lena received threats directed against him because of his role defending the Pope and the Holy See.[234] Regardless of the silence surrounding the process, several things do seem certain as the Pope chooses his attorneys. First, the religious beliefs of these attorneys do not seem relevant. Lena himself was never asked by anyone at the Vatican about his faith before his selection as counsel.[235] Second, the litigation victories that Mr. Lena, Mr. Dunn and others obtained on behalf of their client indicate that whether or not outsiders understand the selection process employed by the Vatican in selection of its attorneys, the process works very well.

V. Conclusion

Why does the Pope need lawyers? His role in the direction of his Church is under attack both historically and presently. That role is and has been misunderstood. His Church and its current and former adherents in the United States are the victims of physical assaults and the objects of verbal attacks.[236] Some of the moral positions of his Church, particularly its views on abortion, fly in the face of the temporal decisions of governments and individuals.[237] He has deep pockets. His Church witnessed horrible wrongs committed by those in the roles of spiritual leaders within his Church. His Church reacted too slowly and has since admitted its mistakes.[238] Calls to strip the Pope of immunity and his nation of its nation status come from many—even from those within his own ranks.[239] He makes mistakes, just like the rest of us. And like the rest of us, he sometimes needs the assistance of a good lawyer.

---

234. Winfield, *supra* note 227.

235. *Id.*

236. *See* Jenkins, *supra* note 98, at 31–33.

237. *See id.* at 70–75.

238. Letter from His Holiness Pope Benedict XVI to the Bishops of the Catholic Church (Mar. 10, 2009), *available at* http://www.npr.org/templates/story/story.php?storyId=101789591.

239. Paisley Dodds, *Pope's Immunity Could be Challenged in Britain*, NBC News (Apr. 4, 2010 12:22 PM), http://www.nbcnews.com/id/36167166/ns/world_news-europe/t/popes-immunity-could -be-challenged-britain/#.VM1U_i6At2g.

C. Our Approach

Throughout this book, where there is a relevant pronouncement issued under the infallibility doctrine, we will include it and refer to it. Where there is no such pronouncement, we will note that fact. And, we will include the position statements on the various issues presented by the United States Conference of Catholic Bishops (USCCB) or other authority.

Still other perspectives regarding the law are offered by Catholic theologians, educators, and lawyers. Just as the law varies in its application and its interpretation, there is also some divergence within these sources of Catholic perspectives. So, just as it is nearly impossible to obtain a unanimous view regarding the application of a particular law, it is also possible that there will be differing interpretations regarding the Catholic position regarding the law. Nonetheless, the important legal and Catholic perspectives can be observed, compared and woven into a broad tapestry offering the reader an appreciation of the common themes and the divergence within these systems.

We start with the assumption that both systems are interested ultimately in the pursuit of justice, and that both systems recognize the imperfect world in which we live. In the face of these imperfections, both systems nonetheless aspire to produce a better, more peaceful, and more just society.

Religion plays an important role in shaping the views of the electorate on current legal issues. For example, a Pew Research poll published September 17, 2010,[2] indicated that 35% of respondents viewed religion as the main influence regarding their view on same sex marriage. Sixty percent of those opposed to same sex marriage identified religion as the most important influence on their view. On another issue, abortion, 45% of abortion opponents listed religion as the most important factor, with 26% overall identifying that reason for their views. Regarding the death penalty, 32% of death penalty opponents cited religion; while overall, 19% found religion to be the most important factor regarding their views. Concerning immigration, 7% cited religion as the most important influence. It is possible that those who learn of the Catholic Church's position on these and other matters might find that source useful in framing or refining their own views.

With this brief background, we turn to examining critical areas where there are important and sometimes conflicting discussions in American society. In Chapter 2, we will consider some issues related to family, namely those of marriage, separation, and divorce. We will examine which relationships should be sanctioned or dissolved, by the State and/or by the Church. We will then take up the question as to what role society should play in critical life and death issues including abortion,

---

2. PEW FORUM ON RELIGION & PUBLIC LIFE, *Few Say Religion Shapes Immigration, Environment Views: Results from the 2010 Annual Religion and Public Life Survey,* at 1 (2010), http://pewforum .org/uploadedFiles/Topics/Issues/Politics_and_Elections/immigration-environment-views -fullreport.pdf.

stem cell research, eugenics and sterilization, euthanasia, and the death penalty, in Chapter 3. Chapter 4 examines immigration issues, revolving around the ultimate question of who is, or should be, allowed to live and work in the United States. These immigration issues continue to shape the very body of people who make up this society. Once we determine who should be allowed to live and work here, what about those who do not have the immediate ability to feed and clothe themselves? In Chapter 5, we consider the current realities concerning need for food and shelter in the form of public and private assistance. Finally, in Chapter 6, we strive to construct some applications of these principles. Our journey begins.

D. For Further Thought

1. Prior to reading this Introduction, what did you understand papal infallibility to mean? Has your understanding of this doctrine changed?

2. Examine briefly the Catechism of the Catholic Church. To what source(s) would you turn in order to clarify the meaning of some of its provisions?

3. Lawyers and law students are familiar with the differing levels of civil authority. We are also aware of the occasional split among the United States Courts of Appeals on issues of law. We understand that while the Supreme Court of the United States is the ultimate arbiter of matters arising under the Constitution and laws of the United States, each of the fifty states has its own legal system. Is there any way to compare this system to the hierarchy of the Catholic Church?

4. As you examine the materials in this book, see if you perceive any differences in the views of the Vatican, American bishops, clergy, theologians, scholars, and laity. Unless the issue is the subject of an *ex cathedra* pronouncement, how can these views be reconciled?

Chapter 2

Family Issues

A. Marriage

The first discussion considering the views of the Church and the legal system must involve the family. Unlike some areas of the law, family issues affect virtually all Catholics. Both the legal system and the Church recognize the importance of marriage. Both establish requirements for entering into, and for withdrawal from, that status. While the requirements and concerns overlap in many regards, there are some critical differences between the approaches to the institution of marriage by the Church and by the secular legal system. In this chapter we will explore these issues beginning with an understanding of how each institution views the nature of the marital relationship. We examine the requirements each institution imposes for entering into a marriage. In this regard we pay particular attention to the relatively recent phenomenon of same-sex marriage. There is an irreconcilable difference between the positions of the Catholic Church and the legal system in this regard. Unfortunately, some marriages break down, and we explore the mechanisms within the Church and the legal system for annulling or dissolving a marriage. We will examine the dilemma, and the solutions, for Catholics who face the trauma of the breakdown of a marriage. We conclude this chapter with a discussion of the role of the Catholic judge or lawyer in family law and divorce proceedings.

1. Marriage and the Legal System

The Supreme Court of the United States has long recognized the importance of the institution of marriage. In 1888, it characterized marriage as "The most important relation in life,"[1] and as, "The foundation of the family and of society, without which there would be neither civilization nor progress. . . ."[2]

The right to marry is considered a fundamental right under the Due Process Clause of the Constitution of the United States.[3] While states generally have the right to identify the qualifications necessary to enter into a marriage, they cannot enact restrictions, such as racial restrictions, which would violate this constitutional principle, and that

---

1. Maynard v. Hill, 125 U.S. 190, 205 (1888).
2. *Id.*
3. Zablocki v. Redhail, 434 U.S. 374, 384 (1978).

of the Equal Protection Clause of the Fourteenth Amendment to the Constitution.[4] Because of the constitutional importance of this right to marry, even incarcerated inmates have a constitutional right to marry.[5] However, they do not have the right to consummate the marriage.[6]

Marriage is afforded a great deal of importance by the legal system because of its impact on, and role in, the formation of societal relationships. While the agreement to marry and live as husband and wife is recognized as involving elements of a contract between the spouses, it has always been viewed as more than just a contract between two people.[7] The State has a direct interest in the creation, maintenance, and dissolution of the marriage relationship because of the concerns associated with children, property, and general good order in society. Thus the State identifies who is eligible to marry, under what circumstances the marriage can be dissolved, and how child custody, visitation, and property allocation and distribution is to occur if the marriage breaks down.[8] One summary of the nature of marriage provides: "Marriage is a unique institution by which those who are married enter into a legally recognized personal relationship."[9]

The legal system, like the Church, imposes qualifications on who can marry. These restrictions are generally left to the States and each state sets its own requirements. Typically, states impose minimum age restrictions for marriage. Also common are prohibitions against marriage between people related by blood, adoption, or between those who are, or who have been, in a stepchild or step-sibling relationship. States require some formalities in creating the marriage relationship. That is, usually the parties are required to obtain a marriage license, have the marriage ceremony performed by an authorized officiant, and then the license must be recorded noting the date and location of the marriage ceremony. These records are usually maintained in the county where the marriage license was issued. Some states allow "common law," or marriages without formalities, and these are discussed below.

Note that the requirements within the legal system for entering into marriage actually have some basis in the Old Testament. For example, in Leviticus 18, there are a series of prohibitions against sexual relations and therefore marriage, between a man and his mother (v.8), his father's wife (v.8), his sister by either his father or mother (v.9), his son's daughter or his daughter's daughter (v.10), daughter of his father's wife (v.10), his father's sister (v.12), his mother's sister (v.13), his father's brother's wife (v.14), his daughter in law (v.15), his brother's wife (v.16), both a woman and her daughter, her son's daughter or her daughter's daughter (v.17), and

---

4. Loving v. Virginia, 388 U.S. 1, 12 (1967).

5. Turner v. Safley, 482 U.S. 78, 94 (1987).

6. *Id.*

7. *See generally* 52 Am. Jur. 2d *Marriage* § 7 (2013).

8. *See generally* 24 Am. Jur. 2d *Divorce and Separation* § 16 (2013).

9. *See generally* 52 Am. Jur. 2d *Marriage* § 1 (2013).

a wife's sister while the wife is living (v.18).[10] A typical state approach to marriage requirements is set out in the Texas Family Code, which provides:

§ 2.001. Marriage License[11]

(a) A man and a woman desiring to enter into a ceremonial marriage must obtain a marriage license from the county clerk of any county of this state.

(b) A license may not be issued for the marriage of persons of the same sex.

The Application for a marriage license form explicitly identifies who is eligible to be married.

§ 2.004. Application Form[12]

(a) The county clerk shall furnish the application form as prescribed by the bureau of vital statistics.

(b) The application form must contain:

(1) a heading entitled "Application for Marriage License, ____ County, Texas";

(2) spaces for each applicant's full name, including the woman's maiden surname, address, social security number, if any, date of birth, and place of birth, including city, county, and state;

(3) a space for indicating the document tendered by each applicant as proof of identity and age;

(4) spaces for indicating whether each applicant has been divorced within the last 30 days;

(5) printed boxes for each applicant to check "true" or "false" in response to the following statement: "I am not presently married and the other applicant is not presently married";

(6) printed boxes for each applicant to check "true" or "false" in response to the following statement: "The other applicant is not related to me as:

(A) an ancestor or descendant, by blood or adoption;

(B) a brother or sister, of the whole or half blood or by adoption;

(C) a parent's brother or sister, of the whole or half blood or by adoption;

(D) a son or daughter of a brother or sister, of the whole or half blood or by adoption;

(E) a current or former stepchild or stepparent; or

---

10. *Leviticus* 18: 8–10, 12–18 (New Cath. Version).
11. Tex. Fam. Code Ann. § 2.001 (West).
12. *Id.* at § 2.004 (West).

(F) a son or daughter of a parent's brother or sister, of the whole or half blood or by adoption."

(7) printed boxes for each applicant to check "true" or "false" in response to the following statement: "I am not presently delinquent in the payment of court-ordered child support.";

(8) a printed oath reading: "I SOLEMNLY SWEAR (OR AFFIRM) THAT THE INFORMATION I HAVE GIVEN IN THIS APPLICATION IS CORRECT.";

(9) spaces immediately below the printed oath for the applicants' signatures;

(10) a certificate of the county clerk that:

(A) each applicant made the oath and the date and place that it was made; or

(B) an applicant did not appear personally but the prerequisites for the license have been fulfilled as provided by this chapter;

(11) spaces for indicating the date of the marriage and the county in which the marriage is performed; and

(12) a space for the address to which the applicants desire the completed license to be mailed.

(c) An applicant commits an offense if the applicant knowingly provides false information under Subsection (b)(1), (2), (3), or (4). An offense under this subsection is a Class C misdemeanor.

(d) An applicant commits an offense if the applicant knowingly provides false information under Subsection (b)(5) or (6). An offense under this subsection is a Class A misdemeanor.

Applicants for a marriage license in Texas must be at least 18 years of age.[13] They can, however, obtain a marriage license if they are emancipated by court order,[14] and provide that order to the county clerk.[15]

Note that while the statutes speak in terms of one man and one woman, the *Obergefell* decision of the Supreme Court of the United States, set out below, prohibits this limitation. Eventually this Texas statute and similar state statutes will be re-written, but for the time being, even though the language of "one man one woman" appears, that restriction cannot be applied.

Review carefully at this point each of the substantive qualifications. Why do you think there are minimum age requirements? Why would parents or a judge grant permission to persons younger than 18 to marry? Why should relatives, within the degrees

---

13. *Id.* at § 2.003 (West).

14. *Id.* at § 2003.a (West).

15. *Id.* at § 2003.b (West).

of the relationships identified in the statute, be precluded from marriage? Regarding this latter question, if there is concern about genetic defects in the offspring of such parties, why would step-children or those who are unable to procreate face this ban?

In addition to the substantive requirements, states impose procedural steps necessary to establishing a marriage. These include the obtaining of a license, the performance of a ceremony by an authorized officiant, and the recording of the license noting the date and location of the marriage ceremony as well as the identity of the officiant. These records are typically maintained in the county records where the marriage license was issued.

Note that in Texas and in some other jurisdictions, people can enter into "common law" marriages without the need for a formal license or ceremony. Again, a Texas statute is illustrative.

§ 2.401. Proof of Informal Marriage[16]

(a) In a judicial, administrative, or other proceeding, the marriage of a man and woman may be proved by evidence that:

(1) a declaration of their marriage has been signed as provided by this subchapter; or

(2) the man and woman agreed to be married and after the agreement they lived together in this state as husband and wife and there represented to others that they were married.

(b) If a proceeding in which a marriage is to be proved as provided by Subsection (a)(2) is not commenced before the second anniversary of the date on which the parties separated and ceased living together, it is rebuttably presumed that the parties did not enter into an agreement to be married.

(c) A person under 18 years of age may not:

(1) be a party to an informal marriage; or

(2) execute a declaration of informal marriage under Section 2.402.

(d) A person may not be a party to an informal marriage or execute a declaration of an informal marriage if the person is presently married to a person who is not the other party to the informal marriage or declaration of an informal marriage, as applicable.

Why would any state allow its residents to marry by this method?

A marriage valid in the state where it is created is generally valid in the other states because of the Full Faith and Credit Clause of the Constitution of the United States.[17]

---

16. *Id.* at § 2.401 (West).

17. U.S. Const. art. IV § 1, cl. 1. ("Full Faith and Credit shall be given in each State to the public Acts, Records, and judicial Proceedings of every other State.").

2. The Catholic Church Views Marriage

The Catholic Church recognizes marriage as one of the seven sacraments. Canon Law indicates that:

> The matrimonial covenant, by which a man and a woman establish between themselves a partnership of the whole of life, is by its nature ordained toward the good of the spouses and the procreation and education of offspring; this covenant between baptized persons has been raised by Christ the Lord to the dignity of a sacrament.[18]

The importance of marriage was underscored by Pope Benedict XVI on February 7, 2007, and on February 22, 2007:

> The family . . . is the "cradle" of life and of every vocation. We are well aware that the family founded on marriage is the natural environment in which to bear and raise children and thereby guarantee the future of all of humanity. However, we also know that marriage is going through a deep crisis and today must face numerous challenges. It is consequently necessary to defend, help, safeguard, and value it in its unrepeatable uniqueness. If this commitment is in the first place the duty of spouses, it is also a priority duty of the Church and of every public institution to support the family by means of pastoral and political initiatives that take into account the real needs of married couples, of the elderly and of the new generations.[19]

> Marriage and the family are institutions that must be promoted and defended from every possible misrepresentation of their true nature, since whatever is injurious to them is injurious to society itself.[20]

The Catholic Bishops of the United States followed, in 2009, with a pastoral letter entitled, *Marriage: Love and Life in the Divine Plan.*

USCCB: Pastoral Letter — Marriage: Love and Life in the Divine Plan (Abridged)[21]

---

18. 1983 CODE c. 1055, http://www.vatican.va/archive/ENG1104/__P3V.HTM (last visited Oct. 2, 2017); *see also* G. Martinez, *Matrimony, Sacrament of,* NEW CATHOLIC ENCYCLOPEDIA, vol. 9, 333–39 (2003) (complete encyclopedic entry).

19. Pope Benedict XVI, *Message at Weekly Angelus* (Feb. 4, 2007), http://www.vatican.va/holy _father/benedict_xvi/angelus/2007/documents/hf_ben-xvi_ang_20070204_en.html (last visited Oct. 2, 2017).

20. Pope Benedict XVI, *Apostolic Exhortation Sacramentum Caritatis* 98 (Feb. 22, 2007), http:// www.vatican.va/holy_father/benedict_xvi/apost_exhortations/documents/hf_ben-xvi_exh _20070222_ sacramentum-caritatis_en.html (last visited Oct. 2, 2017).

21. USCCB, *Love and Life in the Divine Plan* (Nov. 2009), http://www.usccb.org/issues-and -action/marriage-and-family/marriage/love-and-life/upload/Love-and-Life-Abridged-Version .pdf (last visited Oct. 2, 2017).

What Is Marriage?

Marriage is a natural institution established by God the Creator. It is a permanent, faithful, fruitful partnership between one man and one woman, established by their free mutual consent. It has two purposes: the good of the spouses, called the unitive purpose, and the procreation and education of children.

Marriage is not merely a private institution. It is the foundation of the family, where children learn values and virtues that make them good Christians as well as good citizens. Marriage is important for the upbringing of the next generation, and therefore it is important for society.

Men and women are equal as persons. As male and female, they are two different ways of being human. These differences relate them to each other in a total and complementary way. They make possible a unique communion of persons in which spouses give themselves and receive each other in love. This communion of persons has the potential to bring forth human life and thus to produce the family. No other relationship symbolizes life and love as marriage does.

The two purposes of marriage are inseparable; they are two aspects of the same self-giving. The unitive purpose of marriage means that husband and wife participate in God's own self-giving love. The two become one flesh, giving mutual help and service to each other through their intimate union.

The procreative purpose recognizes that married love is by its nature life-giving. The children who result from this union are the supreme gift of marriage. Some couples experience the tragedy of infertility and may be tempted to think that their union is not complete; however, it remains a distinctive communion of persons.

Challenges to Marriage

Contemporary society poses fundamental challenges to the meaning and purposes of marriage. Four of these challenges are discussed here.

(1) Contraception. Each act of intercourse must be open to procreation, because the whole meaning of marriage is expressed in each marital act. Contraception closes off the possibility of procreation and separates the unitive and procreative meanings of marriage. This is objectively wrong and is essentially opposed to God's plan for marriage and proper human development. Deliberately separating these two meanings can damage or destroy the marriage and bring many other negative consequences, both personal and social. Natural family planning (NFP) methods enable a couple to plan their family in accord with God's design.

(2) Same-sex unions. Male-female complementarity is essential to marriage. It makes possible authentic union and the generation of new life. Attempts to make same-sex unions the equivalent of marriage disregard the nature of

marriage. Since marriage and same-sex unions are different realities, it is not unjust discrimination to oppose the legal recognition of same-sex unions. These unions pose a serious threat to the fabric of society that affects all people.

(3) Divorce. Marriage is meant to be a lifelong covenantal union, which divorce claims to break. Troubled couples as well as divorced persons are encouraged to rely on God's help and to use the resources of the Church for support and healing. An annulment is a possibility for some divorced persons. This is a finding by a church tribunal, or court, that no valid marriage bond was formed because the requirements for valid consent were not met at the time of the wedding.

(4) Cohabitation. Many couples live together in a sexual relationship without marriage. This is always wrong and objectively sinful because the complete gift of self can only take place within the public, permanent commitment of marriage. Cohabitation can have negative effects on couples themselves, as well as any children who are part of the relationship.

Marriage as a Christian Sacrament

Although marriage remains a blessing from God, Original Sin has had grave consequences for married life. As a break with God, it ruptured the original communion between man and woman.

Jesus healed this rupture when he raised marriage to the dignity of a sacrament. In marriage a man and woman become one flesh. They love each other as they love themselves and cherish each other's bodies as their own. This union is an image of Christ's love for his Church. Spouses are called to give themselves to each other as fully as Christ gave himself to his Church.

When the baptized spouses exchange their promises of loving and permanent fidelity before the Church, their marriage covenant becomes a participation in the unbreakable covenant between Christ and the Church. The Holy Spirit binds the spouses together and enables them to perform acts of self–giving love to the benefit of themselves, their families, and the whole Church. In this way their marriage does more than symbolize Christ's love; it makes that love present in the world.

In order to imitate Christ's love for his Church, the relationship between man and woman needs healing. Their relationship is not a one-sided subjection of the wife to the husband, but a mutual subjection of husband and wife, following St. Paul's charge to "be subordinate to one another out of reverence for Christ." (Eph. 5:21)

Marriage and Family: A Communion of Love

The Christian married couple, with their children, forms an image of the Trinitarian God: Father, Son, and Holy Spirit. Marriage and family life images the Trinity in two ways. First, like the Trinity, marriage is a communion of love between co-equal persons, beginning with husband and wife and extending to all the members of the family. Second, just as Trinity's love is life-giving, a married couple's love conceives and cares for children.

In addition to reflecting the Trinity, the family is a microcosm of the Church. The ancient expression "domestic church" accurately describes the family because it is a small communion of persons that draws its sustenance from the larger Church and reflects its life in unique ways. Within this domestic church, parents have a special responsibility to teach children the faith and help them to grow in virtue. The family matures as a domestic church by participating in the life and worship of the larger Church, especially Sunday Eucharist. In the Eucharist, members of the family are most fully united to Christ, to one another, and to their brothers and sisters throughout the world.

Christian spouses in a mixed marriage (between a Catholic and a baptized person who is not Catholic) witness to the universality of God's love, even without sharing the Eucharist. They can make an important contribution towards Christian unity. Sometimes, Catholics marry non-Christians. These marriages are not sacramental, although the parties do commit to fidelity, permanence, and openness to children. Both types of unions face particular challenges, especially the religious upbringing of children. The Catholic party needs to take seriously the promise to maintain his or her Catholic faith and to do all in his or her power to have the children baptized and raised Catholic.

Marriage is a vocation, or divine call, as necessary and valuable to the Church as other vocations. Discernment of and preparation for marriage is a process that begins early in life and continues through the engagement period. Because marriage is for the good of the Church and the entire community, the Church and the state have an obligation to help support and sustain marriage.

Growth in Virtue

With God's grace, couples are called to grow in holiness. A holy marriage is made up of many virtues. Fundamentally, the couple lives out the theological virtues of faith, hope, and love. Love is the heart of the vocation of marriage. It calls spouses to imitate Jesus by their willingness to sacrifice themselves in everyday situations for each other and their children. Couples must also grow in the moral virtues of prudence, justice, fortitude, and temperance.

Two virtues that are sometimes overlooked are chastity and gratitude. Marital chastity means that the couple's love is total, faithful, exclusive, and open to life. It protects a great good: the communion of persons and the procreative purpose of marriage.

Marriage is a school of gratitude, in which husband and wife are thankful for the gift of each other. They express their joyous gratitude in giving themselves completely to each other. Their gratitude leads them to be open to children and to be generous towards others.

Growth in virtue is a lifelong journey in which the spouses become more like Christ so that they can more perfectly love each other as Christ loves his Church.

The Eucharist

In the Eucharist Catholic couples meet Christ, the source of their marriage. This encounter moves them to reach out in love to the broader Church and to the world. The Eucharist nourishes the virtue of marital hospitality and helps the couple to recognize God's image in others. This hospitality builds up the Church and makes it a stronger witness to Christ's love in the world.

A marriage that is truly in Christ is a sign of the Kingdom that is coming. At the end of time, at the celebration of the heavenly wedding banquet, the love to which the spouses have been called will find its completion when the entire Church is assumed into the glory of the risen Christ.

Just as with the civil authorities, the Church also identifies certain requirements for marriage. Marriages which do not meet these requirements are considered non-sacramental and invalid. A succinct summary of these requirements appears in Scott P. Richert's note, Can I Get Married in the Catholic Church?[22]

Richert identifies five basic requirements. First, a Catholic can only marry a baptized Christian. A Catholic seeking to marry a non-Catholic Christian must obtain permission from the Catholic's bishop. Second, the parties must not be too closely related. In some cases, though, the Church will allow a dispensation for first cousins to marry. Third, Richert notes, the partners must be free to marry. If either party has been previously married, he or she can only remarry in the Catholic Church if the Church declares the previous marriage "null." Fourth, the parties must be one man and one woman. Finally, the Catholic partner must be in good standing with the Church.

The Catholic Church does not recognize common law marriages, or other informal marriage or marriage like arrangements. This position was made clear in the Vatican's Pontifical Council for the Family, in its statement on Family, Marriage and "De Facto" Unions[23] set out in 2000. The document runs thirty pages, and includes

22. Scott P. Richert, *Can I Get Married in the Catholic Church?* (Apr. 9, 2017), https://www.thoughtco.com/get-married-in-the-catholic-church-542166 (last visited Oct. 2, 2017).
23. Vatican's Pontifical Council for the Family, *Statement on "Family, Marriage and 'De Facto' Unions"* (Jul. 26, 2000), http://www.vatican.va/roman_curia/pontifical_councils/family/documents/rc_pc_family_doc_20001109_de-facto-unions_en.html (last visited Oct. 2, 2017).

extensive analyses of the Church's opposition to recognizing "de facto" unions. A few paragraphs illustrate the Church's position:

==

One very widespread phenomenon that calls strongly upon the conscience of the Christian community today is the growing number of de facto unions in society as a whole, with the disaffection for the stability of marriage that this entails. The Church cannot fail to shed light on this reality in its discernment of the "signs of the times."

. . . .

(2) The term "de facto unions" includes a whole series of many heterogeneous human realities whose common element is that of being forms of cohabitation (of a sexual kind) which are not marriage. De facto unions are characterized precisely by the fact that they ignore, postpone, or even reject the conjugal commitment. Grave consequences are derived from this.

In marriage, through the covenant of conjugal love, all the responsibilities that result from the bond that has been made are taken on publicly. From this public assumption of responsibilities a good results not only for the spouses themselves and for the children in their affective and formational growth, but also for the other members of the family. Therefore, the family based on marriage is a fundamental and precious good for the whole society whose most solid fabric is built on the values that are developed in family relations and guaranteed by stable marriage. The good generated by marriage is basic for the Church which recognizes the family as the "domestic Church." All this is endangered by abandoning the institution of marriage, which is implicit in de facto unions.

(3) Some may wish to, and may use sexuality in a way other than that written by God into human nature and the specifically human end of their acts. This goes against the interpersonal language of love and seriously endangers, through an objective disorder, the true dialogue of life willed by the Creator and Redeemer of humankind. The doctrine of the Catholic Church is well known by public opinion, and it is not necessary to repeat it here. It is the social dimension of the problem that requires greater reflection and makes it possible to point out, especially to those with public responsibilities, the inappropriateness of elevating these private situations to the category of public interest. With the pretext of regulating one context of social and juridical cohabitation, attempts are made to justify the institutional recognition of de facto unions. In this way, de facto unions would turn into an institution, and their rights and duties would be sanctioned by law to the detriment of the family based on marriage. The de facto unions would be put on a juridical level similar to

marriage; moreover, this kind of cohabitation would be publicly qualified as a "good" by elevating it to a condition similar to, or equivalent to marriage, to the detriment of truth and justice. In this way, a very strong contribution would be made toward the breakdown of the natural institution of marriage which is absolutely vital, basic and necessary for the whole social body.

. . . .

(10) Equality before the law must respect the principle of justice which means treating equals equally, and what is different differently: i.e., to give each one his due in justice. This principle of justice would be violated if de facto unions were given a juridical treatment similar or equivalent to the family based on marriage. If the family based on marriage and de facto unions are neither similar nor equivalent in their duties, functions, and services in society, then they cannot be similar or equivalent in their juridical status.

The pretext used for exerting pressure to recognize de facto unions (i.e., their "non-discrimination") implies a real discrimination against the family based on marriage because it would be considered on a level similar to any other form of cohabitation, regardless of whether there is a commitment to reciprocal fidelity and the begetting and upbringing of children or not. The orientation of some political communities today of discriminating against marriage by attributing an institutional status to de facto unions that is similar, or even equivalent to marriage and the family, is a serious sign of the contemporary breakdown in the social moral conscience, of "weak thought" with regard to the common good, when it is not a real and proper ideological imposition exerted by influential pressure groups.

. . . .

(50) Over the ages, the wisdom of peoples, albeit with limitations, has substantially been capable of recognizing the essence and the fundamental and irreplaceable mission of the family based on marriage. The family is a necessary and indispensable good for the whole of society, and it has a real and proper right in justice to be recognized, protected, and promoted by the whole of society. It is this whole of society that is damaged when this precious and necessary good of humanity is wounded in any way. Before the social phenomenon of de facto unions, and the postponing of conjugal love which this implies, society itself cannot remain indifferent. Merely erasing the problem through the false solution of granting them recognition and placing them on a public level similar to, or even equivalent to families based on marriage, is a detrimental comparison to marriage (which further damages this natural institution, that is so necessary today, rather than providing real family policies). Moreover, this implies a profound lack of recognition

of the anthropological truth about the human love between a man and a woman, and its inseparable aspects of stable unity and openness to life. This lack of recognition is still more grave when the essential and very profound difference is ignored between conjugal love, that comes from the institution of marriage, and homosexual relationships. The "indifference" of public administrations toward this aspect is very similar to a kind of apathy with regard to the life or death of society; an indifference about its future projection or its degradation. If suitable remedies are not applied, this "neutrality" would lead to a serious breakdown of the social fabric and of the pedagogy of the future generations.

The under-evaluation of conjugal love and its intrinsic openness to life, with the instability of family life that this entails, is a social phenomenon that requires proper discernment by all those who feel committed to the good of the family, and in a very special way by Christians. This means first of all recognizing the real causes (ideological and economic) of the situation, and not giving in to demagogic pressures by lobbies that do not take the common good of society into consideration. The Catholic Church, in following Jesus Christ, recognizes in the family and in conjugal love a gift of communion of the merciful God with humanity, a precious treasure of holiness and grace that shines in the midst of the world. Therefore, it invites those who are fighting for the cause of man to unite their efforts in promoting the family and its intimate source of life which is the conjugal union.[24]

B. Same-Sex Marriage

1. State Approaches and the Federal Response

Marriage had only been recognized, traditionally, by both the legal system and the Catholic Church as those unions between one man and one woman. However, beginning in the early 90s, a state-by-state approach produced legislation recognizing the validity of same-sex marriages. In 1993, the Hawaii Supreme Court held that limiting marriage to heterosexual couples would be unconstitutional without a compelling state interest. Voters in the State then amended the Constitution to maintain the restriction. In 1996, the Congress of the United States passed, and the President signed into law the Defense of Marriage Act (DOMA).[25] That Act read as follows:

---

24. *Id.*
25. 28 U.S.C. § 1738C.

§ 1738C. Certain Acts, Records, and Proceedings and the Effect Thereof

No State, territory, or possession of the United States, or Indian tribe, shall be required to give effect to any public act, record, or judicial proceedings of any other State, territory, possession, or tribe respecting a relationship between persons of the same sex that is treated as a marriage under the laws of such other State, territory, possession, or tribe, or a right or claim arising from such relationship.

The impetus for the enactment of DOMA was the concern that if some states began to recognize same-sex marriage, other states, even those with constitutional prohibitions against same-sex marriage, would nonetheless be required to recognize the marriage under the Full Faith and Credit Clause of the Constitution of the United States. However, DOMA was declared unconstitutional in the case of *U.S. v. Windsor*, 133 S. Ct. 2675 (2013).

A determination in 1998 in Alaska legalizing same-sex marriage provoked a constitutional amendment overturning the decision. In 1999 the Vermont Supreme Court held that same-sex couples must receive the same treatment as married couples. In 2000, the Vermont Legislature created a "civil union" statute and its legislature enacted a same-sex marriage statute in 2009.

Similarly, in 2005, the State of Connecticut adopted a civil union statute and, in 2008, formally recognized same-sex marriage. In 2004, Massachusetts recognized same-sex marriage as have New Hampshire (2009), the District of Columbia (2009), New York (2011), Illinois (2011), California (2008, 2012), Delaware (2012), Hawaii (2012), and Washington (2012).

On May 2, 2013, Rhode Island became the eleventh jurisdiction in the United States to allow same-sex couples to marry.[26] Governor Lincoln Chafee signed the marriage bill into law after the bills passed overwhelmingly in the House and Senate in the weeks prior.[27]

On March 21, 2013, Gov. John Hickenlooper signed a bill into law to allow same-sex couples to join together in civil union after passing the senate.[28] The law took effect on May 1, 2013.[29]

On September 27, 2013, Superior Court Judge Mary Jacobson in New Jersey ruled in favor of the freedom to marry for same-sex couples in a federal lawsuit challenging the state's civil union law as unconstitutional.[30] On October 18, the New Jersey

---

26. Rhode Island, FREEDOMTOMARRY.ORG, http://www.freedomtomarry.org/states/entry/c /rhode-island (last visited Oct. 2, 2017).

27. *Id.*

28. Colorado, FREEDOMTOMARRY.ORG, http://www.freedomtomarry.org/states/entry/colorado (last visited Oct. 2, 2017).

29. *Id.*

30. New Jersey, FREEDOMTOMARRY.ORG, http://www.freedomtomarry.org/states/entry/new -jersey (last visited Oct. 2, 2017).

Supreme Court denied a request for a stay in the marriage case.[31] Same-sex couples began marrying in New Jersey on October 21, 2013, and just a few hours later, the Christie administration dropped its appeal of the ruling.[32]

The trend of state recognition of same-sex marriage continued. In December, 2013, the Supreme Court of the State of New Mexico determined that New Mexico "is constitutionally required to allow same-gender couples to marry and must extend to them the rights, protections and responsibilities that derive from civil marriage under New Mexico law."[33] Even though no specific statute or constitutional provision addressed the issue of same-sex marriage, county clerks in at least eight of New Mexico's 33 counties had begun to allow same-sex couples to obtain marriage licenses. The resulting confusion in the status of those marriages led to the ultimate determination by the state Supreme Court. In response to that decision, the New Mexico conference of Catholic Bishops observed, "The Catholic Church respects and loves the gay and lesbian members of our community. . . . We will continue to promote Catholic teaching of the biblical definition of marriage to be that of one man and one woman."[34]

Federal courts were active in striking down as unconstitutional bans in states against same-sex marriage. A United States District Judge in Utah held the Utah provisions prohibiting same-sex couples from marrying to be unconstitutional.[35]

Similarly, on February 26, 2014, United States District Judge Orlando Garcia found the Texas constitutional ban on same-sex marriage to be in violation of the Constitution of the United States. Judge Garcia's opinion concluded that, "Without a rational relation to a legitimate governmental purpose, state-imposed inequality can find no refuge in our United States Constitution."[36]

Judge Garcia, however, issued a stay of his decision in order to allow Texas to appeal his decision to the United States Court of Appeals for the fifth circuit in New Orleans. Judge Garcia's determination added the State of Texas to the list of states for same-sex marriage bans which were overturned. Rulings in Oklahoma and Virginia overturned similar bans.[37]

---

31. *Id.*

32. *Id.*

33. Russell Contreras, *New Mexico Same-Sex Marriage Ruling Comes Amid Long Wait, National Trend*, FoxNews.com (Dec. 20, 2013), http://www.foxnews.com/us/2013/12/20/new-mexico-same-sex-marriage-ruling-comes-amid-long-wait-national-trend (last visited Oct. 2, 2017).

34. *Id.*

35. Erik Eckholm, *Federal Judge Rules That Same-Sex Marriage Is Legal in Utah*, NYTimes.com (Dec. 20, 2013), http://www.nytimes.com/2013/12/21/us/utahs-gay-marriage-ban-is-ruled-unconstitutional.html (last visited Oct. 2, 2017).

36. Manny Fernandez, *Federal Judge Strikes Down Texas' Ban on Same-Sex Marriage*, NYTimes.com (Feb. 26, 2014), http://www.nytimes.com/2014/02/27/us/texas-judge-strikes-down-state-ban-on-same-sex-marriage.html (last visited Oct. 2, 2017).

37. National Conference of State Legislators, *Defining Marriage: State Defense of Marriage Laws and Same-Sex Marriage*, NCSL.org (Feb. 26, 2014), http://www.ncsl.org/research/human-services/same-sex-marriage-overview.aspx. Not Available anymore.

A ruling by a federal judge in Kentucky added an additional twist to the concept of the legality or illegality of same-sex marriages. Late in February, 2014, a judge considered whether people who obtained marriage licenses outside of the state of Kentucky and then moved back would have the validity of their marriage recognized in Kentucky. Kentucky did not recognize the validity of same-sex marriages created in that state. U.S. District Judge John G. Heyburn II determined "Assigning a religious or traditional rationale for a law, does not make it constitutional when that law discriminates against a class of people without other reasons."[38] The potential impact of this case would have been to ultimately result in the recognition of the validity of same-sex marriages in all fifty states. Same-sex couples who could not obtain permission to marry in their own state could have nonetheless left that jurisdiction, marry in a state which allows such marriages, and then return to their home state with a marriage which would have to be recognized locally.

Even if states which prohibited same-sex couples from marrying were not required to recognize the validity of out-of-state marriages, the federal government pressed states' attorneys general to stop defending prohibitions against same-sex marriages in the states. This development raised interesting ethical questions and legal questions regarding the roles of the attorneys general. It followed the pattern established when the Attorney General of the United States quit defending DOMA.[39]

Eventually, of course, these matters were resolved by the Supreme Court of the United States in its decision in *Obergefell v. Hodges*, 135 S. Ct. 2584 (2015), which established the constitutional right of same sex couples to marry. The *Obergefell* decision was foreshadowed by the case of *Lawrence v. Texas*,[40] where the Supreme Court of the United States struck down as unconstitutional a Texas statute outlawing homosexual sodomy. In doing so, the Court noted that the case involved adults engaging in homosexual conduct by mutual consent. The Court stated, "Petitioners are entitled to respect for their private lives. The State cannot demean their existence or control their destiny by making their private sexual conduct a crime. The right to liberty under the Due Process Clause gives them the full right to engage in their conduct without intervention of the government. The Texas statute furthers no legitimate state interest which can justify its intrusion into the personal and private life of the individual."[41]

---

38. Dana Ford, *Judge Rules Kentucky Must Recognize Same-Sex Marriages*, CNN.COM (Feb. 12, 2014), http://www.cnn.com/2014/02/12/us/kentucky-same-sex-marriage (last visited Oct. 2, 2017).

39. Office of Public Affairs, The U.S. Dep't of Justice, *Statement of the Attorney General on Litigation Involving the Defense of Marriage Act* (Feb. 23, 2011), http://www.justice.gov/opa/pr/2011/February/11-ag-222.html (last visited Oct. 2, 2017).

40. 539 U.S. 558, 578 (U.S. 2003).

41. *Id.*

The opinion for the majority in the *Lawrence* case was written by Justice Kennedy, a Catholic. Another Catholic, Justice Scalia dissented. He determined that there was no constitutional right to the recognition of the same-sex relationship involved in *Lawrence*. Justice Scalia objected to the majority's language, "When sexuality finds overt expression in intimate contact with another person, the conduct can be but one element in a personal bond that is more enduring." Justice Scalia went on to ask, "What justification could there possibly be for denying the benefits of marriage to homosexual couples exercising 'the liberty protected by the Constitution.' Surely not the encouragement of procreation, since the sterile and elderly are allowed to marry. This case 'does not involve' the issue of homosexual marriage only if one entertains the belief that principle and logic have nothing to do with the decisions of this Court."[42] Justice Scalia accurately predicted that the Supreme Court of the United States would eventually determine that there is a constitutional right for same-sex couples to marry.

Does the *Obergefell* decision mean that the church's teachings will become irrelevant? The church continues to hold that abortion is wrong, even in the face of determinations by the Supreme Court that the Constitution allows the legal system to provide abortions. The Church will undoubtedly continue to teach the value of traditional marriage and will likely do all in its power to try to persuade individuals to reject the choice of same-sex marriage. An examination of the Church's role leading up to *Windsor* and *Obergefell* offers some context.

2. The Catholic Church Opposes Same-Sex Marriage

As might be expected, the Catholic Church took a negative view regarding the creation of a state-sanctioned homosexual marriage. The June 24, 2011 Statement of the Bishops of New York State is illustrative:

> The passage by the Legislature of a bill to alter radically and forever humanity's historic understanding of marriage leaves us deeply disappointed and troubled.

> We strongly uphold the Catholic Church's clear teaching that we always treat our homosexual brothers and sisters with respect, dignity, and love. But we just as strongly affirm that marriage is the joining of one man and one woman in a lifelong, loving union that is open to children, ordered for the good of those children and the spouses themselves. This definition cannot change, though we realize that our beliefs about the nature of marriage will continue to be ridiculed, and that some will even now attempt to enact government sanctions against churches and religious organizations that preach these timeless truths.

---

42. *Id.*

We worry that both marriage and the family will be undermined by this tragic presumption of government in passing this legislation that attempts to redefine these cornerstones of civilization.

Our society must regain what it appears to have lost—a true understanding of the meaning and the place of marriage, as revealed by God, grounded in nature, and respected by America's foundational principles.[43]

On February 23, 2011, President Obama ordered the United States Department of Justice to stop defending DOMA. The Archbishop of New York, Timothy M. Dolan, as president of the USCCB issued the following statement on March 3, 2011:

The announcement on February 23 that the President has instructed the Department of Justice to stop defending the Defense of Marriage Act (DOMA) is an alarming and grave injustice. Marriage, the union of one man and one woman as husband and wife, is a singular and irreplaceable institution. Only a man and a woman are capable of the "two-in-one-flesh" union of husband and wife. Only a man and a woman have the ability to bring children into the world. Along with that ability comes responsibility which society historically reinforces with laws that bind mothers and fathers to each other and their children. This family unit represents the most basic and vital cell of any society, protecting the right of children to know and be known by, to love and be loved by, their mother and father. Thus, marriage represents the bedrock of the common good of society, it's very foundation and future.

Contrary to the Attorney General's statement, DOMA does not single out people based on sexual "orientation" or inclination. Every person deserves to be treated with justice, compassion, and respect, a proposition of natural law and American law that we as Catholics vigorously promote. Unjust discrimination against any person is always wrong. But DOMA is not "unjust discrimination," rather, it merely affirms and protects the time-tested and unalterable meaning of marriage. The suggestion that this definition amounts to "discrimination" is grossly false and represents an affront to millions of citizens in this country.

The decision also does not stand the test of common sense. It is hardly "discrimination" to say that a husband and a wife have a unique and singular

---

43. Archdiocese of New York, *Statement of the Bishops of N.Y. State on SSM* (June 24, 2011), http://www.archny.org/news-events/news-press-releases/?i=20810 (last visited Oct. 2, 2017) (defining marriage as a union between a man and a woman).

relationship that two persons of the same sex—or any unmarried persons—simply do not and cannot have. Nor is it "discrimination" to believe that the union of husband and wife has a distinctive and exclusive significance worthy of promotion and protection by the state. It is not "discrimination" to say that having both a mother and a father matters to and benefits a child. Nor is it "discrimination" to say that the state has more than zero interest in ensuring that children will be intimately connected with and raised by their mother and father.

Protecting the definition of marriage is not merely permissible, but actually necessary as a matter of justice. Having laws that affirm the vital importance of mothers and fathers—laws that reinforce, rather than undermine, the ideal that children should be raised by their own mother and father—is essential for any just society. Those laws serve not only the good of the spouses and their children, but the common good. Those laws are now under relentless attack. If we forget the meaning of marriage, we forget what it means to be a human person, what it means to be a man or a woman. Have we wandered away so far in our society as to forget why men and women matter, and eroded the most central institution for our children and for our future?

The Administration's current position is not only a grave threat to marriage, but to religious liberty and the integrity of our democracy as well. Our nation and government have the duty to recognize and protect marriage, not tamper with and redefine it, nor to caricature the deeply held beliefs of so many citizens as "discrimination." On behalf of the United States Conference of Catholic Bishops, I express my deep disappointment over the Administration's recent decision. I have written of these concerns to the President in separate correspondence, and I pray that he and the Department of Justice may yet make the right choice to carry out their constitutional responsibility, defending the irreplaceable institution of marriage, and in so doing protect the future generations of our children.[44]

Archbishop Dolan followed this up by writing directly to President Barrack Obama on September 20, 2011.[45] He indicated that the Obama Administration's "attack" on DOMA would cause a serious breach in relations between the Catholic Church and

---

44. USCCB, News Release, *Archbishop Dolan Calls Refusal to Defend Defense of Marriage Act an 'Alarming and Grave Injustice'* (Mar. 3, 2011), http://www.usccb.org/news/2011/11-043.cfm (last visited Oct. 2, 2017).

45. Most Rev. Timothy M. Dolan, Letter to President Obama in support of DOMA (Sept. 20, 2011), http://www.usccb.org/issues-and-action/marriage-and-family/marriage/promotion-and-defense-of -marriage/upload/dolan-to-obama-doma-letter-sept-20-2011.pdf (last visited Oct. 2, 2017).

the United States government. He also indicated that such action would undermine marriage in this country. His complete letter follows:

―――――――――――――――――――――

September 20, 2011
President Barack Obama
The White House
1600 Pennsylvania Avenue
Washington, D.C. 20500

Dear Mr. President:

I write with a growing sense of urgency about recent actions taken by your Administration that both escalate the threat to marriage and imperil the religious freedom of those who promote and defend marriage. This past spring the Justice Department announced that it would no longer defend the Defense of Marriage Act (DOMA) in court, a decision strongly opposed by the Catholic Bishops of the United States and many others. Now the Justice Department has shifted from not defending DOMA — which is problem enough, given the duty of the executive branch to enforce even laws it disfavors — to actively attacking DOMA's constitutionality. My predecessor, Cardinal Francis George, OMI, and I have expressed to you in the past our strong disappointment about the direction your Administration has been moving regarding DOMA. Unfortunately the only response to date has been the intensification of efforts to undermine DOMA and the institution of marriage.

The Justice Department's move, in addition to other troubling federal decisions occurring recently, prompts me yet again to register my grave concerns. The content of this letter reflects the strong sentiment expressed at a recent meeting by more than thirty of my brother Bishops who serve on the Administrative Committee of our Episcopal conference. I know they are joined by hundreds of additional Catholic bishops throughout our nation. My observations are offered in the spirit of respectful, but frank dialogue.

The Catholic Bishops stand ready to affirm every positive measure taken by you and your Administration to strengthen marriage and the family. We cannot be silent, however, when federal steps harmful to marriage, the laws defending it, and religious freedom continue apace. Attached you will find an analysis prepared by my staff detailing the various executive activities of late that warrant our increasing apprehension.

Mr. President, your Administration's actions against DOMA and the values it stands for contrast sharply with your excellent Mother's Day and Father's Day proclamations issued earlier this year, which are also referenced in the attached analysis. In these perceptive and heartening statements, you correctly emphasize the critical role played by both a mom and a dad in a child's life, and you rightly call upon society to do all it can to uphold *both* mothers *and* fathers.

I know that you treasure the importance that you and the First Lady, separately and as a couple, share in the lives of your children. The Mother's Day and Father's Day proclamations display a welcome conviction on your part that neither a mom nor a dad is expendable. I believe therefore that you would agree that every child has the right to be loved by both a mother and a father.

The institution of marriage is built on this truth, which goes to the core of what the Catholic Bishops of the United States, and the millions of citizens who stand with us on this issue, want for all children and for the common good of society. That is why it is particularly upsetting, Mr. President, when your Administration, through the various court documents, pronouncements and policies identified in the attached analysis, attributes to those who support DOMA a motivation rooted in prejudice and bias. It is especially wrong and unfair to equate opposition to redefining marriage with either intentional or willfully ignorant racial discrimination, as your Administration insists on doing.

We as Bishops of the Catholic Church recognize the immeasurable personal dignity and equal worth of all individuals, including those with same-sex attraction, and we reject all hatred and unjust treatment against any person. Our profound regard for marriage as the complementary and fruitful union of a man and a woman does not negate our concern for the well-being of all people but reinforces it. While all persons merit our full respect, no other relationships provide for the common good what marriage between husband and wife provides. The law should reflect this reality.

Mr. President, I respectfully urge you to push the reset button on your Administration's approach to DOMA. Our federal government should not be presuming ill intent or moral blindness on the part of the overwhelming majority of its citizens, millions of whom have gone to the polls to directly support DOMAs in their states and have thereby endorsed marriage as the union of man and woman. Nor should a policy disagreement over the meaning of marriage be treated by federal officials as a federal offense — but this will happen if the Justice Department's latest constitutional theory prevails in court. The Administration's failure to change course on this matter will, as the attached analysis indicates, precipitate a national conflict between Church and State of enormous proportions and to the detriment of both institutions.

Thus, on behalf of my brother Bishops, I urge yet again that your Administration end its campaign against DOMA, the institution of marriage it protects, and religious freedom. Please know that I am always ready to discuss with you the concerns raised here and to address any questions that you may have. I am convinced that the door to a dialogue that is strong enough to endure even serious and fundamental disagreements can and must remain open, and I believe that you desire the same. Also please know that you, your family, and your Administration continue to be in my prayers.

Faithfully in Christ,
Most Reverend Timothy M. Dolan,
Archbishop of New York
President, United States Conference of
Catholic Bishops

Attachment:

USCCB Staff Analysis of Recent Federal Threats to Marriage April-August 2011

Early in 2011, the Department of Justice (DoJ) announced its decision to *refuse to defend* the federal Defense of Marriage Act (DOMA) from constitutional challenge,[46] which is a serious problem in its own right given the duty of the executive branch to enforce even laws it disfavors. More recently, however, the Department has begun *actively attacking* DOMA's constitutionality. On July 1, 2011, DoJ filed a brief in *Golinski v. U.S. Office of Personnel Management*, arguing that DOMA should be struck down as a form of sexual orientation discrimination.[47] This escalates yet again the level of hostility shown by DoJ against the definition of marriage codified in DOMA.

The Justice Department's argument in *Golinski* compares DOMA in effect to racially discriminatory laws. According to the government's view, support for a definition of marriage that recognizes that sexual difference is a defining and valuable feature of marriage now constitutes a forbidden intent to harm a vulnerable class of people. The false claim that animus is at work ignores the intrinsic goods of complementarity and fruitfulness found only in the union of man and woman as husband and wife. DoJ's contention thus transforms a moral disagreement into a constitutional violation, with grave practical consequences.

This new, more aggressive position poses a threat reaching well beyond the elimination of the federal DOMA. If successful in federal court, the Justice Department's claim would create a precedent that casts into constitutional doubt all state DOMAs. Also at risk would be any other federal or

---

46. OFFICE OF PUBLIC AFFAIRS, *supra* note 39.

47. Defendants' Brief in Opposition to Motions to Dismiss, Golinski v. U.S. Office Pers. Mgmt., No. C3:10-00257-JSW (N.D. Cal. Filed Feb. 23, 2011).

state policy that applies unique incentives for households where children are raised by a father and a mother who are legally married to each other.

The Justice Department's position also denigrates the considered judgment of the American people. In every state where citizens have been allowed to vote on state constitutional versions of DOMA, twenty-nine states in all, voters by sizable majorities have affirmed marriage as the union of a man and a woman. A total of forty-one states have statutory or constitutional DOMAs on the books. Equating the approval of these state laws with racial bias wrongly treats the millions of voters in those states as if they were bigots, who refuse to redefine marriage only out of hostility against those who experience same-sex attraction. It falsely imputes the same supposed bigotry and hostility to the substantial, bi-partisan majorities in Congress — and to President Clinton — who were responsible for the passage of DOMA only fifteen years ago.

Other steps taken by the Administration in this area also merit grave concern.

1. In May, a White House spokesperson indicated that President Obama supports the imposition of a federal mandate that "ensure[s] adoption rights for all couples and individuals, regardless of their sexual orientation."[48] This statement followed the introduction in Congress of H.R. 1681, Every Child Deserves a Family Act, a bill proposing to punish adoption and foster care agencies that refuse to participate in same-sex adoptions or foster care. The bill would deny access to federal funding and create a federal cause of action for damages. In a May 3 gathering of supporters of the bill, David Hansell of the Administration for Children and Families stated that "[t]he goals of that Act are admirable, and I'm delighted to say that we have already implemented much of what the Act would require of the federal government — specifically, providing technical assistance and guidance on recruiting adoptive and foster parents regardless of sexual orientation or gender identity[.]"[49]

This endorsement of parenting arrangements that, by design, exclude a child from the care of either an adoptive father or an adoptive mother ignores the indispensable role of *both* mothers *and* fathers. It also conflicts with President Obama's Mother's Day and Father's Day proclamations issued in May

---

48. *See* Chris Johnson, *Stark Introduces Adoption Anti-Discrimination Bill*, WASH. BLADE ONLINE (May 3, 2011), http://www.washingtonblade.com/2011/05/03/stark-introduces-adoption -anti-discrimination-bill/ (reporting on statement of White House spokesperson Shin Inouye) (last visited Oct. 3, 2017).

49. OFFICE OF PUBLIC AFFAIRS, ADMIN. FOR CHILDREN & FAMILIES, U.S. DEP'T OF HEALTH & HUMAN SERVICES, *Remarks for David Hansell: Meeting of Parents and Friends of Lesbians and Gays, the National Black Justice Coalition, and the Family Equality Council* (May 3, 2011), http://www.acf .hhs.gov/opa/remarks_050311b.html (ed. note moved to http://letsstrengthenmarriage.org/images /research/LSM-USCCBLettertoPresidentObama-DOMA-9-20-11.pdf).

and June of this year, which appeared to affirm a conviction on the President's part that neither a mom nor a dad is expendable.[50] Regarding mothers, President Obama acknowledged "the extraordinary importance of mothers in our lives," and rightly affirmed that "[m]others are the rocks of our families and a foundation in our communities." Regarding fathers, the President noted that "we honor the men in our lives who have helped shape us for the good, and we recommit to supporting fatherhood in our families, in our communities, and across our Nation." The President observed that "[a] father's absence is felt by children, families, and communities in countless ways, leaving a hole that can have lasting effects." He called on all "to recommit ourselves to making fatherhood, and the support men need to be fathers, a priority in our Nation." These stated commitments to the importance of both a mother and a father cannot be reconciled with a policy that supports adoption by same-sex couples, which are always missing either a mother or a father.

2. It was also reported in June that a push is underway to expand to all federal agencies a sexual orientation "sensitivity training" program created by the U.S. Department of Agriculture for its employees. The training materials advise that support for DOMA is to be treated as an actionable form of "heterosexism," which, employees are told, is "an 'ism' like sexism or racism."[51] The underlying goal of such a program—the elimination of so-called "heterosexism"—puts all federal officials subject to its mandate in an unavoidable bind: carrying out their very duty to uphold and enforce DOMA now would violate their workplace responsibilities. The training also pressures federal employees opposed to redefining marriage to ignore their moral and faith-based convictions.

3. Finally, anticipating the lifting of the "Don't Ask, Don't Tell" military policy, the Office of Navy Chaplains issued in April a directive requiring access to Navy chapels for wedding ceremonies involving two persons of the same sex.[52] The directive acknowledged that "[t]his is a change to previous training that stated that same-sex marriages are not authorized on federal property." The directive also referred to proposed amendments in training materials on the repeal of "Don't Ask, Don't Tell" that open the possibility that two persons of the same sex with a marriage license would have access to military housing on the same basis as married couples. In May, the Navy suspended the chaplaincy directive—but did not reject it outright—and this

50. President Barack Obama, Presidential Proclamation—Mother's Day (May 6, 2011), http://www.presidency.ucsb.edu/ws/index.php?pid=90364; President Barack Obama, Presidential Proclamation—Father's Day (June 17, 2011), http://www.presidency.ucsb.edu/ws/index.php?pid=90552.

51. U.S. Dep't of Agric., *Including Sexual Orientation and Sexual Identity in Diversity*, slides 16–17 (Jan. 2010), http://www.la.nrcs.usda.gov/about/LGBT/GLBT_Training_January_2010.pdf.

52. Memorandum from the Chief of Navy Chaplains to Chaplains and Religious Program Specialists on the Subject of Revision of Chaplain Corps Tier 1 Training (Apr. 13, 2011), http://assets.nationaljournal.com/pdf/2011.05.10.RevisionofChaplainCorpsTier1Training.pdf.

minimal retreat occurred only after strong congressional protests were raised highlighting the conflict with DOMA.[53]

In sum, these recent actions undermine certain fundamental truths about the nature of the human person—the equal importance of mothers *and* fathers to children, and the unchangeable meaning and nature of marriage as a communion of the sexes. They also oppose the deeply rooted consensus among the American people in support of the authentic definition of marriage and laws that reflect it. These actions also harm the common good by imperiling the religious freedom of those who hold these truths and defend these laws.

In particular, the Administration's efforts to change the law—in all three branches of the federal government—so that support for authentic marriage is treated as an instance of "sexual orientation discrimination," will threaten to spawn a wide range of legal sanctions against individuals and institutions within the Catholic community, and in many others as well. Based on the experience of religious entities under some state and local governments already, we would expect that, if the Administration succeeds, we would face lawsuits for supposed "discrimination" in all the areas where the Church operates in service to the common good, and where civil rights laws apply—such as employment, housing, education, and adoption services, to name just a few.

Even if religious entities prevail in such cases, we will face an additional layer of government punishments, such as the cessation of long-standing and successful contracts for the provision of social services, and other forms of withdrawn government cooperation. Society will suffer when religious entities are compelled to remove themselves from the social service network due to their duty to maintain their institutional integrity and not compromise on basic moral principles.

Thus, the comprehensive efforts of the federal government—using its formidable moral, economic, and coercive power—to enforce its new legal definition of "marriage" against a resistant Church would, if not reversed, precipitate a systemic national conflict between Church and State, harming both institutions, as well as our Nation as a whole.

————————————————————————

As with other issues, the view of many Catholics is not completely in accord with that of the Church. On March 24, 2001, an article by Robert P. Jones, CEO of Public Religion Research Institute and contributor to *The Washington Post*, cited several

---

53. Sara Sorcher, *Navy Suspends Guidelines for Same-Sex Marriages on Bases*, NationalJournal .com, May 11, 2011, http://www.nationaljournal.com/nationalsecurity/navy-suspends-guidelines-for -same-sex-marriages-on-bases-20110511.

polls indicating that a majority of Catholics would vote to allow gay and lesbian couples to marry.[54] A Quinnipiac University poll cited in the article indicated that 52% of Catholic voters in New York supported same-sex marriage as did 54% of Catholics in California. Mr. Jones cited an American Values Survey suggesting that 53% of Catholics support same-sex marriage, an even greater percentage (48%) than that of the general public. By 2017, according to a Pew Research poll, while 62% of Americans approved of same-sex marriage, among Catholics, the acceptance level was even higher, with two-thirds indicating approval.[55]

Nonetheless, the Catholic Church will continue to insist on the unity of a man and a woman as the sole basis for marriage.[56] This is an *ex cathedra* pronouncement. In 2007, Pope Benedict reaffirmed the Church's position. In *Sacramentum Caritatis*, the Pope noted that Catholics, particularly Catholic political leaders, had a duty to defend the fundamental values of the Catholic Church stating:

> [T]his is true for all the baptized, yet it is especially incumbent upon those who, by virtue of their social or political position, must make decisions regarding fundamental values, such as respect for human life, its defense from conception to natural death, the family build on marriage between a man and a woman, the freedom to educate one's children, and the promotion of the common good and all its forms. These values are not negotiable. Consequently, Catholic politicians and legislators, conscious of their grave responsibility before society, must feel particularly bound, on the basis of a properly formed conscience, to introduce and support laws inspired by values grounded in human nature.[57]

The clear position of the Catholic Church in this regard can be seen in the approach of the Vatican's Pontifical Council for the Family, in its statement on *Family, Marriage and "De Facto" Unions*.

> *Making homosexual relations equivalent to marriage is much more grave* [than recognizing common law unions among heterosexual couples].

---

54. Robert P. Jones, *Study*: *Strong Catholic Support for Gay Rights*, WASH. POST "GUEST VOICES" BLOG (Mar. 24, 2011), http://www.washingtonpost.com/blogs/guest-voices/post/why-do-catholics-support-gay-rights-when-the-hierarchydoes-not/2011/03/24/AFqObxVB_blog.html (last visited Oct. 3, 2017).

55. Pew Research Center, *Changing Attitudes on Gay Marriage, Public Opinion on same-sex marriage* (June 26, 2017), http://www.pewforum.org/fact-sheet/changing-attitudes-on-gay-marriage/ (last visited Oct. 2, 2017).

56. CATECHISM OF THE CATH. CHURCH, *Article 7*: *The Sacrament of Matrimony*, 1601 (1993), http://www.vatican.va/archive/ccc_css/archive/catechism/p2s2c3a7.htm (last visited Oct. 2, 2017).

"The matrimonial covenant, by which a man and a woman establish between themselves a partnership of the whole of life, is by its nature ordered toward the good of the spouses and the procreation and education of offspring; this covenant between baptized persons has been raised by Christ the Lord to the dignity of a sacrament." (CCC 1601).

57. Pope Benedict XVI, *supra* note 20; *see also* Vatican's Pontifical Council for the Family, *supra* note 23.

(23) The truth about conjugal love also makes it possible to understand the serious social consequences of the institutionalization of homosexual relations: "We can also see how incongruous is the demand to grant 'marital' status to unions between persons of the same sex. It is opposed, first of all, by the objective impossibility of making the partnership fruitful through the transmission of life according to the plan inscribed by God in the very structure of the human being. Another obstacle is the absence of the conditions for that interpersonal complementarity between male and female willed by the Creator at both the physical-biological and the eminently psychological levels." Marriage cannot be reduced to a condition similar to that of a homosexual relationship: this is contrary to common sense. In the case of homosexual relations, which demand to be considered de facto unions, the moral and juridical consequences take on special relevance. "Lastly, 'de facto unions' between homosexuals are a deplorable distortion of what should be a communion of love and life between a man and a woman in a reciprocal gift open to life." However, the presumption to make these unions equivalent to "legal marriage," as some recent initiatives attempt to do, is even more serious. Furthermore, the attempts to legalize the adoption of children by homosexual couples adds an element of great danger to all the previous ones. "The bond between two men or two women cannot constitute a real family and much less can the right be attributed to that union to adopt children without a family." To recall the social transcendence of the truth about conjugal love and consequently the grave error of recognizing or even making homosexual relations equivalent to marriage does not presume to discriminate against these persons in any way. It is the common good of society which requires the laws to recognize, favor and protect the marital union as the basis of the family which would be damaged in this way.[58]

However, there is some indication that Pope Francis is leading a discussion on an evolving Catholic Church position regarding the treatment of LGBT individuals within the church. In July 2013, Pope Francis opined, "If someone is gay and searches for the Lord and has good will, who am I to judge?"[59] On September 30, 2013, Pope Francis was quoted as stating, "A person once asked me, in a provocative manner, if I approved of homosexuality. I replied with another question: 'Tell me: when God looks at a gay person, does he endorse the existence of this person with love, or reject and condemn this person?' We must always consider the person. Here we enter into the mystery of the human being."[60]

---

58. Vatican's Pontifical Council for the Family, *supra* note 23.

59. Christopher J. Hale, *The Pope Francis Statement That Changed the Church on LGBT Issues*, Time.com (Jul. 28, 2015), http://time.com/3975630/pope-francis-lgbt-issues/ (last visited Oct. 15, 2017).

60. *Id.*

The following March, the Pope repeated the traditional position of the church that "marriage is between a man and a woman."[61] However, taking the same position that he had previously taken as Archbishop of Buenos Aires, the Pope argued that there might be some place for civil unions of LGBT people: "We have to look at different cases and evaluate them in their variety."[62]

Nonetheless, the church has not formally revised its position on same-sex marriage, although discussions on the need to include LGBT Catholics in a more formal way within the church continues.

3. Constitutional Issues — The Legal System Recognizes Same-Sex Marriage

While the Catholic Church opposition continued, and notwithstanding the fact that the majority of states did not recognize same-sex marriage, the Supreme Court of the United States has provided definitive determinations regarding the constitutional right to same-sex marriage recognition.

a. DOMA Declared Unconstitutional

In 2013, The Supreme Court found DOMA to violate the 5th Amendment:

---

133 S. Ct. 2675

UNITED STATES, Petitioner

v.

Edith SCHLAIN WINDSOR, In Her Capacity as Executor of the Estate of Thea Clara SPYER, ET AL.

On Writ of Certiorari to the United States Court of Appeals
for the Second Circuit
[June 26, 2013]

KENNEDY, J., delivered the opinion of the Court, in which GINSBURG, BREYER, SOTOMAYOR, and KAGAN, JJ., joined. ROBERTS, C.J., filed a dissenting opinion. SCALIA, J., filed a dissenting opinion, in which THOMAS, J., joined, and in which ROBERTS, C.J., joined as to Part I. ALITO, J., filed a dissenting opinion, in which THOMAS, J., joined as to Parts II and III.

JUSTICE KENNEDY delivered the opinion of the Court.

Excerpt:

. . . .

---

61. *Id.*
62. *Id.*

In 1996, as some States were beginning to consider the concept of same-sex marriage, see, e.g., *Baehr v. Lewin*, 74 Haw. 530, 852 P.2d 44 (1993), and before any State
had acted to permit it, Congress enacted the Defense of Marriage Act (DOMA), 110
Stat. 2419. DOMA contains two operative sections: Section 2, which has not been
challenged here, allows States to refuse to recognize same-sex marriages performed
under the laws of other States. See 28 U.S.C. § 1738C.

Section 3 is at issue here. It amends the Dictionary Act in Title 1, § 7, of the United
States Code to provide a federal definition of "marriage" and "spouse." Section 3 of
DOMA provides as follows:

> "In determining the meaning of any Act of Congress, or of any ruling, regu-
> lation, or interpretation of the various administrative bureaus and agencies of
> the United States, the word 'marriage' means only a legal union between one
> man and one woman as husband and wife, and the word 'spouse' refers only
> to a person of the opposite sex who is a husband or a wife." 1 U.S.C. § 7.

The definitional provision does not by its terms forbid States from enacting laws
permitting same-sex marriages or civil unions or providing state benefits to residents in that status. The enactment's comprehensive definition of marriage for purposes of all federal statutes and other regulations or directives covered by its terms,
however, does control over 1,000 federal laws in which marital or spousal status is
addressed as a matter of federal law. See GAO, D. Shah, Defense of Marriage Act:
Update to Prior Report 1 (GAO–04–353R, 2004).

. . . .

The decision of the Executive not to defend the constitutionality of § 3 in court
while continuing to deny refunds and to assess deficiencies does introduce a complication. Even though the Executive's current position was announced before the
District Court entered its judgment, the Government's agreement with Windsor's
position would not have deprived the District Court of jurisdiction to entertain and
resolve the refund suit; for her injury (failure to obtain a refund allegedly required
by law) was concrete, persisting, and unredressed. The Government's position —
agreeing with Windsor's legal contention but refusing to give it effect — meant that
there was a justiciable controversy between the parties, despite what the claimant
would find to be an inconsistency in that stance. Windsor, the Government, BLAG,
and the amicus appear to agree upon that point. The disagreement is over the standing of the parties, or aspiring parties, to take an appeal in the Court of Appeals and
to appear as parties in further proceedings in this Court.

. . . .

Against this background of lawful same-sex marriage in some States, the design,
purpose, and effect of DOMA should be considered as the beginning point in deciding whether it is valid under the Constitution. By history and tradition the definition
and regulation of marriage, as will be discussed in more detail, has been treated
as being within the authority and realm of the separate States. Yet it is further
established that Congress, in enacting discrete statutes, can make determinations

that bear on marital rights and privileges. Just this Term the Court upheld the authority of the Congress to pre-empt state laws, allowing a former spouse to retain life insurance proceeds under a federal program that gave her priority, because of formal beneficiary designation rules, over the wife by a second marriage who survived the husband. *Hillman v. Maretta*, 569 U.S.___, 133 S. Ct. 1943, ___ L. Ed. 2d ___ (2013); see also *Ridgway v. Ridgway*, 454 U.S. 46, 102 S. Ct. 49, 70 L. Ed. 2d 39 (1981); *Wissner v. Wissner*, 338 U.S. 655, 70 S. Ct. 398, 94 L. Ed. 424 (1950). This is one example of the general principle that when the Federal Government acts in the exercise of its own proper authority, it has a wide choice of the mechanisms and means to adopt. See *McCulloch v. Maryland*, 4 Wheat. 316, 421, 4 L. Ed. 579 (1819). Congress has the power both to ensure efficiency in the administration of its programs and to choose what larger goals and policies to pursue.

. . . .

Though these discrete examples establish the constitutionality of limited federal laws that regulate the meaning of marriage in order to further federal policy, DOMA has a far greater reach; for it enacts a directive applicable to over 1,000 federal statutes and the whole realm of federal regulations. And its operation is directed to a class of persons that the laws of New York, and of 11 other States, have sought to protect. See *Goodridge v. Department of Public Health*, 440 Mass. 309, 798 N.E.2d 941 (2003). . . .

. . . .

The significance of state responsibilities for the definition and regulation of marriage dates to the Nation's beginning; for "when the Constitution was adopted the common understanding was that the domestic relations of husband and wife and parent and child were matters reserved to the States." *Ohio ex rel. Popovici v. Agler*, 280 U.S. 379, 383–84, 50 S. Ct. 154, 74 L. Ed. 489 (1930). Marriage laws vary in some respects from State to State. For example, the required minimum age is 16 in Vermont, but only 13 in New Hampshire. Compare Vt. Stat. Ann., Tit. 18, § 5142 (2012), with N.H. Rev. Stat. Ann. § 457:4 (West Supp.2012). Likewise the permissible degree of consanguinity can vary (most States permit first cousins to marry, but a handful— such as Iowa and Washington, see Iowa Code § 595.19 (2009); Wash. Rev. Code § 26.04.020 (2012)—prohibit the practice). But these rules are in every event consistent within each State.

Against this background DOMA rejects the long-established precept that the incidents, benefits, and obligations of marriage are uniform for all married couples within each State, though they may vary, subject to constitutional guarantees, from one State to the next. Despite these considerations, it is unnecessary to decide whether this federal intrusion on state power is a violation of the Constitution because it disrupts the federal balance. The State's power in defining the marital relation is of central relevance in this case quite apart from principles of federalism. Here the State's decision to give this class of persons the right to marry conferred upon them a dignity and status of immense import. When the State used its historic and essential authority to define the marital relation in this way, its role and its power in making the decision enhanced the recognition, dignity, and protection of the class in their own community. DOMA, because of its reach and extent, departs from this history and tradition of reliance on state law to define marriage. "'[D]iscriminations of an unusual character especially suggest careful consideration to determine whether they are obnoxious to the constitutional provision.'" *Romer v. Evans*, 517 U.S. 620, 633.

. . . .

The Federal Government uses this state-defined class for the opposite purpose—to impose restrictions and disabilities. That result requires this Court now to address whether the resulting injury and indignity is a deprivation of an essential part of the liberty protected by the Fifth Amendment. What the State of New York treats as alike the federal law deems unlike by a law designed to injure the same class the State seeks to protect.

. . . .

The States' interest in defining and regulating the marital relation, subject to constitutional guarantees, stems from the understanding that marriage is more than a routine classification for purposes of certain statutory benefits. Private, consensual sexual intimacy between two adult persons of the same sex may not be punished by the State, and it can form "but one element in a personal bond that is more enduring." *Lawrence v. Texas*, 539 U.S. 558, 567, 123 S. Ct. 2472, 156 L. Ed. 2d 508 (2003). . . . This status is a far-reaching legal acknowledgment of the intimate relationship between two people, a relationship deemed by the State worthy of dignity in the community equal with all other marriages. It reflects both the community's considered perspective on the historical roots of the institution of marriage and its evolving understanding of the meaning of equality.

. . . .

The responsibility of the States for the regulation of domestic relations is an important indicator of the substantial societal impact the State's classifications have in the daily lives and customs of its people. DOMA's unusual deviation from the usual tradition of recognizing and accepting state definitions of marriage here operates to deprive same-sex couples of the benefits and responsibilities that come with the federal recognition of their marriages. This is strong evidence of a law having the purpose and effect of disapproval of that class. The avowed purpose and practical effect of the law here in question are to impose a disadvantage, a separate status, and so a stigma upon all who enter into same-sex marriages made lawful by the unquestioned authority of the States.

. . . .

The history of DOMA's enactment and its own text demonstrate that interference with the equal dignity of same-sex marriages, a dignity conferred by the States in the exercise of their sovereign power, was more than an incidental effect of the federal statute. It was its essence. . . . The stated purpose of the law was to promote an "interest in protecting the traditional moral teachings reflected in heterosexual-only marriage laws." *Ibid*. Were there any doubt of this far-reaching purpose, the title of the Act confirms it: The Defense of Marriage.

The arguments put forward by BLAG are just as candid about the congressional purpose to influence or interfere with state sovereign choices about who may be married. As the title and dynamics of the bill indicate, its purpose is to discourage enactment of state same-sex marriage laws and to restrict the freedom and choice of couples married under those laws if they are enacted. The congressional goal was "to put a thumb on the scales and influence a state's decision as to how to shape its own marriage laws." *Massachusetts* [*v. United States*], 682 F.3d [1], at 12–13 [(1st Cir. 2012)]. The Act's demonstrated purpose is to ensure that if any State decides to recognize same-sex marriages, those unions will be treated as second-class marriages for purposes of federal law. . . . When New York adopted a law to permit same-sex marriage, it sought to eliminate inequality; but DOMA frustrates that objective through a system-wide enactment with no identified connection to any particular area of federal law. DOMA writes inequality into the entire United States Code.

. . . .

The principal purpose is to impose inequality, not for other reasons like governmental efficiency . . . And DOMA contrives to deprive some couples married under the laws of their State, but not other couples, of both rights and responsibilities. By creating two contradictory marriage regimes within the same State, DOMA forces same-sex couples to live as married for the purpose of state law but unmarried for the purpose of federal law, thus diminishing the stability and predictability of basic personal relations the State has found it proper to acknowledge and protect. By this dynamic DOMA undermines both the public and private significance of state-sanctioned same-sex marriages; for it tells those couples, and all the world, that their otherwise valid marriages are unworthy of federal recognition. This places same-sex couples in an unstable position of being in a second-tier marriage. The differentiation demeans the couple, whose moral and sexual choices the Constitution protects, see *Lawrence*, 539 U.S. 558, 123 S. Ct. 2472, and whose relationship the State has sought to dignify. And it humiliates tens of thousands of children now being raised by same-sex couples. The law in question makes it even more difficult for the children to understand the integrity and closeness of their own family and its concord with other families in their community and in their daily lives.

. . . .

DOMA divests married same-sex couples of the duties and responsibilities that are an essential part of married life and that they in most cases would be honored to accept were DOMA not in force.

. . . .

DOMA singles out a class of persons deemed by a State entitled to recognition and protection to enhance their own liberty. It imposes a disability on the class by refusing to acknowledge a status the State finds to be dignified and proper. DOMA instructs all federal officials, and indeed all persons with whom same-sex couples interact, including their own children, that their marriage is less worthy than the marriages of others. The federal statute is invalid, for no legitimate purpose overcomes the purpose and effect to disparage and to injure those whom the State, by its marriage laws, sought to protect in personhood and dignity. By seeking to displace this protection and treating those persons as living in marriages less respected than others, the federal statute is in violation of the Fifth Amendment. This opinion and its holding are confined to those lawful marriages.

The judgment of the Court of Appeals for the Second Circuit is affirmed.

It is so ordered.

———

JUSTICE SCALIA, with whom JUSTICE THOMAS joins, and with whom THE CHIEF JUSTICE joins as to Part I, dissenting.

This case is about power in several respects. It is about the power of our people to govern themselves, and the power of this Court to pronounce the law. Today's opinion aggrandizes the latter, with the predictable consequence of diminishing the former. We have no power to decide this case. And even if we did, we have no power under the Constitution to invalidate this democratically adopted legislation. The Court's errors on both points spring forth from the same diseased root: an exalted conception of the role of this institution in America.

I.

A.

The Court is eager—hungry—to tell everyone its view of the legal question at the heart of this case. Standing in the way is an obstacle, a technicality of little interest to anyone but the people of We the People, who created it as a barrier against judges' intrusion into their lives. They gave judges, in Article III, only the "judicial Power," a power to decide not abstract questions but real, concrete "Cases" and "Controversies." Yet the plaintiff and the Government agree entirely on what should happen in this lawsuit. They agree that the court below got it right; and they agreed in the court below that the court below that one got it right as well. What, then, are we doing here? The answer lies at the heart of the jurisdictional portion of today's opinion, where a single sentence lays bare the majority's vision of our role.

. . . .

We have never before agreed to speak—to "say what the law is"—where there is no controversy before us. In the more than two centuries that this Court has existed as an institution, we have never suggested that we have the power to decide a question when every party agrees with both its nominal opponent and the court below on that question's answer.

. . . .

It may be argued that if what we say is true some Presidential determinations that statutes are unconstitutional will not be subject to our review. That is as it should be, when both the President and the plaintiff agree that the statute is unconstitutional. Where the Executive is enforcing an unconstitutional law, suit will of course lie; but if, in that suit, the Executive admits the unconstitutionality of the law, the litigation should end in an order or a consent decree enjoining enforcement. This suit saw the light of day only because the President enforced the Act (and thus gave Windsor standing to sue) even though he believed it unconstitutional. He could have equally chosen (more appropriately, some would say) neither to enforce nor to defend the statute he believed to be unconstitutional, see Presidential Authority to Decline to Execute Unconstitutional Statutes, 18 Op. Off. Legal Counsel 199 (Nov. 2, 1994)—in which event Windsor would not have been injured, the District Court could not have refereed this friendly scrimmage, and the Executive's determination of unconstitutionality would have escaped this Court's desire to blurt out its view of the law. The matter would have been left, as so many matters ought to be left, to a tug of war between the President and the Congress, which has innumerable means (up to and including impeachment) of compelling the President to enforce the laws it has written.

. . . .

II.

A.

There are many remarkable things about the majority's merits holding. The first is how rootless and shifting its justifications are. For example, the opinion starts with seven full pages about the traditional power of States to define domestic relations—initially fooling many readers, I am sure, into thinking that this is a federalism opinion. But we are eventually told that "it is unnecessary to decide whether this federal intrusion on state power is a violation of the Constitution," and that "[t]he State's power in defining the marital relation is of central relevance in this case quite apart from principles of federalism" because "the State's decision to give this class of persons the right to marry conferred upon them a dignity and status of immense import." But no one questions the power of the States to define marriage (with the concomitant conferral of dignity and status), so what is the point of devoting seven pages to describing how long and well established that power is? Even after the opinion has formally disclaimed reliance upon principles of federalism, mentions of "the usual tradition of recognizing and accepting state definitions of marriage" continue . . . What to make of this? The opinion never explains. My guess is that the majority, while reluctant to suggest that defining the meaning of "marriage" in federal statutes is unsupported by any of the Federal Government's enumerated powers, nonetheless needs some rhetorical basis to support its pretense that today's prohibition of laws excluding same-sex marriage is confined to the Federal Government (leaving the second, state-law shoe to be dropped later, maybe next Term). But I am only guessing.

. . . .

Yet the opinion does not argue that same-sex marriage is "deeply rooted in this Nation's history and tradition," *Washington v. Glucksberg*, 521 U.S. 702, 720–21 (1997), a claim that would of course be quite absurd. So would the further suggestion (also necessary, under our substantive-due-process precedents) that a world in which DOMA exists is one bereft of "'ordered liberty.'" *Id.*, at 721 (quoting *Palko v. Connecticut*, 302 U.S. 319, 325 (1937)). Some might conclude that this loaf could have used a while longer in the oven. But that would be wrong; it is already overcooked. The most expert care in preparation cannot redeem a bad recipe. The sum of all the Court's nonspecific hand-waving is that this law is invalid (maybe on equal-protection grounds, maybe on substantive-due-process grounds, and perhaps with some amorphous federalism component playing a role) because it is motivated by a "'bare . . .' desire to harm" couples in same-sex marriages . . . It is this proposition with which I will therefore engage.

B.

As I have observed before, the Constitution does not forbid the government to enforce traditional moral and sexual norms. See *Lawrence v. Texas*, 539 U.S. 558, 599 (2003) (SCALIA, J., dissenting). . . . [T]he Constitution neither requires nor forbids our society to approve of same-sex marriage, much as it neither requires nor forbids us to approve of no-fault divorce, polygamy, or the consumption of alcohol.

However, even setting aside traditional moral disapproval of same-sex marriage (or indeed same-sex sex), there are many perfectly valid—indeed, downright boring—justifying rationales for this legislation. Their existence ought to be the end of this case. For they give the lie to the Court's conclusion that only those with hateful hearts could have voted "aye" on this Act. And more importantly, they serve to make the contents of the legislators' hearts quite irrelevant: "It is a familiar principle of constitutional law that this Court will not strike down an otherwise constitutional statute on the basis of an alleged illicit legislative motive." *United States v. O'Brien*, 391 U.S. 367, 383 (1968). Or at least it was a familiar principle. By holding to the contrary, the majority has declared open season on any law that (in the opinion of the law's opponents and any panel of like-minded federal judges) can be characterized as mean-spirited.

The majority concludes that the only motive for this Act was the "bare . . . desire to harm a politically unpopular group."

. . . .

But the majority says that the supporters of this Act acted with malice—with the "purpose" . . . "to disparage and to injure" same-sex couples. It says that the motivation for DOMA was to "demean," *ibid.*; to "impose inequality," . . . to "impose . . . a stigma," . . . to deny people "equal dignity," *ibid.*; to brand gay people as "unworthy," . . . and to "humiliat[e]" their children, *ibid.* (emphasis added).

I am sure these accusations are quite untrue. To be sure (as the majority points out), the legislation is called the Defense of Marriage Act. But to defend traditional marriage is not to condemn, demean, or humiliate those who would prefer other arrangements, any more than to defend the Constitution of the United States is to condemn, demean, or humiliate other constitutions. To hurl such accusations so casually demeans this institution. In the majority's judgment, any resistance to its holding is beyond the pale of reasoned disagreement. To question its high-handed invalidation of a presumptively valid statute is to act (the majority is sure) with the purpose to "disparage," "injure," "degrade," "demean," and "humiliate" our fellow human beings, our fellow citizens, who are homosexual. All that, simply for supporting an Act that did no more than codify an aspect of marriage that had been unquestioned in our society for most of its existence—indeed, had been unquestioned in virtually all societies for virtually all of human history. It is one thing for a society to elect change; it is another for a court of law to impose change by adjudging those who oppose it hostes humani generis, enemies of the human race.

. . . .

The penultimate sentence of the majority's opinion is a naked declaration that "[t]his opinion and its holding are confined" to those couples "joined in same-sex marriages made lawful by the State." . . . I have heard such "bald, unreasoned disclaimer[s]" before. *Lawrence*, 539 U.S., at 604. When the Court declared a constitutional right to homosexual sodomy, we were assured that the case had nothing, nothing at all to do with "whether the government must give formal recognition to any relationship that homosexual persons seek to enter." *Id.*, at 578. Now we are told that DOMA is invalid because it "demeans the couple, whose moral and sexual choices the Constitution protects," . . . with an accompanying citation of Lawrence. It takes real cheek for today's majority to assure us, as it is going out the door, that a constitutional requirement to give formal recognition to same-sex marriage is not at issue here—when what has preceded that assurance is a lecture on how superior the majority's moral judgment in favor of same-sex marriage is to the Congress's hateful moral judgment against it. I promise you this: The only thing that will "confine" the Court's holding is its sense of what it can get away with . . . State and lower federal courts should take the Court at its word and distinguish away. In my opinion, however, the view that this Court will take of state prohibition of same-sex marriage is indicated beyond mistaking by today's opinion. As I have said, the real rationale of today's opinion, whatever disappearing trail of its legalistic argle-bargle one chooses to follow, is that DOMA is motivated by "'bare . . . desire to harm'" couples in same-sex marriages. *Supra*, at 18. How easy it is, indeed how inevitable, to reach the same conclusion with regard to state laws denying same-sex couples marital status.

. . . .

In my opinion, however, the view that this Court will take of state prohibition of same-sex marriage is indicated beyond mistaking by today's opinion. As I have said, the real rationale of today's opinion, whatever disappearing trail of its legalistic argle-bargle one chooses to follow, is that DOMA is motivated by "'bare . . . desire to harm'" couples in same-sex marriages. *Supra*, at 18. How easy it is, indeed how inevitable, to reach the same conclusion with regard to state laws denying same-sex couples marital status. Consider how easy (inevitable) it is to make the following substitutions in a passage from today's opinion . . . : "DOMA's *This state law's* principal effect is to identify a subset of state-sanctioned marriages *constitutionally protected sexual relationships*, see *Lawrence*, and make them unequal. The principal purpose is to impose inequality, not for other reasons like governmental efficiency. Responsibilities, as well as rights, enhance the dignity and integrity of the person. And DOMA *this state law* contrives to deprive some couples married under the laws of their State *enjoying constitutionally protected sexual relationships*, but not other couples, of both rights and responsibilities." . . .

. . . .

In sum, that Court which finds it so horrific that Congress irrationally and hatefully robbed same-sex couples of the "personhood and dignity" which state legislatures conferred upon them, will of a certitude be similarly appalled by state legislatures' irrational and hateful failure to acknowledge that "personhood and dignity" in the first place. . . . As far as this Court is concerned, no one should be fooled; it is just a matter of listening and waiting for the other shoe.

By formally declaring anyone opposed to same-sex marriage an enemy of human decency, the majority arms well every challenger to a state law restricting marriage to its traditional definition. Henceforth those challengers will lead with this Court's declaration that there is "no legitimate purpose" served by such a law, and will claim that the traditional definition has "the purpose and effect to disparage and to injure" the "personhood and dignity" of same-sex couples. . . . The result will be a judicial distortion of our society's debate over marriage—a debate that can seem in need of our clumsy "help" only to a member of this institution.

As to that debate: Few public controversies touch an institution so central to the lives of so many, and few inspire such attendant passion by good people on all sides. Few public controversies will ever demonstrate so vividly the beauty of what our Framers gave us, a gift the Court pawns today to buy its stolen moment in the spotlight: a system of government that permits us to rule ourselves. Since DOMA's passage, citizens on all sides of the question have seen victories and they have seen defeats. There have been plebiscites, legislation, persuasion, and loud voices—in other words, democracy. Victories in one place for some, see North Carolina Const., Amdt. 1 (providing that "[m]arriage between one man and one woman is the only domestic legal union that shall be valid or recognized in this State") (approved by a popular vote, 61% to 39% on May 8, 2012), are offset by victories in other places for others, see Maryland Question 6 (establishing "that Maryland's civil marriage laws allow gay and lesbian couples to obtain a civil marriage license") (approved by a popular vote, 52% to 48%, on November 6, 2012). Even in a single State, the question has come out differently on different occasions. Compare Maine Question 1 (permitting "the State of Maine to issue marriage licenses to same-sex couples") (approved by a popular vote, 53% to 47%, on November 6, 2012) with Maine Question 1 (rejecting "the new law that lets same-sex couples marry") (approved by a popular vote, 53% to 47%, on November 3, 2009).

In the majority's telling, this story is black-and-white: Hate your neighbor or come along with us. The truth is more complicated. It is hard to admit that one's political opponents are not monsters, especially in a struggle like this one, and the challenge in the end proves more than today's Court can handle. Too bad. A reminder that disagreement over something so fundamental as marriage can still be politically legitimate would have been a fit task for what in earlier times was called the judicial temperament. We might have covered ourselves with honor today, by promising all sides of this debate that it was theirs to settle and that we would respect their resolution. We might have let the People decide.

I dissent.

---

b. A Constitutional Right to Same-Sex Marriage Announced

The *Windsor* decision, while finding DOMA to be unconstitutional, nonetheless did not require the states to allow the creation of same-sex marriages. The issue whether the Constitution requires the states to allow the creation of such marriages was decided in the 2015 decision in *Obergefell v. Hodges*, 135 S. Ct. 2584 (2015):

---

135 S. Ct. 2584

James OBERGEFELL, et al., Petitioners v. Richard HODGES, Director, Ohio Department of Health, et al.

Decided June 26, 2015

Justice KENNEDY delivered the opinion of the Court, in which JUSTICES GINSBURG, BREYER, SOTOMAYOR and KAGAN joined.

The Constitution promises liberty to all within its reach, a liberty that includes certain specific rights that allow persons, within a lawful realm, to define and express their identity. The petitioners in these cases seek to find that liberty by marrying someone of the same sex and having their marriages deemed lawful on the same terms and conditions as marriages between persons of the opposite sex.

[. . .] From their beginning to their most recent page, the annals of human history reveal the transcendent importance of marriage. The lifelong union of a man and a woman always has promised nobility and dignity to all persons, without regard to their station in life. Marriage is sacred to those who live by their religions and offers unique fulfillment to those who find meaning in the secular realm. Its dynamic allows two people to find a life that could not be found alone, for a marriage becomes greater than just the two persons. Rising from the most basic human needs, marriage is essential to our most profound hopes and aspirations.

The centrality of marriage to the human condition makes it unsurprising that the institution has existed for millennia and across civilizations. Since the dawn of history, marriage has transformed strangers into relatives, binding families and societies together. [. . .] There are untold references to the beauty of marriage in religious and philosophical texts spanning time, cultures, and faiths, as well as in art and literature in all their forms. It is fair and necessary to say these references were based on the understanding that marriage is a union between two persons of the opposite sex.

That history is the beginning of these cases. The respondents say it should be the end as well. To them, it would demean a timeless institution if the concept and lawful status of marriage were extended to two persons of the same sex. Marriage, in their view, is by its nature a gender-differentiated union of man and woman. This view long has been held—and continues to be held—in good faith by reasonable and sincere people here and throughout the world.

The petitioners acknowledge this history but contend that these cases cannot end there. Were their intent to demean the revered idea and reality of marriage, the petitioners' claims would be of a different order. But that is neither their purpose nor their submission. To the contrary, it is the enduring importance of marriage that underlies the petitioners' contentions. This, they say, is their whole point. Far from seeking to devalue marriage, the petitioners seek it for themselves because of their respect—and need—for its privileges and responsibilities. And their immutable nature dictates that same-sex marriage is their only real path to this profound commitment.

[. . .] The ancient origins of marriage confirm its centrality, but it has not stood in isolation from developments in law and society. The history of marriage is one of both continuity and change. That institution—even as confined to opposite-sex relations—has evolved over time.

For example, marriage was once viewed as an arrangement by the couple's parents based on political, religious, and financial concerns; but by the time of the Nation's founding it was understood to be a voluntary contract between a man and a woman. As the role and status of women changed, the institution further evolved. Under the centuries-old doctrine of coverture, a married man and woman were treated by the State as a single, male-dominated legal entity. As women gained legal, political, and property rights, and as society began to understand that women have their own equal dignity, the law of coverture was abandoned. [. . .] These new insights have strengthened, not weakened, the institution of marriage.

[. . .] The Court has long held the right to marry is protected by the Constitution. In *Loving v. Virginia,* 388 U.S. 1, 12, 87 S. Ct. 1817 (1967), [. . .] a unanimous Court held marriage is "one of the vital personal rights essential to the orderly pursuit of happiness by free men." [...] Over time and in other contexts, the Court has reiterated that the right to marry is fundamental under the Due Process Clause. [...] It cannot be denied that this Court's cases describing the right to marry presumed a relationship involving opposite-sex partners. The Court, like many institutions, has made assumptions defined by the world and time of which it is a part.

[...] Still, this Court's cases have expressed constitutional principles of broader reach. [...] And in assessing whether the force and rationale of its cases apply to same-sex couples, the Court must respect the basic reasons why the right to marry has been long protected. [...] This analysis compels the conclusion that same-sex couples may exercise the right to marry. The four principles and traditions to be discussed demonstrate that the reasons marriage is fundamental under the Constitution apply with equal force to same-sex couples.

A first premise of the Court's relevant precedents is that the right to personal choice regarding marriage is inherent in the concept of individual autonomy. This abiding connection between marriage and liberty is why *Loving* invalidated interracial marriage bans under the Due Process Clause. Like choices concerning contraception, family relationships, procreation, and childrearing, all of which are protected by the Constitution, decisions concerning marriage are among the most intimate that an individual can make.

The nature of marriage is that, through its enduring bond, two persons together can find other freedoms, such as expression, intimacy, and spirituality. This is true for all persons, whatever their sexual orientation. There is dignity in the bond between two men or two women who seek to marry and in their autonomy to make such profound choices.

A second principle in this Court's jurisprudence is that the right to marry is fundamental because it supports a two-person union unlike any other in its importance to the committed individuals. (*Griswold v. Connecticut.*)

Marriage responds to the universal fear that a lonely person might call out only to find no one there. It offers the hope of companionship and understanding and assurance that while both still live there will be someone to care for the other. [...] While *Lawrence* confirmed a dimension of freedom that allows individuals to engage in intimate association without criminal liability, it does not follow that freedom stops there. Outlaw to outcast may be a step forward, but it does not achieve the full promise of liberty.

A third basis for protecting the right to marry is that it safeguards children and families and thus draws meaning from related rights of childrearing, procreation, and education.

[...] As all parties agree, many same-sex couples provide loving and nurturing homes to their children, whether biological or adopted. And hundreds of thousands of children are presently being raised by such couples. Most States have allowed gays and lesbians to adopt, either as individuals or as couples, and many adopted and foster children have same-sex parents. This provides powerful confirmation from the law itself that gays and lesbians can create loving, supportive families.

Excluding same-sex couples from marriage thus conflicts with a central premise of the right to marry. Without the recognition, stability, and predictability marriage offers, their children suffer the stigma of knowing their families are somehow lesser. They also suffer the significant material costs of being raised by unmarried parents, relegated through no fault of their own to a more difficult and uncertain family life. The marriage laws at issue here thus harm and humiliate the children of same-sex couples.

[. . .] Fourth and finally, this Court's cases and the Nation's traditions make clear that marriage is a keystone of our social order. [. . .] For that reason, just as a couple vows to support each other, so does society pledge to support the couple, offering symbolic recognition and material benefits to protect and nourish the union. Indeed, while the States are in general free to vary the benefits they confer on all married couples, they have throughout our history made marriage the basis for an expanding list of governmental rights, benefits, and responsibilities. These aspects of marital status include: taxation; inheritance and property rights; rules of intestate succession; spousal privilege in the law of evidence; hospital access; medical decisionmaking authority; adoption rights; the rights and benefits of survivors; birth and death certificates; professional ethics rules; campaign finance restrictions; workers' compensation benefits; health insurance; and child custody, support, and visitation rules. [. . .] There is no difference between same- and opposite-sex couples with respect to this principle. Yet by virtue of their exclusion from that institution, same-sex couples are denied the constellation of benefits that the States have linked to marriage. This harm results in more than just material burdens. It demeans gays and lesbians for the State to lock them out of a central institution of the Nation's society. Same-sex couples, too, may aspire to the transcendent purposes of marriage and seek fulfillment in its highest meaning.

[. . .] The right of same-sex couples to marry that is part of the liberty promised by the Fourteenth Amendment is derived, too, from that Amendment's guarantee of the equal protection of the laws. The Due Process Clause and the Equal Protection Clause are connected in a profound way, though they set forth independent principles. Rights implicit in liberty and rights secured by equal protection may rest on different precepts and are not always co-extensive, yet in some instances each may be instructive as to the meaning and reach of the other. In any particular case one Clause may be thought to capture the essence of the right in a more accurate and comprehensive way, even as the two Clauses may converge in the identification and definition of the right. This interrelation of the two principles furthers our understanding of what freedom is and must become. [. . .] Although *Lawrence* elaborated its holding under the Due Process Clause, it acknowledged, and sought to remedy, the continuing inequality that resulted from laws making intimacy in the lives of gays and lesbians a crime against the State. *Lawrence* therefore drew upon principles of liberty and equality to define and protect the rights of gays and lesbians, holding the State "cannot demean their existence or control their destiny by making their private sexual conduct a crime."

This dynamic also applies to same-sex marriage. [. . .] The marriage laws enforced by the respondents are in essence unequal: same-sex couples are denied all the benefits afforded to opposite-sex couples and are barred from exercising a fundamental right. Especially against a long history of disapproval of their relationships, this denial to same-sex couples of the right to marry works a grave and continuing harm. The imposition of this disability on gays and lesbians serves to disrespect and subordinate them. And the Equal Protection Clause, like the Due Process Clause, prohibits this unjustified infringement of the fundamental right to marry.

These considerations lead to the conclusion that the right to marry is a fundamental right inherent in the liberty of the person, and under the Due Process and Equal Protection Clauses of the Fourteenth Amendment couples of the same-sex may not be deprived of that right and that liberty. The Court now holds that same-sex couples may exercise the fundamental right to marry [. . .] and the State laws challenged by Petitioners in these cases are now held invalid to the extent they exclude same-sex couples from civil marriage on the same terms and conditions as opposite-sex couples.

No union is more profound than marriage, for it embodies the highest ideals of love, fidelity, devotion, sacrifice, and family. In forming a marital union, two people become something greater than once they were. As some of the petitioners in these cases demonstrate, marriage embodies a love that may endure even past death. It would misunderstand these men and women to say they disrespect the idea of marriage. Their plea is that they do respect it, respect it so deeply that they seek to find its fulfillment for themselves. Their hope is not to be condemned to live in loneliness, excluded from one of civilization's oldest institutions. They ask for equal dignity in the eyes of the law. The Constitution grants them that right.

Chief Justice ROBERTS, with whom Justice SCALIA and Justice THOMAS join, dissenting.

Petitioners make strong arguments rooted in social policy and considerations of fairness. They contend that same-sex couples should be allowed to affirm their love and commitment through marriage, just like opposite-sex couples. That position has undeniable appeal. [. . .] But this Court is not a legislature. Whether same-sex marriage is a good idea should be of no concern to us. Under the Constitution, judges have power to say what the law is, not what it should be.

[. . .] Supporters of same-sex marriage have achieved considerable success persuading their fellow citizens—through the democratic process—to adopt their view. That ends today. Five lawyers have closed the debate and enacted their own vision of marriage as a matter of constitutional law. Stealing this issue from the people will for many cast a cloud over same-sex marriage, making a dramatic social change that much more difficult to accept.

The majority's decision is an act of will, not legal judgment. The right it announces has no basis in the Constitution or this Court's precedent. As a result, the Court invalidates the marriage laws of more than half the States and orders the transformation of a social institution that has formed the basis of human society for millennia, for the Kalahari Bushmen and the Han Chinese, the Carthaginians and the Aztecs. Just who do we think we are?

[. . .] As the majority notes, some aspects of marriage have changed over time. [. . .] These changes did not, however, work any transformation in the core structure of marriage as the union between a man and a woman. If you had asked a person on the street how marriage was defined, no one would ever have said, "Marriage is the union of a man and a woman, where the woman is subject to coverture." The majority may be right that the "history of marriage is one of both continuity and change," but the core meaning of marriage has endured.

[. . .] The majority's approach has no basis in principle or tradition, except for the unprincipled tradition of judicial policymaking that characterized discredited decisions such as *Lochner v. New York*, 198 U.S. 45.

To avoid repeating *Lochner*'s error of converting personal preferences into constitutional mandates, our modern substantive due process cases have stressed the need for "judicial self-restraint." Our precedents have required that implied fundamental rights be "objectively, deeply rooted in this Nation's history and tradition," and "implicit in the concept of ordered liberty, such that neither liberty nor justice would exist if they were sacrificed." [*Washington v. Glucksberg*, 521 U.S. 720-721.]

[. . .] Expanding a right suddenly and dramatically is likely to require tearing it up from its roots. Even a sincere profession of "discipline" in identifying fundamental rights does not provide a meaningful constraint on a judge, for "what he is really likely to be 'discovering,' whether or not he is fully aware of it, are his own values," J. Ely, Democracy and Distrust (1980). The only way to ensure restraint in this delicate enterprise is "continual insistence upon respect for the teachings of history, solid recognition of the basic values that underlie our society, and wise appreciation of the great roles [of] the doctrines of federalism and separation of powers." *Grisworld* (Harlan, J., concurring in judgment).

[. . .] Neither *Lawrence* nor any other precedent in the privacy line of cases supports the right that petitioners assert here. Unlike criminal laws banning contraceptives and sodomy, the marriage laws at issue here involve no government intrusion. They create no crime and impose no punishment. Same-sex couples remain free to live together, to engage in intimate conduct, and to raise their families as they see fit. No one is "condemned to live in loneliness" by the laws challenged in these cases — no one. At the same time, the laws in no way interfere with the "right to be let alone."

[. . .] One immediate question invited by the majority's position is whether States may retain the definition of marriage as a union of two people. Although the majority randomly inserts the adjective "two" in various places, it offers no reason at all why the two-person element of the core definition of marriage may be preserved while the man-woman element may not. Indeed, from the standpoint of history and tradition, a leap from opposite-sex marriage to same-sex marriage is much greater than one from a two-person union to plural unions, which have deep roots in some cultures around the world.

[…] In addition to their due process argument, petitioners contend that the Equal Protection Clause requires their States to license and recognize same-sex marriages. […] Absent from this portion of the opinion, however, is anything resembling our usual framework for deciding equal protection cases. […] In any event, the marriage laws at issue here do not violate the Equal Protection Clause, because distinguishing between opposite-sex and same-sex couples is rationally related to the States' "legitimate state interest" in "preserving the traditional institution of marriage." […] The equal protection analysis might be different, in my view, if we were confronted with a more focused challenge to the denial of certain tangible benefits.

[…] If you are among the many Americans—of whatever sexual orientation— who favor expanding same-sex marriage, by all means celebrate today's decision. Celebrate the achievement of a desired goal. Celebrate the opportunity for a new expression of commitment to a partner. Celebrate the availability of new benefits. But do not celebrate the Constitution. It had nothing to do with it.

4. Children of Same-Sex Couples

The legal system recognizes same-sex marriage and the Catholic Church does not. It should come as no surprise then that the way each system views related issues including adoption would vary.

a. Child Custody Suits

The Supreme Court has held the right to have and nurture children is a fundamental liberty,[63] which will be protected against all but the most compelling state interests.[64] In the event of a divorce or legal separation, this protection is endangered

---

63. Stanley v. Illinois, 405 U.S. 645, 651 (1971) ("The private interest . . . , of a man in the children he has sired and raised, undeniably warrants deference and, absent a powerful countervailing interest, protection."); Pierce v. Soc'y of Sisters, 268 U.S. 510, 518 (1924) (stating that parents should have the freedom to guide their child both intellectually and religiously); Meyer v. Nebraska, 262 U.S. 390, 399 (1923) (reasoning that the right to conceive and raise one's child is "essential to the orderly pursuit of happiness by free men").

64. See, e.g., Troxel v. Granville, 530 U.S. 57, 96 (2000) (Kennedy, J., dissenting) (noting that protecting a child from harm provides a "compelling state interest" that overrides a parent's fundamental right to raise his or her own child); Christensen v. State, 468 S.E.2d 188, 190 (Ga.

when parents are unable to agree on child custody arrangements.[65] Therefore courts must step in to make an initial apportionment for the child during marriage dissolutions.[66] The courts are required by statutes[67] and case law[68] to balance the positive and negative characteristics of each party to determine child custody disputes and place the child with the party that is able to best serve the child's needs.[69]

Complicating matters, the "best interests of the child" standard is usually ambiguously defined.[70] In those jurisdictions, judges have expansive discretionary power to safeguard the children presented in their court and can consider practically any factor relevant to the child's best interest.[71] While this flexibility is touted as helping to avoid an arbitrary judgment that may contradict with a child's best interest, it also invites discrimination that may result in the child's best interest being compromised in favor of a judge's own biases.[72]

1996) (holding that the "furtherance of the moral welfare of the public" provides a compelling state interest to prohibit sodomy). *See generally* Sheila Reynolds & Roy B. Lacoursiere, *Interminable Child Neglect/Custody Cases: Are There Better Alternatives?*, 21 J. Fam. L. 239, 264–65, 269–73 (1982–83) (noting that what qualifies as a compelling interest may vary depending on the state).

65. Vicki Parrott, *Pulliam v. Smith*, 19 Campbell L. Rev. 131, 138 (1996). Although a parent has a fundamental right to raise his or her own child, the child's well-being takes precedence over the parent's liberty interest in the course of a custody or visitation dispute. *See, e.g.,* Wasserman v. Wasserman, 671 F.2d 832, 833 (4th Cir. 1982).

66. Parrott, *supra* note 65, at 138. With respect to visitation privileges, courts generally allocate them on a reasonable basis in order to foster the relationship between the child and non-custodial parent. *See, e.g.,* Boswell v. Boswell, 701 A.2d 1153, 1163 (Md. Ct. Spec. App. 1997) (noting that a parent can see his or her child at reasonable times if the child is not in his or her custody), *affd.* 721 A.2d 662 (Md. 1998).

67. *See, e.g.,* Ark. Code Ann. §9–13–101 (Supp. 2002); Conn. Gen. Stat. Ann. §46b-56 (West 1987); Ga. Code Ann. §19–9–3 (1988); Minn. Stat. Ann. §257.025 (West 1988); *see also* Uniform Marriage and Divorce Act §402 (1987).

68. *See, e.g.,* Bull v. Bull, 24 Cal. Rptr. 149, 150 (Cal. Dist. Ct. App. 1962) (stating that between a choice of two households, a child's best interests will be met where he or she will be "better cared for, better trained, more secure and happier"); Finlay v. Finlay, 240 N.Y. 429, 433–34; 148 N.E. 624, 626 (1925) ("The chancellor . . . acts as *parens patriae* to do what is best for the interest of the child. He is to put himself in the position of a 'wise, affectionate and careful parent' . . . , and make provision for the child accordingly."); Wolff v. Wolff, 349 N.W.2d 656, 658 (S.D. 1984).

69. *Developments in the Law: Sexual Orientation and the Law*, 102 Harv. L. Rev. 1508, 1629 (1989) (citing A. Haralambie, Handling Child Custody Cases §§3.06, 7.07 (1983)) [hereinafter *Developments*].

70. For example, many state statutes and case rulings do not provide the judge with a list of factors to consider when determining what is best for the child's welfare. *See supra* note 68.

71. Parrott, *supra* note 65, at 138.

72. Julie Shapiro, *Custody and Conduct: How the Law Fails Lesbian and Gay Parents and Their Children*, 71 Ind. L.J. 623, 647 (1996) ("In addition to . . . genuine concerns, some judges appear to be motivated by general hostility towards lesbian and gay parents and a desire to punish these individuals for living in a manner which the court finds unacceptable."); *see, e.g.,* Ward v. Ward, 742 So. 2d 250, 252–55 (Fla. Dist. Ct. App. 1996) (removing child from custody of lesbian mother and granting custody to the father, who had served an eight-year prison term for the second-degree murder of his first wife); Bottoms v. Bottoms, 457 S.E.2d 102, 108 (Va. 1995) (removing child from

Prior to *Obergefell*, and depending on the jurisdiction, if one of the persons seeking child custody was homosexual, courts utilized a "nexus test" considering homosexuality as one of many factors.[73] (Other factors included the sex and age of the child, the respective home environment of the parties, the characteristics of those seeking custody, and the capacity and interest of each parent to provide for the varying needs of the child.)[74] In addition, courts would consider the health, safety, and general moral and social well-being of the child as a result of the custody decision, as in all other custody determinations. However, subsequent to *Lawrence* and *Obergefell*, it is unlikely that a court which denies custody on the sole fact of the homosexuality of one of the litigants would be upheld.[75] Even prior to these cases however, homosexuality could not be the sole factor in awarding custody unless the homosexual conduct of the parent harmed the child.[76] There is still room for courts to consider behavior of a homosexual parent which harms the child in making custody determinations, just as courts can weigh behavior of a heterosexual parent which harms the child.

The church has not directly addressed custody issues in same-sex couples. However, Pope Francis recently noted during a meeting of the Union of Superiors General at the Vatican in November of 2013, when acknowledging the reality of the growing numbers of children of same-sex unions, divorced, or non-traditional families:

> "How can we proclaim Christ to these boys and girls?" the pope asked. "How can we proclaim Christ to a generation that is changing? We must be careful not to administer a vaccine against faith to them."[77]

b. Gay and Lesbian People as Adoptive Parents in the Legal System

The legal system no longer precludes gay and lesbian people from adopting. See for example, the decision in the case of *V.L. v. E.L.*, 136 S. Ct. 1017 (2016). In that 2016 decision, the Supreme Court reversed an Alabama Supreme Court decision

---

custody of loving and nurturing mother because she engaged in criminal, immoral sexual behavior with her live-in partner). In addition, appellate courts will only reverse a trial court's denial of custody if there is a clear abuse of discretion; therefore, the trial court's decision is generally final. *See Developments*, *supra* note 69, at 1630.

73. *See id.* at 636–37 (noting that the heterosexual father in the *Van Driel* case was not granted custody because he gave no evidence showing that the lesbian mother adversely affected the children's well-being).

74. 64 Am. Jur. 3d *Proof of Facts* 403 (Originally published in 2001).

75. *Id.*

76. Shapiro, *supra* note 72, at 636–37.

77. Jimmy Akin, *What Did Pope Francis Say About the Children of Homosexual Couples? 8 Things to Know and Share*, NCRegister.com (Jan. 4, 2014), http://www.ncregister.com/blog/jimmy-akin/what-did-pope-francis-say-about-the-children-of-homosexual-couples-8-things.

which had failed to recognize the adoption of a child by a same-sex couple from another jurisdiction.

c. The Catholic Church Opposes Adoptions by Same-Sex Couples

The Catholic Church's aversion to homosexuality stems from its Scripture-based[78] view of human life and sexuality.[79] The Bible proclaims that God created man and woman in his own image and likeness.[80] As creations of God, men and women are called to mirror the "inner unity of the Creator" by way of their "complementarity," and must unite with God in the "transmission of life" by "a mutual donation of the self to the other."[81] Homosexual activity, lacking this complementarity, therefore challenges "the rich symbolism and meaning, not to mention the goals, of the Creator's sexual design."[82] Faced with this fundamental conflict in today's world, while the church believes that homosexual *persons* should be accepted with sensitivity, compassion and respect, there are no circumstances under which homosexual *acts* can be approved of by the Catholic Church.[83]

With this understanding, it should be no surprise that the Church has taken a public position against allowing children to be adopted or fostered in households of same-sex couples.[84] Solidifying its position against such practices, in 2003 the Congregation for the Doctrine of the Faith, the "Vatican group charged with promoting and safeguarding Catholic Church doctrine,"[85] released a document titled

---

78. Congregation for the Doctrine of the Faith, Letters to the Bishops of the Catholic Church on the Pastoral Care of Homosexual Persons (Oct. 1, 1986) [hereinafter Letters to the Bishops], http://www.vatican.va/roman_curia/congregations/cfaith/documents/rc_con_cfaith_doc_1986 1001_homosexual-persons_en.html (last visited Oct. 2, 2017). After the fall and the introduction of original sin, the men of Sodom are considered sinners partly due to their homosexual relations. *Genesis* 19:1–11. Meanwhile, those who behave in a homosexual fashion are excluded from the rank of the Chosen People. *Leviticus* 18:22, 20:13. The apostle Paul confirms that those who engage in such behavior shall not enter the Kingdom of God in *1 Corinthians* 6:9, and refers to it as a kind of blindness overcoming mankind in *Romans* 1:18–32.

79. Catechism of the Cath. Church, 2332–33: "Sexuality affects all aspects of the human person in the unity of his body and soul. . . . Everyone, man and woman, should acknowledge and accept his sexual identity.", http://www.vatican.va/archive/ENG0015/__P84.HTM (last visited Oct. 2, 2017). Catechism of the Cath. Church, 2337: "Chastity means the successful integration of sexuality within the person and thus the inner unity of man in his bodily and spiritual being.", 2351–55: "Offenses against chastity include lust, fornication, masturbation, pornography, and prostitution", 2359: "and homosexual persons are called to chastity", http://www.vatican.va /archive/ENG0015/__P85.HTM (last visited Oct. 2, 2017).

80. *Genesis* 1:26–27.

81. Letters to the Bishops, *supra* note 78.

82. *Id.*

83. *Id.*

84. Elisa Y. Lee, *An American Way of Life: Prescription Drug Use in the Modern ADA Workplace*, 45 Colum. J.L. & Soc. Probs. 225, 230–31.

85. The Congregation is the body in the Vatican responsible for promoting and safeguarding Catholic Church doctrine. *See* Pope John Paul II, *Apostolic Constitution*, *Pastor Bonus*, Art. 48

"Considerations Regarding Proposals to Give Legal Recognition to Unions Between Homosexual Persons."[86] This document explicitly stated the Church's position on same-sex couple adoption, that "allowing children to be adopted by persons living in [homosexual] unions would actually mean doing violence to these children," because the absence of "sexual complementarity" in same-sex unions "creates obstacles in the normal development of children who would be placed in the care of such [homosexual] persons."[87] Through the Considerations, the Catholic Church took the view that homosexuality, its unions, and acts are "troubling moral and social phenomen[a]," "against the natural moral law," "serious depravit[ies]," "intrinsically disordered," "immoral," and "evil."[88] Since this document came from the Congregation, its authority necessitates that all Catholics, especially Catholic politicians, have a moral obligation to oppose the legal recognition of same-sex unions.[89]

On March 9, 2006, guided by the Considerations document, Cardinal William Joseph Levada, the current head of the Congregation and former Archbishop of San Francisco released a directive to the Archdiocese of San Francisco requiring it to discontinue placing children available for adoption with same-sex households.[90] Then on March 17, 2006, George Niederauer, the Archbishop of San Francisco, publicized that Catholic Charities would also stop placing children in same-sex households.[91] These actions were almost immediately followed by a response by the San Francisco Board of Supervisors (the Board), the legislative body of the City and County.[92] Just four days later, the Board unanimously passed non-binding Resolution No. 168–06:

> Resolution urging Cardinal William Levada, in his capacity as head of the Congregation for the Doctrine of the Faith at the Vatican, to withdraw his discriminatory and defamatory directive that Catholic Charities of the Archdiocese of San Francisco stop placing children in need of adoption with homosexual households.
>
> WHEREAS, It is an insult to all San Franciscans when a foreign country, like the Vatican, meddles with and attempts to negatively influence this great City's existing and established customs and traditions such as the right of same-sex couples to adopt and care for children in need; and

---

(June 28, 1988), http://www.vatican.va/holy_father/john_paul_ii/apost_constitutions/documents/hf_jp-ii_apc_19880628_pastor-bonus_en.html (last visited Oct. 2, 2017).

86. Congregation for the Doctrine of the Faith, *Considerations Regarding Proposals to Give Legal Recognition to Unions Between Homosexual Persons* (July 31, 2003) [hereinafter *Considerations*], http://www.vatican.va/roman_curia/congregations/cfaith/documents/rc_con_cfaith_doc_20030731_homosexual-unions_en.html (last visited Oct. 2, 2017).

87. *Id.*

88. *Id.*

89. *Id.*

90. Wyatt Buchanan, *Archdiocese Halts Same-Sex Adoptions at Catholic Charities*, S.F. Chron., Feb. 12, 2014, http://articles.sfgate.com/2006-03-21/bay-area/17286860_1_catholic-charities-adoptions-same-sex-couples. Not available anymore.

91. *Id.*

92. Lee, *supra* note 84.

WHEREAS, The statements of Cardinal Levada and the Vatican that "Catholic agencies should not place children for adoption in homosexual households," and "Allowing children to be adopted by persons living in such unions would actually mean doing violence to these children" are absolutely unacceptable to the citizenry of San Francisco; and

WHEREAS, Such hateful and discriminatory rhetoric is both insulting and callous, and shows a level of insensitivity and ignorance which has seldom been encountered by this Board of Supervisors; and

WHEREAS, Same-sex couples are just as qualified to be parents as are heterosexual couples; and

WHEREAS, Cardinal Levada is a decidedly unqualified representative of his former home city, and of the people of San Francisco and the values they hold dear; and

WHEREAS, The Board of Supervisors urges Archbishop Niederauer and the Catholic Charities of the Archdiocese of San Francisco to defy all discriminatory directives of Cardinal Levada; now, therefore, be it

RESOLVED, That the Board of Supervisors urges Cardinal William Levada, in his capacity as head of the Congregation for the Doctrine of the Faith at the Vatican (formerly known as Holy Office of the Inquisition), to withdraw his discriminatory and defamatory directive that Catholic Charities of the Archdiocese of San Francisco stop placing children in need of adoption with homosexual households.[93]

In turn the Catholic Church, through the Catholic League for Religious and Civil Rights, sued the City and County of San Francisco.[94] The case was dismissed by the United States District Court of the Northern District of California for failure to state a claim upon which relief could be granted.[95] On appeal, the Ninth Circuit initially affirmed the district court's dismissal and holding[96] but then voted to rehear the case en banc.[97] The Ninth Circuit affirmed the district court's dismissal.[98]

The Archdiocese responded by withdrawing its financial support with any adoption agency that works to place children with homosexual couples.[99] This reaction mirrors the actions taken by the Catholic Charities of Boston, one of the nation's

---

93. *See* S.F., Cal., Board of Supervisors Res. No. 168–06 (Mar. 21, 2006).

94. Complaint, *Catholic League I*, 464 F. Supp. 2d 938 (N.D. Cal. 2006) (No. C 06-2351).

95. *Catholic League I*, 464 F. Supp. 2d 938 (N.D. Cal. 2006), *aff'd en banc*, 624 F.3d 1043 (9th Cir. 2010).

96. *Catholic League II*, 567 F.3d 595 (9th Cir. 2009), *vacated*, 624 F.3d 1043 (9th Cir. 2010).

97. Catholic League for Religious & Civil Rights v. City & County of S.F., 586 F.3d 1166 (9th Cir. 2009).

98. *Catholic League III*, 624 F.3d 1043 (9th Cir. 2010).

99. CNA, *Catholic Charities in San Francisco Severs Links to Homosexual Adoptions*, Catholic-NewsAgency.com (Oct. 5, 2008), https://www.catholicnewsagency.com/news/catholic_charities _in_san_francisco_severs_links_to_ homosexual_adoptions (last visited Oct. 2, 2017).

oldest adoption agencies. In 2006, the Catholic Charities of Boston faced a difficult choice; violate the Congregation or shut down its adoption services.[100] To be licensed by Massachusetts, the Catholic Charities of Boston would have to allow adoptions by same-sex couples in order to be in compliance with state laws prohibiting "sexual orientation discrimination" or risk losing its license.[101] After being denied a religion exemption the Catholic Charities of Boston chose to close its adoption services.[102]

In April 2017, Representative Mike Enzi introduced the Child Welfare Provider Inclusion Act in the U.S. House of Representatives.[103] The bill would allow adoption agencies and foster care providers to place children based upon the "religious or moral convictions" of the child welfare provider. The bill would penalize states which fail to comply by withholding 15% of federal funds which would otherwise be made available to the state to administer its child welfare programs. In September 2017, a Texas law took effect, providing a defense to faith-based groups if they are named as defendants in litigation regarding child placement, due to their "sincerely-held religious beliefs."[104] Similar laws have recently been enacted in North and South Dakota, Michigan and Virginia.[105]

C. Divorce, Annulment, and Separation

1. The Legal System

Just as states provide the basis and the qualifications for marriage, so too do the states provide the legal requirements for a divorce. Historically, the party seeking the divorce was required to prove that there was fault on the part of the other person in order to obtain a divorce. The most commonly cited ground was that of adultery. Because the parties could not legally agree to procure a divorce without a showing of fault, even if both wanted the divorce, it was not unusual for the parties to collude and obtain a fault-based divorce. It was not uncommon, for example, for an investigator to testify that he had witnessed the husband enter a motel or hotel with some unnamed woman for the period of the evening. Whether or not any adultery occurred, the parties would nonetheless be able to demonstrate the existence of

---

100. USCCB, *Discrimination Against Catholic Adoption Services*, USCCB.ORG, http://www.usccb .org/issues-and-action/religious-liberty/discrimination-against-catholic-adoption-services.cfm (last visited Oct. 2, 2017).

101. *Id.*

102. *Id.*

103. CONGRESS.GOV, Child Welfare Provider Inclusion Act, H.R. 1881 (Apr. 2017), https://www .congress.gov/bill/115th-congress/house-bill/1881 (last visited Oct. 2, 2017).

104. LEGISCAN, Texas House Bill 3859 (passed in Jun. 2017, effective Sept. 1, 2017), https:// legiscan.com/TX/bill/HB3859/2017 (last visited Oct. 2, 2017).

105. Lauren McGaughy, *Texas House passes bill protecting religious adoption agencies that deny services, turn away prospective parents*, DALLASNEWS.COM (May 10, 2017), https://www.dallasnews .com/news/texas-legislature/2017/05/10/texas-house-passes-bill-protectingreligious-adoption -agencies-deny-services-turn-away-prospective-parents (last visited Oct. 2, 2017).

a fault-based reason for a court to enter a finding of divorce. (Isn't it ironic that in these circumstances the parties, who could not cooperate in maintaining the marriage, could cooperate in order to end it?)

Because the basis of obtaining a divorce required the proving of fault of the other parties, the person against whom the divorce was filed could raise defenses to the divorce. If one party had behaved in an inappropriate fashion, and was served with a divorce petition, that party could defend by showing that his or her marital partner had engaged in behavior, usually cruelty or adultery, of the same character. This defense was known as "recrimination." This produced the very curious results that a couple with intense disagreements, even rising to the level of mutual cruelty or adultery, would nonetheless be denied a divorce and forced to remain in a marriage. If one of the parties had engaged in misconduct and the other had forgiven the misconduct, usually by resuming the marital relationship, the forgiving party might be precluded from obtaining a divorce due to the defense of "condonation."

By the late 1960s and early 1970s, states began to create and implement "no fault" provisions in their divorce laws. The Texas version now codified at § 6.001 of the Texas Family Code provides: "Insupportability. On the petition of either party to a marriage, the court may grant a divorce without regard to fault if the marriage has become insupportable because of discord or conflict of personalities that destroys the legitimate ends of the marital relationship and prevents any reasonable expectation of reconciliation." The ground of insupportability, or "incompatibility," or similar grounds in other jurisdictions, now provides the basis for the awarding of most divorces in the United States. Parties no longer have to plead and prove fault. Theoretically, this allows for a less acrimonious dissolution of the marriage. Reducing the hostilities should be of particular benefit when there are minor children of the parties.

Even though states have moved toward a no fault divorce in most instances, alternative fault-based grounds for obtaining a divorce still exist. These grounds are invoked in order to attempt to persuade a court to enter an unequal division of property on behalf of the aggrieved spouse. Fault-based divorce petitions are also used in order to attempt to gain an advantage in child custody matters. Among the fault bases still retained by the State of Texas is that of cruelty, defined as, "cruel treatment toward the complaining spouse of a nature that renders further living together insupportable." [106] Other fault-based grounds in Texas include, adultery, [107] felony conviction,[108] abandonment and remaining away for at least one year,[109] living apart

---

106. Tex. Fam. Code Ann. § 6.002 (West).

107. *Id.* at § 6.003.

108. *Id.* at § 6.004.

109. *Id.* at § 6.005.

without cohabitation for at least three years,[110] or confinement in a mental hospital for at least three years.[111]

Texas has abolished the defenses of recrimination and adultery.[112] Thus, if the petitioner alleges adultery or cruelty, the responding party cannot defend on the basis of the adultery or cruelty of the petitioner. Texas statutes have also allowed condonation to remain as a defense but only if the court finds that there is a reasonable expectation of reconciliation.[113]

In a divorce action, the person seeking the dissolution of the marriage is asking that a court declare an otherwise valid marriage to be dissolved. There may, however, be reasons, including religious reasons, why one party might choose, instead of dissolving the marriage, to have it declared annulled. If an annulment is granted, a court determines that the marriage was voidable when entered into and one of the parties is allowed to have the court declare that the marriage does not exist. In Texas, as in other states, the legislature identifies the specific grounds under which a party can obtain an annulment. Under Texas law, for example, a court may issue an annulment if, "at the time of the marriage, the petitioner was under the influence of alcoholic beverages or narcotics and as a result did not have the capacity to consent to the marriage; and the petitioner has not voluntarily cohabited with the other party to the marriage since the effects of the alcoholic beverages or narcotics ended."[114] A court in Texas can also annul a marriage for impotency as long as "the petitioner did not know of the impotency at the time of the marriage and has not voluntarily cohabited with the other party since learning of the impotency." This ground applies when either party was "permanently impotent" at the time of the marriage.[115]

If a person uses "fraud, duress or force to induce the petitioner to enter in the marriage," in Texas the marriage can be annulled so long as "the petitioner has not voluntarily cohabited with the other party since learning of the fraud or since being released from the duress or force."[116] Other grounds by which one party can obtain an annulment of marriage in Texas include if the respondent has been divorced within 30 days of the marriage and concealed that from the petitioner. This is because there is a 30 day waiting period after the entry of a divorce in Texas before a party can remarry. However, there is an exception in the statute that requires that an annulment action brought under this ground of "concealed divorce" must be filed within one year of the marriage.[117] Similarly, in Texas the parties must wait 72 hours after a marriage license is issued before marrying. If a marriage violates this provision, the

---

110. *Id.* at § 6.006.
111. *Id.* At § 6.007.
112. *Id.* at § 6.008.
113. *Id.*
114. *Id.* at § 6.105.
115. *Id.* at § 6.106.
116. *Id.* at § 6.107.
117. *Id.* at § 6.109.

court can annul the marriage although neither party can bring an action more than 30 days after the marriage under this ground.[118] Annulment statutes typically provide that the enumerated ground for obtaining the annulment makes the marriage voidable. That is, unless someone affirmatively brings an annulment action, the marriage remains valid and in effect.

There is however a category of "void" marriages which means that the marriage never took place in the first place. In Texas, and in other jurisdictions, marriages that are entered into where the parties are within the proscribed parameters of consanguinity are void marriages. In Texas, consanguinity is defined in the Family Code as:

§ 6.201. Consanguinity[119]

A marriage is void if one party to the marriage is related to the other as:

(1) an ancestor or descendant, by blood or adoption;

(2) a brother or sister, of the whole or half blood or by adoption;

(3) a parent's brother or sister, of the whole or half blood or by adoption; or

(4) a son or daughter of a brother or sister, of the whole or half blood or by adoption.

Another basis for obtaining a declaration that the marriage is void is if there is a prior marriage still in effect at the time of the contracting of the offending marriage.[120] Thus if marriage number one is still in effect and one of the parties to that marriages enters into a second "marriage" with someone else, marriage number two is void. What happens, though, if marriage number one is still in effect, marriage two takes place, marriage number one is then dissolved, and after that dissolution, the husband and wife live together and have hold themselves out to others as being husband and wife? In Texas, at least, the second marriage that otherwise would be void becomes valid by operation of law.[121] Marriages in Texas and elsewhere are void if the party is younger than the prescribed age (18 in Texas without a court order) or if the party is a "current or former stepchild or stepparent of the other party."[122] Texas, and approximately 40 other states, also have language in their statutes and/or constitutions prohibiting recognition of same-sex marriages or civil unions.

In many jurisdictions, short of a divorce or an annulment, parties to a marriage are able to obtain a legal separation. The legal separation maintains the legal existence of the marriage but provides for a division of property, might contain orders related to

---

118. *Id.* at § 6.110.
119. *Id.* at § 6.201.
120. *Id.* at § 6.202
121. *Id.*
122. *Id.* at § 6.206.

children and child support, and identifies the property rights in the spouses. Why would a married couple enter into a separation agreement? It might be that for religious reasons the couple feels that a divorce is morally wrong. It might be that the parties are attempting to determine whether the more dramatic step of divorce is necessary, or whether, during a time of separation, the parties might be able to reconcile any differences and resume the marital relationship.

In any event, whether the action is brought as a divorce, annulment, or a separation, states require that legal formalities be followed. There is, in other words, no such thing as a common law divorce, even in states which recognize common law marriages. State statutes prescribe the requirements of residency and venue. They require notice to the other party. In the case of children, courts typically will be required to enter orders regarding visitation and support and ultimately custody, based upon the best interests of the children. Courts have the power to enter protective orders or temporary orders providing for the peaceful transition of the couple from married couple to a divorced or separated couple. Courts can enforce these orders by the contempt power.

Just because the couple is divorced, separated or the marriage annulled, state statutes provide for ongoing supervision of relationships particularly in the areas of child support and sometimes in the area of spousal support. Thus, while the divorce, annulment, or separation proceeding might terminate or reduce the legal relationship between husband and wife, the parties are required to interact peaceably in order to provide as much stability as the court can enforce regarding children.

2. Teachings of the Church Regarding Divorce, Separation, and Annulment

Because the Church views marriage as a sacrament, and of great importance not only to the individuals but to the Church itself, it should come as no surprise that the Catholic Church would take a very restrictive approach to the dissolution of marriage. Canon Law explicitly states: "[a] marriage that is *ratum et consummatum* can be dissolved by no human power and by no cause, except death."[123] A summary of the Church's position in this regard can be found in the *Catholic Encyclopedia*:

> The term *divorce* (*divortium,* from *divertere, divortere,* 'to separate') was employed in pagan Rome for the mutual separation of married people. Etymologically the word does not indicate whether this mutual separation included the dissolution of the marriage bond, and in fact the word is used in the Church and in ecclesiastical law in this neutral signification. Hence we distinguish between *divortium plenum* or *perfectum* (absolute divorce),

---

123. 1983 CODE c. 1141, http://www.vatican.va/archive/ENG1104/__P44.HTM (last visited Oct. 11, 2017).

which implies the dissolution of the marriage bond, and *divortium imperfectum* (limited divorce), which leaves the marriage bond intact and implies only the cessation of common life (separation from bed and board, or in addition separation of dwelling-place). In civil law divorce means the dissolution of the marriage bond; *divortium imperfectum* is called separation (*séparation de corps*).

The Catholic doctrine on divorce may be summed up in the following propositions:

- In Christian marriage, which implies the restoration, by Christ Himself, of marriage to its original indissolubility, there can never be an absolute divorce, at least after the marriage has been consummated;

- Non-Christian marriage can be dissolved by absolute divorce under certain circumstances in favour of the Faith;

- Christian marriage before consummation can be dissolved by solemn profession in a religious order, or by an act of papal authority;

- Separation from bed and board (*divortium imperfectum*) is allowed for various causes, especially in the case of adultery or lapse into infidelity or heresy on the part of husband or wife.[124]

Thus the Church would recognize an absolute divorce only in the rarest of circumstances.

Separation is permitted by the Church. It is permissible for the offended spouse to turn out the adulterer. Although "Canon Law makes it clear that if one party is guilty of adultery, the other has the right to effect a permanent separation, and this indeed without any intervention of ecclesiastical authority. The marriage bond itself remains, however, and precludes remarriage."[125]

The Catechism reflects that "[i]f civil divorce remains the only possible way of ensuring certain legal rights, the care of the children, or the protection of inheritance, it can be tolerated and does not constitute a moral offense."[126] The Archdiocese of Denver explains that "[i]t is critical for all who have undergone a civil divorce to understand that the Church still recognizes the validity of a marriage, even if it is a dissolved union at the civil level; for marriage is first and foremost a physical and spiritual union of a man and a woman."[127] Of course, the Church, just as the civil authorities, would recognize a separation. However, if it was a Catholic

---

124. *Divorce* (in Moral Theology), The Catholic Encyclopedia (Kevin Knight ed., 1993), http://www.newadvent.org/cathen/05054c.htm (last visited Oct. 11, 2017) (Although this text was written 1908–12 and has not been updated, it did receive Nihil Obstat and Imprimatur. The premises represented by this footnote are still current.).

125. *Adultery*, New Catholic Encyclopedia, vol. 1, 131 (2d ed., 2003).

126. Catechism of the Cath. Church, *Article 6: The Sixth Commandment*, 2383 (1993), http://www.vatican.va/archive/ccc_css/archive/catechism/p3s2c2a6.htm (last visited Oct. 11, 2017).

127. Archidocese of Denver, *The Teaching of the Catholic Church on Divorce*, http://www.archden.org/tribunal/documents/divorce.htm (last visited Mar. 19, 2014). Not available anymore.

to Catholic marriage, the divorcees are not free to remarry unless an annulment is granted.

> The declaration of nullity must be carefully distinguished from divorce proper. It can be called divorce only in a very improper sense, because it presupposes that there is and has been no marriage. However, as there is question of an alleged marriage and of a union which is considered by the public as a true marriage, we can understand why a previous ecclesiastical judgment should be required, declaring the presence of a diriment impediment and the consequent invalidity of a supposed marriage, before the persons in question might be free to separate or to enter upon a new marriage. It is only when the invalidity of a marriage becomes publicly known and further cohabitation gives scandal, or when other important reasons render a prompt separation of domicile necessary or advisable, that such a separation should take place at once, to be made definitive by a later judicial sentence. When the invalidity of a marriage is publicly known, official procedure is necessary, and ecclesiastical process of nullification must be introduced. In the case of impediments which refer exclusively to the rights of the husband and wife, and which can be removed by their consent, only the one of the supposed spouses whose right is in question is permitted to impugn the marriage by complaint before the ecclesiastical court, provided it is desired to maintain this right. Such cases are the impediments of fear or violence, of essential error of impotence on the part of the other not fully established, and failure to comply with some fixed condition. In cases of the other possible impediments, every Catholic, even a stranger, may enter a complaint of nullity if he can bring proofs of such nullity. The only plaintiffs excluded are those who, on account of private advantage, were unwilling to declare the invalidity of the marriage before its dissolution by death, or who knew the impediment when the banns or marriage were proclaimed and culpably kept silence. Of course it is allowed to the married parties to disprove the reasons alleged by strangers against their marriage (Wernz, "*Jus decretalium*," IV, n.743).[128]

Although this excerpt received *Imprimatur* a century ago, it offers a good reference point for a discussion on annulments. Generally, the modern Church considers an annulment after a civil divorce is finalized.

> [T]he 1983 [Canon Law] . . . represents a shift towards a more personalistic and less institutional approach to marriage. The old law was conceived with the goal of protecting the indissolubility of marriage even if that meant little attention would be paid to the personal disposition of the parties, such as their mistaken knowledge, their acting under duress, or their lack of maturity. The new law continues to uphold the permanency of marital

---

128. Knight, *supra* note 124.

commitment, but it goes a long way toward providing remedies in case of misguided or defective consent.

The complexity of the procedural norms in nullity cases have been reduced. Provided the diocesan tribunals take advantage of the new rules, the 'trials' can be made more expeditious. The law allows the judges to give more weight to the depositions of the parties, and in exceptional circumstances it allows one (not three, as usual) judge to conduct the case and to decide it. It also permits the substitution of a 'review' of the first sentence instead of a formal trial by an appellate court.[129]

Just as in a civil annulment, the aggrieved party seeking to obtain an annulment must have entered into the marriage without knowledge that the grounds for annulment existed. Moreover, it appears that historically the Church would allow an annulment proceeding to be brought by someone other than a party to the marriage. That could result in the parties defending their marriage in such a proceeding.

Does this sound harsh to modern ears? The Church recognizes that there may be an innocent party to the divorce. That is to say, one party may not desire the divorce but the divorce will proceed even against the person's wishes. The Catechism explains that "It can happen that one of the spouses is the innocent victim of a divorce decreed by civil law; this spouse therefore has not contravened the moral law. There is a considerable difference between a spouse who has sincerely tried to be faithful to the sacrament of marriage and is unjustly abandoned, and one who through his own grave fault destroys a canonically valid marriage."[130]

3. The Dilemma, and the Solutions, for Catholics Who Face the Breakdown of a Marriage

The sad and unfortunate reality is that some marriages, even Catholic marriages, will break down, as the result of many possible factors. Consider the situation where this has occurred, and there is no feasible way, except for recourse to the judicial system, for a Catholic to protect property rights, arrange for custody of minor children and their support, or other similar circumstances. Does the Church preclude divorce in such a circumstance? The answer is, no, it does not. Section 2383 of the Catechism provides, in part, "If civil divorce remains the only possible way of ensuring certain legal rights, the care of the children, or the protection of inheritance, it can be tolerated and does not constitute a moral offense."[131] It is also not a sin for the Catholic who has been divorced by his/her spouse under the circumstances set out in Section 2386: "It can happen that one of the spouses is the innocent victim of a divorce decreed by civil law; this spouse therefore has not contravened the moral

---

129. *Marriage Legislation* (Canon Law), New Catholic Encyclopedia, vol. 9, 206–07 (2d ed., 2003).

130. *Id.*

131. *Id.*

law. There is a considerable difference between a spouse who has sincerely tried to be faithful to the sacrament of marriage and is unjustly abandoned, and one who through his own grave fault destroys a canonically valid marriage."

Under either of the scenarios above, the Catholic has not committed sin and is free to continue to receive the sacraments. Even where the Catholic has brought or caused a divorce, under circumstances outside of these situations, he/she can confess the sin through the sacrament of Reconciliation, and continue to receive the sacraments. The difficulty arises, however, if the divorced Catholic, even those who would be covered under the provisions of 2383 or 2386, remarry. The Church has made clear that unless the first marriage has been annulled by the Church, the parties are not free to remarry, and are thus not free to take the sacraments. See the words of then Cardinal Ratzinger, "Concerning the Reception of Holy Communion by Divorced-and-Remarried Members of the Faithful" the Congregation for the Doctrine of the Faith in a letter to the world's bishops on October 14, 1994:

> I. The mistaken conviction of a divorced-and-remarried person that he may receive Holy Communion normally presupposes that personal conscience is considered in the final analysis to be able, on the basis of one's own convictions, to come to a decision about the existence or absence of a previous marriage and the value of the new union. However, such a position is inadmissible. Marriage, in fact, both because it is the image of the spousal relationship between Christ and his church as well as the fundamental core and an important factor in the life of civil society, is essentially a public reality.[132]

There is one narrow circumstance under which a divorced and remarried Catholic could receive the sacraments. That is the situation where the Catholic and his/her new spouse repent of their sin and live together as brother and sister. "This means, in practice, that when for serious reasons, for example, for the children's upbringing, a man and a woman cannot satisfy the obligation to separate, they take on themselves the duty to live in complete continence, that is, by abstinence from the acts proper to married couples. In such a case they may receive Holy Communion as long as they respect the obligation to avoid giving scandal." (Letter of Cardinal Ratzinger, *ibid.*, paragraph 4.)

Obviously, most Catholics would not view this as a realistic option. And, they view with concern the position of the Church that would treat their attempt to enter into a new and loving marriage, with all the protection afforded to that relationship by the legal system, as the equivalent of unrepentant adultery. Still, there is some hope

---

132. CONGREGATION FOR THE DOCTRINE OF FAITH, http://www.vatican.va/roman_curia/con gregations/cfaith/documents/rc_con_cfaith_doc_14091994_rec-holy-comm-by-divorced_en.html (last visited Oct. 11, 2017).

for these people that the Church's view might be modified to some extent by Pope Francis. In his new book, *On Heaven and Earth,* he states: "Catholic doctrine reminds its divorced members who have remarried that they are not excommunicated—even though they live in a situation on the margin of what indissolubility of marriage and the sacrament of marriage require of them—and they are asked to integrate into the parish life,"[133] Pope Francis continued this theme with a statement to journalists on September 16, 2013. Reuters reported that the Pope: "called for 'another way' of treating divorcees who remarry—a thorny issue since Catholics who wed a second time are currently not allowed to receive Holy Communion at mass. Catholic faithful should 'feel at home' in parishes and those who have remarried should be treated with 'justice' the pope was quoted as saying by Romasette, the local newspaper for the diocese of Rome. 'Our duty is to find another way in justice,' he said."[134]

Pope Francis continued this theme in his apostolic exhortation, *Amoris Laetitia* ("Joy of Love") in 2016. The exhortation drew widespread praise but also drew an accusation of heresy by numerous Catholic theologians. A bit of background at this point will help in an understanding of Pope Francis' teaching on this point and provide some perspective regarding the criticism leveled at him.

In 2014 and 2015, two separate meetings of the Synod of bishops of the Catholic Church considered the issue of marriage and the family. The bishops met in Rome. The website of the USCCB provides an explanation of how the Synod functions: "The Synod of Bishops is a permanent institution of the Catholic Church. It was established by Pope Paul VI in 1965, shortly after the close of the Second Vatican Council, to continue the spirit of collegiality and communion that was present at the Council. The Synod is an assembly of bishops from around the world who assist the Holy Father by providing counsel on important questions facing the Church in a manner that preserves the Church's teaching and strengthens her internal discipline. (See the Vatican website and the Code of Canon Law, canon 342.)"[135]

After these gatherings, and after much prayer and reflection, Pope Francis issued his exhortation. Again, the USCCB offers an explanation: "An apostolic exhortation is a particular kind of papal teaching that communicates the mind of the pope on a certain topic. It is often used to share the conclusions reached by the Holy Father after consideration of the recommendations of a Synod of Bishops. It can also be used

---

133. National Catholic Register, Pope Francis Desires to Draw Remarried People to Christ (May 2, 2013), http://www.ncregister.com/daily-news/pope-francis-desires-to-draw-rema rried-people-to-christ/#ixzz2fkEeH3Pf (last visited Oct. 11, 2017).

134. The Straits Times, Pope calls for 'Another Way' for Catholic Divorcees (Sept. 17, 2013), http://www.straitstimes.com/breaking-news/world/story/pope-calls-another-way-catholic -divorcees-20130917 (last visited Oct. 11, 2017).

135. United States Conference of Catholic Bishops, *Amoris Laetitia*, http://www.usccb.org /issues-and-action/marriage-and-family/amoris-laetitia.cfm (last visited Oct. 15, 2017).

as a way for the pope to exhort (encourage) the faithful to a deeper life of Christian discipleship. . . ."[136]

On July 16, 2017, a group of Catholic theologians challenged the Pope's exhortation as being heretical.[137] Their letter set forth the passages of *Amoris Laetitia* which they believed constitute heresy. Those passages are as follows:

> **AL 295:** 'Saint John Paul II proposed the so-called "law of gradualness" in the knowledge that the human being "knows, loves and accomplishes moral good by different stages of growth". This is not a "gradualness of law" but rather a gradualness in the prudential exercise of free acts on the part of subjects who are not in a position to understand, appreciate, or fully carry out the objective demands of the law.'

> **AL 296:** 'There are two ways of thinking which recur throughout the Church's history: casting off and reinstating. The Church's way, from the time of the Council of Jerusalem, has always been the way of Jesus, the way of mercy and reinstatement. The way of the Church is not to condemn anyone forever.'

> **AL 297:** 'No one can be condemned for ever, because that is not the logic of the Gospel!'

> **AL 298:** 'The divorced who have entered a new union, for example, can find themselves in a variety of situations, which should not be pigeonholed or fit into overly rigid classifications leaving no room for a suitable personal and pastoral discernment. One thing is a second union consolidated over time, with new children, proven fidelity, generous self-giving, Christian commitment, a consciousness of its irregularity and of the great difficulty of going back without feeling in conscience that one would fall into new sins. The Church acknowledges situations "where, for serious reasons, such as the children's upbringing, a man and woman cannot satisfy the obligation to separate [footnote 329: In such situations, many people, knowing and accepting the possibility of living "as brothers and sisters" which the Church offers them, point out that if certain expressions of intimacy are lacking, "it often happens that faithfulness is endangered and the good of the children suffers."] There are also the cases of those who made every effort to save their first marriage and were unjustly abandoned, or of "those who have entered into a second union for the sake of the children's upbringing, and are sometimes subjectively certain in conscience that their previous and irreparably broken marriage had never been valid". Another thing is a new union arising from a recent divorce, with all the suffering and confusion which this

---

136. *Id.*
137. Correctio Filialis, *Correctio filialis de haeresibus propagatis* (Jul. 16, 2017), http://www.correctiofilialis.org/wp-content/uploads/2017/08/Correctio-filialis_English_1.pdf (last visited Oct. 15, 2017).

entails for children and entire families, or the case of someone who has consistently failed in his obligations to the family. It must remain clear that this is not the ideal which the Gospel proposes for marriage and the family. The Synod Fathers stated that the discernment of pastors must always take place "by adequately distinguishing", with an approach which "carefully discerns situations." We know that no "easy recipes" exist.'

AL 299: 'I am in agreement with the many Synod Fathers who observed that "the baptized who are divorced and civilly remarried need to be more fully integrated into Christian communities in the variety of ways possible, while avoiding any occasion of scandal. The logic of integration is the key to their pastoral care, a care which would allow them not only to realize that they belong to the Church as the body of Christ, but also to know that they can have a joyful and fruitful experience in it. They are baptized; they are brothers and sisters; the Holy Spirit pours into their hearts gifts and talents for the good of all. . . . Such persons need to feel not as excommunicated members of the Church, but instead as living members, able to live and grow in the Church and experience her as a mother who welcomes them always, who takes care of them with affection and encourages them along the path of life and the Gospel."'

AL 300: 'Since "the degree of responsibility is not equal in all cases," the consequences or effects of a rule need not necessarily always be the same. [footnote 336] This is also the case with regard to sacramental discipline, since discernment can recognize that in a particular situation no grave fault exists.'

AL 301: 'It is [sic] can no longer simply be said that all those in any "irregular" situation are living in a state of mortal sin and are deprived of sanctifying grace. More is involved here than mere ignorance of the rule. A subject may know full well the rule, yet have great difficulty in understanding "its inherent values, or be in a concrete situation which does not allow him or her to act differently and decide otherwise without further sin."'

AL 303: 'Conscience can do more than recognize that a given situation does not correspond objectively to the overall demands of the Gospel. It can also recognize with sincerity and honesty what for now is the most generous response which can be given to God, and come to see with a certain moral security that it is what God himself is asking amid the concrete complexity of one's limits, while yet not fully the objective ideal.'

AL 304: 'I earnestly ask that we always recall a teaching of Saint Thomas Aquinas and learn to incorporate it in our pastoral discernment: "Although there is necessity in the general principles, the more we descend to matters of detail, the more frequently we encounter defects. . . . In matters of action, truth or practical rectitude is not the same for all, as to matters of detail, but only as to the general principles; and where there is the same rectitude in matters of detail, it is not equally known to all. . . . The principle will be found to fail, according as we descend further into detail." It is true that general rules set forth a good which can never be disregarded or neglected, but in their formulation they cannot provide absolutely for all particular situations.'

AL 305: 'Because of forms of conditioning and mitigating factors, it is possible that in an objective situation of sin—which may not be subjectively culpable, or fully such—a person can be living in God's grace, can love and can also grow in the life of grace and charity, while receiving the Church's help to this end. [footnote 351: In certain cases, this can include the help of the sacraments. Hence, "I want to remind priests that the confessional must not be a torture chamber, but rather an encounter with the Lord's mercy." I would also point out that the Eucharist "is not a prize for the perfect, but a powerful medicine and nourishment for the weak."]'

AL 308: 'I understand those who prefer a more rigorous pastoral care which leaves no room for confusion. But I sincerely believe that Jesus wants a Church attentive to the goodness which the Holy Spirit sows in the midst of human weakness, a Mother who, while clearly expressing her objective teaching, "always does what good she can, even if in the process, her shoes get soiled by the mud of the street."'

AL 311: 'The teaching of moral theology should not fail to incorporate these considerations.'[138]

Catholics worldwide understood that the Pope was extending an element of mercy to divorced and remarried Catholics. On September 5, 2016 bishops in the Buenos Aires area in Argentina issued a statement concerning the application of the Pope's exhortation.[139] They noted that the Pope's exhortation offered the possibility of access which would allow divorced and remarried Catholics, after a process of discernment, to receive the sacraments of reconciliation and communion.[140] The Pope agreed with this assessment in a formal letter to the bishops[141] which gave the authors of Correctio Filialis another point of claimed heresy against the Pope.

---

138. Vatican Press, *Post-Synodal Apostolic Exhortation Amoris Laetitia of the Holy Father Francis* (Mar. 19, 2016), https://w2.vatican.va/content/dam/francesco/pdf/apost_exhortations/documents /papa-francesco_esortazione-ap_20160319_amoris-laetitia_en.pdf (last visited Oct. 11, 2017).

139. CRUX Taking the Catholic Pulse, Guidelines of Buenos Aires bishops on divorced/remarried (Sept. 18, 2016), https://cruxnow.com/global-church/2016/09/18/guidelines-buenos-aires -bishops-divorcedremarried/ (last visited Oct. 15, 2017).

140. *Id.*

141. Holy See Press Office, Carta Del Santo Padre Francisco A Los Obispos De La Región Pastoral De Buenos Aires En Respuesta Al Documento "Criterios Básicos Para La Aplicación Del Capítulo Viii De La Amoris Laetitia" (officially published in Spanish) (Sept. 5, 2016), http://w2.vatican.va/content/francesco/es/letters/2016/documents/papa-francesco_20160905 _regione-pastorale-buenos-aires.html (last visited Oct. 15, 2017).

Pope Francis's exhortation was not issued under an infallible declaration. How-ever, neither is the prohibition regarding the receipt of communion by divorced and remarried Catholics the result of an infallible pronouncement. Thus, the theological implications regarding under what circumstances, if any, divorced and remarried Catholics may resume the sacraments will continue to be a discussion within the Catholic Church.

There is the hope among Catholics that ultimately the Church will find its way to bring back to the sacraments the very many who long for that inclusion. Divorced and divorcing Catholics should also consider resources such as the "Catholic's Divorce Survival Guide," or similar offerings, which attempt to provide some assistance.[142] Finally, I concluded the first edition of *Catholic Legal Perspectives* by noting that then-Cardinal Ratzinger assigned *imprimatur* to the following statement regarding the role of individual conscience:

> Conscience, as "moral judgment" and as "moral imperative," constitutes the final evaluation of an act as good or evil before God. In effect, only God knows the moral value of each human act, even if the Church, like Jesus, can and must classify, judge, and sometimes condemn some kinds of action.[143]

4. The Role of the Catholic Lawyer or Judge in Divorce Proceedings

Given the Catholic Church's clear position regarding the sanctity of marriage, under what circumstances, if any, would a Catholic lawyer or judge be morally permitted to participate in the civil divorce process? This is not a new issue in American jurisprudence. *The American Lawyer* carried reference to just such a dis-cussion in 1905.

Catholics and Divorce

> Can Catholic lawyers and judges consistently with their religious profes-sions serve to secure the annulment of valid marriages is an interesting ques-tions. It was recently propounded to Monsignor Canon Moyes, theologian to the Catholic Archbishop of Westminster, London. He was asked whether a Catholic lawyer can with a safe conscience take part in his professional capacity in divorce cases, and whether a Catholic judge can conscientiously administer a law contrary to the teachings of the Catholic Church.

> Canon Moyes answers by saying that there are authentic decisions in which such action on the part of lawyer and judge is forbidden implicitly or

---

142. THE CATHOLIC'S SURVIVAL GUIDE, http://www.catholicsdivorce.com (last visited Oct. 11, 2017).

143. INT'L THEOLOGICAL COMM'N, *Memory and Reconciliation: The Church and the Faults of the Past* (Dec. 1999), http://www.vatican.va/roman_curia/congregations/cfaith/cti_documents/rc_con_cfaith_doc_20000307_memory-reconc-itc_en.html (last visited Oct. 11, 2017).

indirectly. He says there are many pronouncements by the Apostolic See declaring that Christian marriage is a sacrament, and that the civil power is therefore incompetent to dissolve it. Any affirmation that the bond of marriage is dissolved or any authorization that the parties may marry again is, if referring to the bond itself or to remarriage itself, therefore sinful and immoral. It follows from the ordinary principles of Catholic teaching that no Catholic, whether judge or lawyer, can help in procuring or effecting a divorce is understood. There are, however, special circumstances in which participation in the work of divorce court need not imply co-operation in the evil of divorce in the sense described.[144]

In January 2002, Pope John Paul II spoke to the lawyers and judges participating in the Church's Annulment Body, the Sacra Rota, formerly the Supreme Court of Christendom,[145] the Pope expressed concern that divorce was spreading like the plague.[146] He urged lawyers not to become part of evil, because of the devastating effects of divorce. The Pope declared that:

> . . . *professionals in the field of civil law* should avoid being personally involved in anything that might imply a *cooperation with divorce*. For *judges* this may prove difficult, since the legal order does not recognize a conscientious objection to exempt them from giving sentence.
>
> . . . .
>
> *Lawyers,* as independent professionals, should always decline the use of their profession for an end that is contrary to justice, as is divorce. They can only cooperate in this kind of activity when, in the intention of the client, it is not directed *to the break-up of the marriage,* but *to the securing of other legitimate effects* that can only be obtained through such a judicial process in the established legal order (*cf. Catechism of the Catholic Church,* n.2383). In this way, with their work of assisting and reconciling persons who are going through a marital crises, lawyers truly serve the rights of the

---

144. *Catholics and Divorce*, Am. Lawyer, vol. xiii, Apr. 1905, at 178.

145. Also called the Court of the Rota or simply the Rota, it was formed of twelve members: three from Rome, two from Spain, and one each from Germany, France, Milan, Bologna, Ferrara, Venice, and alternating from Tuscany and Perugia. The Rota's history dates to 1336.

146. The Pope expressed concern that divorce had "spread through the social body like a plague—to use the term of the Second Vatican Council to describe divorce (cf. Gaudium et spes, n.47)—and that . . . [has] a negative influence on the new generations who view as tarnished the beauty of true marriage." (Pope John Paul II, *Address to the Prelate Auditors, Official, and Advocates of the Tribunal of the Roman Rota* ¶ (Jan. 28, 2002), http://www.vatican.va/holy_father/john_paul_ii/speeches/2002/january/documents/hf_jpii_spe_20020128_roman-rota_en.html (last visited Oct. 11, 2017)).

person and avoid becoming mere technicians at the service of any interest whatever.[147]

The Pope reasoned his instruction to the legal practitioner. He stated, in part; "*Marriage 'is' indissoluble:* . . . In this perspective, it is meaningless to speak of an 'imposition' by human law, because human law should reflect and safeguard the natural and divine law that is always a freeing truth."[148] On the other hand, "[f]or grave and proportionate motives they may therefore act *in accord with the traditional principles of material cooperation.* But they too must seek effective means to encourage marital unions, especially through *a wisely handled work of reconciliation.*"[149]

Does this mean that Catholic lawyers and judges must refuse to become involved in divorce actions? Not completely, at least according to John Garvey, former Dean of Boston College Law School. In response to the publicity surrounding Pope John Paul II's remarks, Dean Garvey wrote:

> Let us consider now the case of divorce raised by the pope. This too is a proceeding in which lawyers play many different roles. The church teaches that divorce is a grave offense against the natural law because it introduces disorder into the family and society. For Catholics it is also a breach of a sacramental covenant. This means that a lawyer who helps to cause a divorce cooperates in an evil act. If it is her intention to make this happen, she is guilty of formal cooperation. But this would not be true where the lawyer's Catholic client had already procured an annulment—in that case there is no valid marriage for the divorce to terminate. It would also not be true where a lawyer assisted her client in resisting her spouse's efforts to terminate the marriage.
>
> There may even be cases where a Catholic lawyer can act rightly in moving to bring about a divorce. Canon law sometimes allows spouses to separate, in cases of abuse or adultery. In these cases, though the church's marital bond endures, it may be wise to treat the civil contract differently. Divorce may be the only way, under civil law, to resolve issues like custody of the children, division of assets, alimony, and so on. It would be imprudent for a lawyer to abandon the representation of her client in the resolution of these questions. The Catechism of the Catholic Church #2383 actually addresses this point: 'If civil divorce remains the only possible way of ensuring certain

147. Pope John Paul II, *Address to the Prelate Auditors, Official, and Advocates of the Tribunal of the Roman Rota* ¶ 9 (Jan. 28, 2002), http://www.vatican.va/holy_father/john_paul_ii/speeches/2002/january/documents/hf_jpii_spe_ 20020128_roman-rota_en.html (emphasis in original).

148. *Id.* at ¶ 4; *see also* Francis Kennedy, *Pope Urges Catholic Lawyers to Shun Divorce Work*, THE INDEPENDENT (Sept. 29, 2001) (emphasis in original), http://www.independent.co.uk/news/world/europe/pope-rges-catholic-lawyers-to-shun-divorce-work-671576.html (last visited Oct. 11, 2017) (including quotes from the Pope and Italian political leaders).

149. Pope John Paul II, *supra* note 147.

legal rights, the care of the children, or the protection of inheritance, it can be tolerated and does not constitute a moral offense.'

The pope appreciated this refinement, though most of the media accounts of his remarks did not. He did not say that lawyers should have nothing to do with divorce. He said instead that 'they can only cooperate in this kind of activity when, in the intention of the client, it is not directed to the breakup of the marriage, but to the securing of other legitimate effects that can only be obtained through such a judicial process in the established legal order.'

We should all be alert to the demands our faith makes on us. Sometimes it requires real sacrifice. But we should not be too hasty to assume that our legal system is corrupt, and that the best way to defend our virtue is to steer clear of it. The moral life is more complicated than that.[150]

Pope John Paul II's successor, Pope Benedict XVI, reaffirmed the Church's commitment to the indissolubility of marriage.

The Church wishes to remain utterly faithful to the mandate entrusted to her by her Founder, her Master and Lord, Jesus Christ. She does not cease to repeat with him: "What God has joined together, let not man put asunder!" (Matt. 19:6). The Church did not give herself this mission: she received it.[151]

However, he struck a somewhat compassionate note for those who have gone through a divorce:

To be sure, none can deny that certain families experience trials, sometimes very painful ones. Families in difficulty must be supported, they must be helped to understand the greatness of marriage, and encouraged not to relativize God's will and the laws of life which he has given us. A particularly painful situation, as you know, concerns those who are divorced and remarried. The Church, which cannot oppose the will of Christ, firmly maintains the principle of the indissolubility of marriage, while surrounding with the greatest affection those men and women who, for a variety of reasons, fail to respect it.[152]

Pope Francis' pronouncements, noted above, would also seem relevant to Catholic attorneys who advise Catholic clients in domestic relations matters.

---

150. John Garvey, *Law & Morality: Divorce, the Death Penalty, & the Pope*, COMMONWEAL, vol. 129.8 (Apr. 2002), at 12.

151. Pope Benedict XVI, Meeting with French Episcopal Conference (Sept. 14, 2008), http://www.vatican.va/holy_father/benedict_xvi/speeches/2008/september/documents/hf_ben-xvi_spe_20080914_ lourdes-vescovi_en.html.

152. *Id.*

What about some other issues? Do the same potential constraints that could apply to Catholic attorneys who might represent clients in a divorce involving a heterosexual couple apply if the litigants are parties to a same-sex marriage? And could courts ever require attorneys to represent litigants in same-sex divorces? In 2016, the *Albany Law Review* published this author's article "Opting Out in the Name of God: Will Lawyers be Compelled to Handle Same-Sex Divorces?"

Opting Out in the Name of God: Will Lawyers Be Compelled to Handle Same-Sex Divorces?

Bill Piatt*

I. Introduction

In June 2015 the Supreme Court of the United States determined, by a 5–4 ruling in the case of *Obergefell v. Hodges*,[1] that same-sex couples have a constitutionally guaranteed right to marry.[2] Soon thereafter, a same-sex couple applied for a marriage license in Rowen County, Kentucky.[3] Kim Davis, the Rowen County clerk refused to issue the license, citing her own religious beliefs.[4] The couple brought suit against Ms. Davis, and she was ordered by a federal district judge to issue the license.[5] When she refused, she was held in contempt, and jailed for five days.[6] Ultimately U.S. District Judge David Bunning ordered Ms. Davis' deputies to issue the license in her stead.[7] Ms. Davis' actions brought her a great deal of notoriety.[8] Some of the publicity was positive with her actions being characterized "heroic," while others considered her to be a "homophobe," or a "Hitler."[9] While certainly dramatic, Ms. Davis' case

* Professor of Law and former Dean (1998–2007), St. Mary's University School of Law. I would like to thank my research assistants, Alicia Stoll, Sean Cohen, and Haben Tewelde. I would also like to thank Maria Vega for her line editing and technical assistance.

1. Obergefell v. Hodges, 135 S. Ct. 2584 (2015).
2. *Id.* at 2607.
3. *See* Miller v. Davis, No. 15-44-DLB, 2015 WL 4866729, at *1–2 (E.D. Ky. Aug. 12, 2015).
4. *Id.* at *1, *3.
5. *Id.* at *4, *15.
6. Claire Galofaro, *Kim Davis Back at Work*, U.S. News & World Rep. (Sept. 14, 2015), http://www.usnews.com/news/us/articles/2015/09/14/kentucky-clerk-jailed-over-gay-marriage-to-return-to-work.
7. *Id.*
8. *See id.*
9. *See* Amita Kelly, *Kim Davis' Supporters, In Their Own words: 'Courageous,' 'Heroic,'* NPR (Sept. 26, 2015), http://www.npr.org/sections/itsallpolitics/2015/09/26/443485200/courageous-heroic-meet-kim-daviss-supporters; Emily Shapiro, *Kentucky Clerk Kim Davis Tells ABC News She's Been Called 'Hitler' and 'Homophobe,'* ABC News (Sept. 21, 2015), http://abcnews.go.com/US/kentucky-clerk-kim-davis-tells-abc-news-shes/story?id=33930655.

was not the first time in recent history that courts or administrative bodies have imposed sanctions against citizens or private business operators who declined to provide goods or services to same-sex couples.[10]

In 2013, the Supreme Court of New Mexico considered a matter involving a photographer who had declined to photograph the commitment ceremony of one woman to another.[11] The photographer, Elaine Huguenin, indicated that she was "personally opposed to same-sex marriage and will not photograph any image or event that violates her religious beliefs."[12] The customers filed a discrimination complaint against the photographer with the New Mexico Human Rights Commission.[13] They alleged that the photographer had engaged in discrimination that violated the provisions of the New Mexico Human Rights Act.[14] The Act precludes discrimination by public accommodations on the basis of sexual orientation.[15] The New Mexico Human Rights Commission ruled against the photographer.[16] The photographer appealed, asserting that her constitutionally-protected First Amendment rights to the free exercise of her religion and expression allowed her to decline to participate in the event.[17] A state district judge granted the customer's motion for summary judgment.[18] The New Mexico Court of Appeals affirmed the ruling against the photographer and in favor of her customers, as did the Supreme Court of New Mexico.[19]

Also in 2015, the Bureau of Labor and Industries of the State of Oregon considered a case involving a baker who declined to make a wedding cake for a same-sex couple.[20] The Commissioner determined that the bakery owners had violated the Oregon statute prohibiting discrimination in public accommodations on the basis of sexual orientation.[21] In addition, the Commissioner awarded money damages to the complainants in the total sum of $135,000, signifying compensatory damages for emotional, mental, and physical suffering resulting from the denial of service.[22]

---

10. *See, e.g.*, Elane Photography, LLC v. Willock, 2013-NMSC-040, ¶ 79, 309 P.3d 53, 77 (N.M. 2013); State v. Arlene's Flowers, Inc., No. 13-2-00871-5, 2015 WL 94248, *17 (Wash. Super. Ct. Jan. 7, 2015).

11. *Elane Photography*, 2013-NMSC-040, ¶ 1, 309 P.3d at 59.

12. *Id.* at ¶ 7, 309 P.3d at 59–60.

13. *Id.* at ¶ 9, 309 P.3d at 60.

14. *Id.*

15. *Id.* at ¶ 1, 309 P.3d at 58.

16. *Id.* at ¶ 9, 309 P.3d at 60.

17. *Id.* at ¶ 10, 11, 309 P.3d at 60.

18. *Id.* at ¶ 10, 309 P.3d at 60.

19. *Id.* at ¶¶ 4, 10, 309 P.3d at 59, 60 (citing Elane Photography, LLC v. Willock, 2012-NMCA-086, ¶ 1, 284 P.3d 428, 432 (N.M. Ct. App. 2012)).

20. Melissa Elaine Klein, Nos. 44-14, 45-14, 2015 WL 4868796, at *24 (Or. Bureau of Lab. & Indus. July 5, 2015).

21. *Id.* at *16.

22. *Id.* at *23.

These are but a few of the cases which have been brought against public officials and private individuals who have declined to provide services in the manner described so far.[23] Undoubtedly, more will follow. As Chief Justice Roberts notes in his dissenting opinion in the *Obergefell* case:

> Hard questions arise when people of faith exercise religion in ways that may be seen to conflict with the new right to same-sex marriage — when, for example, a religious college provides married student housing only to opposite-sex married couples, or a religious adoption agency declines to place children with same-sex married couples. Indeed, the Solicitor General candidly acknowledged that the tax exemptions of some religious institutions would be in question if they opposed same-sex marriage. There is little doubt that these and similar questions will soon be before this Court.[24]

The cases which have arisen so far, and the observations by Chief Justice Roberts, raise an important issue for lawyers. Is it possible that attorneys who decline on religious grounds to provide legal services to same-sex individuals seeking divorces will be ordered to provide that representation? Might those attorneys be sanctioned if they fail to do so? An analysis of these issues will involve an examination of the lawyer's role as both a private practitioner and also as an officer of the court. It will involve a discussion as to whether legal services are "public accommodations" for purposes of human rights acts. It will require an examination of legal ethics rules and principles. It will necessitate examination of the power of courts to order attorneys to represent clients. And, of course, it will require an examination of the constitutional and statutory protections afforded to the religious beliefs and practices of attorneys. These are novel and difficult questions, but they are questions that will undoubtedly be raised. Attorneys need to consider them before the questions arise in their practices.

Before examining the potential obligations of attorneys in this controversy, we turn first to a brief exploration of the right of Americans to "opt out" of performing what otherwise would be a legal duty when their religious beliefs preclude that participation. We must also consider limitations on that right. Obviously, emotions run high, as do political considerations, on all sides of this current debate. It might be helpful from the outset, however, to recognize that this is not the first time in American history that we have witnessed a clash between religious beliefs and government duties imposed in a highly-charged environment.[25] The cases are voluminous, and

---

23. *See, e.g.*, Mullins v. Masterpiece Cakeshop, Inc., 2015 COA 115, ¶ 45 (Colo. App. 2015) ("We conclude that the Commission's order merely requires that [defendant] not discriminate against potential customers in violation of [Colorado Anti-Discrimination Act] and that such conduct, even if compelled by the government, is not sufficiently expressive to warrant First Amendment protections."); State v. Arlene's Flowers, Inc., No. 13-2-00871-5, 2015 WL 94248, at *3, *17 (Wash. Super. Ct. Jan. 7, 2015) (ruling against a florist who was sued for not providing services to a same-sex wedding).

24. Obergefell v. Hodges, 135 S. Ct. 2584, 2625–26 (2015) (citations omitted).

25. *See* discussion *infra* Part I.A.

an examination of each is beyond the scope of this article. Nonetheless, we turn to a brief attempt to understand some of this history by quickly considering some areas where religiously-based conscientious objections have been raised to government mandates.

A. *Right to Opt Out?*

1. The Draft

Kim Davis is not the first person from Kentucky to be cast into the national spotlight for refusing to perform a government-required duty because of a religious objection to it. On October 1, 2015, *Sports Illustrated* inaugurated its Muhammad Ali Legacy Award in Ali's Kentucky hometown.[26] Ali was not always regarded in such a positive light. In the Olympic games of 1960, Ali, who was then known by his birth name of Cassius Clay, Jr., won the gold medal in the 175-pound division.[27] Four years later he defeated Sonny Liston and became the heavyweight champion of the world.[28] Clay's victory was surprising, because of his decided underdog status in that fight.[29] He stunned the country again by announcing two days after the fight that he had become a member of the Nation of Islam.[30] Then on March 6, 1964, he announced that hereafter he would be known as Muhammad Ali.[31]

Over the course of the next four years, Ali successfully defended his crown against numerous opponents.[32] However, 1967 found this country in the midst of the Vietnam War and an increasingly unpopular mandatory draft.[33] On April 28, 1967, Ali refused to be inducted into the armed forces of the United States.[34] He cited his religious belief as the basis.[35] Ali's religious claim was made even more controversial by his acknowledgment that while he would fight in an Islamic holy war, he would not fight for the United States in Vietnam.[36] At the time, "conscientious objectors" would only qualify for exemption if they stated that their religious beliefs precluded them from participating in any war.[37]

---

26. Tim Layden, *The Legacy: The Greatest is Still an Inspirational Force*, Sports Illustrated, Oct. 5, 2015, at 61, 62, 64.

27. Thomas Hauser, *Muhammad Ali: American Boxer*, Encyc. Britannica, http://www .britannica.com/biography/Muhammad-Ali-boxer (last updated Dec. 31, 2014).

28. *Id.*

29. *Id.*

30. *Id.*

31. *Id.*

32. *Id.*

33. *Vietnam War Protests*, History.com, http://www.history.com/topics/vietnam-war/vietnam -war-protests (last visited Mar. 20, 2016).

34. Hauser, *supra* note 27.

35. *Id.*

36. *Id.*

37. Clay v. United States, 403 U.S. 698, 700 (1971) ("In order to qualify for classification as a conscientious objector, a registrant must satisfy three basic tests. He must show that he is

Ali's administrative appeal to the Kentucky Appeal Board was denied and the case ultimately reached the Supreme Court of the United States.[38] The Court agreed with Ali.[39] He went on to regain the title that had been stripped from him as a result of his refusal to participate in the draft, but he had lost four years, perhaps the best four years, of his career.[40]

It is important not to understate the intensity of the debate that raged around this case. While the Kim Davis matter has attracted national attention and controversy, at the time of the Ali matter, the country was involved in the increasingly unpopular Vietnam War. College campuses were in turmoil and demonstrations rocked the country.[41] Yet, the Supreme Court upheld the religious based conscientious exemption, and applied it to allow a very high profile sports combatant to decline to participate in military combat.[42] And Ali's case was not the only situation where the Supreme Court recognized the validity of a religious or ethically based objection to induction into the draft.[43]

2. The Workplace

The cases recognizing a religious exemption for workers in various contexts are voluminous, and are based not only on statutory concerns but on the First Amendment's Free Exercise of Religion Clause.[44] Illustrative of the latter is the case of *Sherbert v. Verner*.[45] In *Sherbert*, a claim by a Seventh-Day Adventist for workers compensation benefits in the State of South Carolina was denied.[46] South Carolina barred workers from receiving benefits who failed, "without good cause . . . to accept available suitable work when offered."[47] The worker had refused, because of her religion, to take a job which would have required her to work on Saturdays.[48] The Court concluded that, "[g]overnmental imposition of such a choice puts the same kind of burden upon the free exercise of religion as would a fine imposed against appellant for her Saturday worship."[49] Ultimately, the Court determined that disqualification

---

conscientiously opposed to war in any form." (citing Gillette v. United States, 401 U.S. 437, 443 (1971))); Hauser, *supra* note 27.

38. *See Clay*, 403 U.S. at 700.

39. *See id.* at 705.

40. *See* Hauser, *supra* note 27.

41. *See Student Antiwar Protests and the Backlash*, PBS (Sept. 22, 2005), http://www.pbs.org /wgbh/amex/twodays/peopleevents/e_antiwar.html.

42. *See Clay*, 403 U.S. at 700–01, 705.

43. *See, e.g.*, Welsh v. United States, 398 U.S. 333, 343–344 (1970); United States v. Seeger, 380 U.S. 163, 187–88 (1965).

44. U.S. Const. amend. I ("Congress shall make no law respecting an establishment of religion, or prohibiting the free exercise thereof.").

45. Sherbert v. Verner, 374 U.S. 398 (1963).

46. *Id.* at 399–401, 410.

47. *Id.* at 400–01 (alteration in original).

48. *Id.* at 399–400.

49. *Id.* at 404.

of her benefits imposed a non-constitutionally permissible burden on the free exercise of her religion.[50]

On the other hand, in a 1990 case, the Supreme Court determined that the state of Oregon could criminalize even the religiously inspired use of peyote.[51] It could deny unemployment benefits to employees who were discharged for possession of that drug, even in the face of their claims that the Free Exercise Clause of the First Amendment protected those activities.[52] This case, however, served as impetus three years later for the enactment of the Religious Freedom Restoration Act ("RFRA"),[53] discussed below.

In addition to constitutional protections raised in employment issues, Title VII of the Civil Rights Act of 1964[54] provides in part that it "shall be an unlawful employment practice for an employer . . . to discriminate against any individual with respect to his compensation, terms, conditions, or privileges of employment, because of such individual's race, color, religion, sex, or national origin."[55] In 1972, Congress included the following definition: "The term 'religion' includes all aspects of religious observance and practice, as well as belief, unless an employer demonstrates that he is unable to reasonably accommodate to an employee's or prospective employee's religious observance or practice without undue hardship on the conduct of the employer's business."[56] Courts have reached often conflicting decisions in the application of these provisions.[57] And the provisions do not extend to government officials.[58]

A case considered by the Supreme Court in 2015 involved the issue of whether a private business can prohibit an employee who practices the Muslim faith from wearing religiously-compelled attire to her job.[59] The case was remanded.[60] When that case is ultimately decided, we might have additional guidance on the extent of the

---

50. *Id.* at 410.

51. *See* Emp't Div. v. Smith, 494 U.S. 872, 890 (1990).

52. *Id.*

53. *See* Religious Freedom Restoration Act of 1993, 42 U.S.C. § 2000bb–1 (1993); Holt v. Hobbs, 135 S. Ct. 853, 859 (2015).

54. Civil Rights Act of 1964, Pub. L. No. 88-352, § 703, 78 Stat. 241, 253, 255 (codified as amended at 42 U.S.C § 2000e-2(a)(1) (2014)).

55. § 703, 78 Stat. at 255.

56. 42 U.S.C. § 2000e (j) (2014).

57. *See* Debbie N. Kaminer, *Religious Conduct and the Immutability Requirement: Title VII's Failure to Protect Religious Employees in the Workplace*, 17 Va. J. Soc. Pol'y & L. 453, 467–69 (2010).

58. *See* 42 U.S.C. § 2000e (f) ("[T]he term 'employee' shall not include any person elected to public office in any State or political subdivision of any State by the qualified voters thereof, or any person chosen by such officer to be on such officer's personal staff, or an appointee on the policy making level or an immediate adviser with respect to the exercise of the constitutional or legal powers of the office.").

59. EEOC v. Abercrombie & Fitch Stores, Inc., 135 S. Ct. 2028, 2031 (2015).

60. *Id.* at 2034.

right of employees to opt out of work regulations, and the accommodations which might be required of employers when religious issues arise in the workplace.

3. School Attendance

In 1972 the Supreme Court of the United States considered the case of *Wisconsin v. Yoder*.[61] Yoder refused to send his school-age children to the Wisconsin public schools in violation of a statute requiring such attendance.[62] He argued that his church, Old Order Amish, precluded such public school participation beyond the eighth grade.[63] The Supreme Court agreed that his conviction and the five dollar fine imposed upon him for his noncompliance with the statute violated the First Amendment's Free Exercise Clause.[64]

4. Religious Practice Involving Animal Slaughter

Animal sacrifice is part of the practice of the Santeria religion.[65] In 1993 the Supreme Court struck down as unconstitutional a Florida city's ban on "ritual slaughter" which precluded members of the Church of the Lukumi Babalu Aye from practicing their religion by slaughtering goats within the city limits.[66]

5. Taxation

Not all claims of religious liberty allow an individual to opt out of performing a government-imposed duty. In the case of *United States v. Lee*,[67] the Supreme Court denied to an Amish employer an exemption from compulsory participation in the Social Security system.[68] The employer alleged that such participation violated his free exercise of religion protections.[69] The Court later determined in 1990 that a religious organization would not be allowed to refuse to pay the general sales tax regarding the distribution of religious products and religious literature.[70]

6. Individuals in Government Custody or Control

Inmates have been allowed to exercise dietary and grooming choices, which would otherwise be prohibited, when those inmates demonstrate a religious reason for those choices pursuant to the First Amendment.[71] In the military, however, members

---

61. Wisconsin v. Yoder, 406 U.S. 205 (1972).
62. *Id.* at 207.
63. *Id.*
64. *Id.* at 208, 234.
65. Church of Lukumi Babalu Aye, Inc. v. City of Hialeah, 508 U.S. 520, 525 (1993).
66. *Id.* at 527–28, 547, 550, 551.
67. United States v. Lee, 455 U.S. 252 (1982).
68. *Id.* at 261.
69. *Id.* at 257.
70. Jimmy Swaggart Ministries v. Bd. of Equalization, 493 U.S. 378, 392, 397 (1990).
71. *See, e.g.,* Holt v. Hobbs, 135 S. Ct. 853, 861, 863, 867 (2015) (holding prison grooming policy substantially burdened practicing Muslim prisoner's free exercise of religion under the First Amendment).

of the armed services do not have the right to opt out of the dress code regulations based on a free exercise objection.[72]

7. Government Mandated Provision of Contraception — RFRA

The Congress of the United States enacted the Patient Protection and Affordable Care Act of 2010.[73] In general, that Act mandates that employers with fifty or more full-time employees must offer a group health insurance plan that provides "minimal essential coverage."[74] In regulations implementing the Act, the United States Department of Health and Human Services required employers to provide contraception under the statute, but exempted certain religious non-profit organizations from them.[75] A private employer which did not meet the definition of a religious nonprofit nonetheless challenged the provisions of the Act.[76] The owners of the company believed that life begins at conception and some contraception pills, which were required to be provided by the government, resulted in a termination of the pregnancy after conception had occurred.[77] Being required to provide these pills, they felt, violated their religious beliefs.[78] In deciding the case, the Supreme Court of the United States ruled for the private business owners.[79]

The Court determined that the applicable regulations violated the Religious Freedom Restoration Act of 1993.[80] The Court noted that the RFRA was enacted three years after the decision of the Supreme Court in *Employment Division v. Smith,* cited above.[81] Congress enacted the RFRA to provide additional religious safeguards against government action which infringes upon religious belief.[82] The Court noted that the RFRA provides that, "[g]overnment shall not substantially burden a person's exercise of religion even if the burden results from a rule of general applicability."[83] The Court noted that if the government substantially burdens a person's exercise of religion under the Act, that person is entitled to an exemption from the rule unless the government "demonstrates that application of the burden to the person — (1) is in furtherance of a compelling governmental interest; and (2) is the least restrictive means of furthering that compelling government interest."[84] The Court concluded that there were many other ways that the government could ensure that women have

---

72. Goldman v. Weinberger, 475 U.S. 503, 509–10 (1986).
73. Patient Protection and Affordable Care Act, Pub. L. No. 111–148, 124 Stat. 119 (2010).
74. 26 U.S.C. § 4980H (a), (c)(2)(A) (2014).
75. 45 C.F.R. § 147.131(a) (2015).
76. *See* Burwell v. Hobby Lobby Stores, Inc., 134 S. Ct. 2751, 2759 (2014).
77. *Id.* at 2764–65.
78. *Id.* at 2765.
79. *Id.* at 2785.
80. *Id.*
81. *Id.* at 2760.
82. *Id.* at 2761.
83. *Id.* (internal quotation marks omitted).
84. *Id.* (internal quotation marks omitted).

access to contraception without mandating that it be provided by business owners over their religious objections.[85]

On a similar note, another case has worked its way up to be heard by the Supreme Court in the upcoming Term. That case, *Little Sisters of the Poor v. Burwell*,[86] involves a challenge by a Catholic order of nuns.[87] The nuns had declined not only to provide contraception to their employees, but refused to sign the proposal by the government to authorize a private insurer to issue the contraception in the name of the Little Sisters.[88]

Note that following the enactment of the federal RFRA, states enacted similar versions.[89] However, these typically only provide protection against action by a government.[90] Thus in the *Elane Photography* case, the Supreme Court of New Mexico held that the state's RFRA law did not apply because the government was not a party.[91]

8. Polygamy

In our last quick examination of some of the areas where individual religious beliefs have clashed with government policy, we return to the subject of marriage. In the case of *Reynolds v. United States*,[92] the Supreme Court of the United States determined, over religious objections, that individuals do not have a constitutional right to practice polygamy.[93] This case was decided before the enactment of the RFRA.[94] Undoubtedly the result would be the same even in the post-RFRA environment. Kim Davis' counterparts could lawfully be sanctioned not only for refusing to issue marriage licenses to same-sex couples, but they could be sanctioned under state law for providing licenses to multiple parties within the same marriage, even if the clerks' religious beliefs or those of the applicants permitted or even required polygamy.[95]

B. *The Role of Lawyers in Same-Sex Divorces*

The discussion of the situations where courts have had to decide whether, and to what extent, an individual's religious beliefs permit that person to opt out of compliance with what otherwise would be a government-imposed obligation could be quite lengthy. Nonetheless, it is apparent that while not absolute, the individual right to the free exercise of religion provides an important opportunity to refrain from compliance with many government mandates.[96] Without detailing all of these

---

85. *Id.* at 2759.
86. Little Sisters of the Poor Home for the Aged v. Burwell, 794 F.3d 1151 (10th Cir.), *cert. granted in part*, 136 S. Ct. 446 (2015).
87. *Id.* at 1167.
88. *See id.* at 1167–68, 1170.
89. *See, e.g.,* N.M. STAT. ANN. §§ 28-22-1 to 28-22-6 (West 2015).
90. *Id.* § 28-22-3.
91. Elane Photography, LLC v. Willock, 2013-NMSC-040, ¶ 4, 309 P.3d 53, 59 (N.M. 2013).
92. Reynolds v. United States, 98 U.S. 145 (1878).
93. *Id.* at 166–67.
94. *See* 42 U.S.C. § 2000bb-1 (2014); *Reynolds*, 98 U.S. at 145.
95. *See, e.g.,* UTAH CODE ANN. §§ 30-1-2, 30-1-16 (LexisNexis 2015).
96. *See* discussion *supra* Part I.A.

circumstances, it is apparent that our system recognized an important balance. While "government" necessarily requires that people be governed, there are limits. The free exercise of religion is valued and respected, even to the point of excusing the performance of duties that otherwise would be compelled. Of course, that freedom is not unlimited. These principles serve as the backdrop as we now turn our attention to an area which could potentially affect the readers of this article in their practices and in their judicial determinations. Will lawyers be required to provide legal services, over their religious objections, to individuals seeking same-sex divorces?

Nobody enters into a marriage expecting that it will end in divorce. Yet the cold hard reality is that approximately half of all marriages will end that way.[97] There is no reason to believe that same-sex marriages will be any different. Indeed, even before *Obergefell*, while same-sex couples could not marry in Texas, some same-sex couples who had recently married elsewhere sought to obtain divorces in Texas.[98] Undoubtedly, many of the same-sex couples who celebrate the newly-acquired right to marry by contracting for the services of wedding planners, florists, photographers, bakers and the like will eventually find themselves seeking the services of the legal profession to resolve the property, child custody, and other areas of conflict associated with the breakdown of their marriages.

Many attorneys don't handle divorces because they are not interested in that area of law. Some decline to handle divorces because of religious concerns.[99] Some attorneys might feel a religious compulsion not to represent individuals in a same-sex divorce because doing so would require the assertion that a valid marriage exists. On the other hand, an attorney who is religiously opposed to same-sex marriage actually might be fulfilling his/her view that such individuals should not be married, by assisting in obtaining a divorce. While we will explore these issues below, at this point it seems inevitable that the same type of challenges to pre-wedding service providers who decline, on religious grounds, to provide those services, will be brought against attorneys who decline, on religious grounds, to provide legal services to an individual seeking a same-sex divorce. It is also possible that there could be challenges to attorneys who decline to assist in pre-nuptial planning, or adoptions, for gay couples.

---

97. *See* Nat'l Ctr. for Health Statistics, *FastStats: Marriage and Divorce*, Ctrs. for Disease Control & Prevention, http://www.cdc.gov/nchs/fastats/marriage-divorce.htm (last updated June 19 2014).

98. *See* State v. Naylor, 330 S.W.3d 434, 436 (Tex. App. 2011) (dismissing same-sex divorce action for lack of subject matter jurisdiction); *In re* Marriage of J.B. and H.B., 326 S.W.3d 654, 659 (Tex. App. 2010) (holding Texas courts do not have subject matter jurisdiction over same-sex divorce case). For a further discussion of these cases, see Bill Piatt, Catholic Legal Perspectives 40, 41, 48 (2d ed. 2015).

99. For an examination of the role of a catholic lawyer or judge in divorce proceedings, see Piatt, *supra* note 98, at 78-81.

In trying to determine whether such challenges might succeed, consider first the ethical concerns relating to the role of attorneys. The American Bar Association Model Rules of Professional Conduct ("Model Rules")[100] is an important source for this examination. These are the rules promulgated by the American Bar Association, and adopted with some modifications, from state to state.[101] They serve to establish the norms of conduct required of attorneys, quite separate and apart from other regulatory statutes or theories of civil liability.[102]

The very first sentence of the Preamble to the Model Rules identifies the unique role of attorneys: "A lawyer, as a member of the legal profession, is a representative of clients, an officer of the legal system and a public citizen having special responsibility for the quality of justice."[103] Paragraph 6 of that preamble includes the provision that, "all lawyers should devote professional time and resources and use civic influence to ensure equal access to our system of justice for all those who because of economic or social barriers cannot afford or secure adequate legal counsel."[104] These introductory provisions seem to suggest that the importance of the role of the lawyer in society is probably greater than the role of photographers, bakers, or florists. If that is true, then the obligations of attorneys similarly might be greater than those of photographers, bakers or florists as well.

If a lawyer who has religious concerns regarding same-sex marriage is concerned that his or her role in representing same-sex couples might be construed as an endorsement of same-sex marriage, Model Rule 1.2(b) provides this approach: "A lawyer's representation of a client, including representation by appointment, does not constitute an endorsement of the client's political, economic, social or moral views or activities."[105] Comment 5 to that rule provides: "Legal representation should not be denied to people who are unable to afford legal services, or whose cause is controversial or the subject of popular disapproval. By the same token, representing a client does not constitute approval of the client's views or activities."[106]

Nonetheless, if the attorney's concern is not so much with whether the lawyer's representation will be viewed as an endorsement of same-sex marriage, but rather, because the attorney, for religious reasons finds same-sex marriage repugnant, may the attorney decline the representation under the Model Rules? Model Rule 1.16 is entitled, "Declining or Terminating Representation."[107] Rule 1.16(b)(4) allows an attorney to withdraw from representing a client if "the client insists upon taking

---

100. *See* MODEL RULES OF PROF'L CONDUCT PREFACE (AM. BAR ASS'N 2013).

101. *See About the Model Rules*, AM. BAR ASS'N CTR. FOR PROF'L RESPONSIBILITY, http://www .americanbar.org/groups/professional_responsibility/publications/model_rules_of_professional _conduct.html (last visited Mar. 16, 2016).

102. MODEL RULES OF PROF'L CONDUCT: PMBL AND SCOPE.

103. *Id.* at ¶ 1.

104. *Id.* at ¶ 6.

105. MODEL RULES OF PROF'L CONDUCT r. 1.2(b).

106. *Id.* at r. 1.2 cmt. 5.

107. *Id.* at r. 1.16.

action that the lawyer considers repugnant or with which the lawyer has a fundamental disagreement."[108] Note that the language only speaks to withdrawing from the case on this repugnancy ground and does not directly address the issue of declining the representation in the first place.[109] Comment 7 to that same rule, in referring to withdrawal, allows such withdrawal "where the client insists on taking action that the lawyer considers repugnant or with which the lawyer has a fundamental disagreement."[110] By analogy, if a lawyer would be allowed to withdraw from representing a client whose behavior is considered repugnant, or with which the lawyer fundamentally disagrees, a lawyer should be allowed to decline to represent a client on the same grounds. Indeed, historically attorneys have been viewed as being free from ethical sanction in declining cases,[111] and as we are about to discuss, might have the ability to avoid court appointments on a "repugnancy" ground.

However, consider this scenario. Suppose that in a small town or rural area there are relatively few attorneys. Most of them do not handle divorces. The ones that do represent divorce litigants decline on religious grounds to handle divorces of same-sex couples. A local judge becomes concerned with the inadequate presentation by a same-sex couple attempting to obtain a pro se divorce, because no local attorney will represent them. The judge appoints local attorneys to handle the case. In these circumstances, the provisions of Model Rule 6.2, regarding "Accepting Appointments" apply. That rule provides that: "A lawyer shall not seek to avoid appointment by a tribunal to represent a person except for good cause, such as: the client or the cause is so repugnant to the lawyer as to be likely to impair the client-lawyer relationship or the lawyer's ability to represent the client."[112]

Comment 1 to this rule provides:

> A lawyer ordinarily is not obliged to accept a client whose character or cause the lawyer regards as repugnant. The lawyer's freedom to select clients is, however, qualified. All lawyers have a responsibility to assist in providing pro bono public service. An individual lawyer fulfills this responsibility by accepting a fair share of unpopular matters or indigent or unpopular clients. A lawyer may also be subject to appointment by a court to serve unpopular clients or persons unable to afford legal services.[113]

It begins to appear that under the ethical rules, it is likely that attorneys could be required to represent an individual in a same-sex divorce even where the attorney might have some religious objection to it or might find the client's situation

---

108. *Id.* at r. 1.16 (b)(4).
109. *See id.*
110. *Id.* at r. 1.16 cmt. 7.
111. *See* RONALD D. ROTUNDA & JOHN S. DZIENKOWSKI, PROFESSIONAL RESPONSIBILITY: A STUDENT'S GUIDE § 1.16-1 n.2, at 675 (2011–2012); *but see* Nathanson v. Commonwealth, No. 1999–01657, 2003 Mass. Super. LEXIS 293, at *16 (Mass. Super. Ct. Sept.-16, 2003).
112. MODEL RULES OF PROF'L CONDUCT r. 6.2(c).
113. *Id.* r. 6.2 cmt. 1 (citation omitted).

repugnant. Refusal to accept the appointment and represent the client could result in the attorney, an officer of the court, being sanctioned under the Model Rules.[114] It could also result in a contempt proceeding against the attorney.[115]

Whether appointed or not, attorneys might also face civil liability under applicable human rights statutes in the state or city in which they practice for declining same-sex clients in divorces.[116] It would be difficult for an attorney to convince the body hearing the complaint, or ultimately the courts, that the provision of legal services is somehow not included in the definition of "public accommodations." While we found no cases which directly hold that legal services are a form of public accommodations, other professional services including dental services, and a wide range of other businesses, have been held to be public accommodations.[117] The trend is toward inclusion, rather than exclusion of businesses under those statutes.[118]

Moreover, the ordinances or statutes could easily be amended in the future to include such language so as to resolve any ambiguity. While attorneys view their profession as largely self-regulated, state statutes imposed by the legislatures often add to the professional obligations of attorneys. For example, in Texas, while the Texas Disciplinary Rules of Professional Conduct, Rule 1.05 requires an attorney to maintain client confidences, a state statute requires that attorneys who learn of child abuse—even in client communications—must report it.[119] Barratry statutes in Texas[120] expand upon the professional obligations set out in the Rules. Thus, legislative actions, including human rights statutes, could easily be amended to include

---

114. *Id.* at r. 8.4 cmt. 3.

115. RESTATEMENT (THIRD) OF LAW GOVERNING LAWYERS § 6(6) (AM. LAW INST. 2000).

116. The following is a partial list of states that have sexual orientation anti-discriminatory laws for places of public accommodations: California (CAL. CIV. CODE § 51(b) (West 2015)), Connecticut (CONN. GEN. STAT ANN. § 46a-81d(a) (West 2015)), Iowa (IOWA CODE ANN. § 216.7(1)(a) (West 2014)), Maine (ME. STAT. ANN. tit. 5, § 4592(1) (2015)), Massachusetts (MASS. GEN. LAWS ANN. ch. 272, § 92(A) (West 2015)), Minnesota (MINN. STAT. ANN. § 363A.11(a)(1) (West 2015)), New Hampshire (N.H. REV. STAT. ANN. § 354-A:17 (2015)), New Jersey (N.J. STAT. ANN. § 10:5-4 (West 2015)), New York (N.Y. EXEC. LAW § 296(2)(a) (McKinney 2015)), Vermont (VT. STAT. ANN. tit 9, § 4502(a) (2015)), Washington (WASH. REV. CODE ANN. § 49.60.215(1) (West 2015)), and Wisconsin (WIS. STAT. ANN. § 106.52 (3)(a)(1) (West 2015)).

117. *See* 42 U.S.C. § 12181(7) (2014); D.B. v. Bloom, 896 F. Supp. 166, 169, 170 (D. N.J. 1995) (citing Howe v. Hull, 873 F. Supp. 72, 77 (N.D. Ohio 1994)).

118. *See, e.g.*, Disabled Rights Action Comm. v. Las Vegas Events, Inc., 375 F.3d 861, 865 (9th Cir. 2004) (holding a private group hosting a public event (a rodeo) was a place of accommodation); Martin v. PGA Tour, Inc., 204 F.3d 994, 997 (9th Cir. 2000) (relating to accommodations at a golf course); Nat'l Ass'n for the Deaf v. Netflix, Inc., 869 F. Supp. 2d 196, 201, 202 (D. Mass. 2012) (holding a Netflix website falls within the definition of public accommodation); Cahill v. Rosa, 674 N.E.2d 274, 277 (N.Y. 1996) (holding a dentist's office must comply); Local Fin. Co. v. Mass. Comm'n Against Discrimination, 242 N.E.2d 536, 539 (Mass. 1968) (holding a public accommodation includes a finance company specializing in offering loans).

119. TEX. FAM. CODE ANN. § 261.101(c) (West 2015); TEX. DISCIPLINARY R. OF PROF'L CONDUCT r. 1.05 (2015).

120. TEX. PENAL CODE ANN. §§ 38.12, 38.18 (West 2015).

attorneys as regulated providers, even if there is some ambiguity as to the current wording of those acts.

What then would become of the attorney's argument that his or her right to the free exercise of his or her religion exempts the attorney from performing such services? After the bakery and photography cases, courts relying upon those decisions would have an easy time disposing of any constitutional argument that an attorney might raise. Same-sex divorce litigants could also point to the additional obligations placed upon an attorney as an officer of the court. Those obligations would be heightened if the attorney was court appointed to represent the litigant. Under the order of a court to represent a litigant, the conduct of the attorney moves not only from the bakery and photography realm, but into the Kim Davis realm of state mandated official duties. Ms. Davis' religious beliefs did not save her from jail time. Does this mean that divorce attorneys could ultimately be compelled to handle same-sex divorces? It is beginning to appear that the answer is in the affirmative. Is there any mechanism by which this could be avoided? One approach appears to be that if the lawyer wishes to handle any divorces, the attorney could be compelled to handle same-sex divorces.[121] It would probably be too late for an attorney facing disciplinary sanctions or a civil proceeding for refusing to represent the same-sex individual in the divorce to suddenly determine not to handle any divorces. That approach did not work for Kim Davis and would not work in the other civil cases. If an attorney is seriously opposed on religious grounds to handling a same-sex divorce that attorney should, in advance of any complaint or charge by an individual seeking a same-sex divorce, abandon handling any divorces. That approach avoids the accusation that the attorney is discriminating against same-sex divorces or against an individual based on sexual orientation.

Another approach would be for the attorney to simply decline to handle same-sex divorce and raise the religious objection before the sanctioning body.[122] The attorney would have to be prepared for the possibility that courts would continue to decline to recognize a constitutional right to decline such representation.[123] Under an applicable RFRA, the attorney would demonstrate that representing persons in same-sex divorces "substantially burdens" the attorneys exercise of religion.[124] The attorney would need to bring the action against the state agency that requires his or her participation, in order to avoid a New Mexico-style dismissal for failure to

121. *See generally* note 116 (citing to various state statutory provisions relating to public accommodations that could be enforced against lawyers).

122. *Cf.* Bd. of Prof'l Responsibility of the Sup. Ct. of Tenn. Formal Ethics Op. 96-F-140 (1996) (finding that the appointed attorney could not decline to represent client despite conflicting religious beliefs).

123. *See, e.g.*, Walden v. Ctrs. for Disease Control & Prevention, 669 F.3d 1277, 1280–81, 1283, 1290–91 (11th Cir. 2012).

124. *See* 42 U.S.C. § 2000bb–1(a) (2014).

name the state body as a defendant.[125] Applying the RFRA, the court hearing the attorneys challenge would then require the government to demonstrate its compelling governmental interest in forcing the attorney's participation or penalizing his or her refusal.[126] It would also have to show that the coercion is the least restrictive means of furthering that interest.[127] While access to legal services by all members of the public is a critical and compelling interest of the courts,[128] permitting the attorney to demonstrate that other officers of the court are available to provide the necessary services would satisfy those concerns.[129] That approach of attempted referral was not successful in the bakery or wedding photography cases, but given the unique role of the attorney in client representation, it might be applicable in the legal services cases.

II. Accommodation Not Coercion

In resisting a mandate to represent persons in same-sex marriages, the attorney should hope that eventually our system will reach a model of accommodation between the newly announced right to same-sex marriage and the sincerely held religious beliefs of those who wish not to participate. Accommodation, not coercion, should be the model. Attorneys might point to the concerns of Chief Justice Roberts, who elaborated on the extensive history of traditional marriage in his dissenting opinion in *Obergefell*. He noted with dismay:

> Perhaps the most discouraging aspect of today's decision is the extent to which the majority feels compelled to sully those on the other side of the debate. The majority offers a cursory assurance that it does not intend to disparage people who, as a matter of conscience, cannot accept same-sex marriage. That disclaimer is hard to square with the very next sentence, in which the majority explains that "the necessary consequence" of laws codifying the traditional definition of marriage is to "demea[n] or stigmatiz[e]" same-sex couples. The majority reiterates such characterizations over and over . . . These apparent assaults on the character of fair-minded people will have an effect, in society and in court.[130]

Attorneys should argue that they should not be disparaged; their beliefs should be accommodated.

---

125. *E.g.*, Elane Photography v. Willock, 2013-NMSC-040, ¶¶ 74, 75, 78, 309 P.3d 53, 76, 77 (N.M. 2013).

126. *See* 42 U.S.C. § 2000bb–1(b)(1).

127. *See id.* § 2000bb–1(b)(2).

128. *See e.g.*, N.Y. Comp. Codes R. & Regs. tit. 22, § 51.1(b) (2015).

129. *See* Elizabeth Sepper, *Doctoring Discrimination in the Same-Sex Marriage Debates*, 89 Ind. L.J. 703, 716–17 (2014).

130. Obergefell v. Hodges,135 S. Ct. 2584, 2626 (2015) (Roberts, C.J., dissenting) (first and second alteration in original) (citations omitted).

Attorneys might also note that another difficulty with the model of coercion rather than accommodation is that it is counterproductive. Attempting to force people to do something against their deeply held religious belief will only inflame resistance, as it did in the Kim Davis matter.[131] High profile individuals and people from all walks of life rallied to her defense.[132] In the case of the Oregon bakers, contributions likely exceeding the fine of $135,000 poured into the bakers.[133]

Courts and other adjudicative bodies should also recognize that there will probably need to be time for society to make the necessary adjustments and accommodations. After all, only a few years ago present-day high-profile advocates of same-sex marriage were opposed to it, including then Senator Hillary Clinton and President Barack Obama. [134] Lawyers, by definition are trained in the law. They would be effective adversaries if a coercion model, rather than accommodation model were to be imposed upon the legal profession. Even attorneys who are in favor of same-sex marriage might feel compelled to rally to the sides of their brothers and sisters who were being coerced into providing representation of individuals those attorneys did not want to represent.

What if the attorney is not only opposed to same-sex marriage, but is opposed to representing homosexual clients in other matters? The refusal to provide legal services based upon the sexual orientation of the client would be a clear violation of human rights acts prohibiting such practices.[135] While there are well recognized, religiously-based arguments in support of traditional marriage, there appears to be no valid legal or moral argument for refusing to provide legal services based on the sexual orientation of the client.[136] Courts could easily pierce through a pretext of "religious defense of marriage" argument if it is obvious that the real motivation is the desire not to provide any legal services based on sexual

---

131. *See Ky. clerk: I am being forced to disobey God*, CBS News (Sept. 14, 2015), http://www.cbsnews.com/news/ky-clerk-i-am-being-forced-to-disobey-god/.

132. *See* Elisha Fieldstadt, *Supporters of jailed Kentucky clerk Kim Davis rally to her defense,* MSNBC (Sept. 8, 2015), http://www.msnbc.com/msnbc/supporters-jailed-kentucky-clerk-kim-davis-rally-her-defense.

133. *GoFundMe Nixes Donations for Bakery That Refused to Serve Gay Weddings*, Fox News: Insider (Apr. 27, 2015), http://insider.foxnews.com/2015/04/27/gofundme-blocks-fundraising-oregon-bakery-refused-serve-gay-weddings.

134. GLASSBOOTHdotORG, *Barack Obama on Gay Marriage*, YouTube (Oct. 28, 2008), https://www.youtube.com/watch?v=N6K9dS9wl7U ("I believe that marriage is the union between a man and a woman. Now, for me as a Christian, it's also a sacred union; God's in the mix."). Barack Obama went on to say, "No [he] would not" support a constitutional amendment allowing gay marriage because he believed it should remain a state issue. *Id.* However, Obama says he supports the idea of civil unions as it has been applied to same-sex couples. *Id.; see also* Jvideos8, *Hillary Clinton was against Gay Marriage & for removing Saddam*, YouTube (June 12, 2014), https://www.youtube.com/watch?time_continue=141&v=9TyZBeGfeVM (noting that Hillary Clinton responded to the question of whether or not she thought New York State should recognize gay marriage by flatly saying "no").

135. *See supra* note 116 and accompanying text.

136. *See* Piatt, *supra* note 98, at 14.

orientation. In this regard, though, it is worth noting that neither the New Mexico case nor the Oregon case recognized any distinction.[137] In both instances the providers were willing to serve homosexual customers.[138] Both declined, however, to participate in any activity that would acknowledge the validity of a same-sex marriage.[139] Neither succeeded.[140] Both the Oregon and New Mexico tribunals concluded that the refusal to provide the services for wedding-related matters constituted discrimination based on sexual orientation rather than a conscientious objection to the validity of same-sex marriages.[141]

From an ethics perspective, it would not be possible to justify refusing to serve all homosexual clients on a "repugnancy" basis any more than refusing to serve clients based on race could be justified on a "repugnancy" basis.[142] Still, some lawyers and firms only represent men or women in divorce matters.[143] To this author's knowledge, that method of client selection has not been found to be unlawful or unethical.

But assume that an attorney is not unwilling to serve homosexual clients. He or she in fact represents some gay clients in matters unrelated to a marriage issue. However, that attorney holds a religious view that does not recognize the validity of same-sex marriage. As a result, the attorney declines to represent individuals in same-sex divorces, because such would, in effect, be arguing that a valid marriage is before the court. How might an appropriate accommodation model be implemented to protect the rights of this attorney, others similarly situated, and potential clients?

---

137. Elane Photography, LLC v. Willock, 2013-NMSC-040, ¶¶ 7, 11, 14, 18, 19, 309 P.3d 53, 59–60, 61, 62, 63 (N.M. 2013); Melissa Elaine Klein, Nos. 44-14, 45-14, 2015 WL 4868796, at *19, *24, *25, *51–52 (Or. Bureau of Lab. & Indus. July 5, 2015).

138. *Elane Photography,* 2013-NMSC-040 at ¶ 7, 309 P.3d at 59–60 (refusing to photograph ceremony of same-sex couple); Melissa Elaine Klein, 2015 WL 4868796, at *3 (refusing to provide a wedding cake for same-sex couple).

139. *See Elane Photography,* 2013-NMSC-040 at ¶ 7, 309 P.3d at 59–60; Melissa Elaine Klein, 2015 WL 4868796, at *3.

140. *Elane Photography,* 2013-NMSC-040 at ¶ 79, 309 P.3d at 77; Melissa Elaine Klein, 2015 WL 4868796 at *13.

141. *See Elane Photography,* 2013-NMSC-040 at ¶ 18, 309 P.3d at 62, 70; Melissa Elaine Klein, 2015 WL 4868796 at *19.

142. *See* David B. Wilkins, *Race, Ethics, and the First Amendment: Should a Black Lawyer Represent the Ku Klux Klan?*, 63 GEO. WASH. L. REV. 1030, 1038 (1995) (discussing the possible repercussions facing an African American lawyer that motivated him to accept the Ku Klux Klan as a client); *cf.* Norman W. Spaulding, *Reinterpreting Professional Identity*, 74 U. COLO. L. REV. 1, 20 (2003) ("[O]ne's status as a lawyer, and hence the role itself, is conditioned both by the right of a court to order appointment and the principle that such appointment must be accepted irrespective of the lawyer's opinion of the client.").

143. *See, e.g., Family Law Attorneys for Men*, CORDELL & CORDELL, LLC, http://cordellcordell .com (last visited Mar. 17, 2016); *Nashville Divorce for Men*, DUNN LAW FIRM, http://dunnlawtn .com/tennessee-divorce-for-men/ (last visited Mar. 20, 2016); MEN'S DIVORCE LAW FIRM, http:// www.mensdivorcelaw.com (last visited Mar. 20, 2016); THE LAW FIRM OF VICTORIA, http://www .lawfirmofvictoria.com (last visited Mar. 20, 2016); DIVORCE ATTORNEYS FOR WOMEN, http://www .dawnforwomen.com (last visited Mar. 20, 2016).

Attorneys and judges will need to become aware of the reality that some lawyers hold a deeply held religious belief against same-sex marriage which in many instances is based on religious traditions which pre-date our country by thousands of years. The Catholic Church specifically identifies the religious foundation for traditional marriage, while at the same time extending its love and inclusion of gay Catholics into the church.[144] These issues are discussed in this author's book, *Catholic Legal Perspectives*.[145]

There will also have to be additional legal exploration of the right to the free exercise of religion. Implicit attempts to limit that exercise in political rhetoric and in judicial opinions should be scrutinized. For example, the First Amendment guarantees of free exercise are much broader than the guarantee that President Obama refers to when he characterizes the First Amendment's guarantee as the "freedom of worship."[146] This appears to some observers to be an attempt to seriously limit the First Amendment's Free Exercise clause, which of course, does not limit the guarantee of religious liberty to only "worship."[147] Chief Justice Roberts points out that the majority opinion in *Obergefell* only refers to the right to "advocate" and "teach" that same-sex marriage is inappropriate, "ominously" omitting the right to "exercise" one's religious beliefs.[148] Attorneys will want to ensure that everyone in these discussions understand that the First Amendment protects that "exercise."

On the other hand, participants in same-sex marriages enjoy all the benefits conferred upon any married couple.[149] Property rights, benefits under government programs such as social security, immigration laws, and the tax laws, are among those benefits.[150] In the unfortunate situation where the marriage breaks down, those individuals will have the right to the assistance of the legal system in the resolution of the issues which will arise. If attorneys reject their cases, these rights could be damaged or lost. The anguish associated with divorce will be compounded. If we recognize a right to marriage that can compel a clerk to issue the marriage license, should we not also recognize a right to divorce that would compel state-licensed attorneys to assist?

The market might provide its own accommodation of these issues. If, as this author anticipates, many of the same-sex marriages will end in divorce, it is very likely that the need for legal representation will be eagerly met in a market where recent

---

144. PIATT, *supra* note 98, at 26.

145. *See id.* at 23–31.

146. Randy Sly, *Obama Moves Away From 'Freedom of Religion' Toward 'Freedom of Worship'?*, CATHOLIC ONLINE (July 19, 2010),

147. *See id.*

148. Obergefell v. Hodges, 135 S. Ct. 2584, 2625 (Roberts, C.J., dissenting) (citations omitted). Of course, "the government may . . . accommodate religious practices . . . without violating the Establishment Clause." Hobbie v. Unemp't Appeals Comm'n of Fla., 480 U.S. 136, 144–45 (1987).

149. *See Obergefell*, 135 S. Ct. at 2599, 2601 (majority opinion).

150. *See id.* at 2601.

2 · FAMILY ISSUES   115

graduates are struggling to find employment. In the circumstances where the market does not provide sufficient attorneys, courts should accommodate the religious beliefs of those opposed to same-sex divorce by expanding the additional resources necessary to bring in counsel who are not opposed to handling the divorce. Even where an attorney might nonetheless be ordered to represent a litigant in a same-sex divorce, and where the attorney chooses not to defy the court, the attorney would still have the right, under the First Amendment, to post a disclaimer. The attorney could state that while he/she opposes same-sex marriage, the attorney will nonetheless comply with the order or the anti-discrimination provision.[151]

Accommodation might not happen anytime soon. It might be that there are potential litigants within the same-sex community who would be looking to add lawyers to the list of those who could be required provide services to same-sex couples. It might have been no accident that the same-sex couples bringing the actions against photographers, bakers, and other businesses were well aware that there were others who could have provided the services but chose to pursue the legal claims to establish precedent. As a result, it is possible that future litigants will not be inclined to accept an accommodation model, and will instead press for all possible sanctions in order to dissuade others from refusing to handle same-sex divorces.

In this scenario, a lawyer who opposes same-sex marriage, and has made his or her views known, could become a target of a disciplinary proceeding or civil action. The attorney might expect to lose the initial rounds under the Oregon, New Mexico, and Washington cases cited in this article.[152] The attorney would have to pursue the appeals, perhaps sacrificing his or her ability to practice law and suffering severe economic losses, similar to the career interruption in losses suffered by Muhammad Ali.[153] The attorney might have to be willing to face jail time for contempt, as did Kim Davis, while ultimately hoping that the courts will accommodate his or her religious beliefs.[154]

Perhaps others in the bar might step up. They could volunteer to assist their brothers and sisters in the legal profession. They could take the cases which some attorneys, in the tradition of conscientious objection based upon religious beliefs and in the exercise of their First Amendment rights, decline to handle. In this manner, the rights of same-sex couples to legal representation, and the rights of attorneys to the free exercise of their religion, could best be accommodated.

---

151. Elane Photography, LLC v. Willock, 2013-NMSC-040, ¶ 3, 309 P.3d 53, 59 (N.M. 2013).

152. *See id;* State v. Arlene's Flowers, No. 13-2-00871-5, 2015 WL 720213, at *31 (Wash. Super. Ct. Feb. 18, 2015); Melissa Elaine Klein, Nos. 44-14, 45-14, 2015 WL 4868796, at *23, *24 (Or. Bureau of Lab. & Indus. July 5, 2015).

153. *See* Hauser, *supra* note 27.

154. Galofaro, *supra* note 6.

D. For Further Thought

1. What is or should be the role of a Catholic attorney when a client asks for assistance in a divorce case? Does it make any difference which party is at "fault"? Does the severity of the "fault" make any difference? What if there are children involved? Would the length of the marriage make any difference?

2. In the first problem, would your answers be different depending upon whether the potential client would be seeking the divorce as a petitioner, or had been served with a divorce petition and would be the respondent in the proceeding?

3. Would it make any difference to your answers above if the potential client is not a Catholic? What if the client is Catholic, but the spouse is not? What if they weren't married in the Catholic Church?

4. Suppose a Catholic judge is assigned to a general civil docket, which ordinarily includes family law matters. Should the judge recuse him/herself from all divorce proceedings? Or, should the judge recuse him/herself from only some proceedings? If so, which ones and why?

5. What is or should be the role of the Catholic attorney if one of the parties in a same-sex relationship seeks legal advice regarding pre-nuptial planning?

6. If one of the partners in a same-sex marriage asks a Catholic attorney for representation in a divorce, what should the attorney do?

7. Rule 2.1 of the ABA Model Rules of Professional Conduct provides: "In representing a client, a lawyer shall exercise independent professional judgment and render candid advice. In rendering advice, a lawyer may refer not only to law, but to other considerations such as moral, economic, social and political factors, that may be relevant to the client's situation." What latitude does this give a lawyer meeting with a client in a family law matter?

8. If a Catholic attorney feels morally compelled not to handle many, if any divorce cases, is there another role that attorney could play? Consider the role of mediation, where the mediator seeks to assist couples going through a divorce to reach agreements that might help them maintain some semblance of a working relationship, at least as regards to the children of the marriage. Are there other roles a Catholic attorney might play, assisting couples or individuals who have made the decision to divorce?

9. A Catholic husband and his Catholic wife wish to receive the Eucharist, notwithstanding the fact that they have had been previously married and divorced. Under what circumstances may they do so? What if a Catholic man who has never been married marries a Catholic woman who divorced her first husband? May he receive the Eucharist? May a same-sex married Catholic couple receive the Eucharist? How would the affected people proceed in trying to find answers to these questions?

Chapter 3

Life and Death

A. Abortion

There is a great deal of difference between the position of the Catholic Church regarding abortion, and that of the American legal system. In an *ex cathedra* pronouncement, Pope John Paul II concluded, "I declare that direct abortion, that is, abortion willed as an end or a means, always constitutes a grave moral disorder, since it is the deliberate killing of an innocent human being."[1] His successor, Pope Benedict XVI reiterated this point: "Everyone must be helped to become aware of the intrinsic evil of the crime of abortion. In attacking human life in its very first stages, it is also an aggression against society itself."[2] This view has also been adopted and repeated by the USCCB: "Abortion, the direct killing of an innocent human being is *always* gravely immoral; its victims are the most vulnerable and defenseless of the human family."[3]

On the other hand, the American legal system does not recognize that human life exists from the moment of conception. The court refers instead to "the life of the fetus that may become a child"[4] and it has determined that there is a constitutional right on the part of a mother to obtain an abortion with minimal restrictions, at least up until the point that the preborn child becomes "viable."[5] The view that human life begins at the moment of conception is a position espoused not only by the Catholic Church. Even the Supreme Court notes that many physicians and many non-Catholics adhere to this view.[6]

---

1. Pope John Paul II, *Evangelium Vitae: On the Value and Inviolability of Human Life* ¶ 62 (Mar. 25, 1995), http://www.vatican.va/holy_father/john_paul_ii/encyclicals/documents/hf_jpii_enc_25031995_evangeium-vitae_en.html (last visited Oct. 23, 2017).

2. Pope Benedict XVI, *Address at a Meeting on Family and Life Issues in Latin America* (Dec. 3, 2005), http://www.vatican.va/holy_father/benedict_xvi/speeches/2005/december/documents/hf_ben_xvi_spe_20051203_family-america-latina_en.html (last visited Oct. 23, 2017).

3. USCCB, *Pastoral Plan for Pro-Life Activities: A Campaign in Support of Life*, Introduction (2001), http://www.usccb.org/about/pro-life-activities/pastoral-plan-prolife-activities.cfm (last visited Oct. 23, 2017).

4. Planned Parenthood of Se. Pa. v. Casey, 505 U.S. 833, 846 (1992) "[T]he state interest in potential human life is not an interest in loco parentis, for the fetus is not a person." (*Casey,* 505 U.S. at 914 (Stevens, J., concurring in part and dissenting in part)).

5. *Id.*

6. Roe v. Wade, 410 U.S. 113, 161 (1973).

Thus, there is no way to reconcile the positions of the church and the legal system. What we will be required to do, then, is to attempt to understand both positions and determine whether there will be any reconciliation of these views. As you will see, there is even disagreement regarding the history of abortion and the philosophical views regarding its application throughout history. It should come as no surprise that these moral issues still remain unresolved in the legal system.

As we begin this examination there is a shocking reality. The United States is in a distinct minority among the nations of the world regarding this country's extensive abortion practices. For example, out of 198 nations in the world, only seven of those countries allow abortions after 20 weeks of pregnancy. One of those countries is the United States. The only others include Canada, China, Netherlands, North Korea, Singapore and Vietnam.[7]

1. Catholic Church Position

On March 25, 1995, Pope John Paul II issued his *"Evangelium Vitae"* (Gospel of Life). This lengthy document summarizes the church's position on matters of life, including the death penalty, abortion, and euthanasia, among other life topics. After a lengthy discussion about the morality, or rather the immorality, of the imposition of the death penalty in most instances, the Pope then turned to a discussion of the church's position on abortion. Following are paragraphs 57–62 of this Encyclical:

---

57. If such great care must be taken to respect every life, even that of criminals and unjust aggressors, the commandment "You shall not kill" has absolute value when it refers to the innocent person. And all the more so in the case of weak and defenceless human beings, who find their ultimate defence against the arrogance and caprice of others only in the absolute binding force of God's commandment.

In effect, the absolute inviolability of innocent human life is a moral truth clearly taught by Sacred Scripture, constantly upheld in the Church's Tradition and consistently proposed by her Magisterium. This consistent teaching is the evidence result of that "supernatural sense of the faith" which, inspired and sustained by the Holy Spirit, safeguards the People of God from error when "it shows universal agreement in matters of faith and morals."

---

7. Michelle Ye Hee Lee, *Is the United States one of seven countries that allow elective abortions after 20 weeks of pregnancy?*, Washington Post.com (Oct. 9, 2017), https://www.washingtonpost.com/news/fact-checker/wp/2017/10/09/is-the-united-states-one-of-seven-countries-that-allow-elective-abortions-after-20-weeks-of-pregnancy/?utm_term=.f5dcac34e3d7 (last visited Oct. 16, 2017).

Faced with the progressive weakening in individual consciences and in society of the sense of the absolute and grave moral illicitness of the direct taking of all innocent human life, especially at its beginning and at its end, the Church's Magisterium has spoken out with increasing frequency in defence of the sacredness and inviolability of human life. The Papal Magisterium, particularly insistent in this regard, has always been seconded by that of the Bishops, with numerous and comprehensive doctrinal and pastoral documents issued either by Episcopal Conferences or by individual Bishops. The Second Vatican Council also addressed the matter forcefully, in a brief but incisive passage.

Therefore, by the authority which Christ conferred upon Peter and his Successors, and in communion with the Bishops of the Catholic Church, I confirm that the direct and voluntary killing of an innocent human being is always gravely immoral. This doctrine, based upon that unwritten law which man, in the light of reason, finds in his own heart (*cf.* Rom. 2:14-15), is reaffirmed by Sacred Scripture, transmitted by the Tradition of the Church and taught by the ordinary and universal Magisterium.

The deliberate decision to deprive an innocent human being of his life is always morally evil and can never be licit either as an end in itself or as a means to a good end. It is in fact a grave act of disobedience to the moral law, and indeed to God himself, the author and guarantor of that law; it contradicts the fundamental virtues of justice and charity. "Nothing and no one can in any way permit the killing of an innocent human being, whether a fetus or an embryo, an infant or an adult, an old person, or one suffering from an incurable disease, or a person who is dying. Furthermore, no one is permitted to ask for this act of killing, either for himself or herself or for another person entrusted to his or her care, nor can he or she consent to it, either explicitly or implicitly. Nor can any authority legitimately recommend or permit such an action."

As far as the right to life is concerned, every innocent human being is absolutely equal to all others. This equality is the basis of all authentic social relationships which, to be truly such, can only be founded on truth and justice, recognizing and protecting every man and woman as a person and not as an object to be used. Before the moral norm which prohibits the direct taking of the life of an innocent human being "there are no privileges or exceptions for anyone. It makes no difference whether one is the master of the world or the poorest of the poor on the face of the earth. Before the demands of morality we are all absolutely equal."

"Your eyes beheld my unformed substance" (Ps 139:16): the unspeakable crime of abortion.

58. Among all the crimes which can be committed against life, procured abortion has characteristics making it particularly serious and deplorable.

The Second Vatican Council defines abortion, together with infanticide, as an "unspeakable crime."

But today, in many people's consciences, the perception of its gravity has become progressively obscured. The acceptance of abortion in the popular mind, in behaviour and even in law itself, is a telling sign of an extremely dangerous crisis of the moral sense, which is becoming more and more incapable of distinguishing between good and evil, even when the fundamental right to life is at stake. Given such a grave situation, we need now more than ever to have the courage to look the truth in the eye and to call things by their proper name, without yielding to convenient compromises or to the temptation of self-deception. In this regard the reproach of the Prophet is extremely straightforward: "Woe to those who call evil good and good evil, who put darkness for light and light for darkness" (Isa. 5:20). Especially in the case of abortion there is a widespread use of ambiguous terminology, such as "interruption of pregnancy," which tends to hide abortion's true nature and to attenuate its seriousness in public opinion. Perhaps this linguistic phenomenon is itself a symptom of an uneasiness of conscience. But no word has the power to change the reality of things: procured abortion is the deliberate and direct killing, by whatever means it is carried out, of a human being in the initial phase of his or her existence, extending from conception to birth.

The moral gravity of procured abortion is apparent in all its truth if we recognize that we are dealing with murder and, in particular, when we consider the specific elements involved. The one eliminated is a human being at the very beginning of life. No one more absolutely innocent could be imagined. In no way could this human being ever be considered an aggressor, much less an unjust aggressor! He or she is weak, defenceless, even to the point of lacking that minimal form of defence consisting in the poignant power of a newborn baby's cries and tears. The unborn child is totally entrusted to the protection and care of the woman carrying him or her in the womb. And yet sometimes it is precisely the mother herself who makes the decision and asks for the child to be eliminated, and who then goes about having it done.

It is true that the decision to have an abortion is often tragic and painful for the mother, insofar as the decision to rid herself of the fruit of conception is not made for purely selfish reasons or out of convenience, but out of a desire to protect certain important values such as her own health or a decent standard of living for the other members of the family. Sometimes it is feared that the child to be born would live in such conditions that it would be better if the birth did not take place. Nevertheless, these reasons and others like them, however serious and tragic, can never justify the deliberate killing of an innocent human being.

59. As well as the mother, there are often other people too who decide upon the death of the child in the womb. In the first place, the father of the child

may be to blame, not only when he directly pressures the woman to have an abortion, but also when he indirectly encourages such a decision on her part by leaving her alone to face the problems of pregnancy: in this way the family is thus mortally wounded and profaned in its nature as a community of love and in its vocation to be the "sanctuary of life." Nor can one overlook the pressures which sometimes come from the wider family circle and from friends. Sometimes the woman is subjected to such strong pressure that she feels psychologically forced to have an abortion: certainly in this case moral responsibility lies particularly with those who have directly or indirectly obliged her to have an abortion. Doctors and nurses are also responsible, when they place at the service of death skills which were acquired for promoting life.

But responsibility likewise falls on the legislators who have promoted and approved abortion laws, and, to the extent that they have a say in the matter, on the administrators of the health-care centers where abortions are performed. A general and no less serious responsibility lies with those who have encouraged the spread of an attitude of sexual permissiveness and a lack of esteem for motherhood, and with those who should have ensured-but did not-effective family and social policies in support of families, especially larger families and those with particular financial and educational needs. Finally, one cannot overlook the network of complicity which reaches out to include international institutions, foundations and associations which systematically campaign for the legalization and spread of abortion in the world. In this sense abortion goes beyond the responsibility of individuals and beyond the harm done to them, and takes on a distinctly social dimension. It is a most serious wound inflicted on society and its culture by the very people who ought to be society's promoters and defenders. As I wrote in my Letter to Families, "we are facing an immense threat to life: not only to the life of individuals but also to that of civilization itself." We are facing what can be called a "structure of sin" which opposes human life not yet born.

60. Some people try to justify abortion by claiming that the result of conception, at least up to a certain number of days, cannot yet be considered a personal human life. But in fact, "from the time that the ovum is fertilized, a life is begun which is neither that of the father nor the mother; it is rather the life of a new human being with his own growth. It would never be made human if it were not human already. This has always been clear, and . . . modern genetic science offers clear confirmation. It has demonstrated that from the first instant there is established the programme of what this living being will be: a person, this individual person with his characteristic aspects already well determined. Right from fertilization the adventure of a human life begins, and each of its capacities requires time — a rather lengthy time — to find its place and to be in a position to act." Even if the presence

of a spiritual soul cannot be ascertained by empirical data, the results themselves of scientific research on the human embryo provide "a valuable indication for discerning by the use of reason a personal presence at the moment of the first appearance of a human life: how could a human individual not be a human person?"

Furthermore, what is at stake is so important that, from the standpoint of moral obligation, the mere probability that a human person is involved would suffice to justify an absolutely clear prohibition of any intervention aimed at killing a human embryo. Precisely for this reason, over and above all scientific debates and those philosophical affirmations to which the Magisterium has not expressly committed itself, the Church has always taught and continues to teach that the result of human procreation, from the first moment of its existence, must be guaranteed that unconditional respect which is morally due to the human being in his or her totality and unity as body and spirit: "The human being is to be respected and treated as a person from the moment of conception; and therefore from that same moment his rights as a person must be recognized, among which in the first place is the inviolable right of every innocent human being to life."

61. The texts of Sacred Scripture never address the question of deliberate abortion and so do not directly and specifically condemn it. But they show such great respect for the human being in the mother's womb that they require as a logical consequence that God's commandment "You shall not kill" be extended to the unborn child as well.

Human life is sacred and inviolable at every moment of existence, including the initial phase which precedes birth. All human beings, from their mothers' womb, belong to God who searches them and knows them, who forms them and knits them together with his own hands, who gazes on them when they are tiny shapeless embryos and already sees in them the adults of tomorrow whose days are numbered and whose vocation is even now written in the "book of life" (*cf.* Ps. 139:1, 13–16). There too, when they are still in their mothers' womb — as many passages of the Bible bear witness — they are the personal objects of God's loving and fatherly providence.

Christian Tradition — as the Declaration issued by the Congregation for the Doctrine of the Faith points out so well — is clear and unanimous, from the beginning up to our own day, in describing abortion as a particularly grave moral disorder. From its first contacts with the Greco-Roman world, where abortion and infanticide were widely practised, the first Christian community, by its teaching and practice, radically opposed the customs rampant in that society, as is clearly shown by the Didache mentioned earlier. Among the Greek ecclesiastical writers, Athenagoras records that

Christians consider as murderesses women who have recourse to abortifacient medicines, because children, even if they are still in their mother's womb, "are already under the protection of Divine Providence." Among the Latin authors, Tertullian affirms: "It is anticipated murder to prevent someone from being born; it makes little difference whether one kills a soul already born or puts it to death at birth. He who will one day be a man is a man already."

Throughout Christianity's two thousand year history, this same doctrine has been constantly taught by the Fathers of the Church and by her Pastors and Doctors. Even scientific and philosophical discussions about the precise moment of the infusion of the spiritual soul have never given rise to any hesitation about the moral condemnation of abortion.

62. The more recent Papal Magisterium has vigorously reaffirmed this common doctrine. Pius XI in particular, in his Encyclical *Casti Connubii*,[8] rejected the specious justifications of abortion. Pius XII excluded all direct abortion, i.e., every act tending directly to destroy human life in the womb "whether such destruction is intended as an end or only as a means to an end." John XXIII reaffirmed that human life is sacred because "from its very beginning it directly involves God's creative activity." The Second Vatican Council, as mentioned earlier, sternly condemned abortion: "From the moment of its conception life must be guarded with the greatest care, while abortion and infanticide are unspeakable crimes."

The Church's canonical discipline, from the earliest centuries, has inflicted penal sanctions on those guilty of abortion. This practice, with more or less severe penalties, has been confirmed in various periods of history. The 1917 Code of Canon Law punished abortion with excommunication. The revised canonical legislation continues this tradition when it decrees that "a person who actually procures an abortion incurs automatic (*latae sententiae*) excommunication." The excommunication affects all those who commit this crime with knowledge of the penalty attached, and thus includes those accomplices without whose help the crime would not have been committed. By this reiterated sanction, the Church makes clear that abortion is a most serious and dangerous crime, thereby encouraging those who commit it to seek without delay the path of conversion. In the Church the purpose of the penalty of excommunication is to make an individual fully aware of the gravity of a certain sin and then to foster genuine conversion and repentance.

---

8. Pope Pius XI, *Casti Connubii: Encyclical on Christian Marriage to the Venerable Brethren, Patriarchs, Primates, Archbishops, Bishops, and Other Local Ordinaries Enjoying Peace and Communion With the Apostolic See* (Dec. 31, 1930), http://www.vatican.va/holy_father/pius_xi/encyclicals /documents/hf_p-xi_enc_31121930_casti-connubii_ en.html (last visited Oct. 23, 2017).

Given such unanimity in the doctrinal and disciplinary tradition of the Church, Paul VI was able to declare that this tradition is unchanged and unchangeable. Therefore, by the authority which Christ conferred upon Peter and his Successors, in communion with the Bishops—who on various occasions have condemned abortion and who in the aforementioned consultation, albeit dispersed throughout the world, have shown unanimous agreement concerning this doctrine—I declare that direct abortion, that is, abortion willed as an end or as a means, always constitutes a grave moral disorder, since it is the deliberate killing of an innocent human being. This doctrine is based upon the natural law and upon the written Word of God, is transmitted by the Church's Tradition and taught by the ordinary and universal Magisterium.

No circumstance, no purpose, no law whatsoever can ever make licit an act which is intrinsically illicit, since it is contrary to the Law of God which is written in every human heart, knowable by reason itself, and proclaimed by the Church.[9]

The Catechism of the Catholic Church explains that abortion, unlike the death penalty, is intrinsically evil. The Catechism recites:

2271. Since the first century the Church has affirmed the moral evil of every procured abortion. This teaching has not changed and remains unchangeable. Direct abortion, that is to say, abortion willed either as an end or a means, is gravely contrary to the moral law: You shall not kill the embryo by abortion and shall not cause the newborn to perish. God, the Lord of life, has entrusted to men the noble mission of safeguarding life, and men must carry it out in a manner worthy of themselves. Life must be protected with the utmost care from the moment of conception: abortion and infanticide are abominable crimes.

2272. Formal cooperation in an abortion constitutes a grave offense. The Church attaches the canonical penalty of excommunication to this crime against human life. "A person who procures a completed abortion incurs excommunication *latae sententiae*," "by the very commission of the offense," and subject to the conditions provided by Canon Law. The Church does not thereby intend to restrict the scope of mercy. Rather, she makes clear the gravity of the crime committed, the irreparable harm done to the innocent who is put to death, as well as to the parents and the whole of society.[10]

---

9. Pope John Paul II, *Evangelium Vitae, supra* note 1.
10. CATECHISM OF THE CATHOLIC CHURCH, *Article 5: The Fifth Commandment*, 2271–72 (1993), http://www.vatican.va/archive/ccc_css/archive/catechism/p3s2c2a5.htm (last visited Oct. 23, 2017).

2. Historical Perspectives

Abortion and the ethical and moral concerns surrounding it, are not new topics. Abortions were criminal acts during the time of the Persian Empire.[11] Abortion was practiced in the time of the Greeks and during the Roman Era, but there were powerful voices raised in opposition. A physician named Soranos, an Ephesian, objected to the Roman practice, viewing it as only acceptable to preserve the life of the mother.[12]

Perhaps the most widely recognized abortion critic in the ancient world is Hippocrates, the "Father of Medicine," who lived in the era of approximately 460 B.C. until 377 B.C. He has been described as the "wisest and the greatest practitioner of his art" and the "most important and most complete medical personality of antiquity."[13] The famous Hippocratic Oath, according to the Supreme Court, "represents the apex of the development of strict ethical concepts in medicine, and its influence endures to this day."[14] The Oath includes the following: "I will give no deadly medicine to anyone if asked, nor suggest any such counsel; and in like manner I will not give to a woman a pessary to produce abortion."[15] The view of Hippocrates was consistent with the Pythagorean doctrines which held that "the embryo was animate from the moment of conception, and abortion meant destruction of a living being."[16] Most Greek philosophers approved of the concept of abortion, at least before viability, but none of them had the medical knowledge nor the stature of Hippocrates. It was his view that generally came to be accepted by the developing teachings of Christianity.[17]

The philosophical approaches to abortion leading up to contemporary times included the view that abortion was immoral once human life began. Various disciplines approached this issue by attempting to determine when an embryo "formed" into a recognizable human being. Others attempted to determine when a "person" came into existence as the soul entered the body. While St. Augustine tried to draw a distinction between embryos not yet endowed with a soul, and those that were, he concluded at one point that human powers could not make this determination.[18]

---

11. Roe v. Wade, 410 U.S. 113, 130 n.8 (1973) (referencing ARTURO CASTIGLIONI, HISTORY OF MEDICINE 84 (E. Krumbhaar, trans. and ed., 2d ed. 1947)).

12. *Id.* at 130 n.11 (referencing LUDWIG EDELSTEIN, THE HIPPOCRATIC OATH 12 (1943)).

13. *Id.* at 131 n.13 (referencing ARTURO CASTIGLIONI, HISTORY OF MEDICINE 148 (E. Krumbhaar, trans. and ed., 2d ed. 1947)).

14. *Id.* at 131.

15. *Id.* at 131 n.14 (referencing ARTURO CASTIGLIONI, HISTORY OF MEDICINE 154 (E. Krumbhaar, trans. and ed., 2d ed. 1947)). The Court references a second translation in note 15. (Roe v. Wade, 410 U.S. 113, 131 n.15 (1973) (referencing LUDWIG EDELSTEIN, THE HIPPOCRATIC OATH 3 (1943)).

16. *Roe*, 410 U.S. at 131–32, 132 n.17 (referencing LUDWIG EDELSTEIN, THE HIPPOCRATIC OATH 18 (1943)).

17. *Id.* at 132.

18. *Id.* at 133 n.22. The complete footnote text follows:
Early philosophers believed that the embryo or fetus did not become formed and begin to live until at least 40 days after conception for a male, and 80 to 90 days for a female. *See*, for example,

However, from the first century, early Catholic teaching held that abortion was prohibited as reflected in the Catechism. Theological discussions continued, and in 1869 Pope Pius IX repeated the Catholic Church's position that abortions were immoral, based upon the view that life began at conception.[19] The Church's position in this regard is clear.

The common law, or the law that developed in England and whose principles form the background of American jurisprudence however, generally drew distinctions regarding abortions that involved determining when movement, or "quickening," of the baby occurred. Coke and Blackstone both comment on abortion. Based on studies of the common law, it appears that abortion, even of a quickened fetus, was, at most, a misdemeanor.[20] In 1803 England made the abortion of a quickened fetus a capital crime.[21] It also provided for felony punishment, although not capital punishment, for aborting a fetus that had not yet quickened. Subsequent British statutes continued to criminalize abortion, at least regarding a child that would have been born alive.[22] Abortion is currently legal in England.[23]

Aristotle, Hist. Anim. 7.3.583b; Gen. Anim. 2.3.736, 2.5.741; Hippocrates, Lib. de Nat. Puer., No. 10. Aristotle's thinking derived from his three-stage theory of life: vegetable, animal, rational. The vegetable stage was reached at conception, the animal at 'animation,' and the rational soon after live birth. This theory, together with the 40/ 80 day view, came to be accepted by early Christian thinkers.

The theological debate was reflected in the writings of St. Augustine, who made a distinction between embryo inanimatus, not yet endowed with a soul, and embryo animatus. He may have drawn upon Exodus 21:22. At one point, however, he expressed the view that human powers cannot determine the point during fetal development at which the critical change occurs. *See* Augustine, De Origine Animae 4.4 (Pub. Law 44.527). *See also* W. REANY, THE CREATION OF THE HUMAN SOUL, c.2 and 83–86 (1932); HUSER, THE CRIME OF ABORTION IN CANON LAW 15 (Catholic Univ. of America, Canon Law Studies No. 162, Washington, D.C., 1942).

Galen, in three treatises related to embryology, accepted the thinking of Aristotle and his followers. *Quay* 426–427. Later, Augustine on abortion was incorporated by Gratian into the Decretum, published about 1140. *Decretum Magistri Gratiani* 2.32.2.7 to 2.32.2.10, *in* 1 CORPUS JURIS CANONICI 1122, 1123 (A. Friedberg, 2d ed. 1879). This Decretal and the Decretals that followed were recognized as the definitive body of canon law until the new Code of 1917.

19. Lucinda M. Finley, *Contested Ground: The Story of* Roe v. Wade *and its Impact on American Society, in* CONSTITUTIONAL LAW STORIES 336 (Michael C. Dorf ed., 2d ed. 2009); *Canonical Misconception: Pope Pius IX and the Church's Teaching on Abortion*, Catholics United for Faith (1997), http://www.cuf.org/2004/03/canonical-misconception-pope-pius-ix-and-the-churchs-teaching -on-abortion/ (last visited Oct. 23, 2017).

20. Roe v. Wade, 410 U.S. at 135–36 (1973).

21. Lord Ellenborough's Act, 43 Geo. 3, c. 58 (1803) (Eng.).

22. Infant Life (Preservation) Act, 19 & 20 Geo. 5, c. 34 (1929) (G.B.).

23. *Roe*, 410 U.S. at 137–38. The act that legalized abortion in the majority of the U.K. was the Abortion Act of 1967, 15 & 16 Eliz. 2, c. 87 (Eng., Wales, Scot.). In 1990, the 1967 Act was amended:

(a) that the pregnancy has not exceeded its twenty-fourth week and that the continuance of the pregnancy would involve risk, greater than if the pregnancy were terminated, of injury to the physical or mental health of the pregnant woman or any existing children of her family; or (b) that the termination is necessary to prevent grave permanent injury to the physical or mental health of the pregnant woman; or (c) that the continuance of

The states in the newly-formed United States enacted their own criminal laws, and originally adopted the "quickening" distinctions under the British common law. However, by the late 19th Century this distinction disappeared, and by the end of the 1950's the majority of the states in this country outlawed *all* abortions, regardless of how far along the fetus had developed, except to preserve the life of the mother.[24] The American Medical Association played a major role in the adoption of these strict criminal abortion provisions. The AMA opposed abortions because of the "independent and actual existence of the child before birth, as a living being." In fairness, it is also worth noting that the AMA's strong stance was developed at a time when the AMA itself was attempting to assert itself as the controlling body in American medicine, at a time when there were many alternatives to physicians for medical assistance. Additionally many women's historians have reflected on the AMA's desire to keep women out of the medical practice and to demonize midwives, who commonly performed abortions, as fuel in their fight against abortion-providers.[25] Certainly, data cited by historians has exposed that female midwives performed the greater number of births and abortions compared to medical-school-trained-male-physicians. Whatever their reason, the AMA adopted resolutions "against such unwarrantable destruction of human life."[26] In 1871 the AMA Committee on Criminal Abortion concluded, "[w]e had to deal with human life. In a matter of less importance we could entertain no compromise."[27] Some states relaxed their statues over the next two decades, but by 1973, the majority of states prohibited the performing or obtaining of abortions, criminalizing those acts in various levels of severity, depending upon the law of the individual states.

Notwithstanding the fact that abortion was illegal in most states, an underground abortion industry developed in this country. Following the stock market crash and during the resulting Great Depression, it is estimated by abortion rights advocates that between 600,000 and 800,000 abortions were performed illegally each year. Physicians made money on this practice, and police occasionally ignored it, in many cases because of bribes paid to them by the abortion doctors. By the 1940s, books and articles began to appear encouraging the legalization of abortions in this country.[28]

---

the pregnancy would involve risk to the life of the pregnant woman, greater than if the pregnancy were terminated; or (d) that there is a substantial risk that if the child were born it would suffer from such physical or mental abnormalities as to be seriously handicapped.

Human Fertilisation and Embryology Act, 1990, 38 Eliz. 2, c. 37, § 1) (Eng., Wales, Scot.).

24. *Roe*, 410 U.S. at 139.

25. An excellent and highly readable study on this topic is LESLIE J. REAGAN, WHEN ABORTION WAS A CRIME: WOMEN, MEDICINE, AND LAW IN THE UNITED STATES, 1867–1973 (Univ. of Cal. Press, 1997).

26. *Roe*, 410 U.S. at 141–42 (quoting 12 Trans. of the Am. Med. Assn. 73–78 (1859)).

27. *Id*. at 142 (quoting 22 Trans. of the Am. Med. Assn. 258 (1871)).

28. Finley, *supra* note 19 at 338.

By the 1950s, however, a renewed interest in preventing abortions led to the arrest and conviction of prominent abortion physicians, including a Dr. George Timanus, associated with the Johns Hopkins University Hospital. This renewed interest in limiting abortions drove many physicians away from an abortion practice, and the vacuum was quickly filled by abortion middle-men including "motorcycle mechanics, bartenders, and real-estate agents" who would refer women to "back-alley" providers. Abortion rights advocates estimate that up to 1,000,000 abortions were performed annually in the United States during this time period, and safety concerns were raised regarding the entire abortion industry.[29]

In 1955 Planned Parenthood sponsored a conference on "Abortion in the United States." In 1959 the American Law Institute, an association of judges and lawyers which prepares model statutes for state consideration, proposed relaxing state abortion statutes. In 1968 the American Public Health Association urged that states should recognize a woman's personal right to an abortion. In 1970 the AMA House of Delegates adopted proposals modifying its previous stances. It supported proposals favoring abortion when performed in "the best interests of the patient," involving "informed patient consent," but contrasted that with "mere acquiescence to the patient's demand," and preserved the right of physicians to refuse to participate in abortions on moral grounds.[30]

Some states did relax abortion laws at the urging of abortion activists, but a majority did not. Efforts to obtain state legislative repeals of anti-abortion laws stalled by 1970. An intense legislative battle took place in New York, which relaxed its abortion laws in 1969. Pro-life forces fought back and the legislature rescinded that law in 1971. Noteworthy is the fact that between 1968 and 1971, the actual maternal mortality rate in New York City fell by over half.[31] Governor Rockefeller then vetoed the repeal, and New York narrowly retained its new abortion statute.[32]

The likelihood of sustaining legislative defeats by elected representatives led abortion advocates to consider a new strategy. Rather than relying upon elected officials to change state statutes to provide for a legalization of abortion, abortion rights proponents, and activists determined to take the matter to the federal courts. The reasons for the new strategy involved several considerations. First, federal judges are appointed by the President, confirmed by the Senate, and hold their offices for "good behavior" according to the Constitution. For all practical purposes, this is an appointment for life. Thus, Federal judges are immune from the political interests of any constituents. Looking at it another way, while state legislative officials might fear

---

29. *Id.* at 338–40.

30. *Id.* at 342–48.

31. Lewis H. Roht, M.D., Roger Sherwin, M.D., & Maureen M. Henderson, M.D., *The Impact of Legal Abortion: Redefining the Maternal Mortality Rate*, 89 HEALTH SERVICES REPORTS 211, 268 (1974), http://www.ncbi.nlm.nih.gov/pmc/issues/136079 (In 1968, the Actual Maternal Mortality Rate (total number of maternal deaths/total number of known conceptions) for NYC was 4.1 deaths per 10,000 live births. By 1971, the number had fallen to only 1.7 maternal deaths.).

32. Finley, *supra* note 19, at 347–48.

removal by the electorate for voting to create a right which the majority of their constituents might not favor, federal judges would have no such concern. Second, abortion rights advocates knew that the federal courts could remove the issue of the
abortion debate from the states if those courts recognized a constitutionally protected
right to abortion. Such a constitutional right would override all state laws to the contrary because of the Supremacy Clause of the Constitution of the United States.
Thus, abortion rights advocates decided to shift the abortion strategy away from state
legislatures, which traditionally determine criminal laws in each state, to the federal
courts. In that regard, they decided to ask the courts to utilize the rationale of a 1963
case, *Griswold v. Connecticut*.[33]

Griswold actually had nothing to do with abortion, but it was used as the basic
justification for the creation of an abortion privacy right. In the *Griswold* case, the
Executive Director of the Planned Parenthood League of Connecticut, and another
individual who was a licensed physician serving as a Professor at the Yale Medical
School, were arrested for violating a Connecticut statute. That statute prohibited giving of information, instruction, and medical advice to individuals, including married persons, as a means to prevent conception. The defendants, Griswold and
Buckston, defended on the ground that the statute as applied to them violated the
Fourteenth Amendment to the Constitution of the United States. That amendment,
enacted after the Civil War, provides in part, "No state shall . . . deprive any person
of life, liberty, or property without due process of law." The defendants were found
guilty and fined one hundred dollars each. They appealed their convictions all the
way to the Supreme Court of the United States.

When the *Griswold* case reached the Supreme Court, the Supreme Court
overturned the conviction. It found that the action of the state of Connecticut
violated a constitutionally protected "right to privacy" which was based in the
Due Process Clause of the Fourteenth Amendment. Even though there is no specific right in the Constitution to the contraception information, the Court cited a
number of cases where individuals were held to have rights that are also not specifically mentioned in the Constitution. These include the rights to educate a child
in the school of the parent's choice,[34] the right to study the German language in a
private school,[35] the freedom to teach,[36] and of the entire University community[37] and
others. The Supreme Court concluded "[t]he foregoing cases suggest that specific
guarantees in the Bill Rights have penumbras formed by emanations from those
guarantees that help give them life and substance . . . various guarantees create
zones of privacy."[38]

33. Griswold v. Connecticut, 381 U.S. 479 (1965).
34. Pierce v. Soc'y of Sisters, 268 U.S. 510 (1925).
35. Meyer v. Nebraska, 262 U.S. 390 (1923).
36. Wieman v. Updegraff, 344 U.S. 183, 193 (1952).
37. Sweezy v. New Hampshire, 354 U.S. 234, 248 (1957).
38. *Griswold*, 381 U.S. at 484.

3. *Roe v. Wade*[39]

Abortion rights activists began filing federal suits in an attempt to have a court declare a constitutional right to an abortion. Litigation timing and other circumstances resulted in a Texas case reaching the Supreme Court of the United States in 1971. Attorneys for the lead plaintiff, Norma McCorvey, used the pseudonym "*Roe*" to protect their client's anonymity. McCorvey was pregnant and thought the attorneys would help her obtain an abortion. Her attorneys, who had referred other women to abortion practitioners outside of the country, did not send her away to obtain an abortion. They were concerned that if McCorvey had an abortion, the case would be "moot" and the courts would not hear it. By the time the litigation reached the court, she had given birth. Ironically, the case which granted women a constitutional right to an abortion resulted in *McCorvey*, "*Roe*," giving birth. McCorvey became a pro-life advocate, and regretted her participation in the case. She unsuccessfully asked the Supreme Court, to reconsider its decision.[40]

---

410 U.S. 113 / 93 S. Ct. 705
Supreme Court of the United States
Jane ROE, et al., Appellants,
v.
Henry WADE.
Decided Jan. 22, 1973.

Action was brought for a declaratory and injunctive relief respecting Texas criminal abortion laws which were claimed to be unconstitutional. A three-judge United States District Court for the Northern District of Texas, 314 F. Supp. 1217, entered judgment declaring laws unconstitutional and an appeal was taken. The Supreme Court, Mr. Justice Blackmun, held that the Texas criminal abortion statutes prohibiting abortions at any stage of pregnancy except to save the life of the mother are unconstitutional; that prior to approximately the end of the first trimester the abortion decision and its effectuation must be left to the medical judgment of the pregnant woman's attending physician, subsequent to approximately the end of the first trimester the state may regulate abortion procedure in ways reasonably related to maternal health, and at the stage subsequent to viability the state may regulate and even proscribe abortion except where necessary in appropriate medical judgment for preservation of life or health of mother.

Affirmed in part and reversed in part.

. . . .

---

39. Roe v. Wade, 410 U.S. 113 (1973).
40. Finley, *supra* note 19, at 351–71.

Opinion

Mr. Justice BLACKMUN delivered the opinion of the Court.

This Texas federal appeal and its Georgia companion, *Doe v. Bolton*, 410 U.S. 179, present constitutional challenges to state criminal abortion legislation. The Texas statutes under attack here are typical of those that have been in effect in many States for approximately a century. The Georgia statutes, in contrast, have a modern cast and are a legislative product that, to an extent at least, obviously reflects the influences of recent attitudinal change, of advancing medical knowledge and techniques, and of new thinking about an old issue.

We forthwith acknowledge our awareness of the sensitive and emotional nature of the abortion controversy, of the vigorous opposing views, even among physicians, and of the deep and seemingly absolute convictions that the subject inspires. One's philosophy, one's experiences, one's exposure to the raw edges of human existence, one's religious training, one's attitudes toward life and family and their values, and the moral standards one establishes and seeks to observe, are all likely to influence and to color one's thinking and conclusions about abortion.

In addition, population growth, pollution, poverty, and racial overtones tend to complicate and not to simplify the problem.

Our task, of course, is to resolve the issue by constitutional measurement, free of emotion and of predilection. We seek earnestly to do this, and, because we do, we have inquired into, and in this opinion place some emphasis upon, medical and medical-legal history and what that history reveals about man's attitudes toward the abortion procedure over the centuries. We bear in mind, too, Mr. Justice Holmes' admonition in his now-vindicated dissent in *Lochner v. New York*, 198 U.S. 45, 76 (1905):

> '(The Constitution) is made for people of fundamentally differing views, and the accident of our finding certain opinions natural and familiar, or novel, and even shocking, ought not to conclude our judgment upon the question whether statutes embodying them conflict with the Constitution of the United States.'

I.

The Texas statutes that concern us here are Arts. 1191–1194 and 1196 of the State's Penal Code, Vernon's Ann. P.C. These make it a crime to 'procure an abortion,' as therein defined, or to attempt one, except with respect to 'an abortion procured or attempted by medical advice for the purpose of saving the life of the mother.' Similar statutes are in existence in a majority of the States.

. . . .

II.

Jane Roe, a single woman who was residing in Dallas County, Texas, instituted this federal action in March 1970 against the District Attorney of the county. She sought a declaratory judgment that the Texas criminal abortion statutes were unconstitutional on their face, and an injunction restraining the defendant from enforcing the statutes.

Roe alleged that she was unmarried and pregnant; that she wished to terminate her pregnancy by an abortion 'performed by a competent, licensed physician, under safe, clinical conditions'; that she was unable to get a 'legal' abortion in Texas because her life did not appear to be threatened by the continuation of her pregnancy; and that she could not afford to travel to another jurisdiction in order to secure a legal abortion under safe conditions. She claimed that the Texas statutes were unconstitutionally vague and that they abridged her right of personal privacy, protected by the First, Fourth, Fifth, Ninth, and Fourteenth Amendments. By an amendment to her complaint Roe purported to sue 'on behalf of herself and all other women' similarly situated.

. . . .

V.

The principal thrust of appellant's attack on the Texas statutes is that they improperly invade a right, said to be possessed by the pregnant woman, to choose to terminate her pregnancy. Appellant would discover this right in the concept of personal 'liberty' embodied in the Fourteenth Amendment's Due Process Clause; or in personal marital, familial, and sexual privacy said to be protected by the Bill of Rights or its penumbras; or among those rights reserved to the people by the Ninth Amendment. Before addressing this claim, we feel it desirable briefly to survey, in several aspects, the history of abortion, for such insight as that history may afford us, and then to examine the state purposes and interests behind the criminal abortion laws.

VI.

It perhaps is not generally appreciated that the restrictive criminal abortion laws in effect in a majority of States today are of relatively recent vintage. Those laws, generally proscribing abortion or its attempt at any time during pregnancy except when necessary to preserve the pregnant woman's life, are not of ancient or even of common-law origin. Instead, they derive from statutory changes effected, for the most part, in the latter half of the 19th century.

1. *Ancient attitudes.* These are not capable of precise determination. We are told that at the time of the Persian Empire abortifacients were known and that criminal abortions were severely punished. We are also told, however, that abortion was practiced in Greek times as well as in the Roman Era, and that 'it was resorted to without scruple.' The Ephesian, Soranos, often described as the greatest of the ancient gynecologists, appears to have been generally opposed to Rome's prevailing free-abortion practices. He found it necessary to think first of the life of the mother, and he resorted to abortion when, upon this standard, he felt the procedure advisable. Greek and Roman law afforded little protection to the unborn. If abortion was prosecuted in some places, it seems to have been based on a concept of a violation of the father's right to his offspring. Ancient religion did not bar abortion.

2. *The Hippocratic Oath.* What then of the famous Oath that has stood so long as the ethical guide of the medical profession and that bears the name of the great Greek (460(?)–377(?) B.C.), who has been described as the Father of Medicine, the 'wisest and the greatest practitioner of his art,' and the 'most important and most complete medical personality of antiquity,' who dominated the medical schools of his time, and who typified the sum of the medical knowledge of the past? The Oath varies somewhat according to the particular translation, but in any translation the content is clear: 'I will give no deadly medicine to anyone if asked, nor suggest any such counsel; and in like manner I will not give to a woman a pessary to produce abortion,' or 'I will neither give a deadly drug to anybody if asked for it, nor will I make a suggestion to this effect. Similarly, I will not give to a woman an abortive remedy.'

Although the Oath is not mentioned in any of the principal briefs in this case or in *Doe v. Bolton*, 410 U.S. 179, 93 S. Ct. 739, 35 L. Ed. 2d 201, it represents the apex of the development of strict ethical concepts in medicine, and its influence endures to this day. Why did not the authority of Hippocrates dissuade abortion practice in his time and that of Rome? The late Dr. Edelstein provides us with a theory: The Oath was not uncontested even in Hippocrates' day; only the Pythagorean school of philosophers frowned upon the related act of suicide. Most Greek thinkers, on the other hand, commended abortion, at least prior to viability. For the Pythagoreans, however, it was a matter of dogma. For them the embryo was animate from the moment of conception, and abortion meant destruction of a living being. The abortion clause of the Oath, therefore, 'echoes Pythagorean doctrines,' and '(i)n no other stratum of Greek opinion were such views held or proposed in the same spirit of uncompromising austerity.'

Dr. Edelstein then concludes that the Oath originated in a group representing only a small segment of Greek opinion and that it certainly was not accepted by all ancient physicians. He points out that medical writings down to Galen (A.D. 130–200) 'give evidence of the violation of almost every one of its injunctions.' But with the end of antiquity a decided change took place. Resistance against suicide and against abortion became common. The Oath came to be popular. The emerging teachings of Christianity were in agreement with the Pythagorean ethic. The Oath 'became the nucleus of all medical ethics' and 'was applauded as the embodiment of truth.' Thus, suggests Dr. Edelstein, it is 'a Pythagorean manifesto and not the expression of an absolute standard of medical conduct.'

This, it seems to us, is a satisfactory and acceptable explanation of the Hippocratic Oath's apparent rigidity. It enables us to understand, in historical context, a long-accepted and revered statement of medical ethics.

3. *The common law.* It is undisputed that at common law, abortion performed before 'quickening' — the first recognizable movement of the fetus in utero, appearing usually from the 16th to the 18th week of pregnancy — was not an indictable offense. The absence of a common-law crime for pre-quickening abortion appears to have developed from a confluence of earlier philosophical, theological, and civil and canon law concepts of when life begins. These disciplines variously approached the question in terms of the point at which the embryo or fetus became 'formed' or recognizably human, or in terms of when a 'person' came into being, that is, infused with a 'soul' or 'animated.' A loose consensus evolved in early English law that these events occurred at some point between conception and live birth. This was 'mediate animation.' Although Christian theology and the canon law came to fix the point of animation at 40 days for a male and 80 days for a female, a view that persisted until the 19th century, there was otherwise little agreement about the precise time of formation or animation. There was agreement, however, that prior to this point the fetus was to be regarded as part of the mother, and its destruction, therefore, was not homicide. Due to continued uncertainty about the precise time when animation occurred, to the lack of any empirical basis for the 40- 80-day view, and perhaps to Aquinas' definition of movement as one of the two first principles of life, Bracton focused upon quickening as the critical point. The significance of quickening was echoed by later common-law scholars and found its way into the received common law in this country.

Whether abortion of a quick fetus was a felony at common law, or even a lesser crime, is still disputed. Bracton, writing early in the 13th century, thought it homicide. But the later and predominant view, following the great common-law scholars, has been that it was, at most, a lesser offense. In a frequently cited passage, Coke took the position that abortion of a woman 'quick with childe' is 'a great misprision, and no murder.' Blackstone followed, saying that while abortion after quickening had once been considered manslaughter (though not murder), 'modern law' took a less severe view. A recent review of the common-law precedents argues, however, that those precedents contradict Coke and that even post-quickening abortion was never established as a common-law crime. This is of some importance because while most American courts ruled, in holding or dictum, that abortion of an unquickened fetus was not criminal under their received common law, others followed Coke in stating that abortion of a quick fetus was a 'misprision,' a term they translated to mean 'misdemeanor.' That their reliance on Coke on this aspect of the law was uncritical and, apparently in all the reported cases, dictum (due probably to the paucity of common-law prosecutions for post-quickening abortion), makes it now appear doubtful that abortion was ever firmly established as a common-law crime even with respect to the destruction of a quick fetus.

4. *The English statutory law.* England's first criminal abortion statute came in 1803. It made abortion of a quick fetus, s 1, a capital crime, but in s 2 it provided lesser penalties for the felony of abortion before quickening, and thus preserved the 'quickening' distinction. This contrast was continued in the general revision of 1828. It disappeared, however, together with the death penalty, in 1837, and did not reappear in the Offenses Against the Person Act of 1861, that formed the core of English anti-abortion law until the liberalizing reforms of 1967. In 1929, the Infant Life (Preservation) Act came into being. Its emphasis was upon the destruction of 'the life of a child capable of being born alive.' It made a willful act performed with the

necessary intent a felony. It contained a proviso that one was not to be found guilty of the offense 'unless it is proved that the act which caused the death of the child was not done in good faith for the purpose only of preserving the life of the mother.'

. . . .

5. *The American law.* In this country, the law in effect in all but a few States until mid-19th century was the pre-existing English common law. Connecticut, the first State to enact abortion legislation, adopted in 1821 that part of Lord Ellenborough's Act that related to a woman 'quick with child.' The death penalty was not imposed. Abortion before quickening was made a crime in that State only in 1860. In 1828, New York enacted legislation that, in two respects, was to serve as a model for early anti-abortion statutes. First, while barring destruction of an unquickened fetus as well as a quick fetus, it made the former only a misdemeanor, but the latter second-degree manslaughter. Second, it incorporated a concept of therapeutic abortion by providing that an abortion was excused if it 'shall have been necessary to preserve the life of such mother, or shall have been advised by two physicians to be necessary for such purpose.' By 1840, when Texas had received the common law, only eight American States had statutes dealing with abortion. It was not until after the War Between the States that legislation began generally to replace the common law. Most of these initial statutes dealt severely with abortion after quickening but were lenient with it before quickening. Most punished attempts equally with completed abortions. While many statutes included the exception for an abortion thought by one or more physicians to be necessary to save the mother's life, that provision soon disappeared and the typical law required that the procedure actually be necessary for that purpose.

Gradually, in the middle and late 19th century the quickening distinction disappeared from the statutory law of most States and the degree of the offense and the penalties were increased. By the end of the 1950's a large majority of the jurisdictions banned abortion, however and whenever performed, unless done to save or preserve the life of the mother. The exceptions, Alabama and the District of Columbia, permitted abortion to preserve the mother's health. Three States permitted abortions that were not 'unlawfully' performed or that were not 'without lawful justification,' leaving interpretation of those standards to the courts. In the past several years, however, a trend toward liberalization of abortion statutes has resulted in adoption, by about one-third of the States, of less stringent laws, most of them patterned after the ALI Model Penal Code, s 230.3.

It is thus apparent that at common law, at the time of the adoption of our Constitution, and throughout the major portion of the 19th century, abortion was viewed with less disfavor than under most American statutes currently in effect. Phrasing it another way, a woman enjoyed a substantially broader right to terminate a pregnancy than she does in most States today. At least with respect to the early stage of pregnancy, and very possibly without such a limitation, the opportunity to make this choice was present in this country well into the 19th century. Even later, the law continued for some time to treat less punitively an abortion procured in early pregnancy.

6. *The position of the American Medical Association.* The anti-abortion mood prevalent in this country in the late 19th century was shared by the medical profession. Indeed, the attitude of the profession may have played a significant role in the enactment of stringent criminal abortion legislation during that period.

An AMA Committee on Criminal Abortion was appointed in May 1857. It presented its report to the Twelfth Annual Meeting. That report observed that the Committee had been appointed to investigate criminal abortion 'with a view to its general suppression.' It deplored abortion and its frequency and it listed three causes of 'this general demoralization':

> 'The first of these causes is a wide-spread popular ignorance of the true character of the crime-a belief, even among mothers themselves, that the foetus is not alive till after the period of quickening.

> 'The second of the agents alluded to is the fact that the profession themselves are frequently supposed careless of foetal life. . . .

> 'The third reason of the frightful extent of this crime is found in the grave defects of our laws, both common and statute, as regards the independent and actual existence of the child before birth, as a living being. These errors, which are sufficient in most instances to prevent conviction, are based, and only based, upon mistaken and exploded medical dogmas. With strange inconsistency, the law fully acknowledges the foetus in utero and its inherent rights, for civil purposes; while personally and as criminally affected, it fails to recognize it, and to its life as yet denies all protection.'

The Committee then offered, and the Association adopted, resolutions protesting 'against such unwarrantable destruction of human life,' calling upon state legislatures to revise their abortion laws, and requesting the cooperation of state medical societies 'in pressing the subject.'

In 1871 a long and vivid report was submitted by the Committee on Criminal Abortion. It ended with the observation, 'We had to deal with human life. In a matter of less importance we could entertain no compromise. An honest judge on the bench would call things by their proper names. We could do no less.' It proffered resolutions, adopted by the Association, recommending, among other things, that it 'be unlawful and unprofessional for any physician to induce abortion or premature labor, without the concurrent opinion of at least one respectable consulting physician, and then always with a view to the safety of the child-if that be possible,' and calling 'the attention of the clergy of all denominations to the perverted views of morality entertained by a large class of females-aye, and men also, on this important question.'

Except for periodic condemnation of the criminal abortionist, no further formal AMA action took place until 1967. In that year, the Committee on Human Reproduction urged the adoption of a stated policy of opposition to induced abortion, except when there is 'documented medical evidence' of a threat to the health or life of the mother, or that the child 'may be born with incapacitating physical deformity or mental deficiency,' or that a pregnancy 'resulting from legally established statutory or forcible rape or incest may constitute a threat to the mental or physical health of the patient,' two other physicians 'chosen because of their recognized professional competency have examined the patient and have concurred in writing,' and the procedure 'is performed in a hospital accredited by the Joint Commission on Accreditation of Hospitals.' The providing of medical information by physicians to state legislatures in their consideration of legislation regarding therapeutic abortion was 'to be considered consistent with the principles of ethics of the American Medical Association.' This recommendation was adopted by the House of Delegates. Proceedings of the AMA House of Delegates 40–51 (June 1967).

In 1970, after the introduction of a variety of proposed resolutions, and of a report from its Board of Trustees, a reference committee noted 'polarization of the medical profession on this controversial issue'; division among those who had testified; a difference of opinion among AMA councils and committees; 'the remarkable shift in testimony' in six months, felt to be influenced 'by the rapid changes in state laws and by the judicial decisions which tend to make abortion more freely available'; and a feeling 'that this trend will continue.' On June 25, 1970, the House of Delegates adopted preambles and most of the resolutions proposed by the reference committee. The preambles emphasized 'the best interests of the patient,' 'sound clinical judgment,' and 'informed patient consent,' in contrast to 'mere acquiescence to the patient's demand.' The resolutions asserted that abortion is a medical procedure that should be performed by a licensed physician in an accredited hospital only after consultation with two other physicians and in conformity with state law, and that no party to the procedure should be required to violate personally held moral principles. The AMA Judicial Council rendered a complementary opinion.

7. The position of the American Public Health Association. In October 1970, the Executive Board of the APHA adopted Standards for Abortion Services. These were five in number:

> 'a. Rapid and simple abortion referral must be readily available through state and local public health departments, medical societies, or other non-profit organizations.

> 'b. An important function of counseling should be to simplify and expedite the provision of abortion services; if should not delay the obtaining of these services.

> 'c. Psychiatric consultation should not be mandatory. As in the case of other specialized medical services, psychiatric consultation should be sought for definite indications and not on a routine basis.

> 'd. A wide range of individuals from appropriately trained, sympathetic volunteers to highly skilled physicians may qualify as abortion counselors.

> 'e. Contraception and/ or sterilization should be discussed with each abortion patient.' Recommended Standards for Abortion Services, 61 Am. J. Pub. Health 396 (1971).

. . . .

It was said that 'a well-equipped hospital' offers more protection 'to cope with unforeseen difficulties than an office or clinic without such resources. . . . The factor of gestational age is of overriding importance.' Thus, it was recommended that abortions in the second trimester and early abortions in the presence of existing medical complications be performed in hospitals as inpatient procedures. For pregnancies in the first trimester, abortion in the hospital with or without overnight stay 'is probably the safest practice.' An abortion in an extramural facility, however, is an acceptable alternative 'provided arrangements exist in advance to admit patients promptly if unforeseen complications develop.' Standards for an abortion facility were listed. It was said that at present abortions should be performed by physicians or osteopaths who are licensed to practice and who have 'adequate training.'

8. *The position of the American Bar Association.* At its meeting in February 1972 the ABA House of Delegates approved, with 17 opposing votes, the Uniform Abortion Act that had been drafted and approved the preceding August by the Conference of Commissioners on Uniform State Laws. 58 A.B.A. J. 380 (1972). We set forth the Act in full in the margin. The Conference has appended an enlightening Prefatory Note.

VII.

Three reasons have been advanced to explain historically the enactment of criminal abortion laws in the 19th century and to justify their continued existence.

It has been argued occasionally that these laws were the product of a Victorian social concern to discourage illicit sexual conduct. Texas, however, does not advance this justification in the present case, and it appears that no court or commentator has taken the argument seriously. The appellants and amici contend, moreover, that this is not a proper state purpose at all and suggest that, if it were, the Texas statutes are overbroad in protecting it since the law fails to distinguish between married and unwed mothers.

A second reason is concerned with abortion as a medical procedure. When most criminal abortion laws were first enacted, the procedure was a hazardous one for the woman. This was particularly true prior to the development of antisepsis. Antiseptic techniques, of course, were based on discoveries by Lister, Pasteur, and others first announced in 1867, but were not generally accepted and employed until about the turn of the century. Abortion mortality was high. Even after 1900, and perhaps until as late as the development of antibiotics in the 1940's, standard modern techniques such as dilation and curettage were not nearly so safe as they are today. Thus, it has been argued that a State's real concern in enacting a criminal abortion law was to protect the pregnant woman, that is, to restrain her from submitting to a procedure that placed her life in serious jeopardy.

Modern medical techniques have altered this situation. Appellants and various amici refer to medical data indicating that abortion in early pregnancy, that is, prior to the end of the first trimester, although not without its risk, is now relatively safe. Mortality rates for women undergoing early abortions, where the procedure is legal, appear to be as low as or lower than the rates for normal childbirth.

Consequently, any interest of the State in protecting the woman from an inherently hazardous procedure, except when it would be equally dangerous for her to forgo it, has largely disappeared. Of course, important state interests in the areas of health and medical standards do remain. The State has a legitimate interest in seeing to it that abortion, like any other medical procedure, is performed under circumstances that insure maximum safety for the patient. This interest obviously extends at least to the performing physician and his staff, to the facilities involved, to the availability of after-care, and to adequate provision for any complication or emergency that might arise. The prevalence of high mortality rates at illegal 'abortion mills' strengthens, rather than weakens, the State's interest in regulating the conditions under which abortions are performed. Moreover, the risk to the woman increases as her pregnancy continues. Thus, the State retains a definite interest in protecting the woman's own health and safety when an abortion is proposed at a late stage of pregnancy.

The third reason is the State's interest — some phrase it in terms of duty — in protecting prenatal life. Some of the argument for this justification rests on the theory that a new human life is present from the moment of conception. The State's interest and general obligation to protect life then extends, it is argued, to prenatal life. Only when the life of the pregnant mother herself is at stake, balanced against the life she carries within her, should the interest of the embryo or fetus not prevail. Logically, of course, a legitimate state interest in this area need not stand or fall on acceptance of the belief that life begins at conception or at some other point prior to life birth. In assessing the State's interest, recognition may be given to the less rigid claim that as long as at least potential life is involved, the State may assert interests beyond the protection of the pregnant woman alone.

. . . .

VIII.

The Constitution does not explicitly mention any right of privacy. In a line of decisions, however, going back perhaps as far as [1891], the Court has recognized that a right of personal privacy, or a guarantee of certain areas or zones of privacy, does exist under the Constitution. In varying contexts, the Court or individual Justices have, indeed, found at least the roots of that right in the First Amendment; in the Fourth and Fifth Amendments; in the penumbras of the Bill of Rights; or in the concept of liberty guaranteed by the first section of the Fourteenth Amendment. These decisions make it clear that only personal rights that can be deemed 'fundamental' or 'implicit in the concept of ordered liberty,' are included in this guarantee of personal privacy. They also make it clear that the right has some extension to activities relating to marriage, procreation, contraception, family relationships and child rearing, and education.

This right of privacy, whether it be founded in the Fourteenth Amendment's concept of personal liberty and restrictions upon state action, as we feel it is, or, as the District Court determined, in the Ninth Amendment's reservation of rights to the people, is broad enough to encompass a woman's decision whether or not to terminate her pregnancy. The detriment that the State would impose upon the pregnant woman by denying this choice altogether is apparent. Specific and direct harm medically diagnosable even in early pregnancy may be involved. Maternity, or additional offspring, may force upon the woman a distressful life and future. Psychological harm may be imminent. Mental and physical health may be taxed by child care. There is also the distress, for all concerned, associated with the unwanted child, and there is the problem of bringing a child into a family already unable, psychologically and otherwise, to care for it. In other cases, as in this one, the additional difficulties and continuing stigma of unwed motherhood may be involved. All these are factors the woman and her responsible physician necessarily will consider in consultation.

On the basis of elements such as these, appellant and some amici argue that the woman's right is absolute and that she is entitled to terminate her pregnancy at whatever time, in whatever way, and for whatever reason she alone chooses. With this we do not agree. Appellant's arguments that Texas either has no valid interest at all in regulating the abortion decision, or no interest strong enough to support any limitation upon the woman's sole determination, are unpersuasive. The Court's decisions recognizing a right of privacy also acknowledge that some state regulation in areas protected by that right is appropriate. As noted above, a State may properly assert important interests in safeguarding health, in maintaining medical standards, and in protecting potential life. At some point in pregnancy, these respective interests become sufficiently compelling to sustain regulation of the factors that govern the abortion decision. The privacy right involved, therefore, cannot be said to be absolute. In fact, it is not clear to us that the claim asserted by some amici that one has an unlimited right to do with one's body as one pleases bears a close relationship to the right of privacy previously articulated in the Court's decisions. The Court has refused to recognize an unlimited right of this kind in the past.

We, therefore, conclude that the right of personal privacy includes the abortion decision, but that this right is not unqualified and must be considered against important state interests in regulation.

. . . .

IX.

. . . Appellee argues that the State's determination to recognize and protect prenatal life from and after conception constitutes a compelling state interest. As noted above, we do not agree fully with either formulation.

A.

The appellee and certain amici argue that the fetus is a 'person' within the language and meaning of the Fourteenth Amendment. In support of this, they outline at length and in detail the well-known facts of fetal development. If this suggestion of personhood is established, the appellant's case, of course, collapses, for the fetus' right to life would then be guaranteed specifically by the Amendment. The appellant conceded as much on reargument. On the other hand, the appellee conceded on reargument that no case could be cited that holds that a fetus is a person within the meaning of the Fourteenth Amendment.

The Constitution does not define 'person' in so many words. Section 1 of the Fourteenth Amendment contains three references to 'person.' The first, in defining 'citizens,' speaks of 'persons born or naturalized in the United States.' The word also appears both in the Due Process Clause and in the Equal Protection Clause. 'Person' is used in other places in the Constitution: in the listing of qualifications for Representatives and Senators; in the Apportionment Clause; in the Migration and Importation provision; in the Emolument Clause; in the Electros provisions; in the provision outlining qualifications for the office of President; in the Extradition provisions; and in the Fifth, Twelfth, and Twenty-second Amendments, as well as the Fourteenth Amendment. But in nearly all these instances, the use of the word is such that it has application only postnatally. None indicates, with any assurance, that it has any possible prenatal application.

All this, together with our observation, supra, that throughout the major portion of the 19th century prevailing legal abortion practices were far freer than they are today, persuades us that the word 'person,' as used in the Fourteenth Amendment, does not include the unborn. . . .

This conclusion, however, does not of itself fully answer the contentions raised by Texas, and we pass on to other considerations.

B.

The pregnant woman cannot be isolated in her privacy. She carries an embryo and, later, a fetus, if one accepts the medical definitions of the developing young in the human uterus. The situation therefore is inherently different from marital intimacy, or bedroom possession of obscene material, or marriage, or procreation, or education, with which *Eisenstadt* [*v. Baird*, 405 U.S. 438 (1972)] and *Griswold* [*v. Connecticut*, 381 U.S. 479 (1965)], *Stanley* [*v. Georgia*, 394 U.S. 557 (1969)], *Loving* [*v. Virginia*, 388 U.S. 1 (1967)], *Skinner* [*v. Oklahoma ex rel. Williamson*, 316 U.S. 535 (1942)], *Pierce* [*v. Soc'y of the Sisters of the Holy Names of Jesus & Mary*, 268 U.S. 510 (1925)], and *Meyer* [*v. Nebraska*, 262 U.S. 390 (1923)] were respectively concerned. As we have intimated above, it is reasonable and appropriate for a State to decide that at some point in time another interest, that of health of the mother or that of potential human life, becomes significantly involved. The woman's privacy is no longer sole and any right of privacy she possesses must be measured accordingly.

Texas urges that, apart from the Fourteenth Amendment, life begins at conception and is present throughout pregnancy, and that, therefore, the State has a compelling interest in protecting that life from and after conception. We need not resolve the difficult question of when life begins. When those trained in the respective disciplines of medicine, philosophy, and theology are unable to arrive at any consensus, the judiciary, at this point in the development of man's knowledge, is not in a position to speculate as to the answer.

It should be sufficient to note briefly the wide divergence of thinking on this most sensitive and difficult question. There has always been strong support for the view that life does not begin until live birth. This was the belief of the Stoics. It appears to be the predominant, though not the unanimous, attitude of the Jewish faith. It may be taken to represent also the position of a large segment of the Protestant community, insofar as that can be ascertained; organized groups that have taken a formal position on the abortion issue have generally regarded abortion as a matter for the conscience of the individual and her family. As we have noted, the common law found greater significance in quickening. Physicians and their scientific colleagues have regarded that event with less interest and have tended to focus either upon conception, upon live birth, or upon the interim point at which the fetus becomes 'viable,' that is, potentially able to live outside the mother's womb, albeit with artificial aid. Viability is usually placed at about seven months (28 weeks) but may occur earlier, even at 24 weeks. The Aristotelian theory of 'mediate animation,' that held sway throughout the Middle Ages and the Renaissance in Europe, continued to be official Roman Catholic dogma until the 19th century, despite opposition to this 'ensoulment' theory from those in the Church who would recognize the existence of life from the moment of conception.[41] The latter is now, of course, the official belief of the Catholic Church. As one brief amicus discloses, this is a view strongly held by many non-Catholics as well, and by many physicians. Substantial problems for precise definition of this view are posed, however, by new embryological data that purport to indicate that conception is a 'process' over time, rather than an event, and by new medical techniques such as menstrual extraction, the 'morning-after' pill, implantation of embryos, artificial insemination, and even artificial wombs.

In areas other than criminal abortion, the law has been reluctant to endorse any theory that life, as we recognize it, begins before life birth or to accord legal rights to the unborn except in narrowly defined situations and except when the rights are contingent upon life birth. For example, the traditional rule of tort law denied recovery for prenatal injuries even though the child was born alive. That rule has been changed in almost every jurisdiction. In most States, recovery is said to be permitted only if the fetus was viable, or at least quick, when the injuries were sustained, though few courts have squarely so held. In a recent development, generally opposed by the commentators, some States permit the parents of a stillborn child to maintain an action for wrongful death because of prenatal injuries. Such an action, however, would appear to be one to vindicate the parents' interest and is thus consistent with the view that the fetus, at most, represents only the potentiality of life. Similarly, unborn children have been recognized as acquiring rights or interests by way of inheritance or other devolution of property, and have been represented by guardians *ad litem*. Perfection of the interests involved, again, has generally been contingent upon live birth. In short, the unborn have never been recognized in the law as persons in the whole sense.

---

41. The Catholic Church's position, as reflected in the Catechism and other documents, is that it has held abortion to be wrong since the first century. — Ed.

X.

In view of all this, we do not agree that, by adopting one theory of life, Texas may override the rights of the pregnant woman that are at stake. We repeat, however, that the State does have an important and legitimate interest in preserving and protecting the health of the pregnant woman, whether she be a resident of the State or a non-resident who seeks medical consultation and treatment there, and that it has still another important and legitimate interest in protecting the potentiality of human life. These interests are separate and distinct. Each grows in substantiality as the woman approaches term and, at a point during pregnancy, each becomes 'compelling.'

With respect to the State's important and legitimate interest in the health of the mother, the 'compelling' point, in the light of present medical knowledge, is at approximately the end of the first trimester. This is so because of the now-established medical fact that until the end of the first trimester mortality in abortion may be less than mortality in normal childbirth. It follows that, from and after this point, a State may regulate the abortion procedure to the extent that the regulation reasonably relates to the preservation and protection of maternal health. Examples of permissible state regulation in this area are requirements as to the qualifications of the person who is to perform the abortion; as to the licensure of that person; as to the facility in which the procedure is to be performed, that is, whether it must be a hospital or may be a clinic or some other place of less-than-hospital status; as to the licensing of the facility; and the like.

This means, on the other hand, that, for the period of pregnancy prior to this 'compelling' point, the attending physician, in consultation with his patient, is free to determine, without regulation by the State, that in his medical judgment, the patient's pregnancy should be terminated. If that decision is reached, the judgment may be effectuated by an abortion free of interference by the State.

With respect to the State's important and legitimate interest in potential life, the 'compelling' point is at viability. This is so because the fetus then presumably has the capability of meaningful life outside the mother's womb. State regulation protective of fetal life after viability thus has both logical and biological justifications. If the State is interested in protecting fetal life after viability, it may go so far as to proscribe abortion during that period, except when it is necessary to preserve the life or health of the mother.

. . . .

XI.

To summarize and to repeat:

1. A state criminal abortion statute of the current Texas type, that excepts from criminality only a life-saving procedure on behalf of the mother, without regard to pregnancy stage and without recognition of the other interests involved, is violative of the Due Process Clause of the Fourteenth Amendment.

(a) For the stage prior to approximately the end of the first trimester, the abortion decision and its effectuation must be left to the medical judgment of the pregnant woman's attending physician.

(b) For the stage subsequent to approximately the end of the first trimester, the State, in promoting its interest in the health of the mother, may, if it chooses, regulate the abortion procedure in ways that are reasonably related to maternal health.

(c) For the stage subsequent to viability, the State in promoting its interest in the potentiality of human life may, if it chooses, regulate, and even proscribe, abortion except where it is necessary, in appropriate medical judgment, for the preservation of the life or health of the mother.

2. The State may define the term 'physician,' as it has been employed in the preceding paragraphs of this Part XI of this opinion, to mean only a physician currently licensed by the State, and may proscribe any abortion by a person who is not a physician as so defined.

. . . .

Mr. Justice REHNQUIST, dissenting.

The Court's opinion brings to the decision of this troubling question both extensive historical fact and a wealth of legal scholarship. While the opinion thus commands my respect, I find myself nonetheless in fundamental disagreement with those parts of it that invalidate the Texas statute in question, and therefore dissent.

. . . .

II.

Even if there were a plaintiff in this case capable of litigating the issue which the Court decides, I would reach a conclusion opposite to that reached by the Court. I have difficulty in concluding, as the Court does, that the right of 'privacy' is involved in this case. Texas, by the statute here challenged, bars the performance of a medical abortion by a licensed physician on a plaintiff such as Roe. A transaction resulting in an operation such as this is not 'private' in the ordinary usage of that word. Nor is the 'privacy' that the Court finds here even a distant relative of the freedom from searches and seizures protected by the Fourth Amendment to the Constitution, which the Court has referred to as embodying a right to privacy.

If the Court means by the term 'privacy' no more than that the claim of a person to be free from unwanted state regulation of consensual transactions may be a form of 'liberty' protected by the Fourteenth Amendment, there is no doubt that similar claims have been upheld in our earlier decisions on the basis of that liberty. I agree with the statement of Mr. Justice STEWART in his concurring opinion that the 'liberty,' against deprivation of which without due process the Fourteenth Amendment protects, embraces more than the rights found in the Bill of Rights. But that liberty is not guaranteed absolutely against deprivation, only against deprivation without due process of law. The test traditionally applied in the area of social and economic legislation is whether or not a law such as that challenged has a rational relation to a valid state objective. The Due Process Clause of the Fourteenth Amendment undoubt-edly does place a limit, albeit a broad one, on legislative power to enact laws such as this. If the Texas statute were to prohibit an abortion even where the mother's life is in jeopardy, I have little doubt that such a statute would lack a rational relation to a valid state objective under the test stated in *Williamson, supra*. But the Court's sweep-ing invalidation of any restrictions on abortion during the first trimester is impos-sible to justify under that standard, and the conscious weighing of competing factors that the Court's opinion apparently substitutes for the established test is far more appropriate to a legislative judgment than to a judicial one.

. . . .

The fact that a majority of the States reflecting, after all the majority sentiment in those States, have had restrictions on abortions for at least a century is a strong indi-cation, it seems to me, that the asserted right to an abortion is not 'so rooted in the traditions and conscience of our people as to be ranked as fundamental.' Even today, when society's views on abortion are changing, the very existence of the debate is evidence that the 'right' to an abortion is not so universally accepted as the appel-lant would have us believe.

. . . .

There apparently was no question concerning the validity of this provision or of any of the other state statutes when the Fourteenth Amendment was adopted. The only conclusion possible from this history is that the drafters did not intend to have the Fourteenth Amendment withdraw from the States the power to legislate with respect to this matter.

. . . .

4. Upholding Some Abortion Restrictions

This Federal recognition of a privacy right to an abortion, located in the penum-bras of the rights guarantee by the Bill of Rights, was a dramatic departure from exist-ing law at the time of the decision in *Roe v. Wade*. However, in *Casey*, below, the Supreme Court rejected the trimester scheme announced in *Roe*. In writing for a 5–4 majority, Justice Kennedy upheld Pennsylvania's restrictions on abortion which included the provision of specific information by a doctor coupled with a manda-tory 24-hour waiting period. It also upheld a restriction that allowed the state to require that a minor seeking an abortion obtain parental consent or obtain a judi-cial bypass of that consent. The majority concluded that the spousal notification provision, requiring a pregnant woman to inform her husband of her intent to abort, was an unlawful restriction on the woman's right to choose abortion. While upholding the "essential holding" of *Roe*, including the recognition of the "right of woman to choose to have an abortion before viability and obtain it without undue interference from the state," the majority opinion discarded *Roe*'s trimester approach. In so doing, it refocused on the issue of "viability."

505 U.S. 833 / 112 S. Ct. 2791
Supreme Court of the United States

PLANNED PARENTHOOD OF SOUTHEASTERN PENNSYLVANIA, et al., Petitioners,

v.

Robert P. CASEY, et al., etc. Robert P. CASEY, et al., etc., Petitioners,

v.

PLANNED PARENTHOOD OF SOUTHEASTERN PENNSYLVANIA et al.

Decided June 29, 1992.

Opinion

Justice O'CONNOR, Justice KENNEDY, and Justice SOUTER delivered the opinion of the Court with respect to Parts I, II, and III,

. . . .

After considering the fundamental constitutional questions resolved by *Roe* [*v. Wade*, 410 U.S. 113 (1973)] principles of institutional integrity, and the rule of stare decisis, we are led to conclude this: the essential holding of *Roe v. Wade* should be retained and once again reaffirmed.

It must be stated at the outset and with clarity that *Roe*'s essential holding, the holding we reaffirm, has three parts. First is a recognition of the right of the woman to choose to have an abortion before viability and to obtain it without undue interference from the State. Before viability, the State's interests are not strong enough to support a prohibition of abortion or the imposition of a substantial obstacle to the woman's effective right to elect the procedure. Second is a confirmation of the State's power to restrict abortions after fetal viability, if the law contains exceptions for pregnancies which endanger the woman's life or health. And third is the principle that the State has legitimate interests from the outset of the pregnancy in protecting the health of the woman and the life of the fetus that may become a child. These principles do not contradict one another; and we adhere to each.

. . . .

IV.

From what we have said so far it follows that it is a constitutional liberty of the woman to have some freedom to terminate her pregnancy. We conclude that the basic decision in *Roe* was based on a constitutional analysis which we cannot now repudiate. The woman's liberty is not so unlimited, however, that from the outset the State cannot show its concern for the life of the unborn, and at a later point in fetal development the State's interest in life has sufficient force so that the right of the woman to terminate the pregnancy can be restricted.

That brings us, of course, to the point where much criticism has been directed at *Roe*, a criticism that always inheres when the Court draws a specific rule from what in the Constitution is but a general standard. We conclude, however, that the urgent claims of the woman to retain the ultimate control over her destiny and her body, claims implicit in the meaning of liberty, require us to perform that function. Liberty must not be extinguished for want of a line that is clear. And it falls to us to give some real substance to the woman's liberty to determine whether to carry her pregnancy to full term.

We conclude the line should be drawn at viability, so that before that time the woman has a right to choose to terminate her pregnancy. We adhere to this principle for two reasons. First, as we have said, is the doctrine of stare decisis. Any judicial act of line-drawing may seem somewhat arbitrary, but *Roe* was a reasoned statement, elaborated with great care. We have twice reaffirmed it in the face of great opposition. Although we must overrule those parts of *Thornburgh* and *Akron I* which, in our view, are inconsistent with *Roe* statement that the State has a legitimate interest in promoting the life or potential life of the unborn, the central premise of those cases represents an unbroken commitment by this Court to the essential holding of *Roe* It is that premise which we reaffirm today.

The second reason is that the concept of viability, as we noted in *Roe* is the time at which there is a realistic possibility of maintaining and nourishing a life outside the womb, so that the independent existence of the second life can in reason and all fairness be the object of state protection that now overrides the rights of the woman. Consistent with other constitutional norms, legislatures may draw lines which appear arbitrary without the necessity of offering a justification. But courts may not. We must justify the lines we draw. And there is no line other than viability which is more workable. To be sure, as we have said, there may be some medical developments that affect the precise point of viability, but this is an imprecision within tolerable limits given that the medical community and all those who must apply its discoveries will continue to explore the matter. The viability line also has, as a practical matter, an element of fairness. In some broad sense it might be said that a woman who fails to act before viability has consented to the State's intervention on behalf of the developing child.

The woman's right to terminate her pregnancy before viability is the most central principle of *Roe* It is a rule of law and a component of liberty we cannot renounce.

On the other side of the equation is the interest of the State in the protection of potential life. The *Roe* Court recognized the State's "important and legitimate interest in protecting the potentiality of human life." The weight to be given this state interest, not the strength of the woman's interest, was the difficult question faced in *Roe*. We do not need to say whether each of us, had we been Members of the Court when the valuation of the state interest came before it as an original matter, would have concluded, as the *Roe* Court did, that its weight is insufficient to justify a ban on abortions prior to viability even when it is subject to certain exceptions. The matter is not before us in the first instance, and coming as it does after nearly 20 years of litigation in *Roe*'s wake we are satisfied that the immediate question is not the soundness of *Roe*'s resolution of the issue, but the precedential force that must be accorded to its holding. And we have concluded that the essential holding of *Roe* should be reaffirmed.

Yet it must be remembered that *Roe* speaks with clarity in establishing not only the woman's liberty but also the State's "important and legitimate interest in potential life." That portion of the decision in *Roe* has been given too little acknowledgment and implementation by the Court in its subsequent cases. Those cases decided that any regulation touching upon the abortion decision must survive strict scrutiny to be sustained only if drawn in narrow terms to further a compelling state interest. Not all of the cases decided under that formulation can be reconciled with the holding in *Roe* itself that the State has legitimate interests in the health of the woman and in protecting the potential life within her. In resolving this tension, we choose to rely upon *Roe* as against the later cases.

Roe established a trimester framework to govern abortion regulations. Under this elaborate but rigid construct, almost no regulation at all is permitted during the first trimester of pregnancy; regulations designed to protect the woman's health, but not to further the State's interest in potential life, are permitted during the second trimester; and during the third trimester, when the fetus is viable, prohibitions are permitted provided the life or health of the mother is not at stake. Most of our cases since *Roe* have involved the application of rules derived from the trimester framework.

The trimester framework no doubt was erected to ensure that the woman's right to choose not become so subordinate to the State's interest in promoting fetal life that her choice exists in theory but not in fact. We do not agree, however, that the trimester approach is necessary to accomplish this objective. A framework of this rigidity was unnecessary and in its later interpretation sometimes contradicted the State's permissible exercise of its powers.

Though the woman has a right to choose to terminate or continue her pregnancy before viability, it does not at all follow that the State is prohibited from taking steps to ensure that this choice is thoughtful and informed. Even in the earliest stages of pregnancy, the State may enact rules and regulations designed to encourage her to know that there are philosophic and social arguments of great weight that can be brought to bear in favor of continuing the pregnancy to full term and that there are procedures and institutions to allow adoption of unwanted children as well as a certain degree of state assistance if the mother chooses to raise the child herself. "'[T]he Constitution does not forbid a State or city, pursuant to democratic processes, from expressing a preference for normal childbirth.'" It follows that States are free to enact laws to provide a reasonable framework for a woman to make a decision that has such profound and lasting meaning. This, too, we find consistent with *Roe*'s central premises, and indeed the inevitable consequence of our holding that the State has an interest in protecting the life of the unborn.

We reject the trimester framework, which we do not consider to be part of the essential holding of *Roe*. Measures aimed at ensuring that a woman's choice contemplates the consequences for the fetus do not necessarily interfere with the right recognized in *Roe* although those measures have been found to be inconsistent with the rigid trimester framework announced in that case. A logical reading of the central holding in *Roe* itself, and a necessary reconciliation of the liberty of the woman and the interest of the State in promoting prenatal life, require, in our view, that we abandon the trimester framework as a rigid prohibition on all previability regulation aimed at the protection of fetal life. The trimester framework suffers from these basic flaws: in its formulation it misconceives the nature of the pregnant woman's interest; and in practice it undervalues the State's interest in potential life, as recognized in *Roe*.

. . . .

——— ———

Chief Justice REHNQUIST, with whom Justice WHITE, Justice SCALIA, and Justice THOMAS join, concurring in the judgment in part and dissenting in part.

. . . .

We agree with the Court of Appeals that our decision in *Roe* is not directly implicated by the Pennsylvania statute, which does not prohibit, but simply regulates, abortion. But, as the Court of Appeals found, the state of our post-*Roe* decisional law dealing with the regulation of abortion is confusing and uncertain, indicating that a reexamination of that line of cases is in order. Unfortunately for those who must apply this Court's decisions, the reexamination undertaken today leaves the Court no less divided than beforehand. Although they reject the trimester framework that formed the underpinning of *Roe*. Justices O'CONNOR, KENNEDY, and SOUTER adopt a revised undue burden standard to analyze the challenged regulations. We conclude, however, that such an outcome is an unjustified constitutional compromise, one which leaves the Court in a position to closely scrutinize all types of abortion regulations despite the fact that it lacks the power to do so under the Constitution.

. . . .

We have held that a liberty interest protected under the Due Process Clause of the Fourteenth Amendment will be deemed fundamental if it is "implicit in the concept of ordered liberty." Three years earlier, we referred to a "principle of justice so rooted in the traditions and conscience of our people as to be ranked as fundamental." These expressions are admittedly not precise, but our decisions implementing this notion of "fundamental" rights do not afford any more elaborate basis on which to base such a classification.

In construing the phrase "liberty" incorporated in the Due Process Clause of the Fourteenth Amendment, we have recognized that its meaning extends beyond freedom from physical restraint. In *Pierce v. Society of Sisters*, [268 U.S. 510 (1925)], we held that it included a parent's right to send a child to private school; in *Meyer v. Nebraska*, [262 U.S. 390 (1923)], we held that it included a right to teach a foreign language in a parochial school. Building on these cases, we have held that the term "liberty" includes a right to marry, *Loving v. Virginia*, [388 U.S. 1 (1967)]; a right to procreate, *Skinner v. Oklahoma ex rel. Williamson*, [316 U.S. 535 (1942)]; and a right to use contraceptives, *Griswold* [*v. Connecticut*, 381 U.S. 479 (1965)]. But a reading of these opinions makes clear that they do not endorse any all-encompassing "right of privacy."

In *Roe* the Court recognized a "guarantee of personal privacy" which "is broad enough to encompass a woman's decision whether or not to terminate her pregnancy." We are now of the view that, in terming this right fundamental, the Court in *Roe* read the earlier opinions upon which it based its decision much too broadly. Unlike marriage, procreation, and contraception, abortion "involves the purposeful termination of a potential life." The abortion decision must therefore "be recognized as sui generis, different in kind from the others that the Court has protected under the rubric of personal or family privacy and autonomy." One cannot ignore the fact that a woman is not isolated in her pregnancy, and that the decision to abort necessarily involves the destruction of a fetus.

Nor do the historical traditions of the American people support the view that the right to terminate one's pregnancy is "fundamental." The common law which we inherited from England made abortion after "quickening" an offense. At the time of the adoption of the Fourteenth Amendment, statutory prohibitions or restrictions on abortion were commonplace; in 1868, at least 28 of the then-37 States and 8 Territories had statutes banning or limiting abortion. By the turn of the century virtually every State had a law prohibiting or restricting abortion on its books. By the middle of the present century, a liberalization trend had set in. But 21 of the restrictive abortion laws in effect in 1868 were still in effect in 1973 when *Roe* was decided, and an overwhelming majority of the States prohibited abortion unless necessary to preserve the life or health of the mother. On this record, it can scarcely be said that any deeply rooted tradition of relatively unrestricted abortion in our history supported the classification of the right to abortion as "fundamental" under the Due Process Clause of the Fourteenth Amendment.

. . . .

———————

Justice SCALIA, with whom THE CHIEF JUSTICE, Justice WHITE, and Justice THOMAS join, concurring in the judgment in part and dissenting in part.

[Q]uite simply, the issue in these cases: not whether the power of a woman to abort her unborn child is a "liberty" in the absolute sense; or even whether it is a liberty of great importance to many women. Of course it is both. The issue is whether it is a liberty protected by the Constitution of the United States. I am sure it is not. I reach that conclusion not because of anything so exalted as my views concerning the "concept of existence, of meaning, of the universe, and of the mystery of human life." Rather, I reach it for the same reason I reach the conclusion that bigamy is not constitutionally protected—because of two simple facts: (1) the Constitution says absolutely nothing about it, and (2) the longstanding traditions of American society have permitted it to be legally proscribed.

. . . .

The shortcomings of *Roe* did not include lack of clarity: Virtually all regulation of abortion before the third trimester was invalid. But to come across this phrase in the joint opinion—which calls upon federal district judges to apply an "undue burden" standard as doubtful in application as it is unprincipled in origin—is really more than one should have to bear.

. . . .

The rootless nature of the "undue burden" standard, a phrase plucked out of context from our earlier abortion decisions is further reflected in the fact that the joint opinion finds it necessary expressly to repudiate the more narrow formulations used in Justice O'CONNOR's earlier opinions. Those opinions stated that a statute imposes an "undue burden" if it imposes "absolute obstacles or severe limitations on the abortion decision."

. . . .

To the extent I can discern any meaningful content in the "undue burden" standard as applied in the joint opinion, it appears to be that a State may not regulate abortion in such a way as to reduce significantly its incidence. The joint opinion repeatedly emphasizes that an important factor in the "undue burden" analysis is whether the regulation "prevent[s] a significant number of women from obtaining an abortion," whether a "significant number of women . . . are likely to be deterred from procuring an abortion;" and whether the regulation often "deters" women from seeking abortions. We are not told, however, what forms of "deterrence" are impermissible or what degree of success in deterrence is too much to be tolerated. If, for example, a State required a woman to read a pamphlet describing, with illustrations, the facts of fetal development before she could obtain an abortion, the effect of such legislation might be to "deter" a "significant number of women" from procuring abortions, thereby seemingly allowing a district judge to invalidate it as an undue burden. Thus, despite flowery rhetoric about the State's "substantial" and "profound" interest in "potential human life," and criticism of *Roe* for undervaluing that interest, the joint opinion permits the State to pursue that interest only so long as it is not too successful. As Justice BLACKMUN recognizes (with evident hope) the "undue burden" standard may ultimately require the invalidation of each provision upheld today if it can be shown, on a better record, that the State is too effectively "express[ing] a preference for childbirth over abortion." Reason finds no refuge in this jurisprudence of confusion.

. . . .

The Court's reliance upon stare decisis can best be described as contrived. It insists upon the necessity of adhering not to all of *Roe* but only to what it calls the "central

holding." It seems to me that stare decisis ought to be applied even to the doctrine
of stare decisis, and I confess never to have heard of this new, keep-what-you-want-
and-throw-away-the-rest version. I wonder whether, for example, the new version of
stare decisis would be satisfied if we allowed courts to review the constitutionality of
only those statutes that (like the one in *Marbury* [*v. Madison*, 5 U.S. 137 (1803)]) per-
tain to the jurisdiction of the courts.

I am certainly not in a good position to dispute that the Court has saved the "central holding" of *Roe* since to do that effectively I would have to know what the Court
has saved, which in turn would require me to understand (as I do not) what the
"undue burden" test means. I must confess, however, that I have always thought, and
I think a lot of other people have always thought, that the arbitrary trimester framework, which the Court today discards, was quite as central to *Roe* as the arbitrary
viability test, which the Court today retains. It seems particularly ungrateful to carve
the trimester framework out of the core of *Roe* since its very rigidity (in sharp contrast to the utter indeterminability of the "undue burden" test) is probably the only
reason the Court is able to say, in urging stare decisis, that *Roe* "has in no sense proven
'unworkable.'" I suppose the Court is entitled to call a "central holding" whatever it
wants to call a "central holding" — which is, come to think of it, perhaps one of the
difficulties with this modified version of stare decisis.

      . . . .

The Court's description of the place of *Roe* in the social history of the United
States is unrecognizable. Not only did *Roe* not, as the Court suggests, resolve the
deeply divisive issue of abortion; it did more than anything else to nourish it, by
elevating it to the national level where it is infinitely more difficult to resolve.
National politics were not plagued by abortion protests, national abortion lobbying,
or abortion marches on Congress before *Roe* was decided. Profound disagreement
existed among our citizens over the issue — as it does over other issues, such as the
death penalty — but that disagreement was being worked out at the state level. As
with many other issues, the division of sentiment within each State was not as
closely balanced as it was among the population of the Nation as a whole, meaning
not only that more people would be satisfied with the results of state-by-state resolution, but also that those results would be more stable. Pre-*Roe* moreover, political
compromise was possible.

Roe mandate for abortion on demand destroyed the compromises of the past, rendered compromise impossible for the future, and required the entire issue to be
resolved uniformly, at the national level. At the same time, *Roe* created a vast new
class of abortion consumers and abortion proponents by eliminating the moral
opprobrium that had attached to the act. ("If the Constitution guarantees abortion,
how can it be bad?" — not an accurate line of thought, but a natural one.) Many favor
all of those developments, and it is not for me to say that they are wrong. But to portray *Roe* as the statesmanlike "settlement" of a divisive issue, a jurisprudential Peace
of Westphalia that is worth preserving, is nothing less than Orwellian. *Roe* fanned
into life an issue that has inflamed our national politics in general, and has obscured

with its smoke the selection of Justices to this Court in particular, ever since. And by keeping us in the abortion-umpiring business, it is the perpetuation of that disruption, rather than of any Pax Roeana, that the Court's new majority decrees.

. . . .

But when it is in the mind of a Court that believes the Constitution has an evolving meaning that the Ninth Amendment's reference to "othe[r]" rights is not a disclaimer, but a charter for action; and that the function of this Court is to "speak before all others for [the people's] constitutional ideals" unrestrained by meaningful text or tradition—then the notion that the Court must adhere to a decision for as long as the decision faces "great opposition" and the Court is "under fire" acquires a character of almost czarist arrogance. We are offended by these marchers who descend upon us, every year on the anniversary of *Roe* to protest our saying that the Constitution requires what our society has never thought the Constitution requires. These people who refuse to be "tested by following" must be taught a lesson. We have no Cossacks, but at least we can stubbornly refuse to abandon an erroneous opinion that we might otherwise change—to show how little they intimidate us.

Of course, as THE CHIEF JUSTICE points out, we have been subjected to what the Court calls "'political pressure'" by both sides of this issue. Maybe today's decision not to overrule *Roe* will be seen as buckling to pressure from that direction. Instead of engaging in the hopeless task of predicting public perception—a job not for lawyers but for political campaign managers—the Justices should do what is legally right by asking two questions: (1) Was *Roe* correctly decided? (2) Has *Roe* succeeded in producing a settled body of law? If the answer to both questions is no, *Roe* should undoubtedly be overruled.

In truth, I am as distressed as the Court is—and expressed my distress several years ago—about the "political pressure" directed to the Court: the marches, the mail, the protests aimed at inducing us to change our opinions. How upsetting it is, that so many of our citizens (good people, not lawless ones, on both sides of this abortion issue, and on various sides of other issues as well) think that we Justices should properly take into account their views, as though we were engaged not in ascertaining an objective law but in determining some kind of social consensus.

. . . .

We should get out of this area, where we have no right to be, and where we do neither ourselves nor the country any good by remaining.

———

Casey upheld some state restrictions on abortion. Federal restrictions were upheld in *Carhart*, below.[42] Justice Kennedy, who co-authored the majority opinion in *Casey*,

———
42. Gonzales v. Carhart, 550 U.S. 124 (2007).

wrote the majority opinion in *Carhart*. The opinion contains a graphic description of what actually occurs in the abortion process.

═══════════════════════════

550 U.S. 124 / 127 S. Ct. 1610
Supreme Court of the United States

Alberto R. GONZALES, Attorney General, Petitioner,
v.
Leroy CARHART et al.
Alberto R. Gonzales, Attorney General, Petitioner,
v.
Planned Parenthood Federation of America, Inc., et al.

Decided April 18, 2007.

. . . .

Opinion

Justice KENNEDY delivered the opinion of the Court.

These cases require us to consider the validity of the Partial-Birth Abortion Ban Act of 2003(Act), 18 U.S.C. § 1531 (2000 ed., Supp. IV), a federal statute regulating abortion procedures. In recitations preceding its operative provisions the Act refers to the Court's opinion in *Stenberg v. Carhart*, 530 U.S. 914 (2000), which also addressed the subject of abortion procedures used in the later stages of pregnancy. Compared to the state statute at issue in Stenberg, the Act is more specific concerning the instances to which it applies and in this respect more precise in its coverage. We conclude the Act should be sustained against the objections lodged by the broad, facial attack brought against it.

In No. 05–380 (Carhart) respondents are LeRoy Carhart, William G. Fitzhugh, William H. Knorr, and Jill L. Vibhakar, doctors who perform second-trimester abortions. These doctors filed their complaint against the Attorney General of the United States in the United States District Court for the District of Nebraska. They challenged the constitutionality of the Act and sought a permanent injunction against its enforcement. *Carhart v. Ashcroft*, 331 F. Supp. 2d 805 (2004). In 2004, after a 2-week trial, the District Court granted a permanent injunction that prohibited the Attorney General from enforcing the Act in all cases but those in which there was no dispute the fetus was viable. The Court of Appeals for the Eighth Circuit affirmed. We granted certiorari.

In No. 05–1382 (Planned Parenthood) respondents are Planned Parenthood Federation of America, Inc., Planned Parenthood Golden Gate, and the City and County of San Francisco. The Planned Parenthood entities sought to enjoin enforcement of the Act in a suit filed in the United States District Court for the Northern District of California. *Planned Parenthood Federation of Am. v. Ashcroft*, 320 F. Supp. 2d 957

(2004). The City and County of San Francisco intervened as a plaintiff. In 2004, the District Court held a trial spanning a period just short of three weeks, and it, too, enjoined the Attorney General from enforcing the Act. The Court of Appeals for the Ninth Circuit affirmed. We granted certiorari.

I.

A.

The Act proscribes a particular manner of ending fetal life, so it is necessary here, as it was in Stenberg, to discuss abortion procedures in some detail. Three United States District Courts heard extensive evidence describing the procedures. In addition to the two courts involved in the instant cases the District Court for the Southern District of New York also considered the constitutionality of the Act. It found the Act unconstitutional and the Court of Appeals for the Second Circuit affirmed. The three District Courts relied on similar medical evidence; indeed, much of the evidence submitted to the *Carhart* court previously had been submitted to the other two courts. We refer to the District Courts' exhaustive opinions in our own discussion of abortion procedures.

Abortion methods vary depending to some extent on the preferences of the physician and, of course, on the term of the pregnancy and the resulting stage of the unborn child's development. Between 85 and 90 percent of the approximately 1.3 million abortions performed each year in the United States take place in the first three months of pregnancy, which is to say in the first trimester. The most common first-trimester abortion method is vacuum aspiration (otherwise known as suction curettage) in which the physician vacuums out the embryonic tissue. Early in this trimester an alternative is to use medication, such as mifepristone (commonly known as RU–486), to terminate the pregnancy. The Act does not regulate these procedures.

Of the remaining abortions that take place each year, most occur in the second trimester. The surgical procedure referred to as "dilation and evacuation" or "D & E" is the usual abortion method in this trimester. Although individual techniques for performing D & E differ, the general steps are the same.

A doctor must first dilate the cervix at least to the extent needed to insert surgical instruments into the uterus and to maneuver them to evacuate the fetus. The steps taken to cause dilation differ by physician and gestational age of the fetus. A doctor often begins the dilation process by inserting osmotic dilators, such as laminaria (sticks of seaweed), into the cervix. The dilators can be used in combination with drugs, such as misoprostol, that increase dilation. The resulting amount of dilation is not uniform, and a doctor does not know in advance how an individual patient will respond. In general the longer dilators remain in the cervix, the more it will dilate. Yet the length of time doctors employ osmotic dilators varies. Some may keep dilators in the cervix for two days, while others use dilators for a day or less.

After sufficient dilation the surgical operation can commence. The woman is placed under general anesthesia or conscious sedation. The doctor, often guided by ultrasound, inserts grasping forceps through the woman's cervix and into the uterus to grab the fetus. The doctor grips a fetal part with the forceps and pulls it back through the cervix and vagina, continuing to pull even after meeting resistance from the cervix. The friction causes the fetus to tear apart. For example, a leg might be ripped off the fetus as it is pulled through the cervix and out of the woman. The process of evacuating the fetus piece by piece continues until it has been completely removed. A doctor may make 10 to 15 passes with the forceps to evacuate the fetus in its entirety, though sometimes removal is completed with fewer passes. Once the fetus has been evacuated, the placenta and any remaining fetal material are suctioned or scraped out of the uterus. The doctor examines the different parts to ensure the entire fetal body has been removed.

Some doctors, especially later in the second trimester, may kill the fetus a day or two before performing the surgical evacuation. They inject digoxin or potassium chloride into the fetus, the umbilical cord, or the amniotic fluid. Fetal demise may cause contractions and make greater dilation possible. Once dead, moreover, the fetus' body will soften, and its removal will be easier. Other doctors refrain from injecting chemical agents, believing it adds risk with little or no medical benefit.

The abortion procedure that was the impetus for the numerous bans on "partial-birth abortion," including the Act, is a variation of this standard D & E. The medical community has not reached unanimity on the appropriate name for this D & E variation. It has been referred to as "intact D & E," "dilation and extraction" (D & X), and "intact D & X." . . . For discussion purposes this D & E variation will be referred to as intact D & E. The main difference between the two procedures is that in intact D & E a doctor extracts the fetus intact or largely intact with only a few passes. There are no comprehensive statistics indicating what percentage of all D & Es are performed in this manner.

Intact D & E, like regular D & E, begins with dilation of the cervix. Sufficient dilation is essential for the procedure. To achieve intact extraction some doctors thus may attempt to dilate the cervix to a greater degree. This approach has been called "serial" dilation. Doctors who attempt at the outset to perform intact D & E may dilate for two full days or use up to 25 osmotic dilators.

In an intact D & E procedure the doctor extracts the fetus in a way conducive to pulling out its entire body, instead of ripping it apart. One doctor, for example, testified:

If I know I have good dilation and I reach in and the fetus starts to come out and I think I can accomplish it, the abortion with an intact delivery, then I use my forceps a little bit differently. I don't close them quite so much, and I just gently draw the tissue out attempting to have an intact delivery, if possible.

Rotating the fetus as it is being pulled decreases the odds of dismemberment. A doctor also "may use forceps to grasp a fetal part, pull it down, and re-grasp the fetus at a higher level—sometimes using both his hand and a forceps—to exert traction to retrieve the fetus intact until the head is lodged in the [cervix]."

Intact D & E gained public notoriety when, in 1992, Dr. Martin Haskell gave a presentation describing his method of performing the operation. In the usual intact D & E the fetus' head lodges in the cervix, and dilation is insufficient to allow it to pass. Haskell explained the next step as follows:

"At this point, the right-handed surgeon slides the fingers of the left [hand] along the back of the fetus and "hooks" the shoulders of the fetus with the index and ring fingers (palm down).

"While maintaining this tension, lifting the cervix and applying traction to the shoulders with the fingers of the left hand, the surgeon takes a pair of blunt curved Metzenbaum scissors in the right hand. He carefully advances the tip, curved down, along the spine and under his middle finger until he feels it contact the base of the skull under the tip of his middle finger.

"[T]he surgeon then forces the scissors into the base of the skull or into the foramen magnum. Having safely entered the skull, he spreads the scissors to enlarge the opening.

"The surgeon removes the scissors and introduces a suction catheter into this hole and evacuates the skull contents. With the catheter still in place, he applies traction to the fetus, removing it completely from the patient."

This is an abortion doctor's clinical description. Here is another description from a nurse who witnessed the same method performed on a 26 1/2-week fetus and who testified before the Senate Judiciary Committee:

"Dr. Haskell went in with forceps and grabbed the baby's legs and pulled them down into the birth canal. Then he delivered the baby's body and the arms—everything but the head. The doctor kept the head right inside the uterus. . . .

"The baby's little fingers were clasping and unclasping, and his little feet were kicking. Then the doctor stuck the scissors in the back of his head, and the baby's arms jerked out, like a startle reaction, like a flinch, like a baby does when he thinks he is going to fall.

"The doctor opened up the scissors, stuck a high-powered suction tube into the opening, and sucked the baby's brains out. Now the baby went completely limp. . . .

"He cut the umbilical cord and delivered the placenta. He threw the baby in a pan, along with the placenta and the instruments he had just used."

Dr. Haskell's approach is not the only method of killing the fetus once its head lodges in the cervix, and "the process has evolved" since his presentation. Another doctor, for example, squeezes the skull after it has been pierced "so that enough brain tissue exudes to allow the head to pass through." Still other physicians reach into the cervix with their forceps and crush the fetus' skull. Others continue to pull the fetus out of the woman until it disarticulates at the neck, in effect decapitating it. These doctors then grasp the head with forceps, crush it, and remove it.

Some doctors performing an intact D & E attempt to remove the fetus without collapsing the skull. Yet one doctor would not allow delivery of a live fetus younger than 24 weeks because "the objective of [his] procedure is to perform an abortion," not a birth. The doctor thus answered in the affirmative when asked whether he would "hold the fetus' head on the internal side of the [cervix] in order to collapse the skull" and kill the fetus before it is born. Another doctor testified he crushes a fetus' skull not only to reduce its size but also to ensure the fetus is dead before it is removed. For the staff to have to deal with a fetus that has "some viability to it, some movement of limbs," according to this doctor, "[is] always a difficult situation."

D & E and intact D & E are not the only second-trimester abortion methods. Doctors also may abort a fetus through medical induction. The doctor medicates the woman to induce labor, and contractions occur to deliver the fetus. Induction, which unlike D & E should occur in a hospital, can last as little as 6 hours but can take longer than 48. It accounts for about 5 percent of second-trimester abortions before 20 weeks of gestation and 15 percent of those after 20 weeks. Doctors turn to two other methods of second-trimester abortion, hysterotomy and hysterectomy, only in emergency situations because they carry increased risk of complications. In a hysterotomy, as in a cesarean section, the doctor removes the fetus by making an incision through the abdomen and uterine wall to gain access to the uterine cavity. A hysterectomy requires the removal of the entire uterus. These two procedures represent about 0.07 percent of second-trimester abortions.

B.

After Dr. Haskell's procedure received public attention, with ensuing and increasing public concern, bans on "'partial birth abortion'" proliferated. By the time of the Stenberg decision, about 30 States had enacted bans designed to prohibit the procedure. Congress also acted to ban partial-birth abortion. President Clinton vetoed the congressional legislation, and the Senate failed to override the veto. Congress approved another bill banning the procedure in 1997, but President Clinton again vetoed it. In 2003, after this Court's decision in Stenberg, Congress passed the Act at issue here. On November 5, 2003, President Bush signed the Act into law. It was to take effect the following day. 18 U.S.C. § 1531(a).

The Act responded to *Stenberg* in two ways. First, Congress made factual findings. Congress determined that this Court in *Stenberg* "was required to accept the very questionable findings issued by the district court judge," but that Congress was "not bound to accept the same factual findings." Congress found, among other things, that "[a] moral, medical, and ethical consensus exists that the practice of performing a partial-birth abortion . . . is a gruesome and inhumane procedure that is never medically necessary and should be prohibited."

Second, and more relevant here, the Act's language differs from that of the Nebraska statute struck down in *Stenberg*. The operative provisions of the Act provide in relevant part:

"(a) Any physician who, in or affecting interstate or foreign commerce, knowingly performs a partial-birth abortion and thereby kills a human fetus shall be fined under this title or imprisoned not more than 2 years, or both. This subsection does not apply to a partial-birth abortion that is necessary to save the life of a mother whose life is endangered by a physical disorder, physical illness, or physical injury, including a life-endangering physical condition caused by or arising from the pregnancy itself. This subsection takes effect 1 day after the enactment.

"(b) As used in this section —

"(1) the term 'partial-birth abortion' means an abortion in which the person performing the abortion —

"(A) deliberately and intentionally vaginally delivers a living fetus until, in the case of a head-first presentation, the entire fetal head is outside the body of the mother, or, in the case of breech presentation, any part of the fetal trunk past the navel is outside the body of the mother, for the purpose of performing an overt act that the person knows will kill the partially delivered living fetus; and

"(B) performs the overt act, other than completion of delivery, that kills the partially delivered living fetus; and

"(2) the term 'physician' means a doctor of medicine or osteopathy legally authorized to practice medicine and surgery by the State in which the doctor performs such activity, or any other individual legally authorized by the State to perform abortions: Provided, however, that any individual who is not a physician or not otherwise legally authorized by the State to perform abortions, but who nevertheless directly performs a partial-birth abortion, shall be subject to the provisions of this section.

. . . .

"(d)(1) A defendant accused of an offense under this section may seek a hearing before the State Medical Board on whether the physician's conduct was necessary to save the life of the mother whose life was endangered by a physical disorder, physical illness, or physical injury, including a life-endangering physical condition caused by or arising from the pregnancy itself.

"(2) The findings on that issue are admissible on that issue at the trial of the defendant. Upon a motion of the defendant, the court shall delay the beginning of the trial for not more than 30 days to permit such a hearing to take place.

"(e) A woman upon whom a partial-birth abortion is performed may not be prosecuted under this section, for a conspiracy to violate this section, or for an offense under section 2, 3, or 4 of this title based on a violation of this section."

The Act also includes a provision authorizing civil actions that is not of relevance here.

. . . .

II.

The principles set forth in the joint opinion in *Planned Parenthood of Southeastern Pa. v. Casey*, did not find support from all those who join the instant opinion. Whatever one's views concerning the *Casey* joint opinion, it is evident a premise central to its conclusion—that the government has a legitimate and substantial interest in preserving and promoting fetal life—would be repudiated were the Court now to affirm the judgments of the Courts of Appeals.

Casey involved a challenge to *Roe v. Wade*. The opinion contains this summary:

It must be stated at the outset and with clarity that *Roe* essential holding, the holding we reaffirm, has three parts. First is a recognition of the right of the woman to choose to have an abortion before viability and to obtain it without undue interference from the State. Before viability, the State's interests are not strong enough to support a prohibition of abortion or the imposition of a substantial obstacle to the woman's effective right to elect the procedure. Second is a confirmation of the State's power to restrict abortions after fetal viability, if the law contains exceptions for pregnancies which endanger the woman's life or health. And third is the principle that the State has legitimate interests from the outset of the pregnancy in protecting the health of the woman and the life of the fetus that may become a child. These principles do not contradict one another; and we adhere to each.

Though all three holdings are implicated in the instant cases, it is the third that requires the most extended discussion; for we must determine whether the Act furthers the legitimate interest of the Government in protecting the life of the fetus that may become a child.

To implement its holding, *Casey* rejected both *Roe* rigid trimester framework and the interpretation of *Roe* that considered all previability regulations of abortion unwarranted. On this point *Casey* overruled the holdings in two cases because they undervalued the State's interest in potential life.

We assume the following principles for the purposes of this opinion. Before viability, a State "may not prohibit any woman from making the ultimate decision to terminate her pregnancy." It also may not impose upon this right an undue burden, which exists if a regulation's "purpose or effect is to place a substantial obstacle in the path of a woman seeking an abortion before the fetus attains viability." On the other hand, "[r]egulations which do no more than create a structural mechanism by which the State, or the parent or guardian of a minor, may express profound respect for the life of the unborn are permitted, if they are not a substantial obstacle to the woman's exercise of the right to choose." *Casey*, in short, struck a balance. The balance was central to its holding. We now apply its standard to the cases at bar.

III.

We begin with a determination of the Act's operation and effect. A straightforward reading of the Act's text demonstrates its purpose and the scope of its provisions: It regulates and proscribes, with exceptions or qualifications to be discussed, performing the intact D & E procedure.

. . . .

We conclude that the Act is not void for vagueness, does not impose an undue burden from any overbreadth, and is not invalid on its face.

. . . .

IV.

Under the principles accepted as controlling here, the Act, as we have interpreted it, would be unconstitutional "if its purpose or effect is to place a substantial obstacle in the path of a woman seeking an abortion before the fetus attains viability." The abortions affected by the Act's regulations take place both previability and postviability; so the quoted language and the undue burden analysis it relies upon are applicable. The question is whether the Act, measured by its text in this facial attack, imposes a substantial obstacle to late-term, but previability, abortions. The Act does not on its face impose a substantial obstacle, and we reject this further facial challenge to its validity.

A.

The Act's purposes are set forth in recitals preceding its operative provisions. A description of the prohibited abortion procedure demonstrates the rationale for the congressional enactment. The Act proscribes a method of abortion in which a fetus is killed just inches before completion of the birth process. Congress stated as follows: "Implicitly approving such a brutal and inhumane procedure by choosing not to prohibit it will further coarsen society to the humanity of not only newborns, but all vulnerable and innocent human life, making it increasingly difficult to protect such life." The Act expresses respect for the dignity of human life.

Congress was concerned, furthermore, with the effects on the medical community and on its reputation caused by the practice of partial-birth abortion. The findings in the Act explain:

Partial-birth abortion . . . confuses the medical, legal, and ethical duties of physicians to preserve and promote life, as the physician acts directly against the physical life of a child, whom he or she had just delivered, all but the head, out of the womb, in order to end that life.

There can be no doubt the government "has an interest in protecting the integrity and ethics of the medical profession." Under our precedents it is clear the State has a significant role to play in regulating the medical profession.

. . . .

The Act's ban on abortions that involve partial delivery of a living fetus furthers the Government's objectives. No one would dispute that, for many, D & E is a procedure itself laden with the power to devalue human life. Congress could none-theless conclude that the type of abortion proscribed by the Act requires specific regulation because it implicates additional ethical and moral concerns that justify a special prohibition. Congress determined that the abortion methods it proscribed had a "disturbing similarity to the killing of a newborn infant," and thus it was con-cerned with "draw[ing] a bright line that clearly distinguishes abortion and infanti-cide." The Court has in the past confirmed the validity of drawing boundaries to prevent certain practices that extinguish life and are close to actions that are con-demned. [*Washington v.*] *Glucksberg* [521 U.S. 702 (1997)] found reasonable the State's "fear that permitting assisted suicide will start it down the path to voluntary and perhaps even involuntary euthanasia."

Respect for human life finds an ultimate expression in the bond of love the mother has for her child. The Act recognizes this reality as well. Whether to have an abor-tion requires a difficult and painful moral decision. While we find no reliable data to measure the phenomenon, it seems unexceptionable to conclude some women come to regret their choice to abort the infant life they once created and sustained. Severe depression and loss of esteem can follow.

In a decision so fraught with emotional consequence some doctors may prefer not to disclose precise details of the means that will be used, confining themselves to the required statement of risks the procedure entails. From one standpoint this ought not to be surprising. Any number of patients facing imminent surgical procedures would prefer not to hear all details, lest the usual anxiety preceding invasive medi-cal procedures become the more intense. This is likely the case with the abortion pro-cedures here in issue.

It is, however, precisely this lack of information concerning the way in which the fetus will be killed that is of legitimate concern to the State. The State has an interest in ensuring so grave a choice is well informed. It is self-evident that a mother who comes to regret her choice to abort must struggle with grief more anguished and sor-row more profound when she learns, only after the event, what she once did not know: that she allowed a doctor to pierce the skull and vacuum the fast-developing brain of her unborn child, a child assuming the human form.

It is a reasonable inference that a necessary effect of the regulation and the knowledge it conveys will be to encourage some women to carry the infant to full term, thus reducing the absolute number of late-term abortions. The medical pro-fession, furthermore, may find different and less shocking methods to abort the fetus in the second trimester, thereby accommodating legislative demand. The State's interest in respect for life is advanced by the dialogue that better informs the political and legal systems, the medical profession, expectant mothers, and society as a whole of the consequences that follow from a decision to elect a late-term abortion.

It is objected that the standard D & E is in some respects as brutal, if not more, than the intact D & E, so that the legislation accomplishes little. What we have already said, however, shows ample justification for the regulation. Partial-birth abortion, as defined by the Act, differs from a standard D & E because the former occurs when the fetus is partially outside the mother to the point of one of the Act's anatomical landmarks. It was reasonable for Congress to think that partial-birth abortion, more than standard D & E, "undermines the public's perception of the appropriate role of a physician during the delivery process, and perverts a process during which life is brought into the world." There would be a flaw in this Court's logic, and an irony in its jurisprudence, were we first to conclude a ban on both D & E and intact D & E was overbroad and then to say it is irrational to ban only intact D & E because that does not proscribe both procedures. In sum, we reject the contention that the congressional purpose of the Act was "to place a substantial obstacle in the path of a woman seeking an abortion."

B.

The Act's furtherance of legitimate government interests bears upon, but does not resolve, the next question: whether the Act has the effect of imposing an unconstitutional burden on the abortion right because it does not allow use of the barred procedure where "'necessary, in appropriate medical judgment, for the preservation of the . . . health of the mother.'" The prohibition in the Act would be unconstitutional, under precedents we here assume to be controlling, if it "subject[ed] [women] to significant health risks." In *Ayotte* [*v. Planned Parenthood of N. New England*, 546 U.S. 320 (2006)] the parties agreed a health exception to the challenged parental-involvement statute was necessary "to avert serious and often irreversible damage to [a pregnant minor's] health." Here, by contrast, whether the Act creates significant health risks for women has been a contested factual question. The evidence presented in the trial courts and before Congress demonstrates both sides have medical support for their position.

Respondents presented evidence that intact D & E may be the safest method of abortion, for reasons similar to those adduced in *Stenberg*. Abortion doctors testified, for example, that intact D & E decreases the risk of cervical laceration or uterine perforation because it requires fewer passes into the uterus with surgical instruments and does not require the removal of bony fragments of the dismembered fetus, fragments that may be sharp. Respondents also presented evidence that intact D & E was safer both because it reduces the risks that fetal parts will remain in the uterus and because it takes less time to complete. Respondents, in addition, proffered evidence that intact D & E was safer for women with certain medical conditions or women with fetuses that had certain anomalies.

These contentions were contradicted by other doctors who testified in the District Courts and before Congress. They concluded that the alleged health advantages were based on speculation without scientific studies to support them. They considered D & E always to be a safe alternative.

There is documented medical disagreement whether the Act's prohibition would ever impose significant health risks on women. The three District Courts that considered the Act's constitutionality appeared to be in some disagreement on this central factual question. The District Court for the District of Nebraska concluded "the banned procedure is, sometimes, the safest abortion procedure to preserve the health of women." The District Court for the Northern District of California reached a similar conclusion. The District Court for the Southern District of New York was more skeptical of the purported health benefits of intact D & E. It found the Attorney General's "expert witnesses reasonably and effectively refuted [the plaintiffs'] proffered bases for the opinion that [intact D & E] has safety advantages over other second-trimester abortion procedures." In addition it did "not believe that many of [the plaintiffs'] purported reasons for why [intact D & E] is medically necessary [were] credible; rather [it found them to be] theoretical or false." The court nonetheless invalidated the Act because it determined "a significant body of medical opinion . . . holds that D & E has safety advantages over induction and that [intact D & E] has some safety advantages (however hypothetical and unsubstantiated by scientific evidence) over D & E for some women in some circumstances."

The question becomes whether the Act can stand when this medical uncertainty persists. The Court's precedents instruct that the Act can survive this facial attack. The Court has given state and federal legislatures wide discretion to pass legislation in areas where there is medical and scientific uncertainty. . . .

This traditional rule is consistent with *Casey* which confirms the State's interest in promoting respect for human life at all stages in the pregnancy. Physicians are not entitled to ignore regulations that direct them to use reasonable alternative procedures. The law need not give abortion doctors unfettered choice in the course of their medical practice, nor should it elevate their status above other physicians in the medical community. In *Casey* the controlling opinion held an informed-consent requirement in the abortion context was "no different from a requirement that a doctor give certain specific information about any medical procedure." The opinion stated "the doctor-patient relation here is entitled to the same solicitude it receives in other contexts."

Medical uncertainty does not foreclose the exercise of legislative power in the abortion context any more than it does in other contexts. The medical uncertainty over whether the Act's prohibition creates significant health risks provides a sufficient basis to conclude in this facial attack that the Act does not impose an undue burden.

The conclusion that the Act does not impose an undue burden is supported by other considerations. Alternatives are available to the prohibited procedure. As we have noted, the Act does not proscribe D & E. One District Court found D & E to have extremely low rates of medical complications. Another indicated D & E was "generally the safest method of abortion during the second trimester." In addition the Act's prohibition only applies to the delivery of "a living fetus." If the intact D & E procedure is truly necessary in some circumstances, it appears likely an injection that kills the fetus is an alternative under the Act that allows the doctor to perform the procedure.

The instant cases, then, are different from *Planned Parenthood of Central Mo. v. Danforth*, 428 U.S. 52, 77–79 (1976), in which the Court invalidated a ban on saline amniocentesis, the then-dominant second-trimester abortion method. The Court found the ban in *Danforth* to be "an unreasonable or arbitrary regulation designed to inhibit, and having the effect of inhibiting, the vast majority of abortions after the first 12 weeks." Here the Act allows, among other means, a commonly used and generally accepted method, so it does not construct a substantial obstacle to the abortion right.

. . . .

A zero tolerance policy would strike down legitimate abortion regulations, like the present one, if some part of the medical community were disinclined to follow the proscription. This is too exacting a standard to impose on the legislative power, exercised in this instance under the Commerce Clause, to regulate the medical profession. Considerations of marginal safety, including the balance of risks, are within the legislative competence when the regulation is rational and in pursuit of legitimate ends. When standard medical options are available, mere convenience does not suffice to displace them; and if some procedures have different risks than others, it does not follow that the State is altogether barred from imposing reasonable regulations. The Act is not invalid on its face where there is uncertainty over whether the barred procedure is ever necessary to preserve a woman's health, given the availability of other abortion procedures that are considered to be safe alternatives.

V.

The considerations we have discussed support our further determination that these facial attacks should not have been entertained in the first instance. In these circumstances the proper means to consider exceptions is by as-applied challenge. The Government has acknowledged that preenforcement, as-applied challenges to the Act can be maintained. This is the proper manner to protect the health of the woman if it can be shown that in discrete and well-defined instances a particular condition has or is likely to occur in which the procedure prohibited by the Act must be used. In an as-applied challenge the nature of the medical risk can be better quantified and balanced than in a facial attack.

. . . .

As the previous sections of this opinion explain, respondents have not demonstrated that the Act would be unconstitutional in a large fraction of relevant cases. We note that the statute here applies to all instances in which the doctor proposes to use the prohibited procedure, not merely those in which the woman suffers from medical complications. It is neither our obligation nor within our traditional institutional role to resolve questions of constitutionality with respect to each potential situation that might develop. "[I]t would indeed be undesirable for this Court to consider every conceivable situation which might possibly arise in the application of complex and comprehensive legislation." For this reason, "[a]s-applied challenges are the basic building blocks of constitutional adjudication."

The Act is open to a proper as-applied challenge in a discrete case. No as-applied challenge need be brought if the prohibition in the Act threatens a woman's life because the Act already contains a life exception.

. . . .

—————

Justice THOMAS, with whom Justice SCALIA joins, concurring.

I join the Court's opinion because it accurately applies current jurisprudence, including *Planned Parenthood of Southeastern Pa. v. Casey* [505 U.S. 833 (1992)]. I write separately to reiterate my view that the Court's abortion jurisprudence, including *Casey* and *Roe*, has no basis in the Constitution. . . .

—————

Justice GINSBURG, with whom Justice STEVENS, Justice SOUTER, and Justice BREYER join, dissenting.

In *Planned Parenthood of Southeastern Pa. v. Casey*, the Court declared that "[l]iberty finds no refuge in a jurisprudence of doubt." There was, the Court said, an "imperative" need to dispel doubt as to "the meaning and reach" of the Court's 7-to-2 judgment, rendered nearly two decades earlier in *Roe*. Responsive to that need, the Court endeavored to provide secure guidance to "[s]tate and federal courts as well as legislatures throughout the Union," by defining "the rights of the woman and the legitimate authority of the State respecting the termination of pregnancies by abortion procedures."

. . . .

In reaffirming *Roe*, the *Casey* Court described the centrality of "the decision whether to bear . . . a child," to a woman's "dignity and autonomy," her "personhood" and "destiny," her "conception of . . . her place in society." Of signal importance here, the *Casey* Court stated with unmistakable clarity that state regulation of access to abortion procedures, even after viability, must protect "the health of the woman."

Seven years ago, in *Stenberg v. Carhart* [530 U.S. 914 (2000)], the Court invalidated a Nebraska statute criminalizing the performance of a medical procedure that, in the political arena, has been dubbed "partial-birth abortion." With fidelity to the *Roe-Casey* line of precedent, the Court held the Nebraska statute unconstitutional in part because it lacked the requisite protection for the preservation of a woman's health.

Today's decision is alarming. It refuses to take *Casey* and *Stenberg* seriously. It tolerates, indeed applauds, federal intervention to ban nationwide a procedure found necessary and proper in certain cases by the American College of Obstetricians and Gynecologists (ACOG). It blurs the line, firmly drawn in *Casey* between previability and postviability abortions. And, for the first time since *Roe* the Court blesses a prohibition with no exception safeguarding a woman's health.

I dissent from the Court's disposition. Retreating from prior rulings that abortion restrictions cannot be imposed absent an exception safeguarding a woman's health, the Court upholds an Act that surely would not survive under the close scrutiny that previously attended state-decreed limitations on a woman's reproductive choices.

I.

A.

As *Casey* comprehended, at stake in cases challenging abortion restrictions is a woman's "control over her [own] destiny." "There was a time, not so long ago," when women were "regarded as the center of home and family life, with attendant special responsibilities that precluded full and independent legal status under the Constitution." Those views, this Court made clear in *Casey* "are no longer consistent with our understanding of the family, the individual, or the Constitution." Women, it is now acknowledged, have the talent, capacity, and right "to participate equally in the economic and social life of the Nation." Their ability to realize their full potential, the Court recognized, is intimately connected to "their ability to control their reproductive lives." Thus, legal challenges to undue restrictions on abortion procedures do not seek to vindicate some generalized notion of privacy; rather, they center on a woman's autonomy to determine her life's course, and thus to enjoy equal citizenship stature.

In keeping with this comprehension of the right to reproductive choice, the Court has consistently required that laws regulating abortion, at any stage of pregnancy and in all cases, safeguard a woman's health.

We have thus ruled that a State must avoid subjecting women to health risks not only where the pregnancy itself creates danger, but also where state regulation forces women to resort to less safe methods of abortion. Indeed, we have applied the rule that abortion regulation must safeguard a woman's health to the particular procedure at issue here—intact dilation and evacuation (intact D & E).

In *Stenberg*, we expressly held that a statute banning intact D & E was unconstitutional in part because it lacked a health exception. We noted that there existed a "division of medical opinion" about the relative safety of intact D & E, but we made clear that as long as "substantial medical authority supports the proposition that banning a particular abortion procedure could endanger women's health," a health exception is required. We explained:

The word 'necessary' in *Casey* phrase 'necessary, in appropriate medical judgment, for the preservation of the life or health of the [pregnant woman],' cannot refer to an absolute necessity or to absolute proof. Medical treatments and procedures are often considered appropriate (or inappropriate) in light of estimated comparative health risks (and health benefits) in particular cases. Neither can that phrase require unanimity of medical opinion. Doctors often differ in their estimation of comparative health risks and appropriate treatment. And Casey words 'appropriate medical judgment' must embody the judicial need to tolerate responsible differences of medical opinion. . . .

Thus, we reasoned, division in medical opinion "at most means uncertainty, a factor that signals the presence of risk, not its absence." "[A] statute that altogether forbids [intact D & E] . . . consequently must contain a health exception."

B.

In 2003, a few years after our ruling in *Stenberg*, Congress passed the Partial-Birth Abortion Ban Act—without an exception for women's health. The congressional findings on which the Partial-Birth Abortion Ban Act rests do not withstand inspection, as the lower courts have determined and this Court is obliged to concede. . . .

. . . .

More important, Congress claimed there was a medical consensus that the banned procedure is never necessary. But the evidence "very clearly demonstrate[d] the opposite."

Similarly, Congress found that "[t]here is no credible medical evidence that partial-birth abortions are safe or are safer than other abortion procedures." But the congressional record includes letters from numerous individual physicians stating that pregnant women's health would be jeopardized under the Act, as well as statements from nine professional associations, including ACOG, the American Public Health Association, and the California Medical Association, attesting that intact D & E carries meaningful safety advantages over other methods. No comparable medical groups supported the ban. In fact, "all of the government's own witnesses disagreed with many of the specific congressional findings."

C.

In contrast to Congress, the District Courts made findings after full trials at which all parties had the opportunity to present their best evidence. The courts had the benefit of "much more extensive medical and scientific evidence . . . concerning the safety and necessity of intact D & Es."

During the District Court trials, "numerous" "extraordinarily accomplished" and "very experienced" medical experts explained that, in certain circumstances and for certain women, intact D & E is safer than alternative procedures and necessary to protect women's health.

According to the expert testimony plaintiffs introduced, the safety advantages of intact D & E are marked for women with certain medical conditions, for example, uterine scarring, bleeding disorders, heart disease, or compromised immune systems. Further, plaintiffs' experts testified that intact D & E is significantly safer for women with certain pregnancy-related conditions, such as placenta previa and accreta, and for women carrying fetuses with certain abnormalities, such as severe hydrocephalus.

Intact D & E, plaintiffs' experts explained, provides safety benefits over D & E by dismemberment for several reasons: First, intact D & E minimizes the number of times a physician must insert instruments through the cervix and into the uterus, and thereby reduces the risk of trauma to, and perforation of, the cervix and uterus—the most serious complication associated with nonintact D & E. Second, removing the fetus intact, instead of dismembering it in utero, decreases the likelihood that fetal tissue will be retained in the uterus, a condition that can cause infection, hemorrhage, and infertility. Third, intact D & E diminishes the chances of exposing the patient's tissues to sharp bony fragments sometimes resulting from dismemberment of the fetus. Fourth, intact D & E takes less operating time than D & E by dismemberment, and thus may reduce bleeding, the risk of infection, and complications relating to anesthesia.

Based on thoroughgoing review of the trial evidence and the congressional record, each of the District Courts to consider the issue rejected Congress' findings as unreasonable and not supported by the evidence. The trial courts concluded, in contrast to Congress' findings, that "significant medical authority supports the proposition that in some circumstances, [intact D & E] is the safest procedure."

The District Courts' findings merit this Court's respect. Today's opinion supplies no reason to reject those findings. Nevertheless, despite the District Courts' appraisal of the weight of the evidence, and in undisguised conflict with *Stenberg*, the Court asserts that the Partial-Birth Abortion Ban Act can survive "when . . . medical uncertainty persists." This assertion is bewildering. Not only does it defy the Court's longstanding precedent affirming the necessity of a health exception, with no carve-out for circumstances of medical uncertainty; it gives short shrift to the records before us, carefully canvassed by the District Courts. Those records indicate that "the majority of highly-qualified experts on the subject believe intact D & E to be the safest, most appropriate procedure under certain circumstances.

The Court acknowledges some of this evidence, ante, at 1635, but insists that, because some witnesses disagreed with ACOG and other experts' assessment of risk, the Act can stand. In this insistence, the Court brushes under the rug the District Courts' well-supported findings that the physicians who testified that intact D & E is never necessary to preserve the health of a woman had slim authority for their opinions. They had no training for, or personal experience with, the intact D & E procedure, and many performed abortions only on rare occasions. Even indulging the assumption that the Government witnesses were equally qualified to evaluate the relative risks of abortion procedures, their testimony could not erase the "significant medical authority support[ing] the proposition that in some circumstances, [intact D & E] would be the safest procedure."

II.

A.

The Court offers flimsy and transparent justifications for upholding a nationwide ban on intact D & E sans any exception to safeguard a woman's health. Today's ruling, the Court declares, advances "a premise central to [*Casey's*] conclusion"—i.e., the Government's "legitimate and substantial interest in preserving and promoting fetal life." But the Act scarcely furthers that interest: The law saves not a single fetus from destruction, for it targets only a method of performing abortion. And surely the statute was not designed to protect the lives or health of pregnant women.

As another reason for upholding the ban, the Court emphasizes that the Act does not proscribe the nonintact D & E procedure. But why not, one might ask. Nonintact D & E could equally be characterized as "brutal," involving as it does "tear[ing] [a fetus] apart" and "ripp[ing] off" its limbs. "[T]he notion that either of these two equally gruesome procedures . . . is more akin to infanticide than the other, or that the State furthers any legitimate interest by banning one but not the other, is simply irrational."

Delivery of an intact, albeit nonviable, fetus warrants special condemnation, the Court maintains, because a fetus that is not dismembered resembles an infant. But so, too, does a fetus delivered intact after it is terminated by injection a day or two before the surgical evacuation or a fetus delivered through medical induction or cesarean. Yet, the availability of those procedures — along with D & E by dismemberment — the Court says, saves the ban on intact D & E from a declaration of unconstitutionality. Never mind that the procedures deemed acceptable might put a woman's health at greater risk.

Ultimately, the Court admits that "moral concerns" are at work, concerns that could yield prohibitions on any abortion. Notably, the concerns expressed are untethered to any ground genuinely serving the Government's interest in preserving life. By allowing such concerns to carry the day and case, overriding fundamental rights, the Court dishonors our precedent.

Revealing in this regard, the Court invokes an antiabortion shibboleth for which it concededly has no reliable evidence: Women who have abortions come to regret their choices, and consequently suffer from "[s]evere depression and loss of esteem." Because of women's fragile emotional state and because of the "bond of love the mother has for her child," the Court worries, doctors may withhold information about the nature of the intact D & E procedure. The solution the Court approves, then, is not to require doctors to inform women, accurately and adequately, of the different procedures and their attendant risks. Instead, the Court deprives women of the right to make an autonomous choice, even at the expense of their safety.

This way of thinking reflects ancient notions about women's place in the family and under the Constitution — ideas that have long since been discredited.

Though today's majority may regard women's feelings on the matter as "self-evident," ante, at 1634, this Court has repeatedly confirmed that "[t]he destiny of the woman must be shaped . . . on her own conception of her spiritual imperatives and her place in society."

B.

In cases on a "woman's liberty to determine whether to [continue] her pregnancy," this Court has identified viability as a critical consideration. "[T]here is no line [more workable] than viability," the Court explained in Casey for viability is "the time at which there is a realistic possibility of maintaining and nourishing a life outside the womb, so that the independent existence of the second life can in reason and all fairness be the object of state protection that now overrides the rights of the woman. . . .

In some broad sense it might be said that a woman who fails to act before viability has consented to the State's intervention on behalf of the developing child."

Today, the Court blurs that line, maintaining that "[t]he Act [legitimately] appl[ies] both previability and postviability because ... a fetus is a living organism while within the womb, whether or not it is viable outside the womb." Instead of drawing the line at viability, the Court refers to Congress' purpose to differentiate "abortion and infanticide" based not on whether a fetus can survive outside the womb, but on where a fetus is anatomically located when a particular medical procedure is performed.

One wonders how long a line that saves no fetus from destruction will hold in face of the Court's "moral concerns." The Court's hostility to the right *Roe* and *Casey* secured is not concealed. Throughout, the opinion refers to obstetrician-gynecologists and surgeons who perform abortions not by the titles of their medical specialties, but by the pejorative label "abortion doctor." A fetus is described as an "unborn child," and as a "baby," second-trimester, previability abortions are referred to as "late-term," and the reasoned medical judgments of highly trained doctors are dismissed as "preferences" motivated by "mere convenience." Instead of the heightened scrutiny we have previously applied, the Court determines that a "rational" ground is enough to uphold the Act. And, most troubling, *Casey* principles, confirming the continuing vitality of "the essential holding of *Roe*" are merely "assume[d]" for the moment, rather than "retained" or "reaffirmed."

. . . .

In 2016, a 5–4 majority found two Texas abortion-related provisions to be unconstitutional.

136 S. Ct. 2292
Supreme Court of the United States
WHOLE WOMEN'S HEALTH Et. Al.
v.
HELLERSTEDT, COMMISSIONER, TEXAS DEPARTMENT OF STATE HEALTH SERVICES, Et. Al.
Decided June 27, 2016.

. . . .

Justice BREYER delivered the opinion of the Court, in which Justices KENNEDY, GINSBURG, KAGAN, and SOTOMAYOR joined.

We must here decide whether two provisions of Texas' House Bill 2 violate the Federal Constitution as interpreted in *Casey*. The first provision, which we shall call the "*admitting-privileges requirement*," says that "[a] physician performing or inducing an abortion . . . must, on the date the abortion is performed or induced, have active admitting privileges at a hospital that . . . is located not further than 30 miles from the location at which the abortion is performed or induced." [. . .] The second provision, which we shall call the "*surgical-center requirement*," says that "the minimum standards for an abortion facility must be equivalent to the minimum standards . . . for ambulatory surgical centers."

We conclude that neither of these provisions confers medical benefits sufficient to justify the burdens upon access that each imposes.

[. . .] The rule announced in *Casey*, however, requires that courts consider the burdens a law imposes on abortion access together with the benefits.

[. . .] The Court, when determining the constitutionality of laws regulating abortion procedures, has placed considerable weight upon evidence and argument presented in judicial proceedings. In *Casey*, for example, we relied heavily on the District Court's factual findings and the research-based submissions of *amici*. [And] *Gonzales* [said] that the "*Court retains an independent constitutional duty to review factual findings where constitutional rights are at stake.*" *Ibid.* (emphasis added).

[. . .] The relevant statute here does not set forth any legislative findings. Rather, one is left to infer that the legislature sought to further a constitutionally acceptable objective (namely, protecting women's health). For a district court to give significant weight to evidence in the judicial record in these circumstances is consistent with this Court's case law.

The purpose of the admitting-privileges requirement is to help ensure that women have easy access to a hospital should complications arise during an abortion procedure. But the District Court found that it brought about no such health-related benefit.

[. . .] The evidence upon which the court based this conclusion included, among other things:

- A collection of at least five peer-reviewed studies on abortion complications in the first trimester, showing that the highest rate of major complications—including those complications requiring hospital admission—was less than one-quarter of 1%.

- Figures in three peer-reviewed studies showing that the highest complication rate found for the much rarer second trimester abortion was less than one-half of 1% (0.45% or about 1 out of about 200).

- Expert testimony to the effect that complications rarely require hospital admission, much less immediate transfer to a hospital from an outpatient clinic.

- Expert testimony stating that "it is extremely unlikely that a patient will experience a serious complication at the clinic that requires emergent hospitalization" and "in the rare case in which [one does], the quality of care that the patient receives is not affected by whether the abortion provider has admitting privileges at the hospital."

- Expert testimony stating that in respect to surgical abortion patients who do suffer complications requiring hospitalization, most of these complications occur in the days after the abortion, not on the spot.

- Expert testimony stating that a delay before the onset of complications is also expected for medical abortions, as "abortifacient drugs take time to exert their effects, and thus the abortion itself almost always occurs after the patient has left the abortion facility."

- Some experts added that, if a patient needs a hospital in the day or week following her abortion, she will likely seek medical attention at the hospital nearest her home.

We have found nothing in Texas' record evidence that shows that, compared to prior law, the new law advanced Texas' legitimate interest in protecting women's health.

[. . .] When directly asked at oral argument whether Texas knew of a single instance in which the new requirement would have helped even one woman obtain better treatment, Texas admitted that there was no evidence in the record of such a case.

At the same time, the record evidence indicates that the admitting-privileges requirement places a "substantial obstacle in the path of a woman's choice." *Casey*. [. . .] As of the time the admitting-privileges requirement began to be enforced, the number of facilities providing abortions dropped in half, from about 40 to about 20. Eight abortion clinics closed in the months leading up to the requirement's effective date.

Eleven more closed on the day the admitting-privileges requirement took effect.

[. . .] In our view, the record contains sufficient evidence that the admitting-privileges requirement led to the closure of half of Texas' clinics, or thereabouts. Those closures meant fewer doctors, longer waiting times, and increased crowding.

[. . .] There is considerable evidence in the record supporting the District Court's findings indicating that the statutory provision requiring all abortion facilities to meet all surgical-center standards does not benefit patients and is not necessary.

[. . .] The record makes clear that the surgical-center requirement provides no benefit when complications arise in the context of an abortion produced through medication. That is because, in such a case, complications would almost always arise only after the patient has left the facility. The record also contains evidence indicating that abortions taking place in an abortion facility are safe—indeed, safer than numerous procedures that take place outside hospitals and to which Texas does not apply its surgical-center requirements.

[. . .] Nationwide, childbirth is 14 times more likely than abortion to result in death, but Texas law allows a midwife to oversee childbirth in the patient's own home. Colonoscopy, a procedure that typically takes place outside a hospital (or surgical center) setting, has a mortality rate 10 times higher than an abortion. (The mortality rate for liposuction, another outpatient procedure, is 28 times higher than the mortality rate for abortion.) Medical treatment after an incomplete miscarriage often involves a procedure identical to that involved in a nonmedical abortion, but it often takes place outside a hospital or surgical center. And Texas partly or wholly grandfathers (or waives in whole or in part the surgical-center requirement for) about two-thirds of the facilities to which the surgical-center standards apply. But it neither grandfathers nor provides waivers for any of the facilities that perform abortions.

Moreover, many surgical-center requirements are inappropriate as applied to surgical abortions.

[. . .] The record provides adequate evidentiary support for the District Court's conclusion that the surgical-center requirement places a substantial obstacle in the path of women seeking an abortion. The parties stipulated that the requirement would further reduce the number of abortion facilities available to seven or eight facilities, located in Houston, Austin, San Antonio, and Dallas/Fort Worth. [. . .]

Justice THOMAS, dissenting.

[. . .] Whatever scrutiny the majority applies to Texas' law, it bears little resemblance to the undue-burden test the Court articulated in *Casey*.

First, today's decision requires courts to "consider the burdens a law imposes on abortion access together with the benefits those laws confer." Second, today's opinion tells the courts that, when the law's justifications are medically uncertain, they need not defer to the legislature, and must instead assess medical justifications for abortion restrictions by scrutinizing the record themselves. Finally, even if a law imposes no "substantial obstacle" to women's access to abortions, the law now must have more than a "reasonabl[e] relat[ion] to . . . a legitimate state interest." These precepts are nowhere to be found in *Casey* or its successors, and transform the undue-burden test to something much more akin to strict scrutiny.

Justice ALITO, with whom THE CHIEF JUSTICE and Justice THOMAS join, dissenting.

[. . .] While there can be no doubt that H.B. 2 caused some clinics to cease operation, the absence of proof regarding the reasons for particular closures is a problem because some clinics have or may have closed for [. . .] reasons other than the two H.B. 2 requirements at issue here.

[. . .] Even if the District Court had properly filtered out immaterial closures, its analysis would have been incomplete for a second reason. Petitioners offered scant evidence on the capacity of the clinics that are able to comply with the admitting privileges and ASC requirements, or on those clinics' geographic distribution. Reviewing the evidence in the record, it is far from clear that there has been a material impact on access to abortion.

[. . .] The other potential obstacle to abortion access is the distribution of facilities throughout the State. [. . .] If the only clinics in the State were those that would have remained open if the judgment of the Fifth Circuit had not been enjoined, roughly 95% of the women of reproductive age in the State would live within 150 miles of an open facility (or lived outside that range before H.B. 2).

[. . .] We should decline to hold that these statistics justify the facial invalidation of the H.B. 2 requirements.

---

5. Judicial Bypass

As noted earlier in this discussion, state restrictions prohibiting a minor from obtaining an abortion without parental consent without parental consent or judicial bypass have been upheld. Among the states which have enacted judicial bypass procedures is the State of Texas. The Texas statute is illustrative:

§ 33.003. Judicial Approval, Effective: May 21, 2011[43]

(a) A pregnant minor who wishes to have an abortion without notification to one of her parents, her managing conservator, or her guardian may file an application for a court order authorizing the minor to consent to the performance of an abortion without notification to either of her parents or a managing conservator or guardian.

(b) The application may be filed in any county court at law, court having probate jurisdiction, or district court, including a family district court, in this state.

(c) The application must be made under oath and include:

(1) a statement that the minor is pregnant;

(2) a statement that the minor is unmarried, is under 18 years of age, and has not had her disabilities removed under Chapter 31;

(3) a statement that the minor wishes to have an abortion without the notification of either of her parents or a managing conservator or guardian; and

(4) a statement as to whether the minor has retained an attorney and, if she has retained an attorney, the name, address, and telephone number of her attorney.

(d) The clerk of the court shall deliver a courtesy copy of the application made under this section to the judge who is to hear the application.

---

43. TEX. FAM. CODE ANN. § 33.003 (West).

(e) The court shall appoint a guardian ad litem for the minor. If the minor has not retained an attorney, the court shall appoint an attorney to represent the minor. If the guardian ad litem is an attorney admitted to the practice of law in this state, the court may appoint the guardian ad litem to serve as the minor's attorney.

(f) The court may appoint to serve as guardian ad litem:

(1) a person who may consent to treatment for the minor under Sections 32.001(a)(1)–(3);

(2) a psychiatrist or an individual licensed or certified as a psychologist under Chapter 501, Occupations Code;

(3) an appropriate employee of the Department of Family and Protective Services;

(4) a member of the clergy; or

(5) another appropriate person selected by the court.

(g) The court shall fix a time for a hearing on an application filed under Subsection (a) and shall keep a record of all testimony and other oral proceedings in the action. The court shall enter judgment on the application immediately after the hearing is concluded.

(h) The court shall rule on an application submitted under this section and shall issue written findings of fact and conclusions of law not later than 5 p.m. on the second business day after the date the application is filed with the court. On request by the minor, the court shall grant an extension of the period specified by this subsection. If a request for an extension is made, the court shall rule on an application and shall issue written findings of fact and conclusions of law not later than 5 p.m. on the second business day after the date the minor states she is ready to proceed to hearing. If the court fails to rule on the application and issue written findings of fact and conclusions of law within the period specified by this subsection, the application is deemed to be granted and the physician may perform the abortion as if the court had issued an order authorizing the minor to consent to the performance of the abortion without notification under Section 33.002. Proceedings under this section shall be given precedence over other pending matters to the extent necessary to assure that the court reaches a decision promptly.

(i) The court shall determine by a preponderance of the evidence whether the minor is mature and sufficiently well informed to make the decision to have an abortion performed without notification to either of her parents or a managing conservator or guardian, whether notification would not be in the best interest of the minor, or whether notification may lead to physical, sexual, or emotional abuse of the minor. If the court finds that the minor is mature and sufficiently well informed, that notification would not be in the minor's best interest, or that notification may lead to physical, sexual, or emotional abuse of the minor, the court shall enter an order authorizing the minor to consent to the performance of the abortion without notification to either of her parents or a managing conservator or guardian and shall execute the required forms.

(j) If the court finds that the minor does not meet the requirements of Subsection (i), the court may not authorize the minor to consent to an abortion without the notification authorized under Section 33.002(a)(1).

(k) The court may not notify a parent, managing conservator, or guardian that the minor is pregnant or that the minor wants to have an abortion. The court proceedings shall be conducted in a manner that protects the anonymity of the minor. The application and all other court documents pertaining to the proceedings are confidential and privileged and are not subject to disclosure under Chapter 552, Government Code, or to discovery, subpoena, or other legal process. The minor may file the application using a pseudonym or using only her initials.

(l) An order of the court issued under this section is confidential and privileged and is not subject to disclosure under Chapter 552, Government Code, or discovery, subpoena, or other legal process. The order may not be released to any person but the pregnant minor, the pregnant minor's guardian ad litem, the pregnant minor's attorney, another person designated to receive the order by the minor, or a governmental agency or attorney in a criminal or administrative action seeking to assert or protect the interest of the minor. The Supreme Court may adopt rules to permit confidential docketing of an application under this section.

(m) The clerk of the Supreme Court shall prescribe the application form to be used by the minor filing an application under this section.

(n) A filing fee is not required of and court costs may not be assessed against a minor filing an application under this section.

6. Abortion, Demographics, and Race

One major issue in the abortion controversy is to consider why women would choose to have an abortion. According to a study by the Guttmacher Institute, there are two major reasons. First, women are afraid that they will not be able to provide financially for the child. The second factor is that women do not want to be single mothers because of all of the difficulties that would involve. The Guttmacher study was performed and concluded in August 2008 examining data from 1974 to 2004. That study by Stanley K. Henshaw and Kathryn Kost, entitled *Trends in the Characteristics of Women Obtaining Abortions, 1974–2004*, noted that 49% of pregnancies in the United States during this time period were unintended. Half of those unintended pregnancies ended in abortion. Approximately 1 million abortions are performed each year, and the total number of abortions since *Roe* is in the vicinity of 50 million.[44]

Recently, however, there has been a downward trend in the number of abortions performed in the United States. According to the Guttmacher study abortions declined by 33% between 1974 and 2004. By 2005, the number of abortion providers had fallen to 1,787, down from a high of 2,908 in 1983.[45] It is possible that one of the causes for the reduction in abortion is the changing belief regarding the basic morality of abortion. In May 2009, a Gallup Poll revealed that for the first time in the entire 15 years that the Gallup Poll had asked the question, 51% of Americans identified themselves as believing that abortion was wrong.[46]

In 2014, a subsequent study of abortion rates published by the Guttmacher Institute revealed that the abortion rate in 2011 had fallen to 16.3 per 1,000 women between the ages 15 and 44, down from a high of 29.3 per 1,000 women in 1981. This represents the lowest rate since *Roe* in 1973 (16.3 per 1,000 women.)[47] Between 2008 and 2011, the rate of abortions and the total number of abortions (1.1 million in 2011) both fell by thirteen percent.[48]

According to a news release in 2017 by the Guttmacher Institute, the abortion rate continued its decline, reaching a historic low in 2014. Citing a 2014 study, the rate had dropped to 14.6 abortions for each 1,000 women in the United States between the ages of 15 and 44. That is the lowest rate ever noted. Fewer than one million abortions were performed in both 2013 and 2014. Those were the first years since *Roe v. Wade* that abortionists performed fewer than one million annual abortions in this country. While there were no definitive reasons cited for this decline, the authors of the report speculated that increased access to contraception, and new state-imposed restrictions might have produced the lower abortion rate and numbers.[49]

However, there is disturbing demographic aspect to abortion. The abortion ratio for African-American women is anywhere from 3 to 5 times the rate of white women. According to the 2008 Guttmacher study, African-American women received 37% of all abortions in 2004, non-Hispanic white women received 34% of the abortions, 22% of the abortions were performed upon Hispanic women, and

---

44. Stanley K. Henshaw & Kathryn Kost, *Trends in the Characteristics of Women Obtaining Abortions, 1974 to 2004*, GUTTMACHER INST. 7 (Aug. 2008), http://www.guttmacher.org/pubs/2008 /09/23/TrendsWomenAbortions-wTables.pdf (last visited Oct. 23, 2017).

45. *Id.* at 26-27.

46. Assoc. Press, *Majority of Americans Now 'Pro-Life,' Poll Says*, MSNBC (May 15, 2009), http:// msnbc.msn.com/id/30771408#.TsbazFbrFnA (last visited Oct. 23, 2017).

47. *U.S. Abortion Rate Hits Lowest Level Since 1973*, GUTTMACHER INST. (Feb. 3, 2014), http:// www.guttmacher.org/media/nr/2014/02/03/index.html (last visited Oct. 23, 2017).

48. *Id.*

49. Rebecca Wind, *U.S. Abortion Rate Continues to Decline, Hits Historic Low*, GUTTMACHER INSTITUTE (Jan. 17, 2017), https://www.guttmacher.org/news-release/2017/us-abortion-rate-continues -decline-hits-historic-low (last visited Nov. 4, 2017).

those among other races constituted 8%. Again, according to Guttmacher, the abortion rate among African-Americans was 50 per 1,000 live births, among Hispanics the ratio was 28 for every 1,000 live births, while among white women, 11 abortions were performed for each 1,000 live births.[50] In New York City, in 2012, many more African-American babies were aborted (31,328) than born (24,758).[51]

Some have suggested that this higher rate of abortions among African-Americans is more than coincidence. It appears to some that the proponents of eugenics and those early racist proponents of the legalization of abortion might have created a situation where African-American women are encouraged to receive abortions. Among African-American leaders who have expressed this concern is Ms. Alveda King, the niece of the late Dr. Martin Luther King, Jr. In July 2009, Ms. King wrote: "Let me begin by telling you that 2 of 50 million children taken away by abortionists since 1973 were mine. I can still see them in my mind's eye . . . like many Black women, I once believed the doctor who told me my babies were no more than 'a blob of tissue.' I wanted to believe it. Eventually, I realized I was wrong, that I was a secondary victim of abortion. I repented and found healing through God. Today, I work in the civil rights movement of our century—the right of everyone of every race to live. . . . I am asking you to join me. Let me tell you why. Abortion and racism are evil twins, born of the same lie. Though racism now hides its face in public, abortion is accomplishing the goals of which racism only once dreamed. . . . Abortion has taken a gruesome toll on the Black community. Some 14 million Black babies have been aborted since . . . *Roe.* That's equal to one-third of the number of Blacks living today. . . . Blacks comprise about 13% of the population, yet have 37% of all abortions."[52]

7. Harm to Women

Any woman facing an unintended pregnancy faces an extremely difficult choice. As we have observed, at least up to the point of viability, our legal system gives the woman the choices of either aborting the child or carrying the baby to full term. Either option involves physical and emotional risks to that woman. Most women will have at least some appreciation of the risks associated with the delivery of the child. It appears to many, including state legislators, that most women are not completely informed, however, of the physical and psychological harm that can be associated with an abortion. Doctors performing abortions, just as doctors who are present and assist in a live birth, will generally not inform their patients of all of the procedures

---

50. Henshaw & Kost, *supra* note 44, at 1, 12.

51. Michael W. Chapman, *NYC: More Black Babies Killed by Abortion Than Born*, CNSNews .com (Feb. 20, 2014, 12:31 PM), http://www.cnsnews.com/news/article/michael-w-chapman/nyc -more-black-babies-killed-abortion-born (last visited Oct. 23, 2017).

52. Alveda C. King, *The Abortionist's Eye is on Us: King's Niece Fights this Era's Civil Rights Battle*, Washington Times (July 20, 2009), http://www.washingtontimes.com/news/2009/jul/20/the -abortionists-eye-is-on-us/?page=all (last visited Oct. 23, 2017).

that will be involved. Nonetheless, it appears that in most instances doctors and even abortion counselors do not explain the psychological implications of an abortion. The reality is some women suffer emotionally as the result of an abortion. Whatever this suffering is called, be it post-abortion syndrome, conscience, or any other term, this suffering is so real that even those who generally favor giving women a right to choose abortion are aware of it. For example, in his writing, *The Audacity of Hope*, President Barack Obama identifies "the undeniably difficult issue of abortion and the middle-aged feminist who still mourns her abortion." Further, the Supreme Court of the United States concluded in the *Carhart* case, "[w]hile we have no reliable data to measure the phenomenon, it seems unexceptional to conclude some women come to regret their choice to avoid the infant life they once created and sustained. . . . Severe depression and loss of esteem can follow."[53]

Some argue that if women are truly to be able to exercise a "choice" it should be an informed choice. That means women contemplating an abortion should be provided with the information necessary for them to understand exactly the procedure that will follow. They believe that women should be informed of the physiological risks and psychological risks. Some states, pursuant to *Casey*, have provided various levels of notification and waiting periods. The State of Texas, in August 2011, attempted to implement a program requiring that women be required to undergo a sonogram and be given the opportunity to view the sonogram. However, a federal judge held the law an unconstitutional violation of the physician's First Amendment rights and unconstitutionally vague.[54] The court also determined that:

> The Act does not compel physicians to apprise women of the risks inherent in abortion, inform the women of available alternatives, and facilitate access to additional information if the women wish to review it before making their decisions; existing Texas law already compels such speech by physicians, in conformity with [*Planned Parenthood of S.E. Pennsylvania v.*] *Casey.* Instead, the Act compels physicians to advance an ideological agenda with which they may not agree, regardless of any medical necessity, and irrespective of whether the pregnant women wish to listen.[55]

However, on January 10, 2012, on appeal, a three-judge panel of the Fifth Circuit Court of Appeals overturned the district court's decision and upheld the constitutionality of the Texas Woman's Right to Know statute. TEX. HEALTH & SAFETY CODE ANN. § 171.012 (West 2012). The Fifth Circuit panel clarified the background of the statute:

---

53. Gonzales v. Carhart, 550 U.S. 124, 159 (2007).

54. Texas Med. Providers Performing Abortion Services v. Lakey, No. A–11–CA–486–SS, 2011 WL 3818879, at *1, 23 (W.D. Tex. Aug. 30, 2011).

55. Texas Med. Providers Performing Abortion Services v. Lakey, No. A–11–CA–486–SS, 2011 WL 3818879, at *30 (W.D. Tex. Aug. 30, 2011), *rev'd*, No. 11-50814, 2012 WL 45413, *1 (5th Cir. Jan. 10, 2012).

H.B. 15, passed in May 2011, substantially amended the 2003 Texas Woman's Right to Know Act ("WRKA"). The amendments challenged here are intended to strengthen the informed consent of women who choose to undergo abortions. The amendments require the physician "who is to perform an abortion" to perform and display a sonogram of the fetus, make audible the heart auscultation of the fetus for the woman to hear, and explain to her the results of each procedure and to wait 24 hours, in most cases, between these disclosures and performing the abortion. TEX. HEALTH & SAFETY CODE § 171.012(a)(4). A woman may decline to view the images or hear the heartbeat, § 171.0122(b), (c), but she may decline to receive an explanation of the sonogram images only on certification that her pregnancy falls into one of three statutory exceptions.

Any woman seeking an abortion must also complete a form indicating that she has received the required materials, understands her right to view the requisite images and hear the heart auscultation, and chooses to receive an abortion. § 171.012(a)(5). The physician who is to perform the abortion must maintain a copy of this form, generally for seven years.

If a woman ultimately chooses not to receive an abortion, the physician must provide her with a publication discussing how to establish paternity and secure child support. § 171.0123.

Finally, the Act amended the Texas Occupations Code to deny or revoke a physician's license for violating these provisions. . . .

Texas Med. Providers Performing Abortion Services v. Lakey, 667 F.3d 570, 573 (5th Cir. 2012).

The Court then examined the *Casey* approach:

The law at issue in Casey required an abortion provider to inform the mother of the relevant health risks to her and the "probable gestational age of the unborn child." The woman also had to certify in writing that she had received this information and had been informed by the doctor of the availability of various printed materials "describing the fetus and providing information about medical assistance for childbirth, information about child support from the father, and a list of agencies which provide adoption and other services as alternatives to abortion." Planned Parenthood contended that all of these disclosures operate to discourage abortion and, by compelling the doctor to deliver them, violated the physician's First Amendment free-speech rights. . . .

The *Casey* plurality's opinion concluded that such provisions, entailing "the giving of truthful, nonmisleading information" which is "relevant . . . to the decision," did not impose an undue burden on the woman's right to an abortion and were thus permitted by the Fourteenth Amendment. The requirement that the physician relay the probable age of the fetus furthered the legitimate end of "ensur[ing] that a woman apprehend the full consequences of her decision." In other words, "informed choice need not be defined in such narrow terms that all considerations of the effect on the fetus are made irrelevant." As the Court noted, such information "furthers the legitimate purpose of reducing the risk that a woman may elect an abortion, only to discover later, with devastating psychological consequences, that her decision was not fully informed." . . .

Texas Med. Providers Performing Abortion Services v. Lakey, 667 F.3d at 574-75 (5th Cir 2012).

Finally, applying the principles in *Casey*, the circuit court determined that the Texas Woman's Right to Know statute was a constitutionally valid means of promoting the informed consent approved in *Casey*.

> Applying to H.B. 15 the principles of *Casey*'s plurality, the most reasonable conclusion is to uphold the provisions declared as unconstitutional compelled speech by the district court. To belabor the obvious and conceded point, the required disclosures of a sonogram, the fetal heartbeat, and their medical descriptions are the epitome of truthful, non-misleading information. They are not different in kind, although more graphic and scientifically up-to-date, than the disclosures discussed in *Casey* — probable gestational age of the fetus and printed material showing a baby's general prenatal development stages. Likewise, the relevance of these disclosures to securing informed consent is sustained by *Casey* and *Gonzales*, because both cases allow the state to regulate medical practice by deciding that information about fetal development is "relevant" to a woman's decision-making.

> As for the woman's consent form, that, too, is governed by *Casey*, which approves the practice of obtaining written consent "as with any medical procedure." H.B. 15, § 171.012(a)(5), requires that a pregnant woman certify in writing her understanding that (1) Texas law requires an ultrasound prior to obtaining an abortion, (2) she has the option to view the sonogram images, (3) she has the option to hear the fetal heartbeat, and (4) she is required to hear the medical explanation of the sonogram unless she falls under the narrow exceptions to this requirement.

> . . . .

> For all these reasons, we conclude that the enumerated provisions of H.B. 15 requiring disclosures and written consent are sustainable under *Casey*, are within the State's power to regulate the practice of medicine, and therefore do not violate the First Amendment. . . .

Texas Med. Providers Performing Abortion Services v. Lakey, 667 F.3d at 578, 580 (5th Cir 2012).

Perhaps this educational aspect should be available earlier in life so that women are able to make an informed choice without the immediate pressure of an existing pregnancy. If women, young women, or even teenage girls, were made aware of the emotional and physical challenges that any woman faces in pregnancy, coupled with some realistic assessment of what happens during an abortion and the physical and emotional problems that might result, and including some ability to understand the difficulty of raising children, they might opt to defer pregnancy until circumstances exist which offer the child the best opportunities in life. In this regard, both the legal system and the Catholic Church, operating in their respective roles could assist in an educational program which would reduce the number of unintended pregnancies. However, any government attempt to force the Catholic Church, or entities affiliated with it, to provide contraceptives or abortion services, which are in violation of the fundamental teachings of the church, will likely be met with an uproar. This occurred in January 2012, when the Obama Administration tried, unsuccessfully, to impose such a mandate. See Chapter 5 for a discussion of this recent event.

Is there a possibility that an educational approach could substantially eliminate abortion? Half of the pregnancies in this country today are unintended, and half of those result in abortion. Virtually all abortions occur because of unintended pregnancy. Therefore, abortion could be essentially eliminated by avoiding unplanned pregnancy. Of course, there would be no reason to limit this education to young women and girls. Young men would also benefit from understanding the tremendous responsibility facing pregnant women. They must recognize that men must financially support their children by law and Church mandate. Perhaps most importantly, they must know they will have absolutely no voice in the abortion decision regarding any child they might create.

B. Stem Cell Research

Just as the Catholic Church condemns the practice of abortion, it is also opposed to stem cell research where that research involves the killing of a human embryo. The encyclical *Evangelium Vitae* makes this prohibition explicit in paragraph 63:

> 63. This evaluation of the morality of abortion is to be applied also to the recent forms of intervention on human embryos which, although carried out for purposes legitimate in themselves, inevitably involve the killing of those embryos. This is the case with experimentation on embryos, which is becoming increasingly widespread in the field of biomedical research and is legally permitted in some countries. Although "one must uphold as licit procedures carried out on the human embryo which respect the life and integrity of the embryo and do not involve disproportionate risks for it, but rather are directed to its healing, the improvement of its condition of health, or its individual survival," it must nonetheless be stated that the use of human embryos or fetuses as an object of experimentation constitutes a crime against their dignity as human beings who have a right to the same respect owed to a child once born, just as to every person.

This moral condemnation also regards procedures that exploit living human embryos and fetuses—sometimes specifically "produced" for this purpose by in vitro fertilization—either to be used as "biological material" or as providers of organs or tissue for transplants in the treatment of certain diseases. The killing of innocent human creatures, even if carried out to help others, constitutes an absolutely unacceptable act.[56]

However, it is important to note that the Church is not opposed to stem cell research involving somatic stem cells, that is stem cells collected from adults (bone marrow, tissue, organ mesenchyme), umbilical cord blood, and amniotic fluid. Pope Benedict clearly stated that "somatic stem-cell research . . . deserves approval and encouragement when it felicitously combines scientific knowledge, the most advanced technology in the biological field and ethics that postulate respect for the human being at every stage of his or her existence."[57] In 2010, the Catholic Church entered a joint initiative with NeoStem, an American company developing stem cell therapies through use of adult stem cells.[58] The Church's official position on the matter of stem cell research is:

32. With regard to the ethical evaluation, it is necessary to consider the *methods of obtaining stem cells* as well as *the risks connected with their clinical and experimental use.*

In these methods, the origin of the stem cells must be taken into consideration. Methods which do not cause serious harm to the subject from whom the stem cells are taken are to be considered licit. This is generally the case when tissues are taken from: a) an adult organism; b) the blood of the umbilical cord at the time of birth; c) fetuses who have died of natural causes. The obtaining of stem cells from a living human embryo, on the other hand, invariably causes the death of the embryo and is consequently gravely illicit: "research, in such cases, irrespective of efficacious therapeutic results, is not truly at the service of humanity. In fact, this research advances through the suppression of human lives that are equal in dignity to the lives of other human individuals and to the lives of the researchers themselves. History itself has condemned such a science in the past and will condemn it in the future, not only because it lacks the light of God but also because it lacks humanity."

56. Pope John Paul II, *supra* note 1, at ¶ 62.

57. Pope Benedict XVI, *Address to the Participants in the Symposium on the Theme "Stem Cells: What Future for Therapy?" Organized by the Pontifical Academy for Life* (Sept. 16, 2006), http://www.vatican.va/holy_father/benedict_xvi/speeches/2006/september/documents/hf_ben-xvi_spe_20060916_pav_en.html (last visited Oct. 23, 2017).

58. Press Release, NeoStem, Inc., *Breakthrough: The Pontifical Council for Culture and NeoStem Partner to Advance Adult Stem Cell Research* (May 19, 2010), http://www.prnewswire.com/news-releases/breakthrough-the-pontifical-council-for-culture-and-neostem-partner-to-advance-adult-stem-cell-research 94235474.html (last visited Oct. 23, 2017).

The use of embryonic stem cells or differentiated cells derived from them—even when these are provided by other researchers through the destruction of embryos or when such cells are commercially available—presents serious problems from the standpoint of cooperation in evil and scandal.

There are no moral objections to the clinical use of stem cells that have been obtained licitly; however, the common criteria of medical ethics need to be respected. Such use should be characterized by scientific rigor and prudence, by reducing to the bare minimum any risks to the patient and by facilitating the interchange of information among clinicians and full disclosure to the public at large.

Research initiatives involving the use of adult stem cells, since they do not present ethical problems, should be encouraged and supported.[59]

Removing Barriers to Responsible Scientific Research Involving Human Stem Cells reflects the official policy of the United States Government as ordered by President Obama in 2009.[60] The Executive Order provides:

By the authority vested in me as President by the Constitution and the laws of the United States of America, it is hereby ordered as follows:

Sec. 1. Policy. Research involving human embryonic stem cells and human non-embryonic stem cells has the potential to lead to better understanding and treatment of many disabling diseases and conditions. Advances over the past decade in this promising scientific field have been encouraging, leading to broad agreement in the scientific community that the research should be supported by federal funds.

For the past 8 years, the authority of the Department of Health and Human Services, including the National Institutes of Health (NIH), to fund and conduct human embryonic stem cell research has been limited by Presidential actions. The purpose of this order is to remove these limitations on scientific inquiry, to expand NIH support for the exploration of human stem cell research, and in so doing to enhance the contribution of America's scientists to important new discoveries and new therapies for the benefit of humankind.

Sec. 2. Research. The Secretary of Health and Human Services (Secretary), through the Director of NIH, may support and conduct responsible, scientifically worthy human stem cell research, including human embryonic stem cell research, to the extent permitted by law.

---

59. Congregation for the Doctrine of the Faith, *Instruction Dignitas Personae on Certain Bioethical Questions* ¶ 32 (Sept. 8, 2008), http://www.vatican.va/roman_curia/congregations/cfaith/documents/rc_con_cfaith_doc_20081212_sintesi-dignitas-personae_en.html (last visited Oct. 23, 2017).

60. Exec. Order No, 13505, 74 C.F.R. 10,667–68 (Mar. 11, 2009).

Sec. 3. Guidance. Within 120 days from the date of this order, the Secretary, through the Director of NIH, shall review existing NIH guidance and other widely recognized guidelines on human stem cell research, including provisions establishing appropriate safeguards, and issue new NIH guidance on such research that is consistent with this order. The Secretary, through NIH, shall review and update such guidance periodically, as appropriate. . . . [61]

President Obama's Executive Order revoked that of President George W. Bush, which denied embryonic stem cell research. As a result of President Obama's Order and the subsequent funding guidelines promulgated by NIH, two stem cell researchers filed suit in Federal District Court. The case also provides a thorough discussion on the history of stem cell research in the United States.

766 F. Supp. 2d 1
United States District Court, District of Columbia.

Dr. James L. SHERLEY, et al., Plaintiffs,
v.
Kathleen SEBELIUS, et al., Defendants.

July 27, 2011.

. . . .

Memorandum Opinion

ROYCE C. LAMBERTH, Chief Judge.

. . . .

II. Background

The human body comprises over 200 different cell types—muscle cells, skin cells, nerve cells, and so on—that perform all of its particular functions. These specialized cells, however, are all the descendants of a pool of unspecialized cells in the early human embryo, which divide, grow, and transform into all of the body's cells in a manner whose orderliness and complexity boggles the mind. This case involves those unspecialized cells, called "embryonic stem cells," which can be transformed into any one of the hundreds of cell types found in the human body.

Embryonic stem cells are one of three types of human stem cells, with the other two being adult and induced pluripotent stem cells. Embryonic stem cells are found in human embryos, and are made available for scientific research by a process—called "derivation"—that destroys the embryo. Once embryonic stem cells are derived, they can be used to create "lines" of stem cells that replicate indefinitely and provide a constant source of cells for research purposes. A second type of stem

---

61. *Id.* at 10,667.

cell—adult stem cells—are, unlike embryonic stem cells, "limited to producing only certain types of specialized cells," and "are found in certain tissues in fully developed humans, from babies to adults." The third type of stem cell—induced pluripotent stem cells—are mature cells that have been "reprogrammed" using viruses so that their development reverses course, returning them to a condition similar to that of embryonic stem cells. Like embryonic stem cells, induced pluripotent stem cells can transform into hundreds of specialized human cells, although just how similar induced pluripotent stem cells are to embryonic stem cells remains unknown.

Scientific interest in stem cells is driven by the recognition that, because they can be coaxed into forming particular body tissues, they hold the potential to advance medical science dramatically. Scientists hope to develop treatments for numerous diseases and conditions that continue to plague human beings—such as cancer, diabetes, and cardiovascular disease—by using stem cells to replace or rebuild damaged cells and tissues. *Id.* Since adult stem cells were first discovered in the 1950s, scientists have achieved success using such cells to develop treatments for human disease. But embryonic and induced pluripotent stem cells have only been available for scientific study since 1998, and so proven and safe therapeutic options involving these cell types are likely to require substantial additional research and time. Given the differences between the various stem cell types and their advantages and disadvantages as sources of potential therapies, the National Institutes of Health ("NIH") "believes that it is important to simultaneously pursue all lines of research."

Controversy has surrounded embryonic stem cell research since 1998, when scientists first succeeded in isolating and culturing stem cells from human embryos. In 1999, the NIH, finding that embryonic stem cells were "enormously important to science" and held "great promise for advances in health care," requested public comment on draft guidelines for funding embryonic stem cell research "in an ethical and legal manner." The NIH recognized that the establishment of stem cell lines from embryos had "generated much interest among scientists and the public, particularly among patients and their advocates, especially with regard to the ethical issues related to this research."

Funding embryonic stem cell research with taxpayers' dollars raised legal issues as well. Federal funding potentially conflicted with a Congressional law, first enacted in 1996, known as the "Dickey-Wicker Amendment." That Amendment, reenacted every year since 1996 without alteration, prohibits the NIH from funding:

> (1) the creation of a human embryo or embryos for research purposes; or

> (2) research in which a human embryo or embryos are destroyed, discarded, or knowingly subjected to risk of injury or death greater than that allowed for research on fetuses in utero under 45 CFR 46.204(b) and section 498(b) of the Public Health Service Act (42 U.S.C. 289g(b)).

The Dickey-Wicker Amendment defines "embryo" as "any organism, not protected as a human subject under 45 C.F.R. 46 as of the date of the enactment of this Act, that is derived by fertilization, parthenogenesis, cloning, or any other means from one or more human gametes or human diploid cells."

Aware of possible conflict between the NIH's plan to fund embryonic stem cell research and the Dickey-Wicker Amendment, the Director of the NIH requested a legal opinion in 1998 from the Office of the General Counsel of the Department of Health and Human Services ("HHS") on "whether NIH funds may be used for research using human pluripotent stem cells." The NIH received that opinion in January 1999, in the form of a memorandum from government attorney Harriet S. Rabb. Ms. Rabb concluded that the NIH could legally fund embryonic stem cell research. She wrote that although the Dickey-Wicker Amendment prohibited funding for research involving embryos, embryonic stem cells "are not a human embryo" as defined by the Amendment. Ms. Rabb noted that the Dickey-Wicker Amendment defined an "embryo" as an "organism," and that scientific understanding recognized a distinction between the basic units of living creatures, such as stem cells, that cannot exist independently of the body for long, and organisms themselves, which perform on their own all of the life functions that allow them to grow and reproduce. She determined that stem cells "are not even precursors to human organisms," because stem cells can only develop into different cell types within the human body, while embryos can potentially develop into human organisms. Based on Ms. Rabb's legal advice, the Director of the NIH convened a Working Group of the Advisory Committee to the Director to develop "appropriate guidelines governing . . . research involving the use of pluripotent stem cells derived from early human embryos in excess of clinical need."

The guidelines were published in August 2000. National Institutes of Health Guidelines for Research Using Human Pluripotent Stem Cells. The NIH had received about 50,000 public comments from "members of Congress, patient advocacy groups, scientific societies, religious organizations, and private citizens" in response to its guidelines. Some commenters argued that the guidelines conflicted with the Dickey-Wicker Amendment; that they were too restrictive; that they were unnecessary; or that research on human embryonic stem cells was itself unnecessary because adult stem cells were satisfactory substitutes. In response to commenters who questioned the NIH's decision to fund embryonic stem cell research in addition to adult stem cell research, the NIH concluded that "it is important to simultaneously pursue all lines of promising research," and presented a number of differences between adult and embryonic stem cells that warranted research on the latter. The final guidelines required applicants for NIH grants to provide assurance that the stem cells used in the research were derived from only certain human embryos. Embryos slated for derivation had to be "created for the purposes of fertility treatment" and "in excess of the clinical need of the individuals seeking such treatment." Various other conditions in the guidelines were designed to ensure that the embryo donor's consent was voluntary and informed.

A change in Presidential administrations resulted in a significant change to federal stem cell policy. In August 2001, President George W. Bush stated in an evening address to the nation that "[e]mbryonic stem cell research offers both great promise and great peril." He recognized that this research "could help improve the lives of those who suffer from many terrible diseases." He noted that the United States has a long history of advancing science and medicine, as well as a "proud record of upholding the highest standards of ethics" while expanding science's limits. Embryonic stem cell research, President Bush stated, "raises profound ethical questions" because the derivation process destroys the embryo from which stem cells are derived, therefore "destroy[ing] its potential for life." "Like a snowflake, each of these embryos is unique, with the unique genetic potential of an individual human being."

Torn between his confidence in the healing power of science and his belief that "human life is a sacred gift from our Creator," President Bush made what many have called a "Solomonic" decision: to permit federal funding for embryonic stem cell research, but only for such research as involved stem cells derived from embryos that had already been destroyed, where "the life and death decision has already been made." Like the previous administration, President Bush refused to impose a categorical ban on embryonic stem cell research, but he substituted a temporal limitation in the place of the embryo source and informed consent limitations reflected in the NIH's then-current guidelines. Federal funding was available only for embryonic stem cell research using stem cells derived from embryos that were destroyed before August 9, 2001 — the date of President Bush's address to the nation.

Since President Bush's policy continued to permit some federal funding for embryonic stem cell research, once again there were questions concerning whether even that, more restrictive, policy complied with the Dickey-Wicker Amendment. Dr. Ruth Kirchstein, then Acting Director of the NIH, received a legal opinion on the issue in January 2002 from HHS General Counsel, Alex M. Azar II. Mr. Azar concluded that President Bush's policy was consistent with the plain language of the Dickey-Wicker Amendment. He looked to the ordinary and common meaning of the phrase "research in which" used in the text of the Amendment. *Id*. Mr. Azar cited to a dictionary that defined "in" as meaning "within the confines of; inside"; "within the area covered by"; "during the course of or before the expiration of"; "during or part of the act or process of"; "within the category or class of." He did not specifically define the term "research." Mr. Azar concluded that since President Bush's policy would provide federal funding only for stem cell lines created before his August 9, 2001 address and because it "provides no incentive for the destruction of additional embryos," the policy "does not provide federal funding for 'research in which [during the course of, during or part of the act or process of, or within the category or class of] embryos are destroyed, discarded, or knowingly subjected to risk of injury or death. . . .'"

The winds of federal stem cell policy shifted again in 2008, with the election of Barack Obama as President. In March 2009, President Obama issued an Executive Order nullifying former President Bush's stem cell policy. The Order's purpose was to remove President Bush's limitations on the NIH's ability to fund and conduct human embryonic stem cell research, thereby "enhanc[ing] the contribution of America's scientists to important new discoveries and new therapies for the benefit of humankind." President Obama authorized the NIH to "support and conduct responsible, scientifically worthy human stem cell research, including human embryonic stem cell research, to the extent permitted by law." He directed the NIH to publish new guidelines on human stem cell research consistent with his Order within 120 days.

Several weeks later, the NIH requested public comment on draft guidelines. The NIH stated that the purpose of the draft guidelines was to implement President Obama's Executive Order, "to establish policy and procedures under which NIH will fund research in this area, and to help ensure that NIH-funded research in this area is ethically responsible, scientifically worthy, and conducted in accordance with applicable law." The proposed guidelines would permit funding for embryonic stem cell research using stem cells derived from embryos created for reproductive purposes and no longer needed for that purpose. They also contained provisions ensuring that research funds would only go to research projects using stem cells that were derived from embryos that had been donated with the informed consent of the donor. As such, these proposed guidelines represented a return to the policy and funding approach that existed before President Bush's administration.

The NIH, as it had back in 2000, received nearly 50,000 comments in response to its draft guidelines. In its final Guidelines, the NIH responded to certain categories of public comments that it had received, including comments indicating that the informed consent procedures set out in the draft guidelines were duplicative with existing procedures or too cumbersome, that the allowable sources of embryonic stem cells should be expanded to embryos created solely for research purposes, and that the NIH's mechanisms for ensuring ongoing compliance with the guidelines were lacking.

In the course of responding to comments seeking clarification of its statement in the draft guidelines that embryonic stem cells "are not themselves human embryos," the NIH presented its longstanding interpretation of the Dickey-Wicker Amendment as not prohibiting federal funding for embryonic stem cell research because human embryonic stem cells "are not embryos" as defined by the Amendment. The NIH stated further that the Guidelines "recognize the distinction, accepted by Congress, between the derivation of stem cells from an embryo that results in the embryo's destruction, for which federal funding is prohibited, and research involving [human embryonic stem cells] that does not involve an embryo nor result in an embryo's destruction, for which federal funding is permitted."

The NIH also received numerous comments objecting to any federal funding whatsoever for embryonic stem cell research. Commenters sought a categorical ban on embryonic stem cell research either for ethical or scientific reasons, or both. The NIH did not respond to such comments, believing them to be outside the scope of the rulemaking. The NIH made minor revisions to the draft guidelines in response to certain comments, and then published the final Guidelines, with an effective date of July 7, 2009.

A legal challenge to the Guidelines came swiftly. In August 2009, a group of plaintiffs, including Drs. James L. Sherley and Theresa Deisher—both of whom are scientists performing research involving adult stem cells—filed a lawsuit in this Court against various defendants, including the National Institutes of Health. Plaintiffs claimed that the Guidelines violated the Dickey-Wicker Amendment and were promulgated in violation of the Administrative Procedure Act. Compl. [1] ¶¶ 1, 2. They sought declarations that the Guidelines are not in accordance with law, were promulgated without the observance of required procedures, are arbitrary and capricious, and that past acts by the NIH pursuant to the Guidelines, including previous decisions to fund embryonic stem cell research projects, are null and void. They also sought to enjoin defendants from taking any future actions of any kind pursuant to the Guidelines or otherwise funding embryonic stem cell research. That same day, they filed a Motion for Preliminary Injunction seeking an immediate cessation of actions taken pursuant to the Guidelines.

Defendants filed a Motion to Dismiss, arguing that plaintiffs lacked standing under Article III of the Constitution and that they had failed to state a claim for which relief could be granted. This Court granted defendants' motion, concluding that no plaintiff met all of the requirements of standing and that therefore the Court lacked subject matter jurisdiction over the lawsuit. With respect to Drs. Sherley and Deisher, the Court noted that they had alleged in their Complaint that the Guidelines had increased competition for limited NIH funds and would therefore make it more difficult for them to compete successfully for those funds. The Court found, however, that mere "increased competition for funding is an insufficient injury to impart standing."

Plaintiffs appealed, challenging only this Court's determination that Drs. Sherley and Deisher lacked standing. The Court of Appeals for the District of Columbia reversed, finding that both Dr. Sherley and Dr. Deisher had standing. It held that Drs. Sherley and Deisher suffered an "actual, here-and-now injury" because "the Guidelines have intensified the competition for a share in a fixed amount of money," with the result that "plaintiffs will have to invest more time and resources to craft a successful grant application." The Court reversed this Court's Order dismissing plaintiffs' claims while also reinstating plaintiffs' Motion for Preliminary Injunction.

With plaintiffs' Motion for Preliminary Injunction ripe for decision, this Court promptly ruled and found that "the likelihood of success on the merits, irreparable harm to plaintiffs, the balance of the hardships, and public interest considerations each weigh in favor of a preliminary injunction." In particular, this Court concluded that the Guidelines violated the Dickey-Wicker Amendment's prohibition on federal funding for "research in which a human embryo or embryos are destroyed." This Court determined that the term "research" had "only one meaning, i.e., 'a systematic investigation, including research development, testing and evaluation, designed to develop or contribute to generalizable knowledge.'" Rejecting defendants' argument that "research" meant "a piece of research," this Court found that the

Dickey-Wicker Amendment's prohibition "encompasses all 'research in which' an embryo is destroyed, not just the 'piece of research' in which the embryo is destroyed." After concluding that embryonic stem cell research is research in which an embryo is destroyed according to the Dickey-Wicker Amendment, this Court held that the Guidelines violated that Amendment and that plaintiffs had shown a strong likelihood of success on the merits. This Court applied the other preliminary injunction factors, found them to be satisfied, and granted plaintiffs' motion.

Defendants sought and received a stay of this Court's injunction from the D.C. Circuit, which later vacated the injunction on appeal. Contrary to this Court's conclusion, the Court of Appeals held that "plaintiffs are unlikely to prevail [on the merits] because Dickey-Wicker is ambiguous and the NIH seems reasonably to have concluded that, although Dickey-Wicker bars funding for the destructive act of deriving an [embryonic stem cell] from an embryo, it does not prohibit funding a research project in which an [embryonic stem cell] will be used." The Court determined that the meaning of the word "research" is "flexible enough to describe either a discrete project or an extended process."

. . . While noting that defendants had not defined "research" in so many words, the Court rejected plaintiffs' contention that defendants had not offered an interpretation warranting judicial deference by concluding that NIH's use of the term "research" implicitly gave it a narrow scope. After concluding that the NIH's implicit interpretation was reasonable, the Court held that plaintiffs had failed to show that they were likely to succeed on the merits and that the other preliminary injunction factors weighed against the award of a preliminary injunction.

With the preliminary injunction order vacated by the Court of Appeals, the lawsuit returned to this Court for review of the parties' competing motions for summary judgment.

. . . .

B. Whether the Guidelines Violate the Dickey-Wicker Amendment.

. . . Defendants seek judicial deference to their interpretation of the Dickey-Wicker Amendment under the standard articulated in *Chevron U.S.A. Inc. v. Natural Resources Defense Council, Inc.*, 467 U.S. 837 (1984). The D.C. Circuit has summarized the *Chevron* standard as follows:

Under the *Chevron* analysis, judicial review of an agency's interpretation of a statute under its administration is limited to a two-step inquiry. At the first step, we inquire into whether Congress has directly spoken to the precise question at issue. If we can come to the unmistakable conclusion that Congress had an intention on the precise question at issue, our inquiry ends there; this Court naturally must give effect to the unambiguously expressed intent of Congress.

However, if the statute before us is silent or ambiguous with respect to the specific issue before us, we proceed to the second step. At this stage, we defer to the agency's interpretation of the statute if it is reasonable and consistent with the statute's purpose; we are not free to impose our own construction on the statute, as would be necessary in the absence of an administrative interpretation.

. . . .

1. "Research in which a human embryo or embryos are destroyed . . ."

a. *Chevron* step one.

Chevron requires the Court to consider whether Congress, in the Dickey-Wicker Amendment, has provided an answer to the following question: whether embryonic stem cell research is "research in which a human embryo or embryos are destroyed. . . ." Plaintiffs argue that by funding embryonic stem cell research, the Guidelines violate this provision of the Dickey-Wicker Amendment. They contend that the statute's prohibition against "funding any 'research in which' embryos are destroyed necessarily encompasses all of the research project at issue, not merely a selected 'phase' or 'piece' of research."

. . . .

Therefore the D.C. Circuit's conclusion that the term "research" in the Dickey-Wicker Amendment is ambiguous binds this Court.

b. *Chevron* step two.

Since the Dickey-Wicker Amendment doesn't answer the precise question at issue because "research" has been determined to be ambiguous in the statute, the Court must proceed to step two of *Chevron*, which requires deference to the NIH's interpretation of the Dickey-Wicker Amendment if it is "based on a permissible construction of the statute."

. . . .

The D.C. Circuit's opinion, unfortunately for plaintiffs, has taken the question of deference to the NIH's interpretation off the table. The Court of Appeals considered the question of deference to the NIH's interpretation of the Dickey-Wicker Amendment, and found that deference was due. The Court determined that the NIH's use of the term "research" in the Guidelines implicitly but unequivocally gave [it] a narrow scope, thus ensuring no federal funding will go to a research project in which an embryo is destroyed on the question of whether NIH's implicit, narrower definition of "research" was reasonable, the Court of Appeals looked to the surrounding terms— such as Congress's use of "in which" and "are" instead of "for which" and "were"— as well as Congress's reenactment of the Dickey-Wicker Amendment year after year despite its knowledge that the NIH had been funding embryonic stem cell research since 2001, to conclude that the NIH's interpretation was "entirely reasonable."

. . . .

Therefore this Court, following the D.C. Circuit's reasoning and conclusions, must find that defendants reasonably interpreted the Dickey-Wicker Amendment to permit funding for human embryonic stem cell research because such research is not "research in which a human embryo or embryos are destroyed. . . ."

2. "Research in which a human embryo or embryos are . . . knowingly subjected to risk of injury or death . . ."

Plaintiffs also argue that embryonic stem cell research violates the Dickey-Wicker Amendment's prohibition on funding "research in which a human embryo or embryos are . . . knowingly subjected to risk of injury or death. . . ."

. . . .

Therefore the Court concludes that it must proceed to step two of Chevron because the plain text of the Dickey-Wicker Amendment doesn't answer the question of whether embryonic stem cell research is "research in which a human embryo or embryos are . . . knowingly subjected to risk of injury or death. . . ."

b. *Chevron* step two.

Since the Dickey-Wicker Amendment doesn't answer the question of whether embryonic stem cell research is "research in which a human embryo or embryos are . . . knowingly subjected to risk," the Court must defer to the NIH's interpretation of the Amendment if it is based upon a permissible construction of the statute.

. . . .

The conclusion that the NIH reasonably interpreted the Dickey-Wicker Amendment's "knowingly subjected to risk" language to permit federal funding for embryonic stem cell research follows naturally once "research" is narrowly defined. The NIH reasonably concluded that the Dickey-Wicker Amendment prohibited federal funding for research projects "in which" human embryos are knowingly subjected to risk, such as preimplantation genetic diagnosis, but did not prohibit research projects, such as embryonic stem cell research, that do not involve embryos and so cannot knowingly subject them to risk "in" the research. As stated in the Court's consideration of Chevron step one, Congress had available to it alternative formulations— such as "from which" or "as a result of which"—that would have indicated an intent to prohibit research projects that, while not involving embryos, nevertheless knowingly subjected them to risk. Congress, however, did not choose those words, preferring "in which" and leading the NIH to the reasonable conclusion that the Dickey-Wicker Amendment is only concerned with research involving embryos.

. . . .

The Executive Order is titled "Removing Barriers to Responsible Scientific Research Involving Human Stem Cells." The Order is short, and has five sections. Section 1 (titled "Policy") explains that human stem cell research, including embryonic stem cell research, may lead to advances in medical science and that the purpose of the Order is to remove limitations placed upon embryonic stem cell research by previous Presidential actions. Section 2 (titled "Research") states that the "Secretary of Health and Human Services . . . , through the Director of NIH, may support and conduct responsible, scientifically worthy human stem cell research, including embryonic stem cell research, to the extent permitted by law." Section 3 of the Order ("Guidance") orders the Secretary to issue new guidance on human stem cell research "that is consistent with this order." Section 4 ("General Provisions") states that the Order "shall be implemented consistent with applicable law," and contains some other provisions. Finally, Section 5 ("Revocations") orders that one of former President Bush's statements on stem cell policy would have no further effect and that one of his executive orders concerning embryonic stem cell research is revoked.

The purpose of President Obama's Order, as it clearly states, "is to remove . . . limitations" on the "authority of the Department of Health and Human Services, including the National Institutes of Health," "to fund and conduct human embryonic stem cell research. . . ." The "limitations" President Obama is talking about were the result of "Presidential actions"—specifically, the actions of then-President George W. Bush. President Obama nullified two such actions: (1) President Bush's statement of August 9, 2001, which permitted federal funding only for research using embryonic stem cell lines already in existence at the time of the statement, which supplemented President Bush's August 9, 2001 statement.

It is crucial to note that even President Bush permitted federal funding of embryonic stem cell research. He did not categorically ban such funding, finding necessarily that some forms of embryonic stem cell research are ethically responsible and scientifically worthy. However, President Bush specifically limited the availability of federal funds to embryonic stem cell research projects involving stem cell lines that were already in existence and "where the life and death decision has already been made."

President Obama's Order removes this specific temporal limitation, thereby permitting funding for embryonic stem cell research projects—whether they involve stem cells from already-destroyed embryos or embryos to be destroyed in the future. The Order was not, as plaintiffs suggest, an invitation from President Obama to adopt a policy even more restrictive than his predecessor's by categorically prohibiting funding for any embryonic stem cell research projects. The question of whether embryonic stem cell research should be funded at all was not a question left on the table for the NIH by President Obama's Order. Indeed, had the NIH adopted plaintiffs' views and refused to consider funding any embryonic stem cell research projects, its regulation would have been inconsistent with the Executive Order and unlawful.

The consequences of President Obama's policy as presented in section 1 of the Executive Order are presented in its subsequent sections. Whereas before the Order issued, the NIH was prohibited from supporting human embryonic stem cell research using stem cell lines created after August 9, 2001 (pursuant to then-President Bush's policy), the NIH was now permitted to fund such research without regard to President Bush's temporal limitation. As President Obama stated, the "[NIH] may support and conduct responsible, scientifically worthy stem cell research, including human embryonic stem cell research, to the extent permitted by law." By permitting the NIH to fund "responsible, scientifically worthy . . . human embryonic stem cell research," the Order's language assumes that embryonic stem cell research is, in at least some cases, responsible and scientifically worthy, and grants permission to the NIH to support only such embryonic stem cell research as is "responsible" and "scientifically worthy." The Guidelines' embryo-source and informed consent restrictions—alongside its peer-review process—are, of course, the NIH's means of channeling federal funds to "responsible" and "scientifically worthy" embryonic stem cell research projects.

For these reasons, the NIH reasonably interpreted Executive Order 13,505, and operated consistently with both it and the APA's requirements when it disregarded tens of thousands of public comments that sought an outright ban on embryonic stem cell research. The NIH reasonably concluded, as expressed in the notice of proposed rulemaking, that the fundamental policy question of whether to provide federal funds for embryonic stem cell research wasn't a question for it to decide. That policy question is not answered by any Congressional law, and it has fallen on three Presidential administrations to provide an answer. For all three such administrations, Democratic and Republican, the answer has been to permit federal funding. They have differed only as to the path forward.

. . . .

C. Miscellaneous Life Issues

In 2008 the Congregation for the Doctrine of Faith issued its Instruction entitled *Dignitas Personae*,[62] meaning, the dignity of a person. The Instruction intended that this dignity should be "recognized in every human being from conception to natural death." It speaks to ethical concerns relating to biomedical research. The document was approved by Pope Benedict XVI.

In its second part, concerning "New Problems Concerning Procreation," the Instruction examines a number of new scientific techniques. First, is the topic of In Vitro Fertilization.[63] The Instruction notes that in all such techniques, "the number of embryos sacrificed is extremely high" reaching as high as more than 80%. It condemns the deliberate destruction of embryos in this process as being contrary to the "sacred and inviolable character of every human life from its conception until its natural end."

Another technique examined in the Instruction is that of Intra Cytoplasmic Sperm Injection (ICSI).[64] In this technique, fertilization in the test tube does not occur on its own. Rather, the genetic material of a sperm is injected resulting in fertilization.

---

62. Congregation for the Doctrine of the Faith, *Instruction Dignitas Personae on Certain Bioethical Questions* (June 20, 2008), http://www.vatican.va/roman_curia/congregations/cfaith/documents/rc_con_cfaith_doc_20081208_dignitas-personae_en.html (last visited Oct. 23, 2017).
63. *Id.* at ¶¶ 14-16.
64. *Id.* at ¶ 17.

It is another variety of in vitro procreation. The Instruction deems this technique also to be "morally illicit" because it "causes a complete separation between procreation and the conjugal act."

The Instruction also addresses the practice of freezing of embryos.[65] This process of cryopreservation of embryos at extremely low temperatures, allowing long-term storage, is also held to be illicit. The Instruction indicates that the process "exposes them (embryos) to the serious risk of death or physical harm since a high percentage does not survive the process of freezing and thawing; it deprives them at least temporarily of maternal reception and gestation; it places them in a situation in which they are susceptible to further offense and manipulation." Regarding the large number of frozen embryos which already exist, Pope John Paul II determined that "there seems to be no morally licit solution regarding the human destiny of the thousands and thousands of frozen embryos which are and remain the subjects of essential rights and should therefore be protected by law as human persons."

The Instruction also addressed the issue of freezing of oocytes.[66] The Instruction indicates that the cryopreservation of oocytes "is not in itself immoral." However, if those frozen oocytes are used in the other techniques discussed in the document then it would be considered "morally unacceptable."

Another technique examined in the Instruction is that of preimplantation diagnosis.[67] In this technique, embryos formed *in vitro* are examined for their genetic structure before being implanted in a woman's womb. That diagnosis occurs "in order to ensure that only embryos free from defects or having the desired sex or other particular qualities are transferred." The Instruction condemns treating the human embryo in this fashion. It concludes that this technique is "immoral and unjust."

Other methods of preventing pregnancy which act after the act of fertilization has taken place are condemned by the Instruction. These include both an intrauterine device and "morning after pills."[68] The Instruction notes that not every act of intercourse results in contraception. Nonetheless "anyone who seeks to prevent the implementation of an embryo which may possibly have been conceived and who therefore either requests or prescribes such a pharmaceutical generally intends abortion." The abortion of an embryo which has been implanted falls, according to the Instruction within the sin of abortion.

However, not all assisted fertility techniques are condemned by the Instruction. Those which are held to be permissible are those that "respect the right to life and a physical integrity of every human being, the unity of marriage . . . which means reciprocal respect for the right within marriage to become a father or mother only

---

65. *Id.* at ¶¶ 18-19.
66. *Id.* at ¶ 20.
67. *Id.* at ¶ 22.
68. Congregation for the Doctrine of the Faith, *Instruction Dignitas Personae on Certain Bioethical Questions* at ¶ 23 (June 20, 2008), http://www.vatican.va/roman_curia/congregations/cfaith/documents/rc_con_cfaith_doc_20081208_dignitas-personae_en.html (last visited Oct. 23, 2017).

together with the other spouse . . . and the specifically human values of sexuality which require that the procreation of a new human person come about as the result of a conjugal act specific to the love between a husband and a wife." Thus, "techniques which act as an aid to the conjugal act in its fertility are permitted."

The Instruction discusses the topic of gene therapy, meaning, "techniques of genetic engineering applied to human beings for therapeutic purposes, that is to say, with the aim of curing genetically based diseases, although recently gene therapy has been attempted for diseases which are not inherited, for cancer in particular."[69] The Instruction identifies as licit, somatic gene cell therapy, while condemning germ line cell therapy. The Instruction states:

> In theory, it is possible to use gene therapy on two levels: somatic cell gene therapy and germ line cell therapy. *Somatic cell gene therapy* seeks to eliminate or reduce genetic defects on the level of somatic cells, that is, cells other than the reproductive cells, but which make up the tissue and organs of the body. It involves procedures aimed at certain individual cells with effects that are limited to a single person. *Germ line cell therapy* aims instead at correcting genetic defects present in germ line cells with the purpose of transmitting the therapeutic effects to the offspring of the individual. Such methods of gene therapy, whether somatic or germ line cell therapy, can be undertaken on a fetus *before his or her birth* as gene therapy in the uterus or *after birth* on a child or adult.
>
> 26. For a moral evaluation the following distinctions need to be kept in mind. *Procedures used on somatic cells for strictly therapeutic purposes are in principle morally licit.* Such actions seek to restore the normal genetic configuration of the patient or to counter damage caused by genetic anomalies or those related to other pathologies. Given that gene therapy can involve significant risks for the patient, the ethical principle must be observed according to which, in order to proceed to a therapeutic intervention, it is necessary to establish beforehand that the person being treated will not be exposed to risks to his health or physical integrity which are excessive or disproportionate to the gravity of the pathology for which a cure is sought. The informed consent of the patient or his legitimate representative is also required.
>
> The moral evaluation of *germ line cell therapy* is different. Whatever genetic modifications are effected on the germ cells of a person will be transmitted to any potential offspring. Because the risks connected to any genetic manipulation are considerable and as yet not fully controllable, *in the present state of research, it is not morally permissible to act in a way that may cause possible harm to the resulting progeny.* In the hypothesis of gene therapy on the embryo, it needs to be added that this only takes place

---

69. *Id.* at ¶ 25.

in the context of *in vitro* fertilization and thus runs up against all the ethical objections to such procedures. For these reasons, therefore, it must be stated that, in its current state, germ line cell therapy in all its forms is morally illicit.[70]

Another issue addressed by the Instruction is the utilization of genetic engineering for other purposes. Paragraph 27 states,

> 27. *The question of using genetic engineering for purposes other than medical treatment also calls for consideration.* Some have imagined the possibility of using techniques of genetic engineering to introduce alterations with the presumed aim of improving and strengthening the gene pool. Some of these proposals exhibit a certain dissatisfaction or even rejection of the value of the human being as a finite creature and person. Apart from technical difficulties and the real and potential risks involved, such manipulation would promote a eugenic mentality and would lead to indirect social stigma with regard to people who lack certain qualities, while privileging qualities that happen to be appreciated by a certain culture or society; such qualities do not constitute what is specifically human. This would be in contrast with the fundamental truth of the equality of all human beings which is expressed in the principle of justice, the violation of which, in the long run, would harm peaceful coexistence among individuals. Furthermore, one wonders who would be able to establish which modifications were to be held as positive and which not, or what limits should be placed on individual requests for improvement since it would be materially impossible to fulfill the wishes of every single person. Any conceivable response to these questions would, however, derive from arbitrary and questionable criteria. All of this leads to the conclusion that the prospect of such an intervention would end sooner or later by harming the common good, by favouring the will of some over the freedom of others. Finally it must also be noted that in the attempt to create *a new type of human being* one can recognize *an ideological element* in which man tries to take the place of his Creator.[71]

Continuing with the discussion of controversial scientific experimentation, the Instruction considers, and condemns, human cloning:

> 28. Human cloning refers to the asexual or agametic reproduction of the entire human organism in order to produce one or more "copies" which, from a genetic perspective, are substantially identical to the single original.
>
> Cloning is proposed for two basic purposes: *reproduction*, that is, in order to obtain the birth of a baby, and *medical therapy* or research. In theory, reproductive cloning would be able to satisfy certain specific desires, for example, control over human evolution, selection of human beings with

---

70. *Id.* at ¶¶ 25–26.
71. *Id.* at ¶ 27.

superior qualities, pre-selection of the sex of a child to be born, production of a child who is the "copy" of another, or production of a child for a couple whose infertility cannot be treated in another way. Therapeutic cloning, on the other hand, has been proposed as a way of producing embryonic stem cells with a predetermined genetic patrimony in order to overcome the problem of immune system rejection; this is therefore linked to the issue of the use of stem cells.

Attempts at cloning have given rise to genuine concern throughout the entire world. Various national and international organizations have expressed negative judgments on human cloning and it has been prohibited in the great majority of nations.

Human cloning is intrinsically illicit in that, by taking the ethical negativity of techniques of artificial fertilization to their extreme, it seeks to *give rise to a new human being without a connection to the act of reciprocal self-giving between the spouses* and, more radically, *without any link to sexuality.* This leads to manipulation and abuses gravely injurious to human dignity.

29. If cloning were to be done for *reproduction,* this would impose on the resulting individual a predetermined genetic identity, subjecting him—as has been stated—to a form of *biological slavery,* from which it would be difficult to free himself. The fact that someone would arrogate to himself the right to determine arbitrarily the genetic characteristics of another person represents *a grave offense to the dignity of that person as well as to the fundamental equality of all people.*

The originality of every person is a consequence of the particular relationship that exists between God and a human being from the first moment of his existence and carries with it the obligation to respect the singularity and integrity of each person, even on the biological and genetic levels. In the encounter with another person, we meet a human being who owes his existence and his proper characteristics to the love of God, and only the love of husband and wife constitutes a mediation of that love in conformity with the plan of the Creator and heavenly Father.

30. From the ethical point of view, so-called therapeutic cloning is even more serious. To create embryos with the intention of destroying them, even with the intention of helping the sick, is completely incompatible with human dignity, because it makes the existence of a human being at the embryonic stage nothing more than a means to be used and destroyed. It is *gravely immoral to sacrifice a human life for therapeutic ends.*

The ethical objections raised in many quarters to therapeutic cloning and to the use of human embryos formed *in vitro* have led some researchers to propose new techniques which are presented as capable of producing stem cells of an embryonic type without implying the destruction of true human embryos. These proposals have been met with questions of both a scientific and an ethical nature regarding above all the ontological status of the "product" obtained in this way. Until these doubts have been clarified, the statement of the Encyclical *Evangelium Vitae* needs to be kept in mind: "what is at stake is so important that, from the standpoint of moral obligation, the mere probability that a human person is involved would suffice to justify an absolutely clear prohibition of any intervention aimed at killing a human embryo."[72]

What about the attempts to blend animal genetic structure, with that of a human? The Instruction condemns these hybridization attempts:

33. Recently animal oocytes have been used for reprogramming the nuclei of human somatic cell—this is generally called *hybrid cloning*— in order to extract embryonic stem cells from the resulting embryos without having to use human oocytes.

From the ethical standpoint, such procedures represent an offense against the dignity of human beings on account of *the admixture of human and animal genetic elements capable of disrupting the specific identity of man*. The possible use of the stem cells, taken from these embryos, may also involve additional health risks, as yet unknown, due to the presence of animal genetic material in their cytoplasm. To consciously expose a human being to such risks is morally and ethically unacceptable.[73]

Finally, the Instruction examines "[t]he use of human 'biological material' of illicit origin":

34. For scientific research and for the production of vaccines or other products, cell lines are at times used which are the result of an illicit intervention against the life or physical integrity of a human being. The connection to the unjust act may be either mediate or immediate, since it is generally a question of cells which reproduce easily and abundantly. This "material" is sometimes made available commercially or distributed freely to research centers by governmental agencies having this function under the law. All of this gives rise to *various ethical problems with regard to cooperation in evil and with regard to scandal*. It is fitting therefore to formulate general principles on the basis of which people of good conscience can evaluate and resolve situations in which they may possibly be involved on account of their professional activity.

It needs to be remembered above all that the category of abortion "is to be applied also to the recent forms of *intervention on human embryos* which, although carried out for purposes legitimate in themselves, inevitably involve

---

72. *Id.* at ¶¶ 28–30.
73. *Id.* at ¶ 33.

the killing of those embryos. This is the case with *experimentation on embryos,* which is becoming increasingly widespread in the field of biomedical research and is legally permitted in some countries . . . [T]he use of human embryos or fetuses as an object of experimentation constitutes a crime against their dignity as human beings who have a right to the same respect owed to a child once born, just as to every person." These forms of experimentation always constitute a grave moral disorder.

35. A different situation is created when researchers use "biological material" of illicit origin which has been produced apart from their research center or which has been obtained commercially. The Instruction *Donum Vitae* formulated the general principle which must be observed in these cases: "The corpses of human embryos and fetuses, whether they have been deliberately aborted or not, must be respected just as the remains of other human beings. In particular, they cannot be subjected to mutilation or to autopsies if their death has not yet been verified and without the consent of the parents or of the mother. Furthermore, the moral requirements must be safeguarded that there be no complicity in deliberate abortion and that the risk of scandal be avoided."

In this regard, *the criterion of independence as it has been formulated by some ethics committees is not sufficient.* According to this criterion, the use of "biological material" of illicit origin would be ethically permissible provided there is a clear separation between those who, on the one hand, produce, freeze and cause the death of embryos and, on the other, the researchers involved in scientific experimentation. The criterion of independence is not sufficient to avoid a contradiction in the attitude of the person who says that he does not approve of the injustice perpetrated by others, but at the same time accepts for his own work the "biological material" which the others have obtained by means of that injustice. When the illicit action is endorsed by the laws which regulate healthcare and scientific research, it is necessary to distance oneself from the evil aspects of that system in order not to give the impression of a certain toleration or tacit acceptance of actions which are gravely unjust. Any appearance of acceptance would in fact contribute to the growing indifference to, if not the approval of, such actions in certain medical and political circles.

At times, the objection is raised that the above-mentioned considerations would mean that people of good conscience involved in research would have the duty to oppose actively all the illicit actions that take place in the field of medicine, thus excessively broadening their ethical responsibility. In reality, the duty to avoid cooperation in evil and scandal relates to their ordinary professional activities, which they must pursue in a just manner and by means of which they must give witness to the value of life by their opposition to gravely unjust laws. Therefore, it needs to be stated that there is a duty to refuse to use such "biological material" even when there is no close connection between the researcher and the actions of those who performed the artificial fertilization or the abortion, or when there was no prior agreement with the centers in which the artificial fertilization took place. This duty springs from the necessity to *remove oneself,* within the area of one's own research, *from a gravely unjust legal situation and to affirm with clarity the value of human life.* Therefore, the above-mentioned criterion of independence is necessary, but may be ethically insufficient.

Of course, within this general picture there exist *differing degrees of responsibility.* Grave reasons may be morally proportionate to justify the use of such "biological material." Thus, for example, danger to the health of children could permit parents to use a vaccine which was developed using cell lines of illicit origin, while keeping in mind that everyone has the duty to make known their disagreement and to ask that their healthcare system make other types of vaccines available. Moreover, in organizations where cell lines of illicit origin are being utilized, the responsibility of those who make the decision to use them is not the same as that of those who have no voice in such a decision.

In the context of the urgent need to *mobilize consciences in favour of life,* people in the field of healthcare need to be reminded that "their responsibility today is greatly increased. Its deepest inspiration and strongest support lie in the intrinsic and undeniable ethical dimension of the health-care profession, something already recognized by the ancient and still relevant *Hippocratic Oath*, which requires every doctor to commit himself to absolute respect for human life and its sacredness."[74]

The legal system has had a varied response to the phenomenon of human cloning. There is no blanket prohibition against cloning on a federal level in this country. State legislative schemes vary, depending upon whether the cloning activity is being carried on as research cloning, also referred to as "therapeutic" cloning, or whether it is being performed as reproductive cloning. The website of the National Conference of State Legislatures (NCSL) identifies fifteen states which have enacted laws restricting human cloning. Some of these prohibit both reproductive cloning and therapeutic cloning, while others only restrict reproductive cloning. States explicitly prohibiting reproductive cloning include Arkansas, Connecticut, Indiana, Iowa, Maryland, Massachusetts, Michigan, Rhode Island, New Jersey, North Dakota, South Dakota, and Virginia. Several states prohibit public funding of cloning, including

---

74. Congregation for the Doctrine of the Faith, *Instruction Dignitas Personae on Certain Bioethical Questions* at ¶¶ 34–35 (June 20, 2008), http://www.vatican.va/roman_curia/congregations /cfaith/documents/rc_con_cfaith_doc_20081208_dignitas-personae_en.html (last visited Oct. 23, 2017).

Arizona and Missouri. A table summarizing these state laws is available on the website of the NCSL.[75]

In 2005 the United Nations General Assembly adopted its United Nations Declaration on Human Cloning. The Declaration specifically provides:

(a) Member States are called upon to adopt all measures necessary to protect adequately human life in the application of life sciences;

(b) Member States are called upon to prohibit all forms of human cloning inasmuch as they are incompatible with human dignity and the protection of human life;

(c) Member States are further called upon to adopt the measures necessary to prohibit the application of genetic engineering techniques that may be contrary to human dignity;

(d) Member States are called upon to take measures to prevent the exploitation of women in the application of life sciences;

(e) Member States are also called upon to adopt and implement without delay national legislation to bring into effect paragraphs (a) to (d);

(f) Member States are further called upon, in their financing of medical research, including of life sciences, to take into account the pressing global issues such as HIV/ AIDS, tuberculosis and malaria, which affect in particular the developing countries.[76]

The United States voted in favor of the Declaration on Human Cloning. However, not all of our allies shared our vote.[77]

In Favor of the Declaration

Afghanistan, Albania, Andorra, Australia, Austria, Bahrain, Bangladesh, Belize, Benin, Bolivia, Bosnia and Herzegovina, Brunei, Darussalam, Burundi, Chile, Comoros, Costa Rica, Côte d'Ivoire, Croatia, Democratic Republic of the Congo, Djibouti, Dominican Republic, Ecuador, El Salvador, Equatorial Guinea, Eritrea, Ethiopia, Georgia, Germany, Grenada, Guatemala, Guyana, Haiti, Honduras, Hungary, Iraq, Ireland, Italy, Kazakhstan, Kenya, Kuwait, Lesotho, Liberia, Liechtenstein, Madagascar, Malta, Marshall Islands, Mauritius, Mexico, Micronesia (Federated States of), Monaco, Morocco, Nicaragua, Palau, Panama, Paraguay, Philippines, Poland, Portugal, Qatar, Rwanda, Saint Kitts and Nevis, Saint Lucia, Saint Vincent and the Grenadines, Samoa, San Marino, Sao Tome and Principe,

Continued on next page

---

75. Nat'l Conf. of State Leg. (NCSL), *Human Cloning Laws* (Jan. 2008), http://www.ncsl.org/research/health/genetic-privacy-laws.aspx (last visited Oct. 23, 2017).

76. G.A. Res. 59/280, Annex, U.N. Doc. A/ RES/ 59/ 280 (Mar. 8, 2005), http://www.nrlc.org/uploads/international/UN-GADeclarationHumanCloning.pdf (last visited Oct. 23, 2017).

77. U.N. GAOR, 59th Sess., 82d plen. Mtg., at 2–3, U.N. Doc. A/ 59/ PV.82 (Mar. 8, 2005), http://www.un.org/News/Press/docs/2005/ga10333.doc.htm (last visited Oct. 23, 2017).

Saudi Arabia, Sierra Leone, Slovakia, Slovenia, Solomon Islands, Sudan, Suriname, Switzerland, Tajikistan, the former Yugoslav Republic of Macedonia, Timor-Leste, Trinidad and Tobago, Uganda, United Arab Emirates, United Republic of Tanzania, United States of America, Uzbekistan, Zambia.

Against the Declaration

Belarus, Belgium, Brazil, Bulgaria, Cambodia, Canada, China, Cuba, Cyprus, Czech Republic, Democratic People's Republic of Korea, Denmark, Estonia, Finland, France, Gabon, Iceland, India, Jamaica, Japan, Lao People's Democratic Republic, Latvia, Lithuania, Luxembourg, Netherlands, New Zealand, Norway, Republic of Korea, Singapore, Spain, Sweden, Thailand, Tonga, United Kingdom of Great Britain and Northern Ireland.

Abstained from Voting

Algeria, Angola, Argentina, Azerbaijan, Bahamas, Barbados, Burkina Faso, Cameroon, Cape Verde, Colombia, Egypt, Indonesia, Iran, Israel, Jordan, Lebanon, Malaysia, Maldives, Mongolia, Myanmar, Namibia, Nepal, Oman, Pakistan, Republic of Moldova, Romania, Serbia and Montenegro, Somalia, South Africa, Sri Lanka, Syria, Tunisia, Turkey, Ukraine, Uruguay, Yemen, Zimbabwe.

Absent

Antigua and Barbuda, Armenia, Bhutan, Botswana, Central African Republic, Chad, Congo, Dominica, Fiji, Gambia, Ghana, Greece, Guinea, Guinea-Bissau, Kiribati, Kyrgyzstan, Libya, Malawi, Mali, Mauritania, Mozambique, Nauru, Niger, Nigeria, Papua New Guinea, Peru, Russian Federation, Senegal, Seychelles, Swaziland, Togo, Turkmenistan, Tuvalu, Vanuatu, Venezuela, Vietnam.

Representatives of the Member Nations were given the opportunity to explain their votes on the record. Zhang Yishan, Ambassador from China, explained his country's vote:

> The Chinese delegation voted against the Declaration because the Declaration's wording is too confusing, and the prohibition it contains could be misunderstood as applying to all research into therapeutic cloning. Thus, we cannot accept it. The Declaration is in no way legally binding on China.
>
> However, it should be stressed that the Chinese Government will maintain its stance against reproductive human cloning and will strengthen its regulation and control of research into therapeutic cloning in order to ensure that human dignity and the internationally shared ethical concept of human life will not be undermined.[78]

The British emissary, Sir Emyr Jones Parry, recorded:

> The General Assembly has missed another opportunity to adopt a convention prohibiting reproductive cloning. Why is that so? It is because of

---

78. *Id.* at 4.

the intransigence of those that were not prepared to recognize that other sovereign States, after extensive dialogue and due democratic process, may decide to permit strictly controlled applications of therapeutic cloning.

The United Kingdom is a strong supporter of therapeutic cloning research because it has the potential to revolutionize medicine in this century in the way that antibiotics did in the last. The United Kingdom Government announced this week more than $2 billion in funding over the next three years for biotechnology research, including stem cell research.

The Declaration voted upon today is a weak, nonbinding political statement that does not reflect anything approaching consensus within the General Assembly. Nor will it affect the United Kingdom's strong support of stem cell research.[79]

However, notwithstanding this Declaration, work on both human cloning, and cloning activity involving human-animal hybrids has continued in different locations around the world, including the United States, which thus far has no outright ban on cloning. A British paper, after reporting many such experiments in the United Kingdom, then noted:

Chinese scientists were reportedly the first to successfully create human-animal embryos. In 2003 a team at the Shanghai Second Medical University fused human cells with rabbit eggs. The embryos were allowed to develop for several days in a laboratory dish before being destroyed to harvest their stem cells. Later that same year, a US scientist, Panayiotis Zavos, announced he had created "human-cow" embryos that lived for around a fortnight and could theoretically have been implanted into a woman's womb.

In 2004 researchers at the Mayo Clinic in Minnesota produced pigs with hybrid pig-human blood cells. In 2005 Parkinson's disease researchers at the Salk Institute in San Diego reported they had created mice with 0.01% human cells by injecting about 100,000 human embryonic stem cells per mouse. Last year a Yale researcher, Eugene Redmond, led a project injecting millions of human neural stem cells into the brains of monkeys afflicted with Parkinson's disease. Many countries have banned this human-animal embryo research, including Australia, Canada, France, Germany and Italy.[80]

D. Eugenics and Sterilization

It is difficult to understate the impact that the concepts of eugenics as implemented through sterilization and later, euthanasia, have had in this country and in the world,

---

79. *Id.*

80. David Batty, *Q&A: Hybrid Embryos*, GUARDIAN, (May 19, 2008), http://www.guardian.co .uk/science/2007/may/17/genetics.health1 (last visited Oct. 23, 2017).

particularly during the 20th century. In the early 1900s concerns developed in the United States regarding the immigration of Europeans from eastern or southern Europe. Scholars began to determine that the supposed inferiorities of certain national origin groups would prevent these individuals from being what was considered "100% Americans." Edward Ross, a prominent nativist, characterized these new arrivals as "beaten men from beaten races representing the worst failures in the struggle for existence."[81]

By 1907, Congress established a joint congressional commission. The purpose of that commission, the Dillingham Commission, was to study the impact of immigration. The commission's report in 1911 drew heavily from the pseudo-scientific theories of influential nativists. It concluded that the new arrivals were largely so called "inferior peoples." Around the same time the "Americanization" movement began to take hold in the United States. The goal of limiting new arrivals from inferior national origin groups was accomplished as Congress enacted in 1924 the Nationals Origins Act. That act prohibited immigration from Japan; produced quotas based on the contributions of each nation to the existing U.S. population, and sought to restrain immigration from "inferior" southern and eastern Europeans in favor of immigration from northern Europe. However, those concerned with the appearance and identity of the people of the United States realized that limiting immigration among "inferiors" was only one part of a solution.

During the 1920s, eugenics developed. Eugenicists promoted a "scientific" theory that societal ills including promiscuity, alcoholism, and poverty were genetically transmitted defects. To improve the gene pool, the geneticists determined that those individuals with undesirable traits must be sterilized. Many prominent and wealthy citizens joined the movement including Dr. Clarence Gamble (Proctor & Gamble), James Hanes (Hanes Hosiery), and Margaret Sanger, one of the founders of Planned Parenthood. In 1927, the Supreme Court of the United States upheld a state imposed requirement of forced sterilizations (*see* case below). Justice Holmes, who is one of the most well-known jurists in American legal history, announced, "three generations of imbeciles are enough."[82] *Buck* has not been overturned. In *Buck*, the sterilization involved the involuntary sterilization of individuals with low intelligence.

In July 1933, these theories and practices were implemented in Nazi Germany through the German "Law for the Prevention of Hereditarily Diseased Offspring."[83] This legislation required that all individuals suffering from diseases and conditions

---

81. BILL PIATT, ONLY ENGLISH? LAW & LANGUAGE POLICY IN THE UNITED STATES 16 (1993).

82. Buck v. Bell, 274 U.S. 200, 208 (1927).

83. Dt. Gesetz zur Verhütung erbkranken Nachwuchses [German Law for the Prevention of Hereditarily Diseased Offspring] (July 14, 1933). *See generally "The Law for the Prevention of Hereditarily Diseased Offspring is a Truly Revolutionary Measure: Adolph Hitler, 1934,"* Museum of Contraception & Abortion (Vienna), http://en.muvs.org/topic/the-law-for-the-prevention-of-hereditarily-diseased-offspring-is-a-truly-revolutionary-measure-adolf-hitler-1934 (last visited Oct. 23, 2017) (referencing CLAUDIA ANDREA SPRING: ZWISCHEN KRIEG UND EUTHANASIE— ZWANGSSTERILISATIONEN IN WIEN 1940–1945 [BETWEEN WAR AND EUTHANASIA— FORCED STERILISATION IN VIENNA 1940] (2009)); *Nazi Persecution of the Disabled: Murder of "The Unfit,"* U.S.

believed to be hereditary, including blindness, deafness, alcoholism, mental illness, and severe physical malformation to be sterilized.[84] The disabled were referred to as "life unworthy of life" or "useless eaters."[85] The impact of this forced sterilization program, both in Germany and in the United States, was extensive. Between 1907 and 1939 approximately 30,000 people or more were sterilized in this country, although more than ten times that number were sterilized under the Nazi regime.[86]

However, while we are all too familiar with the horrors of Nazi Germany, the American sterilization continued in this country at least through the 1970s. For example, while the North Carolina Eugenics Board was dissolved in 1977, the official repeal of the involuntary sterilization provisions did not occur until 2003.[87] Between 1929 and 1974, it is estimated that "at least 7,600 people were sterilized by choice, force or coercion under the authority of the [North Carolina] Eugenics Board program."[88] Eighty-five percent of these individuals were female, and race-minority people constituted 40%. Officials of North Carolina estimate that there are still as many as 2,000 victims of forced sterilization still alive. A public hearing was conducted in the summer of 2011 in North Carolina. NBC reported on the North Carolina eugenics program and efforts to locate and compensate victims. In their broadcast, they shared the story of one victim:

> Elaine Riddick was 13 years old when she got pregnant after being raped by a neighbor in Winfall, N.C., in 1967. The state ordered that immediately after giving birth, she should be sterilized. Doctors cut and tied off her fallopian tubes.
>
> . . . .
>
> Riddick was never told what was happening. "Got to the hospital and they put me in a room and that's all I remember, that's all I remember," she said. "When I woke up, I woke up with bandages on my stomach."
>
> Riddick's records reveal that a five-person state eugenics board in Raleigh had approved a recommendation that she be sterilized. The records label Riddick as "feebleminded" and "promiscuous." They said her schoolwork was poor and that she "does not get along well with others."
>
> . . . .

Holocaust Mem'l Museum, https://www.ushmm.org/information/exhibitions/online-exhibitions /special-focus/nazi-persecution-of-the-disabled (last visited Oct. 23, 2017).

84. MICHAEL BURLEIGH, THE THIRD REICH: A NEW HISTORY 354 (2001).

85. U.S. Holocaust Mem'l Museum, *Euthanasia Program*, http://www.ushmm.org/wlc/en /article.php?ModuleId=10005200 (last visited Oct. 23, 2017); U.S. Holocaust Mem'l Museum, *The Murder of the Handicapped*, http://www.ushmm.org/outreach/en/article.php?ModuleId=10007683 (last visited Oct. 23, 2017).

86. *Id.*

87. NC Justice for Sterilization Victims Found., http://www.sterilizationvictims.nc.gov/default .aspx (last visited Oct. 23, 2017).

88. Brochure, N.C. Justice for Sterilization Victims Found. (Oct. 2010), http://www.sterilization-victims.nc.gov/documents/NCJSVF-brochure.pdf (last visited Oct. 23, 2017).

It wouldn't be until Riddick was 19, married and wanting more children, that she'd learn she was incapable of having any more babies. A doctor in New York where she was living at the time told her that she'd been sterilized.

"Butchered. The doctor used that word—I didn't understand what she meant when she said I had been butchered," Riddick said.[89]

The North Carolina provisions were initially designed to control welfare spending, the focus shifted to targeting African Americans. Undoubtedly, the programs in other states operated under the same principle of eugenics.

As a concluding matter to this introduction on the discussion of eugenics and sterilization, some would note that after initiating a forced sterilization program, the German government authorized the performing of eugenic abortions beginning in 1935.[90] Those abortions were authorized to those limited to eugenic purposes and only through the six month of pregnancy. Those in favor of abortion rights in this country continued to cite eugenics as a justification for abortion, even late term abortion. *The New York Times* reported in December 2009 that "abortion rights advocates say the need exists for late term abortions, in cases of extraordinary genetic defects. . . ."[91] This discussion, of course, would move us back into the abortion realm and away from sterilization and eugenics. So, with this brief introduction, we turn to a discussion of the position of the Catholic Church regarding sterilization.

The Catholic Church is profoundly opposed to the practice of eugenics. As Pope Benedict explained:

The disapproval of eugenics used with violence by a state regime or as the result of hatred for a race or a people is so deeply rooted in consciences that it was formally expressed in the *Universal Declaration of Human Rights*. Despite this, still today disturbing manifestations of this odious practice that presents itself with various features are appearing. Of course, the eugenic and racial ideologies that humiliated man in the past and caused tremendous suffering are not being proposed again, but a new mentality is being introduced that tends to justify a different view of life and personal dignity founded on personal desires and individual rights. Hence there is a tendency to give priority to functional ability, efficiency, perfection and physical beauty

89. *Rock Center with Bryan Williams* (NBC television broadcast Nov. 7, 2011), with accompanying article by Michelle Kessel & Jessica Hopper, *Victims Speak Out About North Carolina Sterilization Program, Which Targeted Women, Young Girls and Blacks*, Rock Center—MSNBC (Nov. 7, 2011), http://rockcenter.msnbc.msn.com/_news/2011/11/07/8640744-victims-speak-out-about-north-carolina-sterilization-program-which-targeted-women-young-girls-and-blacks (last visited Oct. 23, 2017) (containing links to videos from the broadcast).

90. Burleigh, *supra* note 84.

91. Monica Davey, *Abortion Battle Shifts to Clinic in Nebraska*, N.Y. Times (Dec. 3, 2009), at A1, http://www.nytimes.com/2009/12/04/us/04abortion.html (last visited Oct. 23, 2017).

to the detriment of life's other dimensions which are deemed unworthy. The respect that is due to every human being, even bearing a developmental defect or a genetic disease that might manifest itself during life, is thus weakened while children whose life is considered not worth living are penalized from the moment of conception.

It is necessary to reiterate that every form of discrimination practised by any authority with regard to persons, peoples or races on the basis of differences traceable to real or presumed genetic factors is an attack on the whole of humanity. What must be strongly reaffirmed is the equal dignity of every human being by the very fact that he has been born. A person's biological, mental and cultural development or state of health must never become a discriminatory factor. On the contrary, it is necessary to consolidate the culture of acceptance and love showing real solidarity toward those who suffer. It must break down the barriers that society often builds by discriminating against those who are disabled or affected by pathologies, or, worse, even reaching the selection and rejection of life in the name of an abstract ideal of health and physical perfection.[92]

The *Catechism* also directly speaks against eugenics. It says:

2268. The fifth commandment forbids *direct and intentional killing* as gravely sinful. The murderer and those who cooperate voluntarily in murder commit a sin that cries out to heaven for vengeance.

Infanticide, fratricide, parricide, and the murder of a spouse are especially grave crimes by reason of the natural bonds which they break. Concern for eugenics or public health cannot justify any murder, even if commanded by public authority.[93]

There can be little doubt that when Pope Pius XI denounced eugenics in 1930, he was specifically prompted by the activities of the American Eugenics Society and the 1927 Supreme Court decision in *Buck v. Bell*. Pope Pius XI simply stated:

66. What is asserted in favor of the social and eugenic "indication" may and must be accepted, provided lawful and upright methods are employed within the proper limits; but to wish to put forward reasons based upon them for the killing of the innocent is unthinkable and contrary to the divine precept promulgated in the words of the Apostle: Evil is not to be done that good may come of it.[94]

---

92. Pope Benedict XVI, *Address to the Members of the Pontifical Academy for Life on the Occasion of the 15th General Assembly* (Feb. 21, 2009), http://www.vatican.va/holy_father/benedict_xvi /speeches/2009/february/documents/hf_ben-xvi_spe_20090221_accademia-vita_en.html (last visited Oct. 23, 2017).
93. CATECHISM OF THE CATH. CHURCH, *supra* note 10.
94. Pope Pius XI, *supra* note 8, at ¶ 66.

274 U.S. 200 / 47 S. Ct. 584
Supreme Court of the United States

BUCK

v.

BELL, Superintendent of State Colony Epileptics and Feeble Minded.

Decided May 2, 1927

Opinion

Mr. Justice HOLMES delivered the opinion of the Court.

This is a writ of error to review a judgment of the Supreme Court of Appeals of the State of Virginia, affirming a judgment of the Circuit Court of Amherst County, by which the defendant in error, the superintendent of the State Colony for Epileptics and Feeble Minded, was ordered to perform the operation of salpingectomy upon Carrie Buck, the plaintiff in error, for the purpose of making her sterile. The case comes here upon the contention that the statute authorizing the judgment is void under the Fourteenth Amendment as denying to the plaintiff in error due process of law and the equal protection of the laws.

Carrie Buck is a feeble-minded white woman who was committed to the State Colony above mentioned in due form. She is the daughter of a feeble-minded mother in the same institution, and the mother of an illegitimate feeble-minded child. She was eighteen years old at the time of the trial of her case in the Circuit Court in the latter part of 1924. An Act of Virginia approved March 20, 1924 recites that the health of the patient and the welfare of society may be promoted in certain cases by the sterilization of mental defectives, under careful safeguard, etc.; that the sterilization may be effected in males by vasectomy and in females by salpingectomy, without serious pain or substantial danger to life; that the Commonwealth is supporting in various institutions many defective persons who if now discharged would become a menace but if incapable of procreating might be discharged with safety and become self-supporting with benefit to themselves and to society; and that experience has shown that heredity plays an important part in the transmission of insanity, imbecility, etc. The statute then enacts that whenever the superintendent of certain institutions including the above named State Colony shall be of opinion that it is for the best interest of the patients and of society that an inmate under his care should be sexually sterilized, he may have the operation performed upon any patient afflicted with hereditary forms of insanity, imbecility, etc., on complying with the very careful provisions by which the act protects the patients from possible abuse.

The superintendent first presents a petition to the special board of directors of his hospital or colony, stating the facts and the grounds for his opinion, verified by affidavit. Notice of the petition and of the time and place of the hearing in the institution is to be served upon the inmate, and also upon his guardian, and if there is no guardian the superintendent is to apply to the Circuit Court of the County to appoint one. If the inmate is a minor notice also is to be given to his parents, if any, with a copy of the petition. The board is to see to it that the inmate may attend the hearings if desired by him or his guardian. The evidence is all to be reduced to writing, and after the board has made its order for or against the operation, the superintendent, or the inmate, or his guardian, may appeal to the Circuit Court of the County. The Circuit Court may consider the record of the board and the evidence before it and such other admissible evidence as may be offered, and may affirm, revise, or reverse the order of the board and enter such order as it deems just. Finally any party may apply to the Supreme Court of Appeals, which, if it grants the appeal, is to hear the case upon the record of the trial in the Circuit Court and may enter such order as it thinks the Circuit Court should have entered. There can be no doubt that so far as procedure is concerned the rights of the patient are most carefully considered, and as every step in this case was taken in scrupulous compliance with the statute and after months of observation, there is no doubt that in that respect the plaintiff in error has had due process at law.

The attack is not upon the procedure but upon the substantive law. It seems to be contended that in no circumstances could such an order be justified. It certainly is contended that the order cannot be justified upon the existing grounds. The judgment finds the facts that have been recited and that Carrie Buck 'is the probable potential parent of socially inadequate offspring, likewise afflicted, that she may be sexually sterilized without detriment to her general health and that her welfare and that of society will be promoted by her sterilization,' and thereupon makes the order. In view of the general declarations of the Legislature and the specific findings of the Court obviously we cannot say as matter of law that the grounds do not exist, and if they exist they justify the result. We have seen more than once that the public welfare may call upon the best citizens for their lives. It would be strange if it could not call upon those who already sap the strength of the State for these lesser sacrifices, often not felt to be such by those concerned, in order to prevent our being swamped with incompetence. It is better for all the world, if instead of waiting to execute degenerate offspring for crime or to let them starve for their imbecility, society can prevent those who are manifestly unfit from continuing their kind. The principle that sustains compulsory vaccination is broad enough to cover cutting the Fallopian tubes. Three generations of imbeciles are enough.

But, it is said, however it might be if this reasoning were applied generally, it fails when it is confined to the small number who are in the institutions named and is not applied to the multitudes outside. It is the usual last resort of constitutional arguments to point out shortcomings of this sort. But the answer is that the law does all that is needed when it does all that it can, indicates a policy, applies it to all within the lines, and seeks to bring within the lines all similarly situated so far and so fast as its means allow. Of course so far as the operations enable those who otherwise must be kept confined to be returned to the world, and thus open the asylum to others, the equality aimed at will be more nearly reached.

Judgment affirmed.

———————

Mr. Justice BUTLER dissents.

[n.b. Justice Butler did not write a dissenting opinion.]

———————

The Supreme Court again addressed the issue of sterilization, this time in the context of criminal behavior, in 1942.

═══════════════════

316 U.S. 535 / 62 S. Ct. 1110
Supreme Court of the United States

SKINNER
v.
STATE OF OKLAHOMA ex rel. WILLIAMSON, Atty. Gen. of Oklahoma

Decided June 1, 1942

. . . .

Opinion

Mr. Justice DOUGLAS delivered the opinion of the Court.

This case touches a sensitive and important area of human rights. Oklahoma deprives certain individuals of a right which is basic to the perpetuation of a race- the right to have offspring. . . .

The statute involved is Oklahoma's Habitual Criminal Sterilization Act. That Act defines an 'habitual criminal' as a person who, having been convicted two or more times for crimes 'amounting to felonies involving moral turpitude' either in an Oklahoma court or in a court of any other State, is thereafter convicted of such a felony in Oklahoma and is sentenced to a term of imprisonment in an Oklahoma penal institution. Machinery is provided for the institution by the Attorney General of a proceeding against such a person in the Oklahoma courts for a judgment that such person shall be rendered sexually sterile. Notice, an opportunity to be heard, and the right to a jury trial are provided. The issues triable in such a proceeding are narrow and confined. If the court or jury finds that the defendant is an 'habitual criminal' and that he 'may be rendered sexually sterile without detriment to his or her general health,' then the court 'shall render judgment to the effect that said defendant be rendered sexually sterile' by the operation of vasectomy in case of a male and of salpingectomy in case of a female. Only one other provision of the Act is material here and that . . . which provides that 'offenses arising out of the violation of the prohibitory laws, revenue acts, embezzlement, or political offenses, shall not come or be considered within the terms of this Act.'

Petitioner was convicted in 1926 of the crime of stealing chickens and was sentenced to the Oklahoma State Reformatory. In 1929 he was convicted of the crime of robbery with fire arms and was sentenced to the reformatory. In 1934 he was convicted again of robbery with firearms and was sentenced to the penitentiary. He was confined there in 1935 when the Act was passed. In 1936 the Attorney General instituted proceedings against him. Petitioner in his answer challenged the Act as unconstitutional by reason of the Fourteenth Amendment. A jury trial was had. The court instructed the jury that the crimes of which petitioner had been convicted were felonies involving moral turpitude and that the only question for the jury was whether the operation of vasectomy could be performed on petitioner without detriment to his general health. The jury found that it could be. A judgment directing that the operation of vasectomy be performed on petitioner was affirmed by the Supreme Court of Oklahoma by a five to four decision.

Several objections to the constitutionality of the Act have been pressed upon us. It is urged that the Act cannot be sustained as an exercise of the police power in view of the state of scientific authorities respecting inheritability of criminal traits. It is argued that due process is lacking because under this Act, unlike the act upheld in *Buck* [*v. Bell*, 274 U.S. 200 (1927),] the defendant is given no opportunity to be heard on the issue as to whether he is the probable potential parent of socially undesirable offspring. It is also suggested that the Act is penal in character and that the sterilization provided for is cruel and unusual punishment and violative of the Fourteenth Amendment. We pass those points without intimating an opinion on them, for there is a feature of the Act which clearly condemns it. That is its failure to meet the requirements of the equal protection clause of the Fourteenth Amendment.

We do not stop to point out all of the inequalities in this Act. A few examples will suffice. In Oklahoma grand larceny is a felony. Larceny is grand larceny when the property taken exceeds $20 in value. Embezzlement is punishable 'in the manner prescribed for feloniously stealing property of the value of that embezzled.' Hence he who embezzles property worth more than $20 is guilty of a felony. A clerk who appropriates over $20 from his employer's till and a stranger who steals the same amount are thus both guilty of felonies. If the latter repeats his act and is convicted three times, he may be sterilized. But the clerk is not subject to the pains and penalties of the Act no matter how large his embezzlements nor how frequent his convictions. A person who enters a chicken coop and steals chickens commits a felony; and he may be sterilized if he is thrice convicted. If, however, he is a bailee of the property and fraudulently appropriates it, he is an embezzler. Hence no matter how habitual his proclivities for embezzlement are and no matter how often his conviction, he may not be sterilized. Thus the nature of the two crimes is intrinsically the same and they are punishable in the same manner. . . .

It was stated in *Buck v. Bell*, that the claim that state legislation violates the Equal Protection Clause of the Fourteenth Amendment is 'the usual last resort of constitutional arguments.' Under our constitutional system the States in determining the reach and scope of particular legislation need not provide 'abstract symmetry.' They may mark and set apart the classes and types of problems according to the needs and as dictated or suggested by experience. . . . Only recently we reaffirmed the view that the Equal Protection Clause does not prevent the legislature from recognizing 'degrees of evil' by our ruling in *Tigner v. Texas*, 310 U.S. 141, 147 [1940], that 'the Constitution does not require things which are different in fact or opinion to be treated in law as though they were the same.' Thus, if we had here only a question as to a State's classification of crimes, such as embezzlement or larceny, no substantial federal question would be raised. . . . As stated in *Buck* 'the law does all that is needed when it does all that it can, indicates a policy, applies it to all within the lines, and seeks to bring within the lines all similarly situated so far and so fast as its means allow.'

But the instant legislation runs afoul of the equal protection clause, though we give Oklahoma that large deference which the rule of the foregoing cases requires. We are dealing here with legislation which involves one of the basic civil rights of man. Marriage and procreation are fundamental to the very existence and survival of the race. The power to sterilize, if exercised, may have subtle, far-reaching and devastating effects. In evil or reckless hands it can cause races or types which are inimical to the dominant group to wither and disappear. There is no redemption for the individual whom the law touches. Any experiment which the State conducts is to his irreparable injury. He is forever deprived of a basic liberty. We mention these matters not to reexamine the scope of the police power of the States. We advert to them merely in emphasis of our view that strict scrutiny of the classification which a State makes in a sterilization law is essential, lest unwittingly or otherwise invidious discriminations are made against groups or types of individuals in violation of the constitutional guaranty of just and equal laws. The guaranty of 'equal protection of the laws is a pledge of the protection of equal laws.' When the law lays an unequal hand on those who have committed intrinsically the same quality of offense and sterilizes one and not the other, it has made as an invidious a discrimination as if it had selected a particular race or nationality for oppressive treatment. Sterilization of those who have thrice committed grand larceny with immunity for those who are embezzlers is a clear, pointed, unmistakable discrimination. Oklahoma makes no attempt to say that he who commits larceny by trespass or trick or fraud has biologically inheritable traits which he who commits embezzlement lacks. Oklahoma's line between larceny by fraud and embezzlement is determined, as we have noted, 'with reference to the time when the fraudulent intent to convert the property to the taker's own use' arises. We have not the slightest basis for inferring that that line has any significance in eugenics nor that the inheritability of criminal traits follows the neat legal distinctions which the law has marked between those two offenses. In terms of fines and imprisonment the crimes of larceny and embezzlement rate the same under the Oklahoma code. Only when it comes to sterilization are the pains and penalties of the law different. The Equal Protection Clause would indeed be a formula of empty words if such conspicuously artificial lines could be drawn. In *Buck v. Bell*, the Virginia statute was upheld though it applied only to feebleminded persons in institutions of the State. But it was pointed out that 'so far as the operations enable those who otherwise must be kept confined to be returned to the world, and thus open the asylum to others, the equality aimed at will be more nearly reached.' Here there is no such saving feature. Embezzlers are forever free. Those who steal or take in other ways are not. If such a classification were permitted, the technical common law concept of a 'trespass' based on distinctions which are 'very largely dependent upon history for explanation' could readily become a rule of human genetics.

. . . .

Reversed.

———————

Mr. Chief Justice STONE and Justice JACKSON, concurring.

. . . .

E. Euthanasia

As might be expected, the Catholic Church is opposed to the practice of euthanasia. In opposing this practice, the Church refers to "an action or omission which of itself and by intention causes death, with the purpose of eliminating all suffering."[95] However, the Church is not opposed to a decision to forgo "aggressive medical treatment."[96] A complete explanation of the Church's position in the regard is found in its *ex cathedra* pronouncement:

> 64. At the other end of life's spectrum, men and women find themselves facing the mystery of death. Today, as a result of advances in medicine and in a cultural context frequently closed to the transcendent, the experience of dying is marked by new features. When the prevailing tendency is to value life only to the extent that it brings pleasure and well-being, suffering seems like an unbearable setback, something from which one must be freed at all costs. Death is considered "senseless" if it suddenly interrupts a life still open to a future of new and interesting experiences. But it becomes a "rightful liberation" once life is held to be no longer meaningful because it is filled with pain and inexorably doomed to even greater suffering.
>
> Furthermore, when he denies or neglects his fundamental relationship to God, man thinks he is his own rule and measure, with the right to demand

———

95. Pope John Paul II, *supra* note 1.
96. *Id.*

that society should guarantee him the ways and means of deciding what to do with his life in full and complete autonomy. It is especially people in the developed countries who act in this way: they feel encouraged to do so also by the constant progress of medicine and its ever more advanced techniques. By using highly sophisticated systems and equipment, science and medical practice today are able not only to attend to cases formerly considered untreatable and to reduce or eliminate pain, but also to sustain and prolong life even in situations of extreme frailty, to resuscitate artificially patients whose basic biological functions have undergone sudden collapse, and to use special procedures to make organs available for transplanting.

In this context the temptation grows to have recourse to euthanasia, that is, to take control of death and bring it about before its time, "gently" ending one's own life or the life of others. In reality, what might seem logical and humane, when looked at more closely is seen to be senseless and inhumane. Here we are faced with one of the more alarming symptoms of the "culture of death," which is advancing above all in prosperous societies, marked by an attitude of excessive preoccupation with efficiency and which sees the growing number of elderly and disabled people as intolerable and too burdensome. These people are very often isolated by their families and by society, which are organized almost exclusively on the basis of criteria of productive efficiency, according to which a hopelessly impaired life no longer has any value.

65. For a correct moral judgment on euthanasia, in the first place a clear definition is required. Euthanasia in the strict sense is understood to be an action or omission which of itself and by intention causes death, with the purpose of eliminating all suffering. "Euthanasia's terms of reference, therefore, are to be found in the intention of the will and in the methods used."

Euthanasia must be distinguished from the decision to forego so-called "aggressive medical treatment," in other words, medical procedures which no longer correspond to the real situation of the patient, either because they are by now disproportionate to any expected results or because they impose an excessive burden on the patient and his family. In such situations, when death is clearly imminent and inevitable, one can in conscience "refuse forms of treatment that would only secure a precarious and burdensome prolongation of life, so long as the normal care due to the sick person in similar cases is not interrupted." Certainly there is a moral obligation to care for oneself and to allow oneself to be cared for, but this duty must take account of concrete circumstances. It needs to be determined whether the means of treatment available are objectively proportionate to the prospects for improvement. To forego extraordinary or disproportionate means is not the equivalent of suicide or euthanasia; it rather expresses acceptance of the human condition in the face of death.

In modern medicine, increased attention is being given to what are called "methods of palliative care," which seek to make suffering more bearable in the final stages of illness and to ensure that the patient is supported and accompanied in his or her ordeal. Among the questions which arise in this context is that of the licitness of using various types of painkillers and sedatives for relieving the patient's pain when this involves the risk of shortening life. While praise may be due to the person who voluntarily accepts suffering by forgoing treatment with pain-killers in order to remain fully lucid and, if a believer, to share consciously in the Lord's Passion, such "heroic" behaviour cannot be considered the duty of everyone. Pius XII affirmed that it is licit to relieve pain by narcotics, even when the result is decreased consciousness and a shortening of life, "if no other means exist, and if, in the given circumstances, this does not prevent the carrying out of other religious and moral duties." In such a case, death is not willed or sought, even though for reasonable motives one runs the risk of it: there is simply a desire to ease pain effectively by using the analgesics which medicine provides. All the same, "it is not right to deprive the dying person of consciousness without a serious reason": as they approach death people ought to be able to satisfy their moral and family duties, and above all they ought to be able to prepare in a fully conscious way for their definitive meeting with God.

Taking into account these distinctions, in harmony with the Magisterium of my Predecessors and in communion with the Bishops of the Catholic Church, I confirm that euthanasia is a grave violation of the law of God, since it is the deliberate and morally unacceptable killing of a human person. This doctrine is based upon the natural law and upon the written word of God, is transmitted by the Church's Tradition and taught by the ordinary and universal Magisterium.

Depending on the circumstances, this practice involves the malice proper to suicide or murder.[97]

The *Catechism* approaches euthanasia directly, stating:

2276 Those whose lives are diminished or weakened deserve special respect. Sick or handicapped persons should be helped to lead lives as normal as possible.

2277 Whatever its motives and means, direct euthanasia consists in putting an end to the lives of handicapped, sick, or dying persons. It is morally unacceptable.

Thus an act or omission which, of itself or by intention, causes death in order to eliminate suffering constitutes a murder gravely contrary to the dignity of the human person and to the respect due to the living God, his Creator. The

97. Pope John Paul II, *supra* note 1.

error of judgment into which one can fall in good faith does not change the nature of this murderous act, which must always be forbidden and excluded.

2278 Discontinuing medical procedures that are burdensome, dangerous, extraordinary, or disproportionate to the expected outcome can be legitimate; it is the refusal of "over-zealous" treatment. Here one does not will to cause death; one's inability to impede it is merely accepted. The decisions should be made by the patient if he is competent and able or, if not, by those legally entitled to act for the patient, whose reasonable will and legitimate interests must always be respected.

2279 Even if death is thought imminent, the ordinary care owed to a sick person cannot be legitimately interrupted. The use of painkillers to alleviate the sufferings of the dying, even at the risk of shortening their days, can be morally in conformity with human dignity if death is not willed as either an end or a means, but only foreseen and tolerated as inevitable. Palliative care is a special form of disinterested charity. As such it should be encouraged.[98]

The Church condemns suicide and the Church is opposed "assisted suicide." A complete understanding of the Church's position can be found by considering Pope John Paul II's words:

66. Suicide is always as morally objectionable as murder. The Church's tradition has always rejected it as a gravely evil choice. Even though a certain psychological, cultural and social conditioning may induce a person to carry out an action which so radically contradicts the innate inclination to life, thus lessening or removing subjective responsibility, suicide, when viewed objectively, is a gravely immoral act. In fact, it involves the rejection of love of self and the renunciation of the obligation of justice and charity towards one's neighbour, towards the communities to which one belongs, and towards society as a whole. In its deepest reality, suicide represents a rejection of God's absolute sovereignty over life and death, as proclaimed in the prayer of the ancient sage of Israel: "You have power over life and death; you lead men down to the gates of Hades and back again." (Wis. 16:13; cf. Tob 13:2).

To concur with the intention of another person to commit suicide and to help in carrying it out through so-called "assisted suicide" means to cooperate in, and at times to be the actual perpetrator of, an injustice which can never be excused, even if it is requested. In a remarkably relevant passage Saint Augustine writes that "it is never licit to kill another: even if he should wish it, indeed if he request it because, hanging between life and death, he begs for help in freeing the soul struggling against the bonds of the body and longing to be released; nor is it licit even when a sick person is no longer able to live." Even when not motivated by a selfish refusal to be burdened with the life of someone who is suffering, euthanasia must be called a false mercy, and indeed a disturbing

---

98. CATECHISM OF THE CATH. CHURCH, *supra* note 10.

"perversion" of mercy. True "compassion" leads to sharing another's pain; it does not kill the person whose suffering we cannot bear. Moreover, the act of euthanasia appears all the more perverse if it is carried out by those, like relatives, who are supposed to treat a family member with patience and love, or by those, such as doctors, who by virtue of their specific profession are supposed to care for the sick person even in the most painful terminal stages.[99]

In 1997, the Supreme Court upheld a Washington statute banning assisted-suicide.

117 S. Ct. 2258

Supreme Court of the United States

WASHINGTON, et al., Petitioners,

v.

Harold GLUCKSBERG et al.

Decided June 26, 1997

. . . .

Opinion

Chief Justice REHNQUIST delivered the opinion of the Court.

The question presented in this case is whether Washington's prohibition against "caus[ing]" or "aid[ing]" a suicide offends the Fourteenth Amendment to the United States Constitution. We hold that it does not.

It has always been a crime to assist a suicide in the State of Washington. In 1854, Washington's first Territorial Legislature outlawed "assisting another in the commission of self-murder." Today, Washington law provides: "A person is guilty of promoting a suicide attempt when he knowingly causes or aids another person to attempt suicide." "Promoting a suicide attempt" is a felony, punishable by up to five years' imprisonment and up to a $10,000 fine. At the same time, Washington's Natural Death Act, enacted in 1979, states that the "withholding or withdrawal of life-sustaining treatment" at a patient's direction "shall not, for any purpose, constitute a suicide."

Petitioners in this case are the State of Washington and its Attorney General. Respondents Harold Glucksberg, M. D., Abigail Halperin, M. D., Thomas A. Preston, M. D., and Peter Shalit, M. D., are physicians who practice in Washington. These doctors occasionally treat terminally ill, suffering patients, and declare that they would assist these patients in ending their lives if not for Washington's assisted-suicide ban. In January 1994, respondents, along with three gravely ill, pseudonymous

---

99. Pope John Paul II, *supra* note 1.

plaintiffs who have since died and Compassion in Dying, a nonprofit organization that counsels people considering physician-assisted suicide, sued in the United States District Court, seeking a declaration that Wash. Rev. Code § 9A.36.060(1) is, on its face, unconstitutional.

The plaintiffs asserted "the existence of a liberty interest protected by the Fourteenth Amendment which extends to a personal choice by a mentally competent, terminally ill adult to commit physician-assisted suicide . . . the District Court agreed and concluded that Washington's assisted-suicide ban is unconstitutional because it "places an undue burden on the exercise of [that] constitutionally protected liberty interest." The District Court also decided that the Washington statute violated the Equal Protection Clause's requirement that "'all persons similarly situated . . . be treated alike.'"

A panel of the Court of Appeals for the Ninth Circuit reversed, emphasizing that "[i]n the two hundred and five years of our existence no constitutional right to aid in killing oneself has ever been asserted and upheld by a court of final jurisdiction." The Ninth Circuit reheard the case en banc, reversed the panel's decision, and affirmed the District Court. Like the District Court, the en banc Court of Appeals emphasized our [*Planned Parenthood of Se. Pennsylvania v.*] *Casey* [505 U.S. 833 (1992)] and *Cruzan* [*by Cruzan v. Dir., Missouri Dept. of Health*, 497 U.S. 261 (1990)] decisions. The court also discussed what it described as "historical" and "current societal attitudes" toward suicide and assisted suicide, and concluded that "the Constitution encompasses a due process liberty interest in controlling the time and manner of one's death — that there is, in short, a constitutionally-recognized 'right to die.'" After "[w]eighing and then balancing" this interest against Washington's various interests, the court held that the State's assisted-suicide ban was unconstitutional "as applied to terminally ill competent adults who wish to hasten their deaths with medication prescribed by their physicians." The court did not reach the District Court's equal protection holding. We granted certiorari and now reverse.

I.

We begin, as we do in all due process cases, by examining our Nation's history, legal traditions, and practices. In almost every State—indeed, in almost every western democracy—it is a crime to assist a suicide. The States' assisted-suicide bans are not innovations. Rather, they are longstanding expressions of the States' commitment to the protection and preservation of all human life. Indeed, opposition to and condemnation of suicide — and, therefore, of assisting suicide — are consistent and enduring themes of our philosophical, legal, and cultural heritages.

. . . .

For the most part, the early American Colonies adopted the common-law approach. For example, the legislators of the Providence Plantations, which would later become Rhode Island, declared, in 1647, that "[s]elf-murder is by all agreed to be the most unnatural, and it is by this present Assembly declared, to be that, wherein he that doth it, kills himself out of a premeditated hatred against his own life or other humor: . . . his goods and chattels are the king's custom, but not his debts nor lands; but in case he be an infant, a lunatic, mad or distracted man, he forfeits nothing." Virginia also required ignominious burial for suicides, and their estates were forfeit to the Crown.

. . . .

Though deeply rooted, the States' assisted-suicide bans have in recent years been reexamined and, generally, reaffirmed. Because of advances in medicine and technology, Americans today are increasingly likely to die in institutions, from chronic illnesses. Public concern and democratic action are therefore sharply focused on how best to protect dignity and independence at the end of life, with the result that there have been many significant changes in state laws and in the attitudes these laws reflect. Many States, for example, now permit "living wills," surrogate health-care decision making, and the withdrawal or refusal of life-sustaining medical treatment. At the same time, however, voters and legislators continue for the most part to reaffirm their States' prohibitions on assisting suicide.

The Washington statute at issue in this case was enacted in 1975 as part of a revision of that State's criminal code. Four years later, Washington passed its Natural Death Act, which specifically stated that the "withholding or withdrawal of life-sustaining treatment . . . shall not, for any purpose, constitute a suicide" and that "[n]othing in this chapter shall be construed to condone, authorize, or approve mercy killing. . . ." In 1991, Washington voters rejected a ballot initiative which, had it passed, would have permitted a form of physician-assisted suicide. Washington then added a provision to the Natural Death Act expressly excluding physician-assisted suicide.

California voters rejected an assisted-suicide initiative similar to Washington's in 1993. On the other hand, in 1994, voters in Oregon enacted, also through ballot initiative, that State's "Death With Dignity Act," which legalized physician-assisted suicide for competent, terminally ill adults. Since the Oregon vote, many proposals to legalize assisted-suicide have been and continue to be introduced in the States' legislatures, but none has been enacted. And just last year, Iowa and Rhode Island joined the overwhelming majority of States explicitly prohibiting assisted suicide. Also, on April 30, 1997, President Clinton signed the Federal Assisted Suicide Funding Restriction Act of 1997, which prohibits the use of federal funds in support of physician-assisted suicide.

. . . .

II.

The Due Process Clause guarantees more than fair process, and the "liberty" it protects includes more than the absence of physical restraint. The Clause also provides heightened protection against government interference with certain fundamental rights and liberty interests. In a long line of cases, we have held that, in addition to the specific freedoms protected by the Bill of Rights, the "liberty" specially protected by the Due Process Clause includes the rights to marry, to have children, to direct the education and upbringing of one's children, to marital privacy, to use contraception, to bodily integrity, and to abortion. We have also assumed, and strongly suggested, that the Due Process Clause protects the traditional right to refuse unwanted lifesaving medical treatment.

But we "ha[ve] always been reluctant to expand the concept of substantive due process because guideposts for responsible decisionmaking in this unchartered area are scarce and open-ended." By extending constitutional protection to an asserted right or liberty interest, we, to a great extent, place the matter outside the arena of public debate and legislative action. We must therefore "exercise the utmost care whenever we are asked to break new ground in this field," lest the liberty protected by the Due Process Clause be subtly transformed into the policy preferences of the Members of this Court.

. . . .

Turning to the claim at issue here, the Court of Appeals stated that "[p]roperly analyzed, the first issue to be resolved is whether there is a liberty interest in determining the time and manner of one's death," or, in other words, "[i]s there a right to die?" Similarly, respondents assert a "liberty to choose how to die" and a right to "control of one's final days," and describe the asserted liberty as "the right to choose a humane, dignified death," and "the liberty to shape death." As noted above, we have a tradition of carefully formulating the interest at stake in substantive-due-process cases. For example, although *Cruzan* is often described as a "right to die" case, we were, in fact, more precise: We assumed that the Constitution granted competent persons a "constitutionally protected right to refuse lifesaving hydration and nutrition." The Washington statute at issue in this case prohibits "aid[ing] another person to attempt suicide," and, thus, the question before us is whether the "liberty" specially protected by the Due Process Clause includes a right to commit suicide which itself includes a right to assistance in doing so.

We now inquire whether this asserted right has any place in our Nation's traditions. Here, we are confronted with a consistent and almost universal tradition that has long rejected the asserted right, and continues explicitly to reject it today, even for terminally ill, mentally competent adults. To hold for respondents, we would have to reverse centuries of legal doctrine and practice, and strike down the considered policy choice of almost every State.

. . . .

The right assumed in *Cruzan*, however, was not simply deduced from abstract concepts of personal autonomy. Given the common-law rule that forced medication was a battery, and the long legal tradition protecting the decision to refuse unwanted medical treatment, our assumption was entirely consistent with this Nation's history and constitutional traditions. The decision to commit suicide with the assistance of another may be just as personal and profound as the decision to refuse unwanted medical treatment, but it has never enjoyed similar legal protection. Indeed, the two acts are widely and reasonably regarded as quite distinct. In *Cruzan* itself, we recognized that most States outlawed assisted suicide — and even more do today — and we certainly gave no intimation that the right to refuse unwanted medical treatment could be somehow transmuted into a right to assistance in committing suicide.

The history of the law's treatment of assisted suicide in this country has been and continues to be one of the rejection of nearly all efforts to permit it. That being the case, our decisions lead us to conclude that the asserted "right" to assistance in committing suicide is not a fundamental liberty interest protected by the Due Process Clause. The Constitution also requires, however, that Washington's assisted-suicide ban be rationally related to legitimate government interests. This requirement is unquestionably met here. As the court below recognized, Washington's assisted-suicide ban implicates a number of state interests.

First, Washington has an "unqualified interest in the preservation of human life." The State's prohibition on assisted suicide, like all homicide laws, both reflects and advances its commitment to this interest.

    . . . .

The State also has an interest in protecting the integrity and ethics of the medical profession. In contrast to the Court of Appeals' conclusion that "the integrity of the medical profession would [not] be threatened in any way by [physician-assisted suicide]," the American Medical Association, like many other medical and physicians' groups, has concluded that "[p]hysician-assisted suicide is fundamentally incompatible with the physician's role as healer." And physician-assisted suicide could, it is argued, undermine the trust that is essential to the doctor-patient relationship by blurring the time-honored line between healing and harming.

Next, the State has an interest in protecting vulnerable groups — including the poor, the elderly, and disabled persons — from abuse, neglect, and mistakes. The Court of Appeals dismissed the State's concern that disadvantaged persons might be pressured into physician-assisted suicide as "ludicrous on its face." We have recognized, however, the real risk of subtle coercion and undue influence in end-of-life situations. Similarly, the New York Task Force warned that "[l]egalizing physician-assisted suicide would pose profound risks to many individuals who are ill and vulnerable. . . . The risk of harm is greatest for the many individuals in our society whose autonomy and well-being are already compromised by poverty, lack of access to good medical care, advanced age, or membership in a stigmatized social group." If physician-assisted suicide were permitted, many might resort to it to spare their families the substantial financial burden of end-of-life health-care costs.

The State's interest here goes beyond protecting the vulnerable from coercion; it extends to protecting disabled and terminally ill people from prejudice, negative and inaccurate stereotypes, and "societal indifference." The State's assisted-suicide ban reflects and reinforces its policy that the lives of terminally ill, disabled, and elderly people must be no less valued than the lives of the young and healthy, and that a seriously disabled person's suicidal impulses should be interpreted and treated the same way as anyone else's.

Finally, the State may fear that permitting assisted suicide will start it down the path to voluntary and perhaps even involuntary euthanasia. The Court of Appeals struck down Washington's assisted-suicide ban only "as applied to competent, terminally ill adults who wish to hasten their deaths by obtaining medication prescribed by their doctors." Washington insists, however, that the impact of the court's decision will not and cannot be so limited. If suicide is protected as a matter of constitutional right, it is argued, "every man and woman in the United States must enjoy it." . . .

. . . .

We need not weigh exactly the relative strengths of these various interests. They are unquestionably important and legitimate, and Washington's ban on assisted suicide is at least reasonably related to their promotion and protection. We therefore hold that Wash. Rev. Code § 9A.36.060(1) (1994) does not violate the Fourteenth Amendment, either on its face or "as applied to competent, terminally ill adults who wish to hasten their deaths by obtaining medication prescribed by their doctors.

. . . .

It is so ordered.

———————

Justice SOUTER, concurring in the judgment.

. . . .

═══════════════

Five states—California, Colorado, Oregon, Vermont and Washington—and the District of Columbia have legalized euthanasia by legislation.[100] Montana has allowed legal physician-assisted suicide via court ruling.[101] A study of the Oregon "Death with Dignity Act"[102] is illustrative:

> *127.805. § 2.01. Who may initiate a written Request for Medication*
>
> (1) An adult who is capable, is a resident of Oregon, and has been determined by the attending physician and consulting physician to be suffering from a terminal disease, and who has voluntarily expressed his or her wish to die, may make a written request for medication for the purpose of ending his or

———————

100. *State-by-State Guide to Physician-Assisted Suicide*, Procon.org (last update Feb. 21, 2017), https://euthanasia.procon.org/view.resource.php?resourceID=000132 (last visited Oct. 17, 2017).

101. *Id.*

102. Or. Rev. Stat. §§ 127.800–.890, 127.895, 127.897 (1997).

her life in a humane and dignified manner in accordance with ORS 127.800 to 127.897.

(2) No person shall qualify under the provisions of ORS 127.800 to 127.897 solely because of age or disability.

127.810. § 2.02. Form of the Written Request

(1) A valid request for medication under ORS 127.800 to 127.897 shall be in substantially the form described in ORS 127.897, signed and dated by the patient and witnessed by at least two individuals who, in the presence of the patient, attest that to the best of their knowledge and belief the patient is capable, acting voluntarily, and is not being coerced to sign the request.

(2) One of the witnesses shall be a person who is not:

(a) A relative of the patient by blood, marriage or adoption;

(b) A person who at the time the request is signed would be entitled to any portion of the estate of the qualified patient upon death under any will or by operation of law; or

(c) An owner, operator or employee of a health care facility where the qualified patient is receiving medical treatment or is a resident.

(3) The patient's attending physician at the time the request is signed shall not be a witness.

(4) If the patient is a patient in a long term care facility at the time the written request is made, one of the witnesses shall be an individual designated by the facility and having the qualifications specified by the Department of Human Services by rule.

127.815. § 3.01. Attending Physician Responsibilities

(1) The attending physician shall:

(a) Make the initial determination of whether a patient has a terminal disease, is capable, and has made the request voluntarily;

(b) Request that the patient demonstrate Oregon residency pursuant to ORS 127.860;

(c) To ensure that the patient is making an informed decision, inform the patient of:

(A) His or her medical diagnosis;

(B) His or her prognosis;

(C) The potential risks associated with taking the medication to be prescribed;

(D) The probable result of taking the medication to be prescribed; and

(E) The feasible alternatives, including, but not limited to, comfort care, hospice care and pain control;

(d) Refer the patient to a consulting physician for medical confirmation of the diagnosis, and for a determination that the patient is capable and acting voluntarily;

(e) Refer the patient for counseling if appropriate pursuant to ORS 127.825;

(f) Recommend that the patient notify next of kin;

(g) Counsel the patient about the importance of having another person present when the patient takes the medication prescribed pursuant to ORS 127.800 to 127.897 and of not taking the medication in a public place;

(h) Inform the patient that he or she has an opportunity to rescind the request at any time and in any manner, and offer the patient an opportunity to rescind at the end of the 15 day waiting period pursuant to ORS 127.840;

(i) Verify, immediately prior to writing the prescription for medication under ORS 127.800 to 127.897, that the patient is making an informed decision;

(j) Fulfill the medical record documentation requirements of ORS 127.855;

(k) Ensure that all appropriate steps are carried out in accordance with ORS 127.800 to 127.897 prior to writing a prescription for medication to enable a qualified patient to end his or her life in a humane and dignified manner; and

(1)(A) Dispense medications directly, including ancillary medications intended to facilitate the desired effect to minimize the patient's discomfort, provided the attending physician is registered as a dispensing physician with the Oregon Medical Board, has a current Drug Enforcement Administration certificate and complies with any applicable administrative rule; or

(B) With the patient's written consent:

(i) Contact a pharmacist and inform the pharmacist of the prescription; and

(ii) Deliver the written prescription personally or by mail to the pharmacist, who will dispense the medications to either the patient, the attending physician or an expressly identified agent of the patient.

(2) Notwithstanding any other provision of law, the attending physician may sign the patient's death certificate.

127.845. § 3.07. Right to Rescind Request

A patient may rescind his or her request at any time and in any manner without regard to his or her mental state. No prescription for medication under

ORS 127.800 to 127.897 may be written without the attending physician offering the qualified patient an opportunity to rescind the request.

127.850. 3.08. Waiting Periods

No less than fifteen (15) days shall elapse between the patient's initial oral request and the writing of a prescription under ORS 127.800 to 127.897. No less than 48 hours shall elapse between the patient's written request and the writing of a prescription under ORS 127.800 to 127.897.

127.860. § 3.10. Residency Requirement

Only requests made by Oregon residents under ORS 127.800 to 127.897 shall be granted. Factors demonstrating Oregon residency include but are not limited to:

(1) Possession of an Oregon driver license;

(2) Registration to vote in Oregon;

(3) Evidence that the person owns or leases property in Oregon; or

(4) Filing of an Oregon tax return for the most recent tax year.

Under the Oregon law, the Oregon Public Health Division is required to maintain statistics and compile annual reports. The 2016 report announced:

Participation Summary and Trends

During 2016, 204 people received prescriptions for lethal medications under the provisions of the Oregon DWDA, compared to 218 during 2015 (see Figure 1 [omitted]). As of January 23, 2017, the Oregon Public Health Division had received reports of 133 people who had died during 2016 from ingesting the medications prescribed under DWDA, compared to 135 during 2015.

Since the law was passed in 1997, a total of 1,749 people have had prescriptions written under the DWDA, and 1,127 patients have died from ingesting the medications. During 2016, the rate of DWDA deaths was 37.2 per 10,000 total deaths.

A summary of DWDA prescriptions written and medications ingested is shown in Figure 2 [omitted]. Of the 204 patients for whom prescriptions were written during 2016, 114 (55.9%) ingested the medication and died without regaining consciousness while 36 (17.6%) did not take the medications and subsequently died of other causes.

Ingestion status is unknown for 54 patients prescribed DWDA medications in 2016. Ten of these patients died, but follow up information is not available. For the remaining 44 patients, both death and ingestion status are pending.

Patient Characteristics

Of the 133 DWDA deaths during 2016, most patients (80.5%) were aged 65 years or older. The median age at death was 73 years. As in previous years, decedents were commonly white (96.2%) and well-educated (50.0% had a least a baccalaureate degree).

Patients' underlying illnesses were similar to those of previous years. Most patients had cancer (78.9%), followed by amyotrophic lateral sclerosis (ALS) (6.8%). Of note, 6.8% of patients had heart disease as their underlying illness, an increase from 2.0% during prior years.

Most (88.6%) patients died at home, and most (88.7%) were enrolled in hospice care. Excluding unknown cases, most (99.2%) had some form of health care insurance, although the percent of patients who had private insurance (29.7%) was lower in 2016 than in previous years (57.1%). The number of patients who had Medicare or Medicaid insurance was higher than in previous years (69.5% compared to 41.5%).

Similar to previous years, the three most frequently mentioned end-of-life concerns were loss of autonomy (89.5%), decreasing ability to participate in activities that made life enjoyable (89.5%), and loss of dignity (65.4%).

DWDA Process

A total of 102 physicians wrote 204 prescriptions during 2016 (1–25 prescriptions per physician). During 2016, no referrals were made to the Oregon Medical Board for failure to comply with DWDA requirements. During 2016, five patients were referred for psychological/psychiatric evaluation.

A procedure revision was made in 2010 to standardize reporting on the follow-up questionnaire. The new procedure accepts information about the time of death and circumstances surrounding death only when the physician or another health care provider was present at the time of death. For 27 patients, either the prescribing physician or another healthcare provider was present at the time of death. Prescribing physicians were present at time of death for 13 patients (10.1%); 14 additional cases had other health care providers present (e.g. hospice nurse). Data on time from ingestion to death are available for only 25 DWDA deaths during 2016. Among those 25 patients, time from ingestion until death ranged from seven minutes to nine hours. For the remaining two patients, the length of time between ingestion and death was unknown.[103]

103. Oregon Public Health Division, *Death with Dignity Act Annual Report Year 19* (Feb. 10, 2017), http://www.oregon.gov/oha/PH/ProviderpartnerRESOURCES/EvaluationResearch/Deathwithdignityact/Documents/year19.pdf (last visited Oct. 17, 2017). For historical records on the Oregon Death with Dignity Act, please visit http://www.oregon.gov/oha/PH/ProviderpartnerRESOURCES/EvaluationResearch/Deathwithdignityact/Pages/ar-index.aspx.

Then-Attorney General John Ashcroft attempted to have Oregon's law struck down as violative of the federal Controlled Substances Act. The Oregon law was upheld by the United States Supreme Court in 2006.

---

546 U.S. 243 / 126 S. Ct. 904
Supreme Court of the United States
Alberto R. GONZALES, Attorney General, et al., Petitioners,
v.
OREGON et al.
Decided Jan. 17, 2006.

. . . .

Opinion
Justice KENNEDY delivered the opinion of the Court.

The question before us is whether the Controlled Substances Act allows the United States Attorney General to prohibit doctors from prescribing regulated drugs for use in physician-assisted suicide, notwithstanding a state law permitting the procedure. As the Court has observed, "Americans are engaged in an earnest and profound debate about the morality, legality, and practicality of physician-assisted suicide." The dispute before us is in part a product of this political and moral debate, but its resolution requires an inquiry familiar to the courts: interpreting a federal statute to determine whether executive action is authorized by, or otherwise consistent with, the enactment.

In 1994, Oregon became the first State to legalize assisted suicide when voters approved a ballot measure enacting the Oregon Death With Dignity Act (ODWDA). ODWDA, which survived a 1997 ballot measure seeking its repeal, exempts from civil or criminal liability state-licensed physicians who, in compliance with the specific safeguards in ODWDA, dispense or prescribe a lethal dose of drugs upon the request of a terminally ill patient.

The drugs Oregon physicians prescribe under ODWDA are regulated under a federal statute, the Controlled Substances Act (CSA or Act). The CSA allows these particular drugs to be available only by a written prescription from a registered physician. In the ordinary course the same drugs are prescribed in smaller doses for pain alleviation.

A November 9, 2001, Interpretive Rule issued by the Attorney General addresses the implementation and enforcement of the CSA with respect to ODWDA. It determines that using controlled substances to assist suicide is not a legitimate medical practice and that dispensing or prescribing them for this purpose is unlawful under the CSA. The Interpretive Rule's validity under the CSA is the issue before us.

I.

A.

We turn first to the text and structure of the CSA. Enacted in 1970 with the main objectives of combating drug abuse and controlling the legitimate and illegitimate traffic in controlled substances, the CSA creates a comprehensive, closed regulatory regime criminalizing the unauthorized manufacture, distribution, dispensing, and possession of substances classified in any of the Act's five schedules. The Act places substances in one of five schedules based on their potential for abuse or dependence, their accepted medical use, and their accepted safety for use under medical supervision. Schedule I contains the most severe restrictions on access and use, and Schedule V the least. Congress classified a host of substances when it enacted the CSA, but the statute permits the Attorney General to add, remove, or reschedule substances. . . .

The present dispute involves controlled substances listed in Schedule II, substances generally available only pursuant to a written, nonrefillable prescription by a physician. A 1971 regulation promulgated by the Attorney General requires that every prescription for a controlled substance "be issued for a legitimate medical purpose by an individual practitioner acting in the usual course of his professional practice."

To prevent diversion of controlled substances with medical uses, the CSA regulates the activity of physicians. To issue lawful prescriptions of Schedule II drugs, physicians must "obtain from the Attorney General a registration issued in accordance with the rules and regulations promulgated by him. The Attorney General may deny, suspend, or revoke this registration if, as relevant here, the physician's registration would be "inconsistent with the public interest." . . .

. . . .

In 2001, John Ashcroft was appointed Attorney General. Perhaps because Mr. Ashcroft had supported efforts to curtail assisted suicide while serving as a Senator, Oregon Attorney General Hardy Myers wrote him to request a meeting with Department of Justice officials should the Department decide to revisit the application of the CSA to assisted suicide. Attorney General Myers received a reply letter from one of Attorney General Ashcroft's advisers writing on his behalf, which stated:

I am aware of no pending legislation in Congress that would prompt a review of the Department's interpretation of the CSA as it relates to physician-assisted suicide. Should such a review be commenced in the future, we would be happy to include your views in that review.

On November 9, 2001, without consulting Oregon or apparently anyone outside his Department, the Attorney General issued an Interpretive Rule announcing his intent to restrict the use of controlled substances for physician-assisted suicide. Incorporating the legal analysis of a memorandum he had solicited from his Office of Legal Counsel, the Attorney General ruled:

[A]ssisting suicide is not a 'legitimate medical purpose' within the meaning of 21 CFR 1306.04 (2001), and that prescribing, dispensing, or administering federally controlled substances to assist suicide violates the Controlled Substances Act. Such conduct by a physician registered to dispense controlled substances may 'render his registration . . . inconsistent with the public interest' and therefore subject to possible suspension or revocation under 21 U.S.C. 824(a)(4). The Attorney General's conclusion applies regardless of whether state law authorizes or permits such conduct by practitioners or others and regardless of the condition of the person whose suicide is assisted.

. . . .

In response the State of Oregon, joined by a physician, a pharmacist, and some terminally ill patients, all from Oregon, challenged the Interpretive Rule in federal court. The United States District Court for the District of Oregon entered a permanent injunction against the Interpretive Rule's enforcement.

. . . .

The structure of the CSA, then, conveys unwillingness to cede medical judgments to an executive official who lacks medical expertise. In interpreting statutes that divide authority, the Court has recognized: "Because historical familiarity and policymaking expertise account in the first instance for the presumption that Congress delegates interpretive lawmaking power to the agency rather than to the reviewing court, we presume here that Congress intended to invest interpretive power in the administrative actor in the best position to develop these attributes." This presumption works against a conclusion that the Attorney General has authority to make quintessentially medical judgments.

The Government contends the Attorney General's decision here is a legal, not a medical, one. This generality, however, does not suffice. The Attorney General's Interpretive Rule, and the Office of Legal Counsel memo it incorporates, place extensive reliance on medical judgments and the views of the medical community in concluding that assisted suicide is not a "legitimate medical purpose." This confirms that the authority claimed by the Attorney General is both beyond his expertise and incongruous with the statutory purposes and design.

The idea that Congress gave the Attorney General such broad and unusual authority through an implicit delegation in the CSA's registration provision is not sustainable. "Congress, we have held, does not alter the fundamental details of a regulatory scheme in vague terms or ancillary provisions—it does not, one might say, hide elephants in mouseholes."

The importance of the issue of physician-assisted suicide, which has been the subject of an "earnest and profound debate" across the country, makes the oblique form of the claimed delegation all the more suspect. Under the Government's theory, moreover, the medical judgments the Attorney General could make are not limited to physician-assisted suicide. Were this argument accepted, he could decide whether any particular drug may be used for any particular purpose, or indeed whether a physician who administers any controversial treatment could be deregistered. This would occur, under the Government's view, despite the statute's express limitation of the Attorney General's authority to registration and control, with

attendant restrictions on each of those functions, and despite the statutory purposes to combat drug abuse and prevent illicit drug trafficking.

. . . .

In deciding whether the CSA can be read as prohibiting physician-assisted suicide, we look to the statute's text and design. The statute and our case law amply support the conclusion that Congress regulates medical practice insofar as it bars
doctors from using their prescription-writing powers as a means to engage in illicit
drug dealing and trafficking as conventionally understood. Beyond this, however,
the statute manifests no intent to regulate the practice of medicine generally. The
silence is understandable given the structure and limitations of federalism, which
allow the States "'great latitude under their police powers to legislate as to the
protection of the lives, limbs, health, comfort, and quiet of all persons.'"

The structure and operation of the CSA presume and rely upon a functioning
medical profession regulated under the States' police powers. The Attorney General
can register a physician to dispense controlled substances "if the applicant is authorized to dispense . . . controlled substances under the laws of the State in which he
practices." . . .

Oregon's regime is an example of the state regulation of medical practice that the
CSA presupposes. Rather than simply decriminalizing assisted suicide, ODWDA limits its exercise to the attending physicians of terminally ill patients, physicians who
must be licensed by Oregon's Board of Medical Examiners. The statute gives attending physicians a central role, requiring them to provide prognoses and prescriptions,
give information about palliative alternatives and counseling, and ensure patients are
competent and acting voluntarily. Any eligible patient must also get a second opinion
from another registered physician, § 127.820, and the statute's safeguards require physicians to keep and submit to inspection detailed records of their actions.

. . . .

In the face of the CSA's silence on the practice of medicine generally and its recognition of state regulation of the medical profession it is difficult to defend the Attorney
General's declaration that the statute impliedly criminalizes physician-assisted suicide. This difficulty is compounded by the CSA's consistent delegation of medical
judgments to the Secretary and its otherwise careful allocation of powers for enforcing the limited objects of the CSA. The Government's attempt to meet this challenge
rests, for the most part, on the CSA's requirement that every Schedule II drug be dis-
pensed pursuant to a "written prescription of a practitioner." A prescription, the Government argues, necessarily implies that the substance is being made available to a
patient for a legitimate medical purpose. The statute, in this view, requires an
anterior judgment about the term "medical" or "medicine." The Government contends ordinary usage of these words ineluctably refers to a healing or curative art,
which by these terms cannot embrace the intentional hastening of a patient's death. It
also points to the teachings of Hippocrates, the positions of prominent medical

organizations, the Federal Government, and the judgment of the 49 States that have not legalized physician-assisted suicide as further support for the proposition that the practice is not 4a-130a.

On its own, this understanding of medicine's boundaries is at least reasonable. The primary problem with the Government's argument, however, is its assumption that the CSA impliedly authorizes an Executive officer to bar a use simply because it may be inconsistent with one reasonable understanding of medical practice. Viewed alone, the prescription requirement may support such an understanding, but statutes "should not be read as a series of unrelated and isolated provisions." The CSA's substantive provisions and their arrangement undermine this assertion of an expansive federal authority to regulate medicine.

. . . .

The judgment of the Court of Appeals is Affirmed.

————————

Justice SCALIA, with whom Chief Justice ROBERTS and Justice THOMAS join, dissenting.

. . . .

————————

Justice THOMAS, dissenting.

. . . .

════════════════

A variation on the theme of the power of the state to terminate life arose in the context of who has the right, and under what circumstances, to determine whether life sustaining measures should cease.

════════════════

885 So. 2d 321
Supreme Court of Florida

Jeb BUSH, Governor of Florida, et al., Appellants,
v.
Michael SCHIAVO, Guardian of Theresa Schiavo, Appellee

Sept. 23, 2004.
Rehearing Denied Oct. 21, 2004
(*cert. denied*, 543 U.S. 1121 (Jan. 25, 2005))

. . . . .

Opinion

PARIENTE, C.J.

....

FACTS AND PROCEDURAL HISTORY

The resolution of the discrete separation of powers issue presented in this case does not turn on the facts of the underlying guardianship proceedings that resulted in the removal of Theresa's nutrition and hydration tube. The underlying litigation, which has pitted Theresa's husband, Michael Schiavo, against Theresa's parents, turned on whether the procedures sustaining Theresa's life should be discontinued. However, the procedural history is important because it provides the backdrop to the Legislature's enactment of the challenged law. We also detail the facts and procedural history in light of the Governor's assertion that chapter 2003–418, Laws of Florida (hereinafter sometimes referred to as "the Act"), was passed in order to protect the due process rights of Theresa and other individuals in her position.

As set forth in the Second District's first opinion in this case, which upheld the guardianship court's final order.

Theresa Marie Schindler was born on December 3, 1963, and lived with or near her parents in Pennsylvania until she married Michael Schiavo on November 10, 1984. Michael and Theresa moved to Florida in 1986. They were happily married and both were employed. They had no children.

On February 25, 1990, their lives changed. Theresa, age 27, suffered a cardiac arrest as a result of a potassium imbalance. Michael called 911, and Theresa was rushed to the hospital. She never regained consciousness.

Since 1990, Theresa has lived in nursing homes with constant care. She is fed and hydrated by tubes. The staff changes her diapers regularly. She has had numerous health problems, but none have been life threatening.

For the first three years after this tragedy, Michael and Theresa's parents, Robert and Mary Schindler, enjoyed an amicable relationship. However, that relationship ended in 1993 and the parties literally stopped speaking to each other. In May of 1998, eight years after Theresa lost consciousness, Michael petitioned the guardianship court to authorize the termination of life-prolonging procedures. By filing this petition, which the Schindlers opposed, Michael placed the difficult decision in the hands of the court.

After a trial, at which both Michael and the Schindlers presented evidence, the guardianship court issued an extensive written order authorizing the discontinuance of artificial life support. The trial court found by clear and convincing evidence that Theresa Schiavo was in a persistent vegetative state and that Theresa would elect to cease life-prolonging procedures if she were competent to make her own decision. This order was affirmed on direct appeal and we denied review.

The severity of Theresa's medical condition was explained by the Second District as follows:

The evidence is overwhelming that Theresa is in a permanent or persistent vegetative state. It is important to understand that a persistent vegetative state is not simply a coma. She is not asleep. She has cycles of apparent wakefulness and apparent sleep without any cognition or awareness. As she breathes, she often makes moaning sounds. Theresa has severe contractures of her hands, elbows, knees, and feet.

Over the span of this last decade, Theresa's brain has deteriorated because of the lack of oxygen it suffered at the time of the heart attack. By mid 1996, the CAT scans of her brain showed a severely abnormal structure. At this point, much of her cerebral cortex is simply gone and has been replaced by cerebral spinal fluid. Medicine cannot cure this condition. Unless an act of God, a true miracle, were to recreate her brain, Theresa will always remain in an unconscious, reflexive state, totally dependent upon others to feed her and care for her most private needs. She could remain in this state for many years.

In affirming the trial court's order, the Second District concluded by stating:

In the final analysis, the difficult question that faced the trial court was whether Theresa Marie Schindler Schiavo, not after a few weeks in a coma, but after ten years in a persistent vegetative state that has robbed her of most of her cerebrum and all but the most instinctive of neurological functions, with no hope of a medical cure but with sufficient money and strength of body to live indefinitely, would choose to continue the constant nursing care and the supporting tubes in hopes that a miracle would somehow recreate her missing brain tissue, or whether she would wish to permit a natural death process to take its course and for her family members and loved ones to be free to continue their lives. After due consideration, we conclude that the trial judge had clear and convincing evidence to answer this question as he did.

Although the guardianship court's final order authorizing the termination of life-prolonging procedures was affirmed on direct appeal, the litigation continued because the Schindlers began an attack on the final order. . . .

        . . . .

The Second District permitted the Schindlers to present evidence to establish by a preponderance of the evidence that the judgment was no longer equitable and specifically held:

To meet this burden, they must establish that new treatment offers sufficient promise of increased cognitive function in Mrs. Schiavo's cerebral cortex — significantly improving the quality of Mrs. Schiavo's life — so that she herself would elect to undergo this treatment and would reverse the prior decision to withdraw life-prolonging procedures.

The Second District required an additional set of medical examinations of Theresa and instructed that one of the physicians must be a new, independent physician selected either by the agreement of the parties or, if they could not agree, by the appointment of the guardianship court.

After conducting a hearing for the purpose set forth in the Second District's decision, the guardianship court denied the Schindlers' motion for relief from judgment. In reviewing the trial court's order, the Second District explained that it was "not reviewing a final judgment in this appellate proceeding. The final judgment was entered several years ago and has already been affirmed by this court." However, the Second District carefully examined the record:

Despite our decision that the appropriate standard of review is abuse of discretion, this court has closely examined all of the evidence in this record. We have repeatedly examined the videotapes, not merely watching short segments but carefully observing the tapes in their entirety. We have examined the brain scans with the eyes of educated laypersons and considered the explanations provided by the doctors in the transcripts. We have concluded that, if we were called upon to review the guardianship court's decision de novo, we would still affirm it.

Finally, the Second District concluded its fourth opinion in the Schiavo case with the following observation:

The judges on this panel are called upon to make a collective, objective decision concerning a question of law. Each of us, however, has our own family, our own loved ones, our own children. From our review of the videotapes of Mrs. Schiavo, despite the irrefutable evidence that her cerebral cortex has sustained the most severe of irreparable injuries, we understand why a parent who had raised and nurtured a child from conception would hold out hope that some level of cognitive function remained. If Mrs. Schiavo were our own daughter, we could not but hold to such a faith.

But in the end, this case is not about the aspirations that loving parents have for their children. It is about Theresa Schiavo's right to make her own decision, independent of her parents and independent of her husband. . . . It may be unfortunate that when families cannot agree, the best forum we can offer for this private, personal decision is a public courtroom and the best decision-maker we can provide is a judge with no prior knowledge of the ward, but the law currently provides no better solution that adequately protects the interests of promoting the value of life. We have previously affirmed the guardianship court's decision in this regard, and we now affirm the denial of a motion for relief from that judgment.

We denied review and Theresa's nutrition and hydration tube was removed on October 15, 2003.

On October 21, 2003, the Legislature enacted chapter 2003–418, the Governor signed the Act into law, and the Governor issued executive order No. 03–201 to stay the continued withholding of nutrition and hydration from Theresa. The nutrition and hydration tube was reinserted pursuant to the Governor's executive order.

On the same day, Michael Schiavo brought the action for declaratory judgment in the circuit court. Relying on undisputed facts and legal argument, the circuit court entered a final summary judgment on May 6, 2004, in favor of Michael Schiavo, finding the Act unconstitutional both on its face and as applied to Theresa. Specifically, the circuit court found that chapter 2003–418 was unconstitutional on its face as an unlawful delegation of legislative authority and as a violation of the right to privacy, and unconstitutional as applied because it allowed the Governor to encroach upon the judicial power and to retroactively abolish Theresa's vested right to privacy.

ANALYSIS

We begin our discussion by emphasizing that our task in this case is to review the constitutionality of chapter 2003–418, not to reexamine the guardianship court's orders directing the removal of Theresa's nutrition and hydration tube, or to review the Second District's numerous decisions in the guardianship case. Although we recognize that the parties continue to dispute the findings made in the prior proceedings, these proceedings are relevant to our decision only to the extent that they occurred and resulted in a final judgment directing the withdrawal of.

The language of chapter 2003–418 is clear. It states in full:

Section 1. (1) The Governor shall have the authority to issue a one-time stay to prevent the withholding of nutrition and hydration from a patient if, as of October 15, 2003:

(a) That patient has no written advance directive;

(b) The court has found that patient to be in a persistent vegetative state;

(c) That patient has had nutrition and hydration withheld; and

(d) A member of that patient's family has challenged the withholding of nutrition and hydration.

(2) The Governor's authority to issue the stay expires 15 days after the effective date of this act, and the expiration of the authority does not impact the validity or the effect of any stay issued pursuant to this act. The Governor may lift the stay authorized under this act at any time. A person may not be held civilly liable and is not subject to regulatory or disciplinary sanctions for taking any action to comply with a stay issued by the Governor pursuant to this act.

(3) Upon issuance of a stay, the chief judge of the circuit court shall appoint a guardian ad litem for the patient to make recommendations to the Governor and the court.

Section 2. This act shall take effect upon becoming a law.

Ch.2003-418, Laws of Fla. Thus, chapter 2003–418 allowed the Governor to issue a stay to prevent the withholding of nutrition and hydration from a patient under the circumstances provided for in subsections (1)(a)–(d). Under the fifteen-day sunset provision, the Governor's authority to issue the stay expired on November 5, 2003. The Governor's authority to lift the stay continues indefinitely.

SEPARATION OF POWERS

The cornerstone of American democracy known as separation of powers recognizes three separate branches of government — the executive, the legislative, and the judicial — each with its own powers and responsibilities. In Florida, the constitutional doctrine has been expressly codified in article II, section 3 of the Florida Constitution, which not only divides state government into three branches but also expressly prohibits one branch from exercising the powers of the other two branches:

Branches of Government. — The powers of the state government shall be divided into legislative, executive and judicial branches. No person belonging to one branch shall exercise any powers appertaining to either of the other branches unless expressly provided herein.

. . . .

In this case, the undisputed facts show that the guardianship court authorized Michael to proceed with the discontinuance of Theresa's life support after the issue was fully litigated in a proceeding in which the Schindlers were afforded the opportunity to present evidence on all issues. This order as well as the order denying the Schindlers' motion for relief from judgment were affirmed on direct appeal. The Schindlers sought review in this Court, which was denied. Thereafter, the tube was removed. Subsequently, pursuant to the Governor's executive order, the nutrition and hydration tube was reinserted. Thus, the Act, as applied in this case, resulted in an executive order that effectively reversed a properly rendered final judgment and thereby constituted an unconstitutional encroachment on the power that has been reserved for the independent judiciary.

. . . .

CONCLUSION

We recognize that the tragic circumstances underlying this case make it difficult to put emotions aside and focus solely on the legal issue presented. We are not insensitive to the struggle that all members of Theresa's family have endured since she fell unconscious in 1990. However, we are a nation of laws and we must govern our decisions by the rule of law and not by our own emotions. Our hearts can fully comprehend the grief so fully demonstrated by Theresa's family members on this record. But our hearts are not the law. What is in the Constitution always must prevail over emotion. Our oaths as judges require that this principle is our polestar, and it alone.

As the Second District noted in one of the multiple appeals in this case, we "are called upon to make a collective, objective decision concerning a question of law. Each of us, however, has our own family, our own loved ones, our own children. . . . But in the end, this case is not about the aspirations that loving parents have for their children." Rather, as our decision today makes clear, this case is about maintaining the integrity of a constitutional system of government with three independent and coequal branches, none of which can either encroach upon the powers of another branch or improperly delegate its own responsibilities.

The continuing vitality of our system of separation of powers precludes the other two branches from nullifying the judicial branch's final orders. If the Legislature with the assent of the Governor can do what was attempted here, the judicial branch would be subordinated to the final directive of the other branches. Also subordinated would be the rights of individuals, including the well established privacy right to self determination. No court judgment could ever be considered truly final and no constitutional right truly secure, because the precedent of this case would hold to the contrary. Vested rights could be stripped away based on popular clamor. The essential core of what the Founding Fathers sought to change from their experience with English rule would be lost, especially their belief that our courts exist precisely to preserve the rights of individuals, even when doing so is contrary to popular will.

The trial court's decision regarding Theresa Schiavo was made in accordance with the procedures and protections set forth by the judicial branch and in accordance with the statutes passed by the Legislature in effect at that time. That decision is final and the Legislature's attempt to alter that final adjudication is unconstitutional as applied to Theresa Schiavo. Further, even if there had been no final judgment in this case, the Legislature provided the Governor constitutionally inadequate standards for the application of the legislative authority delegated in chapter 2003–418. Because chapter 2003–418 runs afoul of article II, section 3 of the Florida Constitution in both respects, we affirm the circuit court's final summary judgment.

It is so ordered.

WELLS, ANSTEAD, LEWIS, QUINCE, CANTERO and BELL, JJ., concur.

Before concluding our discussion of euthanasia, it is important to refer back to the horrors of the 20th century. When the forced sterilization and eugenics program failed to prevent the birth of a disabled child, the Nazis took the next logical step — euthanizing undesirable children. This horror is examined in the website of the United States Holocaust Museum. Basically, in 1939 medical personnel were required by the German government to report those children under the age of three displaying signs of "severe mental or physical disability." These children, and those children whose parents voluntarily surrendered their children, were placed in pediatric wards and killed with lethal doses of medication, or in some instances, starvation. Because of the "success" of this program, the German government took the next logical step of euthanizing undesirable adults.[104] A German psychiatrist, Carl Knab, wrote in 1935 "we have before us in these asylums in addition to idiots on the lowest level, spiritual ruins whose number is not insignificant, notwithstanding all our therapeutic endeavors, patient material which, as mere cost-occasioning ballast, should be eradicated by being killed in a painless fashion."[105] From academic theory to government

---

104. BURLEIGH, *supra* note 84, at 381.
105. *Id.*

implementation, the adult euthanasia program known as "T4" began in 1939. Disabled patients were taken from institutions, killed in gas chambers designed to resemble shower facilities, the bodies were cremated, and urns were returned to the families listing a fictitious cause of death.

Over 70,000 disabled individuals were killed at six gassing centers between January 1940 and August 1941.[106] However, as the realities of the program became obvious opposition appeared led by the Roman Catholic Bishop of Munster. He noted, "[w]e are not dealing with machines, horses, and cows whose only function is to serve mankind, to produce goods for man . . . we are dealing with human beings."[107] Other Catholic priests joined with him. Their courageous opposition led to a formal order to stop the program although it continued, along with the child euthanasia program, in secret resulting in the deaths of more than 200,000 disabled children and adults who were euthanized.

However, despite the individual bravery of many Catholics and Catholic clerics during the Nazi horrors of World War II, critics have charged that Pope Pius XII did not do enough to attempt to alleviate the suffering of the Jews and other victims during the Holocaust.[108]

On March 12, 2000, Pope John Paul II apologized for the Catholic Church's role in the suffering of the Jews. While not specifically mentioning the Holocaust, and over the opposition of some Catholic theologians, the Pope proclaimed: "We are deeply saddened by the behaviour of those who in the course of history have caused these children of yours to suffer, and asking your forgiveness we wish to commit ourselves to genuine brotherhood."[109]

There can be no doubt that a Polish pope was deeply affected and deeply distressed by the reaction of all of Christianity to the atrocities committed by the Nazis. Pope Benedict XVI, a German, made that abundantly clear in his address at Auschwitz.[110] While omitting the words "the Holocaust," Pope Benedict did, nonetheless make it clear that is what he was referencing. The exchange reported by *The Guardian* was actually a passage from prayers offered on the Day of Pardon. The complete prayer is as follows:

IV. Confession of Sins Against the People of Israel

A Representative of the Roman Curia:

Let us pray that, in recalling the sufferings endured by the people of Israel throughout history, Christians will acknowledge the sins committed by not

106. *Id.* at 382–404.
107. *Id.* at 401.
108. *See* Shira Schoenberg, *Pope Pius XII and the Holocaust*, Jewish Virtual Library, http://www.jewishvirtuallibrary.org/jsource/anti-semitism/pius.html (last visited Oct. 23, 2017) (examining the Pope's role in this regard).
109. Rory Carroll, *Pope Says Sorry for Sins of Church*, Guardian (Mar. 13, 2000), http://www.guardian.co.uk/world/2000/mar/13/catholicism.religion (last visited Oct. 23, 2017).
110. Pope Benedict XVI, *Address at Visit to the Auschwitz Camp* (May 28, 2006), http://www.vatican.va/holy_father/benedict_xvi/speeches/2006/may/documents/hf_ben-xvi_spe_20060528_auschwitz-birkenau_en.html (last visited Oct. 23, 2017).

a few of their number against the people of the Covenant and the blessings, and in this way will purify their hearts.

Silent Prayer

The Holy Father:

God of our fathers, you chose Abraham and his descendants to bring your Name to the Nations: we are deeply saddened by the behaviour of those who in the course of history have caused these children of yours to suffer, and asking your forgiveness we wish to commit ourselves to genuine brotherhood with the people of the Covenant. We ask this through Christ our Lord.

R. Amen[111]

However, in a message prepared by Cardinal Ratzinger, now Pope Benedict XVI, the Vatican did express direct remorse:

The relationship between Christians and Jews is one of the areas requiring a special examination of conscience. "The Church's relationship to the Jewish people is unlike the one she shares with any other religion." Nevertheless, "the history of the relations between Jews and Christians is a tormented one. . . . In effect, the balance of these relations over two thousand years has been quite negative." The hostility or diffidence of numerous Christians toward Jews in the course of time is a sad historical fact and is the cause of profound remorse for Christians aware of the fact that "Jesus was a descendent of David; that the Virgin Mary and the Apostles belonged to the Jewish people; that the Church draws sustenance from the root of that good olive tree onto which have been grafted the wild olive branches of the Gentiles (cf. *Rom.* 11:17–24); that the Jews are our dearly beloved brothers, indeed in a certain sense they are 'our elder brothers.'"

The Shoah [Hebrew word for the Holocaust] was certainly the result of the pagan ideology that was Nazism, animated by a merciless anti-Semitism that not only despised the faith of the Jewish people, but also denied their very human dignity. Nevertheless, "it may be asked whether the Nazi persecution of the Jews was not made easier by the anti-Jewish prejudices imbedded in some Christian minds and hearts. . . . Did Christians give every possible assistance to those being persecuted, and in particular to the persecuted Jews?" There is no doubt that there were many Christians who risked their lives to save and to help their Jewish neighbors. It seems, however, also true that "alongside such courageous men and women, the spiritual resistance and concrete action of other Christians was not that which might have been expected from Christ's followers." This fact constitutes a call to the

---

111. The Vatican, *Universal Prayer: Confession of Sins and Asking Forgiveness, Day of Pardon* (Mar. 12, 2000), http://www.vatican.va/news_services/liturgy/documents/ns_lit_doc_20000312 _prayer-day-pardon_en.html (last visited Oct. 23, 2017).

consciences of all Christians today, so as to require "an act of repentance (*teshuva*)," and to be a stimulus to increase efforts to be "transformed by renewal of your mind" (*Rom.* 12:2), as well as to keep a "moral and religious memory" of the injury inflicted on the Jews. In this area, much has already been done, but this should be confirmed and deepened.[112]

F. Death Penalty

In continuing an examination of the Catholic Church's view on the sanctity of life, the last topic involves the theological validity of the death penalty. While the Catholic Church does not condemn the death penalty as intrinsically evil, as it does in the case of abortion, because of the Church's high value of human life, the circumstances under which the death penalty is morally acceptable are rare. *Evangelium Vitae* addresses this issue:

56. This is the context in which to place the problem of the death penalty. On this matter there is a growing tendency, both in the Church and in civil society, to demand that it be applied in a very limited way or even that it be abolished completely. The problem must be viewed in the context of a system of penal justice ever more in line with human dignity and thus, in the end, with God's plan for man and society. The primary purpose of the punishment which society inflicts is "to redress the disorder caused by the offence." Public authority must redress the violation of personal and social rights by imposing on the offender an adequate punishment for the crime, as a condition for the offender to regain the exercise of his or her freedom. In this way authority also fulfills the purpose of defending public order and ensuring people's safety, while at the same time offering the offender an incentive and help to change his or her behaviour and be rehabilitated.

It is clear that, for these purposes to be achieved, the nature and extent of the punishment must be carefully evaluated and decided upon, and ought not go to the extreme of executing the offender except in cases of absolute necessity: in other words, when it would not be possible otherwise to defend society. Today however, as a result of steady improvements in the organization of the penal system, such cases are very rare, if not practically non-existent.

In any event, the principle set forth in the new Catechism of the Catholic Church remains valid: "If bloodless means are sufficient to defend human lives against an aggressor and to protect public order and the safety of

---

112. International Theological Commission, *Memory and Reconciliation: The Church and the Faults of the Past* ¶ 5.4 (Dec. 1999), http://www.vatican.va/roman_curia/congregations/cfaith/cti _documents/rc_con_ cfaith_doc_20000307_memory-reconc-itc_en.html (last visited Oct. 23, 2017) (Imprimatur by Joseph Cardinal Ratzinger).

persons, public authority must limit itself to such means, because they better correspond to the concrete conditions of the common good and are more in conformity to the dignity of the human person."[113]

The Catechism instructs:

> 2266 The State's effort to contain the spread of behaviors injurious to human rights and the fundamental rules of civil coexistence corresponds to the requirement of watching over the common good. Legitimate public authority has the right and duty to inflict penalties commensurate with the gravity of the crime. The primary scope of the penalty is to redress the disorder caused by the offense. When his punishment is voluntarily accepted by the offender, it takes on the value of expiation. Moreover, punishment, in addition to preserving public order and the safety of persons, has a medicinal scope: as far as possible it should contribute to the correction of the offender.

> 2267 The traditional teaching of the Church does not exclude, presupposing full ascertainment of the identity and responsibility of the offender, recourse to the death penalty, when this is the only practicable way to defend the lives of human beings effectively against the aggressor.[114]

The legal system recognizes a broader use of the death penalty than recognized by the Catholic Church. Each of the fifty states and the District of Columbia has a series of criminal statutes, as does the Federal government. While not all of those states provide for a death penalty, many do.

Capital Offenses, by State, 2013[115]

State	Offense
Alabama	Intentional murder (Ala. Stat. Ann. 13A-5-40(a)(1)-(18)) with 10 aggravating factors (Ala. Stat. Ann. 13A-5-49).
Arizona	First-degree murder, including premeditated murder and felony murder, accompanied by at least 1 of 14 aggravating factors (A.R.S. § 13-703(F)).
Arkansas	Capital murder (Ark. Code Ann. § 5-10-101) with a finding of at least 1 of 10 aggravating circumstances; treason (Ark. Code Ann. § 5-51-201).

---

113. Pope John Paul II, *supra* note 1 ¶ 56 (Mar. 2, 1995), http://www.vatican.va/holy_father/john_paul_ii/encyclicals/documents/hf_jp-ii_enc_25031995_evangelium-vitae_en.html (last visited Oct. 23, 2017).

114. Catechism of the Cath. Church, *Article 5: The Fifth Commandment*, 2266–67 (1993), http://www.vatican.va/archive/ENG0015/__P7Z.HTM (last visited Oct. 23, 2017).

115. Bureau of Justice Statistics, Office of Justice Programs, U.S. Dep't of Justice, No. NCJ 248448, *Capital Punishment, 2013—Statistical Tables*, tbl. 1 *Capital offenses, by state, 2013*, at 6. (Dec. 9, 2014), https://www.bjs.gov/content/pub/pdf/cp13st.pdf (last visited Oct. 17, 2017).

California	First-degree murder with special circumstances; sabotage; train wrecking causing death; treason; perjury in a capital case causing execution of an innocent person; fatal assault by a prisoner serving a life sentence.
Colorado	First-degree murder with at least 1 of 17 aggravating factors; first-degree kidnapping resulting in death; treason.
Connecticut	Capital felony with 8 forms of aggravated homicide (C.G.S. § 53a-54b).
Delaware	First-degree murder (11 Del. C. § 636) with at least 1 statutory aggravating circumstance (11 Del. C. § 4209).
Florida	First-degree murder; felony murder; capital drug trafficking; capital sexual battery.
Georgia	Murder with aggravating circumstances; rape, armed robbery, or kidnapping with bodily injury or ransom when the victim dies; aircraft hijacking; treason.
Idaho	First-degree murder with aggravating factors; first-degree kidnapping; perjury resulting in the execution of an innocent person.
Indiana	Murder with 16 aggravating circumstances (IC 35-50-2-9).
Kansas	Capital murder (K.S.A. 21-5401) with 8 aggravating circumstances (K.S.A. 21-6617 and K.S.A. 21-6624).
Kentucky	Capital murder with the presence of at least one statutory aggravating circumstance; capital kidnapping (KRS 532.025).
Louisiana	First-degree murder; treason (La. R.S. 14:30 and 14:113).
Mississippi	Capital murder (Miss. Code Ann. § 97-3-19(2)); aircraft piracy (Miss. Code Ann. § 97-25-55(1)).
Missouri	First-degree murder (565.020 RSMO 2000).
Montana	Capital murder with 1 of 9 aggravating circumstances (Mont. Code Ann. § 46-18-303); aggravated kidnapping; felony murder; capital sexual intercourse without consent (Mont. Code Ann. § 45-5-503).
Nebraska	First-degree murder with a finding of one or more statutory aggravating circumstances.
Nevada	First-degree murder with at least 1 of 15 aggravating circumstances (NRS 200.030, 200.033, and 200.035).
New Hampshire	Murder committed in the course of rape, kidnapping, drug crimes, or home invasion; killing of a police officer, judge, or prosecutor; murder for hire; murder by an inmate while serving a sentence of life without parole (RSA 630:1 and 630:5).
New Mexico	First-degree murder with at least 1 of 7 aggravating factors (NMSA 1978 § 31-20A-5).

New York	First-degree murder with 1 of 13 aggravating factors (NY Penal Law § 125.27).
North Carolina	First-degree murder (N.C.G.S. § 14-17) with the finding of at least 1 of 11 statutory aggravating circumstances (N.C.G.S. § 15A-2000).
Ohio	Aggravated murder with at least 1 of 10 aggravating circumstances (O.R.C. 2903.01, 2929.02, and 2929.04).
Oklahoma	First-degree murder in conjunction with a finding of at least 1 of 8 statutorily-defined aggravating circumstances.
Oregon	Aggravated murder (ORS 163.095).
Pennsylvania	First-degree murder with 18 aggravating circumstances.
South Carolina	Murder with at least 1 of 12 aggravating circumstances (§ 16-3-20(C)(a)).
South Dakota	First-degree murder with 1 of 10 aggravating circumstances.
Tennessee	First-degree murder (Tenn. Code Ann. § 39-13-202) with 1 of 17 aggravating circumstances (Tenn. Code Ann. § 39-13-204).
Texas	Criminal homicide with 1 of 9 aggravating circumstances (Tex. Penal Code § 19.03).
Utah	Aggravated murder (Utah Code Ann. 76-5-202).
Virginia	First-degree murder with 1 of 15 aggravating circumstances (Va. Code § 18.2-31(1-15)).
Washington	Aggravated first-degree murder.
Wyoming	First-degree murder; murder during the commission of sexual assault, sexual abuse of a minor, arson, robbery, burglary, escape, resisting arrest, kidnapping, or abuse of a minor under 16 (W.S.A. § 6-2-101(a)).

Note: Maryland repealed its capital statute effective October 1, 2013. Five men in Maryland remain under a previously imposed sentence of death.

a) Connecticut enacted a prospective repeal of its capital statute as of April 25, 2012. Offenders who committed capital offenses prior to that date are eligible for the death penalty.

b) New Mexico enacted a prospective repeal of its capital statute as of July 1, 2009. Offenders who committed capital offenses prior to that date are eligible for the death penalty.

c) The New York Court of Appeals has held that a portion of New York's death penalty sentencing statute (CPL 400.27) was unconstitutional (*People v. Taylor*, 9 N.Y.3d 129 (2007)). No legislative action has been taken to amend the statute. As a result, capital cases are no longer pursued in New York.

Federal Capital Offenses, by Statute, 2013[116]

Statute	Description
8 U.S.C. 1342	Murder related to the smuggling of aliens.
18 U.S.C. 32-34	Destruction of aircraft, motor vehicles, or related facilities resulting in death.
18 U.S.C. 36	Murder committed during a drug-related drive-by shooting.
18 U.S.C. 37	Murder committed at an airport serving international civil aviation.
18 U.S.C. 115(b)(3)	[by cross-reference to 18 U.S.C. 111] Retaliatory murder of a member of the immediate family of law enforcement officials.
18 U.S.C. 241, 242, 245, 247	Civil rights offenses resulting in death.
18 U.S.C. 351	[by cross-reference to 18 U.S.C. 1111] Murder of a member of Congress, an important executive official, or a Supreme Court Justice.
18 U.S.C. 794	Espionage.
18 U.S.C. 844(d), (f), (i)	Death resulting from offenses involving transportation of explosives, destruction of government property, or destruction of property related to foreign or interstate commerce.
18 U.S.C. 924(i)	Murder committed by the use of a firearm during a crime of violence or a drug-trafficking crime.
18 U.S.C. 930	Murder committed in a federal government facility.
18 U.S.C. 1091	Genocide.
18 U.S.C. 1111	First-degree murder.
18 U.S.C. 1114	Murder of a federal judge or law enforcement official.
18 U.S.C. 1116	Murder of a foreign official.
18 U.S.C. 1118	Murder by a federal prisoner.
18 U.S.C. 1119	Murder of a U.S. national in a foreign country.
18 U.S.C. 1120	Murder by an escaped federal prisoner already sentenced to life imprisonment.

---

116. *Id.* at tbl. 3 *Federal capital offenses, 2013*, at 8 (last visited Oct. 17, 2017).

18 U.S.C. 1121	Murder of a state or local law enforcement official or other person aiding in a federal investigation; murder of a state correctional officer.
18 U.S.C. 1201	Murder during a kidnapping.
18 U.S.C. 1203	Murder during a hostage taking.
18 U.S.C. 1503	Murder of a court officer or juror.
18 U.S.C. 1512	Murder with the intent of preventing testimony by a witness, victim, or informant.
18 U.S.C. 1513	Retaliatory murder of a witness, victim, or informant.
18 U.S.C. 1716	Mailing of injurious articles with intent to kill or resulting in death.
18 U.S.C. 1751	[by cross-reference to 18 U.S.C. 1111] Assassination or kidnapping resulting in the death of the President or Vice President.
18 U.S.C. 1958	Murder for hire.
18 U.S.C. 1959	Murder involved in a racketeering offense.
18 U.S.C. 1992	Willful wrecking of a train resulting in death.
18 U.S.C. 2113	Bank robbery-related murder or kidnapping.
18 U.S.C. 2119	Murder related to a carjacking.
18 U.S.C. 2245	Murder related to rape or child molestation.
18 U.S.C. 2251	Murder related to sexual exploitation of children.
18 U.S.C. 2280	Murder committed during an offense against maritime navigation.
18 U.S.C. 2281	Murder committed during an offense against a maritime fixed platform.
18 U.S.C. 2332	Terrorist murder of a U.S. national in another country.
18 U.S.C. 2332a	Murder by the use of a weapon of mass destruction.
18 U.S.C. 2340	Murder involving torture.
18 U.S.C. 2381	Treason.
21 U.S.C. 848(e)	Murder related to a continuing criminal enterprise or related murder of a federal, state, or local law enforcement officer.
49 U.S.C. 1472–1473	Death resulting from aircraft hijacking.

Does the prohibition in the Constitution of the United States against "cruel & unusual" punishment[117] prohibit the imposition of the death penalty in this

---

117. U.S. Const. amend. VIII.

country? For a brief period of time, in the twentieth century, the answer was yes. However, in 1976, the Supreme Court effectively reinstated the death penalty, in those states which authorized it by statute.

---

428 U.S. 153

Supreme Court of the United States

Troy Leon GREGG, Petitioner,

v.

State of GEORGIA

Decided July 2, 1976

Defendant was convicted in Georgia trial court of armed robbery and murder and was sentenced to death and he appealed. The Georgia Supreme Court, 233 Ga. 117, 210 S.E.2d 659, affirmed except as to imposition of death sentence on robbery charges and certiorari was granted. The United States Supreme Court, Mr. Justice Stewart, Mr. Justice Powell, and Mr. Justice Stevens announcing the judgment of the court and filing an opinion delivered by Mr. Justice Stewart, held that punishment of death for the crime of murder did not, under all circumstances, violate the Eighth and Fourteenth Amendments; that retribution and possibility of deterrence to capital crimes by prospective offenders were not impermissible considerations for legislature to weigh in determining whether the death penalty should be imposed; and that Georgia statutory system under which the punishment and guilt portions of the trial are bifurcated, with the jury hearing additional evidence and argument before determining whether to impose death penalty, under which jury is instructed on statutory factors of aggravation and mitigation, and under which Georgia Supreme Court reviews each sentence of death to determine whether it is disproportionate to the punishment usually imposed in similar cases was constitutional despite contention that it permitted arbitrary and freakish imposition of the death penalty.

. . . .

Opinion

Judgment of the Court, and opinion of Mr. Justice STEWART, Mr. Justice POWELL, and Mr. Justice STEVENS, announced by Mr. Justice STEWART.

The issue in this case is whether the imposition of the sentence of death for the crime of murder under the law of Georgia violates the Eighth and Fourteenth Amendments.

I.

The petitioner, Troy Gregg, was charged with committing armed robbery and murder. In accordance with Georgia procedure in capital cases, the trial was in two stages, a guilt stage and a sentencing stage. The evidence at the guilt trial established that on November 21, 1973, the petitioner and a traveling companion, Floyd Allen, while hitchhiking north in Florida were picked up by Fred Simmons and Bob Moore. Their car broke down, but they continued north after Simmons purchased another vehicle with some of the cash he was carrying. While still in Florida, they picked up another hitchhiker, Dennis Weaver, who rode with them to Atlanta, where he was let out about 11 p.m. A short time later the four men interrupted their journey for a rest stop along the highway. The next morning the bodies of Simmons and Moore were discovered in a ditch nearby.

On November 23, after reading about the shootings in an Atlanta newspaper, Weaver communicated with the Gwinnett County police and related information concerning the journey with the victims, including a description of the car. The next afternoon, the petitioner and Allen, while in Simmons' car, were arrested in Asheville, N. C. In the search incident to the arrest a .25-caliber pistol, later shown to be that used to kill Simmons and Moore, was found in the petitioner's pocket. After receiving the warnings required by *Miranda v. Arizona*, [384 U.S. 436 (1966)], and signing a written waiver of his rights, the petitioner signed a statement in which he admitted shooting, then robbing Simmons and Moore. He justified the slayings on grounds of self-defense. The next day, while being transferred to Lawrenceville, Ga., the petitioner and Allen were taken to the scene of the shootings. Upon arriving there, Allen recounted the events leading to the slayings. His version of these events was as follows: After Simmons and Moore left the car the petitioner stated that he intended to rob them. The petitioner then took his pistol in hand and positioned himself on the car to improve his aim. As Simmons and Moore came up an embankment toward the car, the petitioner fired three shots and the two men fell near a ditch. The petitioner, at close range, then fired a shot into the head of each. He robbed them of valuables and drove away with Allen.

A medical examiner testified that Simmons died from a bullet wound in the eye and that Moore died from bullet wounds in the cheek and in the back of the head. He further testified that both men had several bruises and abrasions about the face and head which probably were sustained either from the fall into the ditch or from being dragged or pushed along the embankment. Although Allen did not testify, a police detective recounted the substance of Allen's statements about the slayings and indicated that directly after Allen had made these statements the petitioner had admitted that Allen's account was accurate. The petitioner testified in his own defense. He confirmed that Allen had made the statements described by the detective, but denied their truth or ever having admitted to their accuracy. He indicated that he had shot Simmons and Moore because of fear and in self-defense, testifying they had attacked Allen and him, one wielding a pipe and the other a knife.

The trial judge submitted the murder charges to the jury on both felony-murder and nonfelony-murder theories. He also instructed on the issue of self-defense but declined to instruct on manslaughter. He submitted the robbery case to the jury on both an armed-robbery theory and on the lesser included offense of robbery by intimidation. The jury found the petitioner guilty of two counts of armed robbery and two counts of murder.

At the penalty stage, which took place before the same jury, neither the prosecutor nor the petitioner's lawyer offered any additional evidence. Both counsel, however, made lengthy arguments dealing generally with the propriety of capital punishment under the circumstances and with the weight of the evidence of guilt. The trial judge instructed the jury that it could recommend either a death sentence or a life prison sentence on each count. The judge further charged the jury that in determining what sentence was appropriate the jury was free to consider the facts and circumstances, if any, presented by the parties in mitigation or aggravation.

Finally, the judge instructed the jury that it "would not be authorized to consider (imposing) the penalty of death" unless it first found beyond a reasonable doubt one of these aggravating circumstances:

> "One. That the offense of murder was committed while the offender was engaged in the commission of two other capital felonies, to-wit the armed robbery of (Simmons and Moore).

> "Two. That the offender committed the offense of murder for the purpose of receiving money and the automobile described in the indictment.

> "Three. The offense of murder was outrageously and wantonly vile, horrible and inhuman, in that they (sic) involved the depravity of (the) mind of the defendant." Tr. 476–477.

Finding the first and second of these circumstances, the jury returned verdicts of death on each count.

The Supreme Court of Georgia affirmed the convictions and the imposition of the death sentences for murder. After reviewing the trial transcript and the record, including the evidence, and comparing the evidence and sentence in similar cases in accordance with the requirements of Georgia law, the court concluded that, considering the nature of the crime and the defendant, the sentences of death had not resulted from prejudice or any other arbitrary factor and were not excessive or disproportionate to the penalty applied in similar cases. The death sentences used for armed robbery, however, were vacated on the grounds that the death penalty had rarely been imposed in Georgia for that offense and that the jury improperly considered the murders as aggravating circumstances for the robberies after having considered the armed robberies as aggravating circumstances for the murders.

We granted the petitioner's application for a writ of certiorari limited to his challenge to the imposition of the death sentences in this case as "cruel and unusual" punishment in violation of the Eighth and the Fourteenth Amendments.

II.

Before considering the issues presented it is necessary to understand the Georgia statutory scheme for the imposition of the death penalty. The Georgia statute, as amended after our decision in *Furman v. Georgia*, 408 U.S. 238 (1972), retains the death penalty for six categories of crime: murder, kidnapping for ransom or where the victim is harmed, armed robbery rape, treason, and aircraft hijacking. The capital defendant's guilt or innocence is determined in the traditional manner, either by a trial judge or a jury, in the first stage of a bifurcated trial.

. . . .

In addition to the conventional appellate process available in all criminal cases, provision is made for special expedited direct review by the Supreme Court of Georgia of the appropriateness of imposing the sentence of death in the particular case. . . .

A transcript and complete record of the trial, as well as a separate report by the trial judge, are transmitted to the court for its use in reviewing the sentence. The report is in the form of a 6 1/2 page questionnaire, designed to elicit information about the defendant, the crime, and the circumstances of the trial. It requires the trial judge to characterize the trial in several ways designed to test for arbitrariness and disproportionality of sentence. Included in the report are responses to detailed questions concerning the quality of the defendant's representation, whether race played a role in the trial, and, whether, in the trial court's judgment, there was any doubt about the defendant's guilt or the appropriateness of the sentence. A copy of the report is served upon defense counsel. Under its special review authority, the court may either affirm the death sentence or remand the case for resentencing. In cases in which the death sentence is affirmed there remains the possibility of executive clemency.

III.

We address initially the basic contention that the punishment of death for the crime of murder is, under all circumstances, "cruel and unusual" in violation of the Eighth and Fourteenth Amendments of the Constitution. In Part IV of this opinion, we will consider the sentence of death imposed under the Georgia statutes at issue in this case.

The Court on a number of occasions has both assumed and asserted the constitutionality of capital punishment. In several cases that assumption provided a necessary foundation for the decision, as the Court was asked to decide whether a particular method of carrying out a capital sentence would be allowed to stand under the Eighth Amendment. But until *Furman v. Georgia*, the Court never confronted squarely the fundamental claim that the punishment of death always, regardless of the enormity of the offense or the procedure followed in imposing the sentence, is cruel and unusual punishment in violation of the Constitution. Although this issue was presented and addressed in *Furman*, it was not resolved by the Court. Four Justices would have held that capital punishment is not unconstitutional per se two Justices would have reached the opposite conclusion; and three Justices, while agreeing that the statutes then before the Court were invalid as applied, left open the question whether such punishment may ever be imposed. We now hold that the punishment of death does not invariably violate the Constitution.

A.

The history of the prohibition of "cruel and unusual" punishment already has been reviewed at length. The phrase first appeared in the English Bill of Rights of 1689, which was drafted by Parliament at the accession of William and Mary. . . .

In the earliest cases raising Eighth Amendment claims, the Court focused on particular methods of execution to determine whether they were too cruel to pass constitutional muster. The constitutionality of the sentence of death itself was not at issue, and the criterion used to evaluate the mode of execution was its similarity to "torture" and other "barbarous" methods.

But the Court has not confined the prohibition embodied in the Eighth Amendment to "barbarous" methods that were generally outlawed in the 18th century. Instead, the Amendment has been interpreted in a flexible and dynamic manner. The Court early recognized that "a principle to be vital must be capable of wider application than the mischief which gave it birth." Thus the Clause forbidding "cruel and unusual" punishments "is not fastened to the obsolete but may acquire meaning as public opinion becomes enlightened by a humane justice."

In *Weems* [v. *United States*, 217 U.S. 349 (1910),] the Court addressed the constitutionality of the Philippine punishment of Cadena temporal for the crime of falsifying an official document. That punishment included imprisonment for at least 12 years and one day in chains at hard and painful labor; the loss of many basic civil rights, and subjection to lifetime surveillance. Although the Court acknowledged the possibility that "the cruelty of pain" may be present in the challenged punishment it did not rely on that factor, for it rejected the proposition that the Eighth Amendment reaches only punishments that are "inhuman and barbarous, torture and the like." Rather, the Court focused on the lack of proportion between the crime and the offense:

"Such penalties for such offenses amaze those who have formed their conception of the relation of a state to even its offending citizens from the practice of the American commonwealths, and believe that it is a precept of justice that punishment for crime should be graduated and proportioned to offense."

Later, in *Trop v. Dulles* [356 U.S. 86 (1958)], the Court reviewed the constitutionality of the punishment of denationalization imposed upon a soldier who escaped from an Army stockade and became a deserter for one day. Although the concept of proportionality was not the basis of the holding, the plurality observed in dicta that "[f]ines, imprisonment and even execution may be imposed depending upon the enormity of the crime."

The substantive limits imposed by the Eighth Amendment on what can be made criminal and punished were discussed in *Robinson v. California*, 370 U.S. 660 (1962). The Court found unconstitutional a state statute that made the status of being addicted to a narcotic drug a criminal offense. It held, in effect, that it is "cruel and unusual" to impose any punishment at all for the mere status of addiction. The cruelty in the abstract of the actual sentence imposed was irrelevant: "Even one day in prison would be a cruel and unusual punishment for the 'crime' of having a common cold." Most recently, in *Furman v. Georgia*, three Justices in separate concurring opinions found the Eighth Amendment applicable to procedures employed to select convicted defendants for the sentence of death.

It is clear from the foregoing precedents that the Eighth Amendment has not been regarded as a static concern. As Mr. Chief Justice Warren said, in an oft-quoted phrase, "(t)he Amendment must draw its meaning from the evolving standards of decency that mark the progress of a maturing society." Thus, an assessment of contemporary values concerning the infliction of a challenged sanction is relevant to the application of the Eighth Amendment. As we develop below more fully, this assessment does not call for a subjective judgment. It requires, rather, that we look to objective indicia that reflect the public attitude toward a given sanction.

But our cases also make clear that public perceptions of standards of decency with respect to criminal sanctions are not conclusive. A penalty also must accord with "the dignity of man," which is the "basic concept underlying the Eighth Amendment." This means, at least, that the punishment not be "excessive." When a form of punishment in the abstract (in this case, whether capital punishment may ever be imposed as a sanction for murder) rather than in the particular (the propriety of death as a penalty to be applied to a specific defendant for a specific crime) is under consideration, the inquiry into "excessiveness" has two aspects. First, the punishment must not involve the unnecessary and wanton infliction of pain. Second, the punishment must not be grossly out of proportion to the severity of the crime.

B.

Of course, the requirements of the Eighth Amendment must be applied with an awareness of the limited role to be played by the courts. This does not mean that judges have no role to play, for the Eighth Amendment is a restraint upon the exercise of legislative power.

. . . .

But, while we have an obligation to insure that constitutional bounds are not overreached, we may not act as judges as we might as legislators.

. . . .

Therefore, in assessing a punishment selected by a democratically elected legislature against the constitutional measure, we presume its validity. We may not require the legislature to select the least severe penalty possible so long as the penalty selected is not cruelly inhumane or disproportionate to the crime involved. And a heavy burden rests on those who would attack the judgment of the representatives of the people.

This is true in part because the constitutional test is intertwined with an assessment of contemporary standards and the legislative judgment weighs heavily in ascertaining such standards. "(I)n a democratic society legislatures, not courts, are constituted to respond to the will and consequently the moral values of the people." . . . Caution is necessary lest this Court become, "under the aegis of the Cruel and Unusual Punishment Clause, the ultimate arbiter of the standards of criminal responsibility . . . throughout the country." A decision that a given punishment is impermissible under the Eighth Amendment cannot be reversed short of a constitutional amendment. The ability of the people to express their preference through the normal democratic processes, as well as through ballot referenda, is shut off. Revisions cannot be made in the light of further experience.

C.

In the discussion to this point we have sought to identify the principles and considerations that guide a court in addressing an Eighth Amendment claim. We now consider specifically whether the sentence of death for the crime of murder is a *Per se* violation of the Eighth and Fourteenth Amendments to the Constitution. We note first that history and precedent strongly support a negative answer to this question.

The imposition of the death penalty for the crime of murder has a long history of acceptance both in the United States and in England. The common-law rule imposed a mandatory death sentence on all convicted murderers. And the penalty continued to be used into the 20th century by most American States, although the breadth of the common-law rule was diminished, initially by narrowing the class of murders to be punished by death and subsequently by widespread adoption of laws expressly granting juries the discretion to recommend mercy.

It is apparent from the text of the Constitution itself that the existence of capital punishment was accepted by the Framers. At the time the Eighth Amendment was ratified, capital punishment was a common sanction in every State. Indeed, the First Congress of the United States enacted legislation providing death as the penalty for specified crimes. The Fifth Amendment, adopted at the same time as the Eighth, contemplated the continued existence of the capital sanction by imposing certain limits on the prosecution of capital cases:

No person shall be held to answer for a capital, or otherwise infamous crime, unless on a presentment or indictment of a Grand Jury . . . ; nor shall any person be subject for the same offense to be twice put in jeopardy of life or limb; . . . nor be deprived of life, liberty, or property, without due process of law. . . .

And the Fourteenth Amendment, adopted over three-quarters of a century later, similarly contemplates the existence of the capital sanction in providing that no State shall deprive any person of "life, liberty, or property" without due process of law.

For nearly two centuries, this Court, repeatedly and often expressly, has recognized that capital punishment is not invalid Per se. In *Wilkerson v. Utah*, 99 U.S. [130 (1878)], where the Court found no constitutional violation in inflicting death by public shooting, it said:

Cruel and unusual punishments are forbidden by the Constitution, but the authorities referred to are quite sufficient to show that the punishment of shooting as a mode of executing the death penalty for the crime of murder in the first degree is not included in that category, within the meaning of the eighth amendment.

Rejecting the contention that death by electrocution was "cruel and unusual," the Court in *In re Kemmler*, 136 U.S. [436 (1890)], reiterated:

[T]he punishment of death is not cruel, within the meaning of that word as used in the Constitution. It implies there something inhuman and barbarous, something more than the mere extinguishment of life.

Again, in *Louisiana ex rel. Francis v. Resweber*, 329 U.S. [459 (1947)], the Court remarked:

The cruelty against which the Constitution protects a convicted man is cruelty inherent in the method of punishment, not the necessary suffering involved in any method employed to extinguish life humanely.

And in *Trop v. Dulles*, Mr. Chief Justice Warren, for himself and three other Justices, wrote:

Whatever the arguments may be against capital punishment, both on moral grounds and in terms of accomplishing the purposes of punishment . . . the death penalty has been employed throughout our history, and, in a day when it is still widely accepted, it cannot be said to violate the constitutional concept of cruelty.

Four years ago, the petitioners in *Furman* and its companion cases predicated their argument primarily upon the asserted proposition that standards of decency had evolved to the point where capital punishment no longer could be tolerated. The petitioners in those cases said, in effect, that the evolutionary process had come to an end, and that standards of decency required that the Eighth Amendment be construed finally as prohibiting capital punishment for any crime regardless of its depravity and impact on society. This view was accepted by two Justices. Three other Justices were unwilling to go so far; focusing on the procedures by which convicted defendants were selected for the death penalty rather than on the actual punishment inflicted, they joined in the conclusion that the statutes before the Court were constitutionally invalid.

The petitioners in the capital cases before the Court today renew the "standards of decency" argument, but developments during the four years since *Furman* have undercut substantially the assumptions upon which their argument rested. Despite the continuing debate, dating back to the 19th century, over the morality and utility of capital punishment, it is now evident that a large proportion of American society continues to regard it as an appropriate and necessary criminal sanction.

The most marked indication of society's endorsement of the death penalty for murder is the legislative response to *Furman*. The legislatures of at least 35 States have enacted new statutes that provide for the death penalty for at least some crimes that result in the death of another person. And the Congress of the United States, in 1974, enacted a statute providing the death penalty for aircraft piracy that results in death. These recently adopted statutes have attempted to address the concerns expressed by the Court in *Furman* primarily (i) by specifying the factors to be weighed and the procedures to be followed in deciding when to impose a capital sentence, or (ii) by making the death penalty mandatory for specified crimes. But all of the post-*Furman* Statutes make clear that capital punishment itself has not been rejected by the elected representatives of the people.

In the only statewide referendum occurring since *Furman* and brought to our attention, the people of California adopted a constitutional amendment that authorized capital punishment, in effect negating a prior ruling by the Supreme Court of California in *People v. Anderson*, 493 P.2d 880 (1972), that the death penalty violated the California Constitution.

The jury also is a significant and reliable objective index of contemporary values because it is so directly involved. The Court has said that "one of the most important functions any jury can perform in making . . . a selection (between life imprisonment and death for a defendant convicted in a capital case) is to maintain a link between contemporary community values and the penal system." It may be true that evolving standards have influenced juries in recent decades to be more discriminating in imposing the sentence of death. But the relative infrequency of jury verdicts imposing the death sentence does not indicate rejection of capital punishment *per se*. Rather, the reluctance of juries in many cases to impose the sentence may well reflect the humane feeling that this most irrevocable of sanctions should be reserved for a small number of extreme cases. Indeed, the actions of juries in many States since *Furman* are fully compatible with the legislative judgments, reflected in the new statutes, as to the continued utility and necessity of capital punishment in appropriate cases. At the close of 1974 at least 254 persons had been sentenced to death since *Furman*, and by the end of March 1976, more than 460 persons were subject to death sentences.

As we have seen, however, the Eighth Amendment demands more than that a challenged punishment be acceptable to contemporary society. The Court also must ask whether it comports with the basic concept of human dignity at the core of the Amendment. Although we cannot "invalidate a category of penalties because we deem less severe penalties adequate to serve the ends of penology," the sanction imposed cannot be so totally without penological justification that it results in the gratuitous infliction of suffering.

The death penalty is said to serve two principal social purposes: retribution and deterrence of capital crimes by prospective offenders.

In part, capital punishment is an expression of society's moral outrage at particularly offensive conduct. This function may be unappealing to many, but it is essential in an ordered society that asks its citizens to rely on legal processes rather than self-help to vindicate their wrongs.

"The instinct for retribution is part of the nature of man, and channeling that instinct in the administration of criminal justice serves an important purpose in promoting the stability of a society governed by law. When people begin to believe that organized society is unwilling or unable to impose upon criminal offenders the punishment they 'deserve,' then there are sown the seeds of anarchy of self-help, vigilante justice, and lynch law."

"Retribution is no longer the dominant objective of the criminal law," but neither is it a forbidden objective nor one inconsistent with our respect for the dignity of men. Indeed, the decision that capital punishment may be the appropriate sanction in extreme cases is an expression of the community's belief that certain crimes are themselves so grievous an affront to humanity that the only adequate response may be the penalty of death.

Statistical attempts to evaluate the worth of the death penalty as a deterrent to crimes by potential offenders have occasioned a great deal of debate.... Although some of the studies suggest that the death penalty may not function as a significantly greater deterrent than lesser penalties, there is no convincing empirical evidence either supporting or refuting this view. We may nevertheless assume safely that there are murderers, such as those who act in passion, for whom the threat of death has little or no deterrent effect. But for many others, the death penalty undoubtedly is a significant deterrent. There are carefully contemplated murders, such as murder for hire, where the possible penalty of death may well enter into the cold calculus that precedes the decision to act. And there are some categories of murder, such as murder by a life prisoner, where other sanctions may not be adequate.

. . . .

In sum, we cannot say that the judgment of the Georgia Legislature that capital punishment may be necessary in some cases is clearly wrong. Considerations of federalism, as well as respect for the ability of a legislature to evaluate, in terms of its particular State, the moral consensus concerning the death penalty and its social utility as a sanction, require us to conclude, in the absence of more convincing evidence, that the infliction of death as a punishment for murder is not without justification and thus is not unconstitutionally severe.

Finally, we must consider whether the punishment of death is disproportionate in relation to the crime for which it is imposed. There is no question that death as a punishment is unique in its severity and irrevocability. When a defendant's life is at stake, the Court has been particularly sensitive to insure that every safeguard is observed. But we are concerned here only with the imposition of capital punishment for the crime of murder, and when a life has been taken deliberately by the offender, we cannot say that the punishment is invariably disproportionate to the crime. It is an extreme sanction, suitable to the most extreme of crimes.

We hold that the death penalty is not a form of punishment that may never be imposed, regardless of the circumstances of the offense, regardless of the character of the offender, and regardless of the procedure followed in reaching the decision to impose it.

IV.

. . . .

Jury sentencing has been considered desirable in capital cases in order "to maintain a link between contemporary community values and the penal system a link without which the determination of punishment could hardly reflect 'the evolving standards of decency that mark the progress of a maturing society.'" But it creates special problems. Much of the information that is relevant to the sentencing decision may have no relevance to the question of guilt, or may even be extremely prejudicial to a fair determination of that question. This problem, however, is scarcely insurmountable. Those who have studied the question suggest that a bifurcated procedure one in which the question of sentence is not considered until the determination of guilt has been made is the best answer. The drafters of the Model Penal Code concluded:

> (If a unitary proceeding is used) the determination of the punishment must be based on less than all the evidence that has a bearing on that issue, such for example as a previous criminal record of the accused, or evidence must be admitted on the ground that it is relevant to sentence, though it would be excluded as irrelevant or prejudicial with respect to guilt or innocence alone. Trial lawyers understandably have little confidence in a solution that admits the evidence and trusts to an instruction to the jury that it should be considered only in determining the penalty and disregarded in assessing guilt.

. . . The obvious solution . . . is to bifurcate the proceeding, abiding strictly by the rules of evidence until and unless there is a conviction, but once guilt has been determined opening the record to the further information that is relevant to sentence. This is the analogue of the procedure in the ordinary case when capital punishment is not in issue; the court conducts a separate inquiry before imposing sentence. . . . When a human life is at stake and when the jury must have information prejudicial to the question of guilt but relevant to the question of penalty in order to impose a rational sentence, a bifurcated system is more likely to ensure elimination of the constitutional deficiencies identified in *Furman*.

But the provision of relevant information under fair procedural rules is not alone sufficient to guarantee that the information will be properly used in the imposition of punishment, especially if sentencing is performed by a jury. Since the members of a jury will have had little, if any, previous experience in sentencing, they are unlikely to be skilled in dealing with the information they are given. . . .

To the extent that this problem is inherent in jury sentencing, it may not be totally correctible. It seems clear, however, that the problem will be alleviated if the jury is given guidance regarding the factors about the crime and the defendant that the State, representing organized society, deems particularly relevant to the sentencing decision.

. . . In summary, the concerns expressed in *Furman* that the penalty of death not be imposed in an arbitrary or capricious manner can be met by a carefully drafted statute that ensures that the sentencing authority is given adequate information and guidance. As a general proposition these concerns are best met by a system that provides for a bifurcated proceeding at which the sentencing authority is apprised of the information relevant to the imposition of sentence and provided with standards to guide its use of the information.

We do not intend to suggest that only the above-described procedures would be permissible under Furman or that any sentencing system constructed along these general lines would inevitably satisfy the concerns of *Furman*, for each distinct system must be examined on an individual basis. Rather, we have embarked upon this general exposition to make clear that it is possible to construct capital-sentencing systems capable of meeting *Furman*'s constitutional concerns.

B.

We now turn to consideration of the constitutionality of Georgia's capital-sentencing procedures. In the wake of *Furman*, Georgia amended its capital punishment statute, but chose not to narrow the scope of its murder provisions.

. . . .

These procedures require the jury to consider the circumstances of the crime and the criminal before it recommends sentence. No longer can a Georgia jury do as *Furman*'s jury did: reach a finding of the defendant's guilt and then, without guidance or direction, decide whether he should live or die. Instead, the jury's attention is directed to the specific circumstances of the crime: Was it committed in the course of another capital felony? Was it committed for money? Was it committed upon a peace officer or judicial officer? Was it committed in a particularly heinous way or in a manner that endangered the lives of many persons? In addition, the jury's attention is focused on the characteristics of the person who committed the crime: Does he have a record of prior convictions for capital offenses? Are there any special facts about this defendant that mitigate against imposing capital punishment (E.g., his youth, the extent of his cooperation with the police, his emotional state at the time of the crime). As a result, while some jury discretion still exists, "the discretion to be exercised is controlled by clear and objective standards so as to produce non-discriminatory application."

. . . .

In short, Georgia's new sentencing procedures require as a prerequisite to the imposition of the death penalty, specific jury findings as to the circumstances of the crime or the character of the defendant. Moreover, to guard further against a situation comparable to that presented in *Furman*, the Supreme Court of Georgia compares each death sentence with the sentences imposed on similarly situated defendants to ensure that the sentence of death in a particular case is not disproportionate. On their face these procedures seem to satisfy the concerns of *Furman*. No longer should there be "no meaningful basis for distinguishing the few cases in which (the death penalty) is imposed from the many cases in which it is not."

The petitioner contends, however, that the changes in the Georgia sentencing procedures are only cosmetic, that the arbitrariness and capriciousness condemned by *Furman* continue to exist in Georgia both in traditional practices that still remain and in the new sentencing procedures adopted in response to *Furman*.

. . . .

3.

Finally, the Georgia statute has an additional provision designed to assure that the death penalty will not be imposed on a capriciously selected group of convicted defendants. The new sentencing procedures require that the State Supreme Court review every death sentence to determine whether it was imposed under the influence of passion, prejudice, or any other arbitrary factor, whether the evidence supports the findings of a statutory aggravating circumstance, and "(w)hether the sentence of death is excessive or disproportionate to the penalty imposed in similar cases, considering both the crime and the defendant.

. . . .

The provision for appellate review in the Georgia capital-sentencing system serves as a check against the random or arbitrary imposition of the death penalty. In particular, the proportionality review substantially eliminates the possibility that a person will be sentenced to die by the action of an aberrant jury. If a time comes when juries generally do not impose the death sentence in a certain kind of murder case, the appellate review procedures assure that no defendant convicted under such circumstances will suffer a sentence of death.

V.

The basic concern of *Furman* centered on those defendants who were being condemned to death capriciously and arbitrarily. Under the procedures before the Court in that case, sentencing authorities were not directed to give attention to the nature or circumstances of the crime committed or to the character or record of the defendant. Left unguided, juries imposed the death sentence in a way that could only be called freakish. The new Georgia sentencing procedures, by contrast, focus the jury's attention on the particularized nature of the crime and the particularized characteristics of the individual defendant. While the jury is permitted to consider any aggravating or mitigating circumstances, it must find and identify at least one statutory aggravating factor before it may impose a penalty of death. In this way the jury's discretion is channeled. No longer can a jury wantonly and freakishly impose the death sentence; it is always circumscribed by the legislative guidelines. In addition, the review function of the Supreme Court of Georgia affords additional assurance that the concerns that prompted our decision in *Furman* are not present to any significant degree in the Georgia procedure applied here.

For the reasons expressed in this opinion, we hold that the statutory system under which Gregg was sentenced to death does not violate the Constitution. Accordingly, the judgment of the Georgia Supreme Court is affirmed.

It is so ordered.

Mr. Justice WHITE, with whom THE CHIEF JUSTICE and Mr. Justice REHNQUIST join, concurring in the judgment.

In *Furman v. Georgia*, this Court held the death penalty as then administered in Georgia to be unconstitutional. That same year the Georgia Legislature enacted a new statutory scheme under which the death penalty may be imposed for several offenses, including murder. The issue in this case is whether the death penalty imposed for murder on petitioner Gregg under the new Georgia statutory scheme may constitutionally be carried out. I agree that it may.

I.

. . . .

Having found an aggravating circumstance, however, the jury is not required to impose the death penalty. Instead, it is merely authorized to impose it after considering evidence of "any mitigating circumstances or aggravating circumstances otherwise authorized by law and any of the (enumerated) statutory aggravating circumstances. . . ." Unless the jury unanimously determines that the death penalty should be imposed, the defendant will be sentenced to life imprisonment. In the event that the jury does impose the death penalty, it must designate in writing the aggravating circumstance which it found to exist beyond a reasonable doubt.

An important aspect of the new Georgia legislative scheme, however, is its provision for appellate review. Prompt review by the Georgia Supreme Court is provided for in every case in which the death penalty is imposed. To assist it in deciding whether to sustain the death penalty, the Georgia Supreme Court is supplied, in every case, with a report from the trial judge in the form of a standard questionnaire. The questionnaire contains, Inter alia, six questions designed to disclose whether race played a role in the case and one question asking the trial judge whether the evidence forecloses "all doubt respecting the defendant's guilt." . . .

II.

Petitioner Troy Gregg and a 16-year-old companion, Floyd Allen, were hitchhiking from Florida to Asheville, N.C., on November 21, 1973. They were picked up in an automobile driven by Fred Simmons and Bob Moore, both of whom were drunk. The car broke down and Simmons purchased a new one a 1960 Pontiac using part of a large roll of cash which he had with him. After picking up another hitchhiker in Florida and dropping him off in Atlanta, the car proceeded north to Gwinnett County, Ga., where it stopped so that Moore and Simmons could urinate. While they were out of the car Simmons was shot in the eye and Moore was shot in the right cheek and in the back of the head. Both died as a result.

On November 24, 1973, at 3 p.m., on the basis of information supplied by the hitchhiker, petitioner and Allen were arrested in Asheville, N.C. They were then in possession of the car which Simmons had purchased; petitioner was in possession of the gun which had killed Simmons and Moore and $107 which had been taken from them; and in the motel room in which petitioner was staying was a new stereo and a car stereo player.

At about 11 p.m., after the Gwinnett County police had arrived, petitioner made a statement to them admitting that he had killed Moore and Simmons, but asserting that he had killed them in self-defense and in defense of Allen. He also admitted robbing them of $400 and taking their car. A few moments later petitioner was asked why he had shot Moore and Simmons and responded: "By God, I wanted them dead."

At about 1 o'clock the next morning, petitioner and Allen were released to the custody of the Gwinnett County police and were transported in two cars back to Gwinnett County. On the way, at about 5 a.m., the car stopped at the place where Moore and Simmons had been killed. Everyone got out of the car. Allen was asked, in petitioner's presence, how the killing occurred. He said that he had been sitting in the back seat of the 1960 Pontiac and was about half asleep. He woke up when the car stopped. Simmons and Moore got out, and as soon as they did petitioner turned around and told Allen: "Get out, we're going to rob them." Allen said that he got out and walked toward the back of the car, looked around and could see petitioner, with a gun in his hand, leaning up against the car so he could get a good aim. Simmons and Moore had gone down the bank and had relieved themselves and as they were coming up the bank petitioner fired three shots. One of the men fell, the other staggered. Petitioner then circled around the back and approached the two men, both of whom were now lying in the ditch, from behind. He placed the gun to the head of one of them and pulled the trigger. Then he went quickly to the other one and placed the gun to his head and pulled the trigger again. He then took the money, whatever was in their pockets. He told Allen to get in the car and they drove away.

When Allen had finished telling this story, one of the officers asked petitioner if this was the way it had happened. Petitioner hung his head and said that it was. The officer then said: "You mean you shot these men down in cold blooded murder just to rob them," and petitioner said yes. The officer then asked him why and petitioner said he did not know. Petitioner was indicted in two counts for murder and in two counts for robbery.

At trial, petitioner's defense was that he had killed in self-defense. He testified in his own behalf and told a version of the events similar to that which he had originally told to the Gwinnett County police. On cross-examination, he was confronted with a letter to Allen recounting a version of the events similar to that to which he had just testified and instructing Allen to memorize and burn the letter. Petitioner conceded writing the version of the events, but denied writing the portion of the letter which instructed Allen to memorize and burn it. In rebuttal, the State called a handwriting expert who testified that the entire letter was written by the same person.

The Jury was instructed on the elements of murder and robbery. The trial judge gave an instruction on self-defense, but refused to submit the lesser included the offense of manslaughter to the jury. It returned verdicts of guilty on all counts.

No new evidence was presented at the sentencing proceeding. However, the prosecutor and the attorney for petitioner each made arguments to the jury on the issue of punishment. The prosecutor emphasized the strength of the case against

petitioner and the fact that he had murdered in order to eliminate the witnesses to
the robbery. The defense attorney emphasized the possibility that a mistake had
been made and that petitioner was not guilty. The trial judge instructed the jury on
their sentencing function and in so doing submitted to them three statutory aggravating circumstances.

. . . .

The jury returned the death penalty on all four counts finding all the aggravating
circumstances submitted to it, except that it did not find the crimes to have been "out-
rageously or wantonly vile," etc.

On appeal the Georgia Supreme Court affirmed the death sentences on the murder counts and vacated the death sentences on the robbery counts. It concluded that
the murder sentences were not imposed under the influence of passion, prejudice,
or any other arbitrary factor; that the evidence supported the finding of a statutory
aggravating factor with respect to the murders; and, citing several cases in which
the death penalty had been imposed previously for murders of persons who had witnessed a robbery, held:

After considering both the crimes and the defendant and after comparing the evidence and the sentences in this case with those of previous murder cases, we are also
of the opinion that these two sentences of death are not excessive or disproportionate to the penalties imposed in similar cases which are hereto attached.

However, it held with respect to the robbery sentences:

Although there is no indication that these two sentences were imposed under the
influence of passing, prejudice or any other arbitrary factor, the sentences imposed
here are unusual in that they are rarely imposed for this offense. Thus, under the
test provided by statute for comparison (Code Ann. § 27-2537(c), (3)), they must be
considered to be excessive or disproportionate to the penalties imposed in similar
cases.

Accordingly, the sentences on the robbery counts were vacated.

III.

The threshold question in this case in whether the death penalty may be carried
out for murder under the Georgia legislative scheme consistent with the decision in
Furman v. Georgia.

. . . .

The Georgia Legislature has made an effort to identify those aggravating factors
which it considers necessary and relevant to the question whether a defendant convicted of capital murder should be sentenced to death. The jury which imposes sentence is instructed on all statutory aggravating factors which are supported by the
evidence, and is told that it may not impose the death penalty unless it unanimously
finds at least one of those factors to have been established beyond a reasonable doubt.
The Georgia Legislature has plainly made an effort to guide the jury in the exercise of
its discretion, while at the same time permitting the jury to dispense mercy on the

basis of factors too intangible to write into a statute, and I cannot accept the naked assertion that the effort is bound to fail. As the types of murders for which the death penalty may be imposed become more narrowly defined and are limited to those which are particularly serious or for which the death penalty is peculiarly appropriate as they are in Georgia by reason of the aggravating-circumstance requirement, it becomes reasonable to expect that juries even given discretion Not to impose the death penalty will impose the death penalty in a substantial portion of the cases so defined. If they do, it can no longer be said that the penalty is being imposed wantonly and freakishly or so infrequently that it loses its usefulness as a sentencing device. There is, therefore, reason to expect that Georgia's current system would escape the infirmities which invalidated its previous system under *Furman*. However, the Georgia Legislature was not satisfied with a system which might, but also might not, turn out in practice to result in death sentences being imposed with reasonable consistency for certain serious murders. Instead, it gave the Georgia Supreme Court the power and the obligation to perform precisely the task which three Justices of this Court, whose opinions were necessary to the result, performed in *Furman*: namely, the task of deciding whether in fact the death penalty was being administered for any given class of crime in a discriminatory, standardless, or rare fashion.

. . . .

Thus in this case the Georgia Supreme Court concluded that the death penalty was so rarely imposed for the crime of robbery that it set aside the sentences on the robbery counts and effectively foreclosed that penalty from being imposed for that crime in the future under the legislative scheme now in existence. Similarly the Georgia Supreme Court has determined that juries impose the death sentence too rarely with respect to certain classes of rape. However it concluded that juries "generally throughout the state" have imposed the death penalty for those who murder witnesses to armed robberies. Consequently it affirmed the sentences in this case on the murder counts. If the Georgia Supreme Court is correct with respect to this factual judgment imposition of the death penalty in this and similar cases is consistent with *Furman*. Indeed, if the Georgia Supreme Court properly performs the task assigned to it under the Georgia statutes, death sentences imposed for discriminatory reasons or wantonly or freakishly for any given category of crime will be set aside. Petitioner has wholly failed to establish, and has not even attempted to establish, that the Georgia Supreme Court failed properly to perform its task in this case or that it is incapable of performing its task adequately in all cases; and this Court should not assume that it did not do so.

Petitioner's argument that there is an unconstitutional amount of discretion in the system which separates those suspects who receive the death penalty from those who receive life imprisonment a lesser penalty or are acquitted or never charged seems to be in final analysis an indictment of our entire system of justice. Petitioner has argued in effect that no matter how effective the death penalty may be as a punishment, government, created and run as it must be by humans, is inevitably incompetent to administer it. This cannot be accepted as a proposition of constitutional law. Imposition of the death penalty is surely an awesome responsibility for any system of justice and those who participate in it. Mistakes will be made and discriminations will occur which will be difficult to explain. However, one of society's most basic tasks is that of protecting the lives of its citizens and one of the most basic ways in which it achieves the task is through criminal laws against murder. I decline to interfere with the manner in which Georgia has chosen to enforce such laws on what is simply an assertion of lack of faith in the ability of the system of justice to operate in a fundamentally fair manner.

. . . .

I therefore concur in the judgment of affirmance.

It is no surprise that the state where the greatest number of death sentences have been carried out in recent years is Texas. However, Texas is by no means alone. The following table represents executions by jurisdiction.

Prisoners sentenced to death and the outcome of the sentence, by jurisdiction, 1973–2013[118]

Jurisdiction	Total sentenced to death, 1973–2011	Executed
U.S. Total	8,466	1,359
Federal	71	3
Alabama	439	56
Arizona	307	36
Arkansas	114	27
California	1,013	13
Colorado	22	1
Connecticut	15	1
Delaware	60	16
Florida	1,040	81
Georgia	325	53
Idaho	42	3
Illinois	307	12
Indiana	103	20
Kansas	13	0
Kentucky	83	3
Louisiana	245	28
Maryland	53	5
Massachusetts	4	0

---

118. Bureau of Justice Statistics, *supra* note 115, at tbl. 17, at 20.

Mississippi	197	21
Missouri	186	70
Montana	15	3
Nebraska	33	3
Nevada	156	12
New Hampshire	1	0
New Jersey	52	0
New Mexico	28	1
New York	10	0
North Carolina	536	43
Ohio	419	52
Oklahoma	353	108
Oregon	63	2
Pennsylvania	417	3
Rhode Island	2	0
South Carolina	204	43
South Dakota	7	3
Tennessee	225	6
Texas	1,075	508
Utah	27	7
Virginia	152	110
Washington	40	5
Wyoming	12	1
Percent of inmates sentenced to death	100%	15.40%

Note: In 1972, the U.S. Supreme Court invalidated capital punishment statutes in several states (*Furman v. Georgia*, 408 U.S. 238 (1972)), effecting a moratorium on executions. Executions resumed in 1977 when the Supreme Court found that revisions to several state statutes had effectively addressed the issues previously held unconstitutional (*Gregg v. Georgia*, 428 U.S. 153 (1976), and its companion cases). Some inmates executed since 1977 or currently under sentence of death were sentenced prior to 1977. For persons sentenced to death more than once, the numbers are based on the most recent death sentence.

While the Supreme Court has upheld the imposition of the death penalty under the circumstances described in *Gregg*, it has prohibited the execution of individuals who commit crimes when under the age of 18.[119] Similarly, the imposition of the death penalty upon mentally incompetent would also be unconstitutional.[120]

119. Roper v. Simmons, 543 U.S. 551 (2005).
120. Atkins v. Virginia, 536 U.S. 304 (2002).

Of course, merely discussing the number of executions by jurisdiction does not give a complete perspective on how the death penalty is administered. A succinct article prepared by the Prosecuting Attorney's office in Clark County, Indiana provides a good overview.[121] Currently five different methods of execution are permitted by various state and federal statutes. These five include lethal injection, electric chair, the gas chamber, firing squad, and death by hanging. Currently sixteen states and the federal government provide for the imposition of the death penalty by injection as the sole method of execution. Twenty other states recognize, as the primary means of execution, the use of lethal injection, but allow for alternative methods with the choice generally given to the condemned prisoner. Ten states provide for the imposition of the death penalty in the electric chair. Four provide for death by a gas chamber. Three states each allow death by firing squad or hanging.

Even identifying the states and the methods of execution don't provide a complete picture. While some of the details are grizzly, it is important to examine the actual execution techniques to obtain a complete understanding of what is happening when the state determines to take a person's life.

Lethal Injection

The protocol employed generally requires the administration of a drug which renders the prisoner unconscious. Next, a muscle relaxant is injected to paralyze the inmate's breathing. Finally a third chemical causes cardiac arrest. Oklahoma was the first state to authorize the injection (1977), but Texas imposed the first lethal injection in 1982. Lethal injection is administered to an inmate strapped to a gurney. A cardiac monitor allows the warden and a licensed physician to determine when death has occurred.

Electric Chair

An inmate is strapped to a wooden chair with sponges and electrodes attached to an ankle and to the inmate's scalp. Typically the inmate's face is concealed by a hood. The purpose of the hood apparently is to minimize the traumatic effect upon the executioners of witnessing the facial contortions and distortions as a lethal amount of electricity pours through the inmate's body. Occasionally the initial shocks do not kill the inmate. Numerous attempts and botched executions prompted the call to move to execution by lethal injection. While no one can be certain what an inmate feels during any of these death procedures, lethal injection appears more placid to observers.

Gas Chamber

In the states that utilize the death chamber, an inmate is strapped in an airtight chamber, to a seat containing cyanide pellets below the chair. During the execution protocol, cyanide falls into a sulfuric acid solution. If the prisoner breathes deeply, he or she will be forced into

---

121. Clark Cnty. Prosecuting Attorney's Office, *Methods of Execution*, http://www .clarkprosecutor.org/html/death/methods.htm (last visited Oct. 23, 2017).

unconsciousness in a relatively short period of time. However, if inmate is able to hold his/her breath, the execution takes much longer and usually results in convulsions. After the inmate is pronounced dead, ammonia is pumped into the gas chamber in order to neutralize the poisonous gas. Exhaust fans remove the gas. After perhaps a half an hour, the inmate's body is removed.

Hanging

A standard military execution chart describes the physics of conducting an effective hanging. If the procedure is not carefully planned, a slow death by strangulation will result. The inmate is required to stand on a trap door. A hood is placed on the inmate's head, again, in order to protect the sensibilities of those witnessing the execution. A knotted rope is fastened around the inmate's neck. The trap door is opened, the inmate drops, and if done properly, death occurs by breaking the neck.

Firing Squad

The most recent executions by firing squads were carried out in Utah in 1996 and 1977. The inmate was restrained in a chair, and a hood was placed over the inmate's head. Again, this served not to protect the inmate, but rather the participants and witnesses. Firing squad members fired their 30-30 caliber rifles at a target placed over the inmate's heart. The five-person firing squad opened fire simultaneously with one member firing a blank. The purpose of the blank apparently was to allow some sort of emotional distance to the members of the squad (although anyone familiar with firing a rifle would be able to tell whether his or her rifle had fired a live shell).

For a complete listing of the methods employed by each state which authorizes the death penalty, (and for graphic details of the mechanics of its imposition), the reader is encouraged to examine the entire article cited above.[122]

G. For Further Thought

1. Assume that at some point in the future, technological advances permit fetal viability to occur earlier. What impact would that have on the relative rights of a pregnant woman to choose abortion and the State to restrict it?

2. Assume that technology would eventually permit an embryo to be extracted from the natural mother and implanted into an artificial womb where a fetus could develop to full term. What would that change mean to relative rights of a pregnant woman to choose abortion and the State to restrict it? Could a state require that a pregnant woman who did not want the child nonetheless be required to undergo

---

122. *Id.*

embryonic extraction and implantation to an artificial womb, with the child then being placed for adoption?

3. If the Supreme Court were to overturn *Roe*, would that mean that abortions would be illegal nationwide? Or, would it mean that the issue of abortion restrictions, like the death penalty, would be returned to the states?

4. Does Justice Scalia believe that a fetus is a "person" for purposes of Due Process and Equal Protection? If not, why is he opposed to the central holding in *Roe*?

5. Pre-born children are not "persons" under the Constitution of the United States. Can you recall other instances where our legal system recognizes as a "person" some categories of individuals now that the same system did not regard as "person" in earlier times? Are there any non-human "persons" recognized as "person" by our legal system? Can you explain?

6. Do you think that science will ever be able to determine when a human being's existence, as such, begins? How did the Catholic Church make that determination?

7. How much information is necessary before a woman can make an informed decision whether to have an abortion? Would it vary depending upon the age, educational level, intelligence, prior experience, economics, and other factors? What might those factors be? Should that same information be provided to any woman before conception? If she's already pregnant, but hasn't approached an abortion provider, should she receive the same information?

8. A young man seeks advice from an attorney. He has just learned his girlfriend is pregnant. He wants to know his legal rights and obligations. What will the attorney tell him? Would the advice be any different if the young man is married to the woman? What should Catholic lawyers and judges do when faced with clients and these issues?

9. Does the Catholic Church oppose the use of science regarding *in vitro* fertilization, genetic research, cloning, and other matters?

10. To what extent should our legal system impose restrictions on scientific research?

11. Can you think of any historical examples where experimentation conducted in the name of science would now be viewed as immoral?

12. Under what circumstances, if any, could involuntary sterilizations be implemented in the United States today?

13. What is the legal difference between assisted suicide and euthanasia? Is there a moral difference?

14. Describe a set of circumstances where the imposition of the death penalty would not violate the teachings of the Catholic Church.

15. Assume that you are in the unfortunate circumstance of representing an inmate on death row who must choose the method of execution. What method would you recommend? Why?

Chapter 4

Who Is Allowed to Live and Work in the U.S.A.? Immigration Issues

A. The Catholic Church Views on Immigration

There is no *ex cathedra* pronouncement by the Catholic Church on the issue of immigration. However, at the "87th World Day of Migration 2001," Pope John Paul II noted, in observing sociological, political, and economic events, that "[t]he interplay of such factors produces the movement of masses from one area of the globe to another. Although in varying forms and degrees, mobility has thus become a general characteristic of mankind. . . . The convergence of races, civilizations, and cultures within one and the same juridical and social order, poses an urgent problem of cohabitation."[1] The Pope continued: "The Church recognizes this right (to immigrate) in every human person, in its dual aspect of the possibility to leave one's country and the possibility to enter another country to look for better conditions of life."[2] However, this right to immigrate is not to be unrestricted by governmental regulation. The Pope explicitly stated: "Certainly, the exercise of such a right (to immigrate) is to be regulated, because practicing it indiscriminately may do harm and be detrimental to the common good of the community that receives the migrant."[3] The Pope identified the necessity for both laws of individual countries, together with "international norms that are capable of regulating everyone's rights, so as to prevent unilateral decisions that are harmful to the weakest."[4]

Two years later, immigration concerns were outlined in a pastoral letter published by the United States Conference of Catholic Bishops and the bishops of Mexico on January 22, 2003.[5] The letter, which was entitled, "Strangers No Longer; Together on the Journey of Hope," recognizes that sovereign nations have the right to control their borders through immigration control, and at the same time individuals have

---

1. Pope John Paul II, *Papal Message for the 87th World Day of Migration 2001* (Feb. 13, 2001), http://www.vatican.va/holy_father/john_paul_ii/messages/migration/documents/hf_jp-ii_mes _20010213_world-migration-day-2001_en.html (last visited Oct. 29, 2017).
2. *Id.*
3. *Id.*
4. *Id.*
5. USCCB & Conferencia del Episcopado Mexicano, *Strangers No Longer: Together on the Journey of Hope* ¶ 36, 37, 38 (Jan. 22, 2003), http://www.usccb.org/issues-and-action/human-life-and -dignity/immigration/strangers-no-longer-together-on-the-journey-of-hope.cfm.

the right to migrate with dignity even when those migrants are not afforded documentation.[6]

These dual objectives, a just policy of border control while recognizing the right to migrate, have operated at the heart of both the Catholic perspectives on immigration and the laws of the United States of America in this regard. It is probably an oversimplification to note that in general, the Catholic Church would afford a right to immigrate into this country on an even broader scale than that recognized by United States law.

How has the United States of America implemented an immigration scheme balancing the interests in regulating the borders against the right of individuals to immigrate? What has been the Catholic Church's response? We turn now to examining these issues, at greater length, beginning with the legal approach.

B. United States Immigration Law and Policy

As you will see, the United States has a very complex immigration scheme. That is because it is not the result of a single, unified approach to immigration. Rather, the policies and laws have been formed over the years, reflecting varying concerns. Nonetheless, the United States admits more legal immigrants each year than any other country in the world.[7] Although the numbers regarding illegal immigration are hard to accurately measure, it appears that the number of people entering the United States each year without proper documentation, or who overstay their visas, exceeds that of any other country in the world. The Department of Homeland Security (DHS) provided the following summary:

> [An] estimated 11.4 million unauthorized immigrants were living in the United States in January 2012 compared to 11.5 million in January 2011. These results suggest little to no change in the unauthorized immigrant population from 2011 to 2012. Of all unauthorized immigrants living in the United States in 2012, 42 percent entered in 2000 or later. Entrants since 2005 accounted for 14 percent of the total. Fifty-nine percent of unauthorized immigrants in 2012 were from Mexico.[8]

---

6. *Id.*

7. U.N., DEP'T OF ECON. & SOC. AFFAIRS, POPULATION DIV. (2011), *World Population Prospects: The 2017 Revision, File MIGR/2: Net number of migrants (both sexes combined) by region, subregion and country, 1950–2100 (thousands) Estimates, 1950—2015* (June 2017), https://esa.un.org/unpd /wpp/Download/Standard/Migration/ (last visited Oct. 29, 2017).

8. DEP'T OF HOMELAND SECURITY, OFFICE OF IMMIGRATION STATISTICS, POLICY DIRECTORATE, ESTIMATES OF THE UNAUTHORIZED IMMIGRANT POPULATION RESIDING IN THE UNITED STATES: JANUARY 2012, 1 (Mar. 2013), https://www.dhs.gov/sites/default/files/publications/Unauthorized%20 Immigrant%20Population%20Estimates%20in%20the%20US%20January%202012_0.pdf (last visited Oct. 23, 2017).

In addition to what appeared to be very strict immigration requirements, throughout our history we have created amnesty programs, waivers of deportation grounds, and other mechanisms that allow people who otherwise would be precluded from living in this country to remain. We create very high qualifications, and then allow immigrants who are most able to establish themselves remain. As this author noted in his immigration law casebook, "what we may have created is a classic model of social Darwinism. We have established a horribly complicated system of laws regarding entry and exclusions. At the same time we periodically offer forms of amnesty. One might conclude after considering the materials to follow . . . that immigrants who are the strongest, and the most able to run a gauntlet of obstacles and establish themselves, and then perhaps make enough money to retain counsel to help themselves remain here will be allowed to stay. It may appear . . . that we send aliens a mixed message: you may or may not be legally permitted to come here. However, if you can figure out how to overcome the obstacles in your path we welcome you."[9] A comprehensive view of American Immigration policy can be found in this author's casebook, *Immigration Law Cases & Materials*.[10] Some background regarding this complex scheme follows.

1. Who Are We?

John F. Kennedy noted, America is "a nation of immigrants."[11] Actually, though, our nation is no different in this regard from any other. People have always migrated in search of better living conditions and will continue to do so. Who are we, then? Consider a brief excerpt from this author's Immigration Law casebook:

> Perhaps the easiest way to identify who we are as a nation and a work force is to clarify who we are not. We are not now, nor have we ever been a monolithic, unilingual, and unicultural nation. Our growth as a nation has occurred as the result of waves of immigrating peoples from many cultural and linguistic backgrounds. Most of this immigration has been voluntary. The exceptions include the reprehensible history of slavery and the annexation of contiguous territories and the people who inhabit them. This process has resulted in the addition of many different people throughout our history. The notion that we might wish to accommodate new arrivals to survive and prosper as a nation, then, is not new. . . . However, immigration patterns have not been a constant progression. During periods of economic downturns or military struggles, the numbers slowed or stopped. In the 1930s, emigration actually exceeded immigration by 85,000. Nor have immigrants been universally welcomed. By the late 1800s, Chinese immigrants in the West were frequently referred to as the "yellow

---

9. Bill Piatt, Immigration Law: Cases and Materials 26 (The Michie Co. 1994).

10. *Id.*

11. John F. Kennedy, *A Nation of Immigrants* (1964).

scourge" or in even more derogatory terms. In the late nineteenth century, citizens of the eastern seaboard feared the loss of national identity as a result of the large number of European arrivals and blamed those immigrants for all manner of vice. Virtually every nationality group has met some opposition initially, and eventually become accepted members of the national community only to have some of their own descendants voice the fear of the dangers to the American union which would result from the addition of foreigners. . . .

. . . .

It is probably accurate to conclude that the majority of economists and historians agree immigration has historically had a positive impact on this country. It is also accurate to say that there is current concern whether the positive impact will continue.[12]

2. Extreme Positions: Bill Piatt, *Immigration Reform from the Outside In*[13]

a. Historical Extremes

The rhetoric associated with the contemporary immigration debate is often harsh. Yet it pales by comparison with the extreme discussions in earlier periods of our history. A brief examination of this history will help us put the current debate and proposals into perspective.

The original European settlers of the colonies were immigrants. By 1639, several colonies, including Massachusetts, Virginia, and Pennsylvania, recognized an "immigration problem" resulting from the English government's policy of deporting felons and vagrants to the colonies. As a result, several colonies enacted legislation precluding criminals and paupers from entering, or requiring their departure. By the early 1700s, other colonies enacted prohibitions against the entry of Catholics. Later, Virginia excluded Quakers. In 1727, Pennsylvania required immigrants to take a loyalty oath.

As time progressed, however, the colonies realized that they needed additional labor in order to clear the lands, settle the wilderness, and protect themselves against Native American tribes and foreign powers, particularly the French. At the same time, the British Crown was determined to restrict immigration to the colonies. By the time of the Declaration of Independence was signed, colonists felt so oppressed by the limitation upon immigration that they cited these restrictions as one of the justifications for armed revolution in the Declaration of Independence. Specifically, the drafters of the Declaration of Independence objected that the King of England

---

12. PIATT, *supra* note 9, at 3–6.
13. Bill Piatt, *Immigration Reform from the Outside In*, 10 SCHOLAR 270, 271–76 (2008) [hereinafter *Immigration Reform*] (internal citations and footnotes omitted).

had "endeavored to prevent the population of these states; for that purpose of obstructing the laws, for naturalization of foreigners; refusing to pass others to encourage their immigrations hither, and raising the conditions of new appropriation of lands." It is hard to imagine a more extreme immigration position than armed revolution and the express willingness to die, if necessary, in the struggle that would ensue.

For the next fifty years, America generally pursued an open immigration policy. The words of Emma Lazarus, inscribed on the Statue of Liberty, were literally true: "Give me your tired, your poor, your huddled masses yearning to breathe free[.]" In general, Americans perceived this "nation to be a refuge for freedom-seeking peoples." However, the arrivals of millions of new immigrants, most of them speaking languages other than English and adhering to different religious viewpoints, created new concerns. Catholic immigrants found themselves in a country consisting mostly of Protestants who were overtly hostile to Catholicism. Societies seeking to preserve the nation's ethnic purity were organized. For example, "[t]he Secret Catholic Order of the Star Spangled Banner and the Know Nothing Party grew out of concern . . . that 'the floodgates of intemperance, populism and crime are thrown open by immigrants and if nothing be done to close them they will carry us back to all of the drunkenness and evil of former times.'"

Violent nativism resulted in "anti-Catholic rioting in New York, Philadelphia and Boston." However, as the Irish and Catholic immigrants assimilated in American life, new immigrants from Eastern Europe became the targets of anti-immigration rhetoric. Edward Ross, a prominent historian, characterized the new arrivals as "beaten men from beaten races representing the worst failures in the struggle for existence."

By the late 1800s, anti-Chinese feelings surfaced as a result of resentment against the Chinese laborers who worked the mines, laid railroad tracks, and occupied positions in which American citizens were apparently unwilling to work. Fears were expressed that the country faced a "yellow scourge." In reaction, Congress enacted the Chinese Exclusion Act in 1882, and its constitutionality was upheld by the Supreme Court of the United States in 1889. The Court noted: "If therefore, the government of the United States, through its legislative department considers the presence of foreigners of a different race in this country, who will not assimilate with us to be dangerous to its peace and security, their exclusion is not to be stayed."

In 1924, after nativist concerns about the influx of "so-inferior peoples," Congress passed the National Origins Act, developing quotas based on the contribution of each nationality to the existing United States population. The theory was that by freezing the percentage of the percentage of those "inferior" peoples, the United States would ultimately be able to prevent from being culturally and ethnically overwhelmed by the immigrants from less-desirable regions of Eastern Europe.

As immigration from Mexico increased in the 1920s and 1930s, nativists became obsessed with what they termed "breeding habits" and "excessive fecundity" of Mexicans. C. M. Goethe, writing in *World's Work* magazine noted that the average American family has three children, while Mexican laborers average between nine and ten children. He asserted that in three generations, the offspring of Mexicans would outnumber Americans 27 to 1, producing a race of "hybrids or *Amerinds*." Samuel J. Holmes borrowed the race suicide theme originally developed by nativists supposing eastern European immigration to declare that a policy of unrestricted immigration "means that to a greater or lesser extent we are going to be replaced by the Mexican." Harry Laughlin worried that the immigration from Mexico was so large, "as to almost reverse the essential consequences of the Mexican War." Roy Garis, a Vanderbilt economics professor asserted, "[w]e cannot postpone the erection of an adequate barrier any longer . . . for it is an invasion, even more serious than if it were military."

Nativists also anxiously contemplated the possibility of miscegenation. Members of Congress John C. Box and Thomas A. Jenkins argued that "because Mexicans themselves were the product of intermarriage among [W]hites, Indians, and [B]lacks . . . they harbored a casual attitude toward interracial unions." To the congressmen, "such a situation will make the blood of all three races flow back and forth between them in the distressing process of mongrelization." Harry Laughlin warned that, "if the time ever comes when men with a small fraction of colored blood can readily find mates among white women, the gates would be thrown open to a final radical race mixture of the whole population."

Subsequent immigration legislation throughout the twentieth century to some extent reflected these anxieties. Concerns related to maintaining an adequate workforce and perhaps a cheap labor force conflicted with nativist, racial and religious concerns as this country hammered out the polyglot of immigration legislation which governs us today. National origins quotas were changed to create immigration preference based on the goals of family unification and work skills rather than national origin.

Still, a very complicated scheme persists which has the effect of limiting immigration from countries with a large percentage of immigrants already in the United States. Indeed, a "lottery" system seeking to allow additional immigrants from northern European countries was enacted with the backing of U.S. Sen. Edward Kennedy and others who were concerned that the immigration system was limiting the influx of northern Europeans.

In 1986, Congress enacted the Immigration Reform and Control Act imposing sanctions for the first time upon employers who hire undocumented workers and providing a limited amnesty program for people who have successfully and illegally run the gauntlet and established themselves in American society. Additional amendments followed, and security concerns became a focus once again following the events of September 11, 2001. The result reflects the extremes of willingness to die for open borders, coupled with the nativist desire to seal those same borders.

b. Contemporary Extremes[14]

Echoes of extreme positions throughout our immigration history reverberate today. This section examines what appears to be the extreme rhetoric in the current immigration debate. These positions really cannot be characterized as "conservative versus liberal." Immigration politics makes strange political bedfellows that defy these over-simplistic labels.

By way of example, a national debate ensued in the 1980s whether to impose sanctions against employers who hire workers who lacked work authorization. Traditional civil rights groups lined up in favor of imposing such sanctions and the resulting decline in job opportunities for undocumented workers. These organizations included the United Farm Workers Union and the National Association for the Advancement of Colored People, both of which would traditionally be viewed as "liberal" organizations. Opposition to the implementation to the employers' sanctions came from agricultural growers, and leaders of industry; these groups and individuals would traditionally be considered "conservative." Employer sanctions were implemented, but political and economic influence, particularly by the agricultural growers in California, lead to the creation of broad amnesty provisions for agricultural workers.

U.S. Sen. Edward Kennedy, a liberal, and U.S. Sen. Alan Simpson, a conservative, co-sponsored legislation to allow more immigration from northern Europe, particularly from Ireland. Sen. Kennedy was concerned that the nation's immigration scheme was resulting in "a pattern of reverse discrimination." The legislation passed, with many categorizing it as a "white man's lottery."

The current debate finds liberals advocating restrictions upon immigration and conservatives proposing "pathways to legalization" for undocumented workers in this country. There are many other examples. Rather than trying to analyze positions as conservative or liberal, it makes more sense to view the extremes from a "closed border" versus an "open border" approach. With the risk of over generalizing, this article will now turn to staking out these positions, identify the underlying assumptions, and attempt to predict why the implementation of either extreme would be disastrous.

(1) Closed Border Approaches[15]

Many anti-immigration voices are demanding a closure of the United States's borders to all illegal immigration, and in some instances, are seeking a shutdown of all but a trickle of legal immigration. In addition, there are some who worry that too many immigrants pose a threat to our national identity and our cultural values. Others express anxiety that immigrants are displacing American workers, particularly those citizens who are at the lower end of the socio-economic scale. A repeated

---

14. *Id.* at 277–78.
15. *Id.* at 278–80.

concern is that the cost of social services and education for immigrants are creating an impossible strain on our economic infrastructure. The solution would be, from this perspective, to deport the twelve million individuals in this country illegally, seal the borders to any further illegal immigration, deny health care and educational benefits to those here without authorization, impose additional sanctions upon employers who hire individuals without work authorization, and implement a number of national and local schemes to discourage additional immigration including restrictions on landlords and hotel operators who rent to unauthorized guests. Finally, official English language statutes would be imposed to help maintain national identity. Some would even go so far as to deny citizenship to those born in the United States.

Implementation of this extreme view would have devastating impact on this nation. It would probably be physically impossible to detain and deport all of the twelve million individuals in this country illegally. We do not have sufficient law enforcement resources or detention facilities to physically round up and detain them. We do not have the judicial infrastructure necessary to process the proceedings and appeals which would be necessary if we wish to maintain our system of due process. There are attempts currently being implemented to seal at least portions of the border with Mexico by the creation of a wall. Again, it is not apparent that we would have the resources to physically seal the southern border and even if we did so, we would leave exposed the northern border of the United States to illegal immigration.

Denying medical benefits to undocumented individuals can be counter-productive. Transmittable diseases that take hold in the immigrant community could spread quickly throughout the general American population. Bacteria and viruses do not distinguish between undocumented and documented individuals.

Depriving immigrant children of an education creates the dangers of the underclass which the Supreme Court of the United States viewed with significant concern in *Plyler v. Doe*.[16]

Employer sanctions enacted with the Immigration and Reform and Control Act of 1986 did not stop illegal immigration. Making it illegal to rent to persons without documentation might only create a black market for such housing and would criminalize otherwise law-abiding citizens who rent to the undocumented.

While every person would acknowledge that to be successful in this country you must be able to speak English, there is a difference between recognizing this reality and imposing this by government fiat.

Attempting to deprive children born in this country of their citizenship would require that Congress repeal the Fourteenth Amendment to the Constitution of the United States. Punishing undocumented children for the immigration sins of their

---

16. Plyler v. Doe, 457 U.S. 202 (1982).

parents in order to prevent illegal immigration raises, in addition to legal concerns, profound moral implications. In addition, the cumulative effect of the imposition of all of these steps would likely have a severe negative impact upon our economy, and would damage our standing in the community of nations.

(2) *Open Border Plus Amnesty*[17]

This position assumes that we cannot stop illegal immigration anyway and we cannot deport the twelve million or so who are already in our presence. It also assumes that Americans will take low-paying jobs that immigrants traditionally and/or currently fill. This view assumes that undocumented workers make economic contributions to our society through taxes they pay and because they require housing, food and services just like any person in this country with documentation requires. It also assumes that humans have a right to move to improve their lot in life.

The main difficulty with this position is that if it were ever implemented, we could expect a huge influx of immigrants. The economy could not guarantee employment to all who would come, just as it cannot now guarantee employment to those that are already here. The burden on health care and educational institutions would be unbearable. As individuals poured across the borders and were unable to find work, there would be a natural human inclination towards theft and crime in order to provide for hungry family members. The experiment could not be undone; if we cannot now deport twelve million, we certainly would not be able to deport the many more millions who would enter. Even granting amnesty to those who are already here illegally creates very difficult problems. Presumably, many of those twelve million are working in lower socio-economic jobs. Their sudden legalization would mean an inclination on their part to move up the economic ladder, thereby creating a vacuum at the lower end of the economy which would draw in many more illegal workers. Even granting amnesty in 1986 did not slow the increase of undocumented workers. Indeed, it appears to have had the opposite effect.

3. Formal Legal Structure

a. Citizenship

Those who enjoy the greatest rights under our immigration scheme are those people who are citizens of the United States. Citizens can live, work, vote, and otherwise enjoy all the benefits of society. They cannot be deported, and they have a greater right to bring their relatives into this country than non-citizens. There are

---

17. *Immigration Reform, supra* note 13, at 280–81.

several ways to acquire U.S. citizenship. These include citizenship at birth and through the process of naturalization.

A person acquires citizenship of the United States if he or she is born in this country, pursuant to the Fourteenth Amendment to the Constitution of the United States of America.[18] The relevant portion reads as follows: "All persons born or naturalized in the United States and subject to the jurisdiction thereof, are citizens of the United States and of the State wherein they reside."[19] The phrase "subject to the jurisdiction thereof" most likely means that the children of foreign diplomats and ambassadors who are born in the United States are not citizens.[20] This citizenship by birth provision is also included in a federal statute,[21] originally enacted as the Civil

---

18. This is also referred to as citizenship "jus soli," meaning the "law of the soil."

19. U.S. Const. amend. XIV, § 1, cl. 1.

20. Interpreting the Fourteenth Amendment, Justice Gray wrote:

This section contemplates two sources of citizenship and two sources only: birth and naturalization. The persons declared to be citizens are 'all persons born or naturalized in the United States, and subject to the jurisdiction thereof.' The evident meaning of these last words is, not merely subject in some respect or degree to the jurisdiction of the United States, but completely subject to their political jurisdiction, and owing them direct and immediate allegiance. And the words relate to the time of birth in the one case, as they do to the time of naturalization in the other. . . . Indians born within the territorial limits of the United States, members of, and owing immediate allegiance to, one of the Indiana tribes, (an alien though dependent power,) although in a geographical sense born in the United States, are no more 'born in the United States and subject to the jurisdiction thereof,' within the meaning of the first section of the fourteenth amendment, than the children of subject of any foreign government born within the domain of that government, or the children born within the United States, of ambassadors or other public ministers of foreign nations.

Elk v. Wilkins, 112 U.S. 94, 101–02 (1884).

21. The following shall be nationals and citizens of the United States at birth:

(a) a person born in the United States, and subject to the jurisdiction thereof;

(b) a person born in the United States to a member of an Indian, Eskimo, Aleutian, or other aboriginal tribe: *Provided*, That the granting of citizenship under this subsection shall not in any manner impair or otherwise affect the right of such person to tribal or other property;

(c) a person born outside of the United States and its outlying possessions of parents both of whom are citizens of the United States and one of whom has had a residence in the United States or one of its outlying possessions, prior to the birth of such person;

(d) a person born outside of the United States and its outlying possessions of parents one of whom is a citizen of the United States who has been physically present in the United States or one of its outlying possessions for a continuous period of one year prior to the birth of such person, and the other of whom is a national, but not a citizen of the United States;

(e) a person born in an outlying possession of the United States of parents one of whom is a citizen of the United States who has been physically present in the United States or one of its outlying possessions for a continuous period of one year at any time prior to the birth of such person;

Rights Act of April 9, 1866.[22] This statute and the constitutional provision guaranteed for the first time that those born in this country would be citizens. The Constitution as originally written contained no such provision. In 1857, the Supreme Court of the United States in one of its most infamous decisions concluded that slaves born in this country would not be citizens.[23] In writing for the majority, Mr. Chief Justice Taney wrote: "The question before us is, whether the class of persons [slaves] described in the plea in abatement compose a portion of this people, and are constituent members of this sovereignty? We think they are not, and that

---

(f) a person of unknown parentage found in the United States while under the age of five years, until shown, prior to his attaining the age of twenty-one years, not to have been born in the United States;

(g) a person born outside the geographical limits of the United States and its outlying possessions of parents one of whom is an alien, and the other a citizen of the United States who, prior to the birth of such person, was physically present in the United States or its outlying possessions for a period or periods totaling not less than five years, at least two of which were after attaining the age of fourteen years: *Provided*, That any periods of honorable service in the Armed Forces of the United States, or periods of employment with the United States Government or with an international organization as that term is defined in section 288 of Title 22 by such citizen parent, or any periods during which such citizen parent is physically present abroad as the dependent unmarried son or daughter and a member of the household of a person (A) honorably serving with the Armed Forces of the United States, or (B) employed by the United States Government or an international organization as defined in section 288 of Title 22, may be included in order to satisfy the physical-presence requirement of this paragraph. This proviso shall be applicable to persons born on or after December 24, 1952, to the same extent as if it had become effective in its present form on that date; and

(h) a person born before noon (Eastern Standard Time) May 24, 1934, outside the limits and jurisdiction of the United States of an alien father and a mother who is a citizen of the United States who, prior to the birth of such person, had resided in the United States.

8 U.S.C. § 1401 (2006).

22. *An Act to protect all Persons in the United States in their Civil Rights, and furnish the Means of their Vindication.*

Be it enacted by the Senate and House of Representatives of the United States of America in Congress assembled, that all persons born in the United States and not subject to any foreign power, excluding Indians not taxed, are hereby declared to be citizens of the United States; and such citizens, of every race and color, without regard to any previous condition of slavery or involuntary servitude, except as a punishment for crime whereof the party shall have been duly convicted, shall have the same right, in every State and Territory in the United States, to make and enforce contracts, to sue, be parties, and give evidence, to inherit, purchase, lease, sell, hold, and convey real and personal property, and to full and equal benefit of all laws and proceedings for the security of person and property, as is enjoyed by white citizens, and shall be subject to like punishment, pains, and penalties, and to none other, any law, statute, ordinance, regulation, or custom, to the contrary notwithstanding.

14 Stat. 27 (*reprinted in* BRUCE FROHNEN, THE AMERICAN NATION: PRIMARY SOURCES, *Ch: Civil Rights Act* (Bruce Frohnen ed., 2008)).

23. Dred Scott v. Sandford, 60 U.S. 393 (1857).

they are not included, and were not intended to be included, under the word 'citizens' in the Constitution, and can therefore claim none of the rights and privileges which that instrument provides for and secures to citizens of the United States."[24]

However, notwithstanding the enactment, of the Fourteenth Amendment and the statutes noted following the Civil War, the Supreme Court of the United States still failed to "get it right." In the 1884 case of *Elk v. Wilkins*,[25] John Elk, a native American, brought suit against the Registrar of a ward of the City of Omaha, Nebraska, for refusing to register him as a qualified voter. Mr. Justice Gray, writing for the Court, stated ". . . the question then is, whether an Indian, born a member of one of the Indian tribes within the United States, is, merely by reason of his birth within the United States, and of his afterwards voluntarily separating himself from his tribe and taking up residency among White citizens, a citizen of the United States, within the meaning of the first section of the Fourteenth Amendment of the Constitution."[26] Mr. Gray answered that question in the negative.[27] He noted that while the Thirteenth Amendment of the Constitution prohibited slavery, and the first section of the Fourteenth Amendment was designed to clarify that slaves born in this country would be citizens, "Indians born within the territorial limits of the United States . . . are no more 'born in the United States and subject to the jurisdiction thereof,' . . . and the children of subjects of any foreign government born within the domain of that government, or the children born within the United States, of ambassadors or other public ministers of foreign nations."[28]

In 1898, in the case of *Wong Kim Ark*,[29] the issue before the Supreme Court was whether a child born in the United States of parents of Chinese descent would be citizens of the United States. The Court finally got it right.[30] It distinguished *Elk v. Wilkins* on the grounds that that case only applied to Indian tribes.[31]

---

24. *Id.* at 404.

25. Elk v. Wilkins, 112 U.S. 94 (1884).

26. *Id.* at 99.

27. *Id.* at 109.

28. *Id.* at 102.

29. United States v. Wong Kim Ark, 169 U.S. 649 (1898).

30. The evident intention, and the necessary effect, of the submission of this case to the decision of the court upon the facts agreed by the parties, were to present for determination the single question, stated at the beginning of this opinion, namely, whether a child born in the United States, of parents of Chinese descent, who, at the time of his birth, are subjects of the emperor of China, but have a permanent domicile and residence in the United States, and are there carrying on business, and are not employed in any diplomatic or official capacity under the emperor of China, becomes at the time of his birth a citizen of the United States. For the reasons above stated, this court is of opinion that the question must be answered in the affirmative. *Id.* at 705.

31. *Id.* at 682 ("The decision in *Elk v. Wilkins* concerned only members of the Indian tribes within the United States, and had no tendency to deny citizenship to children born in the United States of foreign parents of Caucasian, African, or Mongolian descent, not in the diplomatic service of a foreign country.").

Notwithstanding that this issue of citizenship at birth in the United States has been settled, there are new calls to treat the children born in this country, whose parents are undocumented, in a fashion so as to deny them citizenship. In 1985 Peter Schuck and Roger Smith argued in their book, *Citizenship Without Consent: Illegal Aliens in the American Policy*,[32] that the Fourteenth Amendment should be reinterpreted to grant citizenship by birth in this country only to those children whose parents were either U.S. citizens or lawfully admitted. More recently, the issue of how to treat children who were born in this country to parents who did not have legal authorization to be here has been renewed in the immigration debate.[33] At this point, however, it would require amending the Fourteenth Amendment or repealing it in order to do away with the citizenship at birth provision.

Children born in the U.S. are not the only ones who acquire citizenship at birth. Children born in some U.S. territories acquire U.S. citizenship at birth.[34] Still another group of people who acquire citizenship at birth are those who have a blood relationship to a U.S. citizen. This is the Roman law concept of "jus sanguinis," meaning the "law of blood." Generally, a child born outside the U.S. to a U.S. citizen parent is a citizen of the United States, if the parent meets the changing requirements for physical presence in the U.S. prior to the birth of the child.[35] An example of

---

32. Peter Schuck & Roger Smith, *Citizenship Without Consent: Illegal Aliens in the American Policy* (Yale University Press 1985).

33. *E.g.*, H.R. 1940 (Birthright Citizenship Act of 2007), 110th Cong. (Apr. 19, 2007), http://thomas.loc.gov/cgi-bin/query/z?c110:H.R.1940: (last visited Oct. 29, 2017) ("To amend section 301 of the Immigration and Nationality Act to clarify those classes of individuals born in the United States who are nationals and citizens of the United States at birth.").

34. 8 U.S.C. § 1408 (2006).

35. (g) a person born outside the geographical limits of the United States and its outlying possessions of parents one of whom is an alien, and the other a citizen of the United States who, prior to the birth of such person, was physically present in the United States or its outlying possessions for a period or periods totaling not less than five years, at least two of which were after attaining the age of fourteen years: *Provided*, That any periods of honorable service in the Armed Forces of the United States, or periods of employment with the United States Government or with an international organization as that term is defined in section 288 of Title 22 by such citizen parent, or any periods during which such citizen parent is physically present abroad as the dependent unmarried son or daughter and a member of the household of a person (A) honorably serving with the Armed Forces of the United States, or (B) employed by the United States Government or an international organization as defined in section 288 of Title 22, may be included in order to satisfy the physical-presence requirement of this paragraph. This proviso shall be applicable to persons born on or after December 24, 1952, to the same extent as if it had become effective in its present form on that date; . . . .

8 U.S.C. § 1401 (2006).

how complicated these changing laws can be can be found in the cases of *Rogers v. Bellei*[36] and *Matter of Tjerina-Villareal*.[37]

In addition to citizenship at birth, another mechanism for acquiring citizenship is through the process of naturalization. The authority to create these rules is given to Congress in Article I, Section 8 of the U.S. Constitution. Congress has enacted a series of statutes within the current Immigration and Nationality Act (INA) and federal regulations have been implemented to regulate those provisions. In general, a person who wishes to obtain naturalization must first acquire the status of lawful permanent resident (see discussion below). The permanent resident must spend a requisite period of time, usually five years, before applying for citizenship. Citizenship, once acquired through naturalization, can be revoked, pursuant to the INA.[38]

---

36. 401 U.S. 815, 816, 835 (1971). The issue involved a child born in Italy to a natural-born American father. The child sought to claim his American citizenship but it was denied him because of a statute that instructed he "shall lose his citizenship unless, after age 14 and before age 28, he shall come to the United States and be physically present here continuously for at least five years. The child challenged the statute on Fifth and Fourteenth Amendments grounds. (Rogers v. Bellei, 401 U.S. 815, 816 (1971)) The Court held:

> Our National Legislature indulged the foreign-born child with presumptive citizenship subject to subsequent satisfaction of a reasonable residence requirement, rather than to deny him citizenship outright, as concededly it had the power to do, and relegate the child, if he desired American citizenship, to the more arduous requirements of the usual naturalization process. The plaintiff here would force the Congress to choose between unconditional conferment of United States citizenship at birth and deferment of citizenship until a condition precedent is fulfilled. We are not convinced that the Constitution requires so rigid a choice. If it does, the congressional response seems obvious.

Rogers, 401 U.S. 815, 835 (1971).

37. 13 I. & N. Dec. 327 (BIA 1969). Respondent was born in Mexico to a natural-born American father. However, there was a question regarding whether his father was legally capable of delivering respondent American citizenship to the Mexico-born son due to a requirement at section 201(g) of the Nationality Act of 1940. The Act required "in substance that a person born outside of the United States of parents one of whom is a citizen of the United States derives United States citizenship at birth if prior to the birth of such person, the citizen parent resided in the United States or one of its outlying possessions for a period of ten years, at least five of which were after attaining the age of 16 years." (Matter of Tijerina-Villarreal, 13 I. & N. Dec. 327, 329 (BIA 1969)) The Board found that there was not credible evidence to support the claim for derivative citizenship and it was thusly denied. (Matter of Tijerina-Villarreal, 13 I. & N. Dec. 327, 332 (BIA 1969)).

38. Kungys v. United States, 485 U.S. 759, 768 (1988) (considering falsities made on immigration documents by alleged World War II war-criminal about his occupation during the war and his place and date of birth).

> In *Chaunt v. United States*, 364 U.S. 350 (1960), we held that a naturalized citizen who had willfully and falsely stated during the naturalization process that he had never been arrested could nevertheless not be denaturalized pursuant to 8 U.S.C. § 1451. A year later, in *Costello v. United States*, 365 U.S. 265 (1961), we held that a naturalized citizen who had willfully and falsely stated during the naturalization process that his occupation was "real estate," when in fact it would more accurately have been described as "bootlegging," could be denaturalized pursuant to § 1451.

. . . .

b. Permanent Residents

In addition to U.S. citizens, permanent resident aliens (PRAs) may also live and work in this country. PRAs hold a "green card." A highly complex system has been developed by Congress to determine eligibility for PRA status. A gross oversimplification of this system would include four broad categories of people eligible to immigrate: 1) family-sponsored immigrants; 2) employment-based immigrants including investors; 3) diversity immigrants; and, 4) refugees and asylees.

(1) Family Relationships

One of the benefits of being a U.S. citizen or permanent resident is that the citizen or PRA is allowed to bring family members into this country. However, there are preference categories depending on the status of the citizen or PRA, and depending on the nature of the relationship. Immediate relatives of U.S. citizens (children, spouses, parents) are not subject, as a practical matter, to a ceiling. Note that in the case of children, Congress has established a definition of an unmarried person under 21 years of age. A parent can only be brought in by a citizen-child, if that "child" is at least 21 years of age. "Spouses" must be a valid spouse and not one who has entered into a sham marriage.[39]

In addition to immediate relatives, there is a very complicated scheme for allowing other relatives, including married children and even siblings, to immigrate. These preference categories contain numerical limitations in each category and numerical limitations on the countries of origin. Each month, the State Department publishes

---

We hold, therefore, that the test of whether Kungys' concealments or misrepresentations were material is whether they had a natural tendency to influence the decisions of the Immigration and Naturalization Service.

Kungys, 485 U.S. at 768, 772 (1988).

39. *See, e.g.,* Dabaghian v. Civiletti 607 F.2d 868 (9th Cir. 1979).

The INS, it is important to note, never has claimed or proved that Dabaghian's first marriage was a sham or fraud when entered. Instead, the INS moved to rescind on the ground that on January 13, 1972, when the adjustment of status was granted, his marriage was dead in fact even though it was still legally alive. Thus, says the INS, he was not the "spouse" of a United States citizen and was ineligible for the adjustment of status.

607 F.2d at 869.

Bark v. Immigration & Naturalization Serv., 511 F.2d 1200, 1202 (9th Cir. 1975):

The administrative record discloses that the Immigration Judge and Board of the Immigration Appeals did not focus their attention on the key issue: Did the petitioner and his wife intend to establish a life together at the time of their marriage? The inquiry, instead, turned on the duration of their separation, which, as we have pointed out, is relevant to, but not dispositive of the intent issue. Moreover, the determination may have been influenced by the irrelevant fact, cited by respondent to support the Service that 'the wife could and did leave as she pleased when they were together.' The bona fides of a marriage do not and cannot rest on either marital partner's choice about his or her mobility after marriage.

a visa availability chart.[40] That chart lists the date of the first applicant who cannot be reached within the numerical limits. Only those aliens who have a priority date earlier than the cutoff can obtain a visa. Where a "C" appears, the class is "Current" and visas are available for all qualified applicants. Where a "U" appears, the U.S. State Department has determined that visas are "Unavailable." Table 1 (below) is the family preference visa availability chart for November 2017, and Table 2 (further below) is the employment-based chart for that same month.[41]

In 2015, the United States Customs and Immigrations Service and the U.S. Department of State revised the application for adjustment of status (process whereby a person applies while inside the United States to become a permanent resident) to more closely conform to the process followed by the DOS outside of this country:

New Visa Bulletin Charts

The Visa Bulletin will now have two different charts because of the revised procedures. DOS will post two charts per visa preference category in the DOS Visa Bulletin. The charts are:

- Application Final Action Dates (dates when visas may finally be issued); and

- Dates for Filing Applications (earliest dates when applicants may be able to apply).

When USCIS determines there are immigrant visas available for the filing of additional adjustment of status applications, the Dates for Filing Applications chart may be used to determine when to file an adjustment of status application with USCIS. Otherwise, the Application Final Action Dates chart must be used to determine when to file an adjustment of status application with USCIS.

In coordination with the DOS, USCIS will monitor visa numbers each month and post the relevant chart on this page under When to File.[42]

This might have streamlined the process, although it does create some additional confusion. It is necessary to consult the Visa Bulletin each month to determine which is the relevant chart. Further explanation follows in the Visa Bulletin:

---

40. The Visa Bulletin is available at https://travel.state.gov/content/visas/en/law-and-policy/bulletin.html (last visited Oct. 23, 2017).

41. Dep't of State, Bureau of Consular Affairs, Visa Bulletin, No. 11, vol. X, *Visa Bulletin for November 2017*, Table 2, https://travel.state.gov/content/visas/en/law-and-policy/bulletin/2018/visa-bulletin-for-november-2017.html (last visited Oct. 23, 2017).

42. Department of Homeland Security, U.S. Citizenship and Immigration Services, When to File Your Adjustment of Status Application for Family-Sponsored or Employment Based Preference Visas: November 2017, https://www.uscis.gov/visabulletin-nov 17#New%20Visa%20 Bulletin (last visited Oct. 23, 2017).

When to File

Use the Visa Bulletin charts below to determine when to file your adjustment of status application.

To use the charts:

1. Find your visa type in the first column (on the left) of the appropriate chart (Family-sponsored or Employment-based).

2. Stay in that row and move directly to the right to find the corresponding date under the country of your birth (as listed in the boldface columns across the top).

3. If the date on the chart is current ("C") or your priority date is earlier than the date on the chart, you may file your adjustment of status application, if otherwise eligible to do so.

Your priority date is generally the date when your relative or employer properly filed the immigrant visa petition on your behalf with USCIS. If a labor certification is required to be filed with your immigrant visa petition, the priority date is the date the labor certification application was accepted for processing by the Department of Labor.[43]

In November 2017, the relevant Family chart was the "Dates for Filing Family-Sponsored Adjustment of Status Applications," while the Employment chart was the "Final Action Dates for Employment-Based Adjustment of Status Applications."[44]

Table 1

Dates for Filing Family-Sponsored Adjustment of Status Applications:

Family-Sponsored	All Chargeability Areas Except Those Listed	CHINA-mainland born	INDIA	MEXICO	PHILIPPINES
F1	01JAN12	01JAN12	01JAN12	01NOV96	01OCT07
F2A	01NOV16	01NOV16	01NOV16	01NOV16	01NOV16
F2B	01SEP11	01SEP11	01SEP11	01JAN97	01SEP07
F3	01DEC05	01DEC05	01DEC05	01OCT95	15JUN95
F4	15NOV04	15NOV04	22JUN04	08FEB98	01MAR95

---

43. *Id.*
44. *Id.*

Family-Sponsored Preferences

First: (F1) Unmarried Sons and Daughters of U.S. Citizens: 23,400 plus any numbers not required for fourth preference.

Second: Spouses and Children, and Unmarried Sons and Daughters of Permanent Residents: 114,200, plus the number (if any) by which the worldwide family preference level exceeds 226,000, plus any unused first preference numbers:

A. (F2A) Spouses and Children of Permanent Residents: 77% of the overall second preference limitation, of which 75% are exempt from the per-country limit;

B. (F2B) Unmarried Sons and Daughters (21 years of age or older) of Permanent Residents: 23% of the overall second preference limitation.

Third: (F3) Married Sons and Daughters of U.S. Citizens: 23,400, plus any numbers not required by first and second preferences.

Fourth: (F4) Brothers and Sisters of Adult U.S. Citizens: 65,000, plus any numbers not required by first three preferences.

(2) *Employment-Based Immigrants*

The INA also allows people with work-skills needed in this country to immigrate. Again, there is a complicated preference scheme and a visa availability determination. Table 2 is the employment preference visa availability chart for November 2017.[45]

(3) *Diversity Immigrants*

A very labyrinthine system allows individuals from "diversity" areas (countries with low immigration numbers) to immigrate to the U.S. The theoretical and political bases for diversity immigration ARE the reality that family-based immigration has had the result of producing heavy immigration from a relatively small number of countries. The diversity legislation was originally sponsored by then-U.S. Senator Ted Kennedy to enable more Irish immigration, among others.

(4) *Refugees & Asylees*

Refugees are those people outside the U.S. who seek entry because they are persecuted, or have a well-founded fear of persecution on account of race, religion, nationality, membership in a particular social group, or political opinion.

Asylees are persons in the U.S. or at the borders who meet the definition of "refugee." The U.S. recognizes refugee and asylee protection and often PRA for those individuals because of the INA and international treaties to which the U.S. is a party.

---

45. *Id.* at table 3.

Table 2

Final Action Dates for Employment-Based Adjustment of Status Applications:

Employment-Based	All Chargeability Areas Except Those Listed	CHINA-mainland born	El SALVADOR GUATEMALA HONDURAS	INDIA	MEXICO	PHILIPPINES
1st	C	C	C	C	C	C
2nd	C	15JUN13	C	08OCT08	C	C
3rd	C	01FEB14	C	15OCT06	C	15JAN16
Other Workers	C	01APR06	C	15OCT06	C	15JAN16
4th	C	C	01NOV15	C	01APR16	C
Certain Religious Workers	C	C	01NOV15	C	01APR16	C
5th Non-Regional Center (C5 and T5)	C	01JUL14	C	C	C	C
5th Regional Center (I5 and R5)	C	01JUL14	C	C	C	C

Employment-Based Preferences

First: Priority Workers: 28.6% of the worldwide employment-based preference level, plus any numbers not required for fourth and fifth preferences.

Second: Members of the Professions Holding Advanced Degrees or Persons of Exceptional Ability: 28.6% of the worldwide employment-based preference level, plus any numbers not required by first preference.

Third: Skilled Workers, Professionals, and Other Workers: 28.6% of the worldwide level, plus any numbers not required by first and second preferences, not more than 10,000 of which to "Other Workers."

Fourth: Certain Special Immigrants: 7.1% of the worldwide level.

Fifth: Employment Creation: 7.1% of the worldwide level, not less than 3,000 of which reserved for investors in a targeted rural or high-unemployment area, and 3,000 set aside for investors in regional centers by Sec. 610 of Pub. L. 102–395.

c. Non-Immigrant Categories

While U.S. law recognizes that some individuals may become PRAs, it also allows other people to enter for limited times in limited purposes as "non-immigrants." The classifications are complicated. Generally, they require intent on the part of the alien to return to his/her home after the authorized period. The U.S. has treaties with a number of countries allowing their citizens to enter without a formal visa. Regarding the citizens of other countries with which the United States does not have a treaty, the alien must apply for and receive a non-immigrant visa. While a complete listing may be found at INA section 101, a few of the most recognizable non-immigrant categories include tourist (B-2), business (B-1), students (F), exchange visitors (J), fiancé(e) (K), and artists/entertainers (P). Aliens who invest or trade in the U.S., pursuant to a treaty such as the North American Free Trade Agreement (NAFTA), hold the "E" visa.

d. Exclusions & Removals

There is a very complicated scheme which provides grounds for exclusion or removal (deportation) of aliens. There is an equally complicated scheme for attaining relief from deportation. There are also current calls for immigration reform which might involve another "amnesty" for those who are already in this country without documentation and who have family ties and no criminal backgrounds.

C. The American Bishops Respond

1. USCCB: Welcoming the Stranger Among Us: Unity in Diversity [46]

A Statement of the U.S. Catholic Bishops

Summary

On June 2, 2000, the Jubilee Day for Migrants and Refugees, Pope John Paul II celebrated the Eucharist in St. Peter's Square for over 50,000 migrants, refugees, people on the move, and their chaplains from all over the world. The Eucharist drew that great diversity of people into unity in the communion of Father, Son, and Holy Spirit, realizing a Jubilee Year hope for the Church: "to gather into one the dispersed children of God," "to sum up all things in Christ, in heaven and on earth" (Jn. 11:52; Eph. 1:10).

---

46. Statement of the U.S. Catholic Bishops, *Welcoming the Stranger Among Us: Unity in Diversity*, USCCB (Nov. 15, 2000), http://www.usccb.org/issues-and-action/cultural-diversity/pastoral-care-of-migrants-refugees-and-travelers/resources/welcoming-the-stranger-among-us-unity-in-diversity.cfm (last visited Oct. 29, 2017).

Unity in diversity is the vision that we bishops, as pastors of the Church in the United States, offer to our people as they welcome the new immigrants and refugees who come to our shores. In the past thirty-five years the number and variety of immigrants coming to the United States have provided a great challenge for us as pastors. Previous immigrants had come predominantly from Europe or as slaves from Africa, but many of the new immigrants come from Latin America and the Caribbean, Asia and the Pacific Islands, the Middle East, Africa, Eastern Europe, the former Soviet Union and Yugoslavia. Though a good number come as skilled workers and professionals, the greater number come as refugees and immigrants on the edge of survival; large numbers join families already here; others arrive without proper documents. Many were forced to leave their homeland because of a well-founded fear of persecution. This diversity of ethnicity, education, and social class challenges us as pastors to welcome these new immigrants and help them join our communities in ways that are respectful of their cultures and in ways that mutually enrich the immigrants and the receiving Church.

To pursue this vision of unity in diversity, we have chosen the way marked out by Pope John Paul II as he stood beneath the figure of Our Lady of Guadalupe in Mexico City on January 22, 1999, and announced the summary of *Ecclesia in America*: namely, the call to conversion, communion, and solidarity.

The presence of so many people of so many different cultures and religions in so many different parts of the United States has challenged us as a Church to a profound conversion so that we can become truly a sacrament of unity. We reject the anti-immigrant stance that has become popular in different parts of our country, and the nativism, ethnocentricity, and racism that continue to reassert themselves in our communities. We are challenged to get beyond ethnic communities living side by side within our own parishes without any connection with each other. We are challenged to become an evangelizing Church open to interreligious dialogue and willing to proclaim the Gospel to those who wish to hear it. The new immigrants call most of us back to our ancestral heritage as descendants of immigrants and to our baptismal heritage as members of the body of Christ. "For in one Spirit we were all baptized into one body, whether Jews or Greeks, slaves or free persons, and we are all given to drink of one Spirit" (1 Cor. 12:13).

The call to communion goes out to all members of the Church—bishops, priests, deacons, religious, lay leaders, and parishioners—to prepare themselves to receive the newcomers with a genuine spirit of welcome. Simple, grace-filled kindness and concern on the part of all parishioners to newcomers are the first steps. This can be accompanied by language and culture study as well as constant and patient efforts at intercultural communication. The integration of incoming groups is complex because of multiple Mass schedules and lack of personnel or resources, but if the receiving parish staffs and parishioners are open to the newcomers and provide a bridge to join cultures to one another, the newcomers themselves will provide the leadership and show the way to a healthy integration. Both on parish and diocesan levels, the presence of brothers and sisters from different cultures should be celebrated as a gift to the Church through well-prepared liturgies, lay leadership development programs inclusive of all, the appointment of prepared leaders of immigrant communities to parish and diocesan positions, and special efforts to help youth find their way as they experience themselves often torn between two cultures.

One successful model of unity in diversity was Encuentro 2000: Many Faces in God's House, the National Conference of Catholic Bishops' celebration for the Jubilee Year. In the materials prior to the celebration, Encuentro 2000 offered a discussion method called the "mutual invitation process," which maximizes intercultural participation. In the celebration itself, Encuentro 2000 was an experience of the exuberance and vitality, the profound faith and devotional life of the participants. Encuentro 2000 also demonstrated that communion in a multicultural Church is a true possibility for the new millennium.

The call to solidarity can be summed up in Pope John Paul II's Message for World Migration Day 2000: "The Church hears the suffering cry of all who are uprooted from their own land, of families forcefully separated, of those who, in the rapid changes of our day, are unable to find a stable home anywhere. She senses the anguish of those without rights, without any security, at the mercy of every kind of exploitation, and she supports them in their unhappiness" (no. 6). We bishops commit ourselves and all the members of our church communities to continue the work of advocacy for laws that respect the human rights of immigrants and preserve the unity of the immigrant family. We encourage the extension of social services, citizenship classes, community organizing efforts that secure improved housing conditions, decent wages, better medical attention, and appropriate educational opportunities for immigrants and refugees. We advocate reform of the 1996 immigration laws that have undermined some basic human rights for immigrants. We join with others of good will in a call for legalization opportunities for the maximum number of undocumented persons, particularly those who have built equities and otherwise contributed to their communities.

In *Ecclesia in America*, Pope John Paul II calls for a "new evangelization" centered on the person of Jesus Christ. "'The encounter with the living Jesus Christ' is 'the path to conversion, communion and solidarity'" (no. 7). Such an encounter, so central to all our Jubilee Year activities, leads to a daily vision of the risen Lord, present and active in the world, especially in the poor, in the stranger, and in the migrant and refugee. These immigrants, new to our shores, call us out of our unawareness to a conversion of mind and heart through which we are able to offer a genuine and suitable welcome, to share together as brothers and sisters at the same table, and to work side by side to improve the quality of life for society's marginalized members. In so doing, we work to bring all the children of God into a fuller communion, "the communion willed by God, begun in time and destined for completion in the fullness of the Kingdom" (*Ecclesia in America*, no. 33).

. . . .

Conclusion: A Call to a New Evangelization

In *Ecclesia in America*, Pope John Paul II calls for a "new evangelization" centered on the person of Jesus Christ: "'The encounter with the living Jesus Christ' is 'the path to conversion, communion and solidarity'" (no. 7). This personal encounter with the risen Lord, so abundantly recounted in the Gospels, Epistles, and Acts of the Apostles, leads to a daily vision of the Lord present and active in the world, especially in the poor, in the stranger, and in the migrant and refugee. Those most in need draw the members of the Church out of their unawareness to a conversion of heart through which they are able to offer a genuine and suitable welcome, to share together as brothers and sisters at the same table, and to work side by side to improve the quality of life for society's most vulnerable members. All of this is an expression of the Spirit of the risen Jesus being poured out again on his followers.

The Holy Spirit made manifest at Pentecost enabled people of diverse languages and cultures to understand the one message of salvation. The new evangelization means openness to the gifts of the Spirit wherever they might appear. Our response to the new immigration thus is informed by a renewed vision of what it is to be Church, and by a new spirituality, informed by the Spirit of Pentecost present in the sacrament of confirmation, which gives the power to discern the one message of the kingdom in the diverse customs and languages of our immigrant brothers and sisters.

Immigrant communities give ample witness to what it is to be Church—in their desire to worship as a people, in their faith, in their solidarity with one another and with the weakest among them, in their devotion and their faithfulness to the Church of their ancestors. For the Church in the United States to walk in solidarity with newcomers to our country is to live out our catholicity as a Church. The Church of the twenty-first century will be, as it has always been, a Church of many cultures, languages and traditions, yet simultaneously one, as God is one—Father, Son, and Holy Spirit—unity in diversity.

The new immigration is a reminder of the pilgrim state of the Church, made up of all those, regardless of race or class or national origin, who have been called to the wedding banquet and have responded (Lk 14:23). As a pilgrim, the Church encompasses in itself all the reality of human suffering and all the glory of the human spirit infused with the grace of Christ. With its diverse pilgrim peoples, the Church in the United States has known uprootedness and loss, persecution and flight, the search for a better life, and the difficulties and disappointments of that search. The Church has known God's grace as it lifts spirits in times of despair, sustains hope in the face of hopelessness, and revives love despite evils and human frailties. In the one baptism, the Church acknowledges God's call to conversion, while in the sacrament of the Eucharist, she enjoys prefigured the glorious communion of Father and Son in the Holy Spirit. At the Eucharist the Church prefigures the revelation of "a great multitude . . . from every nation, race, people, and tongue" (Rev. 7:9).

In such a Eucharist, on that sunlit Jubilee Day of Migrants and Refugees in St. Peter's Square, Pope John Paul II summed up the challenge and hope for the Church in the United States as it welcomes the immigrants of the new millennium in a very simple but profound image:

Like the disciples of Emmaus, believers, supported by the living presence of the risen Christ, become in turn the traveling companions of their brothers and sisters in trouble, offering them the word which rekindles hope in their hearts. With them they break the bread of friendship, brotherhood and mutual help. This is how to build the civilization of love. This is how to proclaim the hoped-for coming of the new heavens and the new earth to which we are heading. (no. 4)

2. USCCB: Frequently Asked Questions About the Catholic Church's Position on Immigration[47]

• *Why does the church care about immigration policies?*

The Catholic Church has historically held a strong interest in immigration and how public policy affects immigrants seeking a new life in the United States. Based on Scriptural and Catholic social teachings, as well as her own experience as an immigrant Church in the United States, the Catholic Church is compelled to raise her voice on behalf of those who are marginalized and whose God-given rights are not respected.

The Church believes that current immigration laws and policies have often led to the undermining of immigrants' human dignity and have kept families apart. The existing immigration system has resulted in a growing number of persons in this country in an unauthorized capacity, living in the shadows as they toil in jobs that would otherwise go unfilled. Close family members of U.S. citizens and lawful permanent residents must wait years for a visa to be reunited. And, our nation's border enforcement strategies have been ineffective and have led to the death of thousands of migrants.

The Church has a responsibility to shine the message of God on this issue and help to build bridges between all parties so that an immigration system can be created that is just for all and serves the common good, including the legitimate security concerns of our nation.

---

47. Justice for Immigrants, *Frequently Asked Questions About the Catholic Church's Position on Immigration* (Aug. 22, 2005), http://www.justiceforimmigrants.org/facts.shtml. [Ed. Note— this site is no longer available. *See* USCCB, *Tough Questions about Immigration*, https:// justiceforimmigrants.org/what-we-are-working-on/immigration/tough-questions-about-immigration/.]

• Does the Catholic Church support illegal immigration?

The Catholic Bishops do not condone unlawful entry or circumventions of our nation's immigration laws. The bishops believe that reforms are necessary in order for our nation's immigration system to respond to the realities of separated families and labor demands that compel people to immigrate to the United States, whether in an authorized or unauthorized fashion.

Our nation's economy demands foreign labor, yet there are insufficient visas to meet this demand. Close family members of U.S. citizens and lawful permanent residents face interminable separations, sometimes of twenty years or longer, due to backlogs of available visas. U.S. immigration laws and policies need to be updated to reflect these realties.

• Does the Catholic Church support "amnesty"?

The Catholic bishops are proposing an earned legalization for those in this country in an unauthorized status and who have built up equities and are otherwise admissible. "Amnesty," as commonly understood, implies a pardon and a reward for those who did not obey immigration laws, creating inequities for those who wait for legal entry. The bishops' proposal is not an "amnesty."

The Bishops' earned legalization proposal provides a window of opportunity for undocumented immigrants who are already living in our communities and contributing to our nation to come forward, pay a fine and application fee, go through rigorous criminal background checks and security screenings, demonstrate that they have paid taxes and are learning English, and obtain a visa that could lead to permanent residency, over time.

D. Toward Reform

1. USCCB Views Reform

In August, 2013, the USCCB published an update, *"Catholic Church's Position on Immigration Reform"*:[48]

Comprehensive Immigration Reform

According to the Pew Hispanic Center, there are currently 11.2 million unauthorized persons residing in the United States. Each year, approximately 300,000 more unauthorized immigrants enter the country. In large

48. Statement of the U.S. Catholic Bishops, Catholic Church's Position on Immigration Reform, USCCB (Aug. 2013), http://www.usccb.org/issues-and-action/human-life-and-dignity/immigration/churchteachingonimmigrationreform.cfm (last visited Oct. 29, 2017).

part, these immigrants feel compelled to enter by either the explicit or implicit promise of employment in the U.S. agriculture, construction, and service industries, among others. Most of this unauthorized flow comes from Mexico, a nation struggling with severe poverty, where it is often impossible for many to earn a living wage and meet the basic needs of their families.

Survival has thus become the primary impetus for unauthorized immigration flows into the United States. Today's unauthorized immigrants are largely low-skilled workers who come to the United States for work to support their families. Over the past several decades, the demand by U.S. businesses, large and small, for low-skilled workers has grown exponentially, while the supply of available workers for low-skilled jobs has diminished. Yet, there are only 5,000 green cards available annually for low-skilled workers to enter the United States lawfully to reside and work. The only alternative to this is a temporary work visa through the H-2A (seasonal agricultural) or H-2B (seasonal non-agricultural) visa programs which provide temporary status to low-skilled workers seeking to enter the country lawfully. While H-2A visas are not numerically capped, the requirements are onerous. H-2B visas are capped at 66,000 annually. Both only provide temporary status to work for a U.S. employer for one year. At their current numbers, these are woefully insufficient to provide legal means for the foreign-born to enter the United States to live and work, and thereby meet our demand for foreign-born labor.

In light of all of this, many unauthorized consider the prospect of being apprehended for crossing illegally into the United States a necessary risk. Even after being arrested and deported, reports indicate that many immigrants attempt to re-enter the United States once again in the hope of bettering their lives.

Adding to this very human dilemma is the potentially dangerous nature of crossing the Southern border. Smugglers looking to take advantage of would-be immigrants extort them for exorbitant sums of money and then transport them to the U.S. under perilous conditions. Other immigrants have opted to access the U.S. by crossing through the Southwest's treacherous deserts. As a result, thousands of migrants have tragically perished in such attempts from heat exposure, dehydration, and drowning.

Catholic Social Teaching

The Catholic Catechism instructs the faithful that good government has two duties, both of which must be carried out and neither of which can be ignored. The first duty is to welcome the foreigner out of charity and respect for the human person. Persons have the right to immigrate and thus government must accommodate this right to the greatest extent possible, especially financially blessed nations:

"The more prosperous nations are obliged, to the extent they are able, to welcome the foreigner in search of the security and the means of livelihood which he cannot find in his country of origin. Public authorities should see to it that the natural right is respected that places a guest under the protection of those who receive him." Catholic Catechism, 2241.

The second duty is to secure one's border and enforce the law for the sake of the common good. Sovereign nations have the right to enforce their laws and all persons must respect the legitimate exercise of this right: "Political authorities, for the sake of the common good for which they are responsible may make the exercise of the right to immigrate subject to various juridical conditions, especially with regard to the immigrants' duties toward their country of adoption. Immigrants are obliged to respect with gratitude the material and spiritual heritage of the country that receives them, to obey its laws and to assist in carrying civic burdens." Catholic Catechism, 2241.

In January 2003, the U.S. Catholic Bishops released a pastoral letter on migration entitled, "Strangers No Longer: Together on the Journey of Hope." In their letter, the Bishops stressed that, "[w]hen persons cannot find employment in their country of origin to support themselves and their families, they have a right to find work elsewhere in order to survive. Sovereign nations should provide ways to accommodate this right." No. 35. The Bishops made clear that the "[m]ore powerful economic nations . . . have a stronger obligation to accommodate migration flows." No. 36.

USCCB Position

The United States Conference of Catholic Bishops (USCCB) opposes "enforcement only" immigration policies and supports comprehensive immigration reform. In Strangers No Longer: Together on the Journey of Hope, the U.S. Catholic Bishops outlined the elements of their proposal for comprehensive immigration reform. These include:

Earned Legalization: An earned legalization program would allow foreign nationals of good moral character who are living in the United States to apply to adjust their status to obtain lawful permanent residence. Such a program would create an eventual path to citizenship, requiring applicants to complete and pass background checks, pay a fine, and establish eligibility for resident status to participate in the program. Such a program would help stabilize the workforce, promote family unity, and bring a large population "out of the shadows," as members of their communities.

Future Worker Program: A worker program to permit foreign-born workers to enter the country safely and legally would help reduce illegal immigration and the loss of life in the American desert. Any program should include workplace protections, living wage levels, safeguards against the displacement of U.S. workers, and family unity.

Family-based Immigration Reform: It currently takes years for family members to be reunited through the family-based legal immigration system. This leads to family breakdown and, in some cases, illegal immigration. Changes in family-based immigration should be made to increase the number of family visas available and reduce family reunification waiting times.

Restoration of Due Process Rights: Due process rights taken away by the 1996 Illegal Immigration Reform and Immigrant Responsibility Act (IIRIRA) should be restored. For example, the three and ten year bars to reentry should be eliminated.

Addressing Root Causes: Congress should examine the root causes of migration, such as under-development and poverty in sending countries, and seek long-term solutions. The antidote to the problem of illegal immigration is sustainable economic development in sending countries. In an ideal world, migration should be driven by choice, not necessity.

Enforcement: The U.S. Catholic Bishops accept the legitimate role of the U.S. government in intercepting unauthorized migrants who attempt to travel to the United States. The Bishops also believe that by increasing lawful means for migrants to enter, live, and work in the United States, law enforcement will be better able to focus upon those who truly threaten public safety: drug and human traffickers, smugglers, and would-be terrorists. Any enforcement measures must be targeted, proportional, and humane.

In Donald Kerwin's note, *Immigration Reform and the Catholic Church*,[49] Kerwin summarizes the efforts of American Catholic bishops in the pursuit of immigration reform. In his writing, he notes that by 1920, 75% of American Catholics had immigrated to this country. This demographic reality has undoubtedly led to the Church's concern with immigrants and immigration policy. Kerwin observes that,

> The Catholic Church in the United States does not support open borders, illegal immigration, or an "amnesty" that would grant legal status to all unauthorized immigrants. It believes nations have a legitimate responsibility to promote the common good by denying admission to certain migrants and by regulating the flow of all those who are seeking to enter.
>
> However, the church sees the current U.S. immigration system—while generous in many respects—as badly in need of reform. . . .
>
> . . . .
>
> To fix the current system, U.S. bishops support a comprehensive approach. They believe "enforcement only" will exacerbate the current crisis. . . .
>
> . . . .

49. Donald Kerwin, *Immigration Reform and the Catholic Church*, CATHOLIC LEGAL IMMIGRATION NETWORK, INC. (May 1, 2006), http://www.migrationinformation.org/Feature/display.cfm?id=395 (last visited Oct. 29, 2017).

. . . [The Catholic Church] believes a just immigration system would allow immigrants to realize their basic aspirations and, in doing so, would serve the good of all Americans.

How might such a movement toward reform operate? This author offers the following approach.

2. Bill Piatt: Immigration Reform from the Outside In[50]

a. Moving Inward

A majority of American citizens are not satisfied with the current state of immigration laws. The extreme approaches will not work. Constructing a realistic alternative will require the involvement of people from many different backgrounds and all ranges of the political spectrum. It would require a comprehensive analysis of the legal, economic, political, social, religious, and racial issues, rather than the ad hoc responses to the perceived hot-button issues at whatever time policy is being debated. A more comprehensive view which would allow us to find more politically-acceptable middle ground from the extremes would require a thoughtful examination of a number of issues. These issues and the out-lines of a resolution follow.

(1) *Why Do People Want To Come To The United States?*

More people enter this country illegally and legally than any other nation in the world. Political freedom and economic opportunities have drawn people to this nation from the inception of our republic. What do these newcomers need, and what do we as a nation have a right to expect? It is likely that many, if not most, of the new arrivals seek the more immediate benefit of economic prosperity in the United States. The nation, that is the majority of individuals living and working in the United States, has the legitimate right to maintain the sovereignty of this country in order to provide the same blessings of economic prosperity and liberty for their families and for future generations.

(2) *What Impact Do New Arrivals Have On The Economy?*

So far, economists have disagreed on this very important issue. We need to be able to determine the costs and benefits of immigration. It makes no sense to drastically curtail immigration if the nation is experiencing economic benefits from it anymore than it makes sense to open the borders wider if that would cause an economic downturn.

---

50. *Immigration Reform*, *supra* note 13, at 282–87.

(3) *What Would Be The Costs And Benefits Of Attempting To Remove Those Who Are Here Illegally?*

Do we have the resources to identify, detain and remove all those who are here illegally? If not, how would we prioritize enforcement? Should we consider some form of amnesty for these individuals? In this regard, what were the successes and failures of the amnesty provisions enacted in 1986? Would granting amnesty create a vacuum encouraging others to enter illegally? There are many individuals outside of the United States who have applied for an entry visa and who have spent years and even decades awaiting the availability of a visa under our incredibly complex quota system. Is it fair to those who have followed the law to allow those who have broken the law to receive amnesty? If we consider amnesty for those who enter unlawfully, should we consider some form of amnesty for those who have patiently waited in line all these years?

(4) *How Do We Prioritize Immigration Enforcement Efforts?*

Assuming that we cannot physically stop every person who wishes to enter this country illegally from doing so, how do we set priorities for prevention of entry, and for deportation? What role should physical barriers and technology play in this process?

(5) *What Role Should The Federal, State And Local Governments Play?*

Traditionally, immigration enforcement has been left to the federal government. It has become obvious to the governors of the border states and many localities that these immigration enforcement efforts are failing? In fact, several border states have recently enacted their own enforcement schemes. For example, Arizona recently enacted a scheme for employers' sanctions. On the other hand, some state and local governments have declared themselves to be amnesty or sanctuary zones for illegal entrants.

(6) *To What Extent Should We Rely Upon Private Immigration Enforcement?*

The federal government has imposed upon the private sector a large portion of the burden of immigration enforcement through the creation of employer sanctions. Employers currently are prohibited from hiring undocumented workers. Moreover, they must maintain records to prove they are not hiring undocumented workers. An employer who hires someone with documentation but fails to maintain records at the employer's place of business is subject to penalties. The private sector is not compensated for this. To what extent do we want to increase the sanctions thereby breaking the magnet of employment drawing people to our country illegally without providing compensation to these private enforcers? What do we do about private volunteers who seek to enforce the nation's immigration policies? Do we want to encourage them in their efforts or does this lead to at least the perception of vigilante justice when armed, private individuals and groups patrol the borders?

(7) *How Much Are We Willing To Impose Sanctions Upon Citizens In The Name Of Immigration Control?*

To what extent would illegal immigration be curbed if we deny citizenship to children born in the United States to undocumented parents? To what extent do we discourage illegal immigration by enacting English-only rules which affect citizens and non-citizens alike? Will denying educational and health care benefits to illegal entrants curb immigration or will it create more difficulty for citizens and noncitizens alike?

(8) *What Impact Does Immigration Have On Race Relations In The United States?*

Will English-only rules discourage illegal immigration and help to maintain cultural identity? Is the nation or areas of the nation at risk of losing identity by the influx of immigrants? Does the presence of Latino immigrants exacerbate tensions between the African-American and Latino communities? To what extent should race and national origin play a role in immigration policy?

b. Hope for Resolution[51]

It is obvious that attempting to answer these questions will be extremely difficult. We have not been able to successfully address them thus far in the nation's history. That is not to say that the inquiry should not begin. Beginning this process will enable us to start moving inward from the extremes to a more just and politically immigration policy. With principled political leadership much could be accomplished. After all, the heated rhetoric at both ends of the spectrum has been toned down from historical models. Even those who currently adhere to the closed-border approach would likely agree that our immigration policy should allow for the entry of some aliens with exceptional ability. They would probably allow those fleeing persecution to continue to enter this country, particularly those fleeing regimes hostile to the United States. Most of the open-border advocates would nonetheless agree that it makes no sense to allow those into this country who would destroy it. Ultimately, it might be possible, depending upon the result of the studies to the issues raised in the previous section, to come to some more general agreements. The results of those inquiries and the resulting policy might be that immigrants will want to enter the United States because they seek to better their own lot and that of their families. Their motives are likely, in most cases, mixed. They need immediate sustenance and yet they look to provide a better future for their children. This future involves the hope of improved economic circumstances, and the "pursuit of happiness" that is the common goal of people who are already in the United States. We need the skills and labor of some immigrants, and we want to attract the best and brightest to our shores.

---

51. *Id.*

However, we have a right as a nation to admit those who are interested not only in their own economic well-being, but in the political well-being and the sovereignty of this nation. We have the right as a nation to limit entry in terms of absolute numbers and in terms of qualifications of the immigrants. We might choose to continue to allow those with particular work skills to enter our country as well as those who are fleeing persecution. We would also want to allow some immediate family members to accompany those workers. The presence of family members will assist the immigrant in the process of survival and assimilation into the new country, benefiting both the immigrant and the nation. It would likely be cost prohibitive to remove all of those who are now here illegally.

Yet granting a blanket amnesty would likely create a vacuum, drawing others here illegally. It would not be fair to those who have patiently waited, following the legally-ordained process of immigration to the United States, to put those who have "jumped the line" ahead of them. We might strike a balance by creating some opportunities for those who are here illegally to apply for legal entrance. They might have to "stand in line" with the others. They might even have to leave this country for some period of time. For those who are here illegally who do not qualify or who fail to apply for some form of legalization, we might just choose to look the other way. Unless they create negative attention by committing crimes or doing other things that are harmful, we might choose not to spend the resources necessary to uproot them. They would not qualify for the benefits that those who are here lawfully have achieved. At the same time, we would need to provide a safety net for the children of these individuals.

Immigration enforcement efforts should be prioritized with the notion of defense of the nation as the highest priority. Those who pose the greatest threats should be at the top of the enforcement efforts, especially terrorists, and criminals.

Federal, state, and local governments have got to work together to implement effective immigration controls. State and local police officers need to receive training in immigration law and enforcement.

Private enforcement of the nation's immigration laws through employer sanction should be continued with compensation to business owners for the costs associated with this endeavor. Courts should continue to prevent the implementation of private, state and local action which runs contrary to national immigration law and policy. We should not tolerate a plethora of immigration standards on a local basis any more than we would tolerate the minting of currency on a local or private level.

While not all western democracies recognize the concept of citizenship by birth, we do. It is enshrined in the Fourteenth Amendment to the Constitution of the United States. Any attempt to change this would require the effective repeal of the Fourteenth Amendment. Legally and morally, that does not appear to be the right thing to do, just as punishing undocumented children for the sins of their parents should not be condoned.

c. Conclusion[52]

There is no easy approach to immigration reform, yet, it is critical that we attempt it. By following the approaches suggested in this article, a realistic possibility that we would be able to arrive at a better formulation, weighing the economic, sociological, political religions and racial implications of our determinations might be created. In the process, we would quite frankly have to take into account lofty ideals (i.e., human rights, sovereignty) and baser human motivations (i.e., greed, racism). Assuming that no individual, political party or interest group has a monopoly on virtue or vice, seeking common ground from the extremes might increase the likelihood of the formulation of an equitable approach to immigration reform.

3. Voices from the Bishops of the Border Region

In an open letter issued on Thanksgiving Day, November 28, 2013, the bishops of the border region of Mexico, Texas, and New Mexico added their voices to the call for immigration reform. The bishops noted that, "The current immigration system in the United States exacerbates . . . chronically difficult conditions affecting families."[53] The bishops elaborated on the need to respect and preserve family life, while still adhering to the five principles, set out by the Catholic bishops of the United States and Mexico, in the 2003 pastoral letter, "Strangers No Longer":[54]

1. All people have the right to find opportunities for a decent life in their homeland.

2. All people have the right to migrate to support themselves and their families.

3. Nations have the right to control their borders.

4. Refugees and asylum seekers have the right to safety and protection.

5. Undocumented migrants have human rights, which include dignity and the right to participate in civil society.

---

52. *Id.*

53. Catholic Bishops of the Texas-Mexican Border, *Family Beyond Borders: An Open Letter from the Bishops of the Border Region of Mexico, Texas, and New Mexico*, Texas Catholic Conference (Dec. 9, 2013), http://www.txcatholic.org/news/399-catholic-bishops-publish-letter-on-immigration-and-family. Not available anymore.

54. *Id.* (citing Statement of the U.S. Catholic Bishops, *Strangers No Longer: Together on the Journey of Hope. A Pastoral Letter Concerning Migration from the Catholic Bishops of Mexico and the United States*, Ch. 2, (Jan. 22, 2003), http://www.usccb.org/issues-and-action/human-life-and-dignity/immigration/strangers-no-longer-together-on-the-journey-of-hope.cfm).

E. For Further Thought

1. Maria is a citizen of Mexico. She has lived in the United States for the last five years. She is 27 years old, is not married, and has a child, Andrea, who was born in this country three years ago. Maria entered the country on a tourist visa which expired several years ago. The father of Andrea is Charles, a United States citizen. Maria would like to remain in this country. What additional information would you need in order to determine whether there is anything you can do to assist her? What initial advice would you give her? If she asks you whether she should marry Charles, what would you advise? In this regard, consider Rule 1.16(a)(1) of the 2010 American Bar Association's Model Rules of Professional Conduct (Model Rules):

Rule 1.16 Declining or Terminating Representation

(a) Except as stated in paragraph (c), a lawyer shall not represent a client or, where representation has commenced, shall withdraw from the representation of a client if:

(1) the representation will result in violation of the rules of professional conduct or other law;

2. Assume that in the first question Maria marries Charles. Charles engages in acts of domestic violence against Maria. Would she still be able to seek immigrant status? Review the applicable provisions of the Violence Against Women Act of 1994, set out in INA section 240A(b)(2).

Sec. 240A. (b) Cancellation of Removal and Adjustment of Status for Certain Nonpermanent Residents—

(2) Special Rule for Battered Spouse or Child—

(A) Authority—The Attorney General may cancel removal of, and adjust to the status of an alien lawfully admitted for permanent residence, an alien who is inadmissible or deportable from the United States if the alien demonstrates that—

(i)(I) the alien has been battered or subjected to extreme cruelty by a spouse or parent who is or was a United States citizen (or is the parent of a child of a United States citizen and the child has been battered or subjected to extreme cruelty by such citizen parent);

(II) the alien has been battered or subjected to extreme cruelty by a spouse or parent who is or was a lawful permanent resident (or is the parent of a child of an alien who is or was a lawful permanent resident and the child has been battered or subjected to extreme cruelty by such permanent resident parent); or

(III) the alien has been battered or subjected to extreme cruelty by a United States citizen or lawful permanent resident whom the alien intended to marry, but whose marriage is not legitimate because of that United States citizen's or lawful permanent resident's bigamy;

(ii) the alien has been physically present in the United States for a continuous period of not less than 3 years immediately preceding the date of such application, and the issuance of a charging document for removal proceedings shall not toll the 3-year period of continuous physical presence in the United States;

(iii) the alien has been a person of good moral character during such period, subject to the provisions of subparagraph (C);

(iv) the alien is not inadmissible under paragraph (2) or (3) of section 212(a), is not deportable under paragraphs (1)(G) or (2) through (4) of section 237(a), subject to paragraph (5) and has not been convicted of an aggravated felony; and

(v) the removal would result in extreme hardship to the alien, the alien's child, or the alien's parent.

3. A local Catholic parish is interested in providing food and shelter to undocumented poor in the parish. To what extent may parishioners participate? Specifically, could a parishioner donate food and clothing to the church to be distributed to these people? Could a parishioner drive undocumented individuals to church to pick up the food and clothing? Could a parishioner allow the undocumented person to live with the parishioner? Could the parishioner pay the undocumented person to perform household chores? Would it make any difference if the undocumented person was fleeing persecution in his home country, as opposed to moving to the United States to find work? Could the parishioner participate in advocacy efforts aimed at changing the immigration laws? Suppose the parishioner is questioned by law enforcement authorities regarding his/her activities. Must the parishioner respond? What should the parishioner do if it appears that any of his/her activities might run afoul of some legal prohibition? What would your response be if the actor in each of the above matters was a Catholic nun? Would it make any difference if the actor is an attorney?

4. May or must an attorney who learns that someone is in this country without legal authorization report that fact to law enforcement? Would it make any difference if the attorney learns this fact through a discussion with the alien while the alien is seeking legal advice? Review Model Rule 1.6.

Rule 1.6 Confidentiality of Information

(a) A lawyer shall not reveal information relating to the representation of a client unless the client gives informed consent, the disclosure is impliedly authorized in order to carry out the representation or the disclosure is permitted by paragraph (b).

(b) A lawyer may reveal information relating to the representation of a client to the extent the lawyer reasonably believes necessary:

(1) to prevent reasonably certain death or substantial bodily harm;

(2) to prevent the client from committing a crime or fraud that is reasonably certain to result in substantial injury to the financial interests

or property of another and in furtherance of which the client has used or is using the lawyer's services;

(3) to prevent, mitigate or rectify substantial injury to the financial interests or property of another that is reasonably certain to result or has resulted from the client's commission of a crime or fraud in furtherance of which the client has used the lawyer's services;

(4) to secure legal advice about the lawyer's compliance with these Rules;

(5) to establish a claim or defense on behalf of the lawyer in a controversy between the lawyer and the client, to establish a defense to a criminal charge or civil claim against the lawyer based upon conduct in which the client was involved, or to respond to allegations in any proceeding concerning the lawyer's representation of the client; or

(6) to comply with other law or a court order.

5. Some aliens are brought to this country by their parents. These children are raised in the United States, often lose any contacts with their native countries, and attend public schools pursuant to *Plyler v. Doe*.[55] Yet, they remain in undocumented status. What happens and what should happen when they reach adulthood and wish to work or attend institutions of higher learning? Why? See the Texas Dream Act.[56] In November 2014, the Obama administration announced a program by which children who were brought to the United States while they were under age 16 could seek "deferred action." This program, known as Deferred Action for Childhood Arrivals or "DACA," allowed the children to receive a two-year permit to stay and work in the United States. In November 2017, the Trump administration announced the end of the program. It determined to stop reviewing new applications but allowed DACA recipients whose permits would expire before March 5, 2018, the opportunity to seek a 2-year renewal by submitting their applications by October 5, 2017. The Executive Committee of the USCCB, on September 12, 2017 announced:

> In light of many years of failure by Congress, whether controlled by Republicans or Democrats, to address the situation, the Committee urges the Catholic

---

55. Plyler v. Doe, 457 U.S. 202 (1982).

56. *Compare* The Development Relief and Education for Alien Minors Act, or DREAM Act, 77th Leg., R.S., ch. 1392 § 1, 2001 Tex. Sess. Law Serv. 1383 (West) (current version at TEX. EDUC. CODE. ANN. § 54.051(m), .052(j), .0551, .057(a), .060(b)) (The text of the Act is http://www.legis .state.tx.us/tlodocs/77R/billtext/html/HB01403F.htm (last visited Oct. 29, 2017). Complete legislative history is available at http://www.legis.state.tx.us/BillLookup/History.aspx?LegSess=77R&Bill =HB1403, *with* Development, Relief, and Education for Alien Minors Act of 2011 (DREAM Act of 2011), H.R. 1842, 112th Cong. § 1 (2011) (available on Westlaw by searching 2011 CONG US HR 1842) (Federal DREAM Act legislation introduced May, 2001: "To authorize the cancellation of removal and adjustment of status of certain alien students who are long-term United States residents and who entered the United States as children, and for other purposes.").

faithful and all people of goodwill to contact their representatives in Congress to urge the passage of the DREAM Act or similar legislation as a prompt, humane, and durable solution to this problem of greatest urgency. The Executive Committee also notes the tremendous contributions of the DACA youth to date as extraordinary, including the fact that many serve in our military.[57]

6. How long is the wait for would-be immigrants? Nobody knows for certain. However, consider that the unmarried son or daughter from Mexico, of a U.S. citizen, who was seeking a visa based upon that relationship in August, 2011, would find that the F1 category held a priority date of March 15, 1993. By November 2017, almost six years later, that priority date had only moved to April, 1996. At this pace, how many years would it take for that alien to obtain a visa?

7. The Catholic Church and others have called for a legalization program, which would permit those in undocumented status in this country to ultimately become permanent resident aliens and citizens. Consider that many other would-be-immigrants are still in their home countries, have applied for visas, and yet are waiting years for visa eligibility. Discuss the legal and moral implications of a policy that would, in effect, give greater immigration benefits to those who have chosen to break the law and enter this country illegally, than it would to those who have followed our complicated system and have waited years in their own countries for permission to enter this nation legally.

8. What similarities and differences exist between the Catholic Church's position regarding those fleeing upheaval in the countries, and the U.S. policies regarding refugees and asylees? Does the Catholic Church urge that the United States take in all people seeking to escape difficult circumstances in their home countries? Consider the following:

> Because there seems to be no end to poverty, war, and misery in the world, developed nations will continue to experience pressure from many peoples who desire to resettle in their lands. Catholic social teaching is realistic: While people have the right to move, no country has the duty to receive so many immigrants that its social and economic life are jeopardized.

> For this reason, Catholics should not view the work of the federal government and its immigration control as negative or evil. Those who work to enforce our nation's immigration laws often do so out of a sense of loyalty to the common good and compassion for poor people seeking a better life.

---

57. United States Conference of Catholic Bishops, *U.S. Bishops Executive Committee Release Statement on Administration's DACA Decision; Calls on Catholic Faithful to Urge Congress to Pass DREAM Act* (Sept. 12, 2017), http://www.usccb.org/news/2017/17-165.cfm (last visited Oct. 23, 2017).

> In an ideal world, there would be no need for immigration control. The Church recognizes that this ideal world has not yet been achieved.[58]

9. What do you think the result would be if the United States were to conduct a one-year experiment with an "open border" policy, allowing anyone who wants to enter the country to do so?

10. What provisions do you think an ideal immigration reform measure should include?

---

58. United States Conference of Catholic Bishops, *Catholic Social Teaching on Immigration and the Movement of Peoples,* http://www.usccb.org/issues-and-action/human-life-and-dignity/immigration/catholic-teaching-on-immigration-and-the-movement-of-peoples.cfm (last visited Oct. 23, 2017).

Chapter 5

Feeding the Hungry, Sheltering the Homeless, Treating the Sick

A. Feeding the Hungry

The United States and legal systems of all the states provide forms of public assistance which include nutrition programs. These programs are the result of statutory and administrative actions. The Supreme Court has never held that there is a constitutional right to adequate nutrition. The government is under the obligation to feed the people in its custody or under its control (i.e., those imprisoned and those serving in the military).

The Universal Declaration of Human Rights of the General Assembly of the United Nations[1] has proclaimed that nutrition and other matters associated with minimal living standards are a function of basic human rights. The Universal Declaration of Human Rights was approved by 48 votes, with 8 abstentions:

> In favour: Afghanistan, Argentina, Australia, Belgium, Bolivia, Brazil, Burma, Canada, Chile, China, Colombia, Costa Rica, Cuba, Denmark, the Dominican Republic, Ecuador, Egypt, El Salvador, Ethiopia, France, Greece, Guatemala, Haiti, Iceland, India, Iran, Iraq, Lebanon, Liberia, Luxembourg, Mexico, Netherlands, New Zealand, Nicaragua, Norway, Pakistan, Panama, Paraguay, Peru, Philippines, Siam (Thailand), Sweden, Syria, Turkey, United Kingdom, United States, Uruguay, Venezuela.

> Abstaining: Byelorussian SSR, Czechoslovakia, Poland, Saudi Arabia, Ukrainian SSR, Union of South Africa, USSR, Yugoslavia.[2]

Article 25 of the Declaration provides:

> (1) Everyone has the right to a standard of living adequate for the health and well-being of himself and of his family, including food, clothing, housing, and medical care and necessary social services, and the right to security in

---

1. G.A. Res. 217A(III), Universal Declaration of Human Rights, Dec. 10, 1948, U.N. GAOR, 3d Sess., 1st plen. mtg., U.N. Doc. A/810 (Dec. 12, 1948), http://www.un.org/en/universal-declaration-human-rights/index.html (last visited Oct. 29, 2017).

2. U.N.Y.B. 1948, Chapter V. Social, Humanitarian and Cultural Questions, pg. 535, http://www.unhcr.org/cgi-bin/texis/vtx/home/opendocPDFViewer.html?docid=4e1ee7620&query=Indigenous%20Peoples (last visited Oct. 29, 2017).

the event of unemployment, sickness, disability, widowhood, old age or other lack of livelihood in circumstances beyond his control.[3]

Of course, without sustenance, it is difficult to imagine how anyone can exercise any other legal rights.

Pope Benedict XVI described a "scandal of hunger" in November 2010. The USCCB has adopted the view of Pope Benedict in regard to this issue of nutrition, as follows:

Issue

Today, more than 50 million Americans are facing hunger insecurity in the U.S.; 17.2 million of them are children, according to the U.S. Department of Agriculture. This is a substantial increase from 36.2 million in 2008. In addition, an alarming 17.4 million people lived in homes considered to have very low food security, where one or more people in the household went hungry over the course of the year because they were not able to afford enough food. Even before the great recession, the number of people who suffered from hunger due to insufficient food increased, doubling in number in 2008 as compared to 2000. Essential federal programs address hunger and food insecurity, generally through partnerships between the federal and state governments and cooperating organizations. They provide individuals and families in need with access to food, a healthier diet and nutrition education, and they also support agriculture in the United States. A growing number of families facing economic difficulties during the recent recession are helped by these important federal nutrition programs.

Update

The Healthy, Hunger-Free Kids Act (S.3307) was signed into law on December 2, 2010. The legislation is a positive step in promoting nutritional health and hunger security for children. The legislation expands the At-Risk Afterschool Meal Program to all 50 states and the District of Columbia. The program increases access and enhances the Women, Infant and Children (WIC) Program. It improves the Summer Food Service Program by furthering outreach efforts and eliminates limits to the number of non-profits that can participate in the program. The legislation also increases grants to expand school breakfast programs and open access for eligible children to school based meals. Unfortunately, the legislation was not without its weaknesses. The legislation was passed with a reduction in food stamp funding (SNAP) that was included in the stimulus bill. The USCCB wrote Congress

---

3. G.A. Res. 217A(III), Universal Declaration of Human Rights, Dec. 10, 1948, art. 25, U.N. GAOR, 3d Sess., 1st plen. mtg., U.N. Doc. A/810 (Dec. 12, 1948), http://www.un.org/en/universal -declaration-human-rights/index.html (last visited Oct. 29, 2017).

and supported the improvements to the various programs while expressing its concern and commitment to work towards ensuring that the food stamp dollars would be restored in the 112th Congress.

Nutrition Background

The Supplemental Nutrition Assistance Program (SNAP): SNAP, formerly called Food Stamps, is the first line of defense against hunger. It enables low-income families to buy nutritious food. The program serves around 38 million people on a monthly basis, according to USDA estimates. In FY 2009, SNAP served 5.3 million more people, a 22 percent increase, as compared to the previous year. The amount of SNAP benefits given is based on an estimate of how much it costs to buy food to prepare nutritious, low-cost meals for a household. SNAP benefits are expected to supplement a family's food budget. Eligibility is determined by household resources and income.

SNAP benefits have improved and some states have made it easier to apply for benefits. Yet, about 40 percent of those eligible to receive SNAP benefits are not receiving them. Many families leaving welfare may not realize they are eligible for transitional SNAP benefits for at least five months. Both U.S. citizens and some non-citizens are eligible for SNAP benefits. Adult immigrants are eligible only after they have resided in the United States legally for at least five years; legal immigrants who are children or disabled are eligible, regardless of date of entry into the U.S. There are also limits on eligibility for adults 18 to 50 years old without dependent children.

Child and Adult Care Food Program (CACFP): This program provides support for children through nutritious school meals and nutrition assistance for day care, after school and summer programs, and homeless shelters. Charitable and non-profit community organizations feeding children in these programs can receive reimbursement for food and meal preparation, as well as training in the nutritional needs of children. The program is administered at the federal level by the USDA and at the state level through the State Department of Education or Child Nutrition. In 2009, over three million children received nutritious meals and snacks through CACFP programs at child care centers and family child care homes across the country.

WIC Program: The Special Supplemental Nutrition Program for Women, Infants, and Children (WIC) improves the health of mothers and their children by providing supplemental foods, nutrition and breast-feeding education, nutrition screening, and referrals to other social services. WIC serves low-income, nutritionally at risk pregnant women; breast-feeding women; mothers for up to six months after the birth of an infant; infants and children up to their fifth birthday. WIC is a federal grant program that Congress must authorize a specific amount of funds each year. In fiscal year 2009, over nine million women and children participated in WIC.

Food Distribution Programs: Food distribution programs strengthen the nutrition safety net through commodity distribution and other nutrition assistance to low-income families, emergency feeding programs, Indian Reservations, and the elderly. For example, children can receive nutritious food through USDA distribution programs such as the National School Lunch and Breakfast Programs, the CACFP and the Summer Food Service Program. The USDA makes commodity foods available through The Emergency Food Assistance Program (TEFAP), to food banks and soup kitchens, through states and local agencies, allowing low-income people, including elderly people, to receive emergency food and nutrition assistance at no cost. The National School Lunch Program operates in over 101,000 public and non-profit private schools, including Catholic schools, and residential child care institutions. According to USDA, in October 2009, the National School Lunch Program provided nutritionally balanced, low-cost or free lunches to 31.2 million children each school day, and over half of these students were eligible to receive lunch at no cost.

USCCB Position

In November 2010, Pope Benedict XVI spoke of the "scandal of hunger" that pervades our modern age. In *For I Was Hungry and You Gave Me Food*, the U.S. bishops reiterated that a primary goal of food and agricultural policy should be providing basic food and nutrition for all. In *Food Policy in a Hungry World*, the bishops called for strengthening the domestic food assistance programs to ensure that no one in America goes hungry or suffers malnutrition. "When the economy fails to provide the jobs and income necessary to prevent hunger and malnutrition, the various local, state, and national food assistance programs must be funded and expanded to provide food to all in need."

. . . .[4]

In a 2009 article, J.M. Green urged that the United States adopt formal recognition of a right to food.

It is time for the United States to recognize the right to food. Whatever its binding obligations under international law, the United States is at least subject to the non binding Universal Declaration of Human Rights, and for all its speech disparaging international law solutions to food problems, the United States has taken domestic actions that implicitly recognize and seek to implement all the substantive elements of the internationally recognized right to food.[5]

---

4. USCCB, Dep't of Justice, Peace & Human Dev., Office of Domestic Social Dev., *Food & Nutrition Programs* (Feb. 2011), http://www.usccb.org/about/domestic-social-development/resources/upload/food-nutrition-backgrounder-2011.pdf (last visited Oct. 29, 2017).

5. J.M. Greene, *Localization: Implementing the Right to Food*, 14 DRAKE J. AGRIC. L. 377, 383 (2009).

B. Housing

Article 25 of the Universal Declaration of Human Rights explicitly recognizes a right to housing.[6] The USCCB has consistently supported the implementation of a national policy that "includes the preservation and production of quality housing for low income families, the elderly, and other vulnerable people, as well as the participation and partnership of residents, non-profit community groups, and churches to build and preserve affordable housing."[7] While there is no legally recognized right to housing, by statute and administrative regulations the governments of the United States and the states provide assistance in a number of housing programs. A summary of these programs can be found at Benefits.gov under "Housing."[8]

C. Health Care

As noted previously, the Universal Declaration of Human Rights, Article 25, identifies medical care as basic human right.[9] In April, 2006, the USCCB announced its fourth year of participation in the "Cover the Uninsured Week," a nationwide campaign seeking to obtain health insurance for the 46 million Americans without health insurance, at that time. The reason behind this effort is the view that "Catholic teaching supports adequate and affordable health care for all, because health care is a basic human right."[10]

In 2009, the U.S. Congress approved the "Affordable Care Act," referred to by its critics as "ObamaCare" and by its supporters as "ObamaCares." The law is extremely complex, but a summary of its provisions explaining in concise form how this extremely complex law was to operate, were set forth in the government website, HealthCare.gov.

---

6. G.A. Res. 217A(III), Universal Declaration of Human Rights, Dec. 10, 1948, art. 25(1), U.N. GAOR, 3d Sess., 1st plen. mtg., U.N. Doc. A/810 (Dec. 12, 1948), http://www.un.org/en/universal -declaration-human-rights/index.html (last visited Oct. 29, 2017).

7. USCCB, Dep't of Justice, Peace & Human Dev., Office of Domestic Social Dev., *Affordable Housing & the National Housing Trust Fund* (Feb. 2011), http://www.usccb.org/issues-and-action /human-life-and-dignity/housing-homelessness/affordable-housing-and-the-national-housing -trust-fund.cfm (last visited Oct. 29, 2017).

8. Benefits.gov, Housing, https://www.benefits.gov/benefits/browse-by-category/category/19 (last visited Oct. 29, 2017).

9. G.A. Res. 217A(III), Universal Declaration of Human Rights, Dec. 10, 1948, art. 25(1), U.N. GAOR, 3d Sess., 1st plen. mtg., U.N. Doc. A/810 (Dec. 12, 1948), http://www.un.org/en/universal -declaration-human-rights/index.html (last visited Oct. 29, 2017).

10. USCCB, Dep't of Justice, Peace & Human Dev., Office of Domestic Social Dev., *Health Care Reform* (Feb. 2011), http://www.usccb.org/issues-and-action/human-life-and-dignity/health-care /upload/health-care-backgrounder-2011.pdf (last visited Oct. 29, 2017).

2010
New Consumer Protections

• **Putting Information for Consumers Online.** The law provides for an easy-to-use website where consumers can compare health insurance coverage options and pick the coverage that works for them. *Effective July 1, 2010.*

• **Prohibiting Denying Coverage of Children Based on Pre-Existing Conditions.** The health care law includes new rules to prevent insurance companies from denying coverage to children under the age of 19 due to a pre-existing condition. *Effective for health plan years beginning on or after September 23, 2010 for new plans and existing group plans.*

• **Prohibiting Insurance Companies from Rescinding Coverage.** In the past, insurance companies could search for an error, or other technical mistake, on a customer's application and use this error to deny payment for services when he or she got sick. The health care law makes this illegal. After media reports cited incidents of breast cancer patients losing coverage, insurance companies agreed to end this practice immediately. *Effective for health plan years beginning on or after September 23, 2010.*

• **Eliminating Lifetime Limits on Insurance Coverage.** Under the law, insurance companies will be prohibited from imposing lifetime dollar limits on essential benefits, like hospital stays. *Effective for health plan years beginning on or after September 23, 2010.*

• **Regulating Annual Limits on Insurance Coverage.** Under the law, insurance companies' use of annual dollar limits on the amount of insurance coverage a patient may receive will be restricted for new plans in the individual market and all group plans. In 2014, the use of annual dollar limits on essential benefits like hospital stays will be banned for new plans in the individual market and all group plans. *Effective for health plan years beginning on or after September 23, 2010.*

• **Appealing Insurance Company Decisions.** The law provides consumers with a way to appeal coverage determinations or claims to their insurance company, and establishes an external review process. *Effective for new plans beginning on or after September 23, 2010.*

• **Establishing Consumer Assistance Programs in the States.** Under the law, states that apply receive federal grants to help set up or expand independent offices to help consumers navigate the private health insurance system. These programs help consumers file complaints and appeals; enroll in health coverage; and get educated about their rights and responsibilities in group health plans or individual health insurance policies. The programs will also collect data on the types of problems consumers have, and file reports with the U.S. Department of Health and Human Services to identify trouble spots that need further oversight. *Grants Awarded October 2010.* Learn more about Consumer Assistance Programs.

Improving Quality and Lowering Costs

• **Providing Small Business Health Insurance Tax Credits.** Up to 4 million small businesses are eligible for tax credits to help them provide insurance benefits to their workers. The first phase of this provision provides a credit worth up to 35% of the employer's contribution to the employees' health insurance. Small non-profit organizations may receive up to a 25% credit. *Effective now.*

• **Offering Relief for 4 Million Seniors Who Hit the Medicare Prescription Drug "Donut Hole."** An estimated four million seniors will reach the gap in Medicare prescription drug coverage known as the "donut hole" this year. Each eligible senior will receive a one-time, tax free $250 rebate check. *First checks mailed in June 2010, and will continue monthly throughout 2010 as seniors hit the coverage gap. Learn more about the "donut hole" and Medicare.*

• **Providing Free Preventive Care.** All new plans must cover certain preventive services such as mammograms and colonoscopies without charging a deductible, co-pay or coinsurance. *Effective for health plan years beginning on or after September 23, 2010.*

• **Preventing Disease and Illness.** A new $15 billion Prevention and Public Health Fund will invest in proven prevention and public health programs that can help keep Americans healthy — from smoking cessation to combating obesity. *Funding begins in 2010.*

• **Cracking Down on Health Care Fraud.** Current efforts to fight fraud have returned more than $2.5 billion to the Medicare Trust Fund in fiscal year 2009 alone. The new law invests new resources and requires new screening procedures for health care providers to boost these efforts and reduce fraud and waste in Medicare, Medicaid, and CHIP. *Many provisions effective now.*

Increasing Access to Affordable Care

• **Providing Access to Insurance for Uninsured Americans with Pre-Existing Conditions.** The Pre-Existing Condition Insurance Plan provides new coverage options to individuals who have been uninsured for at least six months because of a pre-existing condition. States have the option of running this program in their state. If a state chooses not to do so, a plan will be established by the Department of Health and Human Services in that state. *National program effective July 1, 2010.*

• **Extending Coverage for Young Adults.** Under the law, young adults will be allowed to stay on their parents' plan until they turn 26 years old (in the case of existing group health plans, this right does not apply if the young adult is offered insurance at work). Check with your insurance company or employer to see if you qualify. *Effective for health plan years beginning on or after September 23.*

• **Expanding Coverage for Early Retirees.** Too often, Americans who retire without employer-sponsored insurance and before they are eligible for Medicare see their life savings disappear because of high rates in the individual market. To preserve employer coverage for early retirees until more affordable coverage is available through the new Exchanges by 2014, the new law creates a $5 billion program to provide needed financial help for employment-based plans to continue to provide valuable coverage to people who retire between the ages of 55 and 65, as well as their spouses and dependents. *Applications for employers to participate in the program available June 1, 2010.*

• **Rebuilding the Primary Care Workforce.** To strengthen the availability of primary care, there are new incentives in the law to expand the number of primary care doctors, nurses and physician assistants. These include funding for scholarships and loan repayments for primary care doctors and nurses working in underserved areas. Doctors and nurses receiving payments made under any state loan repayment or loan forgiveness program intended to increase the availability of health care services in underserved or health professional shortage areas will not have to pay taxes on those payments. *Effective 2010.*

• **Holding Insurance Companies Accountable for Unreasonable Rate Hikes.** The law allows states that have, or plan to implement, measures that require insurance companies to justify their premium increases will be eligible for $250 million in new grants. Insurance companies with excessive or unjustified premium exchanges may not be able to participate in the new health insurance Exchanges in 2014. *Grants awarded beginning in 2010.*

• **Allowing States to Cover More People on Medicaid.** States will be able to receive federal matching funds for covering some additional low-income individuals and families under Medicaid for whom federal funds were not previously available. This will make it easier for states that choose to do so to cover more of their residents. *Effective April 1, 2010.*

• **Increasing Payments for Rural Health Care Providers.** Today, 68% of medically underserved communities across the nation are in rural areas. These communities often have trouble attracting and retaining medical professionals. The law provides increased payment to rural health care providers to help them continue to serve their communities. *Effective 2010.*

• **Strengthening Community Health Centers.** The law includes new funding to support the construction of and expand services at community health centers, allowing these centers to serve some 20 million new patients across the country. *Effective 2010.*

2011
Improving Quality and Lowering Costs

• **Offering Prescription Drug Discounts.** Seniors who reach the coverage gap will receive a 50% discount when buying Medicare Part D covered brand-name prescription drugs. Over the next ten years, seniors will receive additional savings on brand-name and generic drugs until the coverage gap is closed in 2020. *Effective January 1, 2011.*

• **Providing Free Preventive Care for Seniors.** The law provides certain free preventive services, such as annual wellness visits and personalized prevention plans for seniors on Medicare. *Effective January 1, 2011.*

• **Improving Health Care Quality and Efficiency.** The law establishes a new Center for Medicare & Medicaid Innovation that will begin testing new ways of delivering care to patients. These methods are expected to improve the quality of care, and reduce the rate of growth in health care costs for Medicare, Medicaid, and the Children's Health Insurance Program (CHIP). Additionally, by January 1, 2011, HHS will submit a national strategy for quality improvement in health care, including by these programs. *Effective no later than January 1, 2011.*

• **Improving Care for Seniors After They Leave the Hospital.** The Community Care Transitions Program will help high risk Medicare beneficiaries who are hospitalized avoid unnecessary readmissions by coordinating care and connecting patients to services in their communities. *Effective January 1, 2011.*

• **Introducing New Innovations to Bring Down Costs.** The Independent Payment Advisory Board will begin operations to develop and submit proposals to Congress and the President aimed at extending the life of the Medicare Trust Fund. The Board is expected to focus on ways to target waste in the system, and recommend ways to reduce costs, improve health outcomes for patients, and expand access to high-quality care. *Administrative funding becomes available October 1, 2011.*

Increasing Access to Affordable Care

• **Increasing Access to Services at Home and in the Community.** The Community First Choice Option allows states to offer home and community based services to disabled individuals through Medicaid rather than institutional care in nursing homes. *Effective beginning October 1, 2011.*

Holding Insurance Companies Accountable

• **Bringing Down Health Care Premiums.** To ensure premium dollars are spent primarily on health care, the law generally requires that at least 85% of all premium dollars collected by insurance companies for large employer plans are spent on health care services and health care quality improvement. For plans sold to individuals and small employers, at least 80% of the premium must be spent on benefits and quality improvement. If insurance companies do not meet these goals, because their administrative costs or profits are too high, they must provide rebates to consumers. *Effective January 1, 2011.*

• **Addressing Overpayments to Big Insurance Companies and Strengthening Medicare Advantage.** Today, Medicare pays Medicare Advantage insurance companies over $1,000 more per person on average than is spent per person in Traditional Medicare. This results in increased premiums for all Medicare beneficiaries, including the 77% of beneficiaries who are not currently enrolled in a Medicare Advantage plan. The law levels the playing field by gradually eliminating this discrepancy. People enrolled in a Medicare Advantage plan will still receive all guaranteed Medicare benefits, and the law provides bonus payments to Medicare Advantage plans that provide high quality care. *Effective January 1, 2011.*

2012
Improving Quality and Lowering Costs

• **Linking Payment to Quality Outcomes.** The law establishes a hospital Value-Based Purchasing program (VBP) in Traditional Medicare. This program offers financial incentives to hospitals to improve the quality of care. Hospital performance is required to be publicly reported, beginning with measures relating to heart attacks, heart failure, pneumonia, surgical care, health-care associated infections, and patients' perception of care. *Effective for payments for discharges occurring on or after October 1, 2012.*

• **Encouraging Integrated Health Systems.** The new law provides incentives for physicians to join together to form "Accountable Care Organizations." These groups allow doctors to better coordinate patient care and improve the quality, help prevent disease and illness and reduce unnecessary hospital admissions. If Accountable Care Organizations provide high quality care and reduce costs to the health care system, they can keep some of the money that they have helped save. *Effective January 1, 2012.*

• **Reducing Paperwork and Administrative Costs.** Health care remains one of the few industries that relies on paper records. The new law will institute a series of changes to standardize billing and requires health plans to begin adopting and implementing rules for the secure, confidential, electronic exchange of health information. Using electronic health records will reduce paperwork and administrative burdens, cut costs, reduce medical errors, and most importantly, improve the quality of care. *First regulation effective October 1, 2012.*

• **Understanding and Fighting Health Disparities.** To help understand and reduce persistent health disparities, the law requires any ongoing or new federal health program to collect and report racial, ethnic and language data. The Secretary of Health and Human Services will use this data to help identify and reduce disparities. *Effective March 2012.*

Increasing Access to Affordable Care

• **Providing New, Voluntary Options for Long-Term Care Insurance.** The law creates a voluntary long-term care insurance program—called CLASS—to provide cash benefits to adults who become disabled. Note: On October 14, 2011, Secretary Sebelius transmitted a report and letter to Congress stating that the Department does not see a viable path forward for CLASS implementation at this time.

2013
Improving Quality and Lowering Costs

• **Improving Preventive Health Coverage.** To expand the number of Americans receiving preventive care, the law provides new funding to state Medicaid programs that choose to cover preventive services for patients at little or no cost. *Effective January 1, 2013.*

• **Expanding Authority to Bundle Payments.** The law establishes a national pilot program to encourage hospitals, doctors, and other providers to work together to improve the coordination and quality of patient care. Under payment "bundling," hospitals, doctors, and providers are paid a flat rate for an episode of care rather than the current fragmented system where each service or test or bundles of items or services are billed separately to Medicare. For example, instead of a surgical procedure generating multiple claims from multiple providers, the entire team is compensated with a "bundled" payment that provides incentives to deliver health care services more efficiently while maintaining or improving quality of care. It aligns the incentives of those delivering care, and savings are shared between providers and the Medicare program. *Effective no later than January 1, 2013.*

Increasing Access to Affordable Care

• **Increasing Medicaid Payments for Primary Care Doctors.** As Medicaid programs and providers prepare to cover more patients in 2014, the Act requires states to pay primary care physicians no less than 100% of Medicare payment rates in 2013 and 2014 for primary care services. The increase is fully funded by the federal government. *Effective January 1, 2013.*

• **Providing Additional Funding for the Children's Health Insurance Program.** Under the law, states will receive two more years of funding to continue coverage for children not eligible for Medicaid. *Effective October 1, 2013.*

2014
New Consumer Protections

• **Prohibiting Discrimination Due to Pre-Existing Conditions or Gender.** The law implements strong reforms that prohibit insurance companies from refusing to sell coverage or renew policies because of an individual's pre-existing conditions. Also, in the individual and small group market, the law eliminates the ability of insurance companies to charge higher rates due to gender or health status. *Effective January 1, 2014.*

• **Eliminating Annual Limits on Insurance Coverage.** The law prohibits new plans and existing group plans from imposing annual dollar limits on the amount of coverage an individual may receive. *Effective January 1, 2014.*

• **Ensuring Coverage for Individuals Participating in Clinical Trials.** Insurers will be prohibited from dropping or limiting coverage because an individual chooses to participate in a clinical trial. Applies to all clinical trials that treat cancer or other life-threatening diseases. *Effective January 1, 2014.*

Improving Quality and Lowering Costs

• **Making Care More Affordable.** Tax credits to make it easier for the middle class to afford insurance will become available for people with income between 100% and 400% of the poverty line who are not eligible for other affordable coverage. (In 2010, 400% of the poverty line comes out to about $43,000 for an individual or $88,000 for a family of four.) The tax credit is advanceable, so it can lower your premium payments each month, rather than making you wait for tax time. It's also refundable, so even moderate-income families can receive the full benefit of the credit. These individuals may also qualify for reduced cost-sharing (copayments, co-insurance, and deductibles). *Effective January 1, 2014.*

• **Establishing Affordable Insurance Exchanges.** Starting in 2014 if your employer doesn't offer insurance, you will be able to buy it directly in an Affordable Insurance Exchange. An Exchange is a new transparent and competitive insurance marketplace where individuals and small businesses can buy affordable and qualified health benefit plans. Exchanges will offer you a choice of health plans that meet certain benefits and cost standards. Starting in 2014, Members of Congress will be getting their health care insurance through Exchanges, and you will be able buy your insurance through Exchanges too. *Effective January 1, 2014.*

• **Increasing the Small Business Tax Credit.** The law implements the second phase of the small business tax credit for qualified small businesses and small non-profit organizations. In this phase, the credit is up to 50% of the employer's contribution to provide health insurance for employees. There is also up to a 35% credit for small non-profit organizations. *Effective January 1, 2014.*

Increasing Access to Affordable Care

• **Increasing Access to Medicaid.** Americans who earn less than 133% of the poverty level (approximately $14,000 for an individual and $29,000 for a family of four) will be eligible to enroll in Medicaid. States will receive 100% federal funding for the first three years to support this expanded coverage, phasing to 90% federal funding in subsequent years. *Effective January 1, 2014.*

• **Promoting Individual Responsibility.** Under the law, most individuals who can afford it will be required to obtain basic health insurance coverage or pay a fee to help offset the costs of caring for uninsured Americans. If affordable coverage is not available to an individual, he or she will be eligible for an exemption. *Effective January 1, 2014.*

• **Ensuring Free Choice.** Workers meeting certain requirements who cannot afford the coverage provided by their employer may take whatever funds their employer might have contributed to their insurance and use these resources to help purchase a more affordable plan in the new health insurance Exchanges. *Effective January 1, 2014.*

2015
Improving Quality and Lowering Costs

• **Paying Physicians Based on Value Not Volume.** A new provision will tie physician payments to the quality of care they provide. Physicians will see their payments modified so that those who provide higher value care will receive higher payments than those who provide lower quality care. *Effective January 1, 2015.*[11]

While the Catholic bishops believed that "providing affordable and accessible health care . . . is a public good, moral, imperative, and urgent national priority,"[12] the Catholic bishops nonetheless opposed final passage of the Act. They objected on the grounds that the federal government would be involved in facilitating abortion by providing coverage for abortions. They also objected to the bill because it "failed to include necessary language to provide essential conscience protections (both within and beyond the abortion context)."[13] They were concerned that undocumented aliens and their families would be excluded from purchasing health coverage in the "new exchanges" even if they use their own funds.

As with most other federal legislation, federal agencies enact regulations to implement statutes. In September 2011, the USCCB objected to a proposed regulation by the Department of Health and Human Services (HHS) which would obligate all health care insurers to pay for sterilizations and FDA approved contraceptives, including those contraceptives known as the "morning after pill."[14] The bishops stated that the regulation would be "'an unprecedented attack on religious liberty' and that even Jesus would not qualify as 'religious' under the proposed regulation's 'religious

---

11. U.S. Dep't of Health & Human Servs., *Provisions of the Affordable Care Act By Year*, http://www.hhs.gov/healthcare/rights/law/index.html (last visited Oct. 29, 2017).

12. USCCB, Dep't of Justice, Peace & Human Dev., Office of Domestic Soc. Dev., *Health Care Reform* (Feb. 2011), http://www.usccb.org/issues-and-action/human-life-and-dignity/health-care/upload/health-care-backgrounder-2011.pdf (last visited Oct. 29, 2017).

13. *Id.*

14. Terence P. Jeffrey, *Catholic Bishops on Obamacare Reg: 'Unprecedented Attack on Religious Liberty,' Even Jesus Wouldn't Qualify as 'Religious,'* Catholic News Serv. (Sept. 25, 2011), http://cnsnews.com/news/article/catholic-bishops-obamacare-reg-unprecedented-attack-religious-liberty-even-jesus (last visited Oct. 29, 2017).

exemption.'"[15] Former HHS Secretary Kathleen Sebelius, former Governor of Kansas, is a Catholic. The Archbishop of Kansas City, Kansas has barred her "from taking communion . . . until she publicly repudiates her support for legalized abortion and goes to confession."[16]

Between September 2011 and January 20, 2012, President Obama engaged in a series of consultation with officials within and from outside the administration regarding the Affordable Care Act. While Catholics urged that the proposed rule not be implemented, other groups, such as Planned Parenthood, urged the White House to include the mandate that all employers provide health care insurance which covered contraception, morning-after pills, and sterilization, free of charge, to all female employees. The original mandate created a narrow exemption for the immediate employees of churches and gave other religious institutions, such as universities and hospitals, a one year extension before the rules would apply to them as well. The Associated Press summarized the response from Catholics and non-Catholics, Republicans and Democrats alike, in an analysis entitled, *Backlash no Surprise, but Ferocity Was,* published in many papers, including the *San Antonio Express-News* on February 12, 2012, at A20. The article noted that within hours of the announcement, the USCCB called the mandate an "affront to religious liberty" placing the Obama Administration "on the wrong side of the Constitution" and urged Catholics to "tell their elected leaders to rescind it." (*Id.*). Bishops prepared letters to read to their congregations from pulpits across the nation. Commentators and editorial writers, both conservative and liberal, condemned the policy. An Op-Ed piece by Charlotte Allen in the *Los Angeles Times* on February 5, 2012 called the policy, "An Affront Catholics Agree On," noting that the policy had outraged even liberal Catholics who had previously supported the Obama Administration. In an editorial published February 11, 2012, Charles Krauthammer summarized the constitutional problems with the Obama approach, concluding that the definition in the new regulation does not include Catholic hospitals in the category of "religious institutions" because such institutions do not, according to the Administration, have the "inculcation of religious values as its purpose." Such an approach, Krauthammer argues allows the Administration to define "religious" on a "whim" in contravention of the Free Exercise Clause of the First Amendment. ("Religious Defined According to Whim," *San Antonio Express-News*, Feb. 11, 2012, B9).

Continuing pressure, including the vocal opposition of some leading Democrats, resulted in the President's determination on February 10, 2011, to attempt to implement what the White House termed a "compromise" which would require health insurers to provide the coverage on their own, rather than having the employers pay for the plan. However, the USCCB remained opposed to the plan. The Bishops urged that Catholic employers must be free to decline to provide access to contraceptive

---

15. *Id.*
16. *Id.*

and abortive services for their employees, because those services run contrary to the teaching of the Church.

From the Catholic Church perspective, these concerns ultimately seem to have been successfully addressed. The constitutionality of the ACA was upheld in 2012 in a 5–4 decision of the Supreme Court in the *NFIB v. Sebelius* case below. In 2014, however, another 5–4 decision concluded that the imposition of a contraceptive mandate over the religious objections of the employer was unlawful under the circumstances in the *Hobby Lobby* case, below. The Little Sisters of the Poor resisted the imposition of millions of dollars of fines threatened by the Obama administration. The order engaged in successful, multi-year litigation which twice reached the Supreme Court and which ultimately resulted in an administrative victory for the Little Sisters. We turn to an examination of these cases.

===================

132 S. Ct. 2566
Supreme Court of the United States

NATIONAL FEDERATION OF INDEPENDENT BUSINESS et al., Petitioners,

v.

Kathleen SEBELIUS, Secretary of Health and Human Services, et al. Department of Health and Human Services, et al., Petitioners,

v.

Florida, et al. Florida, et al., Petitioners,

v.

Department of Health and Human Services et al.

Decided June 28, 2012

Opinion

Today we resolve constitutional challenges to two provisions of the Patient Protection and Affordable Care Act of 2010: the individual mandate, which requires individuals to purchase a health insurance policy providing a minimum level of coverage . . . We do not consider whether the Act embodies sound policies. That judgment is entrusted to the Nation's elected leaders. We ask only whether Congress has the power under the Constitution to enact the challenged provisions.

. . . .

The Federal Government "is acknowledged by all to be one of enumerated powers." That is, rather than granting general authority to perform all the conceivable functions of government, the Constitution lists, or enumerates, the Federal Government's powers. Congress may, for example, "coin Money," "establish Post Offices," and "raise and support Armies." Art. I, § 8, cls. 5, 7, 12. The enumeration of powers is also a limitation of powers, because "[t]he enumeration presupposes something not enumerated." *Gibbons v. Ogden*, 22 U.S. 1, 9 Wheat. 1, 195, 6 L. Ed. 23 (1824). The Constitution's express conferral of some powers makes clear that it does not grant others. And the Federal Government "can exercise only the powers granted to it." *McCulloch, supra*, at 405, 4 Wheat. 316, 4 L. Ed. 579.

. . . .

Indeed, the Constitution did not initially include a Bill of Rights at least partly [2578] because the Framers felt the enumeration of powers sufficed to restrain the Government. As Alexander Hamilton put it, "the Constitution is itself, in every rational sense, and to every useful purpose, A BILL OF RIGHTS." The Federalist No. 84, p. 515 (C. Rossiter ed. 1961). And when the Bill of Rights was ratified, it made express what the enumeration of powers necessarily implied: "The powers not delegated to the United States by the Constitution ... are reserved to the States respectively, or to the people." U.S. Const., amend. X. The Federal Government has expanded dramatically over the past two centuries, but it still must show that a constitutional grant of power authorizes each of its actions. . . .

The same does not apply to the States, because the Constitution is not the source of their power. The Constitution may restrict state governments — as it does, for example, by forbidding them to deny any person the equal protection of the laws. But where such prohibitions do not apply, state governments do not need constitutional authorization to act. The States thus can and do perform many of the vital functions of modern government — punishing street crime, running public schools, and zoning property for development, to name but a few — even though the Constitution's text does not authorize any government to do so. Our cases refer to this general power of governing, possessed by the States but not by the Federal Government, as the "police power." *See, e.g., United States v. Morrison*, 529 U.S. 598, 618–619, 120 S. Ct. 1740, 146 L. Ed. 2d 658 (2000).

"State sovereignty is not just an end in itself: Rather, federalism secures to citizens the liberties that derive from the diffusion of sovereign power." *New York v. United States*, 505 U.S. 144, 181, 112 S. Ct. 2408, 120 L. Ed. 2d 120 (1992) (internal quotation marks omitted). Because the police power is controlled by 50 different States instead of one national sovereign, the facets of governing that touch on citizens' daily lives are normally administered by smaller governments closer to the governed. The Framers thus ensured that powers which "in the ordinary course of affairs, concern the lives, liberties, and properties of the people" were held by governments more local and more accountable than a distant federal bureaucracy. The Federalist No. 45, at 293 (J. Madison). The independent power of the States also serves as a check on the power of the Federal Government: "By denying any one government complete jurisdiction over all the concerns of public life, federalism protects the liberty of the individual from arbitrary power." . . .

This case concerns ... powers that the Constitution does grant the Federal Government, but which must be read carefully to avoid creating a general federal authority akin to the police power. The Constitution authorizes Congress to "regulate Commerce with foreign Nations, and among the several States, and with the Indian Tribes." Art. I, § 8, cl. 3. Our precedents read that to mean that Congress may regulate "the channels of interstate commerce," "persons or things in interstate commerce," and "those activities that substantially affect interstate commerce." *Morrison, supra*, at 609, 120 S. Ct. 1740, 146 L. Ed. 2d 658 (internal quotation marks omitted). The power over activities that substantially affect interstate commerce can be expansive. That power has been held to authorize federal regulation of such seemingly local matters as a farmer's decision to grow wheat for himself and his [2579] livestock, and a loan shark's extortionate collections from a neighborhood butcher shop. *See Wickard v. Filburn*, 317 U.S. 111, 63 S. Ct. 82, 87 L. Ed. 122 (1942); *Perez v. United States*, 402 U.S. 146, 91 S. Ct. 1357, 28 L. Ed. 2d 686 (1971).

. . . .

The reach of the Federal Government's enumerated powers is broader still because the Constitution authorizes Congress to "make all Laws which shall be necessary and proper for carrying into Execution the foregoing Powers." Art. I, § 8, cl. 18. We have long read this provision to give Congress great latitude in exercising its powers: "Let the end be legitimate, let it be within the scope of the constitution, and all means which are appropriate, which are plainly adapted to that end, which are not prohibited, but consist with the letter and spirit of the constitution, are constitutional." *McCulloch*, at 421, 4 L. Ed. 579.

Our permissive reading of these powers is explained in part by a general reticence to invalidate the acts of the Nation's elected leaders. "Proper respect for a coordinate branch of the government" requires that we strike down an Act of Congress only if "the lack of constitutional authority to pass [the] act in question is clearly demonstrated." *United States v. Harris*, 106 U.S. 629, 635, 1 S. Ct. 601, 27 L. Ed. 290, 4 Ky. L. Rptr. 739 (1883). Members of this Court are vested with the authority to interpret the law; we possess neither the expertise nor the prerogative to make policy judgments. Those decisions are entrusted to our Nation's elected leaders, who can be thrown out of office if the people disagree with them. It is not our job to protect the people from the consequences of their political choices.

Our deference in matters of policy cannot, however, become abdication in matters of law . . . Our respect for Congress's policy judgments thus can never extend so far as to disavow restraints on federal power that the Constitution carefully constructed . . . .

. . . .

I

In 2010, Congress enacted the Patient Protection and Affordable Care Act, 124 Stat. 119. The Act aims to increase the number of Americans covered by health insurance and decrease the cost of health care. The Act's 10 titles stretch over 900 pages and contain hundreds of provisions. This case concerns constitutional challenges to two key provisions, commonly referred to as the individual mandate . . . . The individual mandate requires most Americans to maintain "minimum essential" health insurance coverage. 26 U.S.C. § 5000A. The mandate does not apply to some individuals, such as prisoners and undocumented aliens. § 5000A(d). Many individuals will receive the required coverage through their employer, or from a government program such as Medicaid or Medicare. *See* § 5000A(f). But for individuals who are not exempt and do not receive health insurance through a third party, the means of satisfying the requirement is to purchase insurance from a private company. Beginning in 2014, those who do not comply with the mandate must make a "[s]hared responsibility payment" to the Federal Government. § 5000A(b)(1). That payment, which the Act describes as a "penalty," is calculated as a percentage of household income, subject to a floor based on a specified dollar amount and a ceiling based on the average annual premium the individual would have to pay for qualifying private health insurance. § 5000A(c). In 2016, for example, the penalty will be 2.5 percent of an individual's household income, but no less than $695 and no more than the average yearly premium for insurance that covers 60 percent of the cost of 10 specified services (e.g., prescription drugs and hospitalization). Ibid.; 42 U.S.C. § 18022. The Act provides that the penalty will be paid to the Internal Revenue Service with an individual's taxes, and "shall be assessed and collected in the same manner" as tax penalties, such as the penalty for claiming too large an income tax refund. 26 U.S.C. § 5000A(g)(1). The Act, however, bars the IRS from using several of its normal enforcement tools, such as criminal prosecutions and levies. § 5000A(g)(2). And some individuals who are subject to the mandate are nonetheless exempt from the penalty—for example, those with income below a certain threshold and members of Indian tribes. § 5000A(e).

On the day the President signed the Act into law, Florida and 12 other States filed a complaint in the Federal District Court for the Northern District of Florida. Those plaintiffs . . . were subsequently joined by 13 more States, several individuals, and the National Federation of Independent Business. . . .

The Court of Appeals for the Eleventh . . . [held] that the individual mandate exceeds Congress's power . . . [finding] that the individual mandate was not supported by Congress's power to "regulate Commerce . . . among the several States." According to the majority, the Commerce Clause does not empower the Federal Government to order individuals to engage in commerce. . . .

Other Courts of Appeals have also heard challenges to the individual mandate. The Sixth Circuit and the D.C. Circuit upheld the mandate as a valid exercise of Congress's commerce power. . . .

We granted certiorari to review the judgment of the Court of Appeals for the Eleventh Circuit. . . .

III

The Government . . . argues that Congress had the power to enact the mandate under the Commerce Clause. Under that theory, Congress may order individuals to buy health insurance because the failure to do so affects interstate commerce, and could undercut the Affordable Care Act's other reforms. . . .

A

The Government's first argument is that the individual mandate is a valid exercise of Congress's power under the Commerce Clause and the Necessary and Proper Clause. According to the Government, the health care market is characterized by a significant cost-shifting problem. Everyone will eventually need health care at a time and to an extent they cannot predict, but if they do not have insurance, they often will not be able to pay for it. Because state and federal laws nonetheless require hospitals to provide a certain degree of care to individuals without regard to their ability to pay, see, e.g., 42 U.S.C. § 1395dd; Fla. Stat. Ann. § 395.1041, hospitals end up receiving compensation for only a portion of the services they provide. To recoup the losses, hospitals pass on the cost to insurers through higher rates, and insurers, in turn, pass on the cost to policy holders in the form of higher premiums. Congress estimated that the cost of uncompensated care raises family health insurance premiums, on average, by over $1,000 per year. 42 U.S.C. § 18091(2)(F).

In the Affordable Care Act, Congress addressed the problem of those who cannot obtain insurance coverage because of preexisting conditions or other health issues. It did so through the Act's "guaranteed-issue" and "community-rating" provisions. These provisions together prohibit insurance companies from denying coverage to those with such conditions or charging unhealthy individuals higher premiums than healthy individuals. *See* §§ 300gg, 300gg-1, 300gg-3, 300gg-4.

The guaranteed-issue and community-rating reforms do not, however, address the issue of healthy individuals who choose not to purchase insurance to cover potential health care needs. In fact, the reforms sharply exacerbate that problem, by providing an incentive for individuals to delay purchasing health insurance until they become sick, relying on the promise of guaranteed and affordable coverage. The reforms also threaten to impose massive new costs on insurers, who are required to accept unhealthy individuals but prohibited from charging them rates necessary to pay for their coverage. This will lead insurers to significantly increase premiums on everyone. See Brief for America's Health Insurance Plans et al. as Amici Curiae in No. 11-393 etc. 8-9.

The individual mandate was Congress's solution to these problems. By requiring that individuals purchase health insurance, the mandate prevents cost-shifting by those who would otherwise go without it. In addition, the mandate forces into the insurance risk pool more healthy individuals, whose premiums on average will be higher than their health care expenses. This allows insurers to subsidize the costs of covering the unhealthy individuals the reforms require them to accept. The Government claims that Congress has power under the Commerce and Necessary and Proper Clauses to enact this solution.

1

The Government contends that the individual mandate is within Congress's power because the failure to purchase insurance "has a substantial and deleterious effect on interstate commerce" by creating the cost-shifting problem . . . The path of our Commerce Clause decisions has not always run smooth, see *United States v. Lopez*, 514 U.S. 549, 552-559, 115 S. Ct. 1624, 131 L. Ed. 2d 626 (1995), but it is now well established that Congress has broad authority under the Clause. . . . Congress's power, moreover, is not limited to regulation of an activity that by itself substantially affects interstate commerce, but also extends to activities that do so only when aggregated with similar activities of others. See *Wickard* [*v. Filburn*], 317 U.S., at 127-128, 63 S. Ct. 82, 87 L. Ed. 122.

Given its expansive scope, it is no surprise that Congress has employed the commerce power in a wide variety of ways to address the pressing needs of the time. But Congress has never attempted to rely on that power to compel individuals not engaged in commerce to purchase an unwanted product. Legislative novelty is not necessarily fatal; there is a first time for everything. But sometimes "the most telling indication of [a] severe constitutional problem . . . is the lack of historical precedent" for Congress's action. . . .

The Constitution grants Congress the power to "*regulate* Commerce." Art. I, § 8, cl. 3 (emphasis added). The power to regulate commerce presupposes the existence of commercial activity to be regulated. If the power to "regulate" something included the power to create it, many of the provisions in the Constitution would be superfluous. For example, the Constitution gives Congress the power to "coin Money," in addition to the power to "regulate the Value thereof." *Id.*, cl. 5. And it gives Congress the power to "raise and support Armies" and to "provide and maintain a Navy," in addition to the power to "make Rules for the Government and Regulation of the land and naval Forces." *Id.*, cls. 12–14. If the power to regulate the armed forces or the value of money included the power to bring the subject of the regulation into existence, the specific grant of such powers would have been unnecessary. The language of the Constitution reflects the natural understanding that the power to regulate assumes there is already something to be regulated. . . .

Our precedent also reflects this understanding. As expansive as our cases construing the scope of the commerce power have been, they all have one thing in common: They uniformly describe the power as reaching "activity." It is nearly impossible to avoid the word when quoting them. See, e.g., *Lopez, supra*, at 560, 115 S. Ct. 1624, 131 L. Ed. 2d 626 ("Where economic activity substantially affects interstate commerce, legislation regulating that activity will be sustained"); *Perez*, 402 U.S., at 154, 91 S. Ct. 1357, 28 L. Ed. 2d 686 ("Where the *class of activities* is regulated and that *class* is within the reach of federal power, the courts have no power to excise, as trivial, individual instances of the class" (emphasis in original; internal quotation marks omitted)); *Wickard, supra*, at 125, 63 S. Ct. 82, 87 L. Ed. 122 ("[E]ven if appellee's activity be local and though it may not be regarded as commerce, it may still, whatever its nature, be reached by Congress if it exerts a substantial economic effect on interstate commerce"); *NLRB v. Jones & Laughlin Steel Corp.*, 301 U.S. 1, 37, 57 S. Ct. 615, 81 L. Ed. 893 (1937) ("Although activities may be intrastate in character when separately considered, if they have such a close and substantial relation to interstate commerce that their control is essential or appropriate to protect that commerce from burdens and obstructions, Congress cannot be denied the power to exercise that control"). . . .

The individual mandate, however, does not regulate existing commercial activity. It instead compels individuals to become active in commerce by purchasing a product, on the ground that their failure to do so affects interstate commerce. Construing the Commerce Clause to permit Congress to regulate individuals precisely because they are doing nothing would open a new and potentially vast domain to congressional authority. Every day individuals do not do an infinite number of things. In some cases they decide not to do something; in others they simply fail to do it. Allowing Congress to justify federal regulation by pointing to the effect of inaction on commerce would bring countless decisions an individual could potentially make within the scope of federal regulation, and—under the Government's theory—empower Congress to make those decisions for him.

. . . .

Wickard has long been regarded as "perhaps the most far reaching example of Commerce Clause authority over intrastate activity," *Lopez*, . . . but the Government's theory in this case would go much further. Under *Wickard* it is within Congress's power to regulate the market for wheat by supporting its price. But price can be supported by increasing demand as well as by decreasing supply. The aggregated decisions of some consumers not to purchase wheat have a substantial effect on the price of wheat, just as decisions not to purchase health insurance have on the price of insurance. Congress can therefore command that those not buying wheat do so, just as it argues here that it may command that those not buying health insurance do so. The farmer in *Wickard* was at least actively engaged in the production of wheat, and the Government could regulate that activity because of its effect on commerce. The Government's theory here would effectively override that limitation, by establishing that individuals may be regulated under the Commerce Clause whenever enough of them are not doing something the Government would have them do.

Indeed, the Government's logic would justify a mandatory purchase to solve almost any problem. . . . To consider a different example in the health care market, many Americans do not eat a balanced diet. That group makes up a larger percentage of the total population than those without health insurance. . . . The failure of that group to have a healthy diet increases health care costs, to a greater extent than the failure of the uninsured to purchase insurance. . . . Those increased costs are borne in part by other Americans who must pay more, just as the uninsured shift costs to the insured. . . . Congress addressed the insurance problem by ordering everyone to buy insurance. Under the Government's theory, Congress could address the diet problem by ordering everyone to buy vegetables. . . . People, for reasons of their own, often fail to do things that would be good for them or good for society. Those failures — joined with the similar failures of others — can readily have a substantial effect on interstate commerce. Under the Government's logic, that authorizes Congress to use its commerce power to compel citizens to act as the Government would have them act.

. . . .

To an economist, perhaps, there is no difference between activity and inactivity; both have measurable economic effects on commerce. But the distinction between doing something and doing nothing would not have been lost on the Framers, who were "practical statesmen," not metaphysical philosophers. *Industrial Union Dept., AFL-CIO v. American Petroleum Institute*, 448 U.S. 607, 673, 100 S. Ct. 2844, 65 L. Ed. 2d 1010 (1980) (Rehnquist, J., concurring in judgment). . . . The Framers gave Congress the power to regulate commerce, not to compel it, and for over 200 years both our decisions and Congress's actions have reflected this understanding. There is no reason to depart from that understanding now.

. . . .

2

The Government next contends that Congress has the power under the Necessary and Proper Clause to enact the individual mandate because the mandate is an "integral part of a comprehensive scheme of economic regulation" — the guaranteed-issue and community-rating insurance reforms. . . . Under this argument, it is not necessary to consider the effect that an individual's inactivity may have on interstate commerce; it is enough that Congress regulate commercial activity in a way that requires regulation of inactivity to be effective.

The power to "make all Laws which shall be necessary and proper for carrying into Execution" the powers enumerated in the Constitution, Art. I, § 8, cl. 18, vests Congress with authority to enact provisions "incidental to the [enumerated] power, and conducive to its beneficial exercise," *McCulloch*, 17 U.S., at 418, 4 Wheat., at 418, 4 L. Ed. 579. Although the Clause gives Congress authority to "legislate on that vast mass of incidental powers which must be involved in the constitution," it does not license the exercise of any "great substantive and independent power[s]" beyond those specifically enumerated. *Id.*, 17 U.S., at 411, 421, 4 Wheat., at 411, 421, 4 L. Ed. 579. Instead, the Clause is "'merely a declaration, for the removal of all uncertainty, that the means of carrying into execution those [powers] otherwise granted are included in the grant.'" *Kinsella v. United States*, 361 U.S. 234, 247, 80 S. Ct. 297, 4 L. Ed. 2d 268 (1960) (quoting VI Writings of James Madison 383 (G. Hunt ed. 1906)).

. . . .

Applying these principles, the individual mandate cannot be sustained under the Necessary and Proper Clause as an essential component of the insurance reforms. Each of our prior cases upholding laws under that Clause involved exercises of authority derivative of, and in service to, a granted power. . . . The individual mandate, by contrast, vests Congress with the extraordinary ability to create the necessary predicate to the exercise of an enumerated power.

. . . .

[A separate part of Chief Justice Robert's opinion for the Court, joined by Justice Ginsberg, Breyer, Sotomayor, and Kagan, upheld the mandate as within Congress' constitutional power to "lay and collect Taxes, Duties, Imposts, and Excises, to pay the Debts and provide for the common Defense and general Welfare of the United State," U.S. Const., Art. 1, § 8, cl. 1.].

Justice SCALIA, Justice KENNEDY, Justice THOMAS, and Justice ALITO, dissenting [from the judgment upholding the mandate, but agreeing with the Chief Justice's resolution of (though not joining his opinion on) the Commerce Clause and Necessary and Proper Clause issues].

This case is in one respect difficult: it presents . . . questions of first impression. The first of those is whether failure to engage in economic activity (the purchase of health insurance) is subject to regulation under the Commerce Clause. . . .

The case is easy and straightforward, however, in another respect. What is absolutely clear, affirmed by the text of the 1789 Constitution, by the Tenth Amendment ratified in 1791, and by innumerable cases of ours in the 220 years since, is that there are structural limits upon federal power—upon what it can prescribe with respect to private conduct, and upon what it can impose upon the sovereign States. . . .

The striking case of *Wickard v. Filburn*, 317 U.S. 111, 63 S. Ct. 82, 87 L. Ed. 122 (1942), which held that the economic activity of growing wheat, even for one's own consumption, affected commerce sufficiently that it could be regulated, always has been regarded as the ne plus ultra of expansive Commerce Clause jurisprudence. To go beyond that, and to say the failure to grow wheat (which is not an economic activity, or any activity at all) nonetheless affects commerce and therefore can be federally regulated, is to make mere breathing in and out the basis for federal prescription and to extend federal power to virtually all human activity.

. . . .

So the question is, quite simply, whether the exaction here is imposed for violation of the law. It unquestionably is. The minimum-coverage provision is found in 26 U.S.C. § 5000A, entitled "*Requirement* to maintain minimum essential coverage." (Emphasis added.) It commands that every "applicable individual *shall* . . . ensure that the individual . . . is covered under minimum essential coverage." Ibid. (emphasis added). And the immediately following provision states that, "[i]f . . . an applicable individual . . . fails to meet the *requirement* of subsection (a) . . . there is hereby imposed . . . a *penalty*." § 5000A(b) (emphasis added). And several of Congress' legislative "findings" with regard to § 5000A confirm that it sets forth a legal requirement and constitutes the assertion of regulatory power, not mere taxing power. . . .

... [T]o say that the Individual Mandate merely imposes a tax is not to interpret the statute but to rewrite it. Judicial tax-writing is particularly troubling . . . .

Under the Patient Protection and Affordable Care Act of 2010 (ACA), the Department of Health and Human Services (HHS) mandated specific employers' group health plans to provide "preventive care and screenings" for women without "any cost sharing requirements." However, Congress failed to specify what types of preventive care must be covered, instead authorizing the Health Resources and Services Administration to decide.

The ACA required nonexempt employers to provide coverage for the 20 contraceptive methods approved by the Food and Drug Administration, including 4 methods that may prevent an already fertilized egg from attachment to the uterus, thus ceasing development. Religious employers, like churches, were exempted from this contraceptive mandate. Furthermore, HHS exempted religious nonprofit organizations that cited religious objections to provide coverage for contraceptive services.

In the present cases, the owners of three closely held for-profit corporations sued HHS and other federal officials and agencies under the Religious Freedom Restoration Act of 1993 (RFRA) and the Free Exercise Clause, seeking to enjoin enforcement of the contraceptive mandate insofar as it required them to provide health coverage for the four objectionable contraceptives.

---

134 S. Ct. 2751
United States Supreme Court

BURWELL, SECRETARY OF HEALTH AND HUMAN SERVICES, et al.

v.

HOBBY LOBBY STORES, INC., et al.

Nos. 13–354 and 13–356 Argued March 25, 2014 Decided June 30, 2014

ALITO, J., delivered the opinion of the Court, in which ROBERTS, C. J., and SCALIA, KENNEDY, and THOMAS, JJ., joined. KENNEDY, J., filed a concurring opinion. GINSBURG, J., filed a dissenting opinion, in which SOTOMAYOR, J., joined, and in which BREYER and KAGAN, JJ., joined as to all but Part III-C-1.BREYER and KAGAN, JJ., filed a dissenting opinion.

ON WRIT OF CERTIORARI TO THE UNITED STATES COURT OF APPEALS FOR THE TENTH CIRCUIT

Opinion

JUSTICE ALITO delivered the opinion of the Court.

We must decide in these cases whether the Religious Freedom Restoration Act of 1993 (RFRA), 107 Stat. 1488, 42 U.S.C. § 2000bb *et seq.*, permits the United States Department of Health and Human Services (HHS) to demand that three closely held corporations provide health-insurance coverage for methods of contraception that violate the sincerely held religious beliefs of the companies' owners. We hold that the regulations that impose this obligation violate RFRA, which prohibits the Federal Government from taking any action that substantially burdens the exercise of religion unless that action constitutes the least restrictive means of serving a compelling government interest.

In holding that the HHS mandate is unlawful, we reject HHS's argument that the owners of the companies forfeited all RFRA protection when they decided to organize their businesses as corporations rather than sole proprietorships or general partnerships. The plain terms of RFRA make it perfectly clear that Congress did not discriminate in this way against men and women who wish to run their businesses as for-profit corporations in the manner required by their religious beliefs.

Since RFRA applies in these cases, we must decide whether the challenged HHS regulations substantially burden the exercise of religion, and we hold that they do. The owners of the businesses have religious objections to abortion, and according to their religious beliefs the four contraceptive methods at issue are abortifacients. If the owners comply with the HHS mandate, they believe they will be facilitating abortions, and if they do not comply, they will pay a very heavy price—as much as $1.3 million per day, or about $475 million per year, in the case of one of the companies. If these consequences do not amount to a substantial burden, it is hard to see what would.

Under RFRA, a Government action that imposes a substantial burden on religious exercise must serve a compelling government interest, and we assume that the HHS regulations satisfy this requirement. But in order for the HHS mandate to be sustained, it must also constitute the least restrictive means of serving that interest, and the mandate plainly fails that test. There are other ways in which Congress or HHS could equally ensure that every woman has cost-free access to the particular contraceptives at issue here and, indeed, to all FDA-approved contraceptives.

In fact, HHS has already devised and implemented a system that seeks to respect the religious liberty of religious nonprofit corporations while ensuring that the employees of these entities have precisely the same access to all FDA-approved contraceptives as employees of companies whose owners have no religious objections to providing such coverage. The employees of these religious nonprofit corporations still have access to insurance coverage without cost sharing for all FDA-approved contraceptives; and according to HHS, this system imposes no net economic burden on the insurance companies that are required to provide or secure the coverage.

Although HHS has made this system available to religious nonprofits that have religious objections to the contraceptive mandate, HHS has provided no reason why the same system cannot be made available when the owners of for-profit corporations have similar religious objections. We therefore conclude that this system constitutes an alternative that achieves all of the Government's aims while providing greater respect for religious liberty. And under RFRA, that conclusion means that enforcement of the HHS contraceptive mandate against the objecting parties in these cases is unlawful.

As this description of our reasoning shows, our holding is very specific. We do not hold, as the principal dissent alleges, that for-profit corporations and other commercial enterprises can "opt out of any law (saving only tax laws) they judge incompatible with their sincerely held religious beliefs." *Post*, at 1 (opinion of GINSBURG, J.). Nor do we hold, as the dissent implies, that such corporations have free rein to take steps that impose "disadvantages . . . on others" or that require "the general public [to] pick up the tab." *Post*, at 1–2. And we certainly do not hold or suggest that "RFRA demands accommodation of a for-profit corporation's religious beliefs no matter the impact that accommodation may have on . . . thousands of women employed by Hobby Lobby." *Post*, at 2. The effect of the HHS-created accommodation on the women employed by Hobby Lobby and the other companies involved in these cases would be precisely zero. Under that accommodation, these women would still be entitled to all FDA-approved contraceptives without cost sharing.

I

A

Congress enacted RFRA in 1993 in order to provide very broad protection for religious liberty. RFRA's enactment came three years after this Court's decision in *Employment Div., Dept. of Human Resources of Ore. v. Smith*, 494 U.S. 872 (1990), which largely repudiated the method of analyzing free-exercise claims that had been used in cases like *Sherbert v. Verner*, 374 U.S. 398 (1963), and *Wisconsin v. Yoder*, 406 U.S. 205 (1972).

. . . .

Congress responded . . . by enacting RFRA. "[L]aws [that are] 'neutral' toward religion," Congress found, "may burden religious exercise as surely as laws intended to interfere with religious exercise." 42 U.S.C. §2000bb(a)(2); see also §2000bb(a)(4). In order to ensure broad protection for religious liberty, RFRA provides that "Government shall not substantially burden a person's exercise of religion even if the burden results from a rule of general applicability." §2000bb–1(a). If the Government substantially burdens a person's exercise of religion, under the Act that person is entitled to an exemption from the rule unless the Government "demonstrates that application of the burden to the person — (1) is in furtherance of a compelling governmental interest; and (2) is the least restrictive means of furthering that compelling governmental interest." §2000bb–1(b).

. . . .

B

At issue in these cases are HHS regulations promulgated under the Patient Protection and Affordable Care Act of 2010 (ACA), 124 Stat. 119. ACA generally requires employers with 50 or more full-time employees to offer "a group health plan or group health insurance coverage" that provides "minimum essential coverage." 26 U.S.C. § 5000A(f)(2); §§ 4980H(a), (c)(2). Any covered employer that does not provide such coverage must pay a substantial price. Specifically, if a covered employer provides group health insurance but its plan fails to comply with ACA's group-health-plan requirements, the employer may be required to pay $100 per day for each affected "individual." §§ 4980D(a)–(b). And if the employer decides to stop providing health insurance altogether and at least one full-time employee enrolls in a health plan and qualifies for a subsidy on one of the government-run ACA exchanges, the employer must pay $2,000 per year for each of its full-time employees. §§ 4980H(a), (c)(1).

Unless an exception applies, ACA requires an employer's group health plan or group-health-insurance coverage to furnish "preventive care and screenings" for women without "any cost sharing requirements." 42 U.S.C. § 300gg–13(a)(4). Congress itself, however, did not specify what types of preventive care must be covered. Instead, Congress authorized the Health Resources and Services Administration (HRSA), a component of HHS, to make that important and sensitive decision. *Ibid.* The HRSA in turn consulted the Institute of Medicine, a nonprofit group of volunteer advisers, in determining which preventive services to require. See 77 Fed. Reg. 8725–8726 (2012).

In August 2011, based on the Institute's recommendations, the HRSA promulgated the Women's Preventive Services Guidelines. See *id.* at 8725–8726, and n.1; online at http://hrsa.gov/womensguidelines (all Internet materials as visited June 26, 2014, and available in Clerk of Court's case file). The Guidelines provide that nonexempt employers are generally required to provide "coverage, without cost sharing" for "[a]ll Food and Drug Administration [(FDA)] approved contraceptive methods, sterilization procedures, and patient education and counseling." 77 Fed. Reg. 8725 (internal quotation marks omitted). Although many of the required, FDA-approved methods of contraception work by preventing the fertilization of an egg, four of those methods (those specifically at issue in these cases) may have the effect of preventing an already fertilized egg from developing any further by inhibiting its attachment to the uterus. See Brief for HHS in No. 13–354, pp. 9–10, n.4; FDA, Birth Control: Medicines to Help You.

HHS also authorized the HRSA to establish exemptions from the contraceptive mandate for "religious employers." 45 CFR § 147.131(a). That category encompasses "churches, their integrated auxiliaries, and conventions or associations of churches," as well as "the exclusively religious activities of any religious order." See *ibid* (citing 26 U.S.C. §§ 6033(a)(3)(A)(i), (iii)). In its Guidelines, HRSA exempted these organizations from the requirement to cover contraceptive services. See http://hrsa.gov /womensguidelines.

In addition, HHS has effectively exempted certain religious nonprofit organizations, described under HHS regulations as "eligible organizations," from the contraceptive mandate. See 45 CFR § 147.131(b); 78 Fed. Reg. 39874 (2013). An "eligible organization" means a nonprofit organization that "holds itself out as a religious organization" and "opposes providing coverage for some or all of any contraceptive services required to be covered . . . on account of religious objections." 45 CFR § 147.131(b). To qualify for this accommodation, an employer must certify that it is such an organization. § 147.131(b)(4). When a group-health-insurance issuer receives notice that one of its clients has invoked this provision, the issuer must then exclude contraceptive coverage from the employer's plan and provide separate payments for contraceptive services for plan participants without imposing any cost-sharing requirements on the eligible organization, its insurance plan, or its employee beneficiaries. § 147.131(c). Although this procedure requires the issuer to bear the cost of these services, HHS has determined that this obligation will not impose any net expense on issuers because its cost will be less than or equal to the cost savings resulting from the services. 78 Fed. Reg. 39877.

In addition to these exemptions for religious organizations, ACA exempts a great many employers from most of its coverage requirements. Employers providing "grandfathered health plans"—those that existed prior to March 23, 2010, and that have not made specified changes after that date—need not comply with many of the Act's requirements, including the contraceptive mandate. 42 U.S.C. §§ 18011(a), (e). And employers with fewer than 50 employees are not required to provide health insurance at all. 26 U.S.C. § 4980H(c)(2).

All told, the contraceptive mandate "presently does not apply to tens of millions of people." 723 F. 3d 1114, 1143 (CA10 2013). This is attributable, in large part, to grandfathered health plans: Over one-third of the 149 million nonelderly people in America with employer-sponsored health plans were enrolled in grandfathered plans in 2013. Brief for HHS in No. 13–354, at 53; Kaiser Family Foundation & Health Research & Educational Trust, Employer Health Benefits, 2013 Annual Survey 43, 221. The count for employees working for firms that do not have to provide insurance at all because they employ fewer than 50 employees is 34 million workers. See The Whitehouse, Health Reform for Small Businesses: The Affordable Care Act Increases Choice and Saving Money for Small Businesses 1.

II

A

Norman and Elizabeth Hahn and their three sons are devout members of the Mennonite Church, a Christian denomination. The Mennonite Church opposes abortion and believes that "[t]he fetus in its earliest stages . . . shares humanity with those who conceived it."

Fifty years ago, Norman Hahn started a wood-working business in his garage, and since then, this company, Conestoga Wood Specialties, has grown and now has 950 employees. Conestoga is organized under Pennsylvania law as a for-profit corporation. The Hahns exercise sole ownership of the closely held business; they control its board of directors and hold all of its voting shares. One of the Hahn sons serves as the president and CEO.

The Hahns believe that they are required to run their business "in accordance with their religious beliefs and moral principles." 917 F. Supp. 2d 394, 402 (ED Pa. 2013). To that end, the company's mission, as they see it, is to "operate in a professional environment founded upon the highest ethical, moral, and Christian principles." *Ibid.* (internal quotation marks omitted). The company's "Vision and Values Statements" affirms that Conestoga endeavors to "ensur[e] a reasonable profit in [a] manner that reflects [the Hahns'] Christian heritage." App. in No. 13–356, p. 94 (complaint).

As explained in Conestoga's board-adopted "Statement on the Sanctity of Human Life," the Hahns believe that "human life begins at conception." 724 F.3d 377, 382, and n.5 (CA3 2013) (internal quotation marks omitted). It is therefore "against [their] moral conviction to be involved in the termination of human life" after conception, which they believe is a "sin against God to which they are held accountable." *Ibid.* (internal quotation marks omitted). The Hahns have accordingly excluded from the group-health-insurance plan they offer to their employees certain contraceptive methods that they consider to be abortifacients. *Id.* at 382.

The Hahns and Conestoga sued HHS and other federal officials and agencies under RFRA and the Free Exercise Clause of the First Amendment, seeking to enjoin application of ACA's contraceptive mandate insofar as it requires them to provide health-insurance coverage for four FDA-approved contraceptives that may operate after the fertilization of an egg. These include two forms of emergency contraception commonly called "morning after" pills and two types of intrauterine devices.

In opposing the requirement to provide coverage for the contraceptives to which they object, the Hahns argued that "it is immoral and sinful for [them] to intentionally participate in, pay for, facilitate, or otherwise support these drugs." *Ibid.* The District Court denied a preliminary injunction, see 917 F. Supp. 2d at 419, and the Third Circuit affirmed in a divided opinion, holding that "for-profit, secular corporations cannot engage in religious exercise" within the meaning of RFRA or the First Amendment. 724 F. 3d, at 381. The Third Circuit also rejected the claims brought by the Hahns themselves because it concluded that the HHS "[m]andate does not impose any requirements on the Hahns" in their personal capacity. *Id.* at 389.

B

David and Barbara Green and their three children are Christians who own and operate two family businesses. Forty-five years ago, David Green started an arts-and-crafts store that has grown into a nationwide chain called Hobby Lobby. There are now 500 Hobby Lobby stores, and the company has more than 13,000 employees. 723 F.3d at 1122. Hobby Lobby is organized as a for-profit corporation under Oklahoma law.

One of David's sons started an affiliated business, Mardel, which operates 35 Christian bookstores and employs close to 400 people. *Ibid.* Mardel is also organized as a for-profit corporation under Oklahoma law.

Though these two businesses have expanded over the years, they remain closely held, and David, Barbara, and their children retain exclusive control of both companies. *Ibid.* David serves as the CEO of Hobby Lobby, and his three children serve as the president, vice president, and vice CEO. See Brief for Respondents in No. 13–354, p. 8.

Hobby Lobby's statement of purpose commits the Greens to "[h]onoring the Lord in all [they] do by operating the company in a manner consistent with Biblical principles." App. in No. 13–354, pp. 134–135 (complaint). Each family member has signed a pledge to run the businesses in accordance with the family's religious beliefs and to use the family assets to support Christian ministries. 723 F.3d, at 1122. In accordance with those commitments, Hobby Lobby and Mardel stores close on Sundays, even though the Greens calculate that they lose millions in sales annually by doing so. *Id.* at 1122; App. in No. 13–354, at 136–137. The businesses refuse to engage in profitable transactions that facilitate or promote alcohol use; they contribute profits to Christian missionaries and ministries; and they buy hundreds of full-page newspaper ads inviting people to "know Jesus as Lord and Savior." *Ibid.* (internal quotation marks omitted).

Like the Hahns, the Greens believe that life begins at conception and that it would violate their religion to facilitate access to contraceptive drugs or devices that operate after that point. 723 F.3d, at 1122. They specifically object to the same four contraceptive methods as the Hahns and, like the Hahns, they have no objection to the other 16 FDA-approved methods of birth control. *Id.* at 1125. Although their group-health-insurance plan predates the enactment of ACA, it is not a grandfathered plan because Hobby Lobby elected not to retain grandfathered status before the contraceptive mandate was proposed. *Id.* at 1124.

The Greens, Hobby Lobby, and Mardel sued HHS and other federal agencies and officials to challenge the contraceptive mandate under RFRA and the Free Exercise Clause. The District Court denied a preliminary injunction, see 870 F. Supp. 2d 1278 (WD Okla. 2012), and the plaintiffs appealed, moving for initial en banc consideration. The Tenth Circuit granted that motion and reversed in a divided opinion. Contrary to the conclusion of the Third Circuit, the Tenth Circuit held that the Greens' two for-profit businesses are "persons" within the meaning of RFRA and therefore may bring suit under that law.

The court then held that the corporations had established a likelihood of success on their RFRA claim. 723 F.3d, at 1140–1147. The court concluded that the contraceptive mandate substantially burdened the exercise of religion by requiring the companies to choose between "compromis[ing] their religious beliefs" and paying a heavy fee — either "close to $475 million more in taxes every year" if they simply refused to provide coverage for the contraceptives at issue, or "roughly $26 million" annually if they "drop[ped] health-insurance benefits for all employees." *Id.* at 1141.

The court next held that HHS had failed to demonstrate a compelling interest in enforcing the mandate against the Greens' businesses and, in the alternative, that

HHS had failed to prove that enforcement of the mandate was the "least restrictive means" of furthering the Government's asserted interests. *Id.* at 1143–1144 (emphasis deleted; internal quotation marks omitted). After concluding that the companies had "demonstrated irreparable harm," the court reversed and remanded for the District Court to consider the remaining factors of the preliminary-injunction test. *Id.* at 1147.

We granted certiorari. 571 U.S. ___ (2013).

III

A

RFRA prohibits the "Government [from] substantially burden[ing] *a person's* exercise of religion even if the burden results from a rule of general applicability" unless the Government "demonstrates that application of the burden to *the person*— (1) is in furtherance of a compelling governmental interest; and (2) is the least restrictive means of furthering that compelling governmental interest." 42 U.S.C. §§ 2000bb–1(a), (b) (emphasis added). The first question that we must address is whether this provision applies to regulations that govern the activities of for-profit corporations like Hobby Lobby, Conestoga, and Mardel.

HHS contends that neither these companies nor their owners can even be heard under RFRA. According to HHS, the companies cannot sue because they seek to make a profit for their owners, and the owners cannot be heard because the regulations, at least as a formal matter, apply only to the companies and not to the owners as individuals. HHS's argument would have dramatic consequences.

. . . .

As we have seen, RFRA was designed to provide very broad protection for religious liberty. By enacting RFRA, Congress went far beyond what this Court has held is constitutionally required. Is there any reason to think that the Congress that enacted such sweeping protection put small-business owners to the choice that HHS suggests? An examination of RFRA's text, to which we turn in the next part of this opinion, reveals that Congress did no such thing.

As we will show, Congress provided protection for people like the Hahns and Greens by employing a familiar legal fiction: It included corporations within RFRA's definition of "persons." But it is important to keep in mind that the purpose of this fiction is to provide protection for human beings. A corporation is simply a form of organization used by human beings to achieve desired ends. An established body of law specifies the rights and obligations of the *people* (including shareholders, officers, and employees) who are associated with a corporation in one way or another. When rights, whether constitutional or statutory, are extended to corporations, the purpose is to protect the rights of these people. For example, extending Fourth Amendment protection to corporations protects the privacy interests of employees and others associated with the company. Protecting corporations from government seizure of their property without just compensation protects all those who have a stake in the corporations' financial well-being. And protecting the free-exercise rights of corporations like Hobby Lobby, Conestoga, and Mardel protects the religious liberty of the humans who own and control those companies.

In holding that Conestoga, as a "secular, for-profit corporation," lacks RFRA protection, the Third Circuit wrote as follows:

"General business corporations do not, *separate and apart from the actions or belief systems of their individual owners or employees,* exercise religion. They do not pray, worship, observe sacraments or take other religiously-motivated actions separate and apart from the intention and direction of their individual actors." 724 F.3d, at 385 (emphasis added).

All of this is true—but quite beside the point. Corporations, "separate and apart from" the human beings who own, run, and are employed by them, cannot do anything at all.

B

1

As we noted above, RFRA applies to "a person's" exercise of religion, 42 U.S.C. §§ 2000bb–1(a), (b), and RFRA itself does not define the term "person." We therefore look to the Dictionary Act, which we must consult "[i]n determining the meaning of any Act of Congress, unless the context indicates otherwise." 1 U.S.C. § 1.

Under the Dictionary Act, "the wor[d] 'person' . . . include[s] corporations, companies, associations, firms, partnerships, societies, and joint stock companies, as well as individuals." *Ibid.*; see *FCC v. AT&T Inc.*, 562 U.S. ___, ___ (2011) (slip op., at 6) ("We have no doubt that 'person,' in a legal setting, often refers to artificial entities. The Dictionary Act makes that clear."). Thus, unless there is something about the RFRA context that "indicates otherwise," the Dictionary Act provides a quick, clear, and affirmative answer to the question whether the companies involved in these cases may be heard.

. . . .

This concession effectively dispatches any argument that the term "person" as used in RFRA does not reach the closely held corporations involved in these cases. No known understanding of the term "person" includes *some* but not all corporations. The term "person" sometimes encompasses artificial persons (as the Dictionary Act instructs), and it sometimes is limited to natural persons. But no conceivable definition of the term includes natural persons and nonprofit corporations, but not for-profit corporations. Cf. *Clark v. Martinez*, 543 U.S. 371, 378 (2005) ("To give th[e] same words a different meaning for each category would be to invent a statute rather than interpret one.").

2

The principal argument advanced by HHS and the principal dissent regarding RFRA protection for Hobby Lobby, Conestoga, and Mardel focuses not on the statutory term "person," but on the phrase "exercise of religion." According to HHS and the dissent, these corporations are not protected by RFRA because they cannot exercise religion. Neither HHS nor the dissent, however, provides any persuasive explanation for this conclusion.

Is it because of the corporate form? The corporate form alone cannot provide the explanation because, as we have pointed out, HHS concedes that nonprofit corporations can be protected by RFRA. The dissent suggests that nonprofit corporations are special because furthering their religious "autonomy . . . often furthers individual religious freedom as well." *Post*, at 15 (quoting *Corporation of Presiding Bishop of Church of Jesus Christ of Latter-day Saints v. Amos*, 483 U.S. 327, 342 (1987) (Brennan, J., concurring in judgment)). But this principle applies equally to for-profit corporations: Furthering their religious freedom also "furthers individual religious freedom." In these cases, for example, allowing Hobby Lobby, Conestoga, and Mardel to assert RFRA claims protects the religious liberty of the Greens and the Hahns.

If the corporate form is not enough, what about the profit-making objective? In *Braunfeld*, 366 U.S. 599, we entertained the free-exercise claims of individuals who were attempting to make a profit as retail merchants, and the Court never even hinted that this objective precluded their claims. As the Court explained in a later case, the "exercise of religion" involves "not only belief and profession but the performance of (or abstention from) physical acts" that are "engaged in for religious reasons." *Smith*, 494 U.S. at 877. Business practices that are compelled or limited by the tenets of a religious doctrine fall comfortably within that definition. Thus, a law that "operates so as to make the practice of . . . religious beliefs more expensive" in the context of business activities imposes a burden on the exercise of religion. *Braunfeld*, *supra*, at 605; see *United States v. Lee*, 455 U.S. 252, 257 (1982) (recognizing that "compulsory participation in the social security system interferes with [Amish employers'] free exercise rights").

If, as *Braunfeld* recognized, a sole proprietorship that seeks to make a profit may assert a free-exercise claim, why can't Hobby Lobby, Conestoga, and Mardel do the same?

Some lower court judges have suggested that RFRA does not protect for-profit corporations because the purpose of such corporations is simply to make money. This argument flies in the face of modern corporate law. "Each American jurisdiction today either expressly or by implication authorizes corporations to be formed under its general corporation act for *any lawful purpose* or business." 1 J. Cox & T. Hazen, Treatise of the Law of Corporations § 4:1, p. 224 (3d ed. 2010) (emphasis added); see 1A W. Fletcher, Cyclopedia of the Law of Corporations § 102 (rev. ed. 2010). While it is certainly true that a central objective of for-profit corporations is to make money, modern corporate law does not require for-profit corporations to pursue profit at the expense of everything else, and many do not do so. For-profit corporations, with ownership approval, support a wide variety of charitable causes, and it is not at all uncommon for such corporations to further humanitarian and other altruistic objectives. Many examples come readily to mind. So long as its owners agree, a for-profit corporation may take costly pollution-control and energy-conservation measures that go beyond what the law requires. A for-profit corporation that operates facilities in other countries may exceed the requirements of local law regarding working conditions and benefits. If for-profit corporations may pursue such worthy objectives, there is no apparent reason why they may not further religious objectives as well.

HHS would draw a sharp line between nonprofit corporations (which, HHS concedes, are protected by RFRA) and for-profit corporations (which HHS would leave unprotected), but the actual picture is less clear-cut. Not all corporations that decline to organize as nonprofits do so in order to maximize profit. For example, organizations with religious and charitable aims might organize as for-profit corporations because of the potential advantages of that corporate form, such as the freedom to participate in lobbying for legislation or campaigning for political candidates who promote their religious or charitable goals. In fact, recognizing the inherent compatibility between establishing a for-profit corporation and pursuing nonprofit goals, States have increasingly adopted laws formally recognizing hybrid corporate forms. Over half of the States, for instance, now recognize the "benefit corporation," a dual-purpose entity that seeks to achieve both a benefit for the public and a profit for its owners.

In any event, the objectives that may properly be pursued by the companies in these cases are governed by the laws of the States in which they were incorporated—Pennsylvania and Oklahoma—and the laws of those States permit for-profit corporations to pursue "any lawful purpose" or "act," including the pursuit of profit in conformity with the owners' religious principles. 15 Pa. Cons. Stat. § 1301 (2001) ("Corporations may be incorporated under this subpart for any lawful purpose or purposes."); Okla. Stat., Tit. 18, §§ 1002, 1005 (West 2012) ("[E]very corporation, whether profit or not for profit" may "be incorporated or organized . . . to conduct or promote any lawful business or purposes"); see also § 1006(A)(3); Brief for State of Oklahoma as *Amicus Curiae* in No. 13–354.

3

. . . .

4

Finally, HHS contends that Congress could not have wanted RFRA to apply to for-profit corporations because it is difficult as a practical matter to ascertain the sincere "beliefs" of a corporation. HHS goes so far as to raise the specter of "divisive, polarizing proxy battles over the religious identity of large, publicly traded corporations such as IBM or General Electric." Brief for HHS in No. 13–356, at 30.

These cases, however, do not involve publicly traded corporations, and it seems unlikely that the sort of corporate giants to which HHS refers will often assert

RFRA claims. HHS has not pointed to any example of a publicly traded corporation asserting RFRA rights, and numerous practical restraints would likely prevent that from occurring. For example, the idea that unrelated shareholders—including institutional investors with their own set of stakeholders—would agree to run a corporation under the same religious beliefs seems improbable. In any event, we have no occasion in these cases to consider RFRA's applicability to such companies. The companies in the cases before us are closely held corporations, each owned and controlled by members of a single family, and no one has disputed the sincerity of their religious beliefs.

. . . .

HHS and the principal dissent express concern about the possibility of disputes among the owners of corporations, but that is not a problem that arises because of RFRA or that is unique to this context. The owners of closely held corporations may—and sometimes do—disagree about the conduct of business. 1 Treatise of the Law of Corporations § 14:11. And even if RFRA did not exist, the owners of a company might well have a dispute relating to religion. For example, some might want a company's stores to remain open on the Sabbath in order to make more money, and others might want the stores to close for religious reasons. State corporate law provides a ready means for resolving any conflicts by, for example, dictating how a corporation can establish its governing structure. See, *e.g., ibid; id.,* §3:2; Del. Code Ann., Tit. 8, §351 (2011) (providing that certificate of incorporation may provide how "the business of the corporation shall be managed"). Courts will turn to that structure and the underlying state law in resolving disputes.

For all these reasons, we hold that a federal regulation's restriction on the activities of a for-profit closely held corporation must comply with RFRA.

IV

Because RFRA applies in these cases, we must next ask whether the HHS contraceptive mandate "substantially burden[s]" the exercise of religion. 42 U.S.C. §2000bb–1(a). We have little trouble concluding that it does.

A

As we have noted, the Hahns and Greens have a sincere religious belief that life begins at conception. They therefore object on religious grounds to providing health insurance that covers methods of birth control that, as HHS acknowledges, see Brief for HHS in No. 13–354, at 9, n.4, may result in the destruction of an embryo. By requiring the Hahns and Greens and their companies to arrange for such coverage, the HHS mandate demands that they engage in conduct that seriously violates their religious beliefs.

If the Hahns and Greens and their companies do not yield to this demand, the economic consequences will be severe. If the companies continue to offer group health plans that do not cover the contraceptives at issue, they will be taxed $100 per day for each affected individual. 26 U.S.C. §4980D. For Hobby Lobby, the bill

344 5 · FEEDING THE HUNGRY, SHELTERING THE HOMELESS, TREATING THE SICK

could amount to $1.3 million per day or about $475 million per year; for Conestoga, the assessment could be $90,000 per day or $33 million per year; and for Mardel, it could be $40,000 per day or about $15 million per year. These sums are surely substantial.

It is true that the plaintiffs could avoid these assessments by dropping insurance coverage altogether and thus forcing their employees to obtain health insurance on one of the exchanges established under ACA. But if at least one of their full-time employees were to qualify for a subsidy on one of the government-run exchanges, this course would also entail substantial economic consequences. The companies could face penalties of $2,000 per employee each year. § 4980H. These penalties would amount to roughly $26 million for Hobby Lobby, $1.8 million for Conestoga, and $800,000 for Mardel.

B

. . . .

C

In taking the position that the HHS mandate does not impose a substantial burden on the exercise of religion, HHS's main argument (echoed by the principal dissent) is basically that the connection between what the objecting parties must do (provide health-insurance coverage for four methods of contraception that may operate after the fertilization of an egg) and the end that they find to be morally wrong (destruction of an embryo) is simply too attenuated. Brief for HHS in 13–354, pp. 31–34; *post*, at 22–23. HHS and the dissent note that providing the coverage would not itself result in the destruction of an embryo; that would occur only if an employee chose to take advantage of the coverage and to use one of the four methods at issue. *Ibid.*

This argument dodges the question that RFRA presents (whether the HHS mandate imposes a substantial burden on the ability of the objecting parties to conduct business in accordance with *their religious beliefs*) and instead addresses a very different question that the federal courts have no business addressing (whether the religious belief asserted in a RFRA case is reasonable). The Hahns and Greens believe that providing the coverage demanded by the HHS regulations is connected to the destruction of an embryo in a way that is sufficient to make it immoral for them to provide the coverage. This belief implicates a difficult and important question of religion and moral philosophy, namely, the circumstances under which it is wrong for a person to perform an act that is innocent in itself but that has the effect of enabling or facilitating the commission of an immoral act by another. Arrogating the authority to provide a binding national answer to this religious and philosophical question, HHS and the principal dissent in effect tell the plaintiffs that their beliefs are flawed. For good reason, we have repeatedly refused to take such a step. See, *e.g., Smith,* 494 U.S. at 887 ("Repeatedly and in many different contexts, we have warned that courts must not presume to determine . . . the plausibility of a religious claim.");

Hernandez v. Commissioner, 490 U.S. 680, 699 (1989); *Presbyterian Church in U.S. v. Mary Elizabeth Blue Hull Memorial Presbyterian Church*, 393 U.S. 440, 450 (1969).

. . . .

Similarly, in these cases, the Hahns and Greens and their companies sincerely believe that providing the insurance coverage demanded by the HHS regulations lies on the forbidden side of the line, and it is not for us to say that their religious beliefs are mistaken or insubstantial. Instead, our "narrow function . . . in this context is to determine" whether the line drawn reflects "an honest conviction," *id.* at 716, and there is no dispute that it does.

HHS nevertheless compares these cases to decisions in which we rejected the argument that the use of general tax revenue to subsidize the secular activities of religious institutions violated the Free Exercise Clause. See *Tilton v. Richardson*, 403 U.S. 672, 689 (1971) (plurality); *Board of Ed. of Central School Dist. No. 1 v. Allen*, 392 U.S. 236, 248–249 (1968). But in those cases, while the subsidies were clearly contrary to the challengers' views on a secular issue, namely, proper church-state relations, the challengers never articulated a *religious* objection to the subsidies. As we put it in *Tilton*, they were "unable to identify any coercion directed at the practice or exercise of their religious beliefs." 403 U.S. at 689 (plurality opinion); see *Allen, supra*, at 249 ("[A]ppellants have not contended that the New York law in any way coerces them as individuals in the practice of their religion"). Here, in contrast, the plaintiffs do assert that funding the specific contraceptive methods at issue violates their religious beliefs, and HHS does not question their sincerity. Because the contraceptive mandate forces them to pay an enormous sum of money—as much as $475 million per year in the case of Hobby Lobby—if they insist on providing insurance coverage in accordance with their religious beliefs, the mandate clearly imposes a substantial burden on those beliefs.

V

Since the HHS contraceptive mandate imposes a substantial burden on the exercise of religion, we must move on and decide whether HHS has shown that the mandate both "(1) is in furtherance of a compelling governmental interest; and (2) is the least restrictive means of furthering that compelling governmental interest." 42 U.S.C. § 2000bb–1(b).

A

. . . HHS maintains that the mandate serves a compelling interest in ensuring that all women have access to all FDA-approved contraceptives without cost sharing. See Brief for HHS in No. 13–354, at 14–15, 49; see Brief for HHS in No. 13–356, at 10, 48. Under our cases, women (and men) have a constitutional right to obtain contraceptives, see *Griswold v. Connecticut*, 381 U.S. 479, 485–486 (1965),and HHS tells us that "[s]tudies have demonstrated that even moderate copayments for preventive services can deter patients from receiving those services." Brief for HHS in No. 13–354, at 50 (internal quotation marks omitted).

The objecting parties contend that HHS has not shown that the mandate serves a compelling government interest, and it is arguable that there are features of ACA that support that view. As we have noted, many employees—those covered by grandfathered plans and those who work for employers with fewer than 50 employees—may have no contraceptive coverage without cost sharing at all.

. . . .

We find it unnecessary to adjudicate this issue. We will assume that the interest in guaranteeing cost-free access to the four challenged contraceptive methods is compelling within the meaning of RFRA, and we will proceed to consider the final prong of the RFRA test, *i.e.*, whether HHS has shown that the contraceptive mandate is "the least restrictive means of furthering that compelling governmental interest." § 2000bb–1(b)(2).

B

The least-restrictive-means standard is exceptionally demanding, see *City of Boerne*, 521 U.S. at 532, and it is not satisfied here. HHS has not shown that it lacks other means of achieving its desired goal without imposing a substantial burden on the exercise of religion by the objecting parties in these cases. See §§ 2000bb–1(a), (b) (requiring the Government to "demonstrat[e] that application of [a substantial] burden to *the person* . . . is the least restrictive means of furthering [a] compelling governmental interest" (emphasis added)).

The most straightforward way of doing this would be for the Government to assume the cost of providing the four contraceptives at issue to any women who are unable to obtain them under their health-insurance policies due to their employers' religious objections. This would certainly be less restrictive of the plaintiffs' religious liberty, and HHS has not shown, see § 2000bb–1(b)(2), that this is not a viable alternative. HHS has not provided any estimate of the average cost per employee of providing access to these contraceptives, two of which, according to the FDA, are designed primarily for emergency use . . . Nor has HHS provided any statistics regarding the number of employees who might be affected because they work for corporations like Hobby Lobby, Conestoga, and Mardel. Nor has HHS told us that it is unable to provide such statistics. It seems likely, however, that the cost of providing the forms of contraceptives at issue in these cases (if not all FDA-approved contraceptives) would be minor when compared with the overall cost of ACA. According to one of the Congressional Budget Office's most recent forecasts, ACA's insurance-coverage provisions will cost the Federal Government more than $1.3 trillion through the next decade. See CBO, Updated Estimates of the Effects of the Insurance Coverage Provisions of the Affordable Care Act, April 2014, p. 2. If, as HHS tells us, providing all women with cost-free access to all FDA-approved methods of contraception is a Government interest of the highest order, it is hard to understand HHS's argument that it cannot be required under RFRA to pay *anything* in order to achieve this important goal.

. . . .

In the end, however, we need not rely on the option of a new, government-funded program in order to conclude that the HHS regulations fail the least-restrictive-means test. HHS itself has demonstrated that it has at its disposal an approach that is less restrictive than requiring employers to fund contraceptive methods that violate their religious beliefs. As we explained above, HHS has already established an accommodation for nonprofit organizations with religious objections. See *supra*, at 9–10, and nn.8–9. Under that accommodation, the organization can self-certify that it opposes providing coverage for particular contraceptive services. See 45 CFR §§ 147.131(b)(4), (c)(1); 26 CFR §§ 54.9815–2713A(a)(4), (b). If the organization makes such a certification, the organization's insurance issuer or third-party administrator must "[e]xpressly exclude contraceptive coverage from the group health insurance coverage provided in connection with the group health plan" and "[p]rovide separate payments for any contraceptive services required to be covered" without imposing "any cost-sharing requirements . . . on the eligible organization, the group health plan, or plan participants or beneficiaries." 45 CFR § 147.131(c)(2); 26 CFR § 54.9815–2713A(c)(2).

We do not decide today whether an approach of this type complies with RFRA for purposes of all religious claims. At a minimum, however, it does not impinge on the plaintiffs' religious belief that providing insurance coverage for the contraceptives at issue here violates their religion, and it serves HHS's stated interests equally well.

The principal dissent identifies no reason why this accommodation would fail to protect the asserted needs of women as effectively as the contraceptive mandate, and there is none. Under the accommodation, the plaintiffs' female employees would continue to receive contraceptive coverage without cost sharing for all FDA-approved contraceptives, and they would continue to "face minimal logistical and administrative obstacles," *post*, at 28 (internal quotation marks omitted), because their employers' insurers would be responsible for providing information and coverage, see, *e.g.*, 45 CFR §§ 147.131(c)–(d); cf. 26 CFR §§ 54.9815–2713A(b), (d). Ironically, it is the dissent's approach that would "[i]mped[e] women's receipt of benefits by 'requiring them to take steps to learn about, and to sign up for, a new government funded and administered health benefit,'" *post*, at 28, because the dissent would effectively compel religious employers to drop health-insurance coverage altogether, leaving their employees to find individual plans on government-run exchanges or elsewhere. This is indeed "scarcely what Congress contemplated." *Ibid.*

C

HHS and the principal dissent argue that a ruling in favor of the objecting parties in these cases will lead to a flood of religious objections regarding a wide variety of medical procedures and drugs, such as vaccinations and blood transfusions, but HHS has made no effort to substantiate this prediction. HHS points to no evidence that insurance plans in existence prior to the enactment of ACA excluded coverage for such items. Nor has HHS provided evidence that any significant number of employers sought exemption, on religious grounds, from any of ACA's coverage requirements other than the contraceptive mandate.

. . . [O]ur decision in these cases is concerned solely with the contraceptive mandate. Our decision should not be understood to hold that an insurance-coverage mandate must necessarily fall if it conflicts with an employer's religious beliefs. Other coverage requirements, such as immunizations, may be supported by different interests (for example, the need to combat the spread of infectious diseases) and may involve different arguments about the least restrictive means of providing them.

The principal dissent raises the possibility that discrimination in hiring, for example on the basis of race, might be cloaked as religious practice to escape legal sanction. See *post*, at 32–33. Our decision today provides no such shield. The Government has a compelling interest in providing an equal opportunity to participate in the workforce without regard to race, and prohibitions on racial discrimination are precisely tailored to achieve that critical goal.

. . . .

In its final pages, the principal dissent reveals that its fundamental objection to the claims of the plaintiffs is an objection to RFRA itself. The dissent worries about forcing the federal courts to apply RFRA to a host of claims made by litigants seeking a religious exemption from generally applicable laws, and the dissent expresses a desire to keep the courts out of this business. See *post*, at 32–35. In making this plea, the dissent reiterates a point made forcefully by the Court in *Smith*. 494 U.S. at 888–889. But Congress, in enacting RFRA, took the position that "the compelling interest test as set forth in prior Federal court rulings is a workable test for striking sensible balances between religious liberty and competing prior governmental interests." 42 U.S.C.§ 2000bb(a)(5).The wisdom of Congress's judgment on this matter is not our concern. Our responsibility is to enforce RFRA as written, and under the standard that RFRA prescribes, the HHS contraceptive mandate is unlawful.

* * *

The contraceptive mandate, as applied to closely held corporations, violates RFRA. Our decision on that statutory question makes it unnecessary to reach the First Amendment claim raised by Conestoga and the Hahns.

The judgment of the Tenth Circuit in No. 13–354 is affirmed; the judgment of the Third Circuit in No. 13–356 is reversed, and that case is remanded for further proceedings consistent with this opinion.

It is so ordered.

JUSTICE GINSBURG, with whom JUSTICE SOTOMAYOR joins, and with whom JUSTICE BREYER and JUSTICE KAGAN join as to all but Part III–C–1, dissenting.

. . . .

Who are the Little Sisters of the Poor? Why did they end up in litigation with the United States government? Their story is the epitome of a struggle of conscience against a government mandate. These nuns provide hospice care to elderly poor around the globe. Their website identifies who they are:

> The Little Sisters of the Poor are an international congregation of Roman Catholic women religious founded in 1839 by Saint Jeanne Jugan. Together with a diverse network of collaborators, we serve the elderly poor in over 30 countries around the world. Continuing the work of Saint Jeanne Jugan, our MISSION is to offer the neediest elderly of every race and religion a home where they will be welcomed as Christ, cared for as family and accompanied with dignity until God calls them to him . . . . [17]

> By our fourth vow of hospitality we promise God to consecrate ourselves totally to the service of the elderly poor.

> Saint Jeanne Jugan, said it this way, "Never forget that the poor are Our Lord. In caring for the poor say to yourself: This is for my Jesus — what a great grace!"

> Our lives are made up of many humble, hidden tasks. We serve the elderly day and night, striving to meet their physical needs, to make them happy and to minister to them spiritually. We accomplish our mission together as a community, each one bringing her gifts and talents to the work of hospitality.

> The accompaniment and care of the dying is the summit of our vocation. It is a powerful witness of the culture of life. Consecrated hospitality is a witness to the mercy and compassionate love of the heart of Jesus.[18]

Their Catholic faith precludes them from providing contraception to those who work with them. Facing millions of dollars in fines for refusing to provide the contraception, the nuns chose to resist and to challenge the mandate in court.

---

17. Little Sisters of the Poor, *Mission Statement*, http://littlesistersofthepoor.org (last visited Oct. 29, 2017).

18. Little Sisters of the Poor, *Mission Hospitality to the Elderly*, http://littlesistersofthepoor.org/our-life/mission/ (last visited Oct. 29, 2017).

136 S. Ct. 1557, 194 L. Ed. 2d 696 (2016)
Supreme Court of the United States

DAVID A. ZUBIK, et. al.
v.
BURWELL, Secretary of Health and Human Services, et. al.

Nos. 14–1418, 14–1453, 14–1505, 15–35, 15–105, 15–119, and
15–191,

Decided May 16, 2016

Opinion

PER CURIAM.

Petitioners are primarily nonprofit organizations that provide health insurance to their employees. Federal regulations require petitioners to cover certain contraceptives as part of their health plans, unless petitioners submit a form either to their insurer or to the Federal Government, stating that they object on religious grounds to providing contraceptive coverage. Petitioners allege that submitting this notice substantially burdens the exercise of their religion, in violation of the Religious Freedom Restoration Act of 1993, 107 Stat. 1488, 42 U.S.C. § 2000bb *et seq.*

Following oral argument, the Court requested supplemental briefing from the parties addressing "whether contraceptive coverage could be provided to petitioners' employees, through petitioners' insurance companies, without any such notice from petitioners." *Post,* p. 1561. Both petitioners and the Government now confirm that such an option is feasible. Petitioners have clarified that their religious exercise is not infringed where they "need to do nothing more than contract for a plan that does not include coverage for some or all forms of contraception," even if their employees receive cost-free contraceptive coverage from the same insurance company. Supplemental Brief for Petitioners 4. The Government has confirmed that the challenged procedures "for employers with insured plans could be modified to operate in the manner posited in the Court's order while still ensuring that the affected women receive contraceptive coverage seamlessly, together with the rest of their health coverage." Supplemental Brief for Respondents 14–15.

In light of the positions asserted by the parties in their supplemental briefs, the Court vacates the judgments below and remands to the respective United States Courts of Appeals for the Third, Fifth, Tenth, and D.C. Circuits. Given the gravity of the dispute and the substantial clarification and refinement in the positions of the parties, the parties on remand should be afforded an opportunity to arrive at an approach going forward that accommodates petitioners' religious exercise while at the same time ensuring that women covered by petitioners' health plans "receive full and equal health coverage, including contraceptive coverage." *Id.,* at 1. We anticipate that the Courts of Appeals will allow the parties sufficient time to resolve any outstanding issues between them.

The Court finds the foregoing approach more suitable than addressing the significantly clarified views of the parties in the first instance. Although there may still be areas of disagreement between the parties on issues of implementation, the importance of those areas of potential concern is uncertain, as is the necessity of this Court's involvement at this point to resolve them. This Court has taken similar action in other cases in the past. See, *e.g.*, *Madison County v. Oneida Indian Nation of N.Y.*, 562 U.S. 42, 43, 131 S. Ct. 704, 178 L.Ed.2d 587 (2011) (*per curiam*) (vacating and remanding for the Second Circuit to "address, in the first instance, whether to revisit its ruling on sovereign immunity in light of [a] new factual development, and — if necessary — proceed to address other questions in the case consistent with its sovereign immunity ruling"); *Kiyemba v. Obama*, 559 U.S. 131, 132, 130 S. Ct. 1235, 175 L.Ed.2d 1070 (2010) (*per curiam*) (vacating and remanding for the D.C. Circuit to "determine, in the first instance, what further proceedings in that court or in the District Court are necessary and appropriate for the full and prompt disposition of the case in light of the new developments"); *Villarreal v. United States*, 572 U.S. ___, 134 S. Ct. 1939, 188 L.Ed.2d 957 (2014) (vacating and remanding to the Fifth Circuit "for further consideration in light of the position asserted by the Solicitor General in his brief for the United States").

The Court expresses no view on the merits of the cases. In particular, the Court does not decide whether petitioners' religious exercise has been substantially burdened, whether the Government has a compelling interest, or whether the current regulations are the least restrictive means of serving that interest.

Nothing in this opinion, or in the opinions or orders of the courts below, is to affect the ability of the Government to ensure that women covered by petitioners' health plans "obtain, without cost, the full range of FDA approved contraceptives." *Wheaton College v. Burwell*, 573 U.S. ___, ___, 134 S. Ct. 2806, 2807, 189 L. Ed.2d 856 (2014). Through this litigation, petitioners have made the Government aware of their view that they meet "the requirements for exemption from the contraceptive coverage requirement on religious grounds." *Id.*, at ___, 134 S. Ct., at 2807. Nothing in this opinion, or in the opinions or orders of the courts below, "precludes the Government from relying on this notice, to the extent it considers it necessary, to facilitate the provision of full contraceptive coverage" going forward. *Ibid.* Because the Government may rely on this notice, the Government may not impose taxes or penalties on petitioners for failure to provide the relevant notice.

The judgments of the Courts of Appeals are vacated, and the cases are remanded for further proceedings consistent with this opinion.

It is so ordered.

Justice SOTOMAYOR, with whom Justice GINSBURG joins, concurring.

I join the Court's *per curiam* opinion because it expresses no view on "the merits of the cases," "whether petitioners' religious exercise has been substantially burdened," or "whether the current regulations are the least restrictive means of serving" a compelling governmental interest. *Ante*, at 1560–1561. Lower courts, therefore, should not construe either today's *per curiam* or our order of March 29, 2016, as signals of where this Court stands. We have included similarly explicit disclaimers in previous orders. See, *e.g., Wheaton College v. Burwell*, 573 U.S. ___ , 134 S. Ct. 2806, 189 L.Ed.2d 856 (2014) ("[T]his order should not be construed as an expression of the Court's views on the merits"). Yet some lower courts have ignored those instructions. See, *e.g., Sharpe Holdings, Inc. v. Department of Health and Human Servs.*, 801 F.3d 927, 944 (C.A.8 2015) ("[I]n *Wheaton College, Little Sisters of the Poor*, and *Zubik*, the Supreme Court approved a method of notice to HHS that is arguably less onerous than [existing regulations] yet permits the government to further its interests. Although the Court's orders were not final rulings on the merits, they at the very least collectively constitute a signal that less restrictive means exist by which the government may further its interests"). On remand in these cases, the Courts of Appeals should not make the same mistake.

I also join the Court's opinion because it allows the lower courts to consider only whether existing or modified regulations could provide seamless contraceptive coverage "'to petitioners' employees, through petitioners' insurance companies, without any . . . notice from petitioners.'" *Ante,* at 1559. The opinion does not, by contrast, endorse the petitioners' position that the existing regulations substantially burden their religious exercise or that contraceptive coverage must be provided through a "separate policy, with a separate enrollment process." Supp. Brief for Petitioners 1; Supp. Reply Brief for Petitioners 5. Such separate contraceptive-only policies do not currently exist, and the Government has laid out a number of legal and practical obstacles to their creation. See Supp. Reply Brief for Respondents 3–4. Requiring standalone contraceptive-only coverage would leave in limbo all of the women now guaranteed seamless preventive-care coverage under the Affordable Care Act. And requiring that women affirmatively opt into such coverage would "impose precisely the kind of barrier to the delivery of preventive services that Congress sought to eliminate." *Id.,* at 6.

Today's opinion does only what it says it does: "afford[s] an opportunity" for the parties and Courts of Appeals to reconsider the parties' arguments in light of petitioners' new articulation of their religious objection and the Government's clarification about what the existing regulations accomplish, how they might be amended, and what such an amendment would sacrifice. *Ante,* at 1560. As enlightened by the parties' new submissions, the Courts of Appeals remain free to reach the same conclusion or a different one on each of the questions presented by these cases.

The impact of this *"David vs. Goliath"* struggle by the Little Sisters was noted in several media reports.[19]

---

19. David French, *The Little Sisters of the Poor Just Beat the Obama Administration at the Supreme Court*, NATIONAL REVIEW (May 16, 2016), http://www.nationalreview.com/corner/435446/little -sisters-poor-just-beat-obama-administration-supreme-court (last visited Oct. 29, 2017).

From the time of the enactment of the ACA without a single Republican vote in favor of the Act, congressional elections witnessed many Republican candidates pledging, if elected, to repeal and replace Obamacare. However, the presence of a Republican majority in both houses of Congress as a result of the 2016 elections did not result in the promised repeal.

On October 6, 2017, however, the Trump administration took significant administrative actions impacting the ACA. The Department of Health and Human Services extended an exemption to any employer objecting "on the basis of sincerely held religious beliefs or moral convictions" to providing contraception in its insurance plan.[20]

This announcement would insulate the Little Sisters of the Poor, and any similar organization, from the massive fines that would otherwise be imposed upon that charitable, religious order, for its refusal, on religious grounds, to agree to provide contraception to its employees. Media reports greatly exaggerated the impact of this announcement, suggesting that it spelled the end of free contraception. However, by its terms, it only applies to those employers whose religious or moral convictions preclude the provision. Out of perhaps 50 million or more women in the workforce, this announcement would only apply to a small fraction of those employees — perhaps 150,000 — according to early estimates. And of course, state and federal governments are free, should they choose to do so, to make free contraception available.

In addition to the HHS announcement, the Trump administration also announced on October 6, 2017, that the U.S. Justice Department would urge in litigation that a broad exemption exists for individuals and entities claiming a religious objection to other laws. The *New York Times* indicated:

> The twin actions, by the Department of Health and Human Services and the Justice Department, were meant to carry out a promise issued by President Trump five months ago, when he declared in the Rose Garden that "we will not allow people of faith to be targeted, bullied or silenced anymore."[21]

D. Education

There is no constitutional right to an education in this country. Does that mean that if a state chooses to create a public school system, as all states have done, students in that public school system have no Due Process rights? Does it mean that states

---

20. Robert Pear, Rebecca R. Ruiz & Laurie Goodstein, *Trump Administration Rolls Back Birth Control Mandate*, NYTIMES (Oct. 6, 2017), https://www.nytimes.com/2017/10/06/us/politics/trump-contraception-birth-control.html (last visited Oct. 29, 2017).

21. *Id.*

which have created public school systems can exclude undocumented children without running afoul of Equal Protection concerns?

---

419 U.S. 565 / 95 S. Ct. 729
Supreme Court of the United States
Norval GOSS et al., Appellants,
v.
Eileen LOPEZ et al.
Decided Jan. 22, 1975

. . . .

At the outset, appellants contend that because there is no constitutional right to an education at public expense, the Due Process Clause does not protect against expulsions from the public school system. This position misconceives the nature of the issue and is refuted by prior decisions. The Fourteenth Amendment forbids the state to deprive any person of life, liberty, or property without due process of law. Protected interests in property are normally 'not created by the Constitution. Rather, they are created and their dimensions are defined' by an independent source such as state statutes or rules entitling the citizen to certain benefits.

Accordingly, a state employee who under state law, or rules promulgated by state officials, has a legitimate claim of entitlement to continued employment absent sufficient cause for discharge may demand the procedural protections of due process. So may welfare recipients who have statutory rights to welfare as long as they maintain the specified qualifications. . . .

Here, on the basis of state law, appellees plainly had legitimate claims of entitlement to a public education. Ohio Rev. Code Ann. §§ 3313.48 and 3313.64 (1972 and Supp.1973) direct local authorities to provide a free education to all residents between five and 21 years of age, and a compulsory-attendance law requires attendance for a school year of not less than 32 weeks. It is true that § 3313.66 of the Code permits school principals to suspend students for up to 10 days; but suspensions may not be imposed without any grounds whatsoever. All of the schools had their own rules specifying the grounds for expulsion or suspension. Having chosen to extend the right to an education to people of appellees' class generally, Ohio may not withdraw that right on grounds of misconduct absent, fundamentally fair procedures to determine whether the misconduct has occurred.

Although Ohio may not be constitutionally obligated to establish and maintain a public school system, it has nevertheless done so and has required its children to attend. Those young people do not "shed their constitutional rights" at the schoolhouse door. "The Fourteenth Amendment, as now applied to the states, protects the citizen against the state itself and all of its creatures-Boards of Education not excepted." The authority possessed by the State to prescribe and enforce standards of conduct in its schools, although concededly very broad, must be exercised consistently with constitutional safeguards. Among other things, the State is constrained to recognize a student's legitimate entitlement to a public education as a property interest which is protected by the Due Process Clause and which may not be taken away for misconduct without adherence to the minimum procedures required by that Clause.

. . . .

---

457 U.S. 202 / 102 S. Ct. 2382
Supreme Court of the United States

James PLYLER, Superintendent of the Tyler Independent School District and Its Board of Trustees et al., Appellants,

v.

J. and R. DOE et al.

TEXAS, et al., Appellants,

v.

CERTAIN NAMED AND UNNAMED UNDOCUMENTED ALIEN CHILDREN et al.

Decided June 15, 1982.

. . . .

Opinion

Justice BRENNAN delivered the opinion of the Court.

The question presented by these cases is whether, consistent with the Equal Protection Clause of the Fourteenth Amendment, Texas may deny to undocumented school-age children the free public education that it provides to children who are citizens of the United States or legally admitted aliens.

. . . .

II

The Fourteenth Amendment provides that "[n]o State shall . . . deprive any person of life, liberty, or property, without due process of law; nor deny to any person within its jurisdiction the equal protection of the laws." (Emphasis added.) Appellants argue at the outset that undocumented aliens, because of their immigration status, are not "persons within the jurisdiction" of the State of Texas, and that they therefore have no right to the equal protection of Texas law. We reject this argument. Whatever his status under the immigration laws, an alien is surely a "person" in any ordinary sense of that term. Aliens, even aliens whose presence in this country is unlawful, have long been recognized as "persons" guaranteed due process of law by the Fifth and Fourteenth Amendments. . . .

. . . .

Our conclusion that the illegal aliens who are plaintiffs in these cases may claim the benefit of the Fourteenth Amendment's guarantee of equal protection only begins the inquiry. The more difficult question is whether the Equal Protection Clause has been violated by the refusal of the State of Texas to reimburse local school boards for the education of children who cannot demonstrate that their presence within the United States is lawful, or by the imposition by those school boards of the burden of tuition on those children. It is to this question that we now turn.

. . . .

A

Sheer incapability or lax enforcement of the laws barring entry into this country, coupled with the failure to establish an effective bar to the employment of undocumented aliens, has resulted in the creation of a substantial "shadow population" of illegal migrants—numbering in the millions—within our borders. This situation raises the specter of a permanent caste of undocumented resident aliens, encouraged by some to remain here as a source of cheap labor, but nevertheless denied the benefits that our society makes available to citizens and lawful residents. The existence of such an underclass presents most difficult problems for a Nation that prides itself on adherence to principles of equality under law.

The children who are plaintiffs in these cases are special members of this underclass. Persuasive arguments support the view that a State may withhold its beneficence from those whose very presence within the United States is the product of their own unlawful conduct. These arguments do not apply with the same force to classifications imposing disabilities on the minor children of such illegal entrants. At the least, those who elect to enter our territory by stealth and in violation of our law should be prepared to bear the consequences, including, but not limited to, deportation. But the children of those illegal entrants are not comparably situated. Their "parents have the ability to conform their conduct to societal norms," and presumably the ability to remove themselves from the State's jurisdiction; but the children who are plaintiffs in these cases "can affect neither their parents' conduct nor their own status." Even if the State found it expedient to control the conduct of adults by acting against their children, legislation directing the onus of a parent's misconduct against his children does not comport with fundamental conceptions of justice.

"[V]isiting . . . condemnation on the head of an infant is illogical and unjust. Moreover, imposing disabilities on the . . . child is contrary to the basic concept of our system that legal burdens should bear some relationship to individual responsibility or wrongdoing. Obviously, no child is responsible for his birth and penalizing the . . . child is an ineffectual—as well as unjust—way of deterring the parent."

. . . .

Public education is not a "right" granted to individuals by the Constitution. But neither is it merely some governmental "benefit" indistinguishable from other forms of social welfare legislation. Both the importance of education in maintaining our basic institutions, and the lasting impact of its deprivation on the life of the child, mark the distinction. The "American people have always regarded education and [the] acquisition of knowledge as matters of supreme importance." We have recognized "the public schools as a most vital civic institution for the preservation of a democratic system of government," and as the primary vehicle for transmitting "the values on which our society rests." "[A]s . . . pointed out early in our history, . . . some degree of education is necessary to prepare citizens to participate effectively and intelligently in our open political system if we are to preserve freedom and independence." And these historic "perceptions of the public schools as inculcating fundamental values necessary to the maintenance of a democratic political system have been confirmed by the observations of social scientists." In addition, education provides the basic tools by which individuals might lead economically productive lives to the benefit of us all. In sum, education has a fundamental role in maintaining the fabric of our society. We cannot ignore the significant social costs borne by our Nation when select groups are denied the means to absorb the values and skills upon which our social order rests.

In addition to the pivotal role of education in sustaining our political and cultural heritage, denial of education to some isolated group of children poses an affront to one of the goals of the Equal Protection Clause: the abolition of governmental barriers presenting unreasonable obstacles to advancement on the basis of individual merit. Paradoxically, by depriving the children of any disfavored group of an education, we foreclose the means by which that group might raise the level of esteem in which it is held by the majority. But more directly, "education prepares individuals to be self-reliant and self-sufficient participants in society." Illiteracy is an enduring disability. The inability to read and write will handicap the individual deprived of a basic education each and every day of his life. The inestimable toll of that deprivation on the social economic, intellectual, and psychological well-being of the individual, and the obstacle it poses to individual achievement, make it most difficult to reconcile the cost or the principle of a status-based denial of basic education with the framework of equality embodied in the Equal Protection Clause. What we said 28 years ago in *Brown v. Board of Education*, 347 U.S. 483, 493 (1954), still holds true:

Today, education is perhaps the most important function of state and local governments. Compulsory school attendance laws and the great expenditures for education both demonstrate to our democratic society. It is required in the performance of our most basic public responsibilities, even service in the armed forces. It is the very foundation of good citizenship. Today it is a principal instrument in awakening the child to cultural values, in preparing him for later professional training, and in helping him to adjust normally to his environment. In these days, it is doubtful that any child may reasonably be expected to succeed in life if he is denied the opportunity of an education. Such an opportunity, where the state has undertaken to provide it, is a right which must be made available to all on equal terms.

. . . .

VI

If the State is to deny a discrete group of innocent children the free public education that it offers to other children residing within its borders, that denial must be justified by a showing that it furthers some substantial state interest. No such showing was made here. Accordingly, the judgment of the Court of Appeals in each of these cases is

Affirmed.

Justice MARSHALL, concurring.

. . . .

Justice BLACKMUN, concurring.

. . . .

Justice POWELL, concurring.

. . . .

Chief Justice BURGER, with whom Justice WHITE, Justice REHNQUIST, and Justice O'CONNOR join, dissenting.

The Catholic Church has implemented an extensive system of education, from prekindergarten through graduate and professional schools. To what extent may public funds be used to assist or advance the educational programs at Catholic primary and secondary schools?

536 U.S. 639 / 122 S. Ct. 2460
Supreme Court of the United States

Susan Tave ZELMAN, Superintendent of Public Instruction of Ohio, et al., Petitioners,

v.

Doris SIMMONS-HARRIS, et al.

Decided June 27, 2002.

. . . .

Opinion

Chief Justice REHNQUIST delivered the opinion of the Court.

The State of Ohio has established a pilot program designed to provide educational choices to families with children who reside in the Cleveland City School District. The question presented is whether this program offends the Establishment Clause of the United States Constitution. We hold that it does not.

There are more than 75,000 children enrolled in the Cleveland City School District. The majority of these children are from low-income and minority families. Few of these families enjoy the means to send their children to any school other than an inner-city public school. For more than a generation, however, Cleveland's public schools have been among the worst performing public schools in the Nation. In 1995, a Federal District Court declared a "crisis of magnitude" and placed the entire Cleveland school district under State control. Shortly thereafter, the state auditor found that Cleveland's public schools were in the midst of a "crisis that is perhaps unprecedented in the history of American education." The district had failed to meet any of the 18 state standards for minimal acceptable performance. Only 1 in 10 ninth graders could pass a basic proficiency examination and students at all levels performed at a dismal rate compared with students in other Ohio public schools. More than two-thirds of high school students either dropped or failed out before graduation. Of those students who managed to reach their senior year, one of every four still failed to graduate. Of those students who did graduate, few could read, write, or compute at levels comparable to their counterparts in other cities.

It is against this backdrop that Ohio enacted, among other initiatives, its Pilot Project Scholarship Program. The program provides financial assistance to families in any Ohio school district that is or has been "under federal court order requiring supervision and operational management of the district by the state superintendent." Cleveland is the only Ohio school district to fall within that category.

The program provides two basic kinds of assistance to parents of children in a covered district. First, the program provides tuition aid for students in kindergarten through third grade, expanding each year through eighth grade, to attend a participating public or private school of their parent's choosing. Second, the program provides tutorial aid for students who choose to remain enrolled in public school.

The tuition aid portion of the program is designed to provide educational choices to parents who reside in a covered district. Any private school, whether religious or nonreligious, may participate in the program and accept program students so long as the school is located within the boundaries of a covered district and meets statewide educational standards. Participating private schools must agree not to discriminate on the basis of race, religion, or ethnic background, or to "advocate or foster unlawful behavior or teach hatred of any person or group on the basis of race, ethnicity, national origin, or religion." Any public school located in a school district adjacent to the covered district may also participate in the program. Adjacent public schools are eligible to receive a $2,250 tuition grant for each program student accepted in addition to the full amount of per-pupil state funding attributable to each additional student. All participating schools, whether public or private, are required to accept students in accordance with rules and procedures established by the state superintendent.

Tuition aid is distributed to parents according to financial need. Families with incomes below 200% of the poverty line are given priority and are eligible to receive 90% of private school tuition up to $2,250. For these lowest income families, participating private schools may not charge a parental copayment greater than $250. For all other families, the program pays 75% of tuition costs, up to $1,875, with no copayment cap. These families receive tuition aid only if the number of available scholarships exceeds the number of low-income children who choose to participate. Where tuition aid is spent depends solely upon where parents who receive tuition aid choose to enroll their child. If parents choose a private school, checks are made payable to the parents who then endorse the checks over to the chosen school.

The tutorial aid portion of the program provides tutorial assistance through grants to any student in a covered district who chooses to remain in public school. Parents arrange for registered tutors to provide assistance to their children and then submit bills for those services to the State for payment. Students from low-income families receive 90% of the amount charged for such assistance up to $360. All other students receive 75% of that amount. The number of tutorial assistance grants offered to students in a covered district must equal the number of tuition aid scholarships provided to students enrolled at participating private or adjacent public schools.

The program has been in operation within the Cleveland City School District since the 1996–1997 school year. In the 1999–2000 school year, 56 private schools participated in the program, 46 (or 82%) of which had a religious affiliation. None of the public schools in districts adjacent to Cleveland have elected to participate. More than 3,700 students participated in the scholarship program, most of whom (96%) enrolled in religiously affiliated schools. Sixty percent of these students were from families at or below the poverty line. In the 1998–1999 school year, approximately 1,400 Cleveland public school students received tutorial aid. This number was expected to double during the 1999–2000 school year.

The program is part of a broader undertaking by the State to enhance the educational options of Cleveland's schoolchildren in response to the 1995 takeover. That undertaking includes programs governing community and magnet schools. Community schools are funded under state law but are run by their own school boards, not by local school districts. These schools enjoy academic independence to hire their own teachers and to determine their own curriculum. They can have no religious affiliation and are required to accept students by lottery. During the 1999–2000 school year there were 10 startup community schools in the Cleveland City School District with more than 1,900 students enrolled. For each child enrolled in a community school, the school receives state funding of $4,518, twice the funding a participating program school may receive.

. . . .

In July 1999, respondents filed this action in United States District Court, seeking to enjoin the reenacted program on the ground that it violated the Establishment Clause of the United States Constitution. . . . In December 1999, the District Court granted summary judgment for respondents. In December 2000, a divided panel of the Court of Appeals affirmed the judgment of the District Court, finding that the program had the "primary effect" of advancing religion in violation of the Establishment Clause. . . . We granted certiorari and now reverse the Court of Appeals.

The Establishment Clause of the First Amendment, applied to the States through the Fourteenth Amendment, prevents a state from enacting laws that have the "purpose" or "effect" of advancing or inhibiting religion. There is no dispute that the program challenged here was enacted for the valid secular purpose of providing educational assistance to poor children in a demonstrably failing public school system. Thus, the question presented is whether the Ohio program nonetheless has the forbidden "effect" of advancing or inhibiting religion.

To answer that question, our decisions have drawn a consistent distinction between government programs that provide aid directly to religious schools, and programs of true private choice, in which government aid reaches religious schools only as a result of the genuine and independent choices of private individuals. While our jurisprudence with respect to the constitutionality of direct aid programs has "changed significantly" over the past two decades our jurisprudence with respect to true private choice programs has remained consistent and unbroken. Three times we have confronted Establishment Clause challenges to neutral government programs that provide aid directly to a broad class of individuals, who, in turn, direct the aid to religious schools or institutions of their own choosing. Three times we have rejected such challenges.

In *Mueller* [*v. Allen*, 463 U.S. 388 (1983)], we rejected an Establishment Clause challenge to a Minnesota program authorizing tax deductions for various educational expenses, including private school tuition costs, even though the great majority of the program's beneficiaries (96%) were parents of children in religious schools. We began by focusing on the class of beneficiaries, finding that because the class included "*all* parents," including parents with "children [who] attend nonsectarian private schools or sectarian private schools," the program was "not readily subject to challenge under the Establishment Clause." Then, viewing the program as a whole, we emphasized the principle of private choice, noting that public funds were made available to religious schools "only as a result of numerous, private choices of individual parents of school-age children." This, we said, ensured that "no 'imprimatur of state approval'" can be deemed to have been conferred on any particular religion, or on religion generally. We thus found it irrelevant to the constitutional inquiry that the vast majority of beneficiaries were parents of children in religious schools. . . .

In *Witter* [*v. Washington Dept. of Servs. for Blind*, 474 U.S. 481 (1986)], we used identical reasoning to reject an Establishment Clause challenge to a vocational scholarship program that provided tuition aid to a student studying at a religious institution to become a pastor. Looking at the program as a whole, we observed that "[a]ny aid . . . that ultimately flows to religious institutions does so only as a result of the genuinely independent and private choices of aid recipients." We further remarked that, as in *Mueller*, "[the] program is made available generally without regard to the sectarian-nonsectarian, or public-nonpublic nature of the institution benefited." In light of these factors, we held that the program was not inconsistent with the Establishment Clause.

Five Members of the Court, in separate opinions, emphasized the general rule from *Mueller* that the amount of government aid channeled to religious institutions by individual aid recipients was not relevant to the constitutional inquiry. Our holding thus rested not on whether few or many recipients chose to expend government aid at a religious school but, rather, on whether recipients generally were empowered to direct the aid to schools or institutions of their own choosing.

Finally, in *Zobrest* [*v. Catalina Foothills School Dist.*, 509 U.S. 1 (1993)], we applied *Mueller* and *Witters* to reject an Establishment Clause challenge to a federal program that permitted sign-language interpreters to assist deaf children enrolled in religious schools. Reviewing our earlier decisions, we stated that "government programs that neutrally provide benefits to a broad class of citizens defined without reference to religion are not readily subject to an Establishment Clause challenge." Looking once again to the challenged program as a whole, we observed that the program "distributes benefits neutrally to any child qualifying as 'disabled.'" Its "primary beneficiaries," we said, were "disabled children, not sectarian schools."

. . . .

Mueller, Witters, and *Zobrest* thus make clear that where a government aid program is neutral with respect to religion, and provides assistance directly to a broad class of citizens who, in turn, direct government aid to religious schools wholly as a result of their own genuine and independent private choice, the program is not readily subject to challenge under the Establishment Clause. A program that shares these features permits government aid to reach religious institutions only by way of the deliberate choices of numerous individual recipients. The incidental advancement of a religious mission, or the perceived endorsement of a religious message, is reasonably attributable to the individual recipient, not to the government, whose role ends with the disbursement of benefits. . . .

. . . .

We believe that the program challenged here is a program of true private choice, consistent with *Mueller*, *Witters*, and *Zobrest*, and thus constitutional. As was true in those cases, the Ohio program is neutral in all respects toward religion. It is part of a general and multifaceted undertaking by the State of Ohio to provide educational opportunities to the children of a failed school district. It confers educational assistance directly to a broad class of individuals defined without reference to religion, *i.e.*, any parent of a school-age child who resides in the Cleveland City School District. The program permits the participation of *all* schools within the district, religious or nonreligious. Adjacent public schools also may participate and have a financial incentive to do so. Program benefits are available to participating families on neutral terms, with no reference to religion. The only preference stated anywhere in the program is a preference for low-income families, who receive greater assistance and are given priority for admission at participating schools.

There are no "financial incentive[s]" that "ske[w]" the program toward religious schools. Such incentives "[are] not present . . . where the aid is allocated on the basis of neutral, secular criteria that neither favor nor disfavor religion, and is made available to both religious and secular beneficiaries on a nondiscriminatory basis." The program here in fact creates financial disincentives for religious schools, with private schools receiving only half the government assistance given to community schools and one-third the assistance given to magnet schools. Adjacent public schools, should any choose to accept program students, are also eligible to receive two to three times the state funding of a private religious school. Families too have a financial disincentive to choose a private religious school over other schools. Parents that choose to participate in the scholarship program and then to enroll their children in a private school (religious or nonreligious) must copay a portion of the school's tuition. Families that choose a community school, magnet school, or traditional public school pay nothing. Although such features of the program are not necessary to its constitutionality, they clearly dispel the claim that the program "creates . . . financial incentive[s] for parents to choose a sectarian school."

Respondents suggest that even without a financial incentive for parents to choose a religious school, the program creates a "public perception that the State is endorsing religious practices and beliefs." But we have repeatedly recognized that no reasonable observer would think a neutral program of private choice, where state aid reaches religious schools solely as a result of the numerous independent decisions of private individuals, carries with it the *imprimatur* of government endorsement. Any objective observer familiar with the full history and context of the Ohio program would reasonably view it as one aspect of a broader undertaking to assist poor children in failed schools, not as an endorsement of religious schooling in general.

There also is no evidence that the program fails to provide genuine opportunities for Cleveland parents to select secular educational options for their school-age children. Cleveland schoolchildren enjoy a range of educational choices: They may remain in public school as before, remain in public school with publicly funded tutoring aid, obtain a scholarship and choose a religious school, obtain a scholarship and choose a nonreligious private school, enroll in a community school, or enroll in a magnet school. That 46 of the 56 private schools now participating in the program are religious schools does not condemn it as a violation of the Establishment Clause. The Establishment Clause question is whether Ohio is coercing parents into sending their children to religious schools, and that question must be answered by evaluating *all* options Ohio provides Cleveland schoolchildren, only one of which is to obtain a program scholarship and then choose a religious school.

. . . Indeed, by all accounts the program has captured a remarkable cross-section of private schools, religious and nonreligious. It is true that 82% of Cleveland's participating private schools are religious schools, but it is also true that 81% of private schools in Ohio are religious schools. To attribute constitutional significance to this figure, moreover, would lead to the absurd result that a neutral school-choice program might be permissible in some parts of Ohio, such as Columbus, where a lower percentage of private schools are religious schools, but not in inner-city Cleveland, where Ohio has deemed such programs most sorely needed, but where the preponderance of religious schools happens to be greater. Likewise, an identical private choice program might be constitutional in some States, such as Maine or Utah, where less than 45% of private schools are religious schools, but not in other States, such as Nebraska or Kansas, where over 90% of private schools are religious schools.

. . . The constitutionality of a neutral educational aid program simply does not turn on whether and why, in a particular area, at a particular time, most private schools are run by religious organizations, or most recipients choose to use the aid at a religious school. . . .

This point is aptly illustrated here. The 96% figure. . . .

. . . .

In sum, the Ohio program is entirely neutral with respect to religion. It provides benefits directly to a wide spectrum of individuals, defined only by financial need and residence in a particular school district. It permits such individuals to exercise genuine choice among options public and private, secular and religious. The program is therefore a program of true private choice. In keeping with an unbroken line of decisions rejecting challenges to similar programs, we hold that the program does not offend the Establishment Clause.

The judgment of the Court of Appeals is reversed.

It is so ordered.

————————

Justice O'CONNOR, concurring.

. . . .

These cases are different from prior indirect aid cases in part because a significant portion of the funds appropriated for the voucher program reach religious schools without restrictions on the use of these funds. The share of public resources that reach religious schools is not, however, as significant as respondents suggest. . . .

. . . .

. . . [T]he support that the Cleveland voucher program provides religious institutions is neither substantial nor atypical of existing government programs. While this observation is not intended to justify the Cleveland voucher program under the Establishment Clause, it places in broader perspective alarmist claims about implications of the Cleveland program and the Court's decision in these cases.

. . . .

Based on the reasoning in the Court's opinion, which is consistent with the realities of the Cleveland educational system, I am persuaded that the Cleveland voucher program affords parents of eligible children genuine nonreligious options and is consistent with the Establishment Clause.

————————

Justice THOMAS, concurring.

. . . .

II

The wisdom of allowing States greater latitude in dealing with matters of religion and education can be easily appreciated in this context. Respondents advocate using the Fourteenth Amendment to handcuff the State's ability to experiment with education. But without education one can hardly exercise the civic, political, and personal freedoms conferred by the Fourteenth Amendment. Faced with a severe educational crisis, the State of Ohio enacted wide-ranging educational reform that allows voluntary participation of private and religious schools in educating poor urban children otherwise condemned to failing public schools. The program does not force any individual to submit to religious indoctrination or education. It simply gives parents a greater choice as to where and in what manner to educate their children. This is a choice that those with greater means have routinely exercised.

. . . .

————————

Justice STEVENS, dissenting.

Is a law that authorizes the use of public funds to pay for the indoctrination of thousands of grammar school children in particular religious faiths a "law respecting an establishment of religion" within the meaning of the First Amendment? In answering that question, I think we should ignore three factual matters that are discussed at length by my colleagues.

First, the severe educational crisis that confronted the Cleveland City School District when Ohio enacted its voucher program is not a matter that should affect our appraisal of its constitutionality. In the 1999–2000 school year, that program provided relief to less than five percent of the students enrolled in the district's schools. The solution to the disastrous conditions that prevented over 90 percent of the student body from meeting basic proficiency standards obviously required massive improvements unrelated to the voucher program. Of course, the emergency may have given some families a powerful motivation to leave the public school system and accept religious indoctrination that they would otherwise have avoided, but that is not a valid reason for upholding the program.

Second, the wide range of choices that have been made available to students *within the public school system* has no bearing on the question whether the State may pay the tuition for students who wish to reject public education entirely and attend private schools that will provide them with a sectarian education. The fact that the vast majority of the voucher recipients who have entirely rejected public education receive religious indoctrination at state expense does, however, support the claim that the law is one "respecting an establishment of religion." The State may choose to divide up its public schools into a dozen different options and label them magnet schools, community schools, or whatever else it decides to call them, but the State is still required to provide a public education and it is the State's decision to fund private school education over and above its traditional obligation that is at issue in these cases.

Third, the voluntary character of the private choice to prefer a parochial education over an education in the public school system seems to me quite irrelevant to the question whether the government's choice to pay for religious indoctrination is constitutionally permissible. Today, however, the Court seems to have decided that the mere fact that a family that cannot afford a private education wants its children educated in a parochial school is a sufficient justification for this use of public funds.

For the reasons stated by Justice SOUTER and Justice BREYER, I am convinced that the Court's decision is profoundly misguided. Admittedly, in reaching that conclusion I have been influenced by my understanding of the impact of religious strife on the decisions of our forbears to migrate to this continent, and on the decisions of neighbors in the Balkans, Northern Ireland, and the Middle East to mistrust one another. Whenever we remove a brick from the wall that was designed to separate religion and government, we increase the risk of religious strife and weaken the foundation of our democracy.

I respectfully dissent.

Justice SOUTER, with whom Justice STEVENS, Justice GINSBURG, and Justice BREYER join, dissenting.

. . . .

———————

Justice BREYER, with whom Justice STEVENS and Justice SOUTER join, dissenting.

. . . .

=====================

E. Public Assistance

In 1970, the Supreme Court held that continued receipt of welfare benefits is a property right per statute.[22] Because of that right, individual recipients have a due process right to a hearing prior to termination. However, the Court restricted the right in *Mathews v. Eldridge*[23] only six years later:

> The essence of due process is the requirement that "a person in jeopardy of serious loss (be given) notice of the case against him and opportunity to meet it." All that is necessary is that the procedures be tailored, in light of the decision to be made, to "the capacities and circumstances of those who are to be heard," to insure that they are given a meaningful opportunity to present their case. In assessing what process is due in this case, substantial weight must be given to the good-faith judgments of the individuals charged by Congress with the administration of social welfare programs that the procedures they have provided assure fair consideration of the entitlement claims of individuals. This is especially so where, as here, the prescribed procedures not only provide the claimant with an effective process for asserting his claim prior to any administrative action, but also assure a right to an evidentiary hearing, as well as to subsequent judicial review, before the denial of his claim becomes final.

> We conclude that an evidentiary hearing is not required prior to the termination of disability benefits and that the present administrative procedures fully comport with due process.[24]

---

22. Goldberg v. Kelly, 397 U.S. 254 (1970).

23. Mathews v. Eldridge, 424 U.S. 319 (1976).

24. *Id.* at 348–49. *Compare Goldberg* (recognizing entitlement to welfare under state law), *with* Dandridge v. Williams, 397 U.S. 471 (1970) (implicitly rejecting idea that welfare is a fundamental right).

May a state bar the citizen children of undocumented parents from receiving public assistance? This author was the attorney for Plaintiffs in the following case. By way of background, Maria Fuentes was referred to this author by Catholic Charities in Topeka, Kansas. Maria's baby, Dario Fuentes, had been born with a birth defect which had resulted in a deformity in one of his legs. Dario, of course, is a citizen of the United States by virtue of being born in this country. A local physician who had treated the family suggested that a simple procedure could correct the baby's medical problem, but that the baby would need to be admitted to a hospital for the surgery. He wrote a note to the Kansas welfare office, on his prescription pad, asking that the baby be afforded access to public medical assistance. Maria went to Catholic Charities, which then referred her to me. I accompanied Maria to the office, and as set out in the opinion below, Dario was denied assistance because his parents could not prove that they were in this country legally. Maria and I were met with insults for her attempts to obtain medical care for her baby, and for our attempts to ensure that other U.S. citizen children of undocumented parents would not be denied services because of the undocumented status of their parent. We ultimately prevailed.

---

709 F. Supp. 1026
United States District Court, D. Kansas.
Dario FUENTES, et al., Plaintiffs,
v.
Cindy WHITE, et al., Defendants.
March 17, 1989.

. . . .

Opinion MEMORANDUM AND ORDER

ROGERS, District Judge.

This matter is presently before the court upon plaintiffs' counsel's motion for attorney's fees. Plaintiffs' counsel seeks fees because he contends that the plaintiffs were the prevailing party in this litigation. . . .

. . . .

. . . The court has developed the following factual background from the affidavits and exhibits that appear in the file. In March, 1985, plaintiff Maria de Jesus Cerca went to the SRS offices in Topeka, Kansas to make application for public assistance for her minor children. She is Hispanic and is not proficient in the English language. On March 11, 1985, she was informed by defendant Betty Litchfield that her application would be denied unless she provided the following information by March 25, 1985: (1) social security numbers for herself, her husband, and her two children; (2) wage verification from her husband from February 1, 1985 through March 11, 1985; and (3) proof of United States citizenship or current alien registration verification. The application was subsequently denied when

Maria failed to produce the requested information. She was informed by SRS that she did have the right to a hearing if she disagreed with their decision.

On April 5, 1985, Maria contacted counsel and explained her situation. He decided to go with Maria to the SRS office and request a hearing. Plaintiffs' counsel and Maria were told to file a new application and were given new application forms. The applications were filled out by Maria with the aid of an interpreter, and Maria and her counsel returned to the SRS office on April 15, 1985. The application asked only for public assistance for her minor children. Maria and her counsel met with defendant White. White asked Maria for proof of citizenship and social security numbers for her and her husband. Counsel indicated to White that such a request was unlawful. White then stated that she needed to confer with her supervisor, defendant Brad Hamilton. White returned and told Maria and her counsel that the children were disqualified from any public assistance because of the parents' inability and unwillingness to prove they were citizens of the United States. White wrote plainly on the applications: "Parents not legal U.S. citizens." She also noted the following on the application next to the names of the childrens' parents: "Not citizens. No SSN [social security number] reported." Counsel asked for an explanation of SRS policy on this issue. White wrote a memo and gave it to counsel, which reads as follows:

TO: Maria de Jesus Cerca

RE: Denial of application for medical and food stamps

Ms. Cerca's application for medical and food stamps were denied thru the Walk-In procedure on 4/15/85.

Ms. Cerca and her husband David Fuentes are the legal parents of the children they are applying for, but they along with 1 child (Ulisis) are not U.S. Citizens. They were given the opportunity to supply the proof of citizenship and Social Security numbers but refused to provide the information as they thought it unnecessary to provide it. They were verbally told that they could not be left off the cases as they are the legally responsible adults for their children. Consequently the entire household is ineligible.

Counsel returned to his office and prepared a written request for a hearing. In this request, counsel noted that he believed that the position of the SRS requiring citizenship information for the parents of the minor children was unconstitutional as a violation of their equal protection rights. This request for hearing was delivered to the SRS in person on April 17, 1985. Later that day, counsel received a telephone call from defendant Hamilton indicating that counsel had not submitted the correct form for requesting a hearing. [Hamilton had, in fact, refused to provide a form when counsel for Plaintiffs had requested one from him.—Ed.] On April 18, 1985, Maria brought counsel another denial of her original application from defendant Litchfield indicating a denial on April 12, 1985.

Thereafter, counsel decided to file an action in this court. This case was filed on April 24, 1985. In an answer filed on May 15, 1985, the defendants indicated that the plaintiffs' application was neither approved nor denied because the plaintiffs failed to provide sufficient information, including their failure to provide their father's citizenship or legal alien status. On May 17, 1985, counsel for the defendants wrote counsel for the plaintiffs the following letter:

> As discussed in our phone conversation this morning, the Department is willing to set aside the issue of the parents' citizenship or legal resident status and proceed with a determination of eligibility for three of the four Fuentes children. In order to determine what, if any benefits, the citizen children may be entitled we will need the following:
>
> 1. Application forms must be completed with current, accurate information and left with the agency.
>
> 2. Social Security numbers or verification of Social Security numbers for all individuals for whom assistance is sought.
>
> 3. Verification of the parent's income.
>
> 4. The process, including required interviews, must be completed.
>
> If Ms. Cerca requires an interpreter, we will provide one. I repeat that we are eager to provide assistance to which any applicant is entitled and I am available to assist in a speedy resolution of this matter.

On July 9, 1985, counsel for plaintiffs wrote a letter to defendants' counsel, which stated in pertinent part the following:

> I am writing to offer settlement of this case. My clients are willing to dismiss, with prejudice, any money damage claims arising from their dealings with your clients and the Department of Social & Rehabilitation Services if you would: 1. Confirm in writing that in the future, our citizen-children clients will not need to prove citizenship or legal alien status and Social Security numbers for their parents in order to be eligible for benefits from the Department of Social & Rehabilitation Services; and 2. Confirm in writing that there has been some training made available to local SRS workers which has informed them that citizen-children do not need to prove the citizenship or legal alien status and Social Security numbers of their parents in order to be eligible for public assistance.
>
> If these matters are agreeable to you, I would ask that you express acceptance by writing me a letter confirming the above-mentioned matters, executing the enclosed Motion to Dismiss and Order, and sending me your letter together with the Motion and Order. As I indicated to you on the phone and as reflected in the Motion and Order, we would leave a determination as to the allocation of costs, and the awarding of attorneys' fees, if any, to plaintiffs' counsel, for further consideration by the Court. I will file the Motion and present the Order to the Court as soon as possible.

Defendants' counsel responded with the following letter on July 12, 1985, which stated:

> Please be advised that, while the department continues to deny any liability claimed in U.S. District Court, Case Number 85–4162–R, training was provided for all income maintenance workers in the Topeka Area Office on the 29th and 30th of May, 1985. Said training included instruction regarding the issue of citizenship and legal alien status. Specifically, that workers are not to require proof of citizenship, legal alien status or Social Security numbers from non-applicants. Persons who are unable or unwilling to provide proof of citizenship or legal alien status are and will remain ineligible for benefits. Applicants are required to provide proof of citizenship, or legal alien status and Social Security numbers. The department will continue to comply with 7 CFR 273.4 in situations where it applies.
>
> The citizen children who are your clients were not, of course, specifically mentioned in the above-described training but would fall within the guidelines described and would be treated as any other applicants. They need not fear any retaliation or harsh feelings on the part of the department or its agents.
>
> I sincerely hope that, in the future, you and others at the Washburn Legal Clinic will give us the opportunity to respond to any misunderstanding or complaints prior to filing a law suit. It is my belief the same results would have been obtained with a phone call or letter. I enclose your signed motion and order.

This action was dismissed on July 22, 1985 upon the aforementioned agreed order submitted by the parties.

Given this background, the court finds that the plaintiffs have clearly demonstrated that they were the prevailing parties in this litigation. The record before the court clearly demonstrates that the minor children of Maria de Jesus Cerca were denied public assistance benefits because of their parents' inability to demonstrate that they were citizens of the United States or legal aliens. The defendants ultimately agreed to provide benefits without regard to the status of the children's parents. Thus, the settlement of this lawsuit was a "significant catalyst" in prompting the defendants to end their policy. The suggestion by the defendants that the plaintiffs' applications were never denied or were denied because the plaintiffs provided insufficient information is not supported by the facts. The record clearly indicates that the sole reason for the denial of benefits to the minor children was because their parents were not United States citizens or legal aliens. This action ended that policy and, thus, the plaintiffs must be regarded as prevailing parties.

The next question faced by the court is whether the defendants' conduct in response to the lawsuit was required by the Constitution or federal law.

We believe that there is little question that the policy applied by the defendants — not allowing public assistance benefits to children who are United States citizens because their parents are not United States citizens or legal aliens — violates the equal protection clause of the Fourteenth Amendment to the United States Constitution. The defendants have not seriously argued that such a policy would be constitutional and have not provided any compelling reason for such a policy. In sum, we find that the plaintiffs were prevailing parties in this litigation.

. . . .

IT IS THEREFORE ORDERED that plaintiffs' counsel's motion for attorney's fees be hereby granted. Plaintiffs' counsel shall be awarded fees in the amount of $5,392.00. Plaintiffs' interpreter shall be awarded $418.50 in fees and $31.50 in expenses. Plaintiffs shall be awarded costs in the amount of $105.00.

IT IS SO ORDERED.

For a further examination of the issues relating to the treatment of the citizen children of undocumented parents, see Bill Piatt, *Born as Second Class Citizens in the USA: Children of Undocumented Parents*, 63 Notre Dame Law Review 35 (1988).

F. For Further Thought

1. While there is no constitutional "right to food" in the United States, do our current statutes and administrative programs, nonetheless, make it unlikely that people in the country will starve?

2. Do we have a national policy that now allows or encourages people to overeat? What role should government play in the matter? Should the overfeeding of children, to the point of obesity, constitute child abuse?

3. Does the fact that some people in the country do not have health insurance impact the rest of the country? Consider health and economic impacts.

4. Should the government fund sex education? Contraception? Abortion?

Chapter 6

Applications

We have now had the opportunity to examine, compare and contrast the views of the legal system and the Catholic Church in areas of contemporary significance. Does the examination end there? Are there some things that Catholic institutions, organizations and individuals could do or should do with this knowledge? In this concluding chapter we will consider some possible applications of these principles. We will first consider the possible role of Catholic education, educators, and students. Next we will take up the role of Catholic judges and lawyers. We will conclude with a discussion of the role of the Church.

A. The Role of Education and Educators

1. Law Schools

Because Catholic law schools are the institutions most directly involved in the process of providing both a legal education and some exposure to Catholicism, the starting point in the discussion will be a determination of the role these schools, their faculty, and students should play. If these schools teach only the same curriculum as other law schools, is there any real purpose to identifying themselves as Catholic? In other words, is there a mission unique to these schools? How would such law schools provide exposure to Catholic principles without violating the academic freedom of law professors, or appear to be proselytizing? Is there anything wrong with a Catholic institution or its students identifying as Catholic and providing some experience that is unique to Catholic education?

In 1990, Pope John Paul II addressed the issue of Catholic identity in higher education in his letter, "*Ex Corde Ecclesiae*—From the Heart of the Church." The encyclical is a detailed examination of the role the Church should play in its institutions of higher education. The Pope wrote in the introduction:

> BORN FROM THE HEART of the Church, a Catholic University is located in that course of tradition which may be traced back to the very origin of the University as an institution. It has always been recognized as an incomparable centre of creativity and dissemination of knowledge for the good of humanity. By vocation, the *Universitas magistrorum et scholarium* is dedicated to research, to teaching and to the education of students who freely associate with their teachers in a common love of knowledge. With every

other University it shares that *gaudium de veritate,* so precious to Saint Augustine, which is that joy of searching for, discovering and communicating truth in every field of knowledge. A Catholic University's privileged task is "to unite existentially by intellectual effort two orders of reality that too frequently tend to be placed in opposition as though they were antithetical: the search for truth, and the certainty of already knowing the fount of truth."

. . . .

27. Every Catholic University, without ceasing to be a University, has a relationship to the Church that is essential to its institutional identity. As such, it participates most directly in the life of the local Church in which it is situated; at the same time, because it is an academic institution and therefore a part of the international community of scholarship and inquiry, each institution participates in and contributes to the life and the mission of the universal Church, assuming consequently a special bond with the Holy See by reason of the service to unity which it is called to render to the whole Church. One consequence of its essential relationship to the Church is that the *institutional* fidelity of the University to the Christian message includes a recognition of and adherence to the teaching authority of the Church in matters of faith and morals. Catholic members of the university community are also called to a personal fidelity to the Church with all that this implies. Non-Catholic members are required to respect the Catholic character of the University, while the University in turn respects their religious liberty.[1]

Ten years later, Professors David Gregory and Charles Russo of St. John's University School of Law addressed the opposition which Catholic law schools in the United States seemed to be offering to the Pope's letter, in a piercing article: *Proposals to Counter Continuing Resistance to the Implementation of Ex Corde Ecclesiae.*[2] The professors outlined the obstacles being thrown in the Pope's way in Catholic law schools. The Article passionately presents an argument and strategy for implementing the Pope's view of Catholic higher education in American Law Schools, including affirmative action at Catholic law schools for hiring Catholic educators, involving the bishops in the institutions, and creating a culture which promotes, not opposes, the Pope's view. More of Gregory and Russo's observations are noted throughout this chapter.

In November 1999, the USCCB adopted guidelines for implementing *Ex Corde Ecclesiae,* to become effective in May, 2001. The bishops summarized the role of the

---

1. Pope John Paul II, *Ex Corde Ecclesiae: Apostolic Constitution of the Supreme Pontiff John Paul II on Catholic Universities* ¶¶ 1, 27 (Aug. 15, 1990), http://www.vatican.va/holy_father/john_paul_ii/apost_constitutions/documents/hf_jp-ii_apc_15081990_ex-corde-ecclesiae_en.html (last visited Nov. 5, 2017).

2. David L. Gregory & Charles J. Russo, *Proposals to Counter Continuing Resistance to the Implementation of Ex Corde Ecclesiae,* 74 St. John's L. Rev. 629 (2000).

University, Trustees, Administration and Staff, Faculty, and as noted below, the Church itself, in a Catholic institution:

─────────────────────────────

1. The responsibility for safeguarding and strengthening the Catholic identity of the university rests primarily with the university itself. All the members of the university community are called to participate in this important task in accordance with their specific roles: the sponsoring religious community, the board of trustees, the administration and staff, the faculty, and the students.[3] Men and women of religious faiths other than Catholic, on the board of trustees, on the faculty, and in other positions, can make a valuable contribution to the university. Their presence affords the opportunity for all to learn and benefit from each other. The university should welcome them as full partners in the campus community.

2. *The Board of Trustees*

   a. Each member of the board must be committed to the practical implications of the university's Catholic identity as set forth in its mission statement or equivalent document.

   b. To the extent possible, the majority of the board should be Catholics committed to the Church.

   c. The board should develop effective ways of relating to and collaborating with the local bishop and diocesan agencies on matters of mutual concern.[4]

   d. The board should analyze ecclesiastical documents on higher education, such as *Ex Corde Ecclesiae* and this Application, and develop specific ways of implementing them appropriate to the structure and life of the university.

   e. The board should see to it that the university periodically undertakes an internal review of the congruence of its mission statement, its courses of instruction, its research program, and its service activity with the ideals, principles and norms expressed in *Ex Corde Ecclesiae*.

─────────────

3. *Ex Corde Ecclesiae*, II, Art. 4, § 1. In these norms the phrases "board of trustees," "president" and "administration" are used to denote the highest bodies of governance within the university's corporate and operational structure. If, in an individual case, the university's governance uses a different structure or other titles, the norms should be applied accordingly.

4. In individual situations, it may be possible and appropriate to invite the diocesan bishop or his delegate to be a member of the board itself. In other cases, arranging periodic meetings to address the university's Catholic identity and mission may prove more practical and effective.

3. *Administration and Staff*

a. The university president should be a Catholic.[5]

b. The administration should inform faculty and staff at the time of their appointment regarding the Catholic identity, mission and religious practices of the university and encourage them to participate, to the degree possible, in the spiritual life of the university.

c. The administration should be in dialogue with the local bishop about ways of promoting Catholic identity and the contribution that the university can make to the life of the Church in the area.

4. *Faculty*

a. In accordance with its procedures for the hiring and retention of professionally qualified faculty and relevant provisions of applicable federal and state law, regulations and procedures, the university should strive to recruit and appoint Catholics as professors so that, to the extent possible, those committed to the witness of the faith will constitute a majority of the faculty. All professors are expected to be aware of and committed to the Catholic mission and identity of their institutions.

b. All professors are expected to exhibit not only academic competence and good character but also respect for Catholic doctrine.[6] When these qualities are found to be lacking, the university statutes are to specify the competent authority and the process to be followed to remedy the situation.[7]

c. Catholic theology should be taught in every Catholic university, and, if possible, a department or chair of Catholic theology should be

---

5. Upon assuming the office of president for the first time, a Catholic should express his or her commitment to the university's Catholic identity and to the Catholic faith in accordance with 1983 CODE c. 833, § 7, http://www.vatican.va/archive/ENG1104/__P2R.HTM (last visited Nov. 5, 2017). *See also* Congregation for the Doctrine of the Faith, *Formula Professio Fidei et Iusiurandum* (*Profession of Faith and Oath of Fidelity*), 104–06 (July 1, 1988), http://www.vatican.va/roman_curia /congregations/cfaith/documents/rc_con_cfaith_doc_19880701_professio-fidei_en.html (last visited Nov. 5, 2017); Congregation for the Doctrine of the Faith, *Rescriptum ex audientia SS. mi Quod Attinet*, 1169 (Sept. 9, 1989), AAS 81 [1989] 1169. When a candidate who is not a Catholic is being considered for appointment as president of a Catholic university, the university should consult with the competent ecclesiastical authority about the matter. In all cases, the president should express his or her commitment to the university's Catholic mission and identity.

6. The identity of a Catholic university is essentially linked to the quality of its professors and to respect for Catholic doctrine. The Church's expectation of "respect for Catholic doctrine" should not, however, be misconstrued to imply that a Catholic university's task is to indoctrinate or proselytize its students. Secular subjects are taught for their intrinsic value, and the teaching of secular subjects is to be measured by the norms and professional standards applicable and appropriate to the individual disciplines. *See Ex Corde Ecclesiae*, II, Art. 4 § 1; and *supra*, nn.24, 27.

7. 1983 CODE c. 810, § 1, http://www.vatican.va/archive/ENG1104/__P2O.HTM (last visited Nov. 5, 2017).

established. Academic events should be organized on a regular basis to address theological issues, especially those relative to the various disciplines taught in the university.[8]

d. Both the university and the bishops, aware of the contributions made by theologians to Church and academy, have a right to expect them to present authentic Catholic teaching. Catholic professors of the theological disciplines have a corresponding duty to be faithful to the Church's magisterium as the authoritative interpreter of Sacred Scripture and Sacred Tradition. . . . [9]

In 2010, this author published an article regarding the issue of bringing Catholic social thought and theology into the law school classroom:

---

a. *Bill Piatt:* Catholicism and Constitutional Law: More Than Privacy in the *Penumbras*[10]

I. Introduction

Catholic law schools and Catholic law professors have multiple obligations to our students and to our communities. In order to comply with American Bar Association (ABA) accreditation standards, and thereby continue our teaching mission, we must prepare students to pass the bar exam.[1] Yet we fail as Catholic educators if we allow our students to ignore fundamental moral issues, leaving students to conclude that we view our role as only helping to supply the correct selection on a multiple choice bar exam.[2]

---

8. Pope Paul VI, *Declaration on Christian Education*: *Gravissimum Educationis*, 10 (Oct. 28, 1965), http://www.vatican.va/archive/hist_councils/ii_vatican_council/documents/vat-ii_decl_19651028 _gravissimum-educationis_en.html (last visited Nov. 5, 2017).

9. USCCB, *The Application of Ex Corde Ecclesiae: Decree of Promulgation* (2000) [hereinafter USCCB, *The Application of Ex Corde Ecclesiae*], http://www.usccb.org/beliefs-and-teachings/how -we-teach/catholic-education/higher-education/the-application-for-ex-corde-ecclesiae-for-the -united-states.cfm (last visited Nov. 5, 2017).

10. Bill Piatt, *Catholicism and Constitutional Law: More Than Privacy in the Penumbras*, 7 J. OF CATHOLIC SOCIAL THOUGHT 337–52 (2010).

1. ABA STANDARDS AND RULES OF PROCEDURE FOR APPROVAL OF LAW SCH., Standard 301(a) (2009–2010).

2. Both the Multistate Bar Exam (MBE) and the Multistate Professional Responsibility Exam (MPRE) test are in a multiple-choice format. NATIONAL CONFERENCE OF BAR EXAMINERS, THE MBE 2012 INFORMATION BOOKLET 6 (2011), *available at* http://www.law.du.edu/documents/registrar/adv -assign/Johns_LegalAnalysis%20Strategies_MBE-Info-Book.pdf (last visited Nov. 5, 2017); NATIONAL CONFERENCE OF BAR EXAMINERS, THE MPRE 2011 INFORMATION BOOKLET 15 (2010), http://www .ncbex.org/uploads/user_docrepos/2011_MPRE_infobooklet.pdf, (not available anymore).

Some subjects lend themselves more easily to an introduction to Catholic values. When I teach Immigration Law, for example, I notice that the casebooks, although not explicitly citing Catholic social thought, tend to follow it. Students self-select into my immigration classes, generally with a predisposition to concern for the plight of immigrants. In Constitutional Law, however, casebooks and scholarship lean away from even discussing Catholic values in critical areas such as abortion. If Catholic legal education means anything, it should at least include an exposure to Catholic perspectives. The challenge will be to do so in a way that does not prevent our students from learning "the law," nor engender resentment. Other groups of scholars, such as Critical Legal Studies,[3] make their perspectives known in discussions involving the relationship between government and the individual, and our voices should be heard as well.

In this article, I will suggest an approach to bringing Catholic social thought into Constitutional Law by discussing perhaps the most controversial issue: the debate surrounding abortion. Where the Supreme Court finds only privacy in the penumbras of a total eclipse (*e.g., Griswold v. Connecticut,*[4] *Roe v. Wade*[5]), I will outline how we might help our students see something else there—the presence of the Divinity and an overarching set of moral values.

II. The Flow of Five Factors

In determining whether Catholic values can be integrated into law school discussions in any particular subject, the interaction of five factors seems to be at play. We will examine these briefly before analyzing how they might apply to our discussion.

The first factor is the Catholic values themselves. In some areas the values are clear. As discussed below, the Catholic Church views abortion as intrinsically evil. In others, there is general clarity with some nuances. The Church's view on the death penalty and immigration law, also discussed below, are the topic of much Church pronouncement and concern. In some other areas, there are no specific declarations. Secured Transactions comes to mind. Obviously, integrating Catholic values into a law school discussion will more likely occur where the topic is most directly tied to Catholic teaching on that subject.

The second relevant factor is the state of the law. Where the Catholic position and the law most neatly align, there will be ample and comfortable room to discuss this concurrence in a Catholic law school. Where they diverge, as in abortion, the law school discussion will likely be more strained. Where there is no relevant Catholic teaching, "Render to Caesar"[6] might be the teaching norm.

Third, the perspective of the teaching materials is an important factor. Where these materials include Catholic perspectives, even if not identified as such, the flow will

---

3. Mark V. Tushnet, *Perspectives on Critical Legal Studies: Introduction*, 52 Geo. Wash. L. Rev. 239, 239–42 (1984).

4. *Griswold,* 381 U.S. at 484.

5. *Roe,* 410 U.S. at 152 (quoting *Griswold,* 381 U.S. at 484–85).

6. *Mk.* 12:17.

be smoother when discussing underlying moral values. When they do not, the flow might become a swim upstream.

The fourth factor is the pre-receptiveness of the students. Students enroll in Catholic law schools for a number of reasons, many of which have little to do with the expression of Catholic values in the classroom.[7] Once in the Catholic law school, students are required to take some courses and have the right to select others. Whether students are receptive to even considering the Catholic approach to a topic is an important consideration in the integration of those topics.

The professor's willingness to present students with the Catholic perspective is the fifth and probably the most critical factor, particularly where the state of law and teaching materials do not satisfactorily address the Catholic view. The important moral pronouncements of the Church will likely not reach law students in the absence of professor's active involvement in teaching the course.

Some subjects seem to lend themselves to an easy flow of these factors. The probable result is that the majority of the students will accept the Catholic perspective or at least respect it as a legitimate approach to the subject. The area in this regard in which I am most familiar is immigration law. Examining how these factors interact in that subject serves as a backdrop to examining an approach to bringing respect for Catholic values into a discussion of constitutional law topics.

III. Catholic Values Mesh Well With Immigration Law

The Catholic Church has made clear it is concerned not only for the rule of law, but also for the plight of immigrants. These concerns are outlined, for example, in a pastoral letter issued by the Catholic bishops of Mexico and the United States on January 22, 2003.[8] The letter, entitled "Strangers No Longer; Together on the Journey of Hope," outlines the Catholic perspective which recognizes that both the right of sovereign nations to control their borders and the right of individuals to migrate with dignity should be afforded even to those without documentation.[9] The bishops cite Pope John Paul II's "Ecclesia in America":

> In its history, America has experienced many immigrations, as waves of men and women came to its various regions in the hope of a better future. The phenomenon continues even today . . . The Church is well aware of the problems created by this situation and is committed to spare no effort in developing her own pastoral strategy among these immigrant people, in order to help them settle in their new land and to foster a welcoming attitude among

---

7. Based upon this author's experience as Dean and in conversations with students at my law school and others, it appears that students primarily select law schools based on factors, which include the prestige of the school, location, and cost.

8. USCCB & Conferencia del Episcopado Mexicano, *Strangers No Longer: Together on the Journey of Hope* ¶ 33 (2003), *available at* http://www.usccb.org/issues-and-action/human-life-and-dignity/immigration/strangers-no-longer-together-on-the-journey-of-hope.cfm (last visited Nov. 5, 2017).

9. *Id.* at ¶¶ 33-39.

the local population, and the belief that a mutual openness will bring enrichment to all.[10]

More recently, on June 18, 2009, Cardinal Frances George of Chicago, writing on behalf of the United States Catholic Bishops gathered in San Antonio, Texas and urged President Obama and congressional leaders "to work together to fashion and enact comprehensive immigration reform before the end of the year."[11] The bishops wrote:

> We urge respect and observance of all just laws, and we do not approve or encourage the illegal entry of anyone into our country. From a humanitarian perspective, however, our fellow human beings who migrate to support their families, continue to suffer at the hands of immigration policies that separate them from family members and drive them to remote parts of the American desert, sometimes to their deaths. This suffering should not continue.[12]

The bishops went on to note, "[o]ur society should no longer tolerate a status quo that perpetuates a permanent underclass of persons and benefits from their labor without offering them legal protections."[13]

In this regard, the position of the Church mirrors the essence of U.S. immigration law and policy and expected reforms of those laws and policies. For example, just as the bishops condemn a "permanent under-class" so too has the Supreme Court of the United States used the same language in proscribing the efforts of states to exclude undocumented children from the public schools.[14]

Moreover, the teaching materials in this area generally line up with this Catholic perspective. All casebooks, including this author's, include the twin perspectives of national sovereignty and respect for the rights of immigrants.[15] My experience with the students I have taught in my Immigration law classes over the last three decades indicates that most of them are generally receptive to these dual concerns. Finally, based upon my own teaching experience and my contact with other immigration law professors, I am of the impression that virtually every Immigration Law class in the United States is taught from a perspective that mirrors Catholic values, whether or not those are identified as such.

IV. Ditto For the Death Penalty

As with Immigration Law, there is a close fit in most American law school classrooms between Catholic values and academic work regarding the death penalty.

---

10. *Id.* at ¶ 21 (quoting Pope John Paul II, *Ecclesia in America*, No. 65 (Jan. 22, 1999)).

11. News Release, Cardinal Francis George, President, USCCB, *Bishops Ask President Obama, Congress to Enact Comprehensive Immigration Reform Before End of 2009* (June 18, 2009), *available at* http://www.catholicculture.org/news/headlines/index.cfm?storyid=3266. Not available anymore.

12. *Id.*

13. *Id.*

14. Plyler v. Doe, 457 U.S. 202, 218–19 (1982).

15. *See* BILL PIATT, IMMIGRATION LAW: CASES AND MATERIALS (The Michie Co. 1994).

While the Catholic Church does not absolutely prohibit the imposition of the death penalty, it does conclude that its use should be rare. For example, Pope John Paul II announced that the death penalty should only be imposed in the rare circumstances when it would not otherwise be possible to defend society, noting: "Today however, as a result of steady improvements in the organization of the penal system, such cases [where the death penalty is justified] are very rare, if not practically non-existent."[16] In the Catechism of the Catholic Church, while the death penalty is not viewed as an intrinsic evil, the taking of innocent life through an abortion or euthanasia is condemned as *always* evil.[17] While the Catechism does not absolutely prohibit the death penalty, it also urges that the death penalty not be utilized if there are better ways to protect society: "If, however, non-lethal means are sufficient to defend and protect people's safety from the aggressor, authority will limit itself to such means, as these are more in keeping with the concrete conditions of the common good and more in conformity with the dignity of the human person."[18]

The current state of American law allows for a broader use of the death penalty than anticipated under the teachings of the Catholic Church. Thirty-five states and the federal government allow for the imposition of the death penalty.[19] The Supreme Court of the United States has upheld its use.[20] The death penalty statutes apply in broader circumstances than only for the immediate protection of society. However, actual imposition of the sentence is relatively rare, and recent trends are toward limiting or eliminating it.[21]

Regarding the perspective of the teaching materials, virtually all of them present a critique of the death penalty that would be very much consistent with that of the Catholic Church. Students self-select into death penalty defense clinics because they oppose the death penalty. Constitutional Law courses and Criminal Law courses which involve a discussion of the death penalty, however, are often required first year courses.

---

16. USCCB, THE CULTURE OF LIFE AND THE PENALTY OF DEATH, pg. 12 (Dec. 2005), *available at* http://www.usccb.org/issues-and-action/human-life-and-dignity/death-penalty-capital-punish ment/upload/penaltyofdeath.pdf (quoting Pope John Paul II, *Evangelium Vitae* ¶ 56 (1995) (last visited Nov. 6, 2017).

17. CATECHISM OF THE CATH. CHURCH, *Article 5: The 5th Commandment*, ¶ 2277 (1997), *available at* http://www.vatican.va/archive/ccc_css/archive/catechism/p3s2c2a5.htm (last visited Nov. 6, 2017).

18. *Id.* at ¶ 2267.

19. *See* BUREAU OF JUSTICE STATISTICS, CAPITAL PUNISHMENT STATISTICS, *available at* http://www.bjs.gov/index.cfm?ty=tp&tid=18 (last visited Apr. 26, 2014).

20. *See* Gregg v. Georgia, 428 U.S. 153, 177 (1976) (holding in 7–2 decision that imposition of death penalty did not constitute cruel and unusual punishment as prohibited by Eighth and Fourteenth Amendments when statute is applied carefully and judiciously). The Court determined that the jury was given objective criteria in sentencing the defendant and the defendant's personal record was carefully considered in the imposition of such punishment. *Id.* at 205–06.

21. *See* DEATH PENALTY INFORMATION CENTER, *Limiting the Death Penalty*, http://www .deathpenaltyinfo.org/part-ii-history-death-penalty (last visited Nov. 6, 2017).

Regarding the fifth factor (teachers' perspectives) while I am unaware of specific studies in this regard, I would imagine that probably most law professors who teach in this subject present a critique of the death penalty very much consistent with the perspectives of the Catholic Church.

There are other examples of law school subjects, such as Elder Law, Public Assistance, and Labor Law, where although not a perfect fit, the presentation of Catholic values would probably mesh well. That is not to say that much work needs to be done to remind teachers and students alike of this important perspective. Having examined some relatively compatible areas of law and Catholic social policy, we turn now to what is perhaps the most controversial and yet one of the most necessary areas to examine: abortion law.

V. Dissonance: Catholic Values and Abortion Law

There might be no area where the dissonance between Catholic teaching and legal teaching is greater than in the area of abortion. The Catholic teaching in this regard is clear: abortion, unlike the death penalty is intrinsically evil.[22] Pope Benedict XVI declared: "everyone must be helped to become aware of the intrinsic evil of the crime of abortion. In attacking human life in its very first stages, it is also an aggression against society itself."[23] The U.S. Conference of Catholic Bishops declares, "[a]bortion, the direct killing of an innocent human being is *always* gravely immoral; its victims are the most vulnerable and defenseless members of the human family."[24]

By contrast, the law does not recognize the existence of a human life from conception.[25] Instead, what the Catholic Church considers a human life, the Supreme Court considers "the life of the fetus that may become a child."[26]

Regarding the teaching material, anyone who hopes or expects that at least some attention will be given to the Catholic perspective that human life begins at conception and that abortion is intrinsically evil will be disappointed. What about student views? Constitutional Law courses are required at most American law schools. The students do not self-select. If their views mirror those of the general public, it might even be that a slim majority of them are opposed to abortion, at least coming in to

---

22. CATECHISM OF THE CATH. CHURCH, *supra* note 27, at ¶ 2271.

23. Pope Benedict XVI, *Address at a Meeting on Family and Life Issues in Latin America* (Dec. 3, 2005), *available at* https://w2.vatican.va/content/benedict-xvi/en/speeches/2005/december/docum ents/hf_ben_xvi_spe_20051203_family-america-latina.html.

24. USCCB, *Select Quotations on Life Issues from Pope Benedict XVI & the USCCB* (citing Pope John Paul II, *Evangelium Vitae* ¶ 57 (1995)) (emphasis in original), http://www.usccb.org/issues-and -action/human-life-and-dignity/abortion/pope-benedict-xvi-usccb-on-life-issues.cfm (last visited Nov. 6, 2017).

25. *See Casey*, 505 U.S. at 914 (Stevens, J., concurring in part and dissenting in part) ("[T]he state interest in potential human life is not an interest *in loco parentis*, for the fetus is not a person.").

26. *Id.* at 846.

the class.[27] However, regarding the fifth consideration, I would suspect that it is rare, in American law schools, and perhaps even in Catholic law schools, to have teachers voice some moral concerns with *Roe v. Wade* and its progeny.

As law professors in Catholic schools, then, what are we to make of this situation? Should we await jurisprudence that will move closer to the recognition of the right to life of the "fetus"? Should we hope for a change in technology that will bring "viability" earlier into the pregnancy and therefore trigger greater right of state intervention?[28] Should we do nothing and present the material as it would be presented in any other law school classroom in the United States? After all, we try to remain objective as teachers and we should not attempt to force our opinions on our students.[29]

The difficulty is that if we really do believe in the teachings of the Catholic Church then we do not have the luxury of silence. Pope Benedict XVI tells us: "As far as *the right to life* is concerned, we must denounce its widespread violation in our society. . . . Abortion and embryonic experimentation constitute a direct denial of that attitude of acceptance of others which is indispensable for establishing lasting relationships of peace."[30] The U.S. Conference of Catholic Bishops demands: "It is imperative that those who are called to serve the least among us give urgent attention and priority to this issue of justice."[31]

In most American law schools, immigration law professors are probably presenting a perspective on immigration law that is sympathetic to the immigrant and thereby consistent with Catholic social teaching. The same is true in the approach of many to the death penalty. If it is acceptable to express an opinion sympathetic to Catholic principles in these contexts, why should it be objectionable to express an opinion consistent with Catholic principles in the context of abortion? On the other hand, attempting to force a religious perspective on our students is probably going to be counterproductive. It will engender resentment against the individual teacher and against the basic and important moral principle that is being presented if not done in an appropriate fashion. And, of course, as teachers we have the obligation to prepare our students to be able to correctly respond to our exam questions and

---

27. *See generally* POLLINGREPORT.COM, *Abortion*, http://www.pollingreport.com/abortion.htm (last visited Nov. 6, 2017).

28. *Casey*, 505 U.S. at 846.

29. *See generally*, ASS'N OF AMERICAN LAW SCHOOLS, AALS HANDBOOK, *Statement of Good Practices by Law Professors in the Discharge of their Ethical and Professional Responsibilities*, http://www.aals.org/members/other-member-services/aals-statements/ethics/ (last visited Nov. 6, 2017).

30. Pope Benedict XVI, Message for the Celebration of the World Day of Peace: The Human Person, The Heart of Peace (Jan. 1, 2007), *available at* http://www.vatican.va/holy_father/benedict_xvi /messages/peace/documents/hf_ben-xvi_mes_20061208_xl-world-day-peace_en.html (last visited Nov. 6, 2017).

31. USCCB, *Pastoral Plan for Pro-Life Activities: A Campaign in Support of Life* (2001), *available at* http://www.usccb.org/about/pro-life-activities/pastoral-plan-prolife-activities.cfm (last visited Nov. 6, 2017).

client concerns with an accurate statement of the current state of the law even as we hope to improve upon it. An approach to accomplishing these objectives is the topic of the next discussion.

VI. Waxing Astronomical

The Supreme Court of the United States used a curious analogy to expand rights of privacy, leading to the right to obtain an abortion; the astronomical analogy the court selected is that of a "penumbra." How this phenomenon was used to create the right to an abortion and how it can be used to illustrate the need to consider Catholic values in the abortion context follows.

In 1961, the Executive Director of the Planned Parenthood League of Connecticut, and another individual, a licensed physician who served as a professor at the Yale Medical School, were arrested for violating a Connecticut statute prohibiting the giving of information, instruction and medical advice to individuals, including married persons, as a mean to prevent contraception.[32] The defendants, Griswold and Buckston, alleged that the statute as applied to them violated the Fourteenth Amendment.[33] They were found guilty and fined $100.00 each.[34] Their convictions were affirmed and ultimately reached the Supreme Court of the United States.[35]

In overturning the conviction, the Supreme Court found that the action of the state of Connecticut violated a constitutionally protected right to privacy.[36] The Court noted a number of cases where individuals were held to have rights that were not specifically mentioned in the Constitution.[37] These include the rights to educate a child in the school of the parent's choice,[38] the right to study the German language in a private school,[39] the freedom to teach and of the entire university community,[40] among others. The Court concluded, "[t]he foregoing cases suggest that specific guarantees in the Bill of Rights have penumbras formed by emanations from those

---

32. *Griswold*, 381 U.S. at 480.

33. *Id.*

34. *Id.*

35. *Id.*

36. *Id.* at 485–86.

37. *Id.* at 482–83.

38. *See* Pierce v. Soc'y of Sisters, 268 U.S. 510, 534–35 (1925) (noting "the liberty of parents and guardians to direct the upbringing and education of children under their control").

39. *See* Meyer v. Nebraska, 262 U.S. 390, 401 (1923) (explaining that "[p]erhaps it would be highly advantageous if all had ready understanding of our ordinary speech, but this cannot be coerced by methods which conflict with the Constitution").

40. *See, e.g.,* Baggett v. Bullitt, 377 U.S. 360, 369 (1964) (overturning, as vague, state statutes requiring teachers and state employees, as condition of employment, to take loyalty oaths); Barenblatt v. United States, 360 U.S. 109, 112 (1959) (noting education as "constitutionally protected domain"); Sweezy v. New Hampshire, 354 U.S. 234, 249–50 (1957) (finding constitutional protected right to lecture and right to associate); Wiemann v. Updegraff, 344 U.S. 183, 195 (1952) (noting that by restricting educators' freedoms of speech and association there is "an unmistakable tendency to chill that free play of the spirit which all teachers ought especially to cultivate and practice").

guarantees that help give them life and substance . . . Various guarantees create zones of privacy."[41]

In *Roe v. Wade*, the Supreme Court specifically referred to a right to personal, marital, familial, and sexual privacy protected by the Bill of Rights or its penumbras.[42] It concluded that the privacy right was broad enough to encompass a woman's decision whether or not to terminate her pregnancy.[43]

This federal recognition of a privacy right to an abortion, located in the penumbras of the rights guaranteed by the Bill of Rights, was a dramatic departure from existing law at the time of the decision in *Roe v. Wade*.[44] The "essential holding" of *Roe*, including the recognition of the right of a woman to choose to have an abortion before viability and obtain it without undue interference from the state was upheld in *Planned Parenthood v. Casey*.[45] Since the time of the *Roe* decision, an estimated fifty million abortions have been performed in the United States.[46] What are these "penumbras" that have been employed to such dramatic affect?

If our students look up the word "penumbra" in the Merriam Webster online dictionary they will find that the word comes from the Latin "pæne," meaning "almost," and "umbra," meaning "shadow."[47] The definition includes "a space of partial illumination (as in an eclipse) between the perfect shadow on all sides and the full light."[48] Undoubtedly because of *Griswold*, the entry also includes, "a body of rights held to be guaranteed by implication in a civil constitution."[49] A scientific explanation for the phenomenon of the eclipse, which gives rise to a penumbra is: "When you look up in the sky at the sun and the moon, you notice a strange coincidence — both look the same size in the sky."[50] If an observer on earth stands at the point where the moon appears to be covering the sun, or a total eclipse, that person would be standing in the "umbra." If the person were standing slightly to the side where the moon only appeared to partially obscure the sun, that person would be standing in the "penumbra" of the eclipse. In this penumbra, the Supreme Court finds the right to privacy.

---

41. *Griswold*, 381 U.S. at 484 (citation omitted).

42. *Roe*, 410 U.S. at 129.

43. *Id.* at 153.

44. *Id.* at 119.

45. *Casey,* 505 U.S. at 833.

46. *See* Bob Unruh, *Abortion Memorial to Honor 50 Million Dead*, WORLD NET DAILY (Jan. 15, 2009), http://www.wnd.com/index.php?fa=PAGE.view&pageId=86129 (last visited Nov. 6, 2017) (estimating 50 million abortions since 1973 decision of *Roe v. Wade*).

47. MERRIAM-WEBSTER ONLINE DICTIONARY, penumbra. (on-line ed. 2009) http://www.merriam-webster.com/dictionary/penumbra (last visited Nov. 6, 2017).

48. *Id.*

49. *Id.*

50. Ron Hipschman, *Solar Eclipse, Why Eclipses Happen*, EXPLORATORIUM, http://www.exploratorium.edu/eclipse/why.html (last visited Nov. 6, 2017). Updated, quote not available on the website anymore.

Now clearly, in teaching Constitutional Law, we are not teaching astronomy. In addition, in attempting to introduce a view of the Catholic teaching on abortion there are very clear and direct pronouncements by the Pope and by the United States Conference of Catholic Bishops on this point that we can present to our students. However, some students may resist a direct presentation of Catholic dogma. Probably all, or most, however, will be intrigued a bit by the further exploration of the "penumbra" phenomenon, particularly in this, the fortieth anniversary of the first moon landing. A law professor might use this approach to lead into a discussion of the Catholic teachings regarding abortion. In the context of immigration, for example, the USCCB uses a similar analogy:

> The word of God and the Catholic social teaching it inspires illuminate an understanding — one that is ultimately full of hope — that recognizes the lights and shadows that are a part of the ethical, social, political, economic, and cultural dimensions of migrations between our two countries . . . These lights and shadows are seen in faith as part of the dynamics of creation and grace on the one hand, and of sin and death on the other, that form the backdrop of all salvation history.[51]

And, of course, the ultimate expression of the theology of the "Light" can be found in John 8:12. One astronomer has noted:

> There's a striking convergence of rare properties that allow people on Earth to witness perfect solar eclipses. There's no law of physics that would necessitate this. In fact, of the nine planets with their more than sixty-three moons in our solar systems, the Earth's surface is the best place where observers can witness a total solar eclipse and that's only possible for the 'near term' future. What's really amazing is that total eclipses are possible because the sun is four hundred times larger than the moon, but it's also four hundred times further away. It's that incredible coincidence that creates a perfect match. Because of this configuration, and because the Earth is the innermost planet with a moon, observers on Earth can discern finer details in the sun's chromosphere and corona than from any other planet, which make these eclipses scientifically rich.[52]

Solar eclipses have enabled scientists to learn the nature of stars, confirm Einstein's theory that gravity bends light and calculate changes in the Earth's rotation.[53]

The configuration that allows for the only perfect solar eclipse in our solar system — our size and distance from the sun and the effect of the moon in

---

51. USCCB & Conferencia del Episcopado Mexicano, *supra* note 18 at ¶¶ 22-23.
52. Lee Strobel, The Case for a Creator 185–86 (2004).
53. *Id.* at 186.

stabilizing the Earth's tilt—enables life to exist on Earth.[54] Exploring the phenomenon of penumbras then, might offer a glimpse that there is indeed a Creator who signals his presence in many ways, including in the light and shadow of a solar eclipse. God doesn't have to write "Hi, I'm God" on the moon to signal his existence and presence to us. (English might not even be his first language). But the planetary configuration giving rise to solar eclipses and our lives do not appear to be coincidental. The Supreme Court sees the legal justification to abort within a penumbra. As Catholic educators, we can see the presence of the Divinity and the moral basis to protect human life in that same phenomenon.

If the penumbra discussion begins to feel a bit remote to our students, there is an effective way to bring the focus back to earth, back to the classroom, and back to the little human life whose continued existence is at issue. In the spring semester of 2009, one of my pregnant Constitutional Law students allowed me to display the sonogram of her baby taken during the baby's first trimester. Most of the students had never seen a sonogram and were stunned to see the baby's features, including the little hands, fingers, feet and toes. No words could add to that impression; no pronouncements about penumbras could detract from it.

VII. From the Shadows into the Light

As individuals, we will each need to decide whether and to what extent we should introduce Catholic values in our teaching, particularly in a Constitutional Law context, and even more specifically regarding the abortion cases. The first step, as in all other endeavors, should be a period of introspection and prayer. We might want to take a look at the writings of many others who express the importance of introducing Catholic values into the legal and legal education system. We might do well to review Pope John Paul II's exhortation: "The moral implications that are present in each discipline are examined as an integral part of the teaching of that discipline."[55] We might consider Rule 2.1 of the 2008 ABA Model Rules of Professional Conduct: "In rendering advice, a lawyer may refer not only to law but to other considerations such as moral, economic, social and political factors that may be relevant to the

---

54. *See, e.g.,* Larry Cunningham, *Can a Catholic Lawyer Represent a Minor Seeking a Judicial Bypass for an Abortion? A Moral and Canon Law Analysis,* 44 J. Cath. Leg. Stud. 379 (2005); Daniel Gordon, *Ex Corde Ecclesiae: The Conflict Created for American Catholic Law Schools,* 34 Gonz. L. Rev. 125 (1998–1999); Aloysius A. Leopold & Marie E. Kaiser, *The Lord in the Law: Reflections on a Catholic Law School,* 25 St. Mary's L.J. 385 (1993); Michael R. Merz, *Conscience of a Catholic Judge,* 29 U. Dayton L. Rev. 305, 310 (2004); John P. O'Callaghan, *Sacred Monkeys and Seamless Garments: Catholics and Political Engagement,* 2 U. St. Thomas L.J. 352 (2005). For further examples, see the articles and papers published in the Journal of Catholic Social Thought, Catholic University Law Review, Journal of Catholic Legal Studies, and The Catholic Lawyer.

55. Pope John Paul II, *Apostolic Constitution Ex Corde Ecclesia on Catholic Universities* ¶ 20 (1990) *available at* http://www.vatican.va/holy_father/john_paul_ii/apost_constitutions/documents/hf_jp -ii_apc_15081990_ex-corde-ecclesiae_en.html (last visited Nov. 6, 2017).

client's situation."[56] What better way to demonstrate this aspect of professional responsibility to our students than by opening their thoughts to moral factors involved in the abortion debate?

Then, on a practical level, we should prepare an approach to each of the five critical factors discussed at the beginning of this article. Regarding understanding the Catholic values, we, as educators, need to become educated. We should review the relevant pastoral letters, encyclicals, Catechism and other important documents. We might even encourage our schools and our colleagues to assist in this continuing Catholic education process by sponsoring gatherings, formal and informal, to discuss Catholic teaching. Regarding the state of the law in our writings, we are not just reporting the law; rather, we seek to shape it by our scholarship. Why not include the Catholic perspective in our writings in an attempt to influence the development of the law to adopt Catholic values? Regarding teaching materials, why not prepare our own texts, which include a perspective on Catholic values? In the short term, why don't we distribute the writings that we are preparing in order to influence the state of the law, to our students as part of our teaching materials?

Concerning the pre-receptiveness of students, we cannot and should not select students into our classes based upon their Catholic perspective or any other perspective. That is not to say, however, that at the admission stage in our law school we could not seek to include students who express an interest in learning Catholic values. In the classroom itself, we have to be careful. We do not want anyone who has had an abortion to feel singled out for criticism. We do not want those who have serious religious objections to the Catholic perspective to feel that they are being punished for those perspectives. Pope John Paul II observed, "Catholic teaching and discipline are to influence all university activities while the freedom of conscience of each person is to be fully respected."[57] In addition to our classroom work, we can encourage and support student groups focusing on the implementation of Catholic values in our professional lives.

The last factor to consider is the professor's willingness to present students with the Catholic perspective. Why wouldn't a professor in a Catholic school want to do this? Perhaps the religious or political views of individual professors run contrary to Catholic values. Even then, could not those professors at least concede that the moral teachings of the Pope and church leaders, directing the spiritual lives of a billion human beings are worthy of being presented, however briefly, in a Catholic law school setting?

---

56. MODEL RULES OF PROF'L CONDUCT R. 2.1 (2008), *available at* http://www.abanet.org/cpr /mrpc/rule_2_1.html (last visited Nov. 6, 2017).

57. Pope John Paul II, *Apostolic Constitution Ex Corde Ecclesia on Catholic Universities* ¶ 4 (1990) *available at* http://www.vatican.va/holy_father/john_paul_ii/apost_constitutions/documents/hf _jp-ii_apc_15081990_ex-corde-ecclesiae_en.html (last visited Nov. 6, 2017).

Not all Catholics share the same view in the abortion debate. That fact does not constitute an excuse to shy away from presenting this view. Catholic students might not know or embrace these values because they have never been adequately exposed to them. Non-Catholic students are even less likely to be aware of the extent of the Church's view unless it is presented to them. Recent polls indicate that more people in the United States now believe that abortion is wrong than those who believe it is right.[58] The trend is in that direction—towards the position the Church has always held. Our students might be interested in learning why so many Americans are now concluding that abortion is wrong.

Introducing the Catholic perspective on abortion is going to be difficult. There is a real possibility that some of our students will not like teachers who present a perspective with which those students might not be familiar or with which they might strenuously disagree. But, we are teachers. Our job is to expose our students to material and perspectives that are unfamiliar to them. Is that not the essence of education? How much does a student learn after all, if what he or she hears in a classroom is only a reinforcement of what he or she already knows or believes?

We can learn from the recent example of Pope Benedict XVI. On July 17, 2009, the Pope discussed, among other topics, the Church's teachings regarding abortion with a former Constitutional Law professor and current President of the United States Barack Obama. President Obama responded that he "would like to reduce the number of abortions in the United States."[59]

We can also learn from another example. Governor Bill Richardson of New Mexico, who is a Catholic and Democrat, had been a long-time supporter of the death penalty.[60] Archbishop Michael J. Sheehan of Santa Fe assisted in persuading the Governor to change his mind.[61] On March 18, 2009, Governor Richardson signed legislation abolishing the death penalty in New Mexico.[62] He attributed his decision, in

---

58. *See* Associated Press, *Majority of Americans Now "Pro-Life," Poll Says*, MSNBC, May 15, 2009, http://www.msnbc.msn.com/id/30771408 (explaining that in May of 2009, a majority (51%) of Americans identified themselves as pro-life, as opposed to pro-choice, for the first time in the fifteen years that the Gallup poll has posed that question) (last visited Nov. 6, 2017).

59. Hada Messia, *Vatican, White House: Abortion One Topic of Obama-Pope Chat*, CNN, July 10, 2009, *available at* http://www.cnn.com/2009/WORLD/europe/07/10/obama.pope/index.html (last visited Nov. 6, 2017).

60. *See* Cindy Wooden, *State's decision to abolish death penalty marked at Rome's Colosseum*, CATHOLIC NEWS SERV. (Apr. 15, 2009), *available at* http://www.santegidio.org/pageID/64/langID /ro/itemID/6392/State-s-decision-to-abolish-death-penalty-marked-at-Rome-s-Colosseum.html (noting Governor's former position on death penalty) (last visited Nov. 6, 2017).

61. Cindy Wooden, *State's Decision to Abolish Death Penalty Marked at Rome's Colosseum*, CATHOLIC NEWS SERV. (Apr. 15, 2009), *available at* http://www.santegidio.org/pageID/64/langID /ro/itemID/6392/State-s-decision-to-abolish-death-penalty-marked-at-Rome-s-Colosseum.html (explaining event) (last visited Nov. 6, 2017).

62. *Id.* (noting change in Governor Richardson's position).

part, to "the Archbishop and Catholic Church."[63] On April 15, 2009, Richardson was given a Papal audience and witnessed the illumination of the Colosseum in Rome to honor New Mexico's decision.[64]

These examples illustrate that people of good faith can be influenced by the teachings of the Church. Those who suggest that it is impermissible to cite religious beliefs in opposition to abortion or who believe that Catholic teaching should not influence legal decisions can be reminded of the Richardson example regarding the death penalty.

VIII. Conclusion

As educators we are experienced at respecting student opinions on a number of subjects while still being able to introduce them to other opinions and perspectives on that same subject. We say we value diversity. True diversity involves a willingness to tolerate and embrace opinions with which we might not agree. We must show respect to those who have concluded that there should be a right to an abortion; we should require that those same people respect the Church's position that the exercise of that legal right is morally wrong. What is ultimately required from us is the courage to patiently expose students to that concept, while at the same time ensuring that students learn the law sufficiently well to pass the necessary exams and to successfully practice law.

There still might be some discontent when we express the Catholic view on abortion. Yet disapproval of the Church's position shouldn't be sufficient reason in a Catholic law school to overlook that position. Our institutions, law schools, and universities need to stand ready to support these efforts by protecting the academic freedom of Catholic educators as we attempt to expose our students to a critical Catholic value—the sanctity of human life.

Of course, not every Catholic law professor believes that Catholic schools should present a Catholic perspective on the law. The reality is that many law professors at Catholic law schools are not Catholic. Some schools have adopted "hiring for mission" approaches encouraging the hiring of Catholics. In these schools, while non-Catholics are not precluded from employment, the institutions nonetheless place emphasis during the recruitment and selection process on the hiring of those individuals, Catholic and non-Catholic alike, who can assist the school in its mission of providing a Catholic perspective in teaching, research, and service. But as a practical matter, there are no "religious police" to ensure that law professors, even

---

63. *Id.*

64. *Id.* (noting recognition). *See also* Phil Stewart, *Richardson Meets Pope Over Death Penalty Repeal*, THOMSON REUTERS (Apr. 15, 2009), http://www.reuters.com/article/2009/04/15/us-pope -richardson-deathpenalty-idUSTRE53E61J20090415 (last visited Nov. 6, 2017).

Catholic law professors, adhere to the Church's teaching on any particular point. The Academic Freedom provisions of the American Bar Association Standards for Accreditation of Law Schools require that schools adhere to the notion of academic freedom for its faculty members. So, any attempt to enlist only Catholic law professors, or only Catholic law professors who adhere to Catholic views in their teaching, would mean that the law school would likely lose ABA accreditation. The loss of ABA accreditation would mean that graduates of that school would not be eligible to take the bar exam in a state, such as Texas, where graduation from such a school is required.

Moreover, there is a voluntary and prestigious organization of law schools, the Association of American Law Schools, which also requires that its members adhere to the concept of academic freedom for its professors. Catholic schools would not want to give up membership in that institution either. Some Catholic law professors insist that their views on Catholicism and its teachings, even when in disagreement with the Church position, are nonetheless legitimate and important positions to be raised in a Catholic law school.[11]

In some instances it appears that this exercise of academic freedom in Catholic institutions contravenes the basic purposes of a Catholic school. Professors Gregory and Russo recall such an example:

> Constitutional law professor Larry Flynt, notorious *Hustler* magazine publisher and pornographer, begins teaching his class at the Catholic Law School. He opens his first class session, not with a prayer, but by grabbing his crotch and declaring, "the [Catholic Church] has had its hand on our crotch for two thousand years." Hell on earth? Well, yes. Beyond all imagination? Unfortunately, no. Save for the fact that Mr. Flynt does not have a law degree, Mr. Flynt addressed approximately nine hundred Georgetown University students on April 30, 1999, and opened his diatribe with the above remarks and actions. Despite the protestations of Cardinal Hickey and the Archdiocese of Washington, D.C., Georgetown University administrative bureaucrats perversely defended Mr. Flynt's depraved charade as the exercise of protected "academic freedom." In the Spring of 2000, however, the retirement of Georgetown University President, Rev. Leo O'Donovan, S.J., was announced. The Holy Spirit moves in mysterious ways, and God's ways are not man's ways. Pope John Paul II was either correct, or incorrect, regarding the need for the revitalization of the Catholic identity of the Catholic colleges and universities. If he was incorrect, there would have been no need for the promulgation of *Ex Corde Ecclesiae*. Notorious incidents such as those at Georgetown University prove that the Pope was, and is, correct.[12]

---

11. *E.g.*, Michael J. Perry, *Catholics, the Magisterium, and Moral Controversy: An Argument for Independent Judgment (with Particular Reference to Catholic Law Schools)*, 26 U. Dayton L. Rev. 293 (2001).

12. Gregory & Russo, *supra* note 2, at 630–31.

Some of the concerns relating to the struggles over the maintenance of Catholic identity in institutions of higher education are discussed in Peter Steinfel's book, *A People Adrift: The Crisis of the Roman Catholic Church in America*.[13]

The same academic freedom concerns which might limit Catholic law schools from requiring that all professors adhere to, and incorporate Catholic views in teaching, should also allow Catholic professors in public law schools to incorporate some aspect of Catholic teaching into their own classroom teaching and into their writings and public service. The approach could involve a discussion of "morality." It is undeniable that moral concerns underlie much, if not all, of the exercise of the creation of law. The Supreme Court of the United States has explicitly recognized and approved this approach to legislation.

For example, in the case of *Heart of Atlanta Motel, Inc. v. United States*,[14] the owner of the motel challenged the constitutionality of the provisions of Title II of the Civil Rights Act of 1964 which outlawed race discrimination in public accommodation, including motels. The owner of the motel did not deny that he engaged in race discrimination. Rather, he argued, in part, that the legislation was based on morality and was not supported by the interstate commerce clause of the Constitution. The Supreme Court rejected this argument, concluding, "[t]hat Congress was legislating against moral wrongs in many of these areas [i.e., prostitution, gambling, racial discrimination in interstate carriers] rendered its enactments no less valid. In framing Title II, Congress was also dealing with what it considered a moral problem."[15] In *Roe*, the majority opinion explicitly recognized that the abortion controversy involved moral and religious concerns.[16] So, a Catholic law professor should be free to explore, from a Catholic perspective, what moral issues are raised in the discussion of civil rights, including abortion.

In such a discussion, the professor might also note that while the legislative branch is free to enact laws based on morality, at least one view is that the courts should not impose their view of morality in considering cases. In upholding and striking some abortion restrictions enacted by the State of Pennsylvania, Justice O'Connor, writing for a divided Supreme Court noted, "Our obligation is to define the liberty of all, not to mandate our own moral code."[17] So, the professor might note, legislatures can base statutes on morality but courts should be reluctant to impose their own view of morality in deciding cases. Among the areas where it is obvious that morality is the basis for legislation include laws precluding stepchildren from marrying, or even laws which preclude people from using illegal drugs. Some would argue that even laws such as speed limits reflect the moral judgment that the state should intervene in driving

---

13. Peter Steinfels, A People Adrift: The Crisis of the Roman Catholic Church in America (2d ed. Aug. 2003).

14. 379 U.S. 241 (1964).

15. Heart of Atlanta Motel, Inc. v. United States, 379 U.S. 241, 257 (1964).

16. *Roe*, 410 U.S. at 116.

17. *Casey*, 505 U.S. at 850.

practices to save lives, because the morality of protecting human life and safety out-weighs the convenience of faster transportation. All of this is fertile ground for a dis-cussion of what is moral and what is not, and for exploring the sources which might be relevant in determining morality, including the teachings of the Catholic Church. However, the reality is that there are very few Catholic law professors in public schools, and virtually none on the faculties of the "elite" law schools which produce most of the nation's law faculty members. Again, Professors Gregory and Russo note,

> Everyone knows that there are virtually no Catholics teaching at Yale, Har-vard, or the other elite private or public secular law schools. Professor Mary Ann Glendon is tolerated, barely, at Harvard. Judge Guido Calabresi, now serving on the United States Court of Appeals for the Second Circuit, con-tinues to be an adjunct lecturer at the Yale Law School. This spot quiz is an interesting exercise, for it yields a disturbingly short list of prominent Cath-olics who are teaching at elite secular law schools. Anti-Catholicism within the elite law school faculties is the open and notorious "secret" of the legal academy. There are virtually no Catholics on the elite private and public secu-lar law school faculties; there are only a few actively committed non-Catholic Christians.[18]

Another aspect to the creation and maintenance of a Catholic identity within a Catholic law school is the visible display of symbols of that identity. In some instances, schools have chosen to display the cross or other symbols. Yet, even that has proven to be controversial in some institutions. Some faculty members have objected to the display. In one recent instance, a Muslim law professor complained that there are no prayer rooms without a crucifix for Muslims in a Catholic law school.[19]

Obviously, public law schools would run into Establishment of Religion issues if they were to display Catholic religious symbols, unless those symbols were part of a more generalized display. Still Catholic educators and students in public schools retain their Free Exercise rights to wear and display symbols of their Catholic identity.

2. Undergraduate Institutions

Many of the concerns regarding Catholic identity in law schools are also of con-cern in Catholic undergraduate institutions. Courses in the areas of Political Science, Sociology, Education, Psychology, Literature, and others offer opportunities to expose students to the Catholic perspectives in these areas. As in the law schools, the devel-opment of hiring norms, encouragement of the presentation of Catholic views inside and outside of the classroom, and the maintenance of a physical environment which serves to remind all on campus of the unique mission of the institution could be

---

18. Gregory & Russo, *supra* note 2, at 636–37 (2000).
19. Michelle Boorstein, *Catholic University is Sued Over Muslim Students' Rights*, WASH. POST (Oct. 27, 2011), http://www.washingtonpost.com/local/cu-sued-over-muslim-worship/2011/10/27/gIQAidsMNM_story.html (last visited Nov. 6, 2017).

created and supported. Professors Gregory and Russo note that the Catholic identity concerns are as critical in undergraduate schools as in law schools:

> *Ex Corde Ecclesiae*, in its call for a majority of Catholic faculty members, does not distinguish between individual units (or schools) within a college or university. Nothing forbids Catholic institutions from seeking a Catholic majority in each of its schools, colleges, and departments.[20]

3. Student Involvement

In addition to the efforts by Catholic institutions and educators, is there a role for student involvement in the creation and maintenance of a Catholic identity? A statement by the USCCB addressed, in part, the role of students within a Catholic school:

> 5. *Students.* With due regard for the principles of religious liberty and freedom of conscience, students should have the opportunity to be educated in the Church's moral and religious principles and social teachings and to participate in the life of faith.
>
> a. Catholic students have a right to receive from a university instruction in authentic Catholic doctrine and practice, especially from those who teach the theological disciplines. They also have a right to be provided with opportunities to practice the faith through participation in Mass, the sacraments, religious devotions and other authentic forms of Catholic spirituality.
>
> b. Courses in Catholic doctrine and practice should be made available to all students.
>
> c. Catholic teaching should have a place, if appropriate to the subject matter, in the various disciplines taught in the university. Students should be provided with adequate instruction on professional ethics and moral issues.[21]

Catholic schools reflect a variety of student interest in the student organizations they recognize. At this author's school, St. Mary's University in San Antonio, Texas, the list of student organizations include those reflecting the involvement of women students, minority students, political interests, older students, and alumni of the various undergraduate schools from which our students have come. There are also groups and activities, formal and otherwise, focusing on Catholic identity. As a private institution, religious-based student organizations, including a chapter of the Christian Legal Society, flourish without Establishment Clause limitation. To what extent may students in public institutions of higher learning organize and associate in groups seeking to reinforce Catholic and Christian values and perspectives?

---

20. Gregory & Russo, *supra* note 9, at 647.
21. USCCB, *The Application of Ex Corde Ecclesiae, supra* note 9.

130 S. Ct. 2971
Supreme Court of the United States

CHRISTIAN LEGAL SOCIETY CHAPTER OF THE UNIVERSITY OF CALIFORNIA, HASTINGS COLLEGE OF THE LAW, aka HASTINGS CHRISTIAN FELLOWSHIP
v.
Leo P. MARTINEZ et al.

Decided June 28, 2010

. . . .

Opinion

Justice GINSBURG delivered the opinion of the Court.

In a series of decisions, this Court has emphasized that the First Amendment generally precludes public universities from denying student organizations access to school-sponsored forums because of the groups' viewpoints. This case concerns a novel question regarding student activities at public universities: May a public law school condition its official recognition of a student group—and the attendant use of school funds and facilities—on the organization's agreement to open eligibility for membership and leadership to all students?

In the view of petitioner Christian Legal Society (CLS), an accept-all-comers policy impairs its First Amendment rights to free speech, expressive association, and free exercise of religion by prompting it, on pain of relinquishing the advantages of recognition, to accept members who do not share the organization's core beliefs about religion and sexual orientation. From the perspective of respondent Hastings College of the Law (Hastings or the Law School), CLS seeks special dispensation from an across-the-board open-access requirement designed to further the reasonable educational purposes underpinning the school's student-organization program.

In accord with the District Court and the Court of Appeals, we reject CLS's First Amendment challenge. Compliance with Hastings' all-comers policy, we conclude, is a reasonable, viewpoint-neutral condition on access to the student-organization forum. In requiring CLS—in common with all other student organizations—to choose between welcoming all students and forgoing the benefits of official recognition, we hold, Hastings did not transgress constitutional limitations. CLS, it bears emphasis, seeks not parity with other organizations, but a preferential exemption from Hastings' policy. The First Amendment shields CLS against state prohibition of the organization's expressive activity, however exclusionary that activity may be. But CLS enjoys no constitutional right to state subvention of its selectivity.

I.

Founded in 1878, Hastings was the first law school in the University of California public-school system. Like many institutions of higher education, Hastings encourages students to form extracurricular associations that "contribute to the Hastings community and experience." These groups offer students "opportunities to pursue academic and social interests outside of the classroom [to] further their education" and to help them "develo[p] leadership skills."

Through its "Registered Student Organization" (RSO) program, Hastings extends official recognition to student groups. Several benefits attend this school-approved status. RSOs are eligible to seek financial assistance from the Law School, which subsidizes their events using funds from a mandatory student-activity fee imposed on all students. RSOs may also use Law-School channels to communicate with students: They may place announcements in a weekly Office-of-Student-Services newsletter, advertise events on designated bulletin boards, send e-mails using a Hastings-organization address, and participate in an annual Student Organizations Fair designed to advance recruitment efforts. In addition, RSOs may apply for permission to use the Law School's facilities for meetings and office space. Finally, Hastings allows officially recognized groups to use its name and logo.

In exchange for these benefits, RSOs must abide by certain conditions. Only a "non-commercial organization whose membership is limited to Hastings students may become [an RSO]." A prospective RSO must submit its bylaws to Hastings for approval and if it intends to use the Law School's name or logo, it must sign a license agreement. Critical here, all RSOs must undertake to comply with Hastings' "Policies and Regulations Applying to College Activities, Organizations and Students."

The Law School's Policy on Nondiscrimination (Nondiscrimination Policy), which binds RSOs, states:

> [Hastings] is committed to a policy against legally impermissible, arbitrary or unreasonable discriminatory practices. All groups, including administration, faculty, student governments, [Hastings]-owned student residence facilities and programs sponsored by [Hastings], are governed by this policy of nondiscrimination. [Hasting's] policy on nondiscrimination is to comply fully with applicable law.

> [Hastings] shall not discriminate unlawfully on the basis of race, color, religion, national origin, ancestry, disability, age, sex or sexual orientation. This nondiscrimination policy covers admission, access and treatment in Hastings-sponsored programs and activities.

> Hastings interprets the Nondiscrimination Policy, as it relates to the RSO program, to mandate acceptance of all comers: School-approved groups must "allow any student to participate, become a member, or seek leadership positions in the organization, regardless of [her] status or beliefs." Other law schools have adopted similar all-comers policies. . . .

In 2004, CLS became the first student group to do so. At the beginning of the academic year, the leaders of a predecessor Christian organization—which had been an RSO at Hastings for a decade—formed CLS by affiliating with the national Christian Legal Society (CLS-National). CLS-National, an association of Christian lawyers and law students, charters student chapters at law schools throughout the country. CLS chapters must adopt bylaws that require members and officers to sign a "Statement of Faith" and to conduct their lives in accord with prescribed principles. Among those tenets is the belief that sexual activity should not occur outside of marriage between a man and a woman; CLS thus interprets its bylaws to exclude from affiliation anyone who engages in "unrepentant homosexual conduct." CLS also excludes students who hold religious convictions different from those in the Statement of Faith.

On September 17, 2004, CLS submitted to Hastings an application for RSO status, accompanied by all required documents, including the set of bylaws mandated by CLS-National. Several days later, the Law School rejected the application; CLS's bylaws, Hastings explained, did not comply with the Nondiscrimination Policy because CLS barred students based on religion and sexual orientation.

CLS formally requested an exemption from the Nondiscrimination Policy, but Hastings declined to grant one. "[T]o be one of our student-recognized organizations," Hastings reiterated, "CLS must open its membership to all students irrespective of their religious beliefs or sexual orientation." If CLS instead chose to operate outside the RSO program, Hastings stated, the school "would be pleased to provide [CLS] the use of Hastings facilities for its meetings and activities." CLS would also have access to chalkboards and generally available campus bulletin boards to announce its events. In other words, Hastings would do nothing to suppress CLS's endeavors, but neither would it lend RSO-level support for them.

Refusing to alter its bylaws, CLS did not obtain RSO status. It did, however, operate independently during the 2004–2005 academic year. CLS held weekly Bible-study meetings and invited Hastings students to Good Friday and Easter Sunday church services. It also hosted a beach barbeque, Thanksgiving dinner, campus lecture on the Christian faith and the legal practice, several fellowship dinners, an end-of-year banquet, and other informal social activities.

On October 22, 2004, CLS filed suit against various Hastings officers and administrators under 42 U.S.C. § 1983. Its complaint alleged that Hastings' refusal to grant the organization RSO status violated CLS's First and Fourteenth Amendment rights to free speech, expressive association, and free exercise of religion. . . .

. . . .

II.

Before considering the merits of CLS's constitutional arguments, we must resolve a preliminary issue: CLS urges us to review the Nondiscrimination Policy as written — prohibiting discrimination on several enumerated bases, including religion and sexual orientation — and not as a requirement that all RSOs accept all comers. The written terms of the Nondiscrimination Policy, CLS contends, "targe[t] solely those groups whose beliefs are based on religion or that disapprove of a particular kind of sexual behavior," and leave other associations free to limit membership and leadership to individuals committed to the group's ideology. For example, "[a] political . . . group can insist that its leaders support its purposes and beliefs," CLS alleges, but "a religious group cannot."

CLS's assertion runs headlong into the stipulation of facts it jointly submitted with Hastings at the summary-judgment stage. In that filing, the parties specified:

> Hastings requires that registered student organizations allow any student to participate, become a member, or seek leadership positions in the organization, regardless of [her] status or beliefs. Thus, for example, the Hastings Democratic Caucus cannot bar students holding Republican political beliefs from becoming members or seeking leadership positions in the organization.

> . . . .

In light of the joint stipulation, both the District Court and the Ninth Circuit trained their attention on the constitutionality of the all-comers requirement, as described in the parties' accord. We reject CLS's unseemly attempt to escape from the stipulation and shift its target to Hastings' policy as written. This opinion, therefore, considers only whether conditioning access to a student-organization forum on compliance with an all-comers policy violates the Constitution.

III.

A.

In support of the argument that Hastings' all-comers policy treads on its First Amendment rights to free speech and expressive association, CLS draws on two lines of decisions. First, in a progression of cases, this Court has employed forum analysis to determine when a governmental entity, in regulating property in its charge, may place limitations on speech. Recognizing a State's right "to preserve the property under its control for the use to which it is lawfully dedicated."

Second, as evidenced by another set of decisions, this Court has rigorously reviewed laws and regulations that constrain associational freedom. In the context of public accommodations, we have subjected restrictions on that freedom to close scrutiny; such restrictions are permitted only if they serve "compelling state interests" that are "unrelated to the suppression of ideas"—interests that cannot be advanced "through . . . significantly less restrictive [means]." "Freedom of association," we have recognized, "plainly presupposes a freedom not to associate." Insisting that an organization embrace unwelcome members, we have therefore concluded, "directly and immediately affects associational rights."

CLS would have us engage each line of cases independently, but its expressive-association and free-speech arguments merge: Who speaks on its behalf, CLS reasons, colors what concept is conveyed. It therefore makes little sense to treat CLS's speech and association claims as discrete. Instead, three observations lead us to conclude that our limited-public-forum precedents supply the appropriate framework for assessing both CLS's speech and association rights.

First, the same considerations that have led us to apply a less restrictive level of scrutiny to speech in limited public forums as compared to other environments apply with equal force to expressive association occurring in limited public forums. As just noted, speech and expressive-association rights are closely linked. When these intertwined rights arise in exactly the same context, it would be anomalous for a restriction on speech to survive constitutional review under our limited-public-forum test only to be invalidated as an impermissible infringement of expressive association. . . .

Second, and closely related, the strict scrutiny we have applied in some settings to laws that burden expressive association would, in practical effect, invalidate a defining characteristic of limited public forums—the State may "reserv[e] [them] for certain groups."

. . . .

Third, this case fits comfortably within the limited-public-forum category, for CLS, in seeking what is effectively a state subsidy, faces only indirect pressure to modify its membership policies; CLS may exclude any person for any reason if it forgoes the benefits of official recognition. The expressive-association precedents on which CLS relies, in contrast, involved regulations that compelled a group to include unwanted members, with no choice to opt out.

In diverse contexts, our decisions have distinguished between policies that require action and those that withhold benefits. Application of the less-restrictive limited-public-forum analysis better accounts for the fact that Hastings, through its RSO program, is dangling the carrot of subsidy, not wielding the stick of prohibition.

In sum, we are persuaded that our limited-public-forum precedents adequately respect both CLS's speech and expressive-association rights, and fairly balance those rights against Hastings' interests as property owner and educational institution. We turn to the merits of the instant dispute, therefore, with the limited-public-forum decisions as our guide.

B.

As earlier pointed out, we do not write on a blank slate; we have three times before considered clashes between public universities and student groups seeking official recognition or its attendant benefits. . . .

. . . .

In all three cases, we ruled that student groups had been unconstitutionally singled out because of their points of view. "Once it has opened a limited [public] forum," we emphasized, "the State must respect the lawful boundaries it has itself set." The constitutional constraints on the boundaries the State may set bear repetition here: "The State may not exclude speech where its distinction is not reasonable in light of the purpose served by the forum . . . nor may it discriminate against speech on the basis of . . . viewpoint."

C.

. . . .

With appropriate regard for school administrators' judgment, we review the justifications Hastings offers in defense of its all-comers requirement. First, the open-access policy "ensures that the leadership, educational, and social opportunities afforded by [RSOs] are available to all students." Just as "Hastings does not allow its professors to host classes open only to those students with a certain status or belief," so the Law School may decide, reasonably in our view, "that the . . . educational experience is best promoted when all participants in the forum must provide equal access to all students." RSOs, we count it significant, are eligible for financial assistance drawn from mandatory student-activity fees the all-comers policy ensures that no Hastings student is forced to fund a group that would reject her as a member.

Second, the all-comers requirement helps Hastings police the written terms of its Nondiscrimination Policy without inquiring into an RSO's motivation for membership restrictions. . . .

. . . .

Third, the Law School reasonably adheres to the view that an all-comers policy, to the extent it brings together individuals with diverse backgrounds and beliefs, "encourages tolerance, cooperation, and learning among students." And if the policy sometimes produces discord, Hastings can rationally rank among RSO-program goals development of conflict-resolution skills, toleration, and readiness to find common ground.

Fourth, Hastings' policy, which incorporates—in fact, subsumes—state-law proscriptions on discrimination, conveys the Law School's decision "to decline to subsidize with public monies and benefits conduct of which the people of California disapprove." State law, of course, may not command that public universities take action impermissible under the First Amendment. But so long as a public university does not contravene constitutional limits, its choice to advance state-law goals through the school's educational endeavors stands on firm footing.

In sum, the several justifications Hastings asserts in support of its all-comers requirement are surely reasonable in light of the RSO forum's purposes.

3.

The Law School's policy is all the more creditworthy in view of the "substantial alternative channels that remain open for [CLS-student] communication to take place." . . .

In this case, Hastings offered CLS access to school facilities to conduct meetings and the use of chalkboards and generally available bulletin boards to advertise events. Although CLS could not take advantage of RSO-specific methods of communication, the advent of electronic media and social-networking sites reduces the importance of those channels.

Private groups, from fraternities and sororities to social clubs and secret societies, commonly maintain a presence at universities without official school affiliation. Based on the record before us, CLS was similarly situated: It hosted a variety of activities the year after Hastings denied it recognition, and the number of students attending those meetings and events doubled. "The variety and type of alternative modes of access present here," in short, "compare favorably with those in other [limited public] forum cases where we have upheld restrictions on access." It is beyond dissenter's license, we note again, constantly to maintain that nonrecognition of a student organization is equivalent to prohibiting its members from speaking.

4.

CLS nevertheless deems Hastings' all-comers policy "frankly absurd." "There can be no diversity of viewpoints in a forum," it asserts, "if groups are not permitted to form around viewpoints." This catchphrase confuses CLS's preferred policy with constitutional limitation—the advisability of Hastings' policy does not control its permissibility. . . .

CLS also assails the reasonableness of the all-comers policy in light of the RSO forum's function by forecasting that the policy will facilitate hostile takeovers; if organizations must open their arms to all, CLS contends, saboteurs will infiltrate groups to subvert their mission and message. This supposition strikes us as more hypothetical than real. CLS points to no history or prospect of RSO-hijackings at Hastings. Students tend to self-sort and presumably will not endeavor en masse to join—let alone seek leadership positions in—groups pursuing missions wholly at odds with their personal beliefs. And if a rogue student intent on sabotaging an organization's objectives nevertheless attempted a takeover, the members of that group would not likely elect her as an officer.

. . . .

D.

We next consider whether Hastings' all-comers policy is viewpoint neutral.

1.

Although this aspect of limited-public-forum analysis has been the constitutional sticking point in our prior decisions, as earlier recounted, we need not dwell on it here. It is, after all, hard to imagine a more viewpoint-neutral policy than one requiring all student groups to accept all comers. In contrast to Healy, Widmar, and Rosenberger, in which universities singled out organizations for disfavored treatment because of their points of view, Hastings' all-comers requirement draws no distinction between groups based on their message or perspective. An all-comers condition on access to RSO status, in short, is textbook viewpoint neutral.

. . . .

Finding Hastings' open-access condition on RSO status reasonable and viewpoint neutral, we reject CLS' free-speech and expressive-association claims.

. . . .

For the foregoing reasons, we affirm the Court of Appeals' ruling that the all-comers policy is constitutional and remand the case for further proceedings consistent with this opinion.

It is so ordered.

Justice STEVENS, concurring.

. . . .

It is critical, in evaluating CLS's challenge to the Nondiscrimination Policy, to keep in mind that an RSO program is a limited forum—the boundaries of which may be delimited by the proprietor. When a religious association, or a secular association, operates in a wholly public setting, it must be allowed broad freedom to control its membership and its message, even if its decisions cause offense to outsiders. Profound constitutional problems would arise if the State of California tried to "demand that all Christian groups admit members who believe that Jesus was merely human." But the CLS chapter that brought this lawsuit does not want to be just a Christian group; it aspires to be a recognized student organization. The Hastings College of Law is not a legislature. And no state actor has demanded that anyone do anything outside the confines of a discrete, voluntary academic program. Although it may be the case that to some "university students, the campus is their world," it does not follow that the campus ought to be equated with the public square.

The campus is, in fact, a world apart from the public square in numerous respects, and religious organizations, as well as all other organizations, must abide by certain norms of conduct when they enter an academic community. Public universities serve a distinctive role in a modern democratic society. Like all specialized government entities, they must make countless decisions about how to allocate resources in pursuit of their role. Some of those decisions will be controversial; many will have differential effects across populations; virtually all will entail value judgments of some kind. As a general matter, courts should respect universities' judgments and let them manage their own affairs.

The RSO forum is no different. It is not an open commons that Hastings happens to maintain. It is a mechanism through which Hastings confers certain benefits and pursues certain aspects of its educational mission. Having exercised its discretion to establish an RSO program, a university must treat all participants evenhandedly. But the university need not remain neutral—indeed it could not remain neutral—in determining which goals the program will serve and which rules are best suited to facilitate those goals. These are not legal questions but policy questions; they are not for the Court but for the university to make. When any given group refuses to comply with the rules, the RSO sponsor need not admit that group at the cost of undermining the program and the values reflected therein. On many levels, a university administrator has a "greater interest in the content of student activities than the police chief has in the content of a soapbox oration."

In this case, petitioner excludes students who will not sign its Statement of Faith or who engage in "unrepentant homosexual conduct." The expressive association argument it presses, however, is hardly limited to these facts. Other groups may exclude or mistreat Jews, Blacks, and women — or those who do not share their contempt for Jews, Blacks, and women. A free society must tolerate such groups. It need not subsidize them, give them its official *imprimatur*, or grant them equal access to law school facilities.

Justice KENNEDY, concurring.

. . . .

Law students come from many backgrounds and have but three years to meet each other and develop their skills. They do so by participating in a community that teaches them how to create arguments in a convincing, rational, and respectful manner and to express doubt and disagreement in a professional way. A law school furthers these objectives by allowing broad diversity in registered student organizations. But these objectives may be better achieved if students can act cooperatively to learn from and teach each other through interactions in social and intellectual contexts. A vibrant dialogue is not possible if students wall themselves off from opposing points of view.

The school's objectives thus might not be well served if, as a condition to membership or participation in a group, students were required to avow particular personal beliefs or to disclose private, off-campus behavior. Students whose views are in the minority at the school would likely fare worse in that regime. Indeed, were those sorts of requirements to become prevalent, it might undermine the principle that in a university community — and in a law school community specifically — speech is deemed persuasive based on its substance, not the identity of the speaker. The era of loyalty oaths is behind us. A school quite properly may conclude that allowing an oath or belief-affirming requirement, or an outside conduct requirement, could be divisive for student relations and inconsistent with the basic concept that a view's validity should be tested through free and open discussion. The school's policy therefore represents a permissible effort to preserve the value of its forum.

Justice ALITO, with whom THE CHIEF JUSTICE, Justice SCALIA, and Justice THOMAS join, dissenting.

. . . .

The Court bases all of its analysis on the proposition that the relevant Hastings' policy is the so-called accept-all-comers policy. This frees the Court from the difficult task of defending the constitutionality of either the policy that Hastings actually — and repeatedly — invoked when it denied registration, i.e., the school's written Nondiscrimination Policy, or the policy that Hastings belatedly unveiled when it filed its brief in this Court. Overwhelming evidence, however, shows that Hastings denied CLS's application pursuant to the Nondiscrimination Policy and that the accept-all-comers policy was nowhere to be found until it was mentioned by a former dean in a deposition taken well after this case began.

. . . .

Hastings claims that this accept-all-comers policy has existed since 1990 but points to no evidence that the policy was ever put in writing or brought to the attention of members of the law school community prior to the dean's deposition. Indeed, Hastings has adduced no evidence of the policy's existence before that date. And while Dean Kane and Ms. Chapman stated, well after this litigation had begun, that Hastings had such a policy, neither they nor any other Hastings official has ever stated in a deposition, affidavit, or declaration when this policy took effect.

Hastings' effort to portray the accept-all-comers policy as merely an interpretation of the Nondiscrimination Policy runs into obvious difficulties. First, the two policies are simply not the same: The Nondiscrimination Policy proscribes discrimination on a limited number of specified grounds, while the accept-all-comers policy outlaws all selectivity. Second, the Nondiscrimination Policy applies to everything that Hastings does, and the law school does not follow an accept-all-comers policy in activities such as admitting students and hiring faculty.

. . . .

B. The Role of Bench and Bar

1. Lawyers

To what extent may a Catholic lawyer practice his/her faith while at the same time practicing law? Is there an inherent conflict between these two roles?

Each state has created its own set of ethical standards regarding the practice of law. The American Bar Association has promulgated the Model Rules of Professional Conduct. While these Rules are not directly applicable in any state unless and until adopted by the state, they nonetheless serve as an important bench mark for attorney conduct nationwide. Rule 2.1 of the Model Rules provides, in part, "[i]n rendering advice, a lawyer may refer not only to law but to other considerations such as moral, economic, social, and political, factors that may be relevant to the client's situation." In explaining the application of this Rule, comment 2, notes, "It is proper for a lawyer to refer to relevant moral and ethical considerations in giving advice. Although a lawyer is not a moral advisor as such, moral and ethical considerations impinge upon most legal questions and may decisively influence how the law will be applied." Thus, it is clear that the Model Rules permit an attorney to bring his or her Catholic faith into the effective representation of the client.

What happens if a Catholic lawyer encounters a potential client who insists on pursuing a course of conduct which the attorney believes would be inconsistent with his or her Catholic faith? Of course, no attorney is required to take any case, unless ordered to do so by a court. The Model Rules preclude an attorney from commencing or continuing representation if the "representation will result in violation of the Rules of Professional Conduct or other law." [22] Once a representation of a client has been undertaken, however, it is more difficult for the attorney to withdraw from representing such a client. The Model Rules do permit attorney withdrawal if that withdrawal could be accomplished without "material adverse affect on the interest of the client," or if the client "persists on a course of action involving the lawyer's services that the lawyer reasonably believes is criminal or fraudulent." [23] That same Rule also allows an attorney to withdraw if "a client insists upon pursuing an objective that the lawyer considers repugnant or imprudent." [24] Thus, there is an opportunity for an attorney to withdraw if the client's conduct meets these criteria. However, if the matter is in front of a tribunal, and the tribunal declines to give the attorney permission to withdraw, the attorney is required to continue representation. Thus, it is incumbent upon the Catholic attorney to carefully screen clients and cases so that if there appears to be a moral conflict between the course of conduct the client chooses to pursue and the moral standards of the attorney, the attorney can decline the representation rather than risk the potential grievance claims, malpractice claims, or refusal by a tribunal to allow withdrawal once the case is initiated.

Of course, Catholic attorneys are interested in far more than just seeking to avoid disciplinary sanction. Indeed, there are many opportunities for Catholic attorneys to associate with others and share their faith at the same time they participate in the practice of law. One such organization is the International Catholic Lawyers Society. The website of that organization identifies the society as follows:

The International Catholic Lawyers Society is a world-wide society of lawyers, jurists, and others interested in:

- creating a forum where Catholic lawyers and jurists can integrate their faith and beliefs with their individual vocations
- making the Catholic legal tradition culturally present in our time,
- educating lawyers in Church teachings, canon law, and natural law concepts and their relationship to the civil law, and supporting scholarship, research, and publication of works on Catholic issues relevant to the law.

---

22. MODEL RULES OF PROF'L CONDUCT R. 1.16(a)(1) (2011 http://www.americanbar.org/groups/professional_responsibility/publications/model_rules_of_professional_conduct/rule_1_0_terminology.html (last visited Nov. 6, 2017).
23. *Id.* at R. 1.16(b)(1).
24. *Id.* at R. 1.16(b)(3).

The Society was founded in June of 2004, and is headquartered at The Catholic University of America in close association with the University's Columbus School of Law and School of Canon Law.[25]

Another organization of Catholic attorneys is the Catholic Lawyers' Guild. These chapters have been organized in various cities nationwide. One of the largest and most active is the Chicago Catholic Lawyers' Guild. Their website identifies some of their purposes and activities:

- **Prayer.** Providing opportunities for reflection and union with God has been a crucial part of the Guild's life, accomplished through retreats, days of recollection, and the Red Mass.

- **Service.** Some notable services provided by the Guild have been pro bono service to immigrants at the request of Cardinal Samuel Stritch in the 1960s and Cardinal Joseph Bernardin in 1970s, the hearings on sexual abuse conducted at the request of Cardinal Francis George in 2002, and our recent adoption of the Catholic Charities Legal Clinic as a service opportunity for our members.

- **Celebration.** Annually we organize the Red Mass at Holy Name Cathedral, the Mass that has opened the Fall Term for courts since 1245 A.D. asking the Holy Spirit's help for lawyers and judges. In tandem with the Red Mass, we celebrate with a luncheon lawyers who have incarnated Christ in the world through their work.

   For many the phrase lawyer-saint is an oxymoron, a contradiction in terms, but we know better, not only do we have our patrons, St. Thomas More and St. Ivo, but we have seen the lawyer-saints in the courthouses and offices of Chicago, many anonymously practicing charity and law side-by-side, others more visible, holding high office, serving God while also serving their fellow man. It is to sainthood we must all aspire. And the law can be a great helper — for the law hangs on two hinges — love of God and love of neighbor. In as simple a deed as stopping at a stop sign — we submit our wills to a power above us, as we should submit to God's will, and we show our love for the safety and well-being of our neighbor in abiding by the law intended to make the roads safe for all. Thus law and the whole legal profession can lead us to fulfill our glorious twofold duty: to pray and to love.[26]

Still another association of Catholic attorneys is the American Catholic Lawyers Association. Their website identifies their purposes as follows:

   The American Catholic Lawyers Association, Inc., ACLA, is a non-profit religious organization dedicated to the free legal defense of the Faith and the rights of Catholics in America.

---

25. International Catholic Lawyers Society, *About Us* (Aug. 14, 2005), http://www.catholic lawyers.net/aboutus (last visited Nov. 6, 2017).

26. Catholic Lawyer's Guild of Chicago, *About the Guild*, http://www.clgchicago.org/about-clg/ (last visited Nov. 6, 2017).

Conceived and formed in 1990 as a Catholic answer to the American Civil Liberties Union and other left-liberal activist groups, the ACLA engages in a wide range of activities aimed at countering the forces of secularism in our society.

The ACLA's activities include:

> *Pro Bono Federal and State Court Litigation* on behalf of Catholic plaintiffs and defendants whose civil rights are being violated on account of their Catholic Faith in the spheres of pro-life activity, employment and the right to worship God in both private and public manifestations of the Faith.
>
> *Defense of the Faith* in public discourse and debate.
>
> *Catholic Apologetics* explaining the truths of the Catholic Faith and refuting attacks against it in formal debate and apologetical literature.[27]

Catholic lawyers can also find valuable sources of intellectual and scholarly support in the publications by Catholic law schools. Following is a list of some of those schools and publications as they relate to general legal, social, ethical, and human rights topics.

School Name	Publication Name
Ave Maria School of Law (Naples, FL)	*Ave Maria Law Review*
Barry University — Dwayne O. Andreas School of Law (Orlando, FL)	*Barry Law Review*
Boston College Law School (Newton, MA)	*Boston College Law Review*
Creighton University School of Law (Omaha, NE)	*Creighton Law Review*
DePaul University College of Law (Chicago, IL)	*DePaul Journal for Social Justice*
	DePaul Law Review
Duquesne University of the Holy Spirit School of Law (Pittsburgh, PA)	*Duquesne Law Review*
Fordham University School of Law (New York, NY)	*Fordham Law Review*
Georgetown University Law Center (Washington, DC)	*Georgetown Journal of Legal Ethics*
	Georgetown Journal on Poverty Law and Policy
	Georgetown Law Journal
Gonzaga University School of Law (Spokane, WA)	*Gonzaga Law Review*
Loyola Marymount University Law School (Los Angeles, CA)	*Loyola of Los Angeles Law Review*

---

27. American Catholic Lawyers Ass'n, *Statement of Purpose*, http://www.americancatholiclawyers .org (last visited Nov. 6, 2017).

Loyola University Chicago School of Law Philip H. Corboy Law Center (Chicago, IL)	*Loyola University Chicago Law Journal*
Loyola University New Orleans College of Law (New Orleans, LA)	*Loyola Law Review*
Marquette University Law School (Milwaukee, WI)	*Marquette Law Review*
Saint John's University School of Law (Queens, NY)	*St. John's Law Review* *Journal of Catholic Legal Studies*
Saint Louis University School of Law (St. Louis, MO)	*Saint Louis University Law Journal*
Saint Mary's University School of Law (San Antonio, TX)	*St. Mary's Law Journal* *The Scholar: St. Mary's Law Review on Race and Social Justice* *St. Mary's Journal on Legal Malpractice & Ethics*
Saint Thomas University School of Law (Miami Gardens, FL)	*Intercultural Human Rights Law Review* *St. Thomas Law Review*
Santa Clara Law (Santa Clara, CA)	*Santa Clara Law Review*
Seattle University School of Law (Seattle, WA)	*Seattle Journal for Social Justice* *Seattle University Law Review*
Seton Hall University School of Law (Newark, NJ)	*Seton Hall Law Review*
The Catholic University of America — Columbus School of Law (Washington, DC)	*Catholic University Law Review*
University of Dayton School of Law (Dayton, OH)	*University of Dayton Law Review*
University of Detroit Mercy School of Law (Detroit, MI)	*University of Detroit Mercy Law Review*
University of Notre Dame Law School (Notre Dame, IN)	*Notre Dame Journal of Law, Ethics and Public Policy* *The Journal of College and University Law Notre Dame Law Review*
University of Saint Thomas School of Law (Saint Paul, MN)	*St. Thomas Law Review*
University of San Diego School of Law (San Diego, CA)	*The San Diego Law Review* *Journal of Contemporary Legal Issues*

University of San Francisco School of Law
(San Francisco, CA)

The University of San Francisco Law Review

Villanova University School of Law
(Villanova, PA)

Journal of Catholic Social Thought
Villanova Law Review

In addition, *The Catholic Lawyer* of The St. Thomas More Institute for Legal Research is published under the auspices of the *St. John's Law Review*.

Another important educational role that Catholic lawyers and Catholic law schools can fulfill involves continuing legal education. Attorneys are required, as a condition of maintaining their licenses, to receive additional education each year. In conjunction with the Christian Legal Society and St. Mary's University School of Law, the Catholic Lawyers Guild of San Antonio, of which this author was President, began offering a Christian Legal Perspective CLE program beginning in 2015. The program consists of lectures and panel discussions by prominent legal educators, judges, and practicing attorneys. It focuses on the role of faith in the practice of law.

The plan was to offer this program as a one-time, small and local program in San Antonio. However, after meeting resistance from the State Bar of Texas, the entity which accredits such programs, the Christian Legal Perspectives CLE program took on additional significance and drew nationwide attention. While the event would likely have received little attention outside of San Antonio, and might have been quickly forgotten, apparently the Holy Spirit had other plans. We continue to offer the program, and other entities across the country have made plans to implement similar programs.

The story of this struggle and eventual success was detailed by this author in a presentation to the meeting of the Religiously Affiliated Law Schools held at Regent University School of Law in Virginia Beach, Virginia in 2016. In 2017, the Regent University Law Review published the following article, written by this author.

REGENT UNIVERSITY LAW REVIEW
Vol. 29:293

State Bar Efforts to Deny Accreditation to Faith-Based CLE Ethics Programs Sponsored by Religiously-Affiliated Law Schools

Bill Piatt

INTRODUCTION

Religiously affiliated law schools focus on the integration of faith in the formation of future attorneys and leaders. Yet our students are only our students for three years. We can extend our influence and continue to provide a faith-based perspective to them and to other attorneys during the thirty, forty, or more years of their careers by offering continuing legal education (CLE) courses, which bring attorneys and judges together to provide a model for incorporating faith and morality into our professional roles. However, CLE programs must receive accreditation by state authorities if participants are to receive credit for them.[1] Recently, the State Bar of Texas' Minimum Continuing Legal Education (MCLE) Committee refused to accredit such a program, determining that only "secular" programs could receive CLE credit.[2] That committee was forced to reverse itself by virtue of a formal appeal filed by this author, and supported by evangelical Christian and Catholic attorneys and entities, including St. Mary's University School of Law.[3] This Article examines that situation, and provides the framework other schools may use to prevent similar denials from occurring in their states.

I. BACKGROUND

A. The Mission of Our Schools

There is obviously something in the mission of religiously affiliated law schools which differentiates our schools from secular law schools. This difference—the focus on integrating faith in the formation of our future lawyers and leaders—is clearly identified in the mission statements of those respective schools. While the list to follow is not exhaustive, a quick examination of the mission statements of a few of our schools reveals what it is that sets us apart from secular institutions.

"St. Mary's University School of Law, a Catholic Marianist institution, prepares its graduates for the competent and ethical practice of law in a community of faith that encourages and supports educational excellence, scholarship, public service, and the promotion of justice."[4] Similarly, Regent University School of Law states that its "mission is to provide an excellent legal education from a Christian perspective, to nurture and encourage our students toward spiritual maturity, and to engage the world through Christian legal thought and practice."[5] According to Brigham Young University Law School's mission statement:

> The mission of the BYU Law School is to teach the laws of men in the light
> of the laws of God. The Law School strives to be worthy in all respects of the
> name it bears, and to provide an education that is spiritually strengthening,

---

1. *See* St. Bar Tex., State Bar Rules Art. XII, §2(J) (2016), https://www.texasbar.com/AM/Template.cfm?Section=Governing_Documents&Template=/CM/ContentDisplay.cfm&ContentID=11009.

2. Adam Cassandra, *Texas State Bar Demands Secularization of Legal Ethics Training Held at Catholic Law School*, Cardinal Newman Soc'y (Dec. 2, 2015), https://cardinalnewmansociety.org/texas-state-bar-demands-secularization-of-legal-ethics- training-held-at-catholic-law-school/.

3. Bill Piatt, *Catholic Education Before the Texas Bar*, Cardinal Newman Soc'y (Jan. 20, 2016), https://cardinalnewmansociety.org/catholic-education-before-the-texas-bar/.

4. Amy Hardberger, St. Mary's University School Of Law Policies And Practices Manual—Practicing Faculty 2 (2016), https://www.stmarytx.edu/policies/wp-content/uploads/2016/10/law-school-policies-and-practices-manual-for-faculty-2016-07.pdf.

5. *Mission Statement*, Regent U. Sch. L., http://www.regent.edu/acad/schlaw/whyregentlaw/mission.cfm (last visited Jan. 11, 2017).

intellectually enlarging, and character building, thus leading to lifelong learning and service.[6]

"Loyola University Chicago School of Law is a student-focused law center inspired by the Jesuit tradition of academic excellence, intellectual openness, and service to others."[7] Likewise, "Liberty University School of Law exists to equip future leaders in law with a superior legal education in fidelity to the Christian faith expressed through the Holy Scriptures."[8] As a final example, "[t]he mission of Pepperdine University School of Law is to provide highly qualified students with a superior legal education. . . . The school's Christian emphasis leads to a special concern for imbuing students with the highest principles of professional, ethical, and moral responsibility."[9]

Another class of religiously affiliated law schools asks the prospective student to consider the sponsoring university's mission statement. For instance, Baylor University School of Law "shares in the University's mission to educate men and women by integrating academic excellence and Christian commitment within a caring community . . . who are sensitive to the needs of a pluralistic society."[10] Catholic University's Columbus School of Law "advances the aims and goals of the university as a whole . . . . These aims and goals manifest themselves in . . . the dignity of each human person; respect for the inviolability of all human life . . . and the obligation of love for one another."[11] As a final example, St. John's School of Law states that, "[c]onsistent with the Vincentian Mission of St. John's University, St. John's School of Law seeks to: [a]chieve academic excellence through a commitment to rigorous teaching . . . [and] scholarly research . . . [and] [e]ngage students to search out the causes of economic and social injustice . . . ."[12]

The purpose of our schools, and our roles within the American legal education system, have been succinctly set forth in the literature on this topic.[13] Our schools

---

6. *Mission & Goals*, BYU L. Sch., http://www.law2.byu.edu/site/mission/ (last visited Jan. 11, 2017).

7. *Missions, Goals and Objectives*, Loy. U. Chi. Sch. L., http://www.luc.edu/law/about/mission .html (last visited June 7, 2016).

8. *About Liberty School of Law*, Liberty Sch. L., http://www.liberty.edu/law/about-liberty-law -school/ (last visited Jan. 11, 2017).

9. *Mission Statement: About Us*, Pepp. Sch. L., http://law.pepperdine.edu/about/our-story /mission/ (last visited Jan. 11, 2017).

10. *Mission Statement*, Baylor U. Sch. L., http://www.baylor.edu/law/index.php?id=930089 (last visited Jan. 11, 2017).

11. *Columbus School of Law: Mission Statement*, Cath. U. Am.: Columbus Sch. L., http://www .law.edu/missionstatement.cfm (last updated Dec. 18, 2009).

12. *Mission*, St. John's Sch. L., http://www.stjohns.edu/law/about (last visited Jan. 11, 2017).

13. *See, e.g.*, Howard A. Glickstein, *Academic Freedom in Religiously Affiliated Law Schools: A Jewish Perspective*, 11 Regent U. L. Rev. 17, 19 (1998) (quoting *Deuteronomy* 16:20 (New American Standard Version)) (describing the roots of Judaism as a law-based religion in pursuit of justice, and explaining that a law school centered on Judaism should "pursue the command of Deuteronomy: 'Justice, and only justice, you shall pursue'").

have been approved not only by receiving accreditation from the American Bar Association and the Association of American Law Schools,[14] but also by the state supreme courts and bar associations which authorize our graduates to take their respective bar examinations and be admitted to the practice of law.[15]

B. Our Mission Extends Beyond Three Years of Law School

If each school is fulfilling its mission,[16] our students receive at least some exposure for the three years that they are with us to the application of a faith-based approach to the provision of legal services. However, we hope that our contact with and influence upon the careers of our students will not be limited to the three years that they find themselves within our walls. After all, most of our graduates can expect to pursue a career of thirty, forty, or even more years. The potential impact upon their clients in society is immeasurable. As a result, if we are truly focused on influencing their outlook, religiously affiliated law schools should strive to participate post-law school by sponsoring faith-based continuing legal education programs.[17]

---

14. Steven R. Smith, *Accreditation and Religiously Affiliated Law Schools*, 78 Marq. L. Rev. 361, 368 (1995) (discussing the accreditation process of law schools and how the accreditation rules do not interfere significantly with the central mission of religious affiliated law schools).

15. State Bar of Tex., State Bar Rules Art. III, §2 (2016), https://www.texasbar.com/AM /Template.cfm?Section=Governing_Documents&Template=/CM/ContentDisplay.cfm&Content ID=11009.

16. *See generally* Michael Herz, *The Role of One Religiously Affiliated Law School*, 59 J. Legal Educ. 136 (2009) (describing the mission and role of a religiously affiliated law school). Religious affiliation within a law school has become a commitment to ethical standards. A religiously affiliated law school, which speaks of ethics, service, morals and values instead of its source, has domesticated religion into a secularized belief system in an attempt to be more inclusive and diverse. *Id.* at 147. However, students who share the religious beliefs of the law school are free to pursue the law in congruence with their beliefs.

17. *See* Warren E. Burger, *The Role of the Law School in the Teaching of Legal Ethics and Professional Responsibility*, 29 Clev. St. L. Rev. 377, 377 (1980) (explaining that law schools have a duty to teach professional ethics to their students). Chief Justice Burger repeatedly encouraged law schools to provide the ethical foundations for the profession. *Id.* Law schools have a "profound duty" and a "unique opportunity" to fulfill an obligation "[t]o see that higher standards of responsibility permeate the profession." *Id.* He believed law schools, state bars, and the judiciary should collaborate to achieve a common goal. *Id.* His warning is sincere.

> Of course, there are exceptions, but, on the whole, what the law schools have done is to take young men and women and train them in the skills of a professional monopoly, leaving the learning of moral and ethical precepts—which ought to guide the exercise of such an important monopoly—to a vague, undetermined, unregulated, and undefined future . . . .
>
> Some observers argue that character and moral sense are largely molded by the time students get to law school. There is some truth to this. The law school cannot replace the family, the church or synagogue, or the strong role model provided by the classroom teacher during the years of elementary and secondary school. But we know full well that the law school is an immensely powerful force in defining, structuring, and internalizing professional norms, values and attitudes. . . . [L]awyers who know how to think in legal terms, but have not learned how to behave, are a menace to society and a liability, not an asset, to the administration of justice.

Id. at 388, 390 (citations omitted).

C. St. Mary's Struggle to Obtain CLE Accreditation for Faith-Based CLE Programs in Texas

Consistent with these goals, the Catholic Lawyers Guild of San Antonio, of which this author is President, joined with the Christian Legal Society of San Antonio to persuade St. Mary's University School of Law to allow us to conduct the first-ever Christian Legal Perspectives seminar in the San Antonio, Texas area. We approached this with a very modest goal which we did not think would ever be controversial. We hoped that we could re-convince attorneys to incorporate moral and religious considerations in their practices. By way of example, we put together a panel consisting of a former Texas state district judge, a mediator with more than thirty years' experience in the practice of law, and two other attorneys with substantial family law backgrounds to discuss faith, lawyering, and divorce. We believed that it would be important to remind attorneys who are asked to represent clients in divorce proceedings to consider the religious view of the sanctity of marriage.[18] This approach might result in attorneys referring their clients to faith-based counseling in order to determine whether a divorce really would be in the best interests of all parties involved, including children. The hope was that this approach might preserve marriages where possible, and where not possible, that the parties might at least be given a perspective that could enable them to work better together post-divorce in their own best interests and those of the children.[19] These are not radical ideas.

Legal ethics should not be taught by lecturing or tested through memorization. *Id.* at 393. Students and lawyers learn professional responsibility through candid conversations with professionals speaking of ethical issues as they arise in various aspects of their own practice. *Id.* Chief Justice Burger does not expressly state the following, but it seems practical that the CLE was envisioned as this opportunity.

18. *See* Martha Minow, *On Being a Religious Professional: The Religious Turn in Professional Ethics*, 150 U. Pa. L. Rev. 661, 71 (2001) (discussing the benefits and dangers of legal and non-legal professionals relying on their religious beliefs in their practices). Often, religion strengthens individuals who act as professionals. However, "[w]hen there is a conflict between religious and professional norms, . . . are compromises possible? . . . And in the absence of such a conflict, what are the benefits and what are the dangers—for those they serve and for the larger society—if professionals rely on their religions to guide their conduct?" *Id.* A lawyer who chooses to practice in accordance with her faith should disclose her beliefs to the clients. *Id.* at 678–79. For those clients that do not share the lawyer's view or feel they will not be served, a referral is the appropriate measure. *Id.* Furthermore, Title VII provides safeguards for clients. *Id.* at 681 (citing EEOC v. Rinella & Rinella, 401 F. Supp. 175, 179–81 (N.D. Ill. 1975)). A lawyer's duty to the client includes counseling the client and preserving the right to raise moral objections to their desires rather than implementing every desire. *Id.* at 678.

19. Burger, *supra* note 17, at 378. "We have served, and must continue to see our role, as problem-solvers, harmonizers, and peacemakers, the healers—not the promoters—of conflict." *Id.* Lawyers should be able to refuse to work for a client or on a particular issue, if their objection stems from a religious or a sincere conscientious belief. Refusal should not violate discrimination protections of Title VII, nor should their demurral become a platform to grandstand on platitudes. A genuine refusal framed in humility and respect will accommodate the best interests of their client or prospective client. Similarly, the lawyer should not be compelled to serve the client. *Cf.* United States v. Seeger, 380 U.S. 163, 176 (1965) (explaining objection on the basis of sincere religious beliefs in the context of a statute exempting conscientious objectors from military service). For a discussion of

However, the Texas MCLE Committee initially denied accreditation.[20] We asked for reconsideration and the committee reluctantly granted our request.[21] Our program took place on the afternoon of October 21, 2015; however, on November 4, 2015, the MCLE committee abruptly announced that it would not accredit any further ethics programs which we might present that dealt with "religious or moral" themes.[22] They informed us that only "secular" programs would receive such credit. The letter from Nancy R. Smith, Director of the State Bar of Texas MCLE, to this author, stated, in relevant part:

> Dear Mr. Piatt: The MCLE Committee recently evaluated the above-referenced activity to determine if credit can be granted for future similar programs. As discussed, we granted a one-time MCLE accreditation to the above-referenced activity. However, because we were uncertain as to whether this activity would fully satisfy all of the criteria outlined in the accreditation standards, we sent your application and supporting documentation to the MCLE Committee for further review. Upon completion of their evaluation, the Committee found that this activity does not satisfy several of the accreditation criteria and therefore, will not be approved in the future.

> Based upon the course description and materials submitted with the application, it was determined that this activity would be denied accreditation by the definition of legal ethics as outlined in the enclosed Accreditation Standards for CLE Activities. The definition of legal ethics/professional responsibility allows credit only for those topics dealing with matters pertaining specifically to attorney duties and responsibilities and excludes credit for individual religious or moral responsibilities. To be approved for partial credit in the future, the portions devoted to secular law and legal ethics would need to be clearly identified and separate from instruction on religious or moral responsibilities. Otherwise, we would not be able to allow MCLE accreditation for any portion of the program.[23]

While this development was stunning, even more surprising was the fact that other CLE programs proposed by faith-based attorney groups in Texas had also been denied accreditation.[24] After much reflection and prayer we determined that in order to preserve our right to present future post-law school Christian CLE programs, we would need to lodge a formal appeal. This was not an easy decision to reach. The thought

---

appointments, *see* Teresa Stanton Collett, *Professional Versus Moral Duty: Accepting Appointments in Unjust Civil Cases*, 32 WAKE FOREST L. REV. 635, 638–39 (1997) (noting that courts may have inherent or statutorily-created authority to appoint counsel).

20. Cassandra, *supra* note 2.

21. *Id.*

22. Letter from Nancy R. Smith, Director, St. Bar Tex. Minimum Continuing Legal Educ., to Bill Piatt (Nov. 4, 2015) (on file with author).

23. *Id.*

24. Letter from Jimmy Blacklock, General Counsel, Office of Governor Greg Abbott, to Allan DuBois, President, St. Bar Tex. 6 (Dec. 22, 2015) (on file with author).

of challenging the actions of our own State bar in a formal and aggressive fashion caused us some pause. After all, the bar has vast resources. It could undoubtedly rely upon some very high-profile attorneys providing legal services to quash our efforts. Moreover, there were some personal concerns. Some of the decision-makers were our friends. Some were people with whom we had worked. Some were people with whom we would need to continue to work. We reflected upon this, we prayed upon this, and in the end, we were convinced we really had no recourse but to pursue the appeal if we wanted to be able to continue to present faith-based CLE programs in the State of Texas.

As it turned out, we were not alone in our efforts. St. Mary's University School of Law, the Catholic Lawyers' Guild of San Antonio, and eight individual attorneys signed off on the appeal.[25] Numerous other educators, attorneys, and political figures rallied to our support. Our supporters included the national Christian Legal Society as well as some individual chapters of the same, the Dean of Baylor Law School, and the Governor of the State of Texas, Greg Abbott. Our efforts were publicized extensively by The Cardinal Newman Society.[26] Articles also appeared in the *Texas Lawyer*.[27]

Now comes the spoiler alert: We were successful. The State Bar of Texas rescinded its letter of November 4, 2015, on January 12, 2016.[28] The Bar wrote, in part: "It is the MCLE committee's position that MCLE credit, including legal ethics credit, may be granted for training and education on moral and religious topics presented in the context of legal training."[29] While we achieved success in this endeavor, rulings can change depending upon who has the authority to administer CLE accreditation procedures. As of this writing, the State Bar of Texas has not yet formally amended its CLE Rules to recognize the legitimacy of faith- and morality-based CLE ethics programs. As part of the settlement, the State Bar of Texas also agreed to put on an ethics CLE program

---

25. Cassandra, *supra* note 2.

26. *E.g.*, Cassandra, *supra* note 2; Adam Cassandra, *Texas Governor's Office: State Bar Continuing Education Ruling Discriminates Against Religion*, Cardinal Newman Soc'y (Dec. 29, 2015), https://cardinalnewmansociety.org/texas-governors-office-state-bar-continuing-education -ruling-discriminates-against-religion/; Adam Cassandra, *State Bar of Texas Says Discriminatory Ruling Against Christian Law Program a 'Miscommunication,'* Cardinal Newman Soc'y (Jan. 14, 2016), https://cardinalnewmansociety.org/state-bar-of-texas-says-discriminatory-ruling-against -christian-law-program-a-miscommunication/ (discussing MCLE Committee's reversal to deny credit for a continuing legal education program in Christian legal ethics); Piatt, *supra* note 3.

27. Brenda Sapino Jeffreys, *Governor Accuses State Bar of Religious Discrimination in Continuing Legal Education Accreditation Battle*, Tex. Law. (Online), Jan. 7, 2016, LEXIS (discussing Governor Abbott's position on MCLE's denial for credit on a continuing legal education program on Christian legal ethics).

28. Letter from Nancy R. Smith, Director, St. Bar Tex. Minimum Continuing Legal Educ., to Bill Piatt (Jan. 12, 2016) (on file with author).

29. *Id.* at 1. The letter explained that the accreditation requirement for CLE activity is that the activity must directly relate to legal subjects, and that "[t]here is no question that programs which approach those issues from a moral or religious perspective can fully satisfy this 'directly relate' standard, and such programs are routinely approved." *Id.*

at the State Bar Convention in Fort Worth in June 2016 involving the role of faith and morality in the practice of law.[30] While the Bar put together a distinguished panel, it declined this author's offer to participate (this author understands human nature!). Unfortunately, it also declined to include any Catholic attorneys on the panel. Thus, work remains, in Texas and perhaps elsewhere.

In order to help guarantee that our law schools and our graduates can continue to extend a faith-based approach to the practice of law beyond our classrooms, we turn to a summary of the legal authority, arguments, and practical approaches upon which CLE providers may rely as they insist on the right to receive accreditation for faith-based CLE programs.

II. BRINGING A FAITH-BASED APPROACH TO CLE ETHICS PROGRAMMING

A. Applicable Ethics Rules Allow Discussions of Moral Concerns with Clients

Lawyers are required to receive annual training in ethics.[31] One of the ethical rules which law students must learn, and to which attorneys must adhere, involves the rendering of legal advice to a client. Rule 2.1 of the American Bar Association's Model Rules of Professional Conduct provides: "In representing a client, a lawyer shall exercise independent professional judgment and render candid advice. In rendering advice, a lawyer may refer not only to law but to other considerations such as moral, economic, social and political factors, that may be relevant to the client's situation."[32] Comment 2 to this Rule explains the importance of the attorney being encouraged to speak to clients in these terms:

> Advice couched in narrow legal terms may be of little value to a client, especially where practical considerations, such as cost or effects on other people, are predominant. Purely technical legal advice, therefore, can sometimes be inadequate. It is proper for a lawyer to refer to relevant moral and ethical considerations in giving advice. Although a lawyer is not a moral advisor as such, moral and ethical considerations impinge upon most legal questions and may decisively influence how the law will be applied.[33]

While the Rule and Comment do not explicitly use the word "religion," it is clear that "other considerations"[34] in the context of morality and ethics would include such an approach. If attorneys are being encouraged to incorporate such considerations

---

30. St. Bar Tex., Annual Meeting Fort Worth 2016 Registration Brochure 8 (2016), https://www.texasbar.com/Content/NavigationMenu/Events/AnnualMeeting/AnnualMeeting Home/AnnualMeetingRegistrationBrochure.pdf.

31. *See, e.g.*, St. Bar Tex., State Bar Rules Art. XII, §2(J) (2016), https://www.texasbar.com /AM/Template.cfm?Section=Governing_Documents&Template=/CM/ContentDisplay.cfm& ContentID=11009.

32. Model Rules Of Prof'l Conduct r. 2.1 (Am. Bar Ass'n 2016).

33. *Id.* at r. 2.1 cmt. 2.

34. *Id.* at r. 2.1.

in their discussions with clients, it makes sense that attorneys who are continuing in their legal education may be reminded of this fact in a CLE program. Religious attorneys should be offered opportunities to see how such an approach might be implemented in their practices.[35]

As noted above, Governor Greg Abbott of the State of Texas supported our appeal.[36] He noted:

> Studying the interplay between morality, religion, and the law is not a new concept, and educating the legal profession on these issues is not a novel pursuit. In the Supreme Court's words, "We are a religious people whose institutions presuppose a Supreme Being." It should be no surprise, then, that American legal education and scholarship has long sought to better understand how religion and morality interact with the law and with a lawyer's responsibilities.[37]

The Governor went on to cite numerous symposia, books, articles, and the like discussing the role of faith, morality, and religion in the ethical practice of law.[38] And, in a powerful summary, he observed:

> The Committee's position that "legal ethics" and "religious or moral responsibilities" should be — or even can be — completely divorced from each other is entirely without basis. . . . To be honest, the idea that a lawyer's professional ethics have nothing to do with morality sounds more like the start of a bad joke than a serious philosophical or legal proposition. But if our profession has in fact reached the point where its leaders no longer think lawyers need concern themselves with the morality of their professional conduct, we should consider whether the lawyer jokes have it right.[39]

B. There Can Be No "Secular" as Opposed to "Non-Secular" CLE Programs Because Moral and Religious Concerns Factor into the Substantive Law

The Texas State Bar was convinced in its initial rulings that there is some distinction between secular and non-secular CLE programs; it would accredit the former and deny accreditation to the latter.[40] This notion, of course, is absolutely inconsistent with our system of jurisprudence. A discussion of this topic would be quite lengthy. Nonetheless, a quick look at two decisions of the Supreme Court of the United States reveals how important morality and religion are to contemporary jurisprudence.

---

35. The Texas Disciplinary Rules of Professional Conduct do not contain the language of ABA Model Rule 2.1, but do contain, verbatim, as Comment 2 to TDR 2.01, the exact language of Comment 2 to ABA Model Rule 2.1. *Compare* Tex. Disciplinary R. Prof'l Conduct, R. 2.01 (Tex. St. Bar 2017), *with* Model Rules Of Prof'l Conduct r. 2.1 cmt. 2 (Am. Bar Ass'n 2016).

36. Letter from Jimmy Blacklock, *supra* note 24 at 1.

37. *Id.* at 5 (citation omitted) (quoting Zorach v. Clauson, 343 U.S. 306, 313 (1952)).

38. *Id.* at 5–6.

39. *Id.* at 2.

40. Letter from Nancy R. Smith, *supra* note 22.

In 1964, the Supreme Court decided the case of *Heart of Atlanta Motel, Inc. v. United States*.[41] In that case, the owner of the motel brought a challenge to the provisions of Title II of the Civil Rights Act of 1964.[42] That Act outlawed race discrimination in public accommodations, including motels.[43] The owner of the motel did not deny that he was engaging in race discrimination.[44] Rather, he argued that legislation aimed at eliminating racial discrimination was outside of Congress's constitutional power to enact.[45] The Supreme Court rejected his argument.[46] The court concluded, "[t]hat Congress was legislating against moral wrongs in many of these areas [i.e., prostitution, gambling, racial discrimination in interstate carriers] rendered its enactments no less valid. In framing Title II of this Act, Congress was also dealing with what it considered a moral problem."[47]

Similarly, in *Roe v. Wade*,[48] the majority opinion explicitly recognized that the abortion controversy involved moral and religious concerns.[49] Thus, if moral and religious concerns are relevant factors in the creation and interpretation of the law, certainly those same concerns are relevant in a discussion of the role of morality and faith in the practice of law.

C. The First Amendment Guarantees Us the Right to Discuss Issues of Faith and Morality in the Practice of Law, and Precludes the States from Denying Accreditation for Those Presentations

While there are some limits, attorneys do not surrender their First Amendment rights by becoming attorneys. For example, the First Amendment guarantees attorneys the right to advertise within a certain framework.[50] Similarly, attorneys have a First Amendment right to speak at CLE programs and to listen to those

---

41. 379 U.S. 241, 257, 261 (1964) (holding Congress's ability to appropriately regulate intrastate commerce that affects interstate commerce is a legitimate exercise of the power granted to Congress, including enforcing regulations prohibiting moral and social wrongs); *see also* McCulloch v. Maryland, 4 Wheat. 316, 421 (1819); United States v. Darby, 312 U.S. 100, 114 (1940) (discussing the importance of morality and high standards in jurisprudence).

42. *Heart of Atlanta*, 379 U.S. at 243, 247.

43. *Id.* at 247.

44. *Id.* at 243.

45. *Id.* at 243–244.

46. *Id.* at 257.

47. *Id.*

48. 410 U.S. 113 (1973).

49. *Id.* at 116.

50. Bates v. State Bar of Az., 433 U.S. 350, 363–64 (1977). A lawyer's advertising, although lacking cultural, philosophical, or political subject matter, is protected. *Id.* The listener has a substantial interest in hearing the speech. *Id.* at 364. "In short, such speech serves individual and societal interests in assuring informed and reliable decisionmaking." *Id.*; *see also* Va. Pharmacy Bd. v. Va. Citizens Consumer Council, 425 U.S. 748, 761 (1976) (holding that speech does not lose First Amendment protection simply because it is in the form of paid advertisement).

presentations, and to associate with attorneys who share similar interests.[51] Given that the foundation of law concerns morality and at times religion,[52] there is a First Amendment right of attorneys to speak on these issues as they impact the professional obligations of attorneys, especially given that the Model Rules encourage such discussions.[53] State denial of accreditation where attorneys discuss these matters as part of a CLE program would violate the First Amendment guarantees to speak and assemble,[54] and would likely violate comparable state constitutional provisions.[55] It would constitute an unconstitutional prior restraint upon the speech of the organizers, presenters, and potential attendees.[56] And, limiting accreditation to "secular" speech would be an unconstitutionally vague, and at the same time, blunt crushing of any speech deemed not to be "secular."[57]

Similarly, attorneys do not surrender their right to the free exercise of their religion[58] by becoming attorneys. And what does free exercise of religion entail in this context? Free exercise means more than worship. As the Supreme Court has held, "the 'exercise of religion' involves 'not only belief and profession but the performance of (or abstention from) physical acts' that are 'engaged in for religious reasons.'"[59] As Christian attorneys, and as Christian educators, we have the First Amendment right to exercise our religion by participating in CLE programs that explain to our peers various perspectives on law, including an application of moral concepts. Any ban on such activity would violate the Free Exercise Clause of the First Amendment.

---

51. Gibson v. Fla. Legislative Investigation Comm., 372 U.S. 539, 543 (1963) ("This Court has repeatedly held that rights of association are within the ambit of the constitutional protections afforded by the First and Fourteenth Amendments.").

52. *Heart of Atlanta*, 379 U.S. at 257.

53. MODEL RULES OF PROF'L CONDUCT r. 2.1 (AM. BAR. ASS'N 2016).

54. U.S. CONST. amend. I.

55. *See* TEX. CONST. art. I, §8, 27 (containing language similar to the First Amendment to the United States Constitution).

56. *See, e.g.,* Kunz v. New York, 340 U.S. 290, 293 (1951) (holding that an ordinance preventing public worship on the streets without a license constituted an unconstitutional prior restraint on speech); Follett v. Town of McCormick, S.C., 321 U.S. 573, 582 (1944) (upholding the right to publish and distribute religious books); Murdock v. Pennsylvania, 319 U.S. 105, 140 (1943) (holding that there is a right to benefit from religious activities); Cantwell v. Connecticut, 310 U.S. 296, 311 (1940) (holding that there is a First Amendment right to publish and distribute religious material).

57. Wright v. Georgia, 373 U.S. 284, 292 (1963) ("[A] generally worded statute which is construed to punish conduct which cannot constitutionally be punished is unconstitutionally vague to the extent that it fails to give adequate warning of the boundary between the constitutionally permissible and constitutionally impermissible applications of the statute.").

58. U.S. CONST. amend. I.

59. Burwell v. Hobby Lobby Stores, Inc., 134 S. Ct. 2751, 2770 (2014) (quoting Emp't Div., Dep't Human Res. of Or. v. Smith, 494 U.S. 872, 877 (1990) (emphasizing ". . . that a State would be 'prohibiting the free exercise of religion' if it sought to ban such acts or abstentions only when they are engaged in for religious reasons, or only because of the religious belief that they display")).

D. There are Potential Due Process and Equal Protection Problems
Regarding Denial of Accreditation to Faith-Based CLE Programs

Typically, the CLE accreditation process involves the submission of a proposed agenda, teaching materials, and some biographical information regarding the presenters.[60] It is also typical that the accreditation committee requires program organizers to state that approval is pending up to the point where final approval is given.[61] A State Bar official can delay the issuance of final approval,[62] thereby discouraging potential participants from enrolling in the CLE. It is also possible, as was the case in our Texas matter, that an accreditation entity might make a determination to deny accreditation without providing any notice or opportunity to be heard.[63] Either of these approaches would deny presenters and potential participants their rights to Due Process as guaranteed by the Fifth and Fourteenth Amendments to the Constitution of the United States[64] and by comparable provisions in state law.[65] In our case, the Due Process violations were even more egregious—we were denied the right to receive accreditation for any *future* CLE presentations, even though none had been planned or submitted for approval at that point.

In the strange circumstance, again as appeared in Texas, where the state bar accrediting entity will accredit the faith-based CLE presentations of some religions and not others, an obvious Fourteenth Amendment denial of Equal Protection arises.[66]

E. How to Achieve Accreditation of Faith-Based CLE Programs

The first step to putting together an effective faith-based CLE program is to enlist the participation of thoughtful and articulate presenters who bring important and diversified backgrounds to the program. Law school deans and former deans, law professors, experienced attorneys and mediators, and judges all fit the bill. That describes exactly the program we assembled—and yet we were still initially denied accreditation in Texas. Ultimately, however, the strength of our panels would have helped ensure success in the unfortunate event that we were forced into litigation.

Of course, strict compliance with all the technical requirements of the CLE accreditation process is also critical. This involves timely submissions of accreditation requests, careful preparation of materials, and the like. And, because we are educators, our first obligation and challenge will be to educate the accreditation committee

---

60. *See, e.g.*, Sт. Bar Tex., Texas Minimum Continuing Legal Education Regulations, at §§ 10.2(d), 10.2(f) (2015), https://www.texasbar.com/AM/Template.cfm.Section=MCLE_Rules1 &Template=/CM/ContentDisplay.cfm& ContentID=31721 (explaining the procedures necessary to apply for accreditation of CLE activities).

61. *Id.* at § 10.1.8.

62. *Id.* at § 10.1.12.

63. *Id.* at § 10.9.

64. U.S. Const. amend. V; *id.* amend. XIV, § 1.

65. *See* Fla. Const. art. I, § 9 (containing language similar to the Fifth Amendment of the United States).

66. U.S. Const. amend. XIV, § 1; Niemotko v. Maryland, 340 U.S. 268, 284 (1951).

of the validity and the importance of these topics. A succinct and polite summary of some of the themes of this Article would be helpful to a well-intentioned accreditor who is not familiar with the importance of the interplay of law, faith, morality, and ethics. Such a summary would also be helpful if the accreditor turns out to be not-so-well-intentioned. In such a case the summary might assist in convincing that person that it might not be a good idea to have his or her State Bar brought before the courts to resolve the accreditation issue.

In the unfortunate situation where accreditation is denied, sponsors would have several alternatives. One would be to cancel the program. Of course, such an approach, while avoiding conflict, would prevent the spread of the message of incorporating faith into practice. It would reinforce in the minds of the CLE accreditors that their position was correct. It would likely intimidate other providers from any further attempts at creating faith-based CLE programs.

Another approach would be to put on the program, even without accreditation, in order to provide participants the benefits of sharing in the faith-based perspectives. After all, the benefits provided by such a program to the lives of the practitioners, their clients, and the system of justice does not depend upon accreditation. The number of participants who would attend and thereby benefit, however, would likely be reduced if the program does not offer CLE credit.

Soon after our battle over accreditation regarding the St. Mary's CLE program, this author learned that a group of faith-based practitioners had prepared a similar CLE program in Dallas. After putting on their program, which was attended by over sixty attorneys, the program was denied accreditation. When the organizers of that program informed us of their situation, this author urged them, even though the time had passed to request reconsideration, to attach the State Bar's letter of January 21, 2016 to such a request. The sponsors did so. In response, the State Bar then granted accreditation.[67]

In addition to either canceling the program or presenting it without accreditation, there are mechanisms to bring administrative denial of faith-based CLE programs to review by the highest court in the state. State Supreme Courts typically exercise superintending control over licensing and accreditation issues.[68] One potential remedy would be to go straight to the highest court of the state with a request for that body to exercise superintending control and grant accreditation.

Another possible remedy would be to take advantage of applicable civil rights laws. The violation of the First Amendment rights of the CLE presenters could be addressed in an action brought under 42 U.S.C. § 1983.[69]

---

67. Correspondence between Bill Piatt and the organizers of the Dallas CLE program (on file with author).

68. *See CLE FAQs*, AM. BAR ASS'N, http://www.americanbar.org/cle/faqs.html (last visited Feb. 14, 2017) (explaining that state supreme courts grant accreditation through a CLE board or commission).

69. *See* 42 U.S.C. § 1983 (2012) (providing a civil cause of action for the deprivation of constitutional rights).

Remedies could also be sought under applicable state Religious Freedom Restoration (RFRA) statutes.[70] The Texas statute is illustrative. Under that Act, remedies are provided for the violation by the government of the "free exercise of religion."[71] "Free exercise" is defined as "an act or refusal to act that is substantially motivated by sincere religious belief."[72] The person bringing such an action must first give notice to the entity that the free exercise of religion "is substantially burdened by an exercise of the government agency's governmental authority."[73] A person must also identify the particular act or refusal to act that was burdened[74] and the manner in which exercise of governmental authority burdens the act.[75] The government agency would then have to demonstrate "that the application of the burden to the person . . . is in furtherance of a compelling governmental interest [and] is the least restrictive means of furthering that interest."[76] Declaratory relief, compensatory damages, costs, and attorneys' fees are available to the successful claimant.[77]

Our RFRA notice to the State Bar of Texas stated: The undersigned give notice as required by the Texas Religious Freedom Restoration Act that, as set out above, the actions of the MCLE Board and Ms. Smith constitute a substantial burden upon the religious freedom of the undersigned by the exercise of the governmental authority of the Board and Ms. Smith. The manner in which the respondents have acted will preclude the undersigned from organizing, presenting, and attending accredited CLE programs which touch on religious or moral themes. Law and religion are important aspects of the free exercise of the religion of the undersigned, in their respective roles as educators and attorneys. The Notice which is the subject of this appeal and notice should be immediately rescinded.[78]

This, in connection with the other arguments raised in our appeal, caught the attention of the Bar. It is difficult to imagine any "compelling governmental interest" which the Bar could have raised to our attempt to provide CLE courses so clearly aligned with the applicable ethical rules. There seems to be no argument which the Bar could have advanced to show that denying *future* accreditation for programs

---

70. *See, e.g.,* Tex. Civ. Prac. & Rem. Code Ann. § 110.003(a) (West, Westlaw through 2015 Reg. Sess. of the 84th Legislature) (preventing government agencies from placing substantial burdens on the free exercise of religion).

71. *Id.*

72. *Id.* at § 110.001(a)(1).

73. *Id.* at § 110.006(a)(1).

74. *Id.* at § 110.006(a)(2).

75. *Id.* at § 110.006(a)(3). Claimants in Texas ordinarily must give the agency 60 days to correct the violation, although that time limitation can be waived if "(1) the exercise of governmental authority that threatens to substantially burden the person's free exercise of religion is imminent; and (2) the person was not informed and did not otherwise have knowledge of the exercise of the governmental authority in time to reasonably provide the notice." *Id.* at § 110.006(b)(1)–(2).

76. *Id.* at § 110.003(b).

77. *Id.* at § 110.005(a).

78. Letter from Bill Piatt to Nancy R. Smith, Director, St. Bar Tex. Minimum Continuing Legal Educ. (Nov. 18, 2015) (on file with author).

which the Bar had not even seen (and which had not even been submitted) could be the "least restrictive means" of accomplishing any compelling governmental interest. The approach we followed in this regard would be a template for other schools in the unfortunate situation where litigation becomes necessary.

III. CONCLUSION

Religiously affiliated law schools offer our students a faith-based approach to the practice of law. That approach benefits not only our individual students, but their future clients and society. What if we could continue to bring this message to them throughout their careers? The answer is obvious. Faith-based CLE programs will bring this assistance to them and to other attorneys. Our profession, our society, and our economic and political systems will benefit from the infusion of the deeply held moral, ethical, and religious values that brought us into the teaching of law in our unique schools in the first place. We should take the lead in the creation of such programs, and fight, where necessary, with the faith that guides our lives, to receive accreditation for them.

Lawyers can also serve an important role in pushing back against attempts to remove God and prayer from public discourse, by informing private and governmental clients, as well as the public, of the First Amendment right to public religious expression. This right includes public prayers that are explicitly Christian. And, Catholic public officials may make the sign of the cross at the conclusion of a public prayer. The 2014 *Greece v. Galloway*[28] decision of the Supreme Court is illustrative.

In the town of Greece, New York town board meetings were opened with a moment of silence. Beginning in 1999, the newly elected town supervisor introduced a practice of replacing the moment of silence with delivery of an invocation or prayer given by a local clergyman. This practice was inspired by a tradition practiced by Congress and many state legislatures. The prayer program was open to all faiths, but reflected the large majority of Christian congregations in the area. Citizens who regularly attend the town meetings speaking on local issues filed suit alleging that by preferring Christians over other prayer givers the town violated the First Amendment's Establishment Clause by sponsoring sectarian prayers.

Finding no impermissible preference for Christian prayers, on summary judgment, the District Court upheld the existing prayer practices of the town of Greece. The District Court concluded that most of the prayer givers were Christian because most of the town's congregations were of Christian character. There was no evidence of an official policy or practice discriminating against minority faiths. The District Court held that the First Amendment did not instill a duty on the town of Greece to invite clergy from beyond their town limits to achieve religious diversity

---

28. Town of Greece, N.Y. v. Galloway, 134 S. Ct. 1811 (2014).

at its town meeting prayers. Furthermore, the District Court rejected the argument of the respondents that legislative prayer must be nonsectarian to avoid violating the First Amendment. On appeal, the Second Circuit reversed, holding that upon review by a reasonable observer, some aspects of the Greece's prayer program sent the message that Greece was endorsing Christianity. The Supreme Court of the United States granted certiorari on whether the town of Greece imposes an impermissible establishment of religion by opening its monthly board meetings with a prayer.

---

134 S. Ct. 1811
Supreme Court of the United States
TOWN OF GREECE, NEW YORK, Petitioner
v.
Susan GALLOWAY et al.
Decided May 5, 2014

Justice KENNEDY delivered the opinion of the Court, except as to Part II–B.

The Court must decide whether the town of Greece, New York, imposes an impermissible establishment of religion by opening its monthly board meetings with a prayer. It must be concluded, consistent with the Court's opinion in *Marsh v. Chambers*, 463 U.S. 783, 103 S. Ct. 3330, 77 L. Ed. 2d 1019 (1983), that no violation of the Constitution has been shown.

I.

. . . .

Having granted certiorari to decide whether the town's prayer practice violates the Establishment Clause, 569 U.S. ___, 133 S. Ct. 2388, 185 L. Ed. 2d 1103 (2013), the Court now reverses the judgment of the Court of Appeals.

II.

In *Marsh v. Chambers*, 463 U.S. 783, 103 S. Ct. 3330, 77 L. Ed. 2d 1019, the Court found no First Amendment violation in the Nebraska Legislature's practice of opening its sessions with a prayer delivered by a chaplain paid from state funds. The decision concluded that legislative prayer, while religious in nature, has long been understood as compatible with the Establishment Clause. As practiced by Congress since the framing of the Constitution, legislative prayer lends gravity to public business, reminds lawmakers to transcend petty differences in pursuit of a higher purpose, and expresses a common aspiration to a just and peaceful society. See *Lynch v. Donnelly*, 465 U.S. 668, 693, 104 S. Ct. 1355, 79 L. Ed. 2d 604 (1984) (O'Connor, J., concurring); cf. A. Adams & C. Emmerich, A Nation Dedicated to Religious Liberty 83 (1990). The Court has considered this symbolic expression to be a "tolerable acknowledgement of beliefs widely held," *Marsh*, 463 U.S., at 792, 103 S. Ct. 3330, 77 L. Ed. 2d 1019, rather than a first, treacherous step towards establishment of a state church.

The Court's inquiry, then, must be to determine whether the prayer practice in the town of Greece fits within the tradition long followed in Congress and the state legislatures. Respondents assert that the town's prayer exercise falls outside that tradition and transgresses the Establishment Clause for two independent but mutually reinforcing reasons. First, they argue that *Marsh* did not approve prayers containing sectarian language or themes, such as the prayers offered in Greece that referred to the "death, resurrection, and ascension of the Savior Jesus Christ," App. 129a, and the "saving sacrifice of Jesus Christ on the cross," *id.*, at 88a. Second, they argue that the setting and conduct of the town board meetings create social pressures that force nonadherents to remain in the room or even feign participation in order to avoid offending the representatives who sponsor the prayer and will vote on matters citizens bring before the board. The sectarian content of the prayers compounds the subtle coercive pressures, they argue, because the nonbeliever who might tolerate ecumenical prayer is forced to do the same for prayer that might be inimical to his or her beliefs.

A.

. . . .

An insistence on nonsectarian or ecumenical prayer as a single, fixed standard is not consistent with the tradition of legislative prayer outlined in the Court's cases. The Court found the prayers in *Marsh* consistent with the First Amendment not because they espoused only a generic theism but because our history and tradition have shown that prayer in this limited context could "coexis[t] with the principles of disestablishment and religious freedom." 463 U.S., at 786, 103 S. Ct. 3330, 77 L. Ed. 2d 1019. The Congress that drafted the First Amendment would have been accustomed to invocations containing explicitly religious themes of the sort respondents find objectionable. One of the Senate's first chaplains, the Rev. William White, gave prayers in a series that included the Lord's Prayer, the Collect for Ash Wednesday, prayers for peace and grace, a general thanksgiving, St. Chrysostom's Prayer, and a prayer seeking "the grace of our Lord Jesus Christ, &c." Letter from W. White to H. Jones (Dec. 29, 1830), in B. Wilson, Memoir of the Life of the Right Reverend William White, D. D., Bishop of the Protestant Episcopal Church in the State of Pennsylvania 322 (1839); see also New Hampshire Patriot & State Gazette, Dec. 15, 1823, p. 1 (describing a Senate prayer addressing the "Throne of Grace"); Cong. Globe, 37th Cong., 1st Sess., 2 (1861) (reciting the Lord's Prayer). The decidedly Christian nature of these prayers must not be dismissed as the relic of a time when our Nation was less pluralistic than it is today. Congress continues to permit its appointed and visiting chaplains to express themselves in a religious idiom. It acknowledges our growing diversity not by proscribing sectarian content but by welcoming ministers of many creeds. See, e.g., 160 Cong. Rec. S1329 (Mar. 6, 2014) (Dalai Lama) ("I am a Buddhist monk—a simple Buddhist monk—so we pray to Buddha and all other Gods"); 159 Cong. Rec. H7006 (Nov. 13, 2013) (Rabbi Joshua Gruenberg) ("Our God and God of our ancestors, Everlasting Spirit of the Universe . . ."); 159 Cong. Rec. H3024 (June 4, 2013) (Satguru Bodhinatha Veylanswami) ("Hindu scripture declares, without equivocation, that the highest of high ideals is to never knowingly harm any-one"); 158 Cong. Rec. H5633 (Aug. 2, 2012) (Imam Nayyar Imam) ("The final prophet of God, Muhammad, peace be upon him, stated: 'The leaders of a people are a representation of their deeds'").

. . . .

To hold that invocations must be nonsectarian would force the legislatures that sponsor prayers and the courts that are asked to decide these cases to act as super-visors and censors of religious speech, a rule that would involve government in reli-gious matters to a far greater degree than is the case under the town's current practice of neither editing or approving prayers in advance nor criticizing their content after the fact. Cf. *Hosanna-Tabor Evangelical Lutheran Church and School v. EEOC*, 565 U.S. ___, ___, 132 S. Ct. 694, 181 L. Ed. 2d 650 (2012)). Our Government is prohib-ited from prescribing prayers to be recited in our public institutions in order to promote a preferred system of belief or code of moral behavior. *Engel v. Vitale*, 370 U.S. 421, 430, 82 S. Ct. 1261, 8 L. Ed. 2d 601 (1962). It would be but a few steps removed from that prohibition for legislatures to require chaplains to redact the religious con-tent from their message in order to make it acceptable for the public sphere. Gov-ernment may not mandate a civic religion that stifles any but the most generic reference to the sacred any more than it may prescribe a religious orthodoxy. See *Lee v. Weisman*, 505 U.S. 577, 590, 112 S. Ct. 2649, 120 L. Ed. 2d 467 (1992) [28] ("The sug-gestion that government may establish an official or civic religion as a means of avoiding the establishment of a religion with more specific creeds strikes us as a contradiction that cannot be accepted"); [*School District of Abington Twp. v.*] *Schempp*, 374 U.S., at 306, 83 S. Ct. 1560, 10 L. Ed. 2d 844 (Goldberg, J., concurring) (arguing that "untutored devotion to the concept of neutrality" must not lead to "a brooding and pervasive devotion to the secular").

. . . .

In rejecting the suggestion that legislative prayer must be nonsectarian, the Court does not imply that no constraints remain on its content. The relevant constraint derives from its place at the opening of legislative sessions, where it is meant to lend gravity to the occasion and reflect values long part of the Nation's heritage. Prayer that is solemn and respectful in tone, that invites lawmakers to reflect upon shared ideals and common ends before they embark on the fractious business of governing, serves that legitimate function. If the course and practice over time shows that the invocations denigrate nonbelievers or religious minorities, threaten damnation, or preach conversion, many present may consider the prayer to fall short of the desire to elevate the purpose of the occasion and to unite lawmakers in their common effort. That circumstance would present a different case than the one presently before the Court.

. . . .

The tradition reflected in *Marsh* permits chaplains to ask their own God for bless-ings of peace, justice, and freedom that find appreciation among people of all faiths.

That a prayer is given in the name of Jesus, Allah, or Jehovah, or that it makes passing reference to religious doctrines, does not remove it from that tradition. These religious themes provide particular means to universal ends. Prayer that reflects beliefs specific to only some creeds can still serve to solemnize the occasion, so long as the practice over time is not "exploited to proselytize or advance any one, or to disparage any other, faith or belief." *Marsh*, 463 U.S., at 794–95, 103 S. Ct. 3330, 77 L. Ed. 2d 1019.

. . . .

From the earliest days of the Nation, these invocations have been addressed to assemblies comprising many different creeds. These ceremonial prayers strive for the idea that people of many faiths may be united in a community of tolerance and devotion. Even those who disagree as to religious doctrine may find common ground in the desire to show respect for the divine in all aspects of their lives and being. Our tradition assumes that adult citizens, firm in their own beliefs, can tolerate and perhaps appreciate a ceremonial prayer delivered by a person of a different faith. See Letter from John Adams to Abigail Adams (Sept. 16, 1774), in C. Adams, Familiar Letters of John Adams and His Wife Abigail Adams, During the Revolution 37–38 (1876).

. . . .

B.

. . . .

It is an elemental First Amendment principle that government may not coerce its citizens "to support or participate in any religion or its exercise." *County of Allegheny* [*v. ACLU*], 492 U.S., at 659, 109 S. Ct. 3086, 106 L. Ed. 2d 472 (KENNEDY, J., concurring in judgment in part and dissenting in part); see also *Van Orden* [*v. Perry*], 545 U.S., at 683, 125 S. Ct. 2854, 162 L. Ed. 2d 607 (plurality opinion) (recognizing that our "institutions must not press religious observances upon their citizens"). On the record in this case the Court is not persuaded that the town of Greece, through the act of offering a brief, solemn, and respectful prayer to open its monthly meetings, compelled its citizens to engage in a religious observance. The inquiry remains a fact-sensitive one that considers both the setting in which the prayer arises and the audience to whom it is directed.

The prayer opportunity in this case must be evaluated against the backdrop of historical practice. As a practice that has long endured, legislative prayer has become part of our heritage and tradition, part of our expressive idiom, similar to the Pledge of Allegiance, inaugural prayer, or the recitation of "God save the United States and this honorable Court" at the opening of this Court's sessions. See *Lynch*, 465 U.S., at 693, 104 S. Ct. 1355, 79 L. Ed. 2d 604 (O'Connor, J., concurring). It is presumed that the reasonable observer is acquainted with this tradition and understands that its purposes are to lend gravity to public proceedings and to acknowledge the place religion holds in the lives of many private citizens, not to afford government an opportunity to proselytize or force truant constituents into the pews. See *Salazar v. Buono*, 559 U.S. 700, 720–21, 130 S. Ct. 1803, 176 L. Ed. 2d 634 (2010) (plurality opinion); *Santa Fe Independent School Dist. v. Doe*, 530 U.S. 290, 308, 120 S. Ct.

2266, 147 L. Ed. 2d 295 (2000). That many appreciate these acknowledgments of the divine in our public institutions does not suggest that those who disagree are compelled to join the expression or approve its content. *West Virginia Bd. of Ed. v. Barnette*, 319 U.S. 624, 642, 63 S. Ct. 1178, 87 L. Ed. 1628 (1943).

. . . .

The analysis would be different if town board members directed the public to participate in the prayers, singled out dissidents for opprobrium, or indicated that their decisions might be influenced by a person's acquiescence in the prayer opportunity. No such thing occurred in the town of Greece. Although board members themselves stood, bowed their heads, or made the sign of the cross during the prayer, they at no point solicited similar gestures by the public. Respondents point to several occasions where audience members were asked to rise for the prayer. These requests, however, came not from town leaders but from the guest ministers, who presumably are accustomed to directing their congregations in this way and might have done so thinking the action was inclusive, not coercive. See App. 69a ("Would you bow your heads with me as we invite the Lord's presence here tonight?"); *id.*, at 93a ("Let us join our hearts and minds together in prayer"); *id.*, at 102a ("Would you join me in a moment of prayer?"); *id.*, at 110a ("Those who are willing may join me now in prayer"). Respondents suggest that constituents might feel pressure to join the prayers to avoid irritating the officials who would be ruling on their petitions, but this argument has no evidentiary support. Nothing in the record indicates that town leaders allocated benefits and burdens based on participation in the prayer, or that citizens were received differently depending on whether they joined the invocation or quietly declined. In no instance did town leaders signal disfavor toward nonparticipants or suggest that their stature in the community was in any way diminished. A practice that classified citizens based on their religious views would violate the Constitution, but that is not the case before this Court.

In their declarations in the trial court, respondents stated that the prayers gave them offense and made them feel excluded and disrespected. Offense, however, does not equate to coercion. Adults often encounter speech they find disagreeable; and an Establishment Clause violation is not made out any time a person experiences a sense of affront from the expression of contrary religious views in a legislative forum, especially where, as here, any member of the public is welcome in turn to offer an invocation reflecting his or her own convictions. See *Elk Grove Unified School Dist. v. Newdow*, 542 U.S. 1, 44, 124 S. Ct. 2301, 159 L. Ed. 2d 98 (2004) (O'Connor, J., concurring) ("The compulsion of which Justice Jackson was concerned . . . was of the direct sort—the Constitution does not guarantee citizens a right entirely to avoid ideas with which they disagree"). If circumstances arise in which the pattern and practice of ceremonial, legislative prayer is alleged to be a means to coerce or intimidate others, the objection can be addressed in the regular course. But the showing has not been made here, where the prayers neither chastised dissenters nor attempted lengthy disquisition on religious dogma. Courts remain free to review the pattern of prayers over time to determine whether they comport with the tradition of solemn, respectful prayer approved in *Marsh*, or whether coercion is a real and substantial likelihood. But in the general course legislative bodies do not engage in impermissible coercion merely by exposing constituents to prayer they would rather not hear and in which they need not participate. See *County of Allegheny*, 492 U.S., at 670, 109 S. Ct. 3086, 106 L. Ed. 2d 472 (KENNEDY, J., concurring in judgment in part and dissenting in part).

. . . .

Ceremonial prayer is but a recognition that, since this Nation was founded and until the present day, many Americans deem that their own existence must be understood by precepts far beyond the authority of government to alter or define and that willing participation in civic affairs can be consistent with a brief acknowledgment of their belief in a higher power, always with due respect for those who adhere to other beliefs. The prayer in this case has a permissible ceremonial purpose. It is not an unconstitutional establishment of religion.

* * *

The town of Greece does not violate the First Amendment by opening its meetings with prayer that comports with our tradition and does not coerce participation by nonadherents. The judgment of the U.S. Court of Appeals for the Second Circuit is reversed.

It is so ordered.

KENNEDY, J., delivered the opinion of the Court, except as to Part II–B. ROBERTS, C.J., and ALITO, J., joined the opinion in full, and SCALIA and THOMAS, JJ., joined except as to Part II–B. ALITO, J., filed a concurring opinion, in which SCALIA, J., joined. THOMAS, J., filed an opinion concurring in part and concurring in the judgment, in which SCALIA, J., joined as to Part II. BREYER, J., filed a dissenting opinion. KAGAN, J., filed a dissenting opinion, in which GINSBURG, BREYER, and SOTOMAYOR, JJ., joined.

---

2. Judges

Are there unique obligations for Catholic jurists? What happens if the judge is assigned to cases involving areas of great controversy within the Catholic faith, such as abortion, death penalty, divorce, or any of the many other legal issues we have examined to this point? The ABA Model Code of Judicial Conduct requires that "a judge shall hear and decide matters assigned to the judge, except when disqualification is required by Rule 2.11 or other law."[29] Rule 2.11 requires disqualification of a judge where the "judge's impartiality might reasonably be questioned."

---

29. MODEL CODE OF JUD. CONDUCT R. 2.7 (2011).

However, these rules don't allow a judge to decline to hear matters solely because the jurist's Catholic faith has teachings in the area that might run contrary to the law.

One prominent Catholic jurist, Justice Antonin Scalia of the Supreme Court of the United States, expressed the opinion that "I don't think there's any such thing as a Catholic judge. . . . There are good judges and bad judges. The only article in faith that plays any part in my judging is the commandment, 'Thou shalt not lie.'"[30] Justice Scalia believed that his obligation as a jurist was to follow the law and not Catholic teaching. Regarding abortion, for example, he stated "[i]f I genuinely thought the Constitution guaranteed a woman's right to abortion, I would be on the other way . . . it would do nothing with my religion it has to do with me being a lawyer."[31]

While Justice Scalia believed that implementing the law without regard to Catholic faith is required of judges, recall that the Catholic bishops have precluded a federal cabinet secretary, Kathleen Sebelius, from receiving communion based upon her intended promulgation of regulations which would allow for the dissemination of "morning after" pills and the provision of abortion services under the recent health care legislation. What happens if a case comes before a judge that involves not only the application of a principle of Catholic faith, but the potential subjugation of the Catholic Church to a legal judgment? Consider the Catholic Church lawsuits where plaintiffs are alleging that priests and officials of the Catholic Church engaged in or permitted child abuse. Merely being a Catholic would not seem to require that judges recuse themselves from such cases. There had been attempts, however. For example, in a lawsuit against a Cleveland Catholic Diocese, plaintiff's attorney asked to remove Catholic judges from hearing the case and also asked that a non-Catholic Supreme Court justice in Ohio rule on that motion. Following his logic however since more than three-quarters of the local judges where the case was filed and a majority of the members of the Ohio Supreme Court at the time were Catholic, it would have been very difficult to find jurists who could rule on the motion of whether a Catholic judge should be disqualified from hearing a case merely because of his or her religion.[32]

Indeed, removing judges under those circumstances would seem to violate the First Amendment's prohibition against the Establishment of Religion and would interfere with the rights of the individual judges to the Free Exercise of their religion.

These issues are not easily resolved from a theological perspective. Even if the judge continues to hear matters where the law conflicts with Catholic teaching, while the legal requirements might be satisfied, the moral implications are troubling to some.

30. George P. Matysek Jr., *Justice Scalia Urges Christians to Have Courage*, THE CATH. REV. (Jan 19, 2012), https://www.archbalt.org/justice-scalia-urges-christians-to-have-courage/ (last visited Nov. 6, 2017).

31. *Id.*

32. James F. McCarty, *Catholic Judges Unwanted on Case*, CLEVELAND PLAIN DEALER (Sept. 5, 2003), http://www.cleveland.com/abuse/index.ssf?/abuse/more/10627542584070.html. Not available anymore.

For example, Professor Edward Hartnett wrote an article entitled *Catholic Judges and Cooperation in Sin*.[33] He addressed the concerns expressed by some that judges who also happen to be Catholic will ignore Catholic teaching. Others are concerned with the opposite possibility that Catholic judges will apply Catholic teaching and not the law. He addressed the dilemma that Catholic judges will face regarding their obligation to uphold and apply the law and still find peace within their own consciences.[34]

C. The Role of the Church

Pope John Paul II saw a clear role for the bishops in Catholic higher education:

> 28. Bishops have a particular responsibility to promote Catholic Universities, and especially to promote and assist in the preservation and strengthening of their Catholic identity, including the protection of their Catholic identity in relation to civil authorities. This will be achieved more effectively if close personal and pastoral relationships exist between University and Church authorities, characterized by mutual trust, close and consistent cooperation and continuing dialogue. Even when they do not enter directly into the internal governance of the University, Bishops "should be seen not as external agents but as participants in the life of the Catholic University."[35]

Professors Gregory and Russo suggested that American colleges and universities could begin the process of bringing the bishops into the schools with simple strategies such as inviting the bishop to lunch. Other methods of creating a dialogue between bishops and schools could be explored and implemented, including bringing the bishops to the campus from time to time as a visible symbol of the Church's presence.

The USCCB has adopted norms for the application of *Ex Corde Ecclesiae*. It identifies the role of the church as follows:

> 1. *The Local Church*
>
> a. In accordance with Church teaching and the universal law of the Church, the local Bishop has a responsibility to promote the welfare of the Catholic universities in his diocese and to watch over the preservation and strengthening of their Catholic character.[36]

---

33. Edward A. Hartnett, *Catholic Judges and Cooperation in Sin*, 4 U. St. Thomas L.J. 221 (2006).

34. *Id.*

35. Pope John Paul II, *Ex Corde Ecclesiae: Apostolic Constitution of the Supreme Pontiff John Paul II on Catholic Universities* ¶ 28 (Aug. 15, 1990), http://www.vatican.va/holy_father/john_paul_ii /apost_constitutions/documents/hf_jp-ii_apc_15081990_ex-corde-ecclesiae_en.html (last visited Nov. 6, 2017).

36. *Ex Corde Ecclesiae*, Art. 5 § 2. *See also* the responsibilities of the diocesan bishop set forth in canons 392, § 1; 394, § 1; 756, § 2; 810, § 2; 813.

b. Bishops should, when appropriate, acknowledge publicly the service of Catholic universities to the Church and support the institution's Catholic identity if it is unjustifiably challenged.

c. Diocesan and university authorities should commit themselves mutually to regular dialogues to achieve the goals of Ex Corde Ecclesiae according to local needs and circumstances.

d. University authorities and the local diocesan bishop should develop practical methods of collaboration that are harmonious with the university's structure and statutes. Similar forms of collaboration should also exist between the university and the religious institute to which it is related by establishment or tradition.[37]

e. Doctrinal Responsibilities: Approaches to Promoting Cooperation and Resolving Misunderstandings between Bishops and Theologians, approved and published by the National Conference of Catholic Bishops, June 17, 1989, can serve as a useful guide for diocesan bishops, professors of the theological disciplines and administrators of universities to promote informal cooperation and collaboration in the Church's teaching mission and the faithful observance within Catholic universities of the principles of Catholic doctrine.

f. Disputes about Church doctrine should be resolved, whenever possible, in an informal manner. At times, the resolution of such matters may benefit from formal doctrinal dialogue as proposed by Doctrinal Responsibilities and adapted by the parties in question.[38]

---

37. The following are some suggestions for collaboration:
   a. Arranging for the diocesan bishop or his delegate and members of the religious institute to be involved in the university's governance, perhaps through representation on the board of trustees or in some other appropriate manner.
   b. Sharing the university's annual report with the diocesan bishop and the religious institute, especially in regard to matters affecting Catholic identity and the religious institute's charism.
   c. Scheduling regular pastoral visits to the university on the part of the diocesan bishop and the religious institute's leadership and involving the members of the diocese and the institute in campus ministry.
   d. Collaborating on evangelization and on the special works of the religious institute.
   e. Conducting dialogues on matters of doctrine and pastoral practice and on the development of spirituality in accordance with the religious institute's charism.
   f. Resolving issues affecting the university's Catholic identity in accordance with established procedures. (See Ex Corde Ecclesiae, II, Art. 5 §2 and n.51).
   g. Participating together in ecumenical and inter-faith endeavors.
   h. Contributing to the diocesan process of formulating the quinquennial report to the Holy See.

38. See National Conference of Catholic Bishops, Doctrinal Responsibilities: Approaches to Promoting Cooperation and Resolving Misunderstandings between Bishops and Theologians, 16–22 (June 17, 1989) (When such disputes are not resolved within the limits of informal or formal dialogue, they should be addressed in a timely manner by the competent ecclesiastical authority through appropriate doctrinal and administrative actions, taking into account the requirements of the common good and the rights of the individuals and institutions involved.).

g. The National Conference of Catholic Bishops, through an appropriate committee structure, should continue to dialogue and collaborate with the Catholic academic community and its representative associations about ways of safeguarding and promoting the ideals, principles and norms expressed in Ex Corde Ecclesiae.[39]

D. Next Steps

Beyond the Catholic bishops' involvement in the higher education focus of Catholic institutions, the USCCB offered an important overall perspective in a document addressed to all American Catholics. The document is entitled *Forming Consciences for Faithful Citizenship: A Call to Political Responsibility from the Catholic Bishops of the United States.*[40] It is with this perspective that we will conclude our work.

In the newly-released Introduction, the Bishops note that this message "calls Catholics to form their consciences in the light of their Catholic faith and to bring our moral principles to the debate and decisions about candidates and issues."[41] It is explicitly, then, a call to action.

Part I of the document, *Forming Consciences for Faithful Citizenship: The U.S. Bishops' Reflection on Catholic Teaching and Political Life*, includes an acknowledgment of the overlap between the legal system and Church teachings, and the benefit from participation by people of faith:

> . . . [T]he obligation to teach about moral values that should shape our lives, including our public lives, is central to the mission given to the Church by Jesus Christ. Moreover, the United States Constitution protects the right of individual believers and religious bodies to participate and speak out without government interference, favoritism, or discrimination. Civil law should fully recognize and protect the Church's right, obligation, and opportunities to participate in society without being forced to abandon or ignore its central moral convictions. Our nation's tradition of pluralism is enhanced, not threatened, when religious groups and people of faith bring their convictions and concerns into public life.[42]

Part II of the document, *Applying Catholic Teaching to Major Issues: A Summary of Policy Positions of the United States Conference of Catholic Bishops*,[43] identifies

---

39. USCCB, *The Application of Ex Corde Ecclesiae supra* note 9.

40. USCCB, *Forming Consciences for Faithful Citizenship: A Call to Political Responsibility from the Catholic Bishops of the United States* (2011) [hereinafter USCCB, *Forming Consciences for Faithful Citizenship*], http://usccb.org/issues-and-action/faithful-citizenship/upload/forming-consciences-for -faithful-citizenship.pdf *and* http://usccb.org/issues-and-action/faithful-citizenship/forming-con sciences-for-faithful-citizenship-document.cfm (last visited Nov. 6, 2017).

41. *Id.*

42. *Id.* at ¶ 11, 3–4.

43. *Id.* at 19.

specific areas where the Bishops believe that "significant moral dimensions" are involved. In some of these areas, such as "the fundamental right to life," the Bishops conclude that there are principles that can never be violated. Others reflect the Bishops' judgment about the "best way to apply Catholic principles to policy issues."

Part II includes the three broad headings of Human Life, Family Life, Social Justice, and Global Solidarity. In the first paragraph under Part II the bishops summarize their position on life issues:

> Our 1998 statement *Living the Gospel of Life* declares, "**Abortion and euthanasia** have become preeminent threats to human life and dignity because they directly attack life itself, the most fundamental good and the condition for all others" . . . **Abortion**, the deliberate killing of a human being before birth, is never morally acceptable and must always be opposed. **Cloning** and **destruction of human embryos** for research or even for potential cures are always wrong. The purposeful taking of human life by **assisted suicide and euthanasia** is not an act of mercy, but an unjustifiable assault on human life. **Genocide, torture,** and the **direct and intentional targeting of noncombatants in war or terrorist attacks** are always wrong.[44]

The statement goes on to address biotechnology, the use of military force, and the spread of nuclear, chemical, and biological weapons. In the last paragraph in this section, the bishops urge the end of the death penalty. Pending its abolition, they urge that its use be restrained. Use of DNA evidence and issues related to unfairness in the application of the death penalty are included in the list of restraints. And, the bishops specifically include "access to effective counsel" as an important restraint. In this latter regard, see also, Bill Piatt, *Reinventing the Wheel: Constructing Ethical Approaches to State Indigent Legal Defense Systems.*[45]

Also in Part II, the bishops address issues related to "Family Life."[46] Included herein are the topics of the sanctity of marriage, the protection of children, and the right of parents to choose education for their children, including the obligation of the Government to provide tax credits and scholarships to allow parents of modest means to send their children to private schools. The bishops also discuss the necessity of protecting against pornography in the media and over the internet.

Finally, Part II covers Social Justice issues including wages, welfare policy, health care, housing, and access to food.[47] Importantly, the bishops also express concern that faith-based groups be allowed to continue to partner with the Government in providing for the poor. The bishops support conscience clauses, prohibiting

---

44. *Id.* at ¶ 64, 19 (emphasis in original).
45. Bill Piatt, *Reinventing the Wheel: Constructing Ethical Approaches to State Indigent Legal Defense Systems*, 2 ST. MARY'S J. LEGAL MAL. & ETHICS 372 (2012).
46. USCCB, *Forming Consciences for Faithful Citizenship supra* note 40, at 21.
47. *Id.* at 22.

Government from requiring Catholics or Catholic institutions to have to compromise their moral convictions in order to participate in these programs.

Part II's conclusion involves global solidarity, addressing concerns of global poverty, religious liberty, torture, the role of the United States as a supporter of the United Nations and other matters, including the concept of protection of those fleeing persecution.[48]

In Part III, *Goals for Political Life: Challenges for Citizens, Candidates, and Public Officials*,[49] Catholics are urged to challenge candidates and public officials, by asking how they will address ten important issues. The bishops note that not all of these are of equal moral weight. The first goal listed is to "[a]ddress the preeminent requirement to protect the weakest in our midst—innocent unborn children—by restricting and bringing to an end the destruction of unborn children through abortion."[50]

Nine other goals follow. The second includes the need to prevent our country from espousing violence as a means of addressing problems. In this regard the bishops oppose euthanasia, assisted suicide, destruction of human embryos, death penalty, and "imprudent resort to war." The third concerns the institution of marriage, between one man and one woman. The fourth involves comprehensive immigration reform. Fifth is the need to overcome poverty, followed by the sixth, health care. Seven requires opposition to discrimination. The eighth goal includes the need for a partnership between government and individuals and groups to address issues of social concern. The institution of "moral limits on the use of military force" commands the ninth goal. Finally, the bishops urge us in uniting with others on a global level to address liberty and justice, and "care for creation."

Forming Consciences contains a listing of *Major Catholic Statements on Public Life and Moral Issues*.[51] You, the reader of *Catholic Legal Perspectives*, are encouraged to consult the statements on that list in order to continue the work you have begun through this book.

E. For Further Thought

1. What issues should organizations of Catholic attorneys seek to address? How?

2. Would it be proper for Catholic judges to consider the teachings of the Catholic Church in the handling of cases brought before them? Do you think they do?

3. What should a Catholic attorney do if presented with an issue in a case which runs contrary to that attorney's conscience? Consider the definitions of "conscience." The USCCB tells us, "[c]onscience is not something that allows us to justify doing

---

48. *Id.* at 26.
49. *Id.* at 29.
50. *Id.* at 29.
51. *Id.* at 33–36.

whatever we want, nor is it a mere 'feeling' about what we should or should not do. Rather, conscience is the voice of God resounding in the human heart, revealing the truth to us and calling us to do what is good while shunning what is evil. Conscience always requires serious attempts to make sound moral judgments based on the truths of our faith."[52] Cardinal Ratzinger assigned *imprimatur* to the following:

> Conscience, as "moral judgement" and as "moral imperative," constitutes the final evaluation of an act as good or evil before God. In effect, only God knows the moral value of each human act, even if the Church, like Jesus, can and must classify, judge, and sometimes condemn some kinds of action (*cf.* Mt 18:15-18).[53]

4. How should a Catholic judge rule in a case where the law runs contrary to the teachings of the Catholic Church? Would it make any difference if the application of the law would also violate the judge's conscience?

5. In 2014, six of the nine justices on the Supreme Court of the United States were Catholic. These included Chief Justice Roberts, and Justices Alito, Kennedy, Scalia, Sotomayor, and Thomas. Justice Scalia died on February 13, 2016, and his seat was filled in 2017 by Neil Gorsuch. Justice Gorsuch was also raised Catholic, although he also worships with his wife and daughters in the Episcopal Church. Are you aware of any opinions by any of these justices which indicate that the particular Justice(s) applied Catholic principles in arriving at a decision? Are there decisions which, even if not explicitly citing a Catholic source, are nonetheless consistent with the approach of the Church to that particular issue? Are you aware of any written opinions by any of these justices which demonstrate a departure from the Catholic perspectives identified throughout this book? If legislative officials can be denied communion because of their approaches to issues, should judicial officials be treated in a similar manner? Or is there some difference in the actions of the legislative branch as opposed to the judicial branch which might warrant different treatment by the Church?

6. Under what circumstances, if any, could a Catholic, as a matter of conscience, come to a conclusion different than that of the Church on some matter of moral concern?

7. What criteria should be utilized in the hiring, promotion, and retention decisions in Catholic universities? How should these differ if at all, from the criteria at public institutions?

8. To what extent should students in Catholic institutions be exposed to Catholic teachings? Is there a difference whether you are an undergraduate student or graduate student?

---

52. *Id.* at ¶ 18, 7.

53. International Theological Commission, *Memory and Reconciliation: The Church and the Faults of the Past* (Dec. 1999), http://www.vatican.va/roman_curia/congregations/cfaith/cti _documents/rc_con_cfaith_doc_20000307_ memory-reconc-itc_en.html (last visited Nov. 6, 2017).

9. Should the Catholic Church or its officials become involved in attempting to influence government action in any of the areas mentioned in this book?

10. What weight, if any, should political leaders give to the recommendations offered by the Catholic Church or its officials as noted in Question 9?

11. After your reading of the materials in this book, has your understanding of either the law or the Catholic Church's positions in those areas changed? In what way(s)? Will this impact your professional role after graduation? If so, how?

Selected Bibliography

Books

Patrick W. Carey, Catholics in America: A History (2004).

Thomas A. Howard, The Pope and the Professor (2017).

Bill Piatt, ¿Only English? Law and Language Policy in the United States (1993).

Leslie J. Reagan, When Abortion Was a Crime: Women, Medicine, and Law in the United States, 1867–1973 (Univ. of Cal. Press, 1997).

Peter Steinfels, A People Adrift: The Crisis of the Roman Catholic Church in America (2d ed. Aug. 2003).

Articles

Paul Axel-Lute, *Same-Sex Marriage: A Selective Bibliography of the Legal Literature* (last updated Dec. 12, 2007), http://lawevents.rutgers.edu/resources/SSM.php.

Robert H. Bork, *Stop Courts from Imposing Gay Marriage*, Wall St. J. (Aug. 7, 2011), http://www.aei.org/article/13064.

Howard Bromberg, *Pope John Paul II, Vatican II, and Capital Punishment*, 6 Ave Maria L. Rev. 109 (2007).

Daniel Burke, *Kansas Gov. Sebelius Told Not to Take Communion*, USA Today (May 13, 2006), http://www.usatoday.com/news/religion/2008-05-12-communion-abortion_N.htm.

Michael W. Chapman, *NYC: More Black Babies Killed by Abortion Than Born*, CNSNews.com (Feb. 20, 2014, 12:31 PM), http://www.cnsnews.com/news/article/michael-w-chapman/nyc-more-black-babies-killed-abortion-born.

Catholics for Immigration Reduction, Conservative Heritage Times, http://www.conservativetimes.org/Conservative_Resources/CatholicsAgainstAmnesty.htm (last visited Mar. 9, 2014).

Art C. Cody, *The King's Good Servants: Catholics as Participants in Capital Litigation*, 44 J. Cath. Legal Stud. 283 (2005).

Susan A. Cohen, *Abortion and Mental Health: Myths and Realities*, Guttmacher Pol. Rev. (Summer 2006), http://www.guttmacher.org/pubs/gpr/09/3/gpr090308.html.

Bryan Cones, *Catholics Say "I Do" to Gay Marriage*, U.S. CATHOLIC (Mar. 24, 2011), http://www.uscatholic.org/blog/2011/03/catholics-say-i-do-gay-marriage.

Larry Cunningham, *Can a Catholic Lawyer Represent a Minor Seeking a Judicial Bypass for an Abortion? A Moral and Canon Law Analysis*, 44 J. CATH LEGAL STUD. 379 (2005).

Carmen DeNavas-Walt, Bernadette D. Proctor, & Jessica C. Smith, *Income, Poverty, and Health Insurance Coverage in the United States: 2010*, U.S. CENSUS BUREAU (Sept. 2011), http://www.diocese-kcsj.org/_docs/Joint-Pastoral-Health-Care-Reform -08-09.pdf.

To Eliminate "Scandal" of Hunger Pope Says Each Person Can Adjust Consumption, CATH. NEWS AGENCY (Nov. 13, 2006), http://www.catholicnewsagency.com/news /to_help_eliminate_scandal_of_hunger_pope_says_each_person_can_adjust _consumption/.

Euthanasia Program, U.S. HOLOCAUST MEMORIAL MUSEUM, http://www.ushmm.org /wlc/en/article.php?ModuleId=10005200 (last visited Mar. 18, 2014).

Lawrence B. Finer, et al., *Reasons U.S. Women Have Abortions: Quantitative and Qualitative Perspectives*, PERSPECTIVES ON SEXUAL AND REPRODUCTIVE HEALTH, 110 (Sept. 2005), http://www.guttmacher.org/pubs/journals/3711005.pdf.

Maggie Gallagher, *Issues: Marriage and Family*, CATHOLICVOTE.ORG, http://www .catholicvote.org/index.php?/site/issues_details/marriage_and_family/ (last visited Mar. 17, 2014).

John Garvey, *Divorce, the Death Penalty, & the Pope*, COMMONWEAL 10 (Apr. 19, 2002); Garvey, John, *Law & Morality*, COMMONWEAL 129.8 (2002): 10. Academic Search Complete. Web. 20 Mar. 2014.

John H. Garvey & Amy V. Coney, *Catholic Judges in Capital Cases*, 81 MARQ. L. REV. 303 (1998).

Mary Ann Glendon, *Principled Immigration*, FIRST THINGS, 23 (June — July 2006), http://www.firstthings.com/article/2007/12/principled-immigration.

J.M. Greene, *Localization: Implementing the Right to Food*, 14 DRAKE J. AGRIC. L. 377 (2009).

Dave Harmon, *UT Student's Outlook: "I Could Do Anything I Wanted To Do,"* AUSTIN AMERICAN-STATESMAN (Nov. 13, 2011), http://www.utexas.edu/law/clinics /immigration/news_pdfs/UT_students_outlook_statesman_2011_11_13.pdf.

Edward A. Hartnett, *Catholic Judges & Cooperation in Sin*, 4 U. ST. THOMAS L. J. 221 (2006).

HealthCare.gov, *Provisions of the Affordable Care Act By Year*, http://www.healthcare .gov/law/timeline/full.html (last visited Mar. 13, 2014).

Gina Holland, *Justice Scalia Questions Catholic Platform Against Death Penalty*, ASSOC. PRESS (Feb. 5, 2002), http://www.beliefnet.com/Faiths/Catholic/2002/02/Justice -Scalia-Questions-Catholic-Platform-Against-Death-Penalty.aspx.

Immigration Policy Center, *Giving Facts a Fighting Chance*, Am. Immigration Coun. (Oct. 2010), http://www.immigrationpolicy.org/special-reports/giving-facts-fight ing-chance-answers-toughest-immigration-questions.

Terence P. Jeffrey, *Catholic Bishops on Obamacare Reg: 'Unprecedented Attack on Religious Liberty,' Even Jesus Wouldn't Qualify as 'Religious,'* Catholic News Serv. (Sept. 25, 2011), http://cnsnews.com/news/article/catholic-bishops-obamacare-reg -unprecedented-attack-religious-liberty-even-jesus.

Justice for Immigrants, *Frequently Asked Questions About the Catholic Church's Position on Immigration*, (Aug. 22, 2005), http://www.justiceforimmigrants.org/facts .shtml.

Justice for Immigrants, *Immigration and the Economy*, (Dec. 2009), http://www .justiceforimmigrants.org/documents/immigration-and-the-economy.pdf.

Nuala P. Kenny, O.C., *The Good of Health Care: Justice and Health Reform*, Cath. Health Assoc. (Winter 2011), http://files.ctewc.gethifi.com/resources/publi cations/articles/Kenny_and_Miller_articles.pdf.

Donald Kerwin, *Immigration Reform and the Catholic Church*, Catholic Legal Immigration Network, Inc. (May, 2006), http://www.migrationinformation.org /Feature/display.cfm?id=395.

Theodore Kim & Emily Bazar, *Immigration Becomes KKK Rallying Point*, USA Today (Feb. 8, 2007), http://www.usatoday.com/news/nation/2007-02-08-kkk-immig ration_x.htm.

Sophia Kishkovsky, *Russia Enacts Law Opposing Abortion*, N.Y. Times (July 15, 2011), http://www.nytimes.com/2011/07/15/world/europe/15iht-russia15.html?_r=0.

The Knights' Party Platform, *KKK*, http://www.kkk.bz/program.htm (last visited Mar. 14, 2014).

Randy Lee, *Finding Marriage Amidst a Sea of Confusion: A Precursor to Considering the Public Purpose of Marriage*, 43 Cath. Law. 339 (2004).

Augustinus Lehmkuhl, *Divorce (in Moral Theology)*, Catholic Encyclopedia (New Advent ed.), http://www.newadvent.org/cathen/05054c.htm (last visited Mar. 14, 2014).

Adam Liptak, *Supreme Court Is Asked to Rule on Health Care*, N.Y. Times (Sept. 28, 2011), http://www.nytimes.com/2011/09/29/us/justice-dept-asks-supreme-court -for-health-care-ruling.html.

E. Michael McCann, *Opposing Capital Punishment: A Prosecutor's Perspective*, 79 Marq. L. Rev. 649 (1996).

Rev. C.J. McCloskey, III, *Private Charity Versus Government Welfare*, Crisis Magazine (May 10, 2011), http://www.crisismagazine.com/2011/private-charity-versus -government-welfare.

Benjamin Mann, *Bishops' Supporter Sees Misguided Zeal in Anti-Immigrant Push*, Catholic News Agency (May 18, 2011), http://www.catholicnewsagency.com /news/bishops-supporter-sees-misguided-zeal-in-anti-immigrant-push/.

The Murder of the Handicapped, U.S. HOLOCAUST MEMORIAL MUSEUM, http://www
.ushmm.org/outreach/en/article.php?ModuleId=10007683 (last visited Nov. 17,
2011).

Fr. Thomas Nairn, O.F.M., *Catholics Understand Health Care as a Right*, HEALTH
PROGRESS (Mar—Apr. 2010), http://www.chausa.org/docs/default-source/health
-progress/catholics-understand-health-care-as-a-right-pdf.pdf?sfvrsn=0.

Christine Newman, *Catholic Theologian Tells of Pro-Choice Tradition*, IRISH TIMES
(May 27, 2005), http://www.religiousconsultation.org/News_Tracker/Catholic
_theologian_tells_ of_pro-choice_tradition.htm.

Kenneth R. Overberg, S.J., *The Death Penalty: Why the Church Speaks a Counter-
cultural Message*, AMERICAN CATHOLIC, http://www.americancatholic.org/News
letters/CU/ac0195.asp (last visited Mar. 14, 2014).

Philip Pullella, *Catholic Politicians Must Oppose Gay Marriage: Pope*, THOMSON
REUTERS (Mar. 13, 2007), http://www.reuters.com/article/2007/03/13/us-pope
-idUSN1340012320070313.

Report: Catholics Support Gay Rights, UPI (Mar. 23, 2011), http://www.upi.com/Top
_News/US/2011/03/23/Report-Catholics-support-gay-rights/UPI-16541300908919/.

Victor C. Romero, *An "Other" Christian Perspective on* Lawrence v. Texas, 45 J. OF
CATH LEGAL STUDIES 115 (2007).

Robert Ruby & Allison Pond, *An Enduring Majority: Americans Continue to Support
the Death Penalty*, PEW FORUM ON RELIGION & PUBLIC LIFE (Sept. 2010), http://
www.pewforum.org/uploadedFiles/Topics/Issues/Politics_and_Elections/immi
gration-environment-views-fullreport.pdf.

Susan J. Stabile, *Catholic Legal Theory*, 44 J. OF CATH. LEGAL STUDIES 421 (2006).

D. Paul Sullins, *American Catholic and Same-Sex "Marriage,"* 15 CATH. SOC. SCIENCE
REV. 97 (2010), http://cssronline.org/CSSR/Archival/2010/Sullins-Article.pdf.

Phillip Thompson, *Silent Protest: A Catholic Justice Dissents in* Buck v. Bell, 43 CATH.
LAW. 125 (2004).

Patrick Wall, *New York Gay Marriage Bill: Could Catholics Play a Decisive Role?*,
CHRISTIAN SCIENCE MONITOR (June 24, 2011), http://www.csmonitor.com
/USA/Politics/2011/0624/New-York-gay-marriage-bill-Could-Catholics-play-a
-decisive-role.

John Zmirak, *Amnesty Equals Abortion*, CRISIS MAGAZINE (May 12, 2011), http://
www.crisismagazine.com/2011/amnesty-equals-abortion.

Reports

Amnesty International, *Death Sentences and Executions 2010* (Mar. 2011), http://www
.amnestyusa.org/our-work/issues/death-penalty/international-death-penalty
/death- penalty-statistics-2010.

Bureau Of Justice Statistics, Off. Of Justice Programs, U.S. Dep't Of Justice, No. NCJ 248448, *Capital Punishment—Statistical Tables*, 2013, tbl. 1, at 6. (Dec. 2014), https://www.bjs.gov/content/pub/pdf/cp13st.pdf (last visited Oct. 17, 2017).

Catholics for Choice, Truth & Consequences: A Look Behind the Vatican's Ban on Contraception (2008), http://www.catholicsforchoice.org/topics/reform /documents/TruthConsequencesFINAL.pdf.

CBO, The Impact of Unauthorized Immigrants on the Budgets of State and Local Governments (Dec. 2007), http://www.cbo.gov/ftpdocs/87xx/doc8711/12 -6-Immigration.pdf.

Center for Nutrition Pol. & Promotion, The Low-Cost, Moderate-Cost, and Liberal Food Plans 2007, USDA (Nov. 2007), http://www.cnpp.usda.gov/Pub lications/FoodPlans/MiscPubs/FoodPlans2007AdminReport.pdf.

Dep't of Health & Human Servs., 2011 Federal Poverty Guidelines (Jan. 21, 2011), http://aspe.hhs.gov/poverty/11poverty.shtml.

Dep't of Homeland Security, Off. Of Immigration Statistics, Policy Directorate, Estimates of the Unauthorized Immigrant Population Residing in the United States: January 2010, 1 (Feb. 2011), http://www.dhs.gov/xlibrary /assets/statistics/publications/ois_ill_pe_2010.pdf.

Dep't Of State, Bureau Of Consular Affairs, Visa Bulletin, No. 11, Vol. X, Immigrant Numbers for November 2017, tbl. 2 (Nov. 2017), https://travel.state .gov/content/visas/en/law-and-policy/bulletin/2018/visa-bulletin-for-november -2017.html.

Forced Apart (by the Numbers): Non-Citizens Deported for Mostly Non-violent Offenses, Human Rights Watch (Apr. 15, 2009), http://www.hrw .org/reports/2009/04/15/forced-apart-numbers-0.

FRAC (Food Research and Action Center), Cost of Food, http://frac.org/reports -and-resources/cost-of-food/ (last visited Mar. 13, 2014).

FRAC, Food Hardship in America 2010: Data for the Nation, States 100 MSAs, and Every Congressional District (Mar. 2011), http://frac.org/wp-content /uploads/2011/03/food_hardship_report_mar2011.pdf.

FRAC, Poverty Data 2008 (Sept. 2011), http://frac.org/reports-and-resources /hunger-and-poverty/.

FRAC, SNAP/FoodStamp Monthly Participation Data 2011, http://frac.org /reports-and-resources/snapfood-stamp-monthly-participation-data/ (last visited Mar. 14, 2014).

Guttmacher Institute, U.S. Abortion Rate Hits Lowest Level Since 1973 (Feb. 2014), http://www.guttmacher.org/media/nr/2014/02/03/index.html.

Stanley K. Henshaw & Kathryn Kost, Trends in the Characteristics of Women Obtaining Abortions, 1974 to 2004, Guttmacher Inst. (Aug. 2008),

http://www.guttmacher.org/pubs/2008/09/18/Report_Trends_Women_Obtain
ing_Abortions.pdf.

Oregon Public Health Division, Death with Dignity Act Annual Report
Year 13 (Jan. 25, 2011), DeathwithDignityAct/Documents/year13.pdf.

Planned Parenthood Fed. of Am., Fact Sheet: Planned Parenthood by the
Numbers (updated Oct. 2011) http://www.plannedparenthood.org/files/PPFA/PP
_by_the_ Numbers.pdf.

Public Opinion on the Death Penalty, Pew Forum on Religion & Public Life
(Sept. 2011), http://pewforum.org/Death-Penalty/Public-Opinion-on-the-Death
-Penalty.aspx.

Responsible Reform for the Middle Class, The Patient Protection and
Affordable Care Act: Detailed Summary, http://dpc.senate.gov/healthre
formbill/healthbill04.pdf (last visited Nov. 12, 2011).

U.N., Yearbook of the United Nations: 1948–1949, available at http://www.
unhcr.org/cgi-bin/texis/vtx/home/opendocPDFViewer.html?docid=4e1ee
7620&query=Indigenous%20Peoples (providing a history of the Universal Declaration of Human Rights).

U.S. Census Bureau, The 2012 Statistical Abstract: Abortion Statistics
(Sept. 28, 2011), http://www.census.gov/compendia/statab/cats/births_deaths
_marriages_divorces/family_planning_abortions.html (last visited Mar. 15, 2014).

USDA, Official USDA Food Plans: Cost of Food at Four Levels, U.S. Average, June 2011 (July 2011), http://www.cnpp.usda.gov/Publications/FoodPlans
/2011/CostofFoodJun 2011.pdf.

Statements & Press Releases

Office of Public Affairs, *U.S. Dep't of Justice, Statement of the Attorney General on
Litigation Involving the Defense of Marriage Act* (Feb. 23, 2011), http://www.justice
.gov/opa/pr/2011/February/11-ag-222.html.

Office of Public Affairs, Admin. For Children & Families, U.S. Dep't of Health &
Human Services, *Remarks for David Hansell: Meeting of Parents and Friends of
Lesbians and Gays, the National Black Justice Coalition, and the Family Equality
Council* (May 3, 2011), http://letsstrengthenmarriage.org/images/research/LSM
-USCCBLetertoPresidentObama-DOMA-9-20-11.pdf.

President Barack Obama, *Presidential Proclamation — Mother's Day* (May 6, 2011),
http://m.whitehouse.gov/the-press-office/2011/05/06/presidential-proclamation
-mothers-day.

President Barack Obama, *Presidential Proclamation — Father's Day* (June 17, 2011),
http://m.whitehouse.gov/the-press-office/2011/06/17/presidential-proclamation
-fathers-day.

Statement of the Bishops of New York State, *Statement of the Bishops of New York State on same-sex "marriage" vote*, (June 24, 2011), http://www.nyscatholic.org/2011/06/statement-of-the-bishops-of-new-york-state-on-same-sex-marriage-vote/.

USCCB, *Archbishop Dolan Calls Refusal to Defend Defense of Marriage Act an 'Alarming and Grave Injustice,'* (Mar. 3, 2011), http://www.usccb.org/news/archived.cfm?release Number=11-043.

USCCB, *Attacks on DOMA Threaten Marriage, Church-State Relationship, Warns Archbishop Dolan in Letter to President,'* (Sept. 22, 2011), http://www.usccb.org/news/2011/11-179.cfm.

Roman Catholic Church Publications & Documents

Amoris Laetitia, Vatican Press, *Post-Synodal Apostolic Exhortation Amoris Laetitia Of The Holy Father Francis* (Mar. 19, 2016), https://w2.vatican.va/content/dam/francesco/pdf/apost _exhortations/documents/papa-francesco_esortazione-ap_20160319_amoris-laetitia_en.pdf (last visited Oct. 11, 2017).

Archdiocese of Denver, *The Teaching of the Catholic Church on Divorce*, http://www.archden.org/tribunal/documents/divorce.htm (last visited Mar. 14, 2014).

J. Kevin Appleby, *Church Urges Humane, Comprehensive Solution to Immigration Issue*, Faithful Citizenship, http://www.catholicnewsagency.com/resources/politics/issues/church-urges-humane-comprehensive-solution-to-immigration-issue/ (last visited Mar. 14, 2014).

William Biernatski, S. J., Plenaria *'97: Tendencies Within U.S.A. Culture*, Centre for the Study of Communication & Culture (1997), http://www.vatican.va/roman_curia/pontifical_councils/cultr/documents/rc_pc_cultr_01031995_doc_i-1995-ple_en.html#1.

Catechism of the Cath. Church, *The Profession of Faith: Christ's Faithful— Hierarchy, Laity, Consecrated Life*, 2383 (1993), http://www.vatican.va/archive/ENG0015/__P2A.HTM.

Catholic Bishops of the Texas-Mexican Border, *Family Beyond Borders An Open Letter from the Bishops of the Border Region of Mexico, Texas, and New Mexico*, Texas Catholic Conference (Dec. 9, 2013), http://www.txcatholic.org/news/399-catholic-bishops-publish-letter-on-immigration-and-family.

Catechism of the Cath. Church, *Article 5: The Fifth Commandment* (1993), http://www.vatican.va/archive/ENG0015/__P7Z.HTM.

Catechism of the Cath. Church, *Article 6: The Sixth Commandment* (1993), http://www.vatican.va/archive/ccc_css/archive/catechism/p3s2c2a6.htm.

Catechism of the Cath. Church, *Article 7: The Sacrament of Matrimony* (1993), http://www.vatican.va/archive/ccc_css/archive/catechism/p2s2c3a7.htm.

Congregation for the Doctrine of the Faith, *Instruction Dignitas Personae on Certain Bioethical Questions* (June 20, 2008), http://www.vatican.va/roman_curia/con gregations/cfaith/documents/rc_con_cfaith_doc_20081208_dignitas-personae _en.html.

Francis Cardinal George, O.M.I., Archbishop of Chicago, *Letter to President-elect Barack Obama*, USCCB (Jan. 16, 2009), http://www.zenit.org/en/articles/cardinal -george-s-letter-to-obama.

Holy See, *Declaration of the Holy See to the First World Congress on the Death Penalty* (June 2001), http://www.vatican.va/archive/ENG0015/__P7Z.HTM.

Bishop William F. Murphy, *Letter to the United States Senate on Child Tax Credit and the Earned Income Tax Credit*, USCCB, Comm. on Domestic Justice & Human Dev. (Sept. 20, 2010), www.usccb.org/issues-and-action/human-life-and-dignity /federal-budget/upload/2010-20-09-ltr-murphy-taxcredits.pdf.

Bishop William F. Murphy, et al., *Letter to Congressional Leaders*, USCCB, et al. (Aug. 3, 2010), http://www.usccb.org/issues-and-action/human-life-and-dignity /agriculture-nutrition-rural-issues/upload/2010-08-03-ltr-congress-child-nutri -reauthorize.pdf (urging reauthorization of the Child Nutrition bill).

Archibishop Joseph F. Naumann & Bishop Robert W. Finn, *Open Letter to the Faithful: Principles of Catholic Social Teaching and Health Care Reform*, Archdiocese of Kansas City in Kansas and The Dioceses of Kansas City-St. Joseph (Aug. 22, 2009), http://www.diocese-kcsj.org/_docs/Joint-Pastoral-Health-Care-Reform-08-09. pdf.

Pontifical Council for the Family, *Partial Birth Abortions: Reflections by Cardinal Alfonso López Trujillo* (1993), http://www.vatican.va/roman_curia/pontifical _councils/family/documents/rc_pc_family_doc_20030331_partial-birth-abortion _en.html.

Pontifical Council for the Family, Family, *Marriage, & "De Facto" Unions*, VATICAN (Jul. 26, 2000), http://www.vatican.va/roman_curia/pontifical_councils/family /documents/rc_ pc_family_doc_20001109_de-facto-unions_en.html.

Pope Benedict XVI, *Address at a Meeting on Family and Life Issues in Latin America* (Dec. 3, 2005), http://www.vatican.va/holy_father/benedict_xvi/speeches/2005 /december/documents/hf_ben_xvi_spe_20051203_family-america-latina_en .html.

Pope Benedict XVI, *Address to the Participants in the Symposium on the Theme "Stem Cells: What Future for Therapy?,"* Organized by the Pontifical Academy for Life (Sept. 16, 2006), http://www.vatican.va/holy_father/benedict_xvi/speeches/2006 /september/documents/hf_ben-xvi_spe_20060916_pav_en.html.

Pope Benedict XVI, *Message at Weekly Angelus* (Nov. 12, 2006), http://www.vatican .va/holy_father/benedict_xvi/angelus/2006/documents/hf_ben-xvi_ang _20061112_en.html.

Pope Benedict XVI, *Homily* (Jan. 1, 2007), http://www.vatican.va/holy_father /benedict_xvi/homilies/2007/documents/hf_ben-xvi_hom_20070101_world-day -peace_en.html.

Pope Benedict XVI, *Message at Weekly Angelus* (Feb. 4, 2007), http://www.vatican .va/holy_father/benedict_xvi/angelus/2007/documents/hf_ben-xvi_ang _20070204_en.html.

Pope Benedict XVI, *Apostolic Exhortation Sacramentum caritatis* 98 (Feb. 22, 2007), http://www.vatican.va/holy_father/benedict_xvi/apost_exhortations/docu ments/hf_ben-xvi_exh_20070222_sacramentum-caritatis_en.html.

Pope Benedict XVI, *Message at Weekly Angelus* (May 25, 2008), http://www.vatican .va/holy_father/benedict_xvi/angelus/2008/documents/hf_ben-xvi_ang _20080525_en.html.

Pope Benedict XVI, *Meeting with French Episcopal Conference* (Sept. 14, 2008), http:// www.vatican.va/holy_father/benedict_xvi/speeches/2008/september/documents /hf_ben-xvi_spe_20080914_lourdes-vescovi_en.html.

Pope Benedict XVI, *Address to the Members of the Pontifical Academy for Life on the Occasion of the 15th General Assembly* (Feb. 21, 2009), http://www.vatican.va/holy _father/benedict_xvi/speeches/2009/february/documents/hf_ben-xvi_spe _20090221_accademia-vita_en.html.

Pope Benedict XVI, *Encyclical Letter Caritas in Veritate* (June 29, 2009), http://www .vatican.va/holy_father/benedict_xvi/encyclicals/documents/hf_ben-xvi_enc _20090629_caritas-in-veritate_en.html.

Pope Benedict XVI, *Message to Participants in the 25th International Conference* Organized by the Pontifical Council for Health Care Workers (Nov. 15, 2010), http://www.vatican.va/holy_father/benedict_xvi/letters/2010/documents/hf _ben-xvi_let_20101115_op-sanitari_en.html.

Pope John Paul II, *Evangelium Vitae: On the Value and Inviolability of Human Life* (Mar. 1995), http://www.vatican.va/holy_father/john_paul_ii/encyclicals /documents/hf_jp-ii_enc_25031995_evangelium-vitae_en.html.

Pope John Paul II, *Address to the Bishops of the Episcopal Conference of the United States of America* (California, Nevada, and Hawaii) (Oct. 2, 1998), http://www.vatican .va/holy_father/john_paul_ii/speeches/1998/october/documents/hf_jp-ii_spe _19981002_ad-limina-usa_en.html.

Pope John Paul II, *Papal Message for the 87th World Day of Migration 2001* (Feb. 13, 2001), http://www.vatican.va/holy_father/john_paul_ii/messages/migration/docu ments/hf_jp-ii_mes_20010213_world-migration-day-2001_en.html.

Pope John Paul II, *Address to the Prelate Auditors*, Official, and Advocates of the Tribunal of the Roman Rota ¶ 9 (Jan. 28, 2002), http://www.vatican.va/holy_father /john_paul_ii/speeches/2002/january/documents/hf_jp-ii_spe_20020128 _roman-rota_en.html (emphasis in original).

Pope Pius XI, Casti Connubii: *Encyclical on Christian Marriage to the Venerable Brethren, Patriarchs, Primates, Archbishops, Bishops, and Other Local Ordinaries Enjoying Peace and Communion With the Apostolic See* (Dec. 31, 1930), http://www.vatican.va/holy_father/pius_xi/encyclicals/documents/hf_p-xi_enc_31121930_casti-connubii_en.html.

Sacred Congregation for the Doctrine of the Faith, *Declaration on Procured Abortion* (Nov. 18, 1974), http://www.vatican.va/roman_curia/congregations/cfaith/documents/rc_con_cfaith_doc_19741118_declaration-abortion_en.html.

Cynthia M. Smith, Esq., *Issue Briefing Series, Issue #1: Why Don't They Come Here Legally?*, Off. of Migration Pol'y & Pub. Affairs, USCCB, http://www.usccb.org/issues-and-action/human-life-and-dignity/immigration/whydonttheycomeherelegally.cfm (last visited Mar. 15, 2014).

Cynthia M. Smith, Esq., *Issue Briefing Series, Issue #2: Birthright Citizenship: The Real Story*, Off. of Migration Pol'y & Pub. Affairs, USCCB, http://www.usccb.org/issues-and-action/human-life-and-dignity/immigration/whydonttheycomeherelegally.cfm (last visited Mar. 19, 2014).

Statement of the Bishops of N.Y. State, N.Y. State Catholic Conf., June 24, 2011, http://www.nyscatholic.org/2011/06/a-message-to-catholic-new-yorkers-from-the-bishops-of-new-york-state/ (defining marriage as a union between a man and a woman).

USCCB, *Catholic Campaign to End the Use of the Death Penalty* (2005), http://www.usccb.org/issues-and-action/human-life-and-dignity/death-penalty-capital-punishment/upload/5-723DEATHBI.pdf.

USCCB, *Catholic Church's Position on Immigration Reform* (Aug. 2013), http://www.usccb.org/issues-and-action/human-life-and-dignity/immigration/churchteachingonimmigrationreform.cfm.

USCCB, *Cover the Uninsured Week* (2009), http://www.usccb.org/issues-and-action/human-life-and-dignity/health-care/cover-the-uninsured-week.cfm.

USCCB, *The Culture of Life and the Penalty of Death* (2005), http://www.usccb.org/issues-and-action/human-life-and-dignity/death-penalty-capital-punishment/upload/penaltyofdeath.pdf.

USCCB, *Forming Consciences: A Call to Political Responsibility from the Catholic Bishops of the United States* (2011), http://usccb.org/issues-and-action/faithful-citizenship/upload/forming-consciences-for-faithful-citizenship.pdf *and* http://usccb.org/issues-and-action/faithful-citizenship/forming-consciences-for-faithful-citizenship-document.cfm.

USCCB, *Love and Life in the Divine Plan* (Nov. 2009), http://www.usccb.org/issues-and-action/marriage-and-family/marriage/love-and-life/upload/Love-and-Life-Abridged-Version.pdf.

USCCB, *Pastoral Plan for Pro-Life Activities: A Campaign in Support of Life* (2001), http://www.usccb.org/about/pro-life-activities/pastoral-plan-prolife-activities.cfm.

USCCB, *Welcoming the Stranger Among Us: Unity in Diversity* (Nov. 15, 2000), http:// www.usccb.org/issues-and-action/cultural-diversity/pastoral-care-of-migrants -refugees-and-travelers/resources/welcoming-the-stranger-among-us-unity-in -diversity.cfm.

USCCB, Dep't of Justice, Peace & Human Dev., Office of Domestic Social Dev., Affordable Housing and the National Housing Trust Fund (NHTF) (Feb. 2011), http://www.usccb.org/issues-and-action/human-life-and-dignity /housing-homelessness/affordable-housing-and-the-national-housing-trust -fund.cfm.

USCCB, Dep't of Justice, Peace & Human Dev., Office of Domestic Social Dev., Food & Nutrition Programs (Feb. 2011), http://www.usccb.org/about /domestic-social-development/resources/upload/food-nutrition-backgrounder -2011.pdf.

USCCB, Dep't of Justice, Peace & Human Dev., Office of Domestic Social Dev., Foreclosure (Feb. 2011), http://www.usccb.org/issues-and-action/human-life -and-dignity/housing-homelessness/foreclosures-2011.cfm.

USCCB, Dep't of Justice, Peace & Human Dev., Office of Domestic Social Dev., Health Care Reform (Feb. 2011), http://www.usccb.org/issues-and-action /human-life-and-dignity/health-care/upload/health-care-backgrounder-2011 .pdf.

USCCB & Conferencia del Episcopado Mexicano, *Strangers No Longer: Together on the Journey of Hope* (2003), http://www.usccb.org/issues-and-action/human-life -and-dignity/immigration/strangers-no-longer-together-on-the-journey-of -hope.cfm.

Anthony Picarello, Jr. & Michael F. Moses, *Letter to the Centers for Medicare & Medic- aid Services: Dep't of Health and Human Services, Re: Interim Final Rules on Preven- tative Services*, USCCB— Off. of the Gen. Counsel (Aug. 31, 2011), http://www .usccb.org/about/general-counsel/rulemaking/upload/comments-to-hhs-on -preventive-services-2011-08-2.pdf.

Anthony Picarello, Jr. & Michael F. Moses, *Letter to Office of Consumer Information and Insurance Oversight: Dep't of Health and Human Services, Re: Interim Final Rules Relating to Coverage of Preventative Services*, USCCB— Off. of the Gen. Counsel (Sept. 17, 2010), http://www.usccb.org/about/general-counsel/rulemaking/upload /comments-to-hhs-on-preventive-services-2010-09.pdf.

Statutes & Acts

Defense of Marriage Act, 28 U.S.C. § 1738C (2006).

Nationals But Not Citizens of the United States at Birth, 8 U.S.C. § 1408 (2006).

G.A. Res. 217A(III), Universal Declaration of Human Rights, Dec. 10, 1948, U.N. GAOR, 3d Sess., 1st plen. mtg., U.N. Doc. A/810 (Dec. 12, 1948), http://www.un .org/en/documents/udhr/.

Cases

Atkins v. Virginia, 536 U.S. 304 (2002) (holding executions of the mentally retarded unconstitutional).

Buck v. Bell, 274 U.S. 200 (1927) (allowing eugenic sterilization). Case is also infamous for Justice Holmes's quote: "Three generations of imbeciles are enough." (at 207).

Dred Scott v. Sandford, 60 U.S. 393 (1857) (holding African-Americans not citizens; slaves remain property even when transported to fee territory; and finding the Missouri Compromise unconstitutional). Case considered the low-point of Supreme Court jurisprudence.

Elk v. Wilkins, 112 U.S. 94, 101-02 (1884) (refusing to apply Fourteenth Amendment to confer American citizenship on Native American who was born on a reservation in the United States and had renounced his tribal allegiance).

Furman v. Georgia, 408 U.S. 238 (1972) (abolishing the death penalty).

Gonzales v. Carhart, 550 U.S. 124 (2007) (striking down a federal ban on partial-birth abortions).

Gregg v. Georgia, 428 U.S. 153 (1976) (reinstating the death penalty).

Griswold v. Connecticut, 381 U.S. 479 (1965) (holding state law banning contraceptives unconstitutional).

I.N.S. v. Elia-Zacarias, 502 U.S. 478 (1992) (providing no asylum for a refugee whose life was threatened by guerillas if he was returned to his native country).

I.N.S. v. Rios-Pineda, 471 U.S. 444 (1985) (determining that children born in the United States to illegal aliens are American citizens).

Loving v. Virginia, 388 U.S. 1 (1967) (invalidating Virginia's ban on interracial marriage under the Fourteenth Amendment).

Nat'l Fed'n of Indep. Bus. v. Sebelius, 132 S. Ct. 2566, 708 (2012) (allowing Congress's individual health care mandate; striking down an expansion of Medicaid).

Obergefell v. Hodges, 135 S. Ct. 2584 (2015) (legalizing same-sex marriage nationwide).

Planned Parenthood of Se. Pa. v. Casey, 505 U.S. 833 (1992) (recognizing a woman's right to choose an abortion before fetal viability; permitting informed consent; and, denying spousal consent).

Plyler v. Doe, 457 U.S. 202 (1982) (holding that the Fourteenth Amendment applies to illegal aliens).

Roe v. Wade, 410 U.S. 113, 131 (1973) (legalizing abortion).

Roper v. Simmons, 543 U.S. 551 (2005) (abolishing the death penalty for offenders under the age of 18).

Stanford v. Kentucky, 492 U.S. 361 (1989) (permitting death penalty for offenders aged 16–17).

Texas Med. Providers Performing Abortion Services v. Lakey, No. A-11-CA-486-SS, 2011 WL 3818879, at *1 (W.D. Tex. Aug. 30, 2011) (invalidating state law that required women be shown a sonogram prior to physician performing their abortion).

Town of Greece, N.Y. v. Galloway, 134 S. Ct. 1811, 708 (2014) (holding that opening town board meetings with prayer did not violate the First Amendment).

United States v. Flores-Villar, 536 F.3d 990 (9th Cir. 2008) (holding that no American citizenship available to the child born outside the United States of a 16 year old American-citizen father).

United States v. Windsor, 133 S. Ct. 2675 (2013) (holding that DOMA's definition of marriage was unconstitutional under the Fifth Amendment).

United States v. Wong Kim Ark, 169 U.S. 649 (1898) (settling that children born in United States to lawful immigrants are American citizens).

Washington v. Glucksburg, 117 S. Ct. 2258 (1997) (denying a right to assistance in committing suicide under the Due Process Clause).

Whole Women's Health v. Hellerstedt, 136 S. Ct. 2292 (2016) (invalidating two portions of a Texas abortion procedures statute).

Zubik v. Burwell, 136 S. Ct. 1557 (2016) (protecting Little Sisters of the Poor from requirements of contraception provision in the Affordable Care Act).

Blogs & Opinions

Cathy Lynn Grossman, *Key Vote for N.Y. Gay Marriage 'Not Just Catholic,'* USA TODAY, (June 26, 2011), http://content.usatoday.com/communities/Religion/post/2011/06/gay-marriage-passes-ny-religion-/1.

Erich H. Holder & Kathleen Sebelius, *Health Reform Will Survive Its Legal Fight*, WASH. POST OP-ED (Dec. 14, 2010), http://www.washingtonpost.com/wp-dyn/content/article/2010/12/13/AR2010121303816.html.

Huma Khan, *Congress Mulls Cuts to Food Stamps Program Amid Record Number of Recipients*, ABC NEWS BLOG (May 31, 2011 11:48am), http://abcnews.go.com/blogs/politics/2011/05/congress-mulls-cuts-to-food-stamps-program-amid-record-number-of-recipients/.

Rev. Michael P. Orsi, *Bishops Wrong: Health Care Not a Right*, HUMAN EVENTS (July 30, 2009), *available at* http://www.humanevents.com/article.php?id=32911 (Rev. Orsi is a research fellow at Ave Maria School of Law).

Anthony Stevens-Arroyo, *How Will Catholics Approach Immigration Reform?*, WASH. POST BLOG (July 14, 2011), http://www.washingtonpost.com/blogs/catholic

-america/post/how-with-catholics-approach-immigration-reform/2011/07/14
/gIQARqDlEI_blog.html.

Websites Generally

Amnesty International, http://www.amnesty.org (last visited Mar. 19, 2014).

Benefits.gov, Energy Assistance Programs, http://www.benefits.gov/benefits/browse
-by-category/category/ENA (last visited Mar. 19, 2014).

Benefits.gov, Food/Nutrition, http://www.benefits.gov/benefits/browse-by-category/
category/FOO (last visited Mar. 19, 2014).

Benefits.gov, Housing, http://www.benefits.gov/benefits/browse-by-category/cate
gory/HOU (last visited Mar. 19, 2014).

Benefits.gov, Public Assistant Benefits by State, http://www.benefits.gov/benefits
/browse-by-state (last visited Mar. 19, 2014).

Death Penalty Information Center, *Fact Sheet* (Mar. 13, 2014), http://www.death
penaltyinfo.org/documents/FactSheet.pdf (last visited Mar. 19, 2014).

Justice for Immigrants, http://www.justiceforimmigrants.org/index.shtml (last visited Mar. 19, 2014).

USCCB, Committee for the Promotion & Defense of Marriage, http://www.usccb
.org/issues-and-action/marriage-and-family/marriage/promotion-and-defense
-of-marriage/ (last visited Mar. 19, 2014).

USCCB, Housing-Homelessness, http://www.usccb.org/issues-and-action/human
-life-and-dignity/housing-homelessness/ (last visited Mar. 19, 2014).

Vatican, http://www.vatican.va/phome_en.htm (last visited Mar. 19, 2014).

Index